A HIGH PRICE

A HIGH PRICE

THE TRIUMPHS AND FAILURES OF ISRAELI COUNTERTERRORISM

DANIEL BYMAN

OXFORD
UNIVERSITY PRESS

OXFORD
UNIVERSITY PRESS

Oxford University Press, Inc., publishes works that further
Oxford University's objective of excellence
in research, scholarship, and education.

Oxford   New York
Auckland   Cape Town   Dar es Salaam   Hong Kong   Karachi
Kuala Lumpur   Madrid   Melbourne   Mexico City   Nairobi
New Delhi   Shanghai   Taipei   Toronto

With offices in
Argentina   Austria   Brazil   Chile   Czech Republic   France   Greece
Guatemala   Hungary   Italy   Japan   Poland   Portugal   Singapore
South Korea   Switzerland   Thailand   Turkey   Ukraine   Vietnam

© Daniel Byman 2011

Published by Oxford University Press, Inc.
198 Madison Avenue, New York, NY 10016
www.oup.com

Oxford is a registered trademark of Oxford University Press

Library of Congress Cataloging-in-Publication Data
Byman, Daniel, 1967-
A high price : the triumphs and failures of Israeli
counterterrorism / Daniel Byman.
p. cm.
Includes bibliographical references.
ISBN 978-0-19-539182-4 (alk. paper)
1. Terrorism—Israel.   2. Terrorism—Israel—Prevention.
3. Arab-Israeli conflict.   I. Title.
HV6433.I75B96 2010
363.325'16095694—dc22
2010033704

9780195391824

Printed in the United States of America
on acid-free paper

CONTENTS

ACKNOWLEDGMENTS

More than any book I've written, this work benefited from the help of others. At Georgetown University my thanks go to Bruce Hoffman, Ellen McHugh, Carol Lancaster, and Robert Gallucci, now President of the MacArthur Foundation. Through them I received assistance from the Center for Peace and Security Studies and the School of Foreign Service at Georgetown University. I am particularly grateful to the George T. Kalaris Intelligence Studies Fund for its support of this book.

I also received tremendous institutional support from the Saban Center for Middle East Policy at the Brookings Institute. Several of my colleagues at the Saban Center—experts in their own right on this topic—were particularly helpful. Ken Pollack offered invaluable input into the research design and provided many superb suggestions for improving the final manuscript as well as the constant encouragement that is his trademark. I thank Bruce Riedel for his careful reading of my entire manuscript and many thoughtful comments during the research process. Khaled Elgindy, Tamara Wittes and Michael O'Hanlon also provided helpful guidance, and I am grateful to Martin Indyk for lending his expertise and helping me arrange interviews in Israel.

I was also fortunate enough to spend the summer at the Institute for National Security Studies at Tel Aviv University. My thanks to Ambassador Zvi Shtauber for hosting me, as well as to the scholars and staff of INSS. This was an ideal location for my research.

Several friends and colleagues at other institutions played a critical role in assisting my research, serving as a sounding board, reviewing the final product, or otherwise helping make my work stronger. I thank Daphne Barak-Erez, Laura Blumenfeld, Stuart Cohen, Kim Cragin, Keren Fraiman, Boaz Ganor, Emile el-Hokayem, Michael Jacobson, Greg Jaffe, David Johnson, Charles King, David Makovsky, Peter Mansoor, H. R. McMaster, Montgomery Meigs, Ami Pedahzur, Charles Perkins, Arie Perliger, Jeremy Pressman, Yoram Schweitzer, Amit Segal, Brent Sterling, Beryl Taswell, and Victoria Wachino. Eliot Cohen offered an exceptionally helpful review of the entire manuscript, pointing out many weak points and offering his own valuable insights. Matthew Levitt not only read parts of the final manuscript, but also gave generously of his time in helping me get this project started. Pope Ward repeatedly helped me hone my message and the book's structure, transforming an inchoate set of ideas into a coherent set of arguments. Also generous was Adam Stahl, whose help enriched my section on targeted killings.

I thank David McBride of Oxford University Press and my agent, Larry Weissman, for helping shape and refine the manuscript at critical stages. I am grateful to Alexandra Dauler and Michael O'Connor for helping move this book through an often-onerous production process.

During the years I worked on this book I was privileged to have the support of several truly exceptional research assistants. In my efforts to secure interviews and initial research for this book, Chana Solomon-Schwartz provided a staggering amount of assistance, helping me find the most important and most useful people for my research and guiding me from start to finish in the process. Her energy and intelligence made their mark throughout this book. Shai Hazkani not only helped tremendously with the Hebrew-language sources, but, as an expert himself, also served as an in-house expert and critic, finding the faults with my work, suggesting new avenues to explore, and helping me avoid many errors. Eleazar ("Lazar") Berman and Sarah Yerkes also were extremely supportive, digging up sources, critiquing the draft, and helping me make the final product much stronger. Sarah's assistance on the photos is particularly appreciated. I'd also like to thank Zachary Foster, Alex Kennedy, Irena Sargsyan, Emily Solis-Cohen, Kimberly Walker, and Eric Werner for their assistance with research and editing for parts of this book.

Although this book draws on a range of documents, interviews are at its heart. In the end I interviewed more than a hundred people for this work: Israelis, Palestinians, Americans, and others with firsthand knowledge of the events or a strong analytic perspective. Some of those interviewed are cited by name in the narrative. Many of the most important people interviewed—often those in political positions or involved in intelligence, which is central to my book—chose to remain off the record. I understand their reasoning, and the absence of their names should not detract from their importance and my thanks. I thank them all for their time and patience

Finally, and most important, I'd like to thank my wife, Vikki. She plunged in with me to bring the family to Israel in 2008 and supported my research before and after. She was intrepid in the face of amorous Moldovans, sleeping bears, and "The Hokey Pokey" sung loudly in Hebrew and French, shepherding me and our boys from one adventure to the next. In my research she has been a constant inspiration.

Despite the help of so many people, I am solely responsible for this book's contents (and, of course, any remaining errors). Many of those who helped me will disagree with my conclusions, so my thanks to them should not be taken as their endorsement of my findings. This book has been reviewed by the U.S. government to prevent the disclosure of classified information, but nothing in its contents should be seen as asserting or implying U.S. government authentication of my factual points or endorsement of my opinions.

A HIGH PRICE

Settlements Established and Evacuated 1967–2008

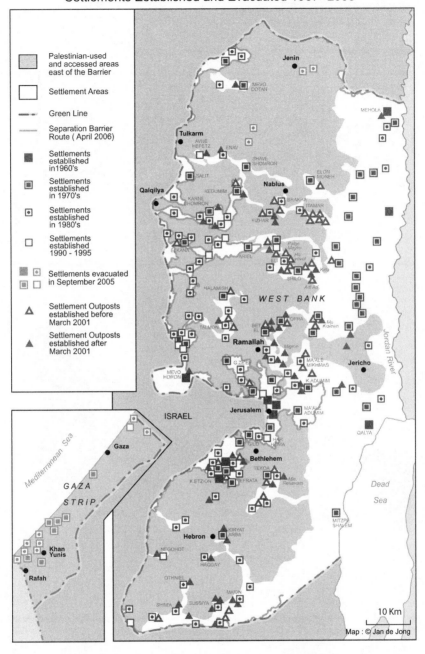

Map of Israeli settlements in the Palestinian territories established and evacuated 1967–2008.
Credit: Foundation for Middle East Peace.

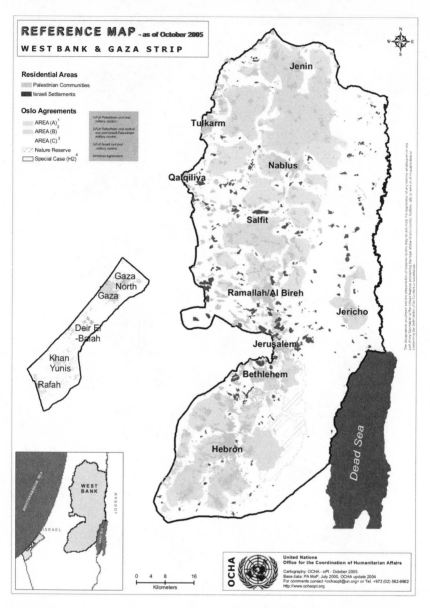

Areas "A," "B", and "C" under the Oslo Accords. The Palestinians had the primary administrative control in Area A, while Israel held control for Area C. Control in area B was shared.

Credit: United Nations

INTRODUCTION

The only thing that matters is that we can exist here on the land
of our forefathers. And unless we show the Arabs that there is a
high price to pay for murdering Jews, we won't survive.
—Advice given to Ariel Sharon, then a special forces commander in
the Israeli Army, by Prime Minister David Ben-Gurion after the
controversial retaliatory raid on Qibya in 1953

IT STARTED as an ordinary day in March. Passengers sat quietly on a bus
traveling from the southern seaside resort town of Eilat to Beersheba.
Some had gone for business, but most had been on vacation and were
now returning with souvenirs and suntans. As the bus snaked its way
along a mountain road, it neared a stone monument. Suddenly there was
chaos. First the Palestinians sprayed the bus with gunfire. Then they
looted the bodies; later a woman was found with no shoes, her ring finger
cut off. Eleven died and two were gravely wounded in the attack. Five-
year-old Miri Firstenberg survived only because a soldier riding on the
bus threw his body in front of her. Afterward the killers fled to safety in a
neighboring Arab state. The Israeli media declared, "The massacre was an
act of war, which can only be met by an act of war on our part."[1]

As the magnitude of the attack became clear, the Israeli prime minister
faced enormous political pressure. His rivals, already deriding him as feck-
less in the face of terrorism, were waiting to pounce should he appear
weak. The Israeli public needed to know their government was fighting
back, and the security elite feared that a feeble reaction would simply
embolden radicals. Everyone agreed that the killers and their supporters
must be held accountable. But how exactly?

The killers hid under the protection of a seemingly sympathetic regime,
one that was simply too weak to take action. The accused government even
offered to help in the investigation, an offer some Israelis derided as insin-
cere. Some Israeli security officials wanted to attack the protector regime's

1

facilities and civilian homes to punish the country and teach its government not to support violence. Others believed that reciprocal violence would only worsen the problem; the regime would then be more likely to support even more raids and paint Israel as the aggressor. Also weighing on the prime minister's mind were past reprisal operations that had killed innocent Arab civilians, leaving Israel condemned by international opinion and its enemies more determined.

Many on the Arab side were quick to point out that the violence was not surprising. One security official in Jordan commented that the local Palestinians had "barely enough for subsistence" and had "nothing to do." In his judgment the raids were "the price the Jews are paying for the brutality with which they liquidated the Arab residents in their country." One of the raiders was even more blunt in his recollections of attacks during this time: "This is what bothered us and made us fight them—they took our homeland, said that you are strangers and you have nothing, and expelled us."

The tragedy of the story is not just the attack, which was brutal, but the fact that similar horrors and conundrums occurred over and over again. This particular massacre occurred in 1954, at Scorpion's Pass. The attackers were Palestinian raiders, probably based in Jordan or Egypt. That time Israel chose not to respond, but this restraint did not prevent further raids and the continued escalation of violence on all sides. With a few small changes the Scorpion's Pass massacre could fit many of the terrorist atrocities that followed: the Palestinian nationalist organization Fatah's 1978 attack on buses that killed thirty-eight along Israel's Coastal Highway; the Palestinian Islamist group Hamas's 1996 attacks on two buses in Jerusalem that killed forty-five Israelis; and Hamas's 2004 strike on buses in Beersheba that killed sixteen.

In these and countless other tragedies Israel is in a no-win situation. On one hand, a failure to respond could embolden its enemies and dishearten its people. On the other hand, tough retaliation could worsen the situation, lead to the deaths of more innocents, and trigger international condemnation. In the more than sixty years of the Jewish state's existence, Israeli governments have tried almost every option in fighting terrorist attacks: negotiations, retaliatory raids, better defenses, and outright invasions of its neighbors. These years saw failures and successes, victories and tragedies. Even today there is no clear-cut solution. The Jewish state has survived and even prospered in the decades after the Scorpion's Pass tragedy, but the price has been painful for its citizens and its Arab neighbors. Israel's history of counterterrorism is marked with boldness, bravery, and mistakes.

In the years following independence Israel became an incubator for new terrorist techniques and had to counter a wide range of foes. When the Palestinians hijacked planes after the 1967 War, people assumed it was an Israeli-only problem, until hijackings spread rapidly across the world. Suicide bombing, invented by Hizballah to fight Israel and its allies, has since metastasized to become a global plague.

Israel has faced virtually every type of foe in the terrorist pantheon. Some of the attackers have been tightly disciplined, others loosely organized. Some were state-backed, others independent. Some operated through small revolutionary cells, others as part of mass movements. Likewise virtually every counterterror instrument that Americans debate today was pioneered by Israelis in their desperate attempt to find some answer to their own terrorism conundrum. As terrorists developed new and more gruesome techniques, Israel countered with hostage rescue missions by elite units, targeted killings of terrorist operatives, aggressive interrogation measures, and administrative detention and other controversial tactics, all, as with the United States today, under the glare of the world media and diplomatic spotlight.

Israel's early successes against terrorists inspired a myth of Israeli brilliance, resolve, and even omnipotence. Some daring Israeli operations lived up to this image, such as the 1976 hostage rescue mission in Entebbe, Uganda. Yet Israeli counterterrorism forces also bungled operations, sometimes because they made mistakes, at other times because of the inherent difficulty of the mission. Less forgivably, political maneuvering, ignorance, and outright hubris have marred counterterrorism policies. Critics point out that Israel has suffered from a terrorism problem since 1948, a record that on the surface seems a stunning failure. Israel's mistakes and track record have thus contributed to a second myth that is perhaps more pernicious: the idea that Israel's methods are disastrous for any who might seek to learn from them.

It is precisely these discordant assumptions that inspired me to write this book. Israel's successes and failures can serve as a blueprint for all countries fighting terrorism. Many have already learned a great deal from the Israelis about how to fight terrorism, yet there is still much more that Israel's military and intelligence services have to teach. By the same token, Israel's failures hold equally important lessons for those seeking to wage war against terrorists, and in the age of al-Qa'ida and the global jihad, that is pretty much everyone except the terrorists themselves.

Both the "brilliance" myth and the "bungle" myth obscure the day-to-day routine of Israeli counterterrorism. While Israel has enjoyed many impressive wins, many of the most important ones did not involve spectacular raids or Bond-like feats, but were the product of routine, grind-it-out intelligence-gathering efforts, solid defense, and the constant disruption of terrorist communications. These more mundane efforts are responsible for Israel's impressive record of preventing and preempting most attacks before they occur. Indeed since 1948 Israel has put several skilled terrorist groups out of business, deterred others and their sponsors, and managed to survive and prosper in the face of ceaseless violence—a record that all countries combating terrorism can envy.

A simple scorecard cannot do justice to Israel's unparalleled experience with counterterrorism—that's why you are holding a book, not a post-card—but it hints at the importance of the story of Israel's many long, shadowy wars on terrorism to the West's struggle with al-Qa'ida and their confederates. On the positive side of the ledger:

- Israeli intelligence services have repeatedly scored coups against terrorist groups, gaining the intelligence necessary to arrest group members, kill group leaders, stop planned attacks, and otherwise disrupt the group. Without this intelligence many more Israelis would have died at the hands of terrorists.
- Israel has at times worked well with Arab states and their leaders, particularly Jordan, at times Egypt, and even the Palestinian Authority, to shut down terrorism. Israel has also successfully deterred some hostile states from supporting terrorism.
- In recent years Israel has successfully used targeted killings to disrupt terrorist groups, reducing their effectiveness and forcing their leaders underground.
- Israeli defensive measures, ranging from sky marshals on airplanes to the security barrier running along Israel's border with Gaza and through much of the West Bank, have made it far harder for terrorists to attack Israel and Israeli targets.
- Israel has wrestled with, and often won, the challenge of how to integrate the rule of law and human rights into counterterrorism. On some issues this took decades, such as with the eventual restrictions on harsh interrogation techniques. Yet Israel's experience shows that counterterrorism and the rule of law go together.
- The Israel Defense Forces and Israeli intelligence services have reorganized successfully to meet emerging forms of terrorism. These changes were often wrenching and costly to other security priorities.
- Throughout decades of terrorist attacks the Israeli public has demonstrated resilience that has enabled the Jewish state to grow and prosper in the face of violence.

Of course Israel has had its share of losses and even "own goals," and these are equally instructive to those willing to learn:

- Israeli leaders often ignore the political consequences of counterterrorism. Israel's killing of terrorist leaders and military operations have at times further radicalized groups that were previously half-hearted in their efforts to go after Israel. Some operations jeopardized important alliances; others actually handed terrorist groups political power.

- Israel has neglected the information and media dimensions of counterterrorism. Its terrorist opponents have long prioritized propaganda, recognizing that the perception of victory and defiance is often more important than the reality. Israel, in contrast, has focused on actual operations, with the result that many successes are perceived as failures and thus increase condemnation of the Jewish state and embolden radicals.

- Many of Israel's problems involve the predictable long-term consequences of its policies. The 1982 invasion of Lebanon, for example, turned into a grueling occupation that created indigenous Lebanese resistance against Israel, the formidable Hizballah.

- Some of Israel's most successful counterterrorism measures, such as its reoccupation of the West Bank in 2002 and building the security barrier, were done without enough focus on the long-term political implications of these measures. As a result a peace deal is far harder to achieve.

- Although Israel has deterred some groups and states, the use of military strikes at times escalated terrorists' response and in one notable case, Lebanon in the 1970s, contributed to state failure and the creation of a de facto sanctuary for terrorists. Because of increased media attention and a growing expectation of proportionality in military operations, punishing attacks are more difficult to carry out today.

- Israel has repeatedly had schizophrenic counterterrorism policies, with its military and intelligence services often working at cross-purposes with its political leadership.

- Israel has a large, and perhaps growing, terrorist problem from Jewish terrorists who have used violence against ordinary Palestinians and Jews seeking peace. Such violence is not only horrible in and of itself, but also increases support for Palestinian terrorist groups and decreases the chance of a peace settlement. Unfortunately the Israeli state often does not act against Jewish violence, and when it does Jewish terrorists are treated more leniently than are Palestinian terrorists.

Many of Israel's problems come down to the issue of tactics versus strategy. The Israelis are usually strong tactically. Indeed raids like the liberation of Israeli hostages in Entebbe and the gathering of intelligence for targeted killings and arrests during the second Intifada at times border on brilliant. At the same time, however, Israel often blunders from crisis to crisis without a long-term plan for how to solve the problem once and for all. The day-to-day maintenance of counterterrorism often does not reflect, and at times is even in opposition to, broader goals, such as a stable peace with the Palestinians, or Israel's diplomatic interests.

Much of the record, however, is gray rather than black and white. Israel often fell short, but just as often it faced only bad options when deciding how to respond to terrorism.

Methods, Caveats, and Structure

Bringing to light the story of Israel's struggle against terrorism is a difficult task. The war itself is waged in the shadows by intelligence services intent on preserving secrecy and violent groups accustomed to a life of hiding—and entirely unaccustomed to Western researchers, let alone written records. One has to dig in many strange places and with every tool available. Consequently it was critical to supplement my research with interviews of Israelis in the military and intelligence services, Arab government personnel, human rights officials, and political leaders. These interviews provided me with a sense not only of what happened but why. For obvious reasons many of these sources preferred to remain anonymous.

Inevitably I did encounter limits. My access to sources was uneven. I secured far more interviews with Israelis than with Arabs. To bridge this gap I have relied on public statements and scholarly work. Nevertheless the gap remains.

In the battle between Israelis and Palestinians words engender bitter fights. For many years leaders on both sides refrained from using the words *Palestinian* and *Israeli* so as not to legitimize their opponents. *Judea* and *Samaria*—administrative names Israelis use for the southern and northern parts of the West Bank, respectively—recall Jewish possession of the lands in biblical times, a claim that Palestinians reject. The same city often has a name in both Arabic and Hebrew, most notably Jerusalem, which is called al-Quds in Arabic. Proponents of the security barrier refer to it as a "fence," suggesting a more bucolic structure, while opponents call it a "wall" to convey an image of cold war Berlin. The barrier itself is both fence and wall; in parts it is a chain-link structure and in other parts concrete. I have chosen to use the word *barrier*, a more neutral term that will no doubt anger both sides.

Suicide bombing and the killing of terrorist leaders are also linguistically contentious. Some Americans prefer *homicide bombing* to emphasize its malignant purpose; Palestinian sympathizers use the term *martyrdom operations* to stress the faith and sacrifices of the bombers. Israelis refer to their killing of terrorist leaders by the cumbersome term *focused prevention operations*, while Palestinians use the more loaded *assassination*. As with the word *barrier*, I usually use more neutral language, and when in doubt I fall back on what is most common in mainstream English sources.

A particularly loaded terminological question that deserves a bit more discussion involves the use of the word *terrorism*. Israelis often use the term *terrorist* loosely, employing the label to mean any Arab not part of an army who is trying to hurt Israelis. Many academic and Western government definitions, however, try to distinguish between terrorism and other forms of violence by nonstate actors, such as guerrilla organizations. For this book I define terrorism as a nonstate actor's use of or threat of violence against noncombatants for political reasons to produce a broader psychological effect. Excluded from this definition are attacks on soldiers in a combat zone. Thus a Hamas suicide bombing against an Israeli bus is terrorism; Hizballah's shooting at Israeli military forces in Lebanon is not terrorism.

Groups like Hamas, Hizballah, and Fatah, however, are difficult to categorize. All regularly use or used terrorism. Yet these groups operate on many levels: they run schools and hospitals, they represent large political movements, and they field hundreds, even thousands, of guerrillas who, in their eyes, are defenders of their people as well as armies to use against Israel's military forces. Finally, they are pseudo-states that control territory and govern people, particularly Hamas in Gaza since 2007. However, to not use the term *terrorist* would miss an important aspect of these groups, one that is particularly important for Western audiences that are struggling with their own terrorism threats. My book is about how Israel fights terrorism. Because these groups deliberately target noncombatants and otherwise act in a way that meets the definition of terrorism, I label these groups as terrorists. For all these groups, however, terrorism is one tool among many. From a counterterrorism point of view, the focus of this book, you cannot fight a terrorist group effectively if you ignore its other activities. Israel's efforts against Hizballah's guerrilla forces or Hamas fundraising are important parts of how Israel fights these organizations that also employ terrorism. Because Israel's policies also address their guerrilla, charitable, and other activities, I also examine these efforts even though they go well beyond a narrow definition of counterterrorism.

Yet this definitional question remains an important one for successful counterterrorism. I believe that Israel's failure to consider the nonterrorist aspects of these groups has often led to the failure of its counterterrorism policy. Israel would benefit from thinking in terms of counterinsurgency, which recognizes the political and social factors that shape violence, rather than in terms of traditional counterterrorism.

In this book I have divided Israeli counterterrorism into different periods according to the nature of the adversary and Israel's response. I begin with the period following the creation of the Israeli state in 1948 and ending with the Oslo peace talks in 1993. The earliest terrorism threat consisted of cross-border attacks from Palestinian raiders, often supported by Israel's enemies, particularly Nasser's Egypt. After the 1967 War independent Palestinian groups like Yasir Arafat's Fatah and leftist groups like the Popular Front for the Liberation of Palestine assumed prominence.

First they fought from the West Bank and Gaza, then from Jordan, and then from Lebanon. Terrorism, raids on Israel, and the Israeli response ultimately triggered a successful Jordanian government crackdown in 1970 and, five years later, contributed to civil war in Lebanon. This was also the period when dramatic international terrorism, such as the 1972 hostage taking at the Munich Olympics and a series of murderous attacks within Israel, put the Palestinian cause on the world map. Israel responded to this wave of terrorism with a campaign of its own, pursuing suspected terrorists around the world and hitting back hard at neighboring states that hosted them. In 1982 Israel invaded Lebanon to drive out the Palestine Liberation Organization. This operation crippled the PLO's military capabilities and eventually contributed to its decision to enter peace negotiations with Israel a decade later.

Then, unexpectedly, the levee broke in 1987 and the West Bank and Gaza Strip, which were pacified after Israel took the territories in 1967, overflowed with unrest in the first Intifada. The shock of this sudden outburst woke most Israeli leaders to the hard reality that Israel could not hold on to the Palestinian territories forever. They opened serious negotiations with the PLO, and in 1993 the Oslo Accords gave Arafat and company control over land within the borders of former Mandatory Palestine for the first time. Fatah would in essence become the core of the Palestinian Authority, a de facto government meant to serve as Israel's counterterrorism partner against Hamas and Palestine Islamic Jihad, the principal groups opposed to the peace process. Unfortunately Arafat's Palestinian Authority was a flawed partner. As a result other terrorist groups regularly struck Israel with devastating results for the ongoing negotiations.

When the peace process collapsed in 2000 terrorism and other forms of violence exploded. Palestinians killed almost a thousand Israeli civilians and security force personnel between September 29, 2000, and the end of 2008; the same period saw almost five thousand Palestinians killed, either by Israeli security forces or by Israeli civilians. Fatah members returned to violence, and Hamas and Palestine Islamic Jihad attacked with all their fury. Israel responded by devastating the Palestinian Authority, reoccupying areas given up in peace negotiations, arresting thousands of suspected terrorists, killing Palestinians in targeted strikes, demolishing homes, and erecting a massive security barrier. These actions shattered groups, but the constant thrust and parry weakened moderate voices among the Palestinians and strengthened rejectionists like Hamas. When Israel withdrew from Gaza in 2005 the terrorist group Hamas emerged as the dominant player there, winning elections in 2006 and seizing full control in 2007. At the end of 2008 the Israeli military launched a massive offensive against Hamas's stronghold in Gaza in which another thousand Palestinians died.

A third period, overlapping with the first two, began after Israel's 1982 invasion of Lebanon and involves a different foe. For even as the invasion devastated the PLO, it gave rise to a new, and more formidable, adversary: Hizballah. Hizballah steadily pushed Israel out of Lebanon, first to a security zone along the border in 1985, then completely out of Lebanon in 2000. After Israel withdrew, Hizballah remained a threat, supporting Palestinian fighters, launching rocket attacks, and kidnapping Israel soldiers—actions that led to war in 2006.

Still another threat, but one that interacts indirectly with others, comes from Jewish terrorists within Israel. They are responsible for numerous terrorist attacks on Palestinians and, most painfully for many Israeli Jews, for killing Prime Minister Yitzhak Rabin in 1995, a murder that devastated the peace process as the murderer intended. Jewish terror also feeds Palestinian terror, providing a further incitement that this conflict does not need.

The final chapters of this book examine broader themes and draw lessons, both for Israel and for counterterrorism in general. Israel is a laboratory: new terrorist techniques are often used against Israel first, and Israel in turn often develops innovative countermeasures before other states do. These chapters explore Israel's use of targeted killings, efforts to improve its defenses, and other counterterrorism measures that other countries are now emulating. Some of these countries should adopt Israel's solutions, but Israel's situation does not apply to all countries, and in some cases its history offers an example of what not to do. Yet whatever the lesson, the Israeli experience is almost always worth studying closely.

I conclude by focusing on two issues: the tension between Israel's need for safety and the demands of long-term peace and the dilemma this creates for peacemaking today. I use my historical analysis to examine what the lessons of Israel's past are for its future and what the United States and other countries can learn as they struggle with terrorism.

SECTION I

THE EARLY YEARS

CHAPTER I

TERROR UPON CREATION
(1948–1956)

THE YISHUV, as the Jewish community in Palestine was known, faced a recurrent threat of Arab violence as it strove to create a state.[1] Anti-Jewish riots swept Palestine in 1920, 1921, and again in 1929. In 1936 Palestine's Arabs revolted en masse, ushering in three years of strife as they tried to end British rule. By the time the tens of thousands of British troops had suppressed the rebellion in 1939, the death toll was massive: perhaps five thousand Arabs died, along with four hundred Jews. For Jewish leaders the violence was no surprise. David Ben Gurion, the leader of the Jewish community and Israel's first prime minister, told the Jewish Agency, "We and they want the same thing: We both want Palestine. And that is the fundamental conflict."[2]

The violence of the Yishuv's early years would continue to plague the new state of Israel in years to come. Yet though the threat remains to the present day, it has changed as the ideologies, societies, and politics of the Arab world fluctuated in the decades after Israel's creation. As the threat changed, so did Israeli counterterrorism.

To defend themselves against Arab strikes, several thousand Jews organized under the Haganah, a paramilitary force that eventually became the nucleus of the Israeli Army. The Zionist leadership created the Haganah after the 1920 riots, and it became far more organized after the 1929 riots. As Arab violence grew in 1936 in the so-called Arab revolt, so did the Haganah. Haganah policy was characterized by self-restraint, which led the British to work with the Jewish community as allies. The British would later support the creation of Jewish units to assist in defending the Mandate area from a German attack.

The Yishuv also created units of Jews from Arab countries who knew Arabic. These units primarily gathered intelligence but also participated in attacks. During the Arab revolt the British officer Charles Orde Wingate, who was deeply sympathetic to the Zionist cause, helped the fledgling Haganah organize "special night squads" that would ambush Arab gangs bent on destruction. The goal was to defend Jewish settlements through offensive action, seeking out the enemy and killing him before he could attack. Even when the enemy could not be killed, the hope was to scare him into passivity. Settlements were also at the heart of the Zionist enterprise; Jewish leaders sought to create facts on the ground that would shape the state's eventual borders.

When Israel became a state, Ben Gurion moved quickly to consolidate the power of the new government, folding in not only his own Haganah but also various underground organizations into the Israeli military and intelligence services. But he also kept much from the prestate period, albeit removing the British label. Many of Israel's legal policies for handling terrorism, for example, grew out of British procedures during the colonial period.

Wingate's legacy in particular remains visible today in how Israel fights its enemies. One aspect is deterrence: the belief that Israel's enemies would remain hostile but that the threat of or demonstrative use of force would stop them from engaging in attacks. Another was an emphasis on offensive operations. Israel's small size, concern over taking casualties, and fears that its infrastructure would be destroyed meant that it could not risk fighting on its own soil, so it sought to bring the war to its enemies. The third part of Wingate's legacy is Israel's emphasis on pre-emption and speed: when possible, strike first, and in doing so keep your adversary off balance.[3]

The prestate period also gave birth to and shaped Israel's intelligence services. In the early 1930s the Haganah established an intelligence unit that became official in 1940. The beginnings were primitive, at least compared to the formidable future of Israeli intelligence, but the fledgling organization already recognized that security depended on understanding potential adversaries and knowing their capabilities. Intelligence officers advised military units on whether local villages were friendly or hostile. Over time Haganah intelligence developed a village portfolio, learning all it could about personal relationships in Arab villages and key leaders there. Such intensive and micro-level information would prove invaluable.

In the years before Israel became a state, several Jewish groups became active in terrorism of their own, striking at both Arab and British targets. Today Israelis and Americans dismiss the idea that the ends justify the means, especially if it involves the deliberate killing of civilians. One future prime minister of Israel, Yitzhak Shamir, did not. Shamir had fled Poland for Palestine in 1935. He quickly joined the militant Irgun, and when it split in 1940 he went over to the even more radical Lehi, also known as "the Stern Gang" after its head, Avraham Stern. The Stern Gang was so anti-British that it even proposed to Nazi officials that they cooperate against the British. (Arab propaganda would later repeat this point endlessly. The future Palestinian leader Mahmud Abbas even wrote about this incident in his PhD dissertation.)[4] After escaping from a prison camp, Shamir became one of the group's leaders in 1943, following Stern's death at British hands in 1942. Both the Irgun and the Stern Gang rejected the policy of restraint. "Strike the British and Arab murderers," one pamphlet declared. "End the passive self-defense! We shall go to the nests of murderers and destroy them."[5]

In 1944 the Stern Gang assassinated Lord Moyne, the British resident minister, who had administrative responsibility for much of the region, and his driver at Moyne's Cairo home. They considered Moyne to be one of the key figures in the British immigration policy that prevented Jews from fleeing Nazi-occupied Europe to Palestine. A local policeman and crowd caught the killers, and they were later tried and executed. Over time, however, these terrorists became lionized as Zionist heroes, and in 1982 the Israeli government issued postage stamps bearing their pictures.

The Stern Gang's violence was the most extreme of the various Zionist organizations, but other groups used terrorism as well. During the Arab Revolt the Irgun—led by another future prime minister, Menachem Begin—had carried out operations against Palestinians, but as the Revolt petered out they turned their eyes on the British, hoping to end their occupation. The Irgun's most famous attack was the bombing of the King David Hotel in Jerusalem, Britain's military and administration headquarters for the occupation of Palestine. Irgun members disguised themselves as Sudanese waiters—the hotel's signature servers—and smuggled in explosives hidden in milk cans. The bombing killed ninety-one people, only twenty-eight of them British, and is still one of the deadliest acts of terrorism the world has seen. The casualties would have been larger had the Irgun not warned Arab kitchen workers to flee and detonated a small bomb in the street near the hotel to keep away passersby. However, casualties would have been smaller if the British had not dismissed an Irgun warning to evacuate. (For many years the British denied such a warning had been given, and the truth of the Irgun's claim to have issued one was confirmed only decades later.)[6]

The attack on the King David Hotel was the most deadly, but the anti-British revolt that followed World War II featured numerous attacks on British soldiers and Arab villagers and other forms of violence that today we call terrorism. Roughly two hundred British security personnel died in these attacks by Jewish organizations. One of the most brutal attacks was an Irgun bombing of an Arab market in Haifa in July 1938 that killed approximately thirty-nine Arabs.[7]

Britain's attempts to suppress Jewish terrorism through mass arrests, curfews, and administrative detentions failed. To stop the violence the British had to deploy almost as many troops as there were adult male Jews in Mandatory Palestine.[8] The violence demoralized British military and security services, and the massive troop deployment depleted the almost empty British treasury. Even more important, it convinced the British public, weary after World War II, that the game was not worth the candle. In the end Jewish terrorism played a major role in convincing the British to leave.

The Haganah both exploited these attacks and tried to conciliate the British. At times the Haganah coordinated with the Irgun and the Stern Gang, but when their violence threatened to derail Ben Gurion's political strategy, the Haganah cooperated with British security services, helping to identify the radicals so they could be jailed. The so-called "hunting season" devastated the ranks of the right-wing organizations.

Begin drew several lessons from the use of violence, ones that, ironically, would haunt Israel and Begin himself when he was prime minister. One lesson involved media coverage. Begin compared Israel to a "glass house," with the world's press gathered to watch and carefully chronicle each small event.[9] The press magnified British problems and abuses and broadcast them to the world. The intense scrutiny often stayed Britain's hand and limited the scope of any crackdown on the Zionist terrorists and on opposition in general. Equally important, Begin developed his strategy based on a fundamental assessment of British humanity. Although the British administration could be quite harsh, they did not murder civilians as the Nazis did. In the infamous Lidice massacre after the killing of SS leader Reinhard Heydrich, the Nazis gunned down the men of the town and shipped the women and children to concentration camps. Begin understood that an assassination of a British leader would provoke a British crackdown, but they would not gun down innocent men and women.

During the war for Israel's independence in 1947–49, violence against civilians on both sides continued together and sometimes in conjunction with military operations. The historian Benny Morris notes, "Arab snipers continuously fired at Jewish houses, pedestrians, and traffic and planted bombs and mines along urban and rural paths and roads."[10] On the day after the UN voted for partition, Palestinians attacked a Jewish bus going from Netanya to Jerusalem, killing three riders. Arab militiamen bombed Jewish areas, particularly in Jerusalem, killing dozens of people in Jerusalem's streets. Jews retaliated with their own brand of terrorism. The Irgun and the Stern Gang were particularly likely to conduct reprisal attacks.

Often violence against civilians degenerated into a brutal tit-for-tat. In December 1947 Irgun and Stern Gang terrorists placed bombs outside Jerusalem's Damascus Gate, and at the same time they lobbed grenades and sprayed machine-gun fire at Arab coffee shops in other parts of Jerusalem. The Stern Gang commander later wrote that the cafés "were jammed with Arabs hatching schemes, sipping coffee, and playing backgammon."[11]

When the war broke out the mainstream Haganah condemned attacks on civilians, but its attitude quickly changed. On December 30, 1947, Irgun operatives threw a grenade into a group of Arab oil refinery workers in Haifa, killing eleven. Arab workers then turned on their Jewish coworkers, slaughtering thirty-nine with knives, crowbars, and hammers. The Haganah avenged the massacre by raiding a nearby village where many refinery workers lived, dragging them from their homes to kill them, leaving several dozen dead.[12]

Attacks on civilians continued as violence escalated, first into outright civil war and then interstate war. Palestinian forces, and later Arab armies, regularly tried to expel Jewish civilians by threatening violence or committing violent acts. Jewish fighters followed suit. Perhaps the most infamous incident was the Irgun and Stern Gang's capture of the village of Deir Yassin after an unexpectedly bitter fight. Villages in the Deir Yassin area were often used as bases for raids on Jewish forces traveling on nearby roads, and the Haganah approved the attack on the village. Having secured control with little resistance, the Jewish forces then proceeded to massacre as many as 110 villagers, including women and children. The survivors of Deir Yassin and Arab regimes spread the story of Jewish atrocities widely, hoping to inspire resistance. The result instead was fear, and afterward, Arab areas often emptied out in advance of or after Jewish military advances.[13] Salah Khalaf, better known as Abu Iyad, who became the deputy head and intelligence director of Fatah—and for many years the terrorist most wanted by Israel—pointed out that fearful Palestinians raced to remove their women from the reach of Zionist soldiers. For these Palestinians, Abu Iyad wrote, "honor . . . is more important than land."[14]

There was no official Israeli state policy of comprehensive expulsion, yet the IDF battle plan permitted expulsions from areas the army occupied, and Ben Gurion told his military commanders "In each attack [against Arabs] it is necessary to give a decisive blow, ruining the place, kicking away the inhabitants."[15] In 1948 Zionist forces expelled civilians in forty-one out of 369 villages, according to the Israeli historian Benny Morris. Arab forces evacuated even more villagers, and some simply fled because they were frightened. Morris also contends that about eight hundred civilians or nonthreatening combatants were killed.[16] Yitzhak Rabin, then the commander of an elite unit, later would write candidly that when asked what to do with the Arab population of Ramleh and Lydda, Ben Gurion gestured and said, "Drive them out!"[17] The war, together with the Jewish conquest of areas the UN had designated Palestinian, created the Palestinian refugee problem that haunts the region today. Both sides saw the other as engaging in deliberate intimidation of and violence against civilians, a perception that would color their actions in the years to come.

Border Wars

For Israelis, the war's end in 1949 did not bring peace.[18] The armistice agreement stated that civilians could not cross fighting areas. Israel interpreted this as a mandate to stop Palestinians from coming back to Israel, whether as raiders or as refugees, and to demand that Arab states stop them from doing so. This interpretation would have a profound impact on the new state's relationship with its enemies.

In all more than 700,000 Palestinians became refugees during the war, a stunning total; the number of Palestinians in what became Israel numbered only around 900,000 before the war. To deal with the problem the UN established the United Nations Relief and Works Agency, a massive and unusual organization that educated and cared for the fleeing Palestinians and, later, their children and grandchildren. The number of Palestinian refugees swelled; today they total almost five million.

Palestinians found life difficult everywhere they went. The Fatah leader Abu Iyad contends that in Jordan "[A]ny political activity, the slightest hint of dissent, was punished by harsh interrogations, arbitrary imprisonment, even torture."[19] Jordan was the best of the host countries; Syria and Lebanon placed severe restrictions on refugees. Future generations of camp residents would swell the ranks of militant organizations.

The situation in Gaza was particularly difficult. More than 200,000 refugees had fled to Gaza, swamping the prewar population of fewer than 100,000. The poor and bitter new arrivals crowded the small area, destroying the traditional hierarchy in Gaza and allowing new leaders to come to the fore, in addition to the traditional clan and family-based elite. The United Nations tried to ameliorate the situation by installing a system of health care, education, and social services to lessen the impact.

Egypt now took charge of Gaza. Egyptian rule was supposed to be temporary, as Gaza was slated to become part of a Palestinian state in accordance with the 1947 UN partition resolution. Nor did Israel make any claims on Gaza. The lack of a peace deal, however, meant that Egypt's temporary rule stretched on indefinitely. Egypt policed this area and at the same time gave lip service to the refugees' right to return to their homes in Israel, even allowing some of them to attempt a return. Both policies alarmed Israel. Under the armistice agreement the size of Egypt's military forces in Gaza was limited, so Egypt instead created units from the local Palestinian population.

Gamal Abd al-Nasser's assumption of power after Egyptian army officers toppled King Farouk on July 23, 1952, electrified the Arab world. The charismatic Nasser championed a pan-Arab agenda, promoting the idea that all Arabs were one people and should act as one. Arab governments came under increasing pressure to prove their dedication to the Arab cause. Allegiance to the Palestinians became the dangerous measure of devotion. This proved to be a double-edged sword: insufficient support would rile the Arab masses and undercut a regime's prestige; aggressive steps to help the Palestinians, however, risked embroiling the regimes in a fight with Israel and the increasingly formidable Israel Defense Forces (IDF). Egypt found the pressure particularly intense. Nasser felt obliged to defend not only Gazan and Egyptian soil but also, as the self-proclaimed leader of the Arab nation, the borders of Jordan and Syria, states that felt the pressure of Israeli raids.

The inter-Arab dynamics at this time were an odd mix of rivalry cloaked in the name of brotherhood. The Jordanian and Egyptian regimes loathed each other, but popular support for Nasser and his anti-Israel stance was high in Jordan, making it difficult for the Hashemite regime there to consistently ignore or defy him. Even though Cairo thought the Hashemites would and should fall, Nasser's pan-Arab rhetoric made it hard for him to turn his back when Jordan was attacked.

After the armistice many refugees tried to get back into Israel. The number of attempted infiltrations peaked in 1952 at sixteen thousand; the attempts fell by more than half in 1953 and continued to fall through the 1956 war. The majority of these refugees came back to visit relatives, harvest crops on their old lands, retrieve their possessions, or steal equipment or money from Jewish areas—not to conduct terrorism. Indeed Israel's Arab population grew by 15 percent in the first five years of the new state, as Israel allowed some returnees to remain in the country.[20] One Israeli military intelligence officer noted in 1951 that most Israeli deaths from refugees at the time were tied to criminal activity.

Not all attempts to cross the border were benign, however. Small numbers, at first organized by the former mufti of Jerusalem and the Muslim Brotherhood, devoted themselves to violence. The number of infiltrators seeking to kill and destroy rather than harvest or steal became pronounced in 1954, when Egypt and Syria began to use Palestinians to attack IDF patrols and Israeli settlements on its borders. In 1950 nineteen Israelis died at the hands of Arab guerrillas and terrorists (often referred to at the time as *fedayeen*),[21] but by 1956 this number rose to fifty-four. For the Israeli government, the small number of terrorists and the larger number of potentially violent thieves became a serious security problem. Although by later definitions most of the fedayeen activities of murder and sabotage qualify them as terrorism, Israel at the time saw this primarily as a guerrilla war, often waged tacitly by neighboring states using the fedayeen as proxies.[22]

Border police and IDF members also often had shoot-to-kill orders and at times even murdered captured infiltrators. In the first few years after the 1948 war this policy led to the death of "several thousand mostly unarmed Arabs," according to the historian Benny Morris.[23] Less dramatic but no less important were the defensive measures Israel began to practice. The IDF armed kibbutz members, mined potential access routes, and installed booby traps in irrigation pipes and water pumps, the favorite targets of raiders. On the other side of the border Arab governments would often shoot at infiltrators to avoid any Israeli retaliation or because they saw those crossing the border as potential Israeli spies.[24] Yet the Palestinians kept coming. One IDF intelligence officer wrote at the time, "Often the infiltrators face a choice between death by hunger and deprivation and possible harm from our forces' fire."[25]

To discourage infiltration, particularly with regard to terrorism or violent crime, the Israeli government conducted retaliatory strikes on the villages and host governments that Israel believed supported the infiltrators. IDF Chief of Staff Moshe Dayan pointed out that the strikes would disturb "the neighboring village tranquility, including the women, children and elderly; then they wake up and complain to the government about border crossings, and in this way the Egyptian and Jordanian governments are motivated to prevent incidents of this nature."[26] Such collective punishment, Dayan contended, was "not justified or moral but effective."[27] The self-restraint of the Mandate period was gone.

Thoughtful Israeli leaders recognized that they could not address the sources of Palestinian discontent. Speaking at the funeral of a soldier killed by infiltrators in 1956, Dayan asked, "Can we argue with their intense hatred for us? For eight years they have been sitting in the refugee camps in Gaza, and before their eyes we are turning the land and the villages in which they and their forefathers lived into our inheritance." Yet for Dayan the solution was not accommodation but vigilance. "This is the choice in our lives—to be prepared and armed, strong and determined, otherwise the sword will fall from our hands and our lives will be obliterated."[28]

The historian Michael Oren (and Israeli ambassador to the United States at the time of this writing) offers three reasons why Israel embraced a policy of retaliation. National morale is one. In 1955, after infiltrators murdered two Israeli watchmen, Prime Minister Moshe Sharett, considered dovish by Israelis at the time, commented, "Rage must be defused, that alone is the logic." Though he did not "believe the reprisal [would] help in any way in terms of national security," he did not hesitate to retaliate.[29] Political leaders needed to assuage the anger of their people and their military forces. In the face of adversity this necessity trumped diplomacy.

The raison d'être of the Jewish state also comes into play, according to Oren. At the core of Zionism is the protection of the Jewish people by the Jewish state. In the early 1950s, with memories of the Holocaust and the bitter strife that attended Israel's birth still vivid in the minds of Israelis, the motto "Jewish blood will not be spilled with impunity" was not abstract. More troubling, however, is the historian Morris's contention that there was a popular Israeli attitude that Jewish life, but not Arab life, is sacred.[30]

Oren says that the final and most important reason for retaliation was simple deterrence: Israel sought to convince neighboring states that allowed fedayeen to cross that they would suffer even more than Israel. Given that at the time Israel had no powerful allies and was not at peace with its neighbors, politicians believed that keeping this fear alive was necessary for the state's survival. Israel felt it had little choice. Too many Palestinians were crossing the border; defensive measures alone would not work. As Dayan said in 1955, "We cannot guard every water pipeline from explosion, and every tree from uprooting. We cannot prevent every murder of a worker in an orchard, or a family in their beds. But it is in our power to set a high price on our blood, a price too high for the Arab community, the Arab army or the Arab government to think it worth paying."[31] Although most raids were organized in refugee camps far from the border, Israel hoped that pressure on local villages would force the host government to crack down on infiltrators rather than support them.

Though the targets of retaliation would vary in the decades to come, the triple logic of assuaging public anger, fear of survival, and deterrence would continue to prevail.

Early on, retaliation initially assumed a somewhat off-the-cuff character, and at times the IDF bungled its attacks. Another future prime minister, Ariel Sharon, made his mark by heading Israel's first special forces unit, Unit 101, which was created in 1953 to conduct raids and reprisals against neighboring states that hosted fedayeen. Unit 101 picked up the spirit of Wingate's special night squads, again trying to defend Israel by hitting Arab areas hard and creating fear within the ranks of the enemy. Ben Gurion told Sharon, "Unless we show the Arabs that there is a high price to pay for murdering Jews, we won't survive."[32]

The IDF itself embraced retaliatory raids, often going far beyond official instructions. In part this independence was deliberate. IDF doctrine gave commanders on the ground considerable autonomy. For Israel's wars, this style paid off handsomely, as commanders seized unexpected opportunities on the battlefield and found creative ways to overcome their enemies. However, local commanders often used problems such as unexpected resistance to expand the scope of a raid, even if they did not have instructions to do so. At times Dayan responded with anger at what he saw as unnecessarily high enemy casualty counts. Nevertheless he tacitly approved them by noting, "I prefer initiative and excessive action, even if they're accompanied by the occasional mistake, over passivity."[33] The more aggressive Israeli raids, however, led to more IDF casualties, a particular risk given Israel's limited manpower reserves and its sensitivity to casualties.

In 1953 the number of fedayeen raids grew. A series of attacks emanating from Jordanian-controlled territory culminated in the October 12 murder of Susan Kanias and her two children when fedayeen threw a grenade into her house in the town of Yehud. On the night of October 14, 1953, Unit 101 raided the village of Qibya in the West Bank, then under Jordanian control. They blew up houses and even a school in retaliation. Israeli forces killed between fifty and seventy civilians, many of them elderly, some of them women and children. Although Sharon later claimed to be surprised and shocked by the deaths of innocents, his actual orders were to demolish houses, "harm their inhabitants, and drive them out of the village."[34] Some sources suggest that the deaths occurred because villagers were too frightened to leave their homes, despite IDF calls to evacuate; others claim that heavy fire forced residents to stay in their homes while grenades were tossed in.[35] The attack was widely condemned, and the unit was disbanded, though Sharon went on to command other elite units that would conduct retaliatory raids. After Qibya Dayan shifted his emphasis to military targets.

The attack on Qibya—controversial, brutal, and bloody—worked. After the raid Jordan arrested more than a thousand would-be infiltrators, and its Arab Legion stepped up its patrolling. Elmo Hutchinson, who oversaw the border commission for the international community, declared, "[After Qibya] I watched Jordan's attitude toward border control change from one of mild interest to a keen determination to put a stop to infiltration."[36]

As Jordan's response suggests, in the first years after Israel's birth retaliation seemed to work. Local governments, despite their sympathy to the refugees, tried to curtail the infiltration. Jordan in particular strove to reduce the problem by punishing infiltrators and dismissing local officials who were not aggressive in stopping them. Egypt did allow a few Palestinians to enter Israel to gather intelligence and conduct sabotage operations, but Egyptian leaders feared Palestinian violence would suck Egypt into a war and destabilize the country. Until 1955 "Egyptian policy had, with few exceptions, consistently opposed infiltration to avoid sparking IDF attacks," notes Morris. [37] One of Fatah's future founders, Khaled al-Wazir, in 1954 organized a raid into Israel from Gaza and found himself arrested by Egyptian security.[38] As a result of this pressure the number of infiltrators, even those crossing into Israel to harvest their lands or to steal, fell.

Israeli retaliation placed Arab governments in a bind from which they never escaped. If a government refused to stop infiltrators, Israeli retaliation could draw them into an even larger military clash that they would lose and that would ultimately prove politically disastrous for them. On the other hand, their own people, and often their own local military commanders charged with policing the border, sympathized with the

Palestinian refugees. When their government failed to support the refugees or respond to Israeli retaliation, they saw their leaders as weak.

This bind was particularly tight for Jordan. The country had a new king, Hussein, who took power in 1953 at age eighteen, after his grandfather was assassinated in 1951 and his father was dismissed because of mental instability. Pan-Arabists inspired by Nasser posed the biggest challenge to King Hussein, so he had to appear pro-Palestinian even as he tried to stop infiltration. Nevertheless he proved adept at balancing Jordan's security realities with popular opinion.

But this precarious calm did not last. Israeli raids had already led Cairo to back away from promised cooperation on the ceasefire agreement, especially the border demarcation plan. Egypt's rhetoric became more heated, and on March 16, 1954, Palestinians from Gaza infiltrated Israel, killing eleven Israelis at Maaleh Akravim. Israel's retaliation led to unrest among Palestinians living in Gaza, which in turn put pressure on local Egyptian troops. After the Egyptians exchanged fire with Israeli positions, a marked deterioration of the ceasefire began. The Egyptian Army also stepped up its direct support of Palestinian infiltration raids that killed Israelis. As raids and mortar exchanges continued,[39] the broader strategic situation also became tense. In February 1955, after an openly pro-Egyptian government took power in Syria, Israelis feared they were encircled.

When Gazan infiltrators murdered an Israeli boy outside Tel Aviv on February 26 and Egypt refused to demarcate the demilitarized zone, Israel stepped up retaliation. Sharon, now with a paratroop unit, led another bloody retaliatory raid on the night of February 28, 1955, called Operation Black Arrow. This time their target was an Egyptian Army camp near Gaza City. Again the death toll was high: eight Israelis died along with thirty-six Egyptian soldiers and two civilians. While the raid, in Ben Gurion's words, gave "the army and the country a feeling of self-confidence," it fostered tremendous bitterness in Gaza. Retaliatory operations against military forces humiliated Arab militaries, on which power depended, and it outraged the Arab people.

New protests erupted in Gaza. Abu Iyad recalled how indignant he and other Palestinian activists were at the Egyptian Army's inability to defend Palestinians and called for military training for Palestinians to defend themselves.[40] Nasser visited Gaza for the first time since taking power and promised "an eye for an eye" retaliation. Egypt actively organized and launched fedayeen raids, dramatically stepping up the pace and brutality of past levels. By the end of 1955 Egypt had six hundred fedayeen under arms. Egyptian officials even worked with criminals who had once crossed over into Israel to steal, telling them, "Instead of being thieves, you will become *fida'iyyin*."[41] Now when Israel responded harshly to attacks, as they did during the Gaza raid, Nasser ordered fedayeen squads from Gaza to murder and destroy in Israel. As the historian Oren argues,

"Thus was created a classic vicious circle: infiltration brought retaliation, causing refugee unrest, which then forced Egypt to support further infiltration and reinforce its troops in the [Gaza] Strip, all of which, in turn, fanned Israel's insecurity and increased its need to retaliate."[42]

Moshe Sharett, Ben Gurion's successor as prime minister, attempted to break the cycle by not responding to Egypt's provocation, reasoning, "[Each raid] ignites afresh a sea of hatred."[43] Dayan, however, threatened to resign, and Ben Gurion, then defense minister and as always an imposing political figure, backed him up. Sharett was forced to endorse major retaliation. Nasser too could not step back, as a host of domestic issues demanded his attention and he could not afford to alienate his key constituents.

Because the fedayeen violence struck at the heart of Israeli morale, Israeli leaders found it difficult to avoid retaliation. The Jordanian military attaché in Cairo described Egypt's goal as "creating an intensive atmosphere of fear" that, over time would "encourage migration from Israel."[44] They were somewhat successful. Israel abandoned several new settlements, and many Israelis near the border lived in constant fear of an attack. "There was great pressure on the government to do something," argues Ariel Merari, an Israeli terrorism expert. As this pressure increased, the Israeli response, particularly against Jordan, began to backfire strategically, pushing the Hashemite Kingdom into open opposition when in reality Amman feared and hated Nasser's regime in Cairo and did not seek a confrontation with Israel.

On August 31, just over a week after a major Egyptian-backed fedayeen raid, an Israeli strike near Khan Yunis in Gaza killed seventy-two Egyptians and Palestinians. For a while Cairo did not resume attacks, fearing more retaliation, and the raid appeared to have succeeded. But on a deeper level it failed. Egypt changed tactics and began to organize Palestinian fedayeen raids from Lebanon, Syria, and Jordan. It was a way of retaliating against Israel yet avoiding Israeli responses against Egypt itself. Egypt also sought out new weapons from the communist bloc to counter Israel's military superiority, a move that quickened the escalation to war when a major deal was announced in 1955. Many Israelis feared that if they did not battle Egypt soon, they would have to contend with a hostile military armed with new and more powerful weapons.

Eventually Egypt returned to fedayeen raids launched from Egypt as well as from Gaza. On April 7, 1956, in response to an Israeli shelling of Gaza, Egypt launched a massive raid with instructions "to ensure sixty dead." The raid resulted in the deaths of two Israeli soldiers and eight or nine civilians (sources disagree), including children and instructors at a local synagogue and school.[45] Israel's attempt to have the UN condemn the raids ended in failure.

In 1956 the pan-Arab agenda championed by Nasser roiled the politics of other Arab countries. "Rise up!" cried the Egypt-controlled radio station Voice of the Arabs when the United States and the United Kingdom tried to recruit Jordan to join the anti-Soviet Baghdad Pact. Palestinians in Jordan rioted. To appease popular opinion, King Hussein dismissed his British officer corps and put in place Arab commanders more sympathetic to Nasser and the Palestinian cause. Jordan's army began to recruit its own fedayeen and allowed Egypt to deploy personnel to launch fedayeen raids from Jordanian territory, thus increasing the overall number of attacks and Israeli reprisals. Operation Samara, for example, led to eighteen IDF deaths and seventy to ninety for the Jordanian Army and security force personnel.

During this tense period Israel also carried out its first targeted killings in the name of counterterrorism. Col. Mustafa Hafez commanded Palestinian fedayeen units for Egyptian intelligence in Gaza. Israeli officials considered sending him a letter bomb or a poisoned fruit basket, but feared that this would harm innocents. Instead, in July 1956 Israeli intelligence deliberately fed false information to a Gazan, Muhammad Suleiman al-Talalka. Al-Talalka masqueraded as an Israeli intelligence source but really was loyal to Egyptian intelligence—duplicity that Israel used to its advantage. The double agent received a supposed codebook with "an important message" to give to another Egyptian, who would use it to spy for Israel. On July 11 al-Talalka duly passed the book directly to Hafez instead, presuming, as Israel knew he would, that the intended recipient was really an Israeli spy. When Hafez opened the book it exploded, mortally wounding him and blinding the agent. The next day Israel sent a book bomb to Lt. Col. Salah Mustafa, Egypt's military attaché in Amman, who organized Palestinians from the West Bank to conduct raids into Israel. He died in the blast.[46] These killings marked the emergence of what would become an important tool for Israel: killing key operatives who organize terrorist attacks.

On October 29, 1956, the years of mounting violence boiled over into war. The so-called Suez Conflict caused more than a thousand Israeli casualties and more than six thousand Egyptian. As part of its military campaign Egypt also launched fedayeen raids that lasted through December; these were the last major raids until Fatah emerged in the mid-1960s. The war ended with an Israeli military victory and brief takeover of Gaza. Afterward many Palestinian fedayeen fled through Israel to the West Bank, but IDF and Israel's domestic intelligence service, the Shin Bet, trapped a large number of them in the strip. The UN estimated that hundreds died in the first few weeks. Later reports would suggest that among the dead were many innocent Palestinian men.

For the first but not the last time, Israel faced the decision of whether to occupy Gaza. Moshe Dayan assessed the dilemma with insight, noting,

"A situation could develop in the Gaza Strip whereby our present problems would appear miniscule compared to the economic, police, and security problems we would inherit if we captured it with its refugees . . . . The next generation might ask us one day: Why were you such fools to change a borderline that you could control with two infantry companies for this hornets nest?"[47]

It is simplistic to say that fedayeen raids and the Israeli retaliation caused the 1956 war. So many other elements played a role: the refusal of Arab leaders to make peace after the 1948 war ended, Nasser's pan-Arab agenda, continuing border disputes, Britain's and France's anger at the Egyptian leader, not to mention Israel's fear of growing Egyptian conventional military power and the hostile climate that the often bloodcurdling rhetoric of Arab leaders engendered. Yet in hindsight it is difficult to believe that the war would have happened without the raids and retaliation. The bloodshed led to a climate of fear and anger that made progress at the negotiating table far more difficult.

Israeli Arabs: The Quiet Success

One of the most important early stories on Israeli counterterrorism involves terrorism that didn't happen. In 1949 the Palestinians in the new state of Israel found themselves strangers in a familiar land. Almost the entire Palestinian Arab elite were now counted among the more than 700,000 refugees. Of those 150,000 or so Palestinians who remained, one-sixth to one-half were internal refugees, separated from their homes and their land. The Arabs remaining in Israel have received far less attention than those who fled or were expelled. Violent conflict between Jews and Palestinians living within Israel's boundaries stopped after the wars of 1947–49. Israeli Arabs, for the most part, were not a fifth column during subsequent Arab-Israeli wars, nor did more than a handful support Palestinian militant groups.

This peacefulness, some would say passivity, is surprising, even in hindsight. The war created tremendous bitterness between the communities, and after Israel's creation Israeli Arabs found themselves treated as second-class citizens. Israel, after all, was a state created for Jews, even though one-sixth of the population was Arab. The civic life of the new state—Independence Day, the Sabbath, Jewish festivals, and other official events—held little meaning for Israeli Arabs. Quite the opposite: the Jewish character of Israel reminded them of their loss of dominance, and the irredentist rhetoric of Israel's Arab neighbors raised additional fears on all sides.

The new Israeli government immediately placed Arab areas under military rule. The military government censored Palestinian newspapers, limited free movement, put suspected radicals under internal exile, and regularly used administrative detention rather than the standard criminal justice system. The government enticed local leaders to cooperate with the Jewish state by leasing abandoned farmland to those who proved loyal, a tremendous perk. Or they allowed those who cooperated to carry a weapon, an important status symbol. The military government also had the power to deprive individuals of their possessions, control contacts among suspected dissidents, require regular check-ins at police stations, and expel people. The government maintained an active intelligence presence in Israeli Arab areas, a presence easy to maintain, as the military government's control of Israeli Arab society gave the Shin Bet, Israel's domestic intelligence service, tremendous leverage. Israeli officials also tried to split off the Druze, Christian, and Bedouin communities from the larger Arab one by giving non-Muslims and the Bedouin special rights and privileges.

In practice the goal was to ensure a quiescent Palestinian community. Ben Gurion told one of the officials in charge of managing the community, "I don't want them to love Israel. They never will. I want them to abide by Israeli law." If fedayeen came to the village, the expectation was not that the villagers would inform on their brethren, but that they would simply chase them out.

Yet a particular success for Israeli security officials was in using Israeli Arabs to stop infiltration. Palestinian infiltrators expected their fellow Arabs, and often fellow villagers and family members, to hide them, not report them, if they wished to remain in Israel. Moreover conditions for Arabs after 1948 were often desperate, and the financial rewards gained through theft and smuggling explained some of the assistance provided. To counter infiltration police and intelligence officials often gave Arabs charged with smuggling or other crimes lenient sentences to get them to talk. At times they went on the offensive, recruiting Israeli Arabs to infiltrate the fedayeen. These recruits then would lead IDF forces to fedayeen bases or would lead the fedayeen into traps. Often they simply killed the fedayeen themselves. Israeli Arabs were also used to recruit their family members living as refugees in various Arab countries.[48]

Israeli Arabs themselves rarely employed terrorism, and the few attempts at subversion were quickly discovered and prevented. Though politically quiescent, Israeli Arabs did not support the established order. Most preferred to live in an Arab state rather than in Israel. Press articles by Israeli Arabs suggested high levels of resentment over land expropriations, economic discrimination, and restrictions on education. Israeli Arab intellectuals and poets were particularly critical of the state.

The brutal exception to this peace was on the Jewish side. On the eve of the 1956 war Israeli soldiers killed forty-seven Israeli Arabs returning to their village of Kafr Qasim from work; the Arabs had been unaware they were violating a last-minute curfew. The soldiers involved were sentenced to up to seventeen years in prison, but none served more than a year. The officer in charge was fined ten *pruta*, a coin worth less than a penny. In their verdict the judges wrote that the fine "express[ed their] view [of] the severity of the charges."[49]

In general, however, violence against Israeli Arabs was rare despite the high level of Jewish suspicion of the community as a whole. Yet the lack of integration and the distinct identity of the Israeli Arabs would prove a constant concern for the Israeli security services.

Several factors led to the end of military government and the lifting of the most onerous restrictions on Israeli Arabs shortly before the 1967 War. Israeli businesses needed more Arab workers, but restrictions on movement made it hard for the workers to participate in the growing economy. Politically the ruling Mapai Party (which would later become the core of the Labor Party) had used its control of the Arab community to ensure that they voted for Mapai, a practice other parties understandably found outrageous. Perhaps most important the success of Israel's security agencies in ensuring peace and quiet reduced perceptions of the threat.

But the government had won the Arab community's loyalty by rendering them powerless, not by integrating them. Politically and culturally Israeli Arabs sympathized with the Palestinians outside Israel and nationalist sentiment grew. This lack of integration appeared to matter little to counterterrorism officials until decades later, when violence would return.

But after the 1956 war Israel's terrorism problem appeared contained. Arab states seemed to have no appetite to resume fedayeen raids, and the feared fifth column of Israeli Arabs at home proved to be little threat in reality. Israeli security officials understandably focused their attention on hostile Arab states and their armies, not realizing that terrorism would soon take a new, and deadly, form.

CHAPTER II

THE RISE OF THE PLO AND THE BIRTH OF INTERNATIONAL TERRORISM (1956-1970s)

"WE are the Palestinians and we have liberated this plane," announced an unexpected voice from the cockpit of El Al Flight 426. On July 22, 1968, three well-dressed Arabs had boarded the plane out of Rome and quickly seized control, brandishing guns and grenades to keep the passengers in line and force the crew to comply. The terrorists diverted the plane to Algeria, sending most passengers from there to France but holding on to twelve Israelis and the crew of ten. Israel, stunned, agreed after forty grueling days to release sixteen Palestinians arrested as terrorists in exchange for the hostages' freedom.[1] Bruce Hoffman, a terrorism expert, would label this hijacking the advent of modern international terrorism.[2]

The hijackers were part of a small but highly skilled Palestinian group, the Popular Front for the Liberation of Palestine (PFLP). Yasir Arafat's Fatah would dominate public perceptions of Palestinian issues, but the PFLP played a tremendously important role in the Palestinian struggle against Israel. The PFLP grew out of the Arab Nationalists Movement, which saw the liberation of Palestine as part of a broader revolutionary and anticolonial struggle. In the movement's sights were conservative Arab regimes that did not embrace revolution. "The road to Tel Aviv passes through Damascus, Baghdad, Amman, and Cairo" was how the PFLP's leader George Habash put it.[3]

The PFLP sought to use spectacular acts of terrorism to draw attention to the Palestinian issue. Dr. Wadi Haddad, for many years the key operational planner of the PFLP and later the leader of a splinter group, put it this way: "These spectacular operations will focus the world's attention on the problem of Palestine. The world will ask, 'What the hell is the problem in Palestine? Who are these Palestinians? Why are they doing these things?'"[4] In only a few short years Haddad's prophecy would be borne out: spectacular terrorism put the Palestinian issue on the world's agenda, though at times with disastrous consequences for the Palestinians themselves. Other terrorist groups would learn from the PFLP that dramatic operations that grabbed media attention could make a once obscure cause a household name.

Hijackings like the PFLP operation initially surprised Israelis, as they thought their terrorism problem was solved, or at least contained. While Arab leaders assured Palestinians that Arab armies would restore their homeland, their militaries had no interest in risking another round with the increasingly formidable IDF. Nor was there a strong Palestinian national movement, and indeed what it meant to be a Palestinian was now an open question. For some, their deepest loyalties lay below the national level, with local clans and families. Other ideologies also competed for Palestinian loyalty; Nasser's pan-Arabism, Islamists, and Marxists all made a claim to the Palestinian cause.

Arab states saw Palestinian groups as a threat as well as an opportunity. Led by Egypt, several Arab states collaborated to create the Palestine Liberation Organization to ensure that the Palestinians remained docile; they believed that by organizing the Palestinians, they could control them and score points with their own peoples. Headed by Ahmad Shuqayri, the PLO promoted the idea that the armies of Arab states, not revolutionary forces, would destroy Israel. Although for Israelis the PLO later became synonymous with terrorism, at first it would convene but do little beyond endorse the wishes of its state masters.

Rendering the PLO impotent did not sit well with the Palestinians, particularly the young and idealistic. The creation in 1959 of the Liberation Movement of the Palestinian Nation, better known as Fatah, was a turning point in the Palestinian movement. "The Palestinian people must retain the power of decision and the role of vanguard," Fatah leaders emphasized, and in so doing, achieve liberation by their own hands.[5] Fatah opposed those who wanted a pan-Arab identity to transcend one that was uniquely Palestinian. "Arab unity will be achieved through the liberation of Palestine," Fatah declared, not the other way around, as Nasser insisted.[6] Fatah's statements emphasized the humiliation and hopelessness of the situation, the abandonment of the Palestinians by Arab states, and sought to restore Palestinian dignity. Fatah rejected the ideology of class struggle embraced by many of its more leftist competitors and did not seek to transform the entire Arab world. Yet it was still in bitter conflict with Shuqayri and others who sought deliverance from Arab armies. For many years Fatah, like almost all Palestinian groups, also sought the return of all of Mandatory Palestine to Palestinian control; the decision to seek only control over the West Bank and Gaza was many years in coming.

Yasir Arafat, whose full name was Muhammad Abdel-Raouf Arafat al-Qudwa al-Husseini, emerged as Fatah's, and thus the Palestinian people's, leader. Arafat would prove the dominant figure in the Palestinian struggle, guiding the Palestinians from defeat to defeat but, at the same time, giving the cause political momentum that had the potential to lead to the creation of a Palestinian state.

Arafat was born on August 4, 1929. He claimed that he was tied to the prominent Husseini family on his mother's side and that after the death of his mother he lived with his uncle in a house right next to the Western Wall and thus grew up watching the bubbling conflict between Arabs and Jews. He also claimed he had fought with the 1948 war hero 'Abd al-Qadir al-Husseini.[7] As with almost everything that surrounded Arafat, the veracity of that claim is uncertain. The scholars Barry Rubin and Judith Colp Rubin claim that Arafat was actually born in Cairo.[8] In contrast to the Marxist and Christian leaders of other rival groups, he felt a strong sense of religious identity. In fact he took the name Abu Ammar as his nom de guerre, a reference to Yasir Abu Ammar, an early Muslim martyr. Arafat first emerged as one of the leaders of the Palestinian Students League in Egypt in the 1950s.

Experience in Egypt was important to another Fatah founder. Khaled al-Wazir, who went by the name of Abu Jihad, first came to prominence fighting with the Egypt-backed fedayeen. He created the beginnings of an organization with key figures such as its security chief, Salah Khalaf (Abu Iyad), and Faruq Qaddumi. Fatah tried to operate initially with a cell-like structure to promote secrecy. Members were required to swear the following oath:

I swear by God the Almighty,
I swear by my honour and my conviction,
I swear that I will be truly devoted to Palestine,
That I will work actively for the liberation of Palestine,
That I will do everything that lies within my capabilities,
That I will not give away Fatah's secrets,
That this is a voluntary oath, and God is my witness.[9]

Fatah rose as the Palestinians' faith in pan-Arabism and Nasser fell. Abu Iyad, Fatah's security chief, recalled that Fatah got its first big break after the 1961 fallout between Syria and Egypt that led to the collapse of the Nasser-led United Arab Republic, which briefly (and largely on paper) had unified the two regimes. Not everyone heeded the call for Palestinians to assume responsibility for their own liberation. Some left-wing groups demurred "out of respect" for Nasser; others claimed they were not yet ready for war.[10]

The revolutionary struggle in Algeria fired up Fatah leaders, offering a compelling if vague model for success. After eight years of a brutal civil war the Algerians had expelled the French. At the end of the war, in 1962, Arafat traveled to Algeria and became convinced that a guerrilla war would work to drive the Jews—in his eyes similar to the European colonialists in Algeria—back to their original homes. Arafat's deputy, Abu Jihad, stayed in Algeria, opening up a Fatah office and military training camp there.

Fatah launched its first attack on December 31, 1964. The attack was meant to involve Palestinians from all neighboring states, but Egyptian security arrested one team that was supposed to infiltrate Israel from Gaza, and Lebanese security detained the other. A second fedayeen team from Lebanon and another from the West Bank did manage to enter Israel, attacking a water pump at Eitan and a farm near Kiryat-Gat. The attackers failed to inflict any losses on Israel, but as Abu Iyad would claim, that was not the point: "We wanted to mount a spectacular operation that would arrest the attention of the Israelis, Palestinians, Arab regimes, and world public opinion."[11] Under the name of al-'Asifah, "the Storm," Fatah issued its first military communiqué a day later, on January 1, 1965. The leaflet justified armed operations "to reiterate to the enemy and the world at large that this people did not die."[12] Fatah from its start cared more about publicity than operational effectiveness.

Almost from the start Fatah attacked civilians. Abu Iyad claimed that at first they prohibited targeting noncombatants, but that Israeli punitive raids that killed Palestinian civilians drove them to attack civilians in turn.[13] Not mentioned, but perhaps more important, attacking the IDF head-on required a level of skill that Fatah did not possess; killing civilians was easier, if less heroic.

Fatah actually encouraged Israeli retaliation. It was a concept vital to the organization's method of operations. According to the scholar Yezid Sayigh, Fatah theorists promoted the idea of "consecutive detonation," so that Fatah action would provoke an Israeli response, which in turn would galvanize the Arab people and the Arab masses. Eventually these actions would force an Arab regime response.[14]

Attacks like those launched by Fatah in the mid-1960s received little attention at the time. Israeli and Arab leaders alike focused on what seemed an imminent clash of armies. For the most part Israeli leaders recognized that infiltration was limited and did not want to encourage a cycle of escalation. But the attacks and the Israeli response worsened an already poisonous atmosphere. From 1965 to the 1967 War Palestinians would launch 113 attacks (Fatah claims three hundred), which resulted in the deaths of eleven Israeli and seven raiders.[15] After a Fatah sabotage attempt sponsored by Syria on November 13, 1966, the IDF did a large-scale raid on the village of Samu in the West Bank that killed fifteen

Jordanian military personnel and five civilians. The attack sparked riots and antiregime demonstrations. It also increased military discontent with the Jordanian regime's efforts to keep the peace with Israel. This raised the pressure on King Hussein and increased his anger at Israel for striking his forces even though Jordan had tried to suppress cross-border attacks. Pressures such as these contributed to Hussein's decision to join the war when it broke out less than a year later.[16] But Arab states, leery of escalation, also acted as forces for restraint. Syria, so often the sponsor of attacks on Israel, had even briefly jailed Yasir Arafat, then a young revolutionary with dreams of ending Israeli rule.

The 1967 Shockwave

In June 1967 Israel's army devastated the combined forces of Egypt, Jordan, and Syria—a victory so swift that the war was dubbed the "Six Day War."[17] The loss alone was painful to Arabs, but the victory was so lopsided that it humiliated Arab regimes. Abu Iyad recalled his feelings after Nasser announced Egypt's defeat: "Nasser had surrendered! Who could ever have imagined such a thing?" Tellingly he concluded, "The Arab armies, all the Arab armies put together, hadn't been capable of keeping the little Israel army at bay."[18]

When Palestinians wanted to resume fedayeen raids, Arab leaders feared another debacle. "You will lose and drag us all along with you in the catastrophe," warned Syria's president Nureddin al-Atassi to Fatah when it sought support for its guerrilla conflict shortly after the war.[19] For young Palestinians who had hoped to gain a state on the backs of Arab armies, there was only one answer: to act on their own.

The first shift was felt in the West Bank and Gaza Strip. After 1967 control of Gaza and in particular the West Bank served Israel's political and military purposes. Some Israeli leaders saw the territories as a bargaining chip with Arab states: if the Hashemite Kingdom wanted the West Bank back, it would have to cut a peace deal. Should peace remain elusive, the new territory had strategic value. Having the Jordan River be the de facto border improved Israel's defensive position, and if Arab armies still got across the river Israel could give up parts of the West Bank before counterattacking.

For many religious and nationalistic Jews, the occupation of the West Bank was the astounding culmination of the Zionist vision; now even more of the biblical land of Israel was under Jewish control. Gen. Shlomo Gazit, the first Israeli coordinator of activities in the territories, notes that from the start Israelis debated whether they were temporarily occupying the territory that in the end belonged to Arabs or liberating historic land that really belonged to the Jews.[20] Even secular Israelis felt that at least part of the territories should remain Israeli for security reasons. In a 1969 interview Foreign Minister Abba Eban recalled, "We said clearly that the Eretz Israel map would never look again as it did on the fourth of June 1967. For it is a matter of security and principles. The June map is seen by us as a token of a lack of security and danger. I would not exaggerate by saying it reminds us of Auschwitz, to some extent."[21] Future prime ministers Begin and Shamir too would use the phrase "Auschwitz borders" to refer to the pre-1967 boundaries of the Jewish state.

Quick Success in the West Bank

Israeli officials tried at first to maintain a light administrative presence in the territories. When Dayan visited the newly captured Western Wall in Jerusalem on June 8, 1967, while the war was still going on, he immediately ordered the Israeli flag removed from the Temple Mount, where two mosques sacred to Muslims stood. Dayan knew that for the Arabs, the flag was a "detested symbol."[22] As defense minister during the occupation, Dayan pushed for similar actions and, because the Defense Ministry and the IDF were charged with managing the day-to-day affairs of the occupation, his requests initially prevailed. Israel flew its flag in few places in the West Bank. Military administration head General Gazit declared the goal to be "that an Arab resident of the area could be born in the hospital, receive his birth-certificate, grow up and get his education, be married, raise his children and his grandchildren and live to a ripe old age, all without the help of an Israeli government employee or clerk, and without even setting eyes on him."[23] For example, only nine Israelis managed the education of almost five thousand Palestinians. The goal, in Dayan's words, was to make the "occupation invisible."[24]

In 1967 the West Bank was hardly fertile ground for revolution, and that helped the IDF keep its presence light. The political establishment in the West Bank was pro-Jordanian, and many leaders saw new groups like the PLO as a threat. These leaders hoped they could find an accommodation with Israel similar to what they had with Jordan and cooperated "out of fear or out of habit," in Gazit's words.[25]

Dayan also worked hard to prevent a Jewish backlash after sporadic Palestinian terrorism. In Jerusalem on August 16, 1968, Palestinians planted grenades in trash cans, wounding fourteen Israelis. Jewish mobs then ransacked parts of the Arab quarter. Afterward Dayan pointedly had coffee in an Arab shop in Jerusalem and told the media who gathered, "The young Jews who ran wild in the city's Arab quarters cooperate with Fatah."[26] The hope was to convince Palestinians that Israel would stop Jewish vigilantism and thus there was no need to turn to militants in their own community.

Dayan, however, sought to balance his behind-the-scenes approach with a swift and severe response to any deliberate abetting of anti-Jewish violence.[27] The granting of work permits, the right to travel, business licenses—anything that required Israeli permission was used to ensure that Israel's intelligence service responsible for the territories, the Shin Bet, could recruit informants in all villages and neighborhoods. Shin Bet worked with petty criminals, offering them a pardon in exchange for information. If it gave collaborators money, it kept the amount small fearing that a suddenly flush agent would flaunt his wealth and expose his ties to the security services. Shin Bet also was involved in hiring and firing principals, teachers, and doctors, among other positions.

Israel deported leaders suspected of helping Palestinian militants or of trying to organize opposition to the Israeli presence. In 1967 Israel deported five Palestinians; that number grew to sixty-nine in 1968, 223 in 1969, and 406 in 1970. By the end of 1971 the cumulative figure would be more than a thousand. Israeli authorities imposed curfews to punish villages and towns that allowed militants to take shelter. Gazit called the curfew "the military government's most potent weapon," as it disrupted local residents' lives and caused tremendous economic losses. And it took place out of sight of TV cameras and reporters.[28] The IDF also destroyed the homes of those who sheltered attackers and at times of those who gave them food or information. The target was a militant's family and the village as a whole. "It proved effective and deterred many," claimed Dayan.[29]

In practice the benefits of the house demolition record was spottier than Dayan's claim suggests. At times Palestinian militant groups offered the family money to rebuild their house, and home owners would often claim ties to such groups after the demolition in order to receive compensation. Often the angry villagers united against the Israelis in support of the family. Demolition also placed cooperative leaders in a bind. The IDF destroyed the home of Dr. Kadri Tokan in Nablus because his son constructed bombs in its basement. Nablus's mayor, however, could not simply ignore the destruction of the home of a prominent citizen and endorsed strikes and demonstrations in response. In the end the bulldozed house became a news image that highlighted Israeli brutality.

Fatah did try to lead a revolt in the territories. In a manifesto distributed throughout the West Bank and Gaza after the Israeli takeover in 1967, Fatah evoked "the legendary resistance of Algeria" and called for establishing "secret resistance cells in every street, village, and neighborhood." They encouraged petty acts of sabotage and even included instructions on how to make a Molotov cocktail.[30] Arafat himself slipped in to try his hand at building an underground network in the West Bank. He and other Fatah leaders in the West Bank and neighboring states organized dozens of "military" operations, usually against farms, factories, and apartment buildings inside Israel.

Yet the seeds of rebellion did not bear fruit. Fatah was still competing with other Palestinian groups for the leadership of Palestinian resistance, and the groups often worked against each other. Even more important, Fatah's amateurish approach was no match for Israel's security forces. Fatah often began operations before setting up a clandestine infrastructure. It often ignored operational security and employed group members who, according to General Gazit, "put their naïve trust in the populace." The consequences were often disastrous.[31] Arafat himself quickly fled the West Bank, barely avoiding arrest. In the first three years of the occupation security forces killed two hundred operatives and arrested thousands. Israeli policy seemed to work. Early on 90 percent of those linked to violence came from the territories themselves, but over time the majority of those arrested came from the diaspora. Fatah leader Abu Iyad notes, "[The initial crackdown] deprived us of hundreds of militants and sympathizers [due to] the efficiency of the Israeli secret service and the carelessness of our fighters."[32]

Fatah's core strategy was also flawed because the Algerian model did not apply. In Algeria the European settlers were French citizens and could return to the French mainland after France relinquished control. But the Israelis had nowhere to go. Palestinians might see the Israelis as part of European imperialism, but for Israelis—with the specter of the Holocaust hanging over them and with virulent anti-Semitism in many Arab countries and around the world—there was no land to return to.

This mix of deportations, restrictions on organization, arrests, and other measures snuffed out anti-Israeli political activity, whether peaceful or violent. In 1972 Israel held municipal elections in the West Bank in the face of Jordanian and fedayeen opposition. The large turnout indicated that, for now, the nationalists did not dominate local politics. As one Palestinian in the West Bank recalled, "We tried petitions, demonstrations, strikes—nothing worked. We tried grenades and sabotage—no use. We are punished and nothing changes. Now we just go about our business and hope something will happen and the Israelis [will] go away."[33]

A Tougher Nut in Gaza

Gaza was far less important in Israeli calculations. It was smaller, less useful as a bargaining chip, offered no additional strategic depth, and had little religious resonance. As a result Gaza policy was often an afterthought.

The Gaza Strip is only twenty-five miles long and between four and seven and a half miles wide, but this narrow stretch of land would prove far more difficult for Israel to control than the much bigger West Bank. The 385,000 or so Gazans who came under Israeli rule in 1967 lived tightly together, with the majority of the population concentrated in one place:

Gaza City. When Egypt took control of Gaza in 1948 it isolated the Gazans almost completely. Unlike Jordan, Cairo's Arab nationalist government did not offer the Palestinians citizenship. Egypt had set up few schools, and local agriculture and industry were limited, leaving Gazans poorer and less educated than Palestinians living in the West Bank.

Because Israel did not deploy large number of troops to Gaza City, militant organizations were able to operate there with greater impunity. Gazans were more resistant to the Israeli occupation than were their West Bank brethren. Many local judges and council members opposed the occupation by refusing to do their duty. Communist groups had already established cells in Gaza, giving them a head start in resistance. Consequently many Gazans avoided cooperating with the occupiers, fearing punishment or ostracism from their own side.

Israel responded harshly to violence in Gaza and made few efforts to win over the locals. The IDF arrested thousands of Gazans and destroyed the homes of suspected militants and their supporters. Violence was high, and Israeli administrators placed Gaza under curfew, deported suspected troublemakers, and used roadblocks to hinder the flow of goods and people, thus adding economic punishment to the mix.

When these measures did not stop the violence, the IDF commander of the Gaza area, Ariel Sharon (now an IDF general and, after his impressive leadership in the 1967 war, a hero to most Israelis), became more aggressive, stepping up detentions and house demolitions. Because Gaza's alleyways were a nightmare for patrolling soldiers, the IDF began to demolish houses to broaden access routes, enabling its forces to close off part of the city and move without peril. Sharon's approach was the opposite of Dayan's. He tried to establish a conspicuous presence and, at the same time, used special operations units to take out Palestinians attacking Israelis. Working with Capt. Meir Dagan, who later went on to head the Mossad when Sharon became prime minister, the two created the Sayeret Rimon unit after Palestinian terrorists threw a bomb into the car of a visiting Israeli family, burning their two children to death. In 1971 the unit began to operate regularly.

Rimon members often went undercover as Arabs, collecting intelligence and at times killing suspected terrorists. The sobriquet Rimon, which means *grenade* in Hebrew, supposedly originated from the time the unit found a large cache of grenades hidden by Fatah members. Rather than seize or destroy them, they altered the grenades' delay mechanisms. Normally a grenade does not explode for several seconds so it can be thrown at an enemy, but the altered grenades exploded immediately, killing the thrower.[34] Like past special forces operations, their goal was to put the terrorists on the defensive and respond creatively to keep them off balance.

Israeli efforts began to pay off. By March 1971 thousands of Palestinians had been imprisoned for security reasons. To stop house demolitions local leaders promised to cooperate against those who attacked Israeli civilians and soldiers. By 1972 Israel had vanquished the Palestinian militants in Gaza. When it became clear that violence was failing and the Israelis were there to stay, local residents began to cooperate more with Israeli security services. As violence in Gaza ended, Israel began to use more moderate methods in Gaza, as they had done in the West Bank.

In both Gaza and the West Bank the human cost of the occupation's early years was considerable. From the 1967 War to 1973 Israel lost 269 people to terrorism and guerrilla attacks. The Palestinians in the West Bank and Gaza lost 327 people, mostly in Gaza. Of those the vast majority died at the hands of Arab militant groups either by accident or as punishment for collaboration.[35] In the first twenty years of the occupation an average of thirty-two Palestinians in the territories would die each year at the hands of Israeli security forces. The number would prove a fraction of the body count after the first Intifada and in particular after the second Intifada in 2000.[36]

Yet by this time Israel's political failure was becoming clearer. In the heady days after the 1967 War Israeli leaders believed that their Arab enemies would be forced to sign a deal simply to get their territory back. The defense minister, Moshe Dayan, famously claimed that he was "waiting for the phone to ring" from Amman, Cairo, and Damascus. The phone never rang. On September 1, 1967, Arab leaders met in Khartoum, Sudan, and declared the famous three no's: no peace with Israel, no recognition of Israel, and no negotiations with Israel. So while the security services' clampdown on the West Bank prevented broader resistance from developing, Israel still lacked a solution for handling the Palestinians under its rule.

The Return of Cross-Border Raids

As the struggle withered in the West Bank and Gaza Strip, Palestinian refugee camps, particularly those in Jordan, became the locus of the resistance movement.[37] Fatah and other groups had perhaps a thousand guerrillas in the Jordan Valley in early 1968. Fatah's base was the town of Karameh, near the border with Israel. Karameh, a name that prophetically means *dignity* in Arabic, would prove a milestone for the Palestinian cause. In March 1968, after a Palestinian terrorist attack on an Israeli school bus, Israel moved to destroy the Fatah presence in Karameh. Jordan's leadership warned the Palestinians to withdraw to avoid destruction.[38] The Palestinians, however, decided to fight. "This is our chance to change the morale of the entire Arab world," Arafat told a confidant. "Even if we die, we have died trying and thousands more will take our place."[39] The battle of Karameh was an indication of how the Palestinians could turn a military failure into a strategic success.

When Israeli troops swept in, the local Jordanian commander, Mashur Haditha, acting without orders from Amman, ordered nearby Jordanian artillery to fire on the Israelis.[40] When I asked Amnon-Lipkin Shahak, who as a young soldier fought at Karameh and decades later became the IDF chief of staff, about the Palestinians' toughness in the battle he quickly corrected me. "The Jordanians fought very well," he said, but the Palestinians mostly ran away.

In the end the military outcome was one-sided: Israel lost twenty-eight fighters with three missing, but Fatah may have lost more than 150, along with a hundred or more prisoners. More than sixty Jordanian soldiers were dead.[41] Arafat quickly fled to Amman, foiling the Israeli paratroopers' attempt to capture him.[42] For Israel, however, thirty-one dead and missing was a heavy loss, and the Israelis also left the field, allowing the Palestinians to claim that Israel yielded the battlefield in the face of stiff resistance. Even though the Jordanian Army deserved most of the credit, the Palestinians paraded destroyed Israeli tanks through the streets.

Karameh came to symbolize defiance and, as its name suggests, dignity. "For the Palestinian masses, jeered at and humiliated for decades, the Karameh victory gave rise to an immense pride and hope," recalled Abu Iyad. "By the thousands, by the tens of thousands, young and old flocked to join Fatah."[43] Throughout the diaspora, in PLO-run schools in refugee camps, the Battle of Karameh became a staple of the curriculum.[44] In Jordan the Palestinian political position became even stronger. Following the Israeli raid King Hussein declared, "We are all *fedayeen*."[45] One theory claims that Arafat's personal security unit, Force 17, was named after the heroic death of seventeen Palestinian fighters at Karameh. Because of Fatah's skillful propaganda, the military defeat was far more useful to their cause than tactical successes that did not make the headlines; this was a pattern for this conflict, where perception was often more important than reality.

With this swell in recruits Fatah and other groups launched attack after attack across the border, and this constant action in turn brought in more fighters. Palestinians claim the number of raids went from twelve per month in 1967 to sixty-two per month in 1968 and up to 279 per month in the beginning of 1970. Arafat insisted that "people aren't attracted to speeches but to bullets."[46] This militant attitude helped him and Fatah wrest the PLO from the hands of Shuqayri and others who took their guidance only from Arab capitals. Control of the PLO, in turn, would help Arafat cement his dominance in Fatah and in the Palestinian movement.

Hijackings and Catastrophe

In 1968, the same year that Palestinian fedayeen and Jordanian forces battled Israel at Karameh, the world saw a new form of Palestinian terrorism that quickly became synonymous with the struggle: airline hijackings. From 1968 to 1976 Palestinian groups hijacked sixteen airplanes and attacked thirty-three aviation targets, such as the El Al offices.[47] Far more than the much bloodier cross-border raids and retaliations, the hijackings would transfix the world and shape attitudes toward the Israeli-Arab dispute.

The Popular Front for the Liberation of Palestine, not Fatah, was often the key mover in these hijackings. In addition to its hatred of Israel and desire to put the Palestinian cause on the political map, rivalry with Fatah drove the PFLP. The group's leftist predecessors had hitched their star to Nasser, but his humiliation in 1967, and the leftists' seeming passivity compared with Fatah, discredited them. They needed to act.

Moreover the PFLP saw Fatah's cross-border approach as a disaster. Israel had put up barriers along the borders with Jordan and Lebanon, mined potential crossing points, installed floodlights, and established a vast intelligence network to detect potential infiltrators. Palestinian organizations lost thousands of activists, and Israel remained unbowed. "[T]rying to get men and weapons across the Jordan is a waste of time and effort," noted the PFLP's operational mastermind, Wadi Haddad. "This is a particular animal, the IDF; we cannot fight it plane for plane, tank for tank, soldier for soldier."[48]

Haddad had a point. IDF records showed that terrorist and guerrilla incidents peaked in 1968, with 1,480 attempts on Israelis by cross-border fire, by planting bombs, and by operatives sent to blow up the Israeli infrastructure. This number declined to 1,373 in 1969 and 1,280 in 1970. In 1971 it would plummet to 533, falling even further, to 173, in 1972, a fraction of the figure only a few years earlier.[49] Over time these sacrifices generated little media attention, which allowed the Palestinian cause to wither.

Even more than Fatah's members, PFLP recruits were idealists. The terrorism scholar Bruce Hoffman observes that this is not unusual; terrorists see themselves as altruists. George Habash was a doctor who served the poor and the elderly, often refusing payment; in contrast to Fatah, PFLP members claimed they did not receive a salary and lived frugally. Also setting the PFLP apart from Fatah, the leftist group invested tremendous resources in training and recruiting the best. Their operational leader, Wadi Haddad, chose candidates who were smart and persistent and had physical stamina. They learned the security procedures at different airports, the laws of each country in case they were caught, and how to fire guns in confined spaces, such as the interior of an airplane, and they even insisted that PFLP members learn Hebrew.[50] Haddad recruited engineers and chemists who developed new explosive technologies so he could hide bombs among ordinary objects such as religious icons and Chianti bottles. He also recognized the skill of Israeli intelligence and regularly suspended operations when he saw even a hint that the plot had been compromised.

For Israeli intelligence, smaller groups like the PFLP were tough targets. The PFLP was composed of "professionals . . . tough people," as one senior intelligence official related to me. They had better training, doctrine, organization, and recruitment. They even studied Israeli interrogation methods and prepared their people for what would come. The former Mossad chief Shabtai Shavit told me that Fatah, in contrast, "was never hard to penetrate."

The PFLP's first operation, the 1968 hijacking of an El Al airplane it diverted to Algiers, blindsided Israel. The PFLP justified El Al as a military target because retired Israeli Air Force pilots flew the planes, and the PFLP claimed it transported ammunition and troops.[51]

The dramatic success encouraged the PFLP to do more hijackings. In 1969, under the leadership of Leila Khaled, a PFLP cell hijacked a TWA flight from Los Angeles bound for Tel Aviv. Khaled—charismatic, articulate, attractive, and (unusually for a Palestinian terrorist) female—soon became a legend in revolutionary circles. When she was four her family had fled Haifa in the 1948 war. She saw the city twenty-one years later, from the air only, when she briefly had the hijacked plane flown over Israel to see the land of her birth (and, in so doing, score propaganda points) before diverting it to Damascus and giving Syria control of the hostages.[52] Syria allowed the non-Israeli passengers to leave but kept two Israelis, releasing them only several months later, after Israel freed several captive Egyptian soldiers.

For the PFLP anything linked to Israel was a target for attack, including hospitals and civilian sites. On February 21, 1970, the PFLP bombed Swissair Flight 330 en route to Israel; the crew tried to make an emergency landing with the wounded aircraft, but an electrical failure resulting from the bomb damage proved fatal. Forty-seven people died, among them fifteen Israelis. World governments were slow to improve security, Khaled recalled: "There were no security measures like now. It was just very easy to go . . . no searching, nothing . . . you just show your passport and pass by."[53]

To make matters harder for Israel, the PFLP began to cooperate with non-Arab groups, both out of revolutionary solidarity and to make their own operations more successful. They trained the infamous Andreas Baader and Ulrika Meinhof, founders of West Germany's Red Army Faction, and individuals linked to Western European groups like Italy's Red Brigades. These connections paid off: in 1969 Baader, Meinhof, and the PFLP collaborated to attack the El Al office in West Berlin. Perhaps the most important connection was with the Japanese Red Army, whose operatives' non-Arab looks made it far easier for them to pass through security. In a brutal attack three Japanese Red Army terrorists working with the PFLP killed twenty-six people when they struck at Ben Gurion Airport on May 30, 1972.

The PFLP mind-set was loosely inspired by revolutionary movements of the time. Habash declared that the Palestinians wanted a "Vietnam

War" in the whole Arab world. "Revolutionary forces [in Arab countries would] rise to our side," he claimed, and in so doing overthrow conservative Arab regimes as well as fight the Zionists.[54] As his words suggest, the PFLP was long on dreams but short on practical plans.

Over time the PFLP focused on freeing captured operatives. When several of Haddad's and the Japanese Red Army's operatives were caught after an attack on a Shell refinery in Singapore and imprisoned in Japan, Haddad's people seized Japan's embassy in Kuwait, forcing Japan to free the captured terrorists.

At first El Al pilots were told to meet a hijacker's demands, but that quickly changed. "If an eighty-year-old woman had pointed a gun on me and demanded that I land in her son-in-law's garden in Algeria, I would have complied," is how one pilot described the initial policy.[55] After the hijackings began, Israel ended this policy of cooperation and put sky marshals on airplanes, introduced rigorous passenger searches and baggage screening, and trained pilots to disrupt a hijacking. Shin Bet also put in place strict passenger and cargo inspection rules for airplanes seeking to travel to or from Israel. At the airports Israelis installed metal detectors, security cameras, X-ray machines, and checkpoints outside terminals, most of which quickly became standard in the West. Israeli embassies became fortresses.

Perhaps the most famous and certainly most consequential PFLP action began on September 6, 1970, when the group hijacked three planes and diverted them to Dawson's Field, a former British airbase, in Jordan. Haddad wanted the Dawson's Field operation to embarrass the Jordanian government, and he also hoped it would lead to the release of prisoners. At the very least he hoped the attack would attract attention to the Palestinian cause and that Israel would strike back hard enough to halt any progress toward a peace deal. Israel's threat to retaliate against Jordan and other regimes that hosted Palestinian militants was, in this case, an incentive for Haddad.

The first two PFLP hijackings, of Swissair and TWA airplanes flying from Europe to New York, went off without a hitch. The third attempt was against an Israeli target, El Al Flight 219, and new Israeli defensive measures foiled the hijackers. Israeli security had turned away two men who were part of a four-person team trying to hijack the El Al flight, correctly identifying them as suspicious. The two remaining operatives, Leila Khaled, who had had plastic surgery to avoid detection, and Patrick Arguello, successfully boarded the plane and tried to continue the operation. Arguello was a left-wing Nicaraguan American doctor who had gone abroad to look for supporters to help with the Nicaraguan Revolution and came into the PFLP's orbit. Khaled and Arguello brandished guns and grenades and tried to take control of the plane. However, the Israeli pilot, operating under the new policy of noncooperation, plunged the plane into a nose-dive. When the terrorists stumbled, a passenger hit Arguello with a whisky bottle. He still managed to shoot and wound one passenger, but an Israeli sky marshal onboard the plane shot and killed him. Other passengers jumped Khaled. The plane made an emergency landing in London, where Khaled was taken into custody.[56]

The two terrorists whom El Al security turned away then casually hijacked another, less vigilant flight (Pan Am Flight 93) and eventually brought it to Dawson's Field. To free Leila Khaled from Britain's clutches, a PFLP sympathizer hijacked yet another plane, a British airliner, and brought it to Dawson's Field; now there were four planes on the ground.

After they all landed, the PFLP let most of the hostages go but kept the Jewish passengers and the flight crews, fifty-six people in all. It later blew up the empty planes as part of a television spectacle. The PFLP operated with an almost contemptuous attitude toward the Jordanian government, highlighting King Hussein's impotence. In the face of this pressure several European governments surrendered hostages, including Khaled and several other PFLP members. It was another public relations coup for the group.

While the hijackings certainly riveted world attention, the PFLP's efforts to "educate" its hostages on its political struggle met with mixed success. Bassam Abu-Sharif, the PFLP spokesman at the time, recalls trying to convince a hostage that they were not in Africa, as the hostage thought. When Abu-Sharif continued with an explanation of the situation, the hostage thought he was talking about Pakistan, not Palestine.[57]

Despite the spectacular nature of the operation, Dawson's Field was a disaster for the Palestinian cause, worsening relations between Palestinian militants and Jordan's King Hussein at a crucial time. The PFLP had gravely overestimated its own strength and underestimated the resolve of Jordan's King Hussein. As with other Arab regimes, the loss in 1967 had dealt a severe blow to the Jordanian regime's prestige. The already large Palestinian refugee population in Jordan swelled as more than 280,000 more refugees came from the West Bank.[58] To mollify critics King Hussein had released jailed Palestinian militants, and Abu Iyad recalled, "He closed his eyes to bases we were establishing along the Jordan River to serve as launching points for the fedayeen."[59] In Palestinian refugee camps Fatah and other militant groups ruled supreme.

At first, as happened at Karameh, the Jordanian Army often supported the Palestinians. King Hussein was particularly reluctant to crack down on cross-border raids because he did not want to jeopardize his support in the West Bank, which he hoped to rule again. But the Palestinians quickly wore out their welcome. Fedayeen established roadblocks in Amman to extort money from merchants. They even attacked police stations to free jailed comrades.[60] By flouting Jordanian laws, leftist Palestinian groups such as the PFLP openly challenged the Jordanian regime's legitimacy and increasingly its sovereignty. In June 1970 PFLP operatives took over the Intercontinental Hotel in Amman, seizing foreign visitors and reporters. The group demanded, successfully, that the Jordanian regime release Palestinian prisoners and remove the head of the army, whom they saw as anti-Palestinian. King Hussein's attempts to placate the guerrillas—he even offered Arafat the position of prime minister, according to some reports—simply emboldened them further. One senior Fatah figure recalls, "We felt there was nobody who could harm us in Jordan."[61]

As in the 1950s Israel once again attacked sites in Jordan to push the regime to crack down on militants, and by 1970 Israeli operations had displaced tens of thousands. Yitzhak Rabin, who was chief of staff, described Israeli attacks on Jordan as trying "to make it clear to Jordan, and to the population collaborating with Fatah, and to Fatah members themselves, that as long as this side of the border will not be quiet, no quiet will prevail on the other side."[62]

On September 1, 1970, militants attacked King Hussein's motorcade in an unsuccessful attempt to assassinate him. Less than one week later the PFLP began the Dawson's Field operation, where they declared that the Jordanian government could not stop them. It proved to be the last provocation Hussein would endure. On September 15 he told the Nixon administration that he was ready to destroy the Palestinian militant presence in his country. The Jordanian government declared martial law and began to shell Palestinian refugee camps.

A series of operations, known as "Black September" for the month they began in 1970 and lasting through much of 1971, led to the destruction of the Palestinian militant presence in Jordan. The fighting was brutal; Jordan even requested American military intervention when it looked as if Syria might intervene on behalf of the fedayeen.[63] In all perhaps three thousand Palestinians died (some place the totals much higher), ten thousand were wounded, and thousands were taken to prison. Palestinians also claim that Jordan tortured, mutilated, and executed their leaders. In 1971 some seventy Palestinians chose to cross the Jordan River and surrender to Israel rather than face Jordanian justice, a sign of just how desperate the fedayeen were.

Palestinian groups had dreams of a mass uprising, but they did not have a military infrastructure in place to resist the tanks and organized infantry of the Jordanian Army. "We were totally unprepared," Abu Iyad later commented.[64] Recriminations followed between groups and within them. Wadi Haddad, the mastermind behind the hijackings that sparked the crackdown, was often singled out. The PFLP even agreed to stop hijacking operations and eventually moved to halt international operations, causing a fissure within the organization and Haddad's departure.

After Black September, cross-border attacks from Jordan plummeted, and much of the Palestinian militant cadre would move to Lebanon. Europe became another battleground. In 1973 Haddad's group tried unsuccessfully to assassinate Lord Joseph Sieff, the head of the famous department store Marks and Spencer, who was also a supporter of Israel. In 1975 it hit a London branch of an Israeli bank. George Habash, the PFLP head, justified these attacks in the name of publicity. "To kill a Jew far from the battlefield has more effect than killing a 100 of them in battle; it attracts more attention. And when we set fire to a store in London those few flames are worth the burning down of two kibbutzim. Because we force people to ask what is going on." He added, "World opinion has never been either with us or against us; it has just kept on ignoring us."[65] As Habash intended, the PFLP's attacks changed this: the Palestinians would no longer be ignored.

The Black September Organization

The PFLP's use of international terrorism created a dilemma for Fatah and Arafat.[66] Though Fatah was making political gains despite its losses on the ground, terrorism lessened support for his movement in America and Europe and in many Arab capitals. At the same time terrorism could be used to exact revenge on unfriendly regimes and rival countries, and it focused world attention on the Palestinian cause. Arafat did not want to surrender this trump card. Perhaps most important, if Arafat abandoned terrorism completely in favor of cross-border raids, he risked being out-flanked in the vital realm of media attention by more radical groups that were continuing international terrorist attacks.

The result was Arafat's ploy to have his cake and eat it too. The PLO moved away from terrorism publicly but, at the same time, created the Black September Organization in 1971. The BSO took its name from the month in 1970 when Jordan cracked down on the Palestinians. Under the leadership of Ali Hassan Salameh, the BSO was charged with carrying out high-profile international attacks. On November 28, 1971, the group conducted its first operation, gunning down Wasfi Tal in a hotel in Egypt. Wasfi Tal had served as Jordan's prime minister and defense minister during the suppression of the Palestinian revolt there. After shooting him, one assassin kneeled and lapped up Tal's blood, a grisly image meant to convey the implacability of the new group.

Although Arafat and other Fatah leaders publicly claimed ignorance of the BSO, the CIA quickly learned that it was run by Fatah's intelligence organization, that it used "Fatah funds, facilities, and personnel," and that "for all intents and purposes, no significant distinction now can be made between the BSO and Fatah."[67] The BSO had perhaps three hundred to five hundred full-time members, and it struck primarily at Jordanian and Israeli targets.

On May 8, 1972, the BSO hijacked a plane from the Belgian national airline, Sabena, and landed it at Tel Aviv's airport. The four hijackers demanded the release of more than three hundred Palestinian prisoners.

Israel had no intention of granting their release—it had learned after the 1968 El Al hijacking that releasing hostages begets more hostage-taking attempts—but stretched out negotiations so that its top special forces unit, Sayeret Matkal, could prepare a rescue mission. Disguised as flight technicians, Israeli commandos surprised the hijackers, killing two and wounding the two others; one hostage was also killed.[68] Though the Red Cross had acceded to the hijackers' demand to search the supposed mechanics, the commandos had hidden their weapons in toolboxes, which they then retrieved after the search. Future prime minister Ehud Barak led the rescue, and another future prime minister, Benjamin Netanyahu, was also on the team.

Success against the BSO would be short-lived. The group's seizure of Israeli athletes at the 1972 Munich Olympics ranked as the most infamous terrorist attack ever until the al-Qa'ida attacks of September 11, 2001. For Munich, Black September supposedly chose fifty young fedayeen, all from refugee families with relatives in Israeli jails, and then winnowed the numbers down with a rigorous training and selection process. Posing as Brazilians, two of the team arrived early in Munich to scout out the territory. One got a job as a waiter in an Olympic village cafeteria. A member of the Israeli delegation even helped show the scouts around the Israeli housing facility.[69] Another team member, posing as a businessman, smuggled weapons in. Increased border security measures before the Olympics almost led to the plot's early demise: a customs inspector opened one of the supposed businessman's trunks, which was filled with women's clothes, but did not open the other two that had weapons packed inside. In general, however, security at the games was lax, a deliberate measure on the part of the German government, which sought to label the 1972 games "the Carefree Games," contrasting it with the 1936 Olympics in Berlin that Hitler used to glorify the Nazi state.

Before the operation commenced, one of the leaders told the team, "From now on, consider yourself dead. As killed in action for the Palestinian cause."[70] The team scaled the fence to the Olympic village, with unwitting help from some American athletes who had slipped out for some late-night drinking. When the attackers entered the Israeli facility Yossef Gutfreund, a weightlifting judge who weighed almost three hundred pounds, saw the barrels of several weapons and threw his bulky frame against the door while shouting a warning. An Israeli coach fled to safety before the BSO team pushed through the door. Another potential hostage escaped when the wrestling coach Moshe Weinberg tried to seize the gun of one of the terrorists.

After the BSO team seized the hostages, chaos ensued. The terrorists demanded the release of more than two hundred prisoners in Israeli jails as well as the German terrorists Andreas Baader and Ulrike Meinhof. Haphazard negotiations followed, accompanied by farcical German attempts at counterterrorism. Early in the crisis the Germans tried to infiltrate a police team into the building, but this move was foiled because they did not realize TV cameras were broadcasting the police movements live.

Bungling continued, turning farce into tragedy. The German government allowed the terrorists to go to the airport, supposedly to fly to Cairo. In reality Germany planned to storm the terrorists and free the hostages. From the start things went wrong. Some of the German assault team abandoned the rescue mission on their own, without asking for orders. German armored personnel carriers vital to the operation got stuck in traffic. The sharpshooters lacked basic equipment, such as two-way radios. Most critically the Germans deployed only five sharp-shooters to take out eight terrorists, making it impossible to make a quick, clean kill simultaneously. Making this worse, several of the five were not positioned correctly, which prevented them from shooting effectively.[71]

Inevitably some of the gunmen survived the sharpshooters, and a shootout ensued. One terrorist broke free and threw a grenade into a helicopter where some of the athletes were held, blowing it up and killing those aboard. Another terrorist jumped aboard another chopper and machine-gunned the remaining hostages. Eleven Israelis and one German police officer died, along with five of the terrorists. Though privately critical of the Germans' lack of professionalism, Prime Minister Golda Meir made a point of publicly thanking Germany for its willingness to "employ force" to fight terrorism.[72]

Munich failed in its ostensible purpose of forcing Israel to release Palestinian prisoners. Yet, as was so often the case, the primary goal of the terrorists was to generate publicity. The "Will of the Munich Guerrillas," a testament supposedly issued by the attackers before the operation, explained that the operation was "for the world to understand and realize the ugly role played by the Zionist occupation of [their] country."[73] And, as Abu Iyad claimed, "world opinion was forced to take note of the Palestinian drama."[74]

Only two years later Arafat would address the UN General Assembly, dressed in guerrilla fatigues and wearing an (empty) holster, declaring to a standing ovation, "Today I have come bearing an olive branch and a freedom fighter's gun. Do not let the olive branch fall from my hand." At the 1974 Arab summit in Rabat Arafat persuaded the Arab world to grant the PLO the status of being the "sole, legitimate representative" of the Palestinians. The European left steadily embraced the cause of the Palestinians and the romance of the fedayeen; Arafat was hailed as "the Palestinian 'Che'" and the Palestinians compared favorably to the Viet Cong. By the decade's end the PLO would enjoy more diplomatic recognition than the state of Israel.[75]

The BSO continued to operate after Munich. Its operatives struck the Israeli embassy in Bangkok on December 28, 1972, and other PLO operatives tried to assassinate Golda Meir when she visited the pope in Rome. The BSO even attacked Western targets, which Fatah had avoided in the past. In 1973 the group seized the Saudi embassy in Khartoum, taking ten diplomats hostage and later killing three of them, including the American ambassador Cleo Noel. Arafat disclaimed responsibility and even tried to play the role of mediator with the BSO, even though, according to the U.S. Department of State, "the Khartoum operation was planned and carried out with the full knowledge and personal approval of Yasir Arafat."[76] In August 1973 two BSO operatives attacked passengers in Athens boarding a flight to New York (the terrorists thought they were Jews going to Israel), killing five, including three Americans. Less than a year later the Greek government freed the killers after sympathizers seized a Greek freighter in Karachi and demanded their release. Such bloody operations, and the weak international response, made the United States more willing to turn a blind eye to Israeli revenge attacks.

The Athens airport strike was the last public BSO attack; in 1973 Arafat began the process of dismantling the BSO, in part to assuage Arab governments and because its international operations were damaging the diplomatic progress the PLO had made after Munich. At the same time the PLO also began to walk on the road of compromise, agreeing in 1974 to establish a state in the West Bank and Gaza, albeit supposedly only as a first step toward regaining all of historic Palestine. Fatah's direct involvement in terrorism against non-Israeli targets would cease at this point. However, spectacular terrorist acts, such as the 1976 hijacking of an Air France flight to Entebbe Airport in Uganda, kept alive a strong association between terrorism and the Palestinians, even though the perpetrators were not Fatah members.

Dismantling the BSO proved tricky. As the terrorism expert Bruce Hoffman explains, BSO members were a highly committed elite, and after years of pumping them up to use terrorism, turning them away from violence in the name of political expediency would not wash. The solution for pacifying a ferocious fighter was both obvious and inspired: marriage. PLO leaders found attractive young Palestinian women and invited them to a mixer in Beirut. BSO members who married were given three thousand dollars, a furnished apartment, and a job with the PLO that did not involve violence. If they had a baby they received another five thousand dollars. Quickly the newly married lions became lambs; the PLO would test them by asking them to go abroad on a peaceful mission, but the once-fearless terrorists would refuse, fearing that they would be arrested and leave their families bereft.[77]

As is usually the case, the shift away from extremism produced a splinter movement. In this case the new group was the Fatah Revolutionary Council, better know as the Abu Nidal Organization (ANO) after the nom de guerre of its leader, Sabri al-Banna.[78] With the support of Iraqi President Saddam Hussein, Abu Nidal took over the PLO infrastructure in Iraq and created a new organization, which warred as much against the PLO as it did other groups. Intelligence services found it hard to penetrate the ANO because it recruited largely from within certain families, and Abu Nidal would brutally punish an entire family if one member defected.

In the end Abu Nidal's paranoia would prove fatal for the ANO. A concerted CIA campaign against the group in the late 1980s yielded only a few genuine intelligence penetrations, but the terrorist leader became convinced his organization was riddled with spies. In 1987 he began a brutal purge, machine-gunning hundreds of operatives and burying others alive. The group was effectively defunct by the early 1990s and Abu Nidal eventually found refuge in Baghdad. In 2002, when the United States began to beat the drum of war against Iraq,[79] Saddam Hussein had Abu Nidal killed in what was probably a desperate attempt to clean his résumé of ties to terrorism.

During the 1980s PLO groups continued international terrorist attacks, primarily against Israeli and U.S. targets. In a particularly horrific attack, on October 8, 1985, terrorists from the Palestine Liberation Front, a group affiliated with the PLO, seized the passenger ship *Achille Lauro* after passing themselves off as passengers. The team initially tried to divert the ship to Syria, which, probably fearing Israeli retaliation and the opprobrium associated with high-profile terrorism, refused to accept them. They then shot Leon Klinghoffer, a sixty-nine-year-old American Jew who was wheelchair-bound, and pushed him overboard. The head of the PLF then persuaded the four hijackers to free the hostages and leave the ship in Egypt. The terrorists abandoned the ship after they were promised safe conduct to Tunis, but on their flight to Tunis U.S. Navy planes forced their airplane to land at a NATO base in Sicily and surrounded it. Italy eventually tried the terrorists, though several were freed on parole after only a few years in jail. The court justified rather lenient sentences for the terrorists because they were "soldiers fighting for ideals."[80]

Terrorism helped invigorate the Palestinian national movement by creating heroes and strengthening Palestinian identity and the Palestinians' right to speak for themselves in their struggle against Israel. The price of terrorism, however, was considerable. Operationally terrorism led to Israeli responses that cost the PLO its bases in Jordan and later Lebanon. Internationally terrorism harmed the legitimacy of the Palestinian cause while strengthening that of Israel. Among Americans in particular, media images of brutal attacks on children and old people tainted the Palestinian struggle.

A Cause Disunited

No single cause united the Arab people more than their desire for justice for the Palestinians. Yet no single cause created as much finger-pointing, strife, and outright violence between Arabs. Palestinians regularly fought one another, and Arab states exploited these rivalries for their own purposes.

After the 1967 War and the discrediting of the old-line PLO leadership, new groups emerged, old groups faded away or merged with others, and many of the groups coexisted in a state of constant conflict. The Popular Front for the Liberation of Palestine, for example, was born in December 1967 after several preexisting left-wing groups merged under the leadership of George Habash. Almost immediately after its formation, Ahmad Jibril splintered off to form the PFLP General Command (PFLP-GC) and Ahmad Zaarour formed the Palestine Arab Organization. In 1969 Nayef Hawatmeh broke away to form the Marxist-oriented Democratic Front for the Liberation of Palestine (DFLP). In 1972 the PFLP again split, when the head of its terrorist operations, Wadi Haddad, seceded from the group. When he died in 1978, probably at the hands of the Mossad, the smaller group again splintered into two.[81] Making these reorganizations even more bewildering, old friendships and personal animosities often outweighed group identities, leading to cooperation or competition when least expected. To outsiders the Palestinian militant world seemed like an alphabet soup of similar names, similar causes, and bitter rivalries. In terms of size Fatah was always the dominant player, and for most of its history counted as many militants as all the other groups put together.[82]

Often small groups would attack targets to stop Fatah or other groups from moving toward more moderate positions. The violence often led to Israeli reprisals, which in turn led more moderate elements of Fatah and other groups to back away from even a hint of negotiations. Smaller groups also were often responsible for some of the most horrific terrorist attacks. In 1974 three DFLP terrorists infiltrated Israel from Lebanon. They first attacked a passing van, killing a female passenger and mortally wounding another (both Israeli Arabs). The terrorists then moved on to the town of Ma'alot, where they immediately killed Yosef and Fortuna Cohen (pregnant at the time) and their young son Eliahu. They continued to a nearby elementary school and took eighty-five students and four adults hostage. They threatened to blow up the school unless Israel released prisoners. Israel's elite Sayeret Matkal army unit tried to rescue the hostages. The operation faltered from the start, when a sniper only wounded Ziad Rahim, the cell's leader, allowing him to return fire at the advancing soldiers and then run back to the classrooms. Other members of the rescue team accidentally went to the wrong floor. In the chaos Rahim opened fire on the children and threw a grenade into the small classroom. Only after his weapon jammed were the commandos able to shoot him.[83] Twenty-five Israeli children and teachers died.

Arab states also set the cause back. Still stinging from the 1967 debacle, Egypt's military chief, Gen. Ali Amir, instructed all Arab governments to crush Fatah to avoid giving "Israel an excuse to attack the Arab countries." Some factions within the Syrian regime at first aided Fatah, but when a new faction, led by Hafez al-Asad, came to power they briefly imprisoned Arafat.[84] Syria also tried to convince Fatah to attack from the West Bank so Jordan would bear the brunt of any retaliation. In 1968 the Syrian regime arrested several PFLP leaders, including Habash, and shut down most of the PFLP facilities, fearing not only Israeli reprisals but also that the group was working with antiregime Syrian forces. It was a harbinger that Fatah's first casualty on an anti-Israel raid came from Jordanian bullets; after an infiltrator had escaped Israel he was shot on returning to Jordan.[85]

Yet even as Arab states repressed fedayeen activity at home, they continued to pour money into these groups, using them to harass Israel and foster their rivalry with one another. Algeria, Fatah's first base, provided arms and training after the 1967 War. Saudi Arabia was immensely helpful, deducting money from the wages of the huge Palestinian workforce in the kingdom and offering matching funds to finance Fatah. King Faisal and other Saudi leaders genuinely supported the Palestinians, but they also coldly calculated that an independent Fatah was more in the kingdom's interest than one controlled by Egypt, Syria, or another rival. Every Arab government seemed able to break off part of the movement and use it for its own ends. The group al-Saiqa formed with Syrian backing, and Iraq helped create the Arab Liberation Front and closed down Fatah's office in Baghdad to help form the Abu Nidal Organization. Iraq, Libya, and South Yemen worked with the DFLP, and Syria aided the PFLP-GC. The PFLP itself often enjoyed support from these states as well.[86] This aid allowed each Arab state a voice in the Palestinian struggle against Israel, and it served as a hedge to ensure that the Palestinian issue did not cause unrest at home.

Abu Iyad bitterly expressed how stunned he and other Palestinians were when they first encountered these raw power politics: "We thought, for example, that Egypt would be with us forever; that Syria would never, not even briefly, side with the Christian right against us in Lebanon. We never imagined that Iraq, whatever our political differences, would stoop to having our most eminent militants abroad assassinated!"[87]

Politically these internal and external rivalries were a nightmare for Fatah and the PLO. As intended, attacks like those of the DFLP at the Ma'alot elementary school struck fear in the hearts of Israelis—but they also convinced Israel not to compromise with the Palestinians. Israel continued to conduct fierce retaliations, often against groups like Fatah rather than just the DFLP. Indeed Fatah could not control the pace or nature of attacks on Israel. Nor did it control whether the movement would target "imperialist" powers like the United States and Europe or continue relations with host states like Jordan. Even more devastating, horrific DFLP attacks like Ma'alot tarnished the PLO as well. Much of the world saw little difference among these Palestinian groups, particularly when Arafat refused to condemn the violence. Abu Iyad lamented that when the Arab Liberation Front or al-Saiqa kidnapped or killed someone from Lebanon, media would denounce the "terrorism of the Palestinians" rather than recognize that those responsible were only a minority faction, and one backed by a state often hostile to Fatah. Yet the PLO found it hard to denounce these groups because it did not want to break openly with Syria or Iraq, nor did they wish to be seen as a tool of Israel or the West. Abu Iyad is correct in his conclusion that the small groups "practically strangled" the Palestinian cause.[88]

Israel Strikes Back

On October 29, 1972, a Black September team hijacked a Lufthansa flight from Beirut. Faced with the terrorists' demand that they would blow up the plane if Germany did not release "the three heroes" held in jail after the Munich massacre, Germany quickly caved. "I was literally physically sickened [by the decision]," Prime Minister Golda Meir would later recall.[89]

Outraged, she demanded that the Mossad "send forth the boys."[90] So began Operation Wrath of God, a campaign to assassinate BSO and PLO operatives involved in the Munich massacre. Depicted in Steven Spielberg's blockbuster *Munich*, Wrath of God marked a return to the offensive for Israel: it would hunt down terrorists around the world. Retaliation went beyond punishing the Munich attackers. Israel conducted high-profile raids in Lebanon and staged a dramatic and heroic hostage-rescue mission deep into faraway Uganda. These aggressive, imaginative, and lethal operations gave Israel and in particular the Mossad and the IDF's elite military units the larger-than-life reputation they still enjoy in many quarters today.

Israeli leaders felt compelled to respond aggressively. And despite statements that justified the strikes as a way to deter future attacks and disrupt existing groups, revenge played an important role as well. Attacks like Munich and Ma'alot outraged Israelis, and they pushed their government to respond in kind. Polls taken in the 1970s showed terrorism to be a dominant concern among Israelis. Many supported harsh measures like house demolitions, cross-border strikes, and targeted killings, and overwhelming majorities saw terrorism as a reason not to recognize the PLO.[91] After Munich the influential and slightly left-wing newspaper *Haaretz* even called on the government to form assassination squads "that were not bound by the historical limitations of various authorities."[92]

Wrath of God marked the first time Israel used targeted killings as a campaign rather than simply a one-time operation against a particular individual. "We decided we had to go after the nerve centers and the perpetrators themselves," says Aharon Yariv, a former head of Israeli military intelligence.[93] To oversee the operation Prime Minister Meir formed and headed Committee X, which, after consulting with the attorney general, approved the Mossad's list of potential names. In all the Committee agreed to kill more than twenty suspected terrorists. In theory the Mossad was using the killings to instill fear and deter future attacks—to terrorize the terrorists—but in reality revenge often drove the operations. As Yariv later noted, "We went back to the old biblical rule of an eye for an eye."[94]

Israel struck first in Rome in 1972, killing Abdel Wael Zwaiter, the PLO representative in Italy, after he returned home from dinner. In the same year a Mossad explosives team put a bomb under the desk of Dr. Mahmud Hamshari, whom Israel believed to be the BSO leader in France. Pretending to be a journalist, a Mossad operative called the house and asked in Arabic, "Is that you, Mr. Hamshari?" After confirming his identity, he detonated the bomb and mortally wounded him.[95] The following year Israeli operatives hit suspected BSO terrorists in Cyprus and Lebanon. The Mossad also would call up other suspected BSO and PLO terrorists and tell them the identities of their families and where they went to work: a clear message that it would kill them if they did not desist.[96]

Years later some Israelis would say the Mossad made mistakes. Aaron Klein, the author of a book on Wrath of God, contends that the Mossad's intelligence work on Zwaiter was sloppy and that he may have been the wrong man. He also claims that many of the core BSO Munich team hid out in Eastern European or Arab capitals, beyond Israel's reach. Israel thus hit less important or more political types who were unprotected in Europe simply because they were within reach. One senior Mossad officer told Klein, "Our blood was boiling. When there was information implicating someone, we didn't inspect it with a magnifying glass."[97] The PLO magnified the importance of these targets in order to praise them as martyrs, furthering the image of Mossad omniscience.

Long after the Munich attack, and long after Black September disbanded, Israel continued to hunt the operatives. On July 21, 1973, Israel tried to kill the BSO leader and head of Fatah security Ali Hassan Salameh, the so-called "Red Prince," in Lillehammer, Norway. Instead of killing Salameh, however, they gunned down Ahmed Bouchiki, an innocent Moroccan waiter. The Lillehammer hit exhibited sloppy tradecraft at all levels, with Mossad operatives ignoring several clues that Bouchiki was not their man. Turning tragedy into farce, the Mossad operatives bungled the escape and enraged not only Norway but also Canada, whose passports they used. Some of the Mossad operatives quickly caved under questioning, giving up details of Mossad operations throughout Europe. Facing international outrage and embarrassment at home, Meir called off the hunt for the BSO. Only in 1996 would Israel express regret for the mistake and offer compensation to Bouchiki's family.

On January 22, 1979, the Mossad finally caught up with Ali Hassan Salameh in Beirut. The Mossad claimed Salameh was the BSO leader and responsible for Munich, but several Fatah leaders claim that although he was involved in many terrorist attacks he was not part of the strike on the Olympic team. Salameh's indulgent lifestyle was his undoing: he enjoyed whisky, women, and other pleasures as well as plotting terror. Shortly before his death he took Georgina Rizak, a former Miss Universe, as his second wife. He was an easy target as he traveled from the home of his first wife to his second, with occasional stops at his health club.

In April 1978 a woman with a British passport, presumably a Mossad agent, rented an apartment overlooking the intersection close to the apartment of Salameh's second wife. Salameh regularly visited his mother, another vulnerability, as it enabled the Mossad to plant a bomb along the route he would take. On January 22, 1979, Mossad agents parked a Volkswagen near the intersection, fitting it with sheets of steel that would ensure that when it exploded the blast would go outward. When Salameh's station wagon passed the car, the explosives detonated, mortally wounding him.[98] Four innocent bystanders, including a German nun, also perished in the blast.

Salameh was more than just a terrorist and a playboy. In 1974, when Arafat sought to improve ties with the United States, Fatah and the CIA arranged a nonaggression pact.[99] In the days of horror in Lebanon's civil war in 1975–76 Fatah tried to protect American diplomats in Beirut, often guarding their residences and facilities. The PLO also stopped a Libyan-backed group from attacking the U.S. embassy in Rome. Salameh was one of Arafat's key aides in this effort, and a grateful CIA reportedly took him to Walt Disney World as a thank you. Some American observers believe that Israel killed Salameh not only out of revenge, but also to destroy any relationship between the PLO and the United States.[100]

With operations like Wrath of God, a shadow war commenced. Black September would place a spring-activated firing pin in a bomb and enclose it in an envelope mailed to various Israeli official facilities.[101] When the unsuspecting victim opened it and relieved pressure on the bomb's wrapping, the bomb would explode. The Mossad then sent out letter bombs and other booby-trapped objects to Palestinian leaders in Beirut, Algiers, Cairo, Tripoli, Bonn, and Copenhagen. Mossad operatives shot some suspected terrorists, bombed the homes and offices of others, and in general tried to terrify its enemy. In response Black September continued its attacks, killing Baruch Cohen, a Mossad agent, in Madrid, briefly seizing the Israeli embassy in Thailand, and even killing Israel's air force attaché in the United States, Col. Yosef (Joe) Alon.

Entebbe and Thunderbolt

Operation Thunderbolt, better known as the Entebbe Raid, remains legendary in the annals of counterterrorism, and justly so. On June 27, 1976, terrorists from the PFLP splinter lead by Wadi Haddad and two German left-wing sympathizers affiliated with the Red Army Faction seized Air France Flight 139, which had originated in Israel, after it took off from Athens. Security at the Athens airport was poor. In this instance, the metal detector was not even manned.[102]

The hijackers diverted the plane at first to Libya and then to Entebbe Airport in Uganda, a country then controlled by the psychopathic dictator Idi Amin, a man infamous for eating his enemies. The hijackers released all the passengers but the Jews, threatening to kill them if fifty-three terrorists held in five countries (forty in Israel) were not released. One passenger, a concentration camp survivor, remembered, "I felt myself back 32 years when I saw German officers and saw the waving guns. I imagined the shuffling lines of prisoners and the harsh cries of 'Jews to the right.'" As the news leaked out that the terrorists held only the Jewish passengers, Israeli newspapers printed the German word *Selektion* as their headline, a painful word for Jews. The heroic Capt. Michel Bacos and his crew chose to remain behind as prisoners, leaving 106 in total. (Air France would later reprimand and temporarily suspend Captain Bacos for not leaving with the other hostages.)[103] One passenger later recalled, "We were trapped in their hands like a mouse in a cat's paws."[104]

The freed non-Jewish hostages, however, provided the Mossad with a trove of vital information. One of them was a retired French paratroop officer, who had meticulously observed and then described the building structure, the terrorists' appearances, and other information vital for the rescue attempt. Unbeknown to the hijackers, an Israeli firm had constructed the building where the hostages were held; they provided the blueprints to the Mossad. Other crucial information came from a Mossad operative who rented a plane in Kenya. He flew it to Entebbe and radioed the tower that a malfunction was forcing him to stay in the air; he photographed all the while, the Ugandans suspecting nothing.[105] The Israeli government negotiated with the hijackers in a bid to stall for time while Israeli commandos prepared for the rescue.

In a stunning raid elite Israeli fighters surreptitiously infiltrated Uganda and surprised the Ugandan forces and the hijackers. One team stormed the airport building, killing the seven hijackers along with forty-five Ugandan soldiers. Two hostages died in the assault, as did one of the commandos, Yonatan Netanyahu, the brother of the future prime minister Benjamin Netanyahu and one of the assault's leaders. A third hostage, seventy-five-year-old Dora Block, had earlier been hospitalized after choking on a piece of meat; Amin's secret police later dragged her screaming from her hospital bed, and she was never seen alive again. The fighters herded the hostages into waiting planes and quickly flew them home to safety.

In another stunning operation Israel eventually caught up with Wadi Haddad, the architect of Entebbe and other dramatic hijackings. According to Ami Pedahzur, an expert on Israeli intelligence, Israel had almost killed Haddad in Beirut, so he fled to Iraq. Baghdad was far from Israel, and the Iraqi police state made it hard for anyone to get in or out unnoticed. Haddad, however, loved fine chocolates, a delicacy rare in 1970s Iraq. Israel arranged for a Palestinian plant in his own organization to deliver him fine Belgian chocolates coated with poison, guessing that Haddad would jealously guard the trove before devouring it. Haddad fell sick and died in agony in an East German hospital. Israel justified killing Haddad not only as revenge, but also because he planned attacks; killing him today prevented terrorism tomorrow.[106]

Israel also attacked other terrorist group leaders when it found the opportunity. On July 15, 1979, Israel caught up with Zuheir Muhsin, who led al-Saiqa, Syria's Palestinian proxy, on the French Riviera. He died mysteriously, and as the former Mossad leader Shabtai Shavit told me, "No one has heard of Saiqa since."

The same mix of revenge, deterrence, and disruption motivated Israel to kill Abu Jihad in Tunis in 1988. Abu Jihad was a top aide to Arafat and for a while commanded Al-'Asifah ("the Storm"), Fatah's military wing. He ran a range of military and terrorist operations, including the 1975 hostage taking at the Savoy Hotel in Tel Aviv that led to the deaths of eight hostages, and a 1978 bus hijacking that killed thirty-eight Israelis, including thirteen children. Abu Jihad also led Fatah's efforts to control the first Intifada, which had broken out in 1987, providing money and other support to Fatah sympathizers in the West Bank and Gaza.

Mossad agents gathered information on the layout of Abu Jihad's home in Tunisia and his daily routine. Israeli commandos led by Moshe (Bogi) Yaalon, who would continue to rise to prominence in the IDF, and then Israeli politics journeyed by sea and landed secretly on the beach, where Mossad operatives met them. Meanwhile Deputy Chief of Staff Ehud Barak, the future prime minister, issued orders from a seaborne operations center.

A commando team sped to Abu Jihad's home in Tunis. The team was efficient and merciless. Two fighters, dressed as women, shot Abu Jihad's bodyguard as he lay sleeping in a car. They then shot a Tunisian maintenance man who had the bad luck to be in the garden. Making their way into the house, the commandos shot Abu Jihad repeatedly at close range while his wife and son looked on. Not willing to bypass intelligence collection as well, the commandos also raided his study, collecting the documents safe before returning to their boats.

Israelis would later question the logic of Abu Jihad's killing. The PLO was moving from bitter foe to potential peace partner, and the loss of a practical and strategic leader like Abu Jihad had costs for Israel too. Israeli writer Yossi Melman, for example, argues, "It is clear to many that his death left Arafat alone at the leadership level of the PLO," a void that would be felt keenly in the years to come.[107]

Israel would conduct many such raids to fight Palestinian groups and would also continue trying to coerce Arab neighbors into cracking down on militant attacks. After Jordan's crackdown on Black September, many of the important raids would occur in Lebanon. For Israel, however, the raids did not do enough, and they tried to oust the PLO from Lebanon in 1982 once and for all. There they did destroy the Palestinian "military option," but this success cost Israel dearly and operations there ultimately proved counterproductive.

CHAPTER III

DEBACLE IN LEBANON (1970s-1993)

ON APRIL 10, 1973, Israeli commandos took boats from Haifa to the Lebanese coast near Beirut, where Mossad agents waited for them. Among the commandos were two women, a blonde and a brunette.[1] Ehud Barak, Israel's future prime minister and the commander of the elite Sayeret Matkal unit at the time, was the brunette, with hand grenades instead of breasts in his bra. "We decided maybe some of us will go like women. It will reduce the suspicions," Barak recalled. "We put everything in place. A wig, and a breast, and everything. And I had my lieutenant Muki Betser, he was kind of a half a head taller than me. And we were a couple."[2] The "couple" even brushed against Lebanese policemen as they walked but attracted no suspicion.

In an operation Israel dubbed Spring of Youth, Israeli commandos sought to kill senior Palestinian leaders who lived in three apartments, two in the same building and one nearby. The commandos split up into three units, while a guard unit waited outside to stop any Lebanese police or Palestinian reinforcements. Barak and his lieutenant, arm in arm, approached the first building like lovers. As they neared, they first shot the PLO building guard with a silencer. The operation had begun.

Barak recalls when the commandos approached the apartment of Kamal Adwan, the PLO's chief of operations. "The moment that they opened the door, the terrorist was there with his Kalashnikov and an AK-47 in his hands," says Barak. "And it was only the split second of hesitation of the terrorist when he sees that it's civilian people that ended up our officer shooting the terrorist and not the other way around." The Israelis shot Adwan fifty-five times while his young daughter stood by. "Glass was being shattered on our heads," she said years later. "And he just fell. And his face was somehow turned like that. And I was telling my brother, 'They're playing cowboys and Indians here.'"[3] During the raid, nearby Lebanese police did try to come to the Palestinians' rescue, leading to a firefight. A Mossad official got on the phone and impersonated a Lebanese police officer in order to divert additional Lebanese police from coming to the scene, telling them that the shooting was simply score-settling among Palestinians. Other Mossad officials claimed to be Lebanese army officials and told Beirut's police chief that the army was investigating the fighting. Thirty minutes after landing the commandos returned to their boats and headed for home.

As the Sayeret Matkal team carried out its mission, a team of paratroopers led by future chief of staff Amnon Lipkin-Shahak struck at Popular Democratic Front for the Liberation of Palestine (which would later drop the "Popular" from its name) headquarters in the Sabra refugee camp near Beirut. Lipkin-Shahak's team met stiffer resistance, but they still left the headquarters a pile of rubble.

Israel lost two soldiers in the raid on the PDFLP headquarters; Palestinian groups lost more in firefights with the commandos, in addition to the leaders the commandos killed. The Israeli forces killed two Lebanese police officers, as well as the wife of one of the terrorists and an Italian woman who lived in the building who had the misfortune to open her door on the apartment landing at the wrong time. Later hundreds of thousands of Lebanese turned out to mourn those killed. Still, the message was clear: terrorists cannot hide.

Lebanon became a battleground after the Palestinian catastrophe in 1970 in Jordan. Israeli pressure had played a role in ending their presence in the Hashemite Kingdom, but Fatah and other Palestinian groups reestablished themselves in Lebanon. Both Israel and the Palestinians found themselves confronting the same problems they had in Jordan. Once again Israel needed to drive the Palestinians out of a base in a neighboring country, while the Palestinians were forced to deal with internal rivalries, Israeli pressure, and inter-Arab competition. This new base proved disastrous for the Palestinian revolutionary cause, for Lebanon, and for Israel.

At first Lebanon seemed an ideal operating base for Fatah and other Palestinian groups—too ideal perhaps. Like Jordan, Syria, and Egypt, Lebanon bordered Israel. But unlike these states, its government was in disarray and its armed forces and intelligence services weak. Palestinian factions, particularly Fatah, inserted themselves into the void, carving out an autonomous area in the south that was quickly dubbed "Fatahland." At the end of 1969 the Lebanese government agreed to the Cairo Accords, which allowed the Palestinian resistance groups, not the government, to control the refugee camps. As a result the camps became a state within a state, with the Palestinians in charge of essential government functions such as employment, justice, and education.[4] The PLO alone had a large, undisciplined paramilitary force of twenty-two thousand to thirty thousand men. Other Palestinian groups, many supported by rival Arab states, also maintained their own forces in an uneasy mix of ostensible cooperation and hidden competition.

From their bases in Lebanon various Palestinian groups launched a series of devastating attacks across the border. Among the most disturbing was the strike several months before Black September, in May 1970, when the PFLP-GC attacked a school bus on the road to Moshav Avivim near the border with Lebanon, killing twelve, including nine children. The PFLP-GC struck again in April 1974, killing eighteen residents (and again nine children) in an apartment building in Kiryat Shemona, also near the border with Lebanon. Just over a month later the DFLP struck Ma'alot, about five miles from the border with Lebanon, killing twenty-one children on a school trip along with five others. In May 1975 Fatah terrorists struck the Savoy Hotel in Tel Aviv and took hostages; eight of the hostages died and three of Israel's special forces were killed in a rescue attempt. These groups and others, such as the BSO, used Lebanon as a base for training terrorists and fighters and for planning worldwide operations—including infamous attacks such as the 1972 Munich Olympics operation.[5]

Now the PLO was able to extend its attacks to northern Israel without leaving Lebanon. Using a mix of rockets, mortars, and small arms fire they harassed Israelis living near the border—before the 1982 Israeli invasion, the PLO shelled Israel over 1,000 times from Lebanon. In response Israel created a six-mile-long "dead zone," clearing trees and shrubs, planting mines, and increasing the border patrol in order to stop infiltration and push the guerrillas farther back into Lebanon. Israel also set up an electronic fence along its border with Lebanon to hinder infiltration. With the dead zone, a mix of defensive measures, and pressure on neighboring regimes, the number of Israeli casualties plummeted.

While Palestinian groups continued to use Lebanon to attack Israel with cross-border raids, terrorist strikes, and rockets, they steadily became enmeshed in Lebanese politics. Under a system that began under French colonial rule, the Maronite Christians played a dominant role in Lebanon. Because Christians were supposedly a majority in Lebanon, they were rewarded with the presidency. And the Maronites, as the largest Christian community, got the top post. A Sunni Muslim would take the less important position of prime minister, and a Shi'a Muslim the even less important post of speaker of Parliament. Other groups, like the Druze and Armenian Christians, also were given slices of the pie. Over time, though Muslims clearly outnumbered Christians and Shi'as outnumbered Sunnis, the system never changed. Many Christians had emigrated, and the ones that remained had a lower birth rate than Muslims.

To preserve their dominance Maronite Christians steadily began to arm and mobilize, and Muslim and leftist groups rose to challenge them. Lebanon became a microcosm of the larger regional political landscape as Marxist and pan-Arab groups overlapped ethnic and sectarian factions. The thousands of Palestinian fighters that arrived from Jordan further undermined the already precarious state. Sunni Muslim Arabs saw the Palestinians as natural allies, as did leftist groups. Moreover, to carve out freedom to operate against Israel the Palestinians resisted the Lebanese state, weakening its authority even more. In 1975 a civil war broke out in Lebanon; it lasted until 1990 and led to well over 150,000 deaths.

A core belief of leftist groups like the PFLP was that the Arab people would be truly liberated only if the old hidebound regimes were thrust out. Many left-leaning Palestinians sided with Lebanese factions against the Maronite Christian leadership as they carried on their war against Israel. With a weak government dominated by pro-Western Christians, Lebanon seemed like an easy plum to pluck. Abu Iyad noted that the "road to Palestine" might go through Junya, a Maronite stronghold.[6]

Yet ideology and operational needs obscured a more fundamental source of the PLO's involvement in Lebanon: corruption. Rashid Khalidi, an American academic, noted "the spectacle of individual Palestinian officials who had grown rich, or had obtained a luxurious apartment, expensive car, and armed bodyguards."[7] In southern sections of the country PLO operatives acted like petty gangsters, extorting money and support from the locals. Pierre Gemayel, a leader of the Maronite Christian community, which saw the Palestinians as a grave threat, declared them the "filthiest of people" and contended, "We offered them a half a loaf and they took the other half."[8] Musa al-Sadr, the charismatic Shi'a leader who founded the group Amal and mobilized much of Lebanon's Shi'a community, was initially sympathetic to the Palestinians. Later his judgment of the PLO was quite harsh: "It is not a revolution. . . . It is a military machine that terrorizes the Arab world."[9] Abu Iyad, pointedly using the passive voice, admits, "Excesses were committed, innocent people were killed."[10]

As the Palestinian groups schemed to expand their power in Lebanon, Israel began to strike at Palestinian targets there in an attempt to disrupt the groups. Such raids in themselves were nothing new. After the 1968 Palestinian attack on an El Al plane in Athens, Israeli commandos raided Beirut and blew up thirteen Arab airplanes in the airport there; the raid had little effect on the Palestinian groups but did much to discredit the government of Lebanon. Major raids such as Spring of Youth continued as the PLO consolidated its presence in Lebanon.

At the same time Israel continued with numerous less spectacular, low-level acts of warfare as they consistently pursued PLO targets along the Israeli-Lebanon border in southern Lebanon. After the bombing of a bus in Jerusalem Israeli artillery units pounded Palestinian strongholds in southern Lebanon, and Israeli aircraft struck suspected Palestinian training bases.[11] At times Israel conducted more massive attacks deep into Lebanon. When the PLO shelled northern Israel in 1981, the Israeli Air Force bombed PLO buildings in Beirut. Several hundred civilians died in the bombings, and Israel was condemned internationally.

These strikes did intimidate some groups, such as Fatah, but the deterrent impact could not overcome the internal rivalries driving many operations. Over time, and as Israeli pressure heated up (particularly before the 1982 Israeli invasion), Palestinian leaders wanted to enforce a truce. However, Fatah and its rivals were engaged in a bitter struggle for mastery of the Palestinian cause, and attacks on Israel served this struggle well. The battle against Israel was secondary to Fatah's desire for control of the Palestinian movement. A failure to strike Israel meant that, over time, Fatah would lose recruits and money to groups that continued attacks. So a temporary pause was possible, but a complete cessation was not.

Israel also tried to make local civilians pay a heavy price for supporting Palestinian militant groups. This policy worked up to a point. Many Shi'as came to loath the Palestinians. They saw them as corrupt and brutal, outsiders who left destruction in their wake. Yet these Shi'as had no ability to force the Palestinians to halt their attacks on Israel. Nor was the Lebanese government able to crack down on the Palestinians. When the Lebanese Army tried to shut down Palestinian activities, it failed. It was simply too weak.

Israel also tried to back the PLO's Maronite Christian rivals in Lebanon. The Christians, like the Israelis, hated the PLO and saw its Arab nationalist agenda as a threat to their hegemony there. Over the years Israel spent perhaps 150 million dollars to support the Maronites and their thuggish militias, particularly the Phalange of Bashir Gemayel. It was a vast sum given Israel's limited budget and the small size of the Lebanese economy. In part because of Israeli money and arms, Bashir Gemayel became the dominant military leader of Lebanon's Christian community. But this community was only one of many, and it could not impose its will on the rest of the country.

The Mossad's promotion of the Maronites prejudiced their intelligence, and as a result they underplayed the role of other communities, particularly the Shi'as. The Maronites had their own agenda, one that went beyond that of their Israeli partners. Israel's allies in the Phalange sought not only to weaken the Palestinians, but also to dominate other Christian groups to ensure their dominance over all of Lebanon. When the Maronites took over the Karantina and Tel al-Za'atar areas in Beirut in 1976, they shelled, shot, or hacked to death thousands of Palestinians, including many civilians who had given themselves up to the militias. The London *Times* captured the horror well: "Dozens of terrified men, woman and children emerged weeping with arms raised from corrugated iron shacks as the Phalangists advance continued. Some carried white flags, but otherwise they brought nothing. . . . They would not be returning to Karantina. As each group of dwellings was evacuated it was systematically set on fire. Then a bulldozer arrived to begin work amid the flames. . . . All around, flames spread, and the sky was blackened by thick smoke. The dead were left in the middle of the streets."[12] This pattern of slaughter and expulsion would be repeated as the civil war continued.

Israel even tolerated a major Syrian military deployment in Lebanon in the hope that Damascus would use its own brand of brutality to end the PLO presence. In 1976, with no small amount of irony, the self-proclaimed socialist champion of Arab nationalism, Damascus, intervened in the Lebanese civil war on the side of the ultraconservative, pro-Western Christians against the PLO and its Sunni Arab allies. Syria feared that the ascendance of radical forces in Lebanon could destabilize Syria itself or lead to a war with Israel—a war that Damascus would lose. By the end of Lebanon's civil war in 1990 Syria had worked with every faction in Lebanon in constant attempts to ensure that it remained the country's powerbroker.

After Syria's intervention began, Israel drew a several-kilometers-long "red line" into the Lebanese side of the border where it would not allow Syrian troops to deploy. True to the law of unintended consequences that constantly plagued Israeli policy in Lebanon, Damascus adhered to the red line, with disastrous results for Israel. Syria, despite cracking down on Palestinians in the Lebanese civil war, did not interfere with their operations along the Lebanese-Israel border. But the situation grew worse in April 1981. Israel shot down two Syrian helicopters to protect the Maronites from a Syrian attack (by this time, Syria was no longer backing the Maronites). In response Syria deployed surface-to-air missiles to stop Israelis from easily overflying Lebanon and, in so doing, enabling Damascus to keep using helicopters to suppress militia groups it opposed in Lebanon. Palestinian groups, however, now enjoyed a Syrian air defense umbrella under which to attack Israel with less fear of reprisal from the Israeli Air Force. As Yitzhak Rabin put it, "Israel's sworn foes found asylum under an Israeli 'deterrent umbrella' intended against the Syrians."[13] For Syria, this balance was fine: the PLO would be contained but would still be a thorn in Israel's side. The result, however, was that Israel was less able to strike at the PLO for fear of escalation into a war with Syria—not the last unintended consequence for Israel in Lebanon.

Operation Litani

The limits of Israel's policies became clear on March 11, 1978, when eleven Palestinian terrorists from Fatah used rubber dinghies to launch a daring raid on Israel. (One of the terrorists' boats capsized, and two of the attackers drowned.) Dalal al-Maghrabi led the raid, establishing her later as a hero for many Palestinians. When they landed on the beach in Israel, they first encountered Gail Rubin, an American nature photographer, whom Maghrabi murdered: "We were worried she'd tell on us."[14] They then seized two buses, transferring all the passengers to one bus. The Israelis attempted to kill the terrorists with grenades when they forced the bus to stop at a roadblock, but the grenades exploded and the bus caught fire. Nine of the terrorists died, as did thirty-five Israelis and one American; seventy-one Israelis were injured. Thirteen of the dead were children. To this day Arab media sources glorify Maghrabi.[15]

The scale of the violence in the so-called Coastal Road massacre, and the deaths of so many children, infuriated the Israeli government. Three days later, in response to the attack, Israel launched its most ambitious military operation in Lebanon yet: Operation Litani. Israel sought to push the PLO back from the Israeli border, but Israeli leaders must have known that the PLO would return as soon as Israeli forces withdrew. In short, the operation was meant to demonstrate strength at home and abroad but had little strategic purpose. Twenty-five thousand IDF troops temporarily penetrated several kilometers into Lebanon to destroy PLO safe areas. Operation Litani resulted in several hundred Lebanese deaths and produced more than 200,000 temporary refugees.[16]

When the IDF left Lebanon it carved out a small border zone and put it under the control of their Lebanese Christian ally Maj. Sa'ad Haddad, whose force later became known as the South Lebanon Army. Israel provided the SLA with money—SLA soldiers received ten times the average pay of Lebanese males living in the same area—and military support.[17] Haddad's forces were often brutal, destroying villages that they believed supported the Palestinians.[18]

It would be more than twenty years before Israel finally quit Lebanon.

In response to the war, the United Nations passed Resolutions 425 and 426, authorizing a UN deployment in Lebanon, and called for a complete Israeli withdrawal. Even by the low standards of UN deployments, the United Nations Interim Force in Lebanon, always referred to as UNIFIL, was useless. UNIFIL did not stop or even try to stop the conflict. It merely recorded violations and, from an Israeli point of view, served as human shields behind which Palestinian (and later Hizballah) attackers could strike.

Operation Litani and UNIFIL did not stop Samir Kuntar, a name that would haunt Israel decades later, when Hizballah claimed him as one of their own. Kuntar was a Druze born in a village on Mount Lebanon and a member of the Palestine Liberation Front. He traced his anger to Israeli raids on Lebanon. "I remember Israel's attack on the Beirut airport," he would later recall. "I stood on my house's porch and watched. I could not forget the flames. I was a small child then. That was the start. They told me, 'You see, these are the Israelis.' Later I started connecting to the Palestinian issue."[19]

On April 22, 1979, Kuntar and three other members of his cell infiltrated Israel by sea. After killing an Israeli police officer, they broke into the Haran family home. The mother, Smadar, and her two-year-old daughter, Yael, hid with a neighbor in a crawlspace, but Kuntar and his followers kidnapped the father, Danny, and his four-year-old daughter, Einat, and tried to bring them back to their boat. "Our whole objective was to take hostages to Lebanon," Kuntar would later claim at his trial.[20] Encountering IDF soldiers blocking their way, Kuntar shot Danny Haran and bashed Einat's skull against a rock with his rifle butt.[21] Yael suffocated to death as her mother tried to keep her quiet so the terrorists would not hear them. Kuntar was wounded and then captured along with another terrorist.[22]

Kuntar was not alone in threatening Israel: hundreds of Palestinian fighters returned to their bases in southern Lebanon after Operation Litani. The various Palestinian groups continued planning and conducting terrorist attacks against Israeli targets, but now they also began to launch rockets, which neither the UN force nor the SLA buffer zone did anything to prevent. From July 14 to 21, 1981, rocket strikes panicked Israeli civilians and led many to flee to safer parts of the country. Near the border Kiryat Shemona became a ghost town after more than 60 percent of its fifteen thousand residents fled for safer parts of the country. One reporter wrote, "There is an atmosphere of genuine fear and mounting despair which is being increased by a daily catalogue of human tragedies. Yesterday a 14-year-old boy who was already on his way to the safety of the Mediterranean port of Ashdod was killed by a random Katyusha rocket and his mother badly hurt. . . . Those few civilians who remain move furtively and quickly when outside their homes or bomb shelters, often looking skywards as if trying to detect where the next salvo of rockets is going to come from."[23] The panic was so great, and proved such a political problem, that Prime Minister Begin was forced to negotiate a U.S.-brokered ceasefire with the PLO to end them. (Readers should imagine Margaret Thatcher making a similar deal with the Irish Republican Army to understand how difficult this was for Begin.)

Into the Maelstrom

Israel's 1982 invasion of Lebanon stemmed from the failures of its counterterrorism policy in that country and Begin and Defense Minister Ariel Sharon's belief (naïve in hindsight) that they could impose their will on

Lebanon. Even when Israel achieved a ceasefire and stopped rocket attacks, as it had after Begin's capitulation in 1981, the ceasefire itself soon became part of the problem. The ceasefire applied to Palestinian attacks across the Lebanese border, but it did not prevent international terrorism, violence in the West Bank or cross-border attacks from other areas. And because many of these attacks were planned and supported in Lebanon, the PLO sanctuary there remained a tremendous threat. Israel also thought an invasion would reshape Palestinian politics outside Lebanon. Itamar Rabinovich, a scholar and senior Israeli negotiator with Syria, argues that Sharon hoped that devastating the PLO in Lebanon would "browbeat the now leaderless Palestinians in the West Bank and Gaza Strip into accepting Israeli rule, thus paving the way for eventual Israeli annexation."[24]

None of these measures helped. But Israel's strategic ambitions are only part of the story. Begin in particular found the threat of constant attacks emanating from Lebanon unacceptable. As he told U.S. Secretary of State Alexander Haig before the invasion, "The man has not been born who will ever obtain from me consent to let Jews be killed by a blood-thirsty enemy."[25] All Israeli political parties rallied behind Begin.

Israel's initially stated goal was to drive the PLO forty kilometers from the Lebanon-Israel border to make their short-range rockets useless and to prevent cross-border infiltration. Sharon reportedly told Cabinet members, "Beirut is out of the picture."[26] Israel's campaign, however, soon proved so ambitious that it included the imposition of a friendly Lebanese government that would make peace with Israel and end the Syrian military presence in the country. Two leading Israeli reporters, Ze'ev Schiff and Ehud Ya'ari, argued, and many in Israel agree, that Defense Minister Sharon embraced these ambitious goals from the beginning.[27] According to this view, Sharon sold the limited operation to the Cabinet and then, when there was no turning back, convinced the members to approve each escalating stage of his grand campaign.[28]

The trick, however, was stopping a repeat of what happened in Operation Litani, when the PLO simply returned to "Fatahland" after Israeli forces departed. To this end Israel sought to play kingmaker, crowning Bashir Gemayel, the Maronite Christian leader of the Phalange militia, president. The Israelis should have known that this approach was doomed even before it began. Phalange leaders told Israeli officials that they did not want to be viewed as "traitors" to the Lebanese and Arab cause and thus could not negotiate a peace with the Jewish state. And as they promised, their contribution to the actual war was minimal. As the Israeli analyst General Shlomo Gazit told me, it was "a totally lunatic plan."

Unless Israel had some justification, Washington would not support the invasion, and Israel would not act without U.S. support. Ironically, just as Israel wanted to go into Lebanon, the PLO began behaving itself. In the months before the invasion the ceasefire held. Israel's justification came on June 3, 1982, in London when the Abu Nidal Organization, Fatah's bitter enemy, shot and severely wounded Shlomo Argov, Israel's ambassador to the United Kingdom. Iraq was behind the ANO operation, hoping to provoke a war in Lebanon and thus divert Iran, Iraq's bitter enemy, to focus on Israel. The attackers went directly from the shooting to the Iraqi embassy. The attack left Argov paralyzed for life.

Israeli intelligence correctly surmised that the killers were members of the ANO rather than the PLO, but Begin lumped them all together. "They're all PLO," he declared. Then Chief of Staff Rafael Eitan made the government's position even clearer: "Abu Nidal, Abu Shmidal. We have to strike at the PLO."[29] For many Israelis, it was clear that Argov's shooting was a pretext. Shlomo Gazit recalls having lunch with Argov himself a week before in London, and the two "wondered what the pretext would be" for war.

Meeting little effective opposition, the IDF swept through Lebanon.[30] The PLO had around fifteen thousand full-time military personnel, with roughly six thousand near the border with Israel. They also had a token tank force and several hundred pieces of artillery. Former Israeli intelligence officers told me that Israel had spent years gathering intelligence on the Palestinian presence and Syria's capabilities in Lebanon and knew precisely where its forces were and their weaknesses. Within days Israel had pushed through these forces and surrounded Beirut. Israel engaged the Syrian Air Force, downing eighty-six aircraft while losing none of its own, a humiliating loss for Damascus. The Israeli Air Force also put on a stunning performance when it destroyed the Syrian air defenses in the Bekaa Valley.[31]

Seen only through the narrow prism of Israel's war against the PLO, the invasion can be deemed a success. Israel helped install a new government in Lebanon that agreed to a peace treaty. The PLO was forced to evacuate its armed presence from Lebanon and set up its new headquarters in Tunis, far from Israel's borders, under the supervision of a U.S., French, and Italian multinational force. The PLO never recovered operationally. Although Israel had tried to kill Arafat during the war itself, it did not kill him when it had a chance at the end of the hostilities. During the evacuation of Beirut an Israeli sniper even had Arafat in his sights. But Israeli leaders saw Arafat as already humiliated, and Begin gave a direct order not to kill him while the world media watched.[32]

Israel's successes against the PLO came at a bloody price. Perhaps seventeen thousand people died in the invasion of Lebanon; the Syrian Army lost more than a thousand soldiers and the PLO perhaps three thousand, but most of the dead were civilians. When Israel besieged PLO-dominated refugee slums in Beirut, the IDF shelled the area, resulting in thousands of deaths, civilian as well as military.

It was not only the Israelis that destroyed the PLO in Lebanon. In 1983 the Syrian government turned decisively against Arafat and backed a PLO splinter, Fatah Uprising, led by Abu Musa, Arafat's lieutenant. The result was a civil war within the Palestinian community in Lebanon. Other radical leftist groups, such as the PFLP-GC, joined Abu Musa, and with strong Syrian military support they hounded Arafat loyalists out of the country.

Nor did Lebanese groups, despite their many differences and hatred of Israel, seek a return of the PLO. In 1985, with Syrian support, the Lebanese Shi'a militia Amal began "the war of the camps," launching a series of clashes with Palestinian groups that lasted for almost two years and led to thousands of Palestinian deaths. (More precise numbers on Arab state or faction killing of Palestinians and on Palestinian internecine violence are often elusive because it attracts far less media attention than Israeli-Palestinian violence.) Amal especially tried to prevent Fatah from returning, as it did not want Palestinians to again incite Israeli retaliations on Shi'a areas or, as Amal put it, to fight "until the last southerner."[33] In addition to the death toll, the Palestinians were forced to endure humiliations during the long siege. One Palestinian woman recalled that as she and others would cross checkpoints in order to buy food, "groups of women would have their hair shorn by soldiers as crowds of Lebanese gathered to jeer and taunt."[34]

Even as Israel succeeded against the PLO, its broader plans to transform Lebanon quickly collapsed. Israel installed a friendly government led by Bashir Gemayel. To intimidate Gemayel's supporters and anyone else who might cooperate with the invasion, on September 14 pro-Syrian agents bombed Phalangist headquarters and killed him. Former Israeli intelligence officers told me that with Gemayel's death, so ended the hopes of the Mossad that the Maronites would hold on to power and make a durable peace with Israel. Bashir's brother and successor, Amin, signed an "alliance agreement" that protected Israeli interests in Lebanon. The civil strife intensified, with pro-Israeli forces quickly losing ground. In March 1984 the Lebanese government cancelled the treaty with Israel. As the months dragged on, Israel's allies were stalemated and defeated, while the IDF suffered from steady attrition in a war that no longer had a clear purpose.

Although IDF leaders knew the Phalangists wanted revenge for Bashir Gemayel's assassination they did not stop Phalangist militiamen from entering Palestinian refugee camps and even abetted their operations in the infamous cases of the Sabra and Shatila camps. Israeli forces lit up the camp with flares—it looked like "a sports stadium lit up for a football game" according to a Dutch nurse—and allowed Phalangists to enter under the guise of clearing the camps of Palestinian guerrillas. Investigations after the massacre, however, found few weapons in the camp, and the Phalangists encountered little resistance. The IDF initially told the Phalangists not to harm civilians, but as the Phalangists went in, Israeli commanders ignored reports of atrocities and even turned back fleeing civilians. One IDF lieutenant heard a Phalangist ask the Maronite commander Elie Hobeika what to do with civilians he had rounded up. Hobeika replied, "This is the last time you're going to ask me a question like that; you know exactly what to do."[35] One female survivor recalled being marched with other Palestinians through the camp: "Suddenly, they told the men to stop and ordered us to go on. We started to scream and weep. They said, 'If you go on screaming we'll kill you too.' We had hardly gone a few meters farther when we heard shots, and we understood that we were lost." Another woman recalled carrying her two-year-old son when a militiaman fired several shots at her. "I heard him cry, 'Yaba [Father]!' just before his skull exploded. I got two bullets in the back of my shoulder. The traces of his brain are still on the wall—and of his little sister too, who was on the shoulder of her big sister and also got a bullet in the head." One survivor recalled a militiaman explaining why killing children was justified: "When they grow up, they'll become fighters—we have to kill them." From September 16 to 18 Phalangists massacred up to thirty-five hundred Palestinians in the Sabra and Shatila refugee camps. Some estimates are even higher, but the true figures will never be known; in the words of one Phalangist militiaman, "You'll find out if they ever build a subway in Beirut."[36]

As the reports of atrocities grew and international criticism spread, the Israeli government came under withering criticism at home. At first Begin and the Cabinet tried to deny the reports. "Goyim kill other goyim and then accuse the Jews," was how Begin put it, while the Cabinet compared the charges of IDF complicity to the blood libel.[37] Reports of women and children massacred in camps resonated painfully among many Israelis. On September 25, 1982, Peace Now held the "400,000 demonstration," calling for an inquiry into the massacres. The protest was the largest demonstration held in Israel until Rabin's assassination more than a decade later. The Kahan Commission, which investigated the massacre, found that the IDF was indirectly responsible for the massacre and that Defense Minister Sharon bore personal responsibility for "not taking appropriate measures to prevent bloodshed."[38] Sharon's career appeared finished. Beyond the moral price Israel suffered politically and diplomatically as the world condemned the Jewish state. Even decades later criticism of the IDF role in Lebanon remains intense in Israel and abroad, memorialized in such films as *Waltz with Bashir*.

Had Israel confined itself to a quick operation to oust the PLO and not tried to transform Lebanon, it might have succeeded. Again, however, Israel's strategic thinking was flawed or absent. The PLO would undoubtedly have attempted to return from Tunis to a Lebanon without an Israeli presence. But inserting themselves into Lebanon once again would have been difficult. One thing all the Lebanese factions agreed on was their hatred of the Palestinians. Israel made a grave mistake in trying to transform Lebanon; it quickly outwore its welcome, and the result was the emergence of a new group, one far more dangerous than the PLO: Hizballah.

The Road to Oslo

Though it was difficult to recognize at the time, the invasion proved decisive in leading the PLO to peace talks with Israel by the end of the decade. From Tunis the PLO could do little but fulminate against the Israelis and launch the occasional terrorist attack, usually done with personnel from outside Lebanon. For the first time the Palestinians had no ability to strike Israel from any of the front-line states in the Israeli-Arab conflict: Egypt, Jordan, Syria, and Lebanon. International terrorism against Jewish and Israeli targets continued, but in contrast to the heady days after the 1967 War, leaders within the PLO knew they had no hope of military victory and began to explore a political deal.

Fatah's control over the Palestinian diaspora fell, and new movements, including those within the West Bank and Gaza Strip, began to gain strength. Since the birth of Israel, the refugee community had dominated the Palestinian nationalist movement. Now the PLO's relevance to Palestinians on the West Bank and Gaza declined. In the 1980s new, home-grown leaders such as Marwan Barghouti for Fatah and the Islamist Sheikh Ahmed Yasin emerged and became key players in Palestinian politics. Although they supported much of what the exiled PLO stood for with regard to Israel, it was crystal clear to Arafat, always hypersensitive to inter-Palestinian disputes and power plays, that the players in the game were changing.

Yet for many this change was of academic interest only. After all, the heart of the Palestinian cause had always been in exile. Israelis meanwhile complimented themselves that Palestinians living on the West Bank and Gaza Strip had apparently made their peace with Israeli rule. Indeed successive Israeli governments had highlighted the educational and economic gains Palestinians had made, creating a false sense among Israelis that the occupation had gained support in the territories. Under leaders like Shamir, who refused to budge when the United States prodded him to make concessions in the name of peace, it seemed as if the status quo would go on forever.

Quietly but steadily, however, Palestinian nationalism had grown in the West Bank and Gaza. Despite the hopes of Israelis, national sentiment grew even as the occupation benefited Palestinians economically. Israelis taught Palestinians new farming techniques, helped introduce fertilizer, and improved irrigation, leading to the tripling of West Bank agricultural production in the first five years of the occupation. By 1973 one-third of the Arab labor force worked in Israel at much higher pay than before.

"If they're picking strawberries in Israel, they're not throwing grenades in Gaza," explained one Israeli official.[39] Educational institutions blossomed. New universities were founded and old ones expanded.

Now that higher paying jobs were available in Israel, poorer Palestinians no longer depended on traditional landowners, who had often cooperated with Israel. Open education meant that new ideas and knowledge were now available to more than a chosen few. Universities became hotbeds of Palestinian nationalism—and later, Islamist senti-ment.[40] The light touch Dayan emphasized slowly became heavier. Israel's tax and customs policies and economic policy tied the Palestinian economy to that of Israel, giving Israel tremendous influence over the daily lives of Palestinians. Violence emanating from the West Bank led to more onerous security measures and an open display of Israel's military presence.[41]

Israel's political policies also helped the PLO cement its position. The Begin government's embrace of Jewish settlements in the West Bank led many Palestinians to conclude that Israel had no intention of leaving the territories. The settlements also went against Dayan's dictum of minimizing the visibility of the Israeli presence. Ariel Sharon, now a minister in Begin's government, even told settlers, "Don't build fences around your settlements. If you put up a fence, you put a limit to your expansion."[42] By the end of the 1980s Israeli flags would flutter throughout the West Bank above Israeli facilities and settlements—110 settlements in the West Bank, fifteen in Gaza.[43] Paradoxically Israel wanted Palestinians to govern themselves but also wanted to quash Palestinian nationalist sentiment. Israel refused to give local Palestinian leaders enough power or make concrete concessions to give them real power, which enabled the PLO to label them quislings.[44] Israel never squared these circles.

Israel often used Palestinians without ties to the PLO as intermediaries. As former Israeli senior policy advisor Nimrod Novik contends, "We Israelis try to appoint our Palestinian counterpart." Sharon tried the same approach by working with Palestinian villagers against the supposedly more politicized city dwellers. Moshe Arens attempted to create a Palestinian middle class that would be tied to prosperity rather than politics, and to undermine the PLO Shimon Peres tried to develop ties to "authentic Palestinians" (meaning non-PLO-affiliated traditional leaders) in the West Bank and Gaza. In 1986 Israel made it illegal even for its citi-zens to meet with members of the PLO. All of these efforts did little to diminish the political dominance of the PLO, which waged an all-out campaign against potential Palestinian rivals.[45]

The failure of Israel's efforts to win over the Palestinians became clear to the world on December 8, 1987, when an IDF truck in Gaza ran into and killed four Palestinians returning home from work in Israel and seriously injured seven others. The accident outraged Palestinians, who believed the killings were a deliberate response to the killing of an Israeli businessman in Gaza the previous day. On December 9 Hatan Alsis, a seventeen-year-old Palestinian, threw a Molotov cocktail at an IDF soldier patrolling in Gaza. The IDF killed Alsis in response, and an uprising, quickly dubbed the *intifada* (from the Arabic, meaning "to shake off" or "to wake up"), began.

No group led the Intifada initially, though Fatah claimed credit once it received favorable international press, and Israel was quick to assume that Fatah was indeed behind it. For the PLO, the Intifada came as a complete surprise.[46] Local leaders on the West Bank and Gaza would emerge in the Intifada, figures ostensibly part of Fatah but distinct from and often resentful of the Tunis-based leadership around Arafat. A new group, Hamas, also emerged at the outbreak of the Intifada, joining the much smaller Palestine Islamic Jihad as another growing source of terrorism against Israel. For Israel, the locus of the problem switched from outside its borders to territory it controlled.

At first the Intifada primarily consisted of demonstrations, stone throwing, and roadblocks. In 1988, though, local Palestinian leaders began to coordinate civil resistance. Ten months into the Intifada only five Israelis had died, and this number did not grow substantially in the first two years.[47] Yitzhak Rabin was defense minister for most of the Intifada, and because it took place in areas under IDF control, he was the key government minister responsible for it. Rabin claimed that 85 percent of the violence of the Intifada involved stone throwing and another 10 percent was burning tires to build roadblocks. Stabbings or firebombs were only 5 percent of the violence.[48] Effective Israeli policing, and the Jordanian and Egyptian governments' sealing of their borders, meant that few Palestinians had weapons.

Over time the Intifada degenerated into a series of feuds within Palestinian society, a constant problem for Palestinians, and one the Israelis at times heightened. By 1989 vengeance exacted on Palestinians suspected of collaborating with Israel constituted one-third of total attacks. In the years preceding Oslo Palestinian vigilantes executed more than a thousand Palestinians for suspected collaboration; some Palestinian sources say the number is higher than those killed by Israeli security forces at the time, and that some Palestinians exploited the atmosphere of anger and paranoia to settle financial and family disputes with charges of spying for Israel.[49]

Although the violence was limited by later standards, Rabin declared, "We will break their legs so they won't be able to walk and break their hands so they won't throw stones." He initiated a policy of "force, might, and beatings" to end the violence, with troops using truncheons and rubber bullets to put down demonstrators.[50] "Our purpose is to increase the number of [wounded] among those who take part in violent activities but not to kill them," he elaborated.[51] Nevertheless people died. Israeli soldiers did on occasion use live ammunition, Palestinian infants did accidentally die from tear gas, and rubber bullets did sometimes prove lethal. A U.S. State Department report contended, "Soldiers frequently used gunfire in situations that did not present mortal danger to troops, causing many avoidable deaths and injuries."[52] The journalists Ze'ev Schiff and Ehud Ya'ari put it more vividly: "There were countless instances in which young Arabs were dragged behind walls or deserted buildings and systematically beaten all but senseless. The clubs descended on limbs, joints, and ribs until they could be heard to crack."[53] The civilian suffering was considerable, and in contrast to past Israeli policing actions on the West Bank and in Gaza, the violence was well covered by the world media— Palestine again was a glass house. Thousands of Palestinians were arrested; thirteen thousand were imprisoned in 1989 alone.[54] From 1987 to 1990 more than six hundred Palestinians died at the hands of Israeli security forces, a figure comparable to the entire first twenty years of the occupation.[55]

Israeli soldiers had been trained to fight in wars against their enemies. Now soldiers were manning checkpoints, using truncheons against teenagers, and otherwise engaging in activities that seemed far from the purity of arms that traditional IDF military doctrine emphasized. Inevitably occupation duties led to abuses. "Every soldier manning a roadblock is a little god," commented one IDF member.[56] On February 5, 1988, IDF soldiers in the West Bank ordered four Palestinian youths to lie down on the road. A bulldozer dumped dirt on them, and the bulldozer driver was then ordered to run over the youths, but he refused. The soldiers soon left, and nearby Palestinians dug out the four youths. Ten days later the IDF arrested the soldiers. "Even in my worst dreams, I would never imagine such a thing," said Major General Amram Mitzna, the military commander of the West Bank, who had cautioned, "There is no military solution for the intifada" and advocated a political settlement.[57] All responsible voices in Israel condemned the brutality, but the story suggested to many that the IDF was out of control.[58] In another infamous incident, in January 1988 Colonel Yehuda Meir told his troops to round up twenty residents of nearby Palestinian villages and "break their arms and legs," interpreting Rabin's rhetoric literally.[59] One soldier recalled what happened if they caught someone they suspected of stone throwing in Gaza: "We made him play backgammon, and whoever won would get to beat the hell out of him."[60] A young soldier, Yigal Amir—the future assassin of Rabin—would pull down washing lines between houses as a lark.[61] Though few in number, some young soldiers protested the abuses by refusing to carry out orders.

The abuses shook the Israeli public and caused a seismic shift in the country's hitherto near-unanimous support for the IDF's activities.

Television programs and newspapers showed pictures of Palestinian demonstrators armed with only stones confronting Israeli tanks. Israel had long portrayed itself as little David standing up to the Goliath of Arab armies; this time Israel was Goliath, not David. In contrast to Israel's wars and past counterterrorism missions, it was not reacting to an Arab military attack or a terrorist strike. Instead it was fighting against Palestinian intellectuals like Sari Nusseibeh, who, in an attempt to speak directly to the Israeli conscience, was articulating a message of self-determination and freedom.[62] As one scholar observed, by the end of the Intifada "many Israelis perceived the occupation as morally indefensible, socially deleterious, economically ruinous, and politically and militarily harmful."[63]

Israel still used many of its old tools to try to limit the violence, even as the uprising began to fizzle after its first few years. In December 1992 Hamas killed five Israeli soldiers and Nissam Toledano, a border policeman whom Hamas had kidnapped a few days earlier. On December 17, 1992, Israel deported 415 Palestinian militants, mostly from Hamas, to Lebanon.

Deportations were nothing new. From the time it assumed control over the West Bank and Gaza Israel had deported more than a thousand Palestinians. The 1992 deportations, however, were far larger in scale than anything Israel had seen since the early 1970s. It was also the middle of winter, and television cameras filmed every move of the deportees. The Lebanese Army refused to allow the deportees to go beyond the edge of the Israeli security zone in Lebanon. During the media circus the Israeli Supreme Court began a series of hearings on the deportations, and the IDF began to backtrack, claiming that several deportees would be allowed to return. Under international pressure, including that of the United States, Israel began to cave. After the initial Supreme Court decision sixteen deportees returned, and in the ensuing months all of the original deportees came back—as heroes.[64]

In addition to the public relations disaster, the deportations also gave the militants from the West Bank and Gaza who did not know one another a chance to coordinate their own activities. Now they became acquainted with "external" leaders based in Jordan and Lebanon. Hamas leaders forged ties to the Lebanese Hizballah, which made a great show of caring for their compatriots during exile. In contrast Fatah's organization in Lebanon did little to help its fellow Palestinians. Hizballah may have also familiarized Hamas with suicide bombings and how bombers could use living wills to publicize their martyrdom.[65] How to best deploy suicide bombers to cause maximum casualties and how to exploit their deaths for propaganda purposes are challenges that other deadly groups, such as al-Qa'ida, would also wrestle with.

Although the first Intifada was a political victory for the Palestinian nationalist cause, it was far more mixed for the PLO as an organization.

New leaders were arising in the West Bank and Gaza, and the heart of the struggle was with them. Hamas, then a shadow of what it would become, was steadily growing, particularly in Gaza, and the deportations gave the organization increased credibility. In Gaza in July 1992 Hamas and Fatah supporters fought each other in street battles.[66]

So in the end the PLO turned to peace, not out of strength, but out of weakness. On November 15, 1988, the Palestinian National Council met in Algiers and gave tacit approval to the idea of recognizing Israel. On December 13 Arafat said the magic words. Recognizing "the distance between the reality and the dream," the chairman told the UN that the PLO "reaffirmed its rejection of terrorism."[67] The stage was set for bringing the Palestinians into formal peace negotiations.

As Fatah moved toward negotiations other PLO groups proved less amenable. The Palestine Liberation Front, a member group of the PLO responsible for the 1985 *Achille Lauro* hijacking, was one. In the summer of 1990 PLF raiders landed on a beach outside Tel Aviv. Though it was disrupted, it was clearly a terrorist raid. Arafat refused to condemn it, insisting it was an Iraqi operation, but Washington suspended dialogue with the PLO.[68] In 1991 Abu Iyad was assassinated. In 1988 he had declared, "If you give me the West Bank and Gaza—I will take it; and if you give me less than that—I will take it too."[69] The Abu Nidal Organization, outraged by Abu Iyad's move toward moderation, killed him in Tunis. Israel had hunted the man responsible for Munich and other attacks for two decades, but he would die at the hands of fellow Palestinians.

Concurrently the PLO's misplaced diplomacy led it to disaster. In 1990 Arafat sided with Saddam Hussein when Iraq invaded Kuwait. This made him a pariah to the United States, setting back hopes of U.S. recognition of the PLO, a switch that became even more important with the collapse of the Soviet Union, the PLO's superpower patron. Money began to dry up. Oil-rich Gulf states, outraged by the PLO's betrayal in supporting Saddam, forced many Palestinian workers to leave. To punish the PLO further they either stopped supporting the organization or directed their money to its rivals.[70] Said Abu Ali, who became governor of Ramallah, recalls that this cash crisis made the Palestinians vulnerable to pressure. By 1991 they were forced to remove up to half of their members from the payroll in Lebanon. This financial and political weakness made the PLO desperate for remedies, including even peace talks with Israel.

Israel did not go quietly toward the peace tables either. The George H. W. Bush administration threatened to withhold loan guarantees, a powerful symbol of American displeasure, if Israel did not attend the U.S.-brokered Madrid conference on peace. This would prove to be the most serious use of U.S. pressure to force Israel on the peace process.

In January 1993 secret negotiations began between Israeli and Palestinian interlocutors in Oslo. Secret contacts, as well as informal public meetings such as academic conferences, had long allowed the two sides to exchange views, but Oslo was different: it actually led to a negotiating framework. The revelation of Oslo shocked almost everyone—Israelis, Palestinians, and Americans alike.

Prime Minister Rabin, who took power after defeating Shamir in the 1992 elections, accepted Oslo not out of enthusiasm for a Palestinian state or respect for Yasir Arafat but because of his views on demographic realities and the emergence of Hamas. Within Israel the Intifada had shown that the Palestinians would not acquiesce to rule by Israel; for Israel to be a Jewish state, and a democratic one at that, it could not continue to rule over vast numbers of Palestinians. For Rabin, sovereignty over all of biblical Israel was "an illusion" that would result in "a racist Jewish state" or a binational one that was no longer truly Jewish given the huge numbers of Palestinians who lived in the West Bank and Gaza.[71] Rabin also believed that the eventual alternative to the PLO was not a gentler Palestinian leadership but Islamic radicalism.

Even as peace talks gathered steam the Intifada never really seemed to end. As late as March 1993 fifteen Israelis died violently, along with twenty-eight Palestinians. Rabin announced that he would "take Gaza out of Tel Aviv" and closed off the West Bank and Gaza to Israel. He also ordered the construction of a security barrier around the Gaza Strip. The IDF arrested thousands of Palestinians and blew up houses, and undercover units penetrated into Palestinian areas to take out militants. Ending the more restrictive rules of engagement for dealing with Palestinian demonstrators, an Israeli border policeman told a reporter, "If you see someone holding a cinderblock, Molotov cocktail, or an iron bar, you shoot him without making any bones of the matter."[72] Although these measures seemed tough and against the spirit of negotiations, Rabin used them as political cover for a deal that would give Palestinians control of Gaza and, as a token presence in the West Bank, Jericho: the so-called Oslo Accords.

Both sides believed the status quo was untenable, and both believed that through negotiations they could get what they wanted—for Israelis, security, and for the Palestinians, their own state. However, the Oslo period, which began with such hope, would soon prove to be another episode of disappointment, anger, and violence for both the Palestinians and the Israelis.

SECTION II

FROM OSLO THROUGH THE SECOND INTIFADA

CHAPTER IV

THE FALSE PROMISE OF OSLO (1993-1996)

MOHAMMAD DAHLAN was born in a refugee camp in Gaza. He first came to Israel's attention as one of the new, young Fatah leaders of the Intifada. Israel jailed him and then expelled him in 1988. Afterward he joined the PLO in Tunis, where he continued to orchestrate protests in Gaza. Jibril Rajoub too had been an Israeli prisoner, in his case for throwing a grenade at a convoy of soldiers. Israel also expelled him in 1988. Yet six years later Dahlan and Rajoub were working closely with Israel's security services to fight terrorism. The two Palestinians led the Preventive Security Force, the largest of the domestic intelligence services of the new Palestinian entity created under the Oslo Accords. As Dahlan and Rajoub's elevation suggests, Oslo had turned the world of Israeli counterterrorism upside down.

On September 13, 1993, PLO chairman Yasir Arafat and Israeli prime minister Yitzhak Rabin signed the Oslo Accords in a White House ceremony. The Accords paved the way for Palestinian self-rule to begin in Gaza and parts of the West Bank beginning in 1994. Rabin, the chief of staff in the 1967 War that led to the conquest of the West Bank and Gaza Strip and the man who authorized harsh policies against the Palestinians in the first Intifada, was on the hook to deliver a state to the Palestinians; Arafat, the man who had been the very face of terrorism for Israelis, would lead it. Politics, as well as counterterrorism, was upside down.

Yet true peace would remain elusive.[1] During the 1990s Hamas eclipsed Fatah and other traditional nationalist groups as the primary Palestinian terrorist threat to Israel. Hamas was a different creature from Fatah, far more determined, far more competent, and far less corrupt. Unlike Fatah, Hamas had little faith in negotiations or the value of international legitimacy. Hamas even embraced suicide bombings, heretofore the province of Hizballah. Hamas and Palestine Islamic Jihad launched four attacks in 1994 and another four in 1995. In 1994 sixty-five Israelis died, the country's bloodiest year in terrorism since 1974.[2] All told, in the period between the Oslo agreement and the beginning of the al-Aqsa Intifada in 2000, Palestinian terrorist groups killed 262 Israelis, and Israeli security forces killed approximately 385 Palestinians.[3]

In another twist the counterterrorism challenge now involved three forces: Israel, the Arafat-led Palestinian Authority (PA), which governed part of the territories, and the terrorist groups themselves. In an attempt to wreak havoc that would undermine the peace process, Hamas used whatever means available. Predictably Israel attempted to arrest and kill Hamas leaders. Arafat, on the other hand, had his own agenda, sometimes exploiting Hamas attacks to extract Israeli concessions and sometimes helping Israel to keep Hamas in check. Israel worked with the PA but also initiated its own arrests and even struck directly against Hamas without consulting Arafat or his lieutenants.

Rabin and his successors continued negotiations in the face of terrorism, but the continuing attacks and the PA's refusal to confront Hamas poisoned the atmosphere. Israelis saw Arafat, their erstwhile partner for peace, as a murderer and a liar.

For a brief moment, however, hope flourished. The possibilities of the Oslo agreement seemed to signal the end of perhaps the world's most intractable conflict. The words Rabin uttered after signing the deal are poignant: "We who have come from a land where parents buried their children, we who have fought against you, the Palestinians, we say to you today, in a loud and clear voice, enough of blood and tears, enough!"[4] Aaron David Miller, one of the U.S. peace negotiators at the time, recalls the White House signing ceremony: "I was convinced we'd reached a point of no return."[5] Oslo was meant as the beginning; over time confidence would grow "like deposits in a bank," Miller told me, and the parties would draw upon this trust as they moved toward peace.

From the start Rabin tried to insulate the Oslo negotiations from terrorism. Ben Gurion had famously justified a policy of simultaneously cooperating with the British occupiers against the Nazis and opposing Britain's restrictive immigration policies to Mandatory Palestine—a difficult circle to square. Echoing Ben Gurion's famous phrasing, Rabin declared, "We shall fight terrorism as if there is no peace process, and pursue the peace process as if there is no terrorism." Indeed although the Oslo Declaration of Principles allowed the Palestinians to create "a strong police force," the agreement itself had little to say about counterterrorism. Rabin pressed to make sure that Israel, not the Palestinians, held responsibility for counterterrorism.

On July 1, 1994, Arafat triumphantly returned from exile in Tunis to what was presumed to be the territory of an eventual Palestinian state. Palestinians in Gaza and the West Bank greeted his return with jubilation. At last, it seemed, years of struggle would pay off. Unfortunately Arafat also brought back from exile many members of the Fatah establishment who were corrupt and, adding insult to injury, were hopelessly out of touch with the people in the West Bank and Gaza Strip.

The details of Arafat's return trip augured poorly for counterterrorism. When he first came to Gaza Arafat smuggled in from Egypt people wanted by Israel and weapons. Israel was particularly upset that he brought in Jihad Amarin, who allegedly had planned the 1974 attack on a school in Ma'alot that killed twenty-two Israeli students. Ehud Ya'ari, a leading Israeli correspondent, recounts one young soldier telling another, "'Gee, I didn't know Arafat was so tall.' Arafat had arrived in a Mercedes and his *kaffiyah* was scraping the ceiling of the car. You have to be an NBA player for that to happen. It turned out that Arafat was sitting on somebody whom he was smuggling in—Jihad Amarin—and Mamduh Nofal, the former military commander of the Democratic Front, was hiding in the trunk. They also had a few Kalashnikov rifles and night-vision equipment in the car."[6] It was Arafat's way of showing his people that even though he made concessions at the negotiating table, he was not Israel's stooge.

Arafat was a master of double talk, delivering one message to the peacemakers and another to his home audience. He left the Israelis guessing as to whether he really wanted to end terrorism and make peace. In a speech in South Africa in May 1994 he compared the Oslo Accords to a truce the Prophet Mohammad agreed to but later violated, the Treaty of Hudaybiyyah, once his power grew greater.[7] Throughout the negotiations Israelis would point to such statements as an indication that Arafat did not want to end violence once and for all.

Arafat's attempts to counter the street power of Hamas and Palestine Islamic Jihad after Oslo also made Israelis doubt that he was committed to peace. He sanctioned the creation of the Tanzim ("the Organization") as a militia that would be allied with Fatah and indirectly with the PA. The Tanzim began with Fatah youths who had been active in the First Intifada, and its ranks swelled as thousands of Palestinians eventually joined. At the heart of the Tanzim were local PLO figures, like its leader on the West Bank, Marwan Barghouti, who made their mark before and during the First Intifada, often through political action rather than violence. The Tanzim offered Fatah street power outside the official organizations. Part of its purpose was to maintain "street cred" with younger radicals who were attracted to the more militant Islamists and supported resistance. Local leaders often guided the Tanzim, and the central Fatah leadership did not exercise tight control.

As Fatah and the PA nominally embraced peace, some Tanzim leaders wanted Fatah to remain a strong nationalist movement independent of the PA. They resented the dominance of the Fatah old guard who held power in the PA, most of whom had long been in exile. They denounced the corruption and incompetence of the PA and called for more democracy and transparency within the organization. The Tanzim itself had internal elections and had far more grassroots strength than the PA.

When he found it convenient, Arafat used the Tanzim as a tool to foment violence, which he then used to enhance his negotiating position with Israel. He claimed that he did not control the movement and that Tanzim's pressure was forcing him toward a more militant position.[8]

Despite this poor beginning, Israelis favoring negotiations believed that self-rule would remove grievances regarding political rights, nationalism, and the daily humiliations inherent in the Israeli occupation. Many Israelis intuitively recognized the importance of these grievances in fomenting terrorism as they began to accept the reality of Palestinian nationalism. Ehud Barak, who had led special forces raids to kill wanted terrorists, even declared in 1997, when he was the Labor Party leader, "If I was [a Palestinian] at the right age, at some stage I would have entered one of the terror organizations and have fought from there."[9] More cynically Israelis also hoped that leaders linked to the Palestinian Authority would embrace peace because a return to violence risked jeopardizing their perks and positions.

Israeli Counterterrorism after Oslo

Israelis hoped Oslo would transform Palestinian security organizations into an arm of Israel's police and intelligence services. They would monitor suspects, arrest and jail terrorists, and otherwise fulfill the functions that Shin Bet and other Israeli services performed during the years of occupation. Indeed in many ways the Palestinians were expected to do the job far better than the Israelis would. For all Israel's technical competence and skilled intelligence personnel, and for all the failings of the Palestinian security services, the Palestinians knew their own community far better than Israel ever could. So people like Dahlan and Rajoub, however unsavory their backgrounds and methods—indeed, because of their unsavory pasts—became vital partners. At the same time Israelis recognized that Palestinian security services were untrained, disorganized, and politicized. They would require time to become effective. Thus Israel also reserved the right to act on its own with its military and intelligence forces. And because Israeli intelligence had penetrated Fatah's political core, it possessed a deep well of political intelligence on the Palestinian leadership. (Shimon Peres, when he would meet Arafat in Ramallah, reportedly would speak to Arafat's desk, knowing that Israeli intelligence intercepted the meetings from there.)

From a counterterrorism point of view, however, intelligence was always scanty. The Israeli withdrawal from Gaza and other Palestinian areas was devastating for Israeli intelligence. Chief of Staff Amnon Lipkin-Shahak declared in January 1995 that Israel had "no response for dealing with suicide bombers" due to a lack of intelligence. The head of the military intelligence research division, Brigadier General Yaakov Amidror, was even more blunt: "Israel's intelligence capacity in the Gaza Strip has dropped to zero."[10] Palestinian self-rule had fundamentally altered Israel's intelligence posture. During the First Intifada Israel ran approximately seven thousand informers in the West Bank and Gaza, a huge number given the small populations there.[11] This network became harder to run when Israel no longer controlled daily aspects of Palestinian life as it did before the PA came into being.

To gain intelligence Israel constantly exploited any conceivable means to elicit information. Many Palestinians had relatives in Jordan or elsewhere in the diaspora, and Israel used "family reunification" permits to extract information. All means were used: the offer of a job, entrance to a university in Israeli areas of control, medical treatment for a sick child at an Israeli hospital, a business permit to import electronics, a contract involving the Israeli government, and the time-honored intelligence tool of money.

Palestinians claimed that Israeli intelligence deliberately entrapped young Palestinians in compromising positions by videotaping them and threatening to expose them. Particularly onerous were homosexual and adulterous liaisons, which were condemned in traditional Palestinian society. One former agent handler admitted, "It's a dirty game."

The permits that controlled entry into Israel also became a means of gathering intelligence. For Gazans especially it became increasingly difficult to work in Israel, to make plans for a doctor's visit, or otherwise to have the certainty that Israeli authorities would allow them entry. PA officials embraced this system, as it enabled them to play the role of middleman, seeking out and approving permits from their side of the border and putting forth names of Palestinians to Israel for approval on the Israeli side—enriching themselves and consolidating their power in the process.

As Shin Bet and the IDF focused on Palestinian rejectionists, one of the biggest blows to peace early on came from a Jewish terrorist. On February 25, 1994, Baruch Goldstein, an American émigré and doctor, entered a mosque in the Cave of the Patriarchs in Hebron and gunned down twenty-nine Palestinian Muslims as they prayed. "The peace process stopped in its tracks," according to a U.S. peace negotiator, Martin Indyk, as the Arab world united in outrage.[12]

Although the peace process soon resumed, Hamas announced that its first successful suicide attack in April 1994 was a response to Goldstein's murders. Hamas of course was seeking to disrupt the peace process in any event. In 1993 Hamas had tried three suicide attacks (and Palestine Islamic

Jihad one), all of which failed to kill anyone except the bomber. The Goldstein attack enabled Hamas to claim that its actions were defensive, a response to Israeli aggression, and their record of bungling changed quickly.[13] A series of five Hamas and Palestine Islamic Jihad suicide bombings in 1994 were a constant backdrop to the negotiations, killing forty Israelis and wounding 144.[14]

In addition to the suicide bombings, the kidnapping of an IDF soldier, Nachson Wachsman, in October 1994 showed that Rabin could not simply paper over the threat Palestinian terrorism posed to the peace process. Hamas members in a car, wearing *kippot,* speaking Hebrew, and playing Hassidic music, picked Wachsman up when he was on leave from his commando unit and hitchhiking (common in Israel) to attend a training course in the north. Hamas announced his abduction and threatened to execute him unless Israel released two hundred Palestinian prisoners. Israelis throughout the country responded with prayer vigils and demonstrations of support.

Rabin sealed Gaza (wrongly thinking that Wachsman had been taken there, when he was actually in the West Bank) and insisted that Arafat locate him. PA security services cracked down hard, not only arresting dozens of Hamas officials but also stopping Hamas demonstrations. It was Shin Bet, however, that caught a break, when they detained a Hamas suspect in the West Bank. This led to the discovery that Wachsman was held in Bir Nabala, a village just north of Jerusalem. Elite IDF forces tried to rescue him, but the attempt did not succeed: Wachsman died along with one rescuer. With bitter irony the Nobel Peace Prize winners were announced on the very day of the rescue attempt: Rabin, Peres, and Arafat all shared the prize.

Sealing the border became an increasingly important Israeli counterterrorism tool. Since the 1967 War Palestinians living in the West Bank and Gaza had been allowed to travel into Israel as well as back and forth from the West Bank to Gaza. During the First Intifada Israel began to require identity cards for Gazans, and during the first Gulf War in 1991 Israel changed the rules and denied Palestinians the right to go to Israel freely. However, there were many exceptions (workers could go for jobs, merchants to sell goods, and so on), and the rules were often not enforced.[15] All this changed after Oslo, when the rules became tighter and closures occurred after terrorist attacks. In 1994 the territories were closed for forty-three days; this number soared to more than a hundred in 1996, making normal life and economic activity almost impossible for Gazans.[16] Closing Gaza both looked tough as a response to a terrorist attack and, because of its economic effects, was one way of pushing Arafat to act against Hamas.

While negotiations continued, Israel reportedly killed several suspected terrorists. On November 2, 1994, Hani' Abed, leader of Palestine Islamic

Jihad, died when his car was blown up, probably by Israeli operatives. In April 1995 a senior figure from the Qassam Brigade (Hamas's military wing), Kamal Kheil, died along with another cell member and a young boy, in an explosion in their building where they were apparently working on bombs.[17]

In hindsight Rabin's approach of separating peace talks and counter-terrorism was unrealistic. Part of the purpose of Oslo—indeed, in the eyes of many Israelis, the *primary* purpose—was to end terrorist violence. Yet Rabin was perhaps too eager to make peace. He tolerated a level of violence that was politically unsustainable and gave Arafat the impression that bloodshed could continue without cost. Ironically Rabin's approach reduced Arafat's incentive to go after groups like Hamas. If Arafat did not suffer at the negotiating table, why would this consummately cautious leader risk a confrontation with Hamas or any other violent group?

Rabin's policy began to change in April 1995, when he declared that the PA would have to go after the terrorist infrastructure for the peace process to continue. At the same time he told U.S. negotiators that politically he could not move forward in peace talks if the violence continued. Rabin was only catching up to political reality: no Israeli government could make progress toward peace so long as terrorism remained rampant. Meanwhile terrorism continued. In July and August 1995 Palestine Islamic Jihad killed six civilians in a suicide bombing attack on a bus in Ramat Gan; later they killed three Israelis and one American when they bombed a bus in Jerusalem.

In September 1995, shortly before Rabin's assassination, Oslo II was signed. The treaty expanded Palestinian autonomy, so it appeared to be yet another marker on the road to peace. In contrast to the first Oslo deal, there was a detailed security protocol. In 1996 the West Bank was divided into three areas that were blandly named A, B, and C. Area A, where 26 percent of Palestinians lived, remained under full Palestinian control. Israelis were given full control of Area C, including areas where settlements are located. The remaining 70 percent of the population lived in Area B under joint Israeli military and Palestinian civil control. Before the Second Intifada broke out in 2000 Area A was 17 percent of the total area, while Areas B and C were 24 and 59 percent, respectively. Oslo II required Palestinians to "act systematically against all expressions of violence and terror" and cooperate closely with Israel security services.[18] The ceiling on the size of the security force also grew.

Oslo II was a high point in the peace talks, but again Jewish terrorism struck, this time in a blow that in hindsight many see as fatal to the peace process. Yigal Amir, a Jew incensed at Rabin's betrayal in surrendering land he believed God gave the Jews, shot and killed the prime minister at a pro-peace rally on November 4, 1995. Rabin's assassination would set back the peace process irretrievably. U.S. peace negotiator Martin Indyk told me, "Jewish and Palestinian terrorism, together, derailed the peace process."

Looking back we can see that although the period after the signing of the Oslo Accords was among the most hopeful in the history of Israeli-Palestinian relations, terrorism was already beginning to doom the peace talks and lay the groundwork for later violence. Courageous leaders like Rabin had forged on in the face of terrorist attacks, but the constant attacks were souring Israelis on peace, and the slow pace of progress made Palestinians increasingly skeptical as well.

CHAPTER V

CLOUDS ON THE HORIZON: THE NETANYAHU PERIOD (1996–1999)

IN THE hotly contested 1996 elections, terrorism—both Jewish and Palestinian—was the dominant issue. At rallies for the Likud candidate Benjamin ("Bibi") Netanyahu political posters superimposed Rabin's face on the bodies of Hitler and Arafat. Another poster depicted Rabin shaking Arafat's hand, but the image was manipulated so it appeared that the prime minister was handing Arafat a gun. Underneath the poster was a slogan: "Do not give them guns!" The Labor Party candidate, Shimon Peres, campaigned as Rabin's successor. He portrayed Rabin's assassination as part of a climate of extremism that defined the right wing in Israel. In the mix he included the politics of Netanyahu.

Netanyahu's most effective advertisement was footage of Arafat and Peres walking hand in hand, an image that morphed into a montage of blown-up buses and dead Israelis. During the 1996 election Likud political posters included such slogans as "Danger! What is good for the PLO and the Palestinians is not good for the Jews. They chose Peres. We say: Only Netanyahu! Netanyahu is good for the Jews." Netanyahu won by less than 1 percent of the total vote, and terrorism made all the difference. One study found that in the area where a terror attack occurred, support for right-wing candidates increased significantly. These attacks influenced political outcomes in 1988 and 1996, both occasions when Likud narrowly won out over Labor.[1]

Palestinians did not see Netanyahu as a partner for peace. Wafa Amr, a Palestinian journalist who knew Arafat well, believes the chairman began to lose faith in the peace process after Rabin's assassination. In personal interviews many Palestinians date their lack of faith in the peace process to the assassination and the Netanyahu victory.

The Clinton administration openly endorsed Peres. Clinton himself told members of the American Israel Public Affairs Committee that Peres was a "true and reliable friend of our country, and a true and reliable leader of his own."[2] Administration officials feared (correctly) that Netanyahu would not prove eager to make peace. His campaign, and his subsequent electoral alliance with ultraorthodox parties, left American officials dismayed. Clinton's White House spokesman Joe Lockhart declared him "one of the most obnoxious individuals you're going to come into—just a liar and a cheat."[3]

From the start Netanyahu stressed security issues and ran on the slogan "Making a Safe Peace." He was skeptical of the peace process, and he made it quite clear that it would not go forward if terrorist attacks continued. Upon victory Netanyahu rejected Rabin's policy of divorcing terrorism from the peace process.

Tunnel Riots

After taking power in June 1996 the Netanyahu government looked to contrast itself with Rabin's conciliatory approach to the Palestinians. They turned to the Temple Mount, the most sensitive issue for religious Jews and Muslims, to make the point. For years Muslim authorities had tried to block the excavation of the Hasmonean Tunnel and Israeli attempts to connect it to the Western Wall tunnel. The latter runs along the Western Wall and thus the Temple Mount, where the Dome of the Rock and the al-Aqsa Mosque, two sites holy to Islam, are located. Rumors had spread that Israel was plotting to use the tunnel excavation to destroy the holy sites of Islam and rebuild the Temple of Solomon or, at the very least, wipe out the Muslim Quarter of Jerusalem.

In September 1996 the Israeli government restarted excavations of the Hasmonean Tunnel. In a gift to Palestinian propagandists, Israel unsealed a walled gate, the main area of contention, in the middle of the night. The restarted excavation resulted in three days of riots, not only in Jerusalem but in several cities in the West Bank; it was the worst fighting since Oslo was concluded. The demonstrations were coordinated, and Israeli military intelligence came to believe that Arafat had deliberately preserved an infrastructure for violence for just such occasions.[4] Arafat himself appeared to support the riots, claiming that Israel was using the tunnel to undermine the holy sites on the Temple Mount.[5]

Even worse, the Palestinian security forces that Israelis believed would be their partners in stopping violence joined the demonstrators. Palestinian police often stood beside rock-throwing civilians, and the IDF found itself unprepared for the mix of demonstrators and hostile security personnel. Casualties were high, with fifty-eight Palestinians and fifteen Israeli soldiers killed. Some Israeli military and intelligence officials claim the Palestinian police had orders from the top to fire; others contend that the police participation in the violence was not a planned response, but rather their own reaction to the situation.[6]

The violence and subsequent uproar was felt at the negotiating table, and some observers believe Netanyahu, facing heavy U.S. pressure, felt compelled to make concessions after the bloodshed in order to keep the peace process alive.[7] In the Protocol Concerning the Redeployment in Hebron, signed on January 17, 1997, Netanyahu's government made concessions on Palestinian autonomy and transferred control of 80 percent of Hebron to the Palestinian Authority, retaining the remaining 20 percent in the area where several hundred Jewish settlers lived. It was to be the first land-for-peace deal Netanyahu signed. The prime minister gamely tried to sell the transfer, noting, "We are not leaving Hebron; we are redeploying in a part of Hebron," but Israelis and Palestinians all saw the move as a concession to the Palestinians.[8] Beyond the importance of the transfer itself, Hebron was the burial place of Abraham, Isaac, Jacob, Sarah, and numerous other Jewish patriarchs and matriarchs. It was also a town where Arabs had conducted a brutal pogrom against their Jewish neighbors in 1929, killing sixty-seven. Its ancient and modern history made it a symbol for religious Israelis and right-wing nationalists, core constituencies for Netanyahu. Some further progress on the peace process occurred with the signing of the Wye Memorandum on October 23, 1998, which further expanded the areas under Palestinian control in exchange for the PA's honoring additional security requirements. As a result of the Hasmonean Tunnel incident, the United States stepped up security assistance and increased the CIA's role in helping train and equip Palestinian forces.

From Arafat's point of view, the tunnel violence was an unqualified success. The Palestinian journalist Wafa Amr believes that Arafat learned the whole world would intervene when violence intensified and that Israel would be forced to make more concessions. The director of Israeli military intelligence, Gen. Amos Malka, also concluded that Arafat's use of the tunnel incident showed that the chairman employed violence to "instill a sense of urgency" in negotiations.[9] In the eyes of younger Palestinian leaders, the violence paid off not only in negotiations, but also in their rivalry with the Fatah old guard. Tanzim's leader Marwan Barghouti later referred to the tunnel riots as a way of "kick-starting" Oslo and reminding the world that the Palestinian masses could not be ignored.[10]

For Israelis the legacy of the tunnel riots and the subsequent negotiations was bitter. First, they recognized that in the event of violence, their ostensible Palestinian partners might once more turn against them. "We felt betrayed [after the police opened fire]," remembers the former IDF chief of staff Amnon Lipkin-Shahak. Second, they determined that they would never again allow Palestinians to be rewarded politically for fomenting violence. Third, and perhaps most important, their distrust of Arafat, always great, became even greater.

Israel Digs In Its Heels

Despite the progress under the Hebron and Wye agreements, the atmosphere remained poisonous. As part of the Wye Accords Netanyahu attained guarantees that Israeli withdrawals and other steps forward were now contingent on several specific Palestinian security promises.[11] In Wye's aftermath he cited a lack of effort on the part of Palestinian security cooperation, and Israel did not implement a second redeployment out of territories promised to Palestinians: they did not construct the safe route reconnecting the West Bank and Gaza, they did not fulfill an agreement that would free Palestinian prisoners, they did not return confiscated lands used as settlements, and they otherwise thwarted attempts to move forward on talks.[12] Meanwhile the much-reviled Ariel Sharon had become Netanyahu's foreign minister and declared that he would never shake Arafat's hand. Deadlines came and went with little progress. Martin Indyk, the former U.S. ambassador to Israel, concludes, "Both sides observed Oslo in the breach." Trust, in particular, was lacking. Although violence diminished, support for violence did not. A 1998 report by the International Committee of the Red Cross found that more than in any other country it had studied, in Israel support for attacks on civilians was high.[13]

Settlement activity in particular was a visible sign that Israel would remain in the West Bank. After Hebron Netanyahu tried to regain his right-wing credibility by announcing that Israel would build the Har Homa settlement in Arab East Jerusalem. In Palestinian eyes Har Homa would be the last in a chain of settlements that encircled Jerusalem. Cooperation between the PA security forces and Israel temporarily ceased.[14] One analyst pointed out that "the noise of the bulldozers" drowned out all the peace talks and political activities.

Terrorism dominated media coverage even though violence had fallen in the Netanyahu years. Nahum Barnea, one of Israel's leading journalists, points out acidly that terrorist attacks are magnets for the media—the ultimate in photo ops. From a reporter's point of view, "you get great pictures, you don't have to travel, and you don't have to be embedded. You can get your Pulitzer Prize by sitting in your own air conditioning." Media pressure became stronger, as Israeli media had gone from unquestioning support for the IDF to near-constant and often scathing criticism.[15]

Bungling in Amman: The Mishal Assassination

Poor planning, politics, and the chaos of Israeli decision making came together in perhaps the biggest counterterrorism blunder of the first Netanyahu administration: the bungled attempt to kill Hamas leader Khaled Mishal in Jordan.

"I never thought Jordan would be a place for assassinations because of its relationship with Israel," Mishal later recalled.[16] He was then a senior Hamas leader, but compared to Sheikh Ahmed Yasin, the head of Hamas, he was not a household name in the Middle East. It took Israel's failed attempt to kill him to make him famous.

Netanyahu felt tremendous political pressure to respond after two suicide bombers struck the Mahane Yehuda market in Jerusalem on July 30, 1997, killing sixteen and wounding 178. At first he took the usual steps, closing off access to Palestinian areas and temporarily stopping tax transfer to the PA. There were few obvious targets to strike in the West Bank and Gaza, however, and at the time counterterrorism cooperation between Israel and the PA seemed to be going well. Netanyahu appealed to the head of the Mossad for potential retaliatory targets, and Mishal's name popped up. Mishal seemed relatively unprotected in Jordan, largely because the Jordan-Israel peace treaty made the Hashemite Kingdom a sanctuary. As one intelligence official told me, the Mossad head Danny Yatom "was eager to put a notch in his belt."

On September 25, 1997, two Mossad agents pretending to be Canadian tourists intercepted Mishal as he walked to his office in Jordan. One agent put a device near Mishal's ear that poisoned him with a modified version of the painkiller fetanyl. According to the plan, Mishal would be dead within forty-eight hours, and there would be no trace of the poison left in his system. The agents, however, bungled the getaway and got lost in the warren of Amman's tangled streets. Mishal's bodyguard pursued the agents and finally cornered them. Not only did the assassination fail, but the capture of the two Mossad officers (as well as the four trapped inside the Israeli embassy) left the Netanyahu government in a very public bind.[17]

As Mishal moved closer to death, Israel initially refused to provide the antidote. Outraged, Jordan's King Hussein called President Clinton, who then demanded Israel deliver it. The Clinton administration feared that King Hussein would abrogate Jordan's peace treaty with Israel because of the assassination attempt and ultimately prevailed on Israel to deliver the antidote that saved Mishal's life.

In his book *Kill Khalid* the Australian journalist Paul McGeough relates that King Hussein had just conveyed an offer from Hamas leaders to Netanyahu that Hamas was considering a thirty-year truce. The head of Jordanian intelligence said, "[Radicals like Mishal] will be sixty years old by the time this expires—maybe they'll fade away."[18] Instead the attempted assassination transformed Mishal from "a third-rate leader," according to Mossad chief Shabtai Shavit, to a household name. Jordan threatened to abrogate the peace treaty and try the Mossad agents as murderers. To placate Hussein, Israel released Sheikh Yasin. Killing Mishal was meant to weaken Hamas and cause a leadership crisis. Instead the organization emerged stronger.

For Israel, the biggest disaster of the Mishal incident was Hussein's loss of confidence in the Netanyahu government. The king was one of Israel's few friends in the Arab world. "Jordanians are excellent partners for counterterrorism," one Israeli intelligence official told me. Prior to the Mishal incident Jordan shared the information they received on Hamas and constantly monitored the activities of Hamas leaders. Indeed Jordanian intelligence officials told me that the assassination attempt shattered their relationship with the Mossad for several years. Efraim Halevy, who later became the head of Mossad and helped broker and maintain the peace deal, believes that King Hussein felt betrayed.[19] Hussein never again saw Netanyahu as a true partner.

Israelis differ in their reactions to the assassination attempt. Foreign policy advisor Uzi Arad points out that "sometimes you have to seize opportunities" and that the problem was really the implementation rather than the result. The Mossad chief Shabtai Shavit believes that the mistake was not the decision to kill Mishal, but rather to do so in Amman, in the territory of a friendly government. Yet most Israelis I spoke to said the Mishal poisoning was a sign that operations had trumped strategic common sense. To kill a second-tier leader Israel had jeopardized one of its most important strategic relationships. As one senior Israeli defense official put it, King Hussein was a responsible and wise leader, "more responsible than Netanyahu."

The contretemps over the attempted Mishal assassination and the release of Yasin did more than just highlight the bungled operation. It also signaled a significant shift in Israeli counterterrorism policy, from a focus on the more secular Fatah to emphasizing Islamist groups like Hamas and Palestine Islamic Jihad. These were the groups that helped derail the peace process before Rabin's murder and made negotiations far more difficult in the years that followed.

CHAPTER VI

HAMAS'S RISE AND SEEMING FALL (1993-2000)

YAHYA AYYASH, a leader of Hamas's military wing and its chief bomb maker, was one of the deadliest opponents of peace. Ayyash planned many of the attacks and built the bombs used in almost all of Hamas's major attacks in 1993 and 1994. Ninety Israelis died as a result of his work. He also built bombs for Hamas's ideological bedfellow—and sometimes rival—Palestine Islamic Jihad.[1]

Nicknamed "the Engineer," Ayyash was a skilled craftsman and mechanic, able to repair televisions and other devices, even as a boy. Like many Palestinians who joined resistance organizations, he had some education, but he found his path to higher education blocked. Ayyash wanted to get his master's degree in Jordan, but Israel denied him an exit visa. Furious, he joined Hamas. Yaakov Peri, who headed Israel's domestic security service Shin Bet until 1994, later sighed, "If we had known that he was going to do what he did, we would have given him permission to travel along with a million dollars."[2]

As his role in the bombings became clear, Shin Bet's hunt for Ayyash grew all-consuming. Efforts to get the Palestinian security services to arrest him failed, with Arafat often claiming he was not in Gaza. Israel even arrested family members and cut off services to his village. To elude his pursuers Ayyash constantly changed his appearance and most nights slept in different houses. Rabin darkly joked about this, saying, "I am afraid he might be sitting between us here in the Knesset."[3] The former

Shin Bet director Carmi Gillon told me, "I admired him. He was very professional. He didn't make any mistakes."

But one mistake cost him his life. On January 5, 1996, Shin Bet tracked down Ayyash and killed him while he was staying at the house of his friend and fellow Hamas member, Osama Hammad. Shin Bet had recruited his friend's cousin Kemal Hammad, and to keep him loyal threatened to inform Hamas that he was working with them. They then handed Hammad a cell phone, claiming only that it was bugged so Israeli intelligence could monitor Ayyash's activities. Unbeknown to Hammad, it also contained fifteen grams of the explosive RDX. As Ayyash took what he was told was a call from his father, an Israeli airplane monitored the conversation to confirm that Ayyash himself was on the other end. "Father, don't call me on the mobile telephone" were reportedly his last words as the phone blew up in his hand and killed him.[4] One Hamas official said later, "It was a quiet explosion, and they got what they desired—his head."[5]

Hamas and Palestine Islamic Jihad retaliated with a series of devastating attacks. PIJ had appreciated Ayyash's help with bombs and was eager for revenge after Israel had killed its leader, Fathi Shiqaqi, in Malta in October 1995.[6] On February 25, 1996, Hamas launched two suicide bombers, the first killing twenty-six Israelis on a bus in Jerusalem and the second killing one Israeli at a hitchhiking post near Ashkelon. On March 3 another suicide bomber killed nineteen in a bus attack in Jerusalem, and a day later thirteen more Israelis died and another seventy-five or so were wounded when a suicide bomber detonated a nail bomb outside of the Dizengoff Center in Tel Aviv. Both Hamas and PIJ claimed responsibility for this most recent atrocity. The dead and wounded included children wearing costumes to celebrate the Purim holiday. The attacks were so devastating that President Clinton, French Prime Minister Chirac, British Prime Minister Major, Russian President Yeltsin, and other world leaders gathered with Prime Minister Peres and leaders of fourteen Arab countries at Sharm al-Shaykh in Egypt to condemn the violence.

Because Ayyash's assassination initiated a new cycle of violence it is easy to see it as a mistake or as counterproductive. Certainly the timing was poor. Some claim Arafat had just forged a truce with Hamas wherein the organization pledged not to embarrass Arafat or the PA—a truce Ayyash's death quickly ended.[7] The solidity of this truce was questionable, however, even without the Ayyash killing. A later investigation found that the bus bombings were planned before Ayyash was killed, suggesting that revenge was not the motivation.[8] As the former Shin Bet director Ami Ayalon argues, bombers were part of Hamas's doctrine. Ayyash simply would have launched more attacks had he remained alive. Moreover, as Ayalon's predecessor Gillon points out, killing Ayyash did not affect counterterrorism cooperation, and in fact his death was probably a relief to Fatah even though Arafat publicly paid tribute to "the martyr, Yahya Ayyash."[9]

Although critics accused Peres of using the killing to bolster his position in the polls, any Israeli leader would have done the same thing. The former U.S. ambassador to Israel Martin Indyk points out that Peres was only following Rabin's logic of fighting terror as if there were no peace process. However, in the end, Indyk concludes, "Peres failed his government" by provoking a retaliation that cost him his position and derailed the peace process.

The Birth of Hamas

Ayyash died, but Hamas lived. In the years before Ayyash's death the Islamist movement became stronger and stronger. Hamas is the offspring of the Muslim Brotherhood, the Arab world's preeminent Islamist organization, which has its roots in Egypt. Egypt had repressed the Muslim Brotherhood when it took control over Gaza in 1949 after the war with Israel, fearing that the Brothers were conspiring against the regime.

Ironically in light of events to come, the Muslim Brotherhood flourished in Gaza after the Israeli takeover in 1967. At first the organization was weak compared with groups like Fatah, pro-Nasser Arab nationalists, and Marxists. Yet the 1967 debacle discredited all these ideologies, and political Islam began to fill the void. Gaza, along with the Muslim world in general, was experiencing a religious revival. In 1967 Gaza had seventy-seven mosques, but by 1989 there were two hundred.[10] Most of the mosques linked to the Muslim Brotherhood also had schools and clinics associated with them. Muslim Brotherhood activists soon dominated the student body of the Islamic University in Gaza, which for many years was the largest in the territories. The surge in oil wealth of conservative Islamist states like Saudi Arabia strengthened the Islamists by supplying funding.

An able leader rode this surge in resources and religiosity to build a movement that would eventually control Gaza and prove a formidable challenge for Israel: Sheikh Ahmed Ismail Hassan Yasin. In 1948 Yasin fled with his family to Gaza from their home in Jorat Askalan, near Ashkelon. Yasin was a quadriplegic and almost blind as the result of an accident as a boy. Despite his handicaps, he was an impressive leader. Palestinians saw him as brave and wise, and his asceticism contrasted sharply with the excesses of Fatah leaders. Hamas offered Yasin a monthly stipend of one thousand dollars, but he instead took only six hundred dollars, which he believed was more than sufficient. Other Hamas members followed his example. In a striking contrast with Fatah's members, no one joined Hamas to get rich.

In 1976 Yasin set up the Islamic Center to support schools, mosques, and medical facilities and to promote Islamist values, in particular resisting what they felt was the cultural corruption that came with the Israeli occupation. Yasin brought together many of Hamas's future leaders and founders, such as Abdel Aziz al-Rantisi, Saleh Shehada, and Ibrahim al-Yazuri. Initially he reasoned that confrontation with Israel should wait until an Islamic state was established, because only then would the Muslim community be free of the weakness that he believed attends a secular society, a process that he thought would take many years.[11]

Israeli officials viewed the Islamists with suspicion, recognizing that they bore no love for the Jewish state. Yet in the 1970s the Islamists were not engaging in violence but simply building a broader social movement. Khaled Mishal, a longtime activist who eventually became a Hamas leader, recalls that proselytizing and social work were the focus of the Palestinian Islamic movement in these early days.[12] Israel's primary enemies at the time were violent leftist and nationalist Palestinian groups. The Islamists and the leftists were bitter rivals, competing for recruits and money in student groups, professional organizations, and Palestinian society as a whole. Islamists initially criticized the leftists simply for abandoning God, but over time, as the PLO moved toward embracing negotiations, Yasin criticized them for their willingness to engage politically with Israel. These clashes sometimes became violent as each group fought to dominate Palestinian politics.

Israel's complicity in Hamas's rise is the subject of great controversy and many conspiracy theories. The Muslim Brotherhood, Hamas's parent organization, needed Israel's permission to establish many of its organizations, so its success in doing so is often viewed as a sign that Israel was behind Hamas's creation. However, Israel took several years to approve the establishment of the Islamic movement from which Hamas grew, suggesting that Israel was not eager for the organization to be established. Avraham Sela, a leading Israeli scholar on the Palestinians and former intelligence officer, claims that Israel did not assist the Brotherhood directly. Barak Ben Zur, a former Israeli intelligence official, told me, "Israel is not stupid."

Yet Israel should not be let off the hook, its complicity was passive rather than active. While Israeli authorities tried to suppress any movement suspected of a link to Fatah or leftist groups, religious groups were allowed to flourish, and Israel knew it was opening space for Islamist rivals to groups like Fatah and the PFLP. So if Israel helped the Muslim Brotherhood, it was by changing the playing field rather than by direct support. Matti Steinberg, another Israeli scholar on the Palestinians and a former advisor to Shin Bet, claims that although Israel did not directly support the Muslim Brotherhood, it often ignored its activities. Israel did not understand the importance of the network of proselytizing and social services that allowed the Muslim Brotherhood and later Hamas to establish a firm foundation. As a result Israel allowed money to flow from the Persian Gulf to the Islamists but tried to stop it when it went to secular forces. Barak Ben Zur notes that unfortunately Israel believed "Words can't harm us," even if the talk is about killing Jews.

Having put in place a social and missionary network, Yasin began to set up a military infrastructure in the 1980s, arranging for weapons to be smuggled into Gaza to a group known as the Palestinian mujahedin. The initial decision was prompted in part after Alan Goodman, an American Jew, fired on Muslims worshiping in the al-Aqsa Mosque in Jerusalem in 1982, a provocation that was exacerbated when IDF soldiers killed two Islamists at Birzeit University in 1983.

The military wing of the Islamist movement initially focused on Palestinian drug dealers, suspected informants, and a variety of internal foes, yet Hamas also wanted arms to be collected to be used against Israel when the time was right.[13] The eventual goal, in Yasin's words, was "anything which would give the Israelis sleepless nights."[14] In 1984 future Hamas leaders, including Yasin and Shehada, would spend time in Israeli jails, charged with possessing weapons and establishing an armed organization. Yasin was released in the 1985 prisoner exchange that Israel conducted with the PFLP-GC in exchange for three of its kidnapped soldiers.

Hamas itself formally emerged when the First Intifada erupted in December 1987. The Intifada surprised the Brotherhood as it had Fatah. For years Fatah and leftist groups had taunted the Islamists as unpatriotic. Now Hamas could no longer risk sitting on the sidelines. PIJ and Fatah's Islamist faction were already plotting attacks against Israeli targets, and Islamist Palestinians in the diaspora pressed them for action. As protest swirled around them the Islamist leaders were forced to act or be left behind.

Hamas's first leaflet declared that the Intifada was a "rejection of the occupation and its pressures, land confiscation and the planting of settlements, and the policy of subjugation by the Zionists," and then went on to blast those in the PLO who were for "gasping after a sick peace."[15] Violence—"military action"—was how Hamas would liberate Palestine, a position similar to that of nationalist Palestinian groups.[16]

Like Fatah in the years after its founding, Hamas is a nationalist organization that seeks to end Jewish control of all of historic Palestine, not just the West Bank and Gaza. Unlike Fatah, Hamas is also an Islamist group, justifying its actions in the name of the Palestinian nation and in the name of religion. Its primary goal is the creation of an Islamic Palestinian state, and it has many facets: "an Islamic movement, a nationalist movement, a militant movement, a political movement—in addition to its cultural and social dimensions, its service functions, and its institution building," is how future leader Khaled Mishal described it.[17]

Hamas leaders also embrace the anti-Zionist stance of all Palestinian resistance and many are openly anti-Semitic, declaring Jews to be "sons of apes and swine." Its founding covenant is a hateful document, full of calls for jihad against the Jews as well as a mix of conspiracy theories that nineteenth century European anti-Semites would recognize at once. Article Twenty-Eight of the covenant contends, "[Zionism is behind] the Freemasons, The Rotary and Lions clubs, and other sabotage groups. All these organizations, whether secret or open, work in the interest of Zionism and according to its instructions. They aim at undermining societies, destroying values, corrupting consciences, deteriorating character and annihilating Islam. It is behind the drug trade and alcoholism in all its kinds so as to facilitate its control and expansion."[18]

In contrast to groups like al-Qa'ida, however, Hamas limits its struggle to one part of the Muslim world: historic Palestine.[19] Learning from Fatah's mistakes in alienating international audiences, Hamas does not strike at Israeli targets in Europe or at Israel's allies, such as the United States. Hamas's base is in Gaza, among Palestinians under Israeli occupation, not refugee camps in neighboring Arab states.

Much of Hamas's agenda involves social behavior; its members oppose moral permissiveness, favor Islamic law over secular law, and are dedicated to eradicating corruption. To these ends Hamas's charitable and political arms are vital to the organization. The founders care about Islamic education, feeding the hungry, and providing health care for the poor. These are core beliefs that further the goal of creating a true Islamic society, which in turn will lay the groundwork for an Islamic state. Politics, communications, and all charity work are considered important forms of resistance.[20]

Nevertheless it is a mistake to fully separate Hamas's spiritual and humanitarian commitment from violence. The same networks Hamas established to proselytize, to educate, and to care for the poor are also used to solicit recruits for violence. Donations for charitable activities are at times siphoned off to support the group's military wing. Clinics can be used to procure chemicals used for explosives, and the mosques can be natural meeting places in which to plan attacks or even store weapons.[21] Every time a poor Palestinian family sends a child to a Hamas school or receives food, Hamas gains public support.

Hamas struck first against suspected collaborators, killing dozens in the first few years of the Intifada. In February 1989 Hamas's military cell kidnapped and killed an Israeli soldier; three months later they kidnapped and killed another soldier, and in late 1990 they stabbed three Israelis. After Hamas began going after Israelis, Israel quickly arrested more than a thousand members, including Sheikh Yasin and all of the top leadership, forcing Hamas to restructure its militant wing to survive.[22] Yasin was imprisoned in 1989 and remained in jail until 1997, when the botched assassination attempt on Khaled Mishal in Jordan forced Israel to free him. (Yasin claims that Israel deprived him of sleep during his incarceration and that they beat his son Abdulhamid in front of him, which eventually led Yasin to confess.) Israel eventually released many of those arrested, deeming them harmless.

Prison would prove an asset for Hamas and for Palestinian militants, and over the years many of its leaders directed the movement from Israeli jails.[23] As the former Mossad director Efraim Halevy contends, Israeli jails were hotbeds for terrorist planning and inspiration.[24] The journalist Amira Hass reports that prison was "a grueling shared rite of passage that forged lifelong bonds among a sizable number of Palestinians."[25]

Hamas still faced an uphill climb for popularity. In 1989 fewer than 3 percent of Palestinians in Gaza, where Hamas would prove strongest, supported the organization.[26] In the days before the Oslo Accords were signed in 1993 only 16.6 percent of Palestinians in Gaza identified with Hamas politically, and only 10 percent in the West Bank; this figure was much smaller when it came to active supporters.[27] The journalist Zaki Chehab claimed that Hamas's military wing only had twenty machine guns when it began its campaign of terrorism as the Intifada wound down.[28] For much of the 1990s the military wing never reached a hundred total fighters.

Israeli arrests in 1989 and 1990 devastated Hamas and revealed the obvious to its leaders: zeal was no substitute for professionalism when it came to clandestine violence. Musa Abu Marzuq, a Hamas leader who studied in the United States and helped lead its military wing from afar until he was deported, helped revive the organization. Fortunately for Marzuq Hamas's political and social wings supplied new recruits to replace the losses. The military wing, known as the Martyr Izz ad-Din al-Qassam Brigades, now sought members who not only professed religious zeal but were highly competent. "Hamas is not an organization with angels for members," notes one observer.[29] Yet even with these improvements Hamas found it hard going. To improve their chances of survival, the Qassam Brigades developed a cell structure and a decentralized command. That made it harder for Israel to penetrate the movement, but also made it difficult for the central leadership to control the Brigades.

The Challenge of Oslo and the Emergence of Suicide Bombing

"Oslo was a major blow to Hamas," the Hamas expert Avraham Sela related to me. Mishal described Oslo as "the funeral of the Palestinian cause," for it surrendered the Palestinian patrimony.[30] Yet despite objections from Hamas and other ideological purists, the prospect of peace was popular at first: it meant the possibility of a Palestinian state, even if truncated from the original Palestinian Mandate territory, as well as an end to the chaos that had characterized Palestinian existence since 1948. International aid poured into PA coffers, and the Fatah-dominated PA bought the allegiances of many local leaders and power brokers.[31]

For both Fatah and Hamas everything now depended on the success of the peace talks. Hamas positioned itself as the anti-peace opposition party; its strength would rise and fall inversely with the peace process, and it used terrorism to help make the talks fail. As hopes soared with Oslo, Hamas's resistance found little support. It would justify its attacks in the name of revenge for Israeli killings of its operatives or of Palestinians, but even this method did not sell. Seventy percent of Palestinians opposed Hamas's 1996 suicide bombing campaign, and overall Palestinian support for the organization fell to 6 percent in that year.[32]

As the Oslo period commenced, Hamas moved swiftly beyond the primitive stabbings that characterized its early days to bring the horror of suicide bombing directly to Israel's people. Israel was already familiar with suicide bombing from Hizballah's devastating attacks against IDF soldiers and intelligence officers deployed in Lebanon. But Hamas did not just go after military targets. Its operatives aimed for civilians inside Israel, especially in places where large numbers congregated—in buses, restaurants, and shopping malls. Hamas and PIJ killed forty-five Israelis in 1993, sixty-five in 1994, twenty-nine in 1995, and fifty-six in 1996: enough to slow the momentum of negotiations but not to stop them altogether.[33]

Hamas botched its first suicide bombing, in April 1993, at Mehola Junction when a flawed bomb design led the blast to go up instead of out, killing only the bomber and an innocent Palestinian worker. It took almost another year for Hamas to succeed. On April 6, 1994, a Hamas suicide bomber pulled his car loaded with four hundred pounds of explosives next to a bus in Afula and detonated it: eight passengers died and forty were wounded.

Hamas justified its attacks on civilians with a number of excuses. Sheikh Yasin claimed that Hamas did not deliberately try to kill Israeli women and children, but the killings were "an eye for an eye, a nose for a nose." As one Hamas bomber dispatcher put it, "If a mother cries here, a mother has to cry there too."[34] Yasin's deputy, Abdel Aziz al-Rantisi, contended, "If we had weapons like F-16s and Apaches, we would use them, but we haven't." The only response, he said, was to duplicate the destruction, using suicide bombings instead.[35] Many rationalized violence by claiming that because Israel is a nation at arms all its citizens are really soldiers, and therefore legitimate targets.[36] Yusuf al-Qardawi, a leading ideologue in the Muslim Brotherhood, argues that suicide bombers' attacks are justified because "Israeli society is a military society. Its men and women are soldiers in its army and can be summoned up for service at any moment. If a child or an old person is killed in these operations, this is not intentional but accidental."[37]

Hamas achieved success by first recruiting the right people. The overwhelming majority of secular militants, and most Islamist ones, came from activist families. They joined youth movements, which are natural breeding grounds for radicalization, and the schools that Hamas ran developed an educated cadre. "Put Hamas leaders in a row and you see the best of the best," says the former Israeli intelligence official Barak Ben Zur. Hamas was also increasingly cool. One arrested youth explained his decision to fight Israel simply by saying, "Everyone was joining."[38] Many Hamas fighters had little direct contact with Israelis. Their impressions came from seeing Israeli soldiers and propaganda that stressed Israeli brutality and inhumanity.

Also vital to the movement was the recruitment of Israeli spies and collaborators. If Hamas discovered a spy, he might be offered a choice: execution as a traitor, with the shame spreading to his entire extended family, or a chance to go out as a martyr against Israel. Sheikh Yasin told an Israeli researcher, Anat Berko, "If a Muslim loses his true path it is important for him to find it again, because otherwise his wife will be labeled 'wife of a traitor,' and his son, 'son of a traitor.'"[39]

Saleh Shehada, the first commander of Hamas's military wing, elaborated on Hamas's approach to its recruitment of suicide bombers. Bombers, he said, were chosen not only for their faith, but also for how that person's death would affect his family. Children, the head of a family, and the elderly were avoided when possible.[40] The bomber himself is usually a volunteer. The suicide vest he wears costs only around $150, but fulfilling the rest of the mission costs up to fifty thousand dollars.[41] Hamas must buy a car, assemble documents, and provide support for the family of the bomber after his death.[42] And the bomber is not alone. Other group members survey the target and film it, after which senior Hamas operatives approve it. Others must train the bomber. As the American terrorism expert Matthew Levitt contends, "Behind every successful suicide bombing lies a network of recruiters, trainers, bomb makers, facilitators, and financiers."[43] The bomber is often the cheapest and least important part of this entire network.

In Western cultures the notion of martyring oneself in this day and age is inconceivable. Because this notion is so strange, and because the destruction wrought is so vast, myths have grown up around suicide bombing. Perhaps the most rampant is that the people involved are poor, unemployed, or otherwise economically disadvantaged. Another myth is that the bombers were misfits that terrorist masterminds exploited. A Shin Bet study done during the height of the Second Intifada found that no simple profile fit: some bombers had wives, and others did not; some were childless, and others had children; some were educated and religious, and others gave their faith only lip service and did not finish high school—and there were many other variations.[44] Bombers appear to be no richer or poorer than other Palestinians. Similarly, though many of the bombers are observant, they are rarely fanatics.[45] In most cases they see themselves as warriors and are treated as such. They believe their actions are akin to charging an enemy machine-gun nest so that their comrades can advance. From the group's point of view, the bombings are desirable simply because they are cheap and effective.[46] Nor should their propaganda impact be dismissed. The notes and videos suicide bombers leave behind are meant to terrorize their enemies and to inspire fellow Palestinians to follow them. And they do.

Even in the mid-1990s, when suicide bombing was rare, bombers and others who attacked Israel could draw on several layers of support. The Palestinian people, even those who were not members of Hamas or PIJ, made up the first circle. Society has long lauded resistance, and portraits and praise for martyrs to the cause are ubiquitous. Even when hopes for peace were strongest, support for attacks on civilians often hovered between 15 and 20 percent, a level that suggests Hamas attacks retained the support of a substantial minority of Palestinians.[47]

Future suicide bombers sustained themselves with the respect and adulation accorded to people of high status. The terrorists were admired; their deeds were praised in mosques and community centers, and their families enjoyed more respect than those of youths who did not take up the struggle. Money also matters. By 2001 Hamas was giving over two million dollars a month to the families of suicide bombers and Hamas prisoners.

Hamas tried to increase its support by going beyond violence. Starting in 1994 some Hamas members formed Khalas, a political movement that published a newspaper and helped spread Hamas ideas throughout Palestinian society. Hamas forged links in the Palestinian diaspora with leaders like Musa Abu Marzuq, who was in the United States, Jordan, and finally Syria, and Khaled Mishal, who was in Kuwait until 1990 and then in Jordan and eventually Syria. During much of the 1990s Hamas leaders from inside the West Bank and Gaza were in Israeli jails, so outside figures often made the key decisions. Because of the Israeli and PA sweeps of Hamas members in the West Bank and Gaza, the outside or "external" leadership, people such as Marzuq and later Mishal, moved to the center of Hamas's organization, with the exact power balance shifting depending on circumstances. Outside of Gaza, in Kuwait, Amman, Damascus, and the United States, they were relatively safe. From those countries Hamas leaders could organize, recruit, and raise money without Israel disrupting their efforts. To avoid laws in the United States directed at stopping financial support for terrorism, sympathizers would raise money for Hamas organizations and initiatives that did not bear the organization's name. Sometimes governments provided funds directly, particularly after Arafat betrayed Gulf leaders by siding with Saddam Hussein after his 1990 Kuwait invasion.

Despite this foreign support Hamas was its own master. The group received money and at times arms and training from various foreign sponsors, but unlike Palestine Islamic Jihad or leftist movements like al-Saiqa it remained independent.

Palestine Islamic Jihad: Hamas's Lesser Sibling

Hamas was not the only rival to Fatah. Palestine Islamic Jihad, which began operations in 1981, was also in the mix. PIJ too was an Islamist group that believed violence was a necessary step toward defeating Israel and creating an Islamic Palestinian state. But PIJ did not seek social change from below: it made only a token effort to run hospitals, schools, and social welfare organizations. Its goal was power, and its ideologues believed a vanguard, not a mass movement, was key to an Islamic state. Although it was small, its very presence led to pressure on Hamas as well as on the peace process. The PIJ leader Fathi al-Shiqaqi broke from the Muslim Brotherhood in 1981 because it would not endorse an armed struggle to liberate Palestine. From the start PIJ wanted war first, while the Muslim Brotherhood wanted mass support first.[48] However, PIJ helped force the Brotherhood's hand, declaring that while the PLO had taken "the path of jihad" without belief, the Muslim Brotherhood had wrongly taken "the path of belief" without jihad.[49] Part of the reason the Brotherhood embraced violence was to counteract this image. PIJ has played second fiddle to Hamas since the latter emerged in 1987. "If you are not accepted by Hamas, you join PIJ" is how one Israeli intelligence official put it to me.

PIJ depended heavily on its founder and longtime leader, Fathi al-Shiqaqi. He was the core of the organization—the recruiter, the fund-raiser, and the planner. Shiqaqi spent most of his time hiding out in Damascus, and Israel did not target him there for fear of jeopardizing ongoing negotiations with Syria. But on October 26, 1995, he stopped in Malta after returning from a meeting in Libya. When Israel learned that he was traveling outside a protective Arab state they had what one senior Israeli security official, Uzi Arad, described as a "once-in-a-lifetime opportunity." Two men drove by in a motorcycle, repeatedly firing a gun with a silencer into his head as Shiqaqi stood in front of his hotel.[50]

This killing devastated the group, leaving it leaderless for several years. The former Mossad head Shabtai Shavit contends, "Shiqaqi was Islamic Jihad and Islamic Jihad was Shiqaqi." Shiqaqi's successor, Ramadan Shalah, left his teaching responsibilities at the University of South Florida to lead the group, but the difference between Shalah and Shiqaqi was "night and day." Shalah had less support within Hamas and did not have the same skill at operations, making PIJ far less effective.

Shiqaqi's death, the PA and Israeli crackdown on PIJ operatives, and the continued popular hope that negotiations would succeed, all combined to decrease support for PIJ. Because the group did not have Hamas's massive social mission to complement its violent activities, it began to draw on Iran for support, though it preferred to remain independent.[51] During the 1990s Iran offered PIJ a bonus for each attack on Israel, and PIJ's budget came almost entirely from Tehran.[52] The PIJ attack on the Dizengoff Center before the Purim holiday in 1996 occurred when Israel-Syria peace talks appeared on the edge of a breakthrough. When PIJ claimed credit for the attack from its Damascus office, Israel suspended negotiations with Syria.[53] For Iran, this disruption was a victory.

PIJ did not get back on its feet until the Second Intifada, when violence of this sort came back in vogue.

The Rise in Security Cooperation and the Decline of Hamas

Rabin, who championed negotiations, has rightly gone down in history as a martyr for peace, particularly in the United States. Yet this hagiography ignores that the man who authorized "force, might, and beatings" during the First Intifada did not seek to make peace with a Palestinian Gandhi. "If we find a partner for peace with the Palestinians," Rabin said shortly after the Palestinians began to govern themselves, "they will run their internal affairs without the High Court of Justice, B'Tselem [an Israeli human rights organization], or all sorts of groups of mothers and fathers and bleeding hearts."[54] In other words, civil liberties would not fetter the new Palestinian government when it fought terrorism.

Amnesty International reported that the PA soon had hundreds of political prisoners and that many detainees were tortured, including such senior Hamas figures as Dr. Mahmud al-Zahhar, Hamas's leader in Gaza after Israel imprisoned Yasin. Zahhar's Palestinian captors broke his arm, and in an effort to humiliate him shaved his head and beard. PA security agencies found numerous ways to torture suspected Palestinian opponents: they suspended them from hooks, beat them with cables, dripped molten plastic on their bodies, and burned them with cigarettes.[55] Rabin, it seems, had got his wish.

The PA's successes against Hamas and PIJ often came at the expense of the rule of law, a violation that Israel and the United States deliberately ignored. But often the PA let the most guilty go free, as they had connections, instead detaining lower-level figures or distant supporters to intimidate Fatah's rivals and satisfy the Israelis that the PA was indeed trying hard. Using counterterrorism as an excuse to weaken its opposition, the PA arrested political foes and peaceful critics of its own abuses. On November 18, 1994, PA security forces prevented a Hamas march in Gaza, provoking a series of riots that killed fourteen Hamas supporters. Although this crackdown was effective in the short term, such repression eventually weakened the PA's legitimacy.

In contrast to the Israelis, Palestinian security services had the "capability to reach into every terrorist headquarters and every terrorist's home," according to Major General Uri Saguy, who headed military intelligence in the mid-1990s. Arafat amassed vast forces, sixty thousand in total security personnel by the late 1990s.[56] From Hamas's point of view, this force could be devastating. In FBI recordings of alleged Hamas-affiliated individuals in the United States, they complained that Fatah officials viewed the Islamic movement as a greater enemy than the Jews.[57]

Yet rather than try to crush Hamas completely, Arafat struck a deal with the devil. For its part, Hamas tried to continue resistance without openly challenging Arafat's leadership. In December 1995 Hamas and PA officials met in Cairo and agreed on a tacit truce. Hamas's leader in Gaza, Mahmud al-Zahhar, said that the truce would allow Arafat to move forward with negotiations, but Hamas would not formally renounce violence "because this . . . would be akin to cancelling prayers."[58] Khaled Mishal, one of Hamas's leaders in exile, justified the agreement as a way to avoid "internecine fighting."[59]

Allowing Hamas to keep its weapons and operate illustrated all the Israelis' frustrations with the PA as a partner. In particular Arafat demanded that Hamas attacks not occur from areas under direct PA control: Gaza and Area A in the West Bank. As the PLO leader in the talks declared, "We see it as sufficient to oblige Hamas not to embarrass the PA, which is responsible for security in the areas it has received." In exchange the PA would turn a blind eye to attacks in Palestinian areas that Israel still controlled.[60] For Israelis this was particularly troubling, as much of the recruitment, fundraising, and leadership of the organization was in PA-controlled areas, even if the cell launching an actual attack was not. Many Israeli security officials came to believe that Area A was "a safe haven for Palestinian terror organizations."[61] The killing of Ayyash would soon render the truce irrelevant, but for Israelis it was a sign of Arafat's attempts to play both sides on terrorism.

Palestinian security cooperation with Israel reached its peak in the spring of 1996, when Arafat arrested twelve hundred Hamas activists after the Hamas and PIJ bombings that followed Ayyash's death. In Gaza the PA conducted mass arrests of Hamas and PIJ supporters, detaining them for months. Prisoners were often beaten or burned or had their heads covered in filthy sacks for days.[62] As they had with Zahhar, PA security forces shaved off half the beards of several Hamas members. One of the security chiefs, Jibril Rajoub, reportedly shot several Hamas activists in Ramallah himself. When Hamas took power in Gaza a decade later it would remember its brutal treatment at the hands of its fellow Palestinians and abuse Fatah members in their turn. Hamas suffered frequent losses. The BBC journalist Zaki Chehab describes a Hamas fighter as living "dangerously, audaciously, and briefly."[63]

Cooperation between Israel and the PA surged in part because Arafat recognized that Shimon Peres, Rabin's dovish successor, was weak electorally and that Hamas was gaining in strength. U.S. pressure was heavy, and Palestinian security chiefs knew that without security, peace talks would go nowhere. For the PA leaders, delivering on security was necessary for them to win their gamble on peace talks. Arafat did make good on controlling Fatah, which, before Oslo, was Israel's key enemy and did not use the organization to strike Israel directly.

Yet for much of this period the PA's relationship with Israel was adversarial, and Hamas exploited this tension. Israel repeatedly demanded the arrests of Hamas leaders, but the PA demurred, claiming incapacity or ignorance of their whereabouts. At times PA security services used a revolving-door system, arresting some terrorist suspects and releasing others (or even the same ones) a few days later. In one instance the PA arrested Awad Silmi, a wanted terrorist, after Israel imposed a closure on Gaza. However, the security services did not arrest the three other Hamas members with him because Israel did not specifically demand it. In a strange twist of logic the PA justified Silmi's arrest to Palestinians as a way of protecting him from the Israelis. Senior IDF officials claim that Silmi's detention was comfortable: he kept his pistol, he stayed in a private home, and he left the house during the day as he pleased.

Israelis claimed that the PA also gave tacit support to Hamas attacks as a way of ratcheting up pressure against Israel. At the very least Arafat was not willing to take the political risk of splitting the Palestinian community. The former Shin Bet director Carmi Gillon judges Arafat "half and half" on stopping terror in this period.

The personal relationships that dominate Palestinian politics also shape Palestinian security agencies. A Shin Bet official noted that if the PA arrested a Hamas or PIJ member, everyone knew who was involved, and the arresting officials feared retaliation. Gaza in particular is heavily clan-based, and each clan has its own members in the security services. Each would favor its own clan, ignoring or abetting their crimes. If they wished, clans could put heavy pressure on a security official, going so far as to threaten his and his family's lives. Sometimes members of the PA and Hamas had either gone to university or grown up together or were comrades in arms, according to Israeli intelligence officials. Rajoub, the PA security chief, had a brother who was a Hamas leader; another PA security head, Mohammad Dahlan, and the Hamas leader Rantisi grew up in the same refugee camp. Later Dahlan told Arafat why arresting Rantisi was out of the question: "I am scared of my mother who adores Sheikh Abdul Aziz Rantisi."[64] Dahlan would at times inform Hamas members beforehand when he heard rumors that Israel planned to kill them.

The security organizations were political, and they were reluctant to get ahead of Palestinian popular opinion, particularly without Arafat's backing. No one wanted to be branded as a collaborator. So they would provide information if they knew a bomb was planted, but not go after recruiters, fundraisers, and other vital members of the support network. Their cooperation moreover was conditional on progress in the peace process. The Palestinian chief of intelligence Major General Amin al-Hindi justified working with Israel by saying, "[The] agreement is in the interest of the Palestinian people [and] we and the Israeli security organs have to prevent those people from aborting the peace process."[65] Polls of Palestinians consistently showed that support for violence fell when belief in the peace process was strong.[66] Some Israeli defense officials now argue that part of the reason cooperation peaked in 1996 was that signed interim agreements proved the benefits of a peace deal.

The opposite was also true. As peace talks faltered and as polls showed that support for violence was increasing, the security organizations feared for their reputations. When Israel built settlements or resisted pullbacks from Palestinian areas, PA security leaders retaliated by releasing suspected terrorists or dragging their feet on investigations, making it clear that cooperation was dependent upon political progress. Indeed Arafat's advisor and peace negotiator Ghaith al-Omari notes that these releases were often timed to impress not only Israel but also foreign audiences, particularly those in the United States.

It angered Israeli security officials—but did not surprise any intelligence official elsewhere in the world—that the Palestinian security services often tried to use Israeli information to seek out and neutralize the person who provided the information rather than the terrorist the source fingered. Every intelligence agency loathes informers, and for the Palestinians hatred was particularly intense given the losses they suffered at Israel's hands. Despite promises to leave the informers alone, hundreds if not thousands were simply arrested without any charges. Suspected informers were regularly killed. Sometimes their murderers would hammer nails into their knees or pour molten plastic into their ears first.[67] Khaled Husseini, a Palestinian arrested by the PA for informing, claims he was dangled by a rope from the ceiling with his toes barely touching the floor for twenty-six days; his interrogators also put out their cigarettes on his flesh, urinated on him, beat him, and shoved a bottle into his anus, as well as threatened to rape his sisters and mother.[68] Israel offered the equivalent of a witness protection program for informers, but few wanted to leave Palestinian areas entirely and live in Israel.

The hunt for informers was only a small part of the broader problem. Omari notes that Palestinian security forces drew on Fatah's military wing. These leaders were revolutionaries, not intelligence professionals, and their instincts were highly political. Arafat often co-opted militants into the security services, an approach that worked in good times but contributed to violence later on. One Shin Bet official compared it to "deciding to take a small crocodile in your house."

Ineptitude explained part of the problem, though understandably Palestinians were reluctant to admit this and few Israelis would credit incompetence over malevolence. Arafat exacerbated the problem by deliberately fragmenting the security leadership. Key security bodies included the General Intelligence Service, the Preventive Security Organization, the Presidential Guard (also known as Force 17), and the much smaller Special Security Force. There were a dozen security forces in total. Orders often conflicted, and information was rarely shared. Fatah also kept its own security institutions and military wing, even though these closely overlapped with those of the PA.

Arafat's relations with Hamas mirrored his relationship with Israel: in neither case would he openly and consistently declare his loyalty. Even though PA security services often cracked down harshly on Hamas, they would, much to the anger of Israelis, honor Yasin's request to release a prisoner. Arafat's behavior with Hamas was equally duplicitous. Arafat had offered Hamas membership in the PLO before Oslo but also tried to exclude the organization from real power. He solicited Yasin's advice and invited him to meetings, even as he attempted to undercut him. Arafat thought he could crush Hamas at any time he chose. In a private speech he once described Hamas members as "ants," and that scorn led him to believe he could control the Islamists.[69]

Hamas again tried to cut a deal with the PA, limiting but not ending its violence in exchange for toleration. Part of the reason was ideological: Yasin strongly feared divisions (*fitna*, or strife among the believers) in the Palestinian community even though many Hamas members resented Fatah's leadership. Because Arafat was the dominant figure, Yasin did not believe Hamas should challenge him directly. Moreover open opposition to Arafat would be political suicide, to say nothing of the PA crackdown that would follow if Hamas made a bid for power. After Hamas and the PA skirmished in Gaza, the Hamas leader Mahmud al-Zahhar declared that the group would not respond, saying, "Civil war is a 'red line' for Hamas."[70] In 1998 Israel successfully targeted two leaders of Hamas's military wing on the West Bank, the Awadallah brothers Imad and Adil, and Hamas accused the PA of collusion. During the operation the Israelis found an archive of the brothers' messages to Hamas commanders, in which the brothers had asked Yasin for guidance on how to behave regarding the PA security services. Yasin replied that the PA services had public support to target Hamas, and thus Hamas members should not fight back even during an arrest attempt. His instructions reflect both his concern about strife within the Palestinian community and his fear that Hamas's support was too weak to risk alienating public opinion further. Lower-level Hamas officials, however, were less fearful of *fitna* and often challenged the PA; indeed Palestinian officials claim that Hamas tried to kill Arafat with a roadside bomb.[71]

Hamas Stalls during the Netanyahu Period

Despite Palestinian mistrust of Netanyahu, progress on peace negotiations such as the so-called Wye Accords helped security cooperation continue. A U.S. State Department evaluation of Palestinian compliance with its peace process commitments declared that "security cooperation was generally good."[72] Uzi Arad, a close advisor to Netanyahu, believes that the Palestinian image of Netanyahu made Arafat more willing to cooperate on counterterrorism, as he feared that Netanyahu would make good on his threats.

However, Ami Ayalon, who ran Shin Bet in the second half of the 1990s, believes progress on the peace process was the key. The PA security services, he says, "were willing to crush their brothers in Hamas for the price of freedom," but at the same time they "didn't want to be Israeli collaborators." They told Ayalon, "We are doing it for ourselves, not for you." Matti Steinberg, an expert on the Palestinians, told me that the successes in this period do not get the credit they deserve because they were politically driven rather than operational in origin. Palestinian security services believed that they were on the road to a political deal, and as such were willing to cooperate. For a while Palestinian political leaders had convinced the Palestinian people that negotiations would work and that Hamas's violence was stopping Palestinians from getting their own state. As Steinberg contended in a media interview, the decline of terrorism happened "in spite of Netanyahu."[73]

Palestinian and Israeli security officials even conducted joint operations in 1999. For example, Ayalon explains that if they received information that there was an apartment in Nablus where a Hamas member was planning an attack, Shin Bet would pass the information to Palestinian officials in the West Bank, and together they would locate the apartment. The Palestinians would conduct the actual arrests, but both sides would share the information.

Although Israel regularly complained that the PA was not doing enough to crush Hamas, from Hamas's point of view the security cooperation was stifling. The documents discovered in the Awadallah operation made it clear that Palestinian intelligence, not Israeli actions, was the key barrier to Hamas operations. Khaled Mishal, who became a top Hamas leader in the 1990s, admits, "There was severe security harassment, a number of our brothers were assassinated or killed in prison." Although the movement was not defeated, it was "hemorrhaging."[74] After being released from prison in 1997 the Hamas leader Sheikh Yasin even spoke of the possibility of a truce.[75]

The numbers tell a similar story. During the Netanyahu administration the Israeli death toll steadily decreased: in 1996 fifty-six Israelis died; in 1997 forty-one; in 1998 only sixteen; and in 1999 only eight. Indeed this progress continued up until the outbreak of the Second Intifada. At the end of September, before the Second Intifada began in 2000, only one Israeli died from terrorism that year.[76] The numbers of Palestinians killed in the occupied territory dropped dramatically as well; in 1988 Israeli security forces killed 290 Palestinians; the number fell to 112 in 1994 and plunged to eighteen in 1997.[77]

While the Israelis maintained a dim view of the security situation—they saw only the continued risk to their citizens—the Palestinians viewed Israeli intelligence as all-powerful. For Palestinian militants, life was difficult. Israel would raid their homes, harass their friends, and constantly force them to be on the run, creating a tremendous strain on their daily lives. Before the Second Intifada Hamas was a battered organization, a shadow of its future self. Its military wing had perhaps a handful of full-time operatives.[78]

The United States, Egypt, and Jordan nurtured the PA-Israeli security partnership. These countries helped supply and train Palestinian security services, which bolstered Arafat's standing with his own people. Jordan also clamped down on Hamas activities in the country after bombings. In August 1999 Jordan's new king, Abdallah, closed down the Hamas offices and arrested many of the staff. Abdallah feared Hamas might radicalize Islamists in Jordan, and he also wanted to placate Israel and the United States, both of which had long pressed for a crackdown.[79]

With Rabin dead and Peres replaced by Netanyahu, Arafat saw that U.S. relations with Israel were becoming visibly strained, and he looked to the United States for support. He was rewarded by Clinton's historic visit to the Gaza Strip in December 1998. To make sure the United States was fully on board, however, Arafat knew the PA would have to act on terrorism, according to U.S. negotiator Martin Indyk. The U.S. effort helped keep the two parties working together even in the absence of a political process. Still, as one involved U.S. official noted, you can't have true security without a political deal, "not in a hundred Sundays."

Despite the relatively low level of terrorism, many Israelis believed that Arafat chose not to deliver the coup de grace to Hamas and PIJ or to the more militant parts of the Fatah-linked Tanzim. Israeli security officials complained that the PA often warned suspects, and even in cases of arrests it continued the revolving-door policy. After several suicide attacks in

1998 there was no help from the Palestinian side. Fatah needed to maintain its militant street cred. One of Dahlan's deputies participated in an attack in Gaza, and in the West Bank the elite Fatah unit Force 17 also led operations. Fatah itself sponsored military training through its youth wings.[80] It supported "summer camps" that trained tens of thousands of young Palestinians to handle weapons and learn the basics of guerrilla war.[81] In the end Israeli security officials grew more and more convinced that Arafat and the Palestinian leaders were not committed to ending terrorism.

Arafat's rhetoric toward Israel remained hostile. He did not try to court the Israeli people, as President Anwar Sadat of Egypt had done so successfully with his dramatic visit to Jerusalem. "Oslo was a deal of elites," the Palestinian journalist Wafa Amr notes, and the leaders did not prepare the people to make the necessary political sacrifices for peace. So there was not a shift in mind-set, making it hard to sustain cooperation when progress on talks faltered. One issue of particular concern to Israelis was Palestinian textbooks, which were filled with anti-Israeli references. Israel was excluded from the regional maps, and Zionists were referred to as "aggressive, dangerous infiltrators."[82]

Many observers, particularly Palestinians, point to politics to explain Arafat's weak efforts. Although Arafat was the unquestioned leader of the Palestinians, his star was fading, and his coterie of advisors was more despised than admired by the Palestinian people. Hamas and other rejectionists had criticized Oslo from the start, but now their arguments became more pointed: not only did the occupation continue, but Jewish settlements expanded, the economic situation had worsened, and thousands of Palestinians remained in Israeli jails.[83] Arafat did not call elections or otherwise try to legitimate his leadership. Instead he tried to co-opt his critics so he could be seen as tough on Israel, even as he negotiated. Arafat's advisor Ghaith al-Omari thinks that many Israelis, particularly in the security establishment, did not appreciate, or chose not to appreciate, the complexity of Palestinian politics. They believed that most political explanations of problems were lies, deliberate attempts to disguise a decision not to cooperate.

Resistance also remained popular, and stagnation on peace talks fed its popularity. One Palestinian observer told me that all the leading Palestinian factions embrace "a legitimate right to armed resistance." In particular "the oppressed, occupied, and expelled have a right to resist." This may go by the name *jihad* for Islamists, *revolution* for Marxists, and so on, but all Palestinians pass on stories of resistance through the generations. Several observers note that even peaceful Palestinian activists are reluctant to condemn armed resistance for fear of being branded as collaborators.

Israelis believe that Arafat kept the option of force open for strategic, not political reasons. The manipulative method he used to exact concessions at Hebron after the 1996 tunnel violence became a model for him. The Israeli military intelligence official Amos Malka contends that Arafat deliberately allowed the groups to stay alive in order to use them against Israel at the right moment, a viewpoint several other U.S. and Israeli intelligence officials share.[84] The future army chief of staff Bogi Yaalon believes that Arafat used terrorism as a stick and counterterrorism cooperation as a carrot. Another former chief of staff, Amnon Lipkin-Shahak, is more cautious, but he too believes that Arafat wanted to keep Hamas's weapons and cells in reserve in case fighting with Israel resumed. The Hamas leader Khaled Mishal recalls that the group even offered to allow the PA to exploit Hamas attacks as leverage during negotiations.[85]

Yasin and Arafat both believed that they would grow stronger against each other as time went on, Arafat because he could consolidate his power by controlling the PA government, and Yasin because his movement steadily made inroads into society. By the end of the decade Arafat appeared to be the winner. The election of Ehud Barak in 1999 breathed new life into the peace process, and the hope of peace sustained and improved security cooperation. Neither Yasin nor Arafat would have predicted that within a few years Hamas would be ascendant.

CHAPTER VII

INTO THE ABYSS: THE SECOND INTIFADA (2000)

THE MORIBUND peace process suddenly took on new life in 1999, after Ehud Barak defeated Netanyahu at the polls. In Barak's first speech to the Knesset as prime minister, he called for a "comprehensive peace in the Middle East" and went so far as to declare, "I know not only the suffering of my people, but also recognize the suffering of the Palestinian people."[1] Shortly after this speech Barak and Arafat met and agreed to a number of steps forward, including prisoner releases. Arafat declared "renewed hope" for a peace deal.[2] Few guessed that this auspicious start would lead to a horrific explosion of violence: the Second, or al-Aqsa, Intifada was about to begin.[3]

Ehud Barak is the most decorated soldier in Israeli history. Before he rose to become IDF chief of staff he served for years as a commando, running daring operations behind enemy lines. In May 1972 he and his fellow soldiers rescued ninety-seven hostages from Sabena Flight 572 and raided Beirut to kill several Palestinian terrorist leaders. Barak also helped design the 1976 Entebbe raid, in which IDF troops rescued passengers from the hijacked Air France Flight 139, as well as the long-standing campaign against the Black September Organization members Israel deemed responsible for murdering Israeli athletes at the 1972 Munich Olympics. In 1988, when Israeli forces killed Abu Jihad, Arafat's number two, in Tunis, Barak was in the command post on an offshore boat.

In 1999 Barak ran for prime minister. Despite his military background, or perhaps because of it, he campaigned as a man of peace, evoking the spirit of Rabin as a warrior-peacemaker. Unlike Shimon Peres, no one could deride Barak as soft on terrorists. He came into office politically empowered; he was popular among Israelis and had carefully assembled a large coalition, freeing his hand to make bold moves.

The outbreak of the Second Intifada is also intertwined with the story of another Israeli hero-soldier: Ariel Sharon. Palestinians loathed Sharon as the sword-bearer of Israel's reprisal strategy in the 1950s, as a father of Israel's settlement policy, and as the butcher of Palestinians in Lebanon after Israel's 1982 invasion. So when Sharon planned to visit the Temple Mount on September 28, 2000, to emphasize Jewish claims to the site, it spelled trouble. The Temple Mount, controlled by Israel since the 1967 War, is the most contested real estate in the world. It is the site of the first and second temples, the latter destroyed by the Romans in 70 CE as punishment for a Jewish revolt. Indeed Jews gather to pray at one of the retaining walls for the second temple, the Western or "Wailing" Wall, because of its proximity to this holiness. Built on top of the Mount, however, are two mosques, the Al-Aqsa Mosque and the Dome of the Rock, the latter of which is supposedly built over the "holy of holies," the inner sanctum of the ancient Jewish temple. For Muslims around the world, the mosques' antiquity and the holiness of Jerusalem in the Islamic tradition make the Temple Mount's status a source of constant concern. Jewish control of the Mount is particularly galling.

Months before Sharon's visit, as Barak and Arafat negotiated the Mount's status at Camp David, the fate of the site dominated the news. Radicals, and even moderates, on each side feared their leaders would make unforgivable concessions to clinch a deal. Sharon's visit was his way of dramatically demonstrating his opposition to any concessions. Palestinian officials, Israeli police, and Israeli intelligence all predicted that blood would flow if Sharon went forward with his visit. Dennis Ross, the U.S. envoy to the peace talks, warned the Israeli interior minister Shlomo Ben-Ami about the visit, "I can think of a lot of bad ideas, but I can't think of a worse one."[4] Before Sharon's visit Arafat and Barak had dinner together at Barak's home in Kochav Yair. As Arafat left he warned Barak about the risks of Sharon's planned visit. Barak, however, felt he could not block Sharon; it was his right as an Israeli to visit the site, and any interference would be seen as politically motivated.

Sharon's visit itself was peaceful, but, as anticipated, it sparked widespread protests and riots, which the Israeli police put down with tear gas and rubber bullets. The following day twenty thousand Palestinians came to the Temple Mount to pray. Some threw stones at Jews who had gathered to pray at the Western Wall on the eve of Rosh Hashanah, the Jewish New Year. Rioters also stoned Israeli police who tried to intervene.[5] At first the police responded with rubber bullets. However, one well-aimed stone hit the head of a police officer in Jerusalem, knocking him unconscious. The police then started to use rubber bullets from close range, which can be lethal, while snipers fired live ammunition at targets believed to be more dangerous. By the end of the day seven Palestinians lay dead and one hundred were wounded. Rumors flew that there had been a massacre on the Temple Mount.

From there the violence escalated, each round drawing more blood. The following day protests erupted throughout Gaza and the West Bank. Militants fired on the IDF from within crowds of demonstrators, and the IDF returned fire, killing ten more Palestinians. Although Palestinian leaders quickly dubbed the violence "the Second Intifada," the body count was far higher than its more peaceful predecessor. By the end of November the Palestinians counted 247 dead. UN officials claimed that almost ten thousand Palestinians were injured in this period, almost half of whom were children.[6]

Terrorism was at the core of the Palestinian struggle against Israel during this period, but the Second Intifada involved far more than terrorism. The Palestinians targeted Israeli soldiers as well as civilians. Israel, for its part, found itself having to struggle in dimensions outside of traditional counterterrorism. To root out the terrorists it had to uproot groups like Hamas that did far more than terrorism, expanding the scope and scale of the struggle in the process. Political, diplomatic, and financial tools all proved important, though at times neglected.

It is difficult to say when the Intifada ended, but Israeli security officials claim that through the end of 2008 Palestinians carried out some fifteen thousand terrorist attacks. Some figures are lower and others are much higher, depending on what is counted as terrorism and as an attack. But no matter what definition is used, more Israeli civilians died from terrorism during this period than had died in terrorist attacks in the entire history of the state. B'Tselem, the Israeli human rights organization, counts over one thousand Israelis, two thirds of them civilians, killed by Palestinians between September 29, 2000, and the end of 2008. The toll on the Palestinian side is far higher: Israeli security forces or civilians killed five thousand Palestinians during the same period.[7]

The Second Intifada was also an economic disaster. Israel's per capita GDP fell successively in 2001, 2002, and 2003, losing 8 percent in total and not recovering until 2004.[8] For the Palestinians, the economic price was even more devastating: the violence and Israel's tightening of security kept Palestinian workers from higher paying jobs in Israel; tourism and foreign investment plummeted; local businesses collapsed; and unemployment and poverty abounded.

Why did the violence explode when peace seemed so near? Although Sharon's visit sparked the fire, the conflagration can be explained only by looking at the broader political environment. Many Palestinians considered the original Oslo deal a surrender that legitimated Israel's control of

Mandatory Palestine. Even a deal that matched the 1967 Green Line border meant that Palestinians would accept losing 78 percent of their claimed patrimony. By the fall of 2000 the peace process appeared to have failed to gain the Palestinians sovereignty over the remaining sliver. In Palestinian eyes Israel was not honoring the spirit of Oslo. Writing several months before the outbreak of the violence, a group of Palestinian activists and intellectuals warned that the settlements, land expropriation, checkpoints, and other problems were creating a disastrous situation. From 1993 to 2000 the settler population rose from 115,000 to 200,000 on the West Bank, and much of that expansion occurred after Barak was elected.[9] Shortly after the Second Intifada broke out, the former U.S. senator George Mitchell headed an investigation that revealed most Palestinians believed that delays in the peace process were "the result of an Israeli attempt to prolong and solidify the occupation."[10] As the Palestinian scholar Hussein Agha and the U.S. peace negotiator Rob Malley note, "Seen from Gaza and the West Bank, Oslo's legacy read like a litany of promises deferred or unfulfilled. Six years after the agreement, there were more Israeli settlements, less freedom of movement, and worse economic conditions."[11] Hamas's dire propaganda on the occasion of Oslo's signing seemed prophetic.

By 2000 Israelis would use similar words, or harsher ones, to describe their erstwhile Palestinian partners. Israelis increasingly believed that the Palestinian Authority in general, and Arafat in particular, had never truly embraced peace despite signing the Oslo agreements. Unlike Egypt's Anwar Sadat or Jordan's King Hussein, Arafat always seemed ready to return to violence. Israelis pointed out that he released suspected terrorists from detention and allowed Palestinian groups to hoard weapons. Some officials also believed he knowingly allowed terrorist attacks on Israel. Rhetoric also remained hostile, and Arafat did not try to prepare his people for peace.

In hindsight the distrust on both sides demonstrates a fundamental flaw in the peace process. Oslo was meant to generate mutual concessions that would promote confidence and even affection, which in turn would move both parties toward a final settlement. However, negotiations over an endless series of incremental steps gave each side the opportunity to feel betrayed over and over again, making the next move even harder.

To most, the Second Intifada came as a shock. It occurred shortly after the Camp David talks, which had held out the tantalizing hope of a deal that would complete the peace process. However, the differences at Camp David and follow-up rounds at Taba were profound. Aaron David Miller, one of the U.S. negotiators there, said, "Anyone who believes that the Israelis and Palestinians came 'this close' to an agreement at any recent negotiation, including Camp David and Taba, has spent too much time with the peace-process tooth fairy."[12]

Israelis and Palestinians took many lessons from the Camp David failure that shaped the Second Intifada and the Israeli response. Many Israelis found Arafat's rejection of Barak's proposals at Camp David outrageous. Barak claimed he had offered the Palestinians the equivalent of the moon; among other concessions, he offered over 90 percent of the pre-1967 West Bank and Gaza Strip, territorial swaps to make up some of the difference, and a Palestinian capital in Jerusalem. Arafat rejected the offer and refused to give a counteroffer. Still he managed to walk away from the deal as a hero to his people, which infuriated Israelis, who had long questioned his commitment to peace. Barak himself saw the rejection as more than simple disagreement on the ultimate location of boundaries or other contentious issues—it was proof to him that "Arafat simply and fundamentally refused to recognize Israel as a Jewish state, period." Barak also believed that the Palestinian people too did not seek peace.[13] Israelis on the left as well as the right believed that Barak was beyond generous on both the hypersensitive issue of Jerusalem and on the total territory promised with no reciprocity.

"[Israel's] 'generous offer' was an illusion in the mind of those offering it," according to Mohammad Dajani of al-Quds University.[14] In Palestinian eyes Barak did not agree to Palestinian sovereignty over the Temple Mount and several core East Jerusalem neighborhoods, and the land swaps legitimated Israel's annexationist policies. For them, this perfidy exposed the peace process as a sham. Polls in late July showed most Palestinians believed that Arafat had already compromised too much on key issues like refugees and Jerusalem, and 60 percent supported violent confrontations if no agreement was reached soon.[15] The Hamas leader Khaled Mishal noted that Arafat reconciled with the Israelis, was welcomed at the White House, and even received the Nobel Peace Prize, but in the end "they didn't give him what they said they would."[16] When Arafat returned home without an agreement many Palestinians feared that peace would never come and the occupation would continue indefinitely. "This left the Palestinians in darkness," Matti Steinberg, an Israeli expert on the Palestinians, believes. In contrast to 1996, when Hamas attacks were widely condemned, surveys taken in the aftermath of Camp David suggested that Palestinians now saw violence as a reasonable way to achieve statehood.[17]

Although U.S. official statements praised both leaders after Camp David, in a separate interview with Israeli television Clinton charged Arafat with wanting to "completely defeat" Israel on issues such as Jerusalem.[18] Clinton later expressed his assessment of blame on Arafat more clearly. In a statement released at the time of Arafat's death, he stated, "I regret that in 2000 he missed the opportunity to bring that nation into being."[19] While Israelis distrusted Barak's explanation for the negotiating failure (as they would that of any other Israeli politician), they did trust Clinton, so when he appeared to publicly blame Arafat, Barak's story became gospel. Nahum Barnea, one of Israel's most respected journalists, points out that Clinton, seen as "an outside, even-handed judge" who was also pro-Israel, gave validity to the argument that Arafat never truly sought peace.

Internal Palestinian dynamics contributed to the outbreak of violence. Younger Palestinian leaders, including many in Fatah, resented the corruption and political dominance of the Tunis crowd who had come in from exile to take over leadership. Security Chief Mohammad Dahlan, for example, enjoyed limousines and a mansion. This resentment was particularly acute among leaders of the Fatah-linked Tanzim, who would lead the Second Intifada in its early years. As time wore on and the occupation continued, they faulted both the leadership and its strategy of negotiations.[20] Tanzim leader Marwan Barghouti told his followers, "The only thing the Israelis understand is force," and they sought to "increase the costs of the occupation to Israel."[21] For both the Tanzim and Fatah rivals like Hamas, violence also offered them a way to challenge the old guard of the PA for leadership of the Palestinian community.

The Israeli withdrawal from Lebanon in May 2000 only made the Tanzim's argument more compelling. Hizballah's victory, according to Hamas, proved that "*jihad,* resistance, blood and sacrifices extract rights."[22] Barghouti later pointed out, "The thinking of the entire new Palestinian generation is influenced by the experiences of our brothers in Hizballah and by Israel's retreat from Lebanon."[23] Demonstrations turned into violent riots on "Nakba Day" on May 15, 2000, the day when Palestinians mark their loss in the 1948 war with Israel, the same day Jewish Israelis celebrate Yom Ha'Atzmaut, or the Day of Independence. Members of Fatah and Palestinian security forces shot at the IDF, though the violence quickly ended. Barghouti and the Tanzim were sending a message to Arafat not to sideline them, a message ignored by Arafat and the Israelis alike.[24]

The Enigma of Arafat

Known by many Palestinians as the *rais* (chairman), by his nom de guerre, Abu Ammar, or affectionately as "the old man," only Arafat had the prestige and charisma to cut a deal and bring the Palestinian people with him. Bassam Abu Sharif, a PFLP member who later became an advisor to Arafat, wrote admiringly of Arafat's "brilliant mind" and "generous nature" and declared, "His genuine passion for Palestine was what drove him day by day, night by night."[25] For almost forty years even rivals such as Hamas's Sheikh Yasin accepted him as the face of the Palestinian people. He had transformed Fatah from an obscure bunch of dreamers to the world's leading revolutionary organization.

From the start Arafat was "indispensable" to any agreement between Israel and the PLO, argues Ephraim Sneh, one of the first Israeli negotiators with the PLO. A senior U.S. official referred to Arafat as "the great decider": his people would not act without his support, and they would not go against him. The U.S. negotiator Robert Malley concluded that even though Palestinians more than anyone else knew of his many failings, "Arafat literally embodied the nation. In the eyes of countless Palestinians, he had taken a dispersed, stateless people, given them dignity and a name, put them on the map, evaded recurring attempts at Arab subjugation, and both built and preserved a national movement. For that, they were prepared to forgive in abundance and in perpetuity." [26]

Arafat is often blamed for orchestrating the violence, a perception that many Israelis share to this day. Supporting this judgment, Israeli military intelligence wrote an assessment a year before the Second Intifada predicting its outbreak, almost to the day. Yossi Kuperwasser, who was head of the Research Department of the IDF's Directorate of Military Intelligence from 2001 to 2006, noted, "We saw what was coming in detail—it is rare that intelligence is that good." The Israeli academic and former intelligence official Matti Steinberg also forecast that an intifada would erupt and even named September as the date. These stunning predictions proved, for many, that the Second Intifada was not spontaneous but instead was planned by Arafat.

A closer look, however, suggests that Arafat did not plan the Second Intifada's outbreak. Those prescient intelligence judgments were made assuming that Arafat would unilaterally declare a Palestinian state in September 2000, a declaration he never gave because the United States and other countries pressed him not to do so.[27] Palestinian negotiators even tried to block Sharon's visit to the Temple Mount, recognizing that it might precipitate violence, and Arafat himself warned Barak against the visit.[28]

One of the officials involved in the Israeli military intelligence assessment notes that it was just an analytic assessment and that there were no indicators at the time that Arafat was actually preparing for violence. Ami Ayalon, who headed Shin Bet until just before the Second Intifada began, declared, "Yasser Arafat neither prepared nor triggered the violence," and Shin Bet interviews with captured militants back up the argument that there was no initial central guidance.[29]

Part of the confusion also stems from three similar but quite distinct charges made against Arafat: first, that he prepared to launch the Intifada; second, that he orchestrated the violence when it broke out; and third, that he tolerated and exploited the bloodshed. On the first charge Gen. Bogi Yaalon claims that "Palestinian chairman Yasser Arafat was preparing for war" even as he negotiated at Camp David.[30] Arafat's preparation, however, did not lead directly to the Intifada's outbreak. Yet Arafat should not be absolved; though he did not directly light the fire that sparked the Second

Intifada, he created a combustible environment. The investigation headed by George Mitchell blamed Arafat for not doing enough to stop the violence but added, "We have no basis on which to conclude that there was a deliberate plan by the PA to initiate a campaign of violence."[31] Thus Arafat did not initiate the Second Intifada, but when violence broke out, he was ready to exploit it.

The chairman's actions, and Israeli hostility toward him, were at the heart of the Second Intifada. Some Israelis think that even if Arafat did not deliberately light the fire in September 2000 he would have done so eventually. Such a charge misses the essence of the man: he thought in contingencies and sought flexibility. Long-term planning, whether for good or for evil, was beyond him.

But why did Arafat undermine the very process he had legitimated? Yaalon described Arafat as "both the pyromaniac and the firefighter."[32] This captures the contradiction of the man; flexibility was his hallmark. He had repeatedly learned from Jordan, Syria, and other Arab states that his ally today might try to kill him the next day, and again be his ally the day after that. Within the Palestinian community he saw former comrades turn against him but also converted rivals and enemies to friends. So he would strengthen one faction to keep another off balance. He also deliberately chose not to act while recognizing that his inaction would enable others to act; thus he achieved his ends without bearing responsibility. He was a master manipulator.

Arafat had built an image of himself as a revolutionary who would deliver his people, and in so doing created an image from which he could not, or would not, escape. The Palestinian leader often wore a uniform and bragged to visitors that he was the only undefeated Arab general ("a general like you," he would tell the American general Anthony Zinni, who served as a mediator in 2002).

U.S. negotiators used a variety of words to describe Arafat, few of them flattering. Sam Lewis, the U.S. ambassador to Israel during the Carter administration, saw him as a "wily bastard." Martin Indyk, the U.S. ambassador during the Clinton administration, described him as "erratic, mercurial, manipulative, yet artful."[33] Elliott Abrams, George W. Bush's point man for the Middle East, was even more blunt, labeling Arafat a "political criminal." In his final hours as president Clinton summoned incoming secretary of state Colin Powell to warn him about Arafat: "Don't you ever trust that son of a bitch. He lied to me and he'll lie to you."[34] Syrian Defense Minister Mustafa Tlas put his feelings about Arafat most colorfully, calling him the "son of sixty thousand whores," a sentiment shared by many other Arab leaders.[35]

Yet some believe that Arafat actually wanted peace. The Palestinian journalist Wafa Amr, who knew him well, contends that he had made a strategic decision to seek peace, and the Israeli expert Matti Steinberg too believes Arafat was ready for a deal if the payoff was right. Unfortunately, though he may have wanted to make peace, when push came to shove, he was unwilling to make the painful concessions that peace demanded. Arafat decided that he would rather go down as a defiant leader of a failed revolution than a pragmatist who could be charged with giving up the fundamental rights of the Palestinians.[36] He feared for his own personal and political survival, and concessions in the name of peace could jeopardize both.

Among the Israeli public Arafat's image vacillated. After decades as the face of terrorism, he was briefly rehabilitated after Oslo. In 1996 an Israeli television show, *HaChartzufim*, used puppets to satirize Israeli and other politicians, and Arafat's puppet was a kindly grandfather. The producer, Avi Cohen, explained, "We merely reflected what we felt at that time, the wish of the entire country, that was so blinding that we adapted the reality to it. So, naturally, Arafat turned into a non-dangerous elder, a kind of party activist in Israeli politics, because this is how we wanted him to be."[37] As the show was popular and the Arafat puppet was the most beloved, it briefly changed public attitudes toward Arafat.[38] Ahmad Tibi, an Israeli Arab member of Parliament who also advised Arafat, recalled, "I told him that the show does him good, that it humanizes him in front of the Israeli audience, and that there are some right-wingers who are angry because the show depicts him as a kind, sweet uncle. This made him laugh."[39] Israel's right wing was indeed furious. One activist fumed, "For God's sake, if the *Chartzufim* existed in the time of the Holocaust, someone would have, probably, make a Hitler muppet."[40] The show went off the air in 1999.[41]

As the Second Intifada spread, Arafat tried to exploit the violence but also keep a lid on it. To mollify the Tanzim he quickly authorized the organization to create the National and Islamic Higher Committee for the Follow-up of the Intifada; it was a way to ensure that Hamas and other Islamists did not seize the momentum and use it for their own ends and to protect his flank within Fatah from younger activists baying for blood. He also allowed local Fatah and Tanzim militias to fight back against Israeli forces from Palestinian areas, which eventually led to the formation of local groups such as the al-Aqsa Martyrs Brigade in late 2000 and the Popular Resistance Committees in Gaza. Arafat wanted to make sure Fatah was in the game but also wanted to keep the hands of the PA police force clean. Most saw through the deception. Few Israelis, and even fewer Palestinians, saw a distinction between the PA and Fatah on the ground.[42]

More important than any action, however, was Arafat's deliberate inaction. In the first weeks of the Second Intifada he issued statements calling for restraint at the behest of U.S. officials, while the Tanzim leaders called for escalating the violence.[43] One senior Arab diplomat told Martin Indyk that during a summit held by President Clinton with Barak and Arafat in Sharm el-Sheikh in October 2000, Arafat sent a directive to the

Tanzim, —"Continue to do what you have to do," as the violence raged.[44] Palestinian security officials, conscious of their own political position, refused to act. Palestinian security officials had always felt they had to justify their collaboration with Israel in fighting militants, but when the peace process collapsed they had no way to justify their aid to their people's enemy. Arafat himself refused to use his credibility to support a crackdown or contain the violence.[45] The Israeli analyst Gen. Giora Eiland said, "We can compare Yasser Arafat to the manager of a zoo who opens the cages to let the wild animals, all the lions and snakes, do what lions and snakes do."[46]

Arafat apparently believed that the violence would pay off at the negotiating table and shore up his position among disenchanted Palestinians. Wafa Amr contends that in the end Arafat believed that suffering would move Israelis to make concessions, just as it had in 1996, after the riots over the tunnel along the Western Wall. Arafat recognized and exploited a difference between the Israelis and Palestinians when he told Terje Roed-Larsen, the UN representative to the Middle East, "[The Israelis] suffer because of casualties. I don't. My people are glorified as martyrs." The scholar Yezid Sayigh goes one step further, saying, "Arafat's instinctive reaction was to maintain this advantage, which in a crude sense required a daily death toll."[47]

Arafat's theory was not beyond belief. As the flames rose higher and the international community condemned Israel, Barak steadily offered more concessions. During the Sharm el-Sheikh summit in 2000, organized to end the violence, Arafat offered little on counterterrorism. Still, on December 23, the United States issued the "Clinton parameters," outlining the U.S. solution. The parameters called for 94 to 96 percent of the West Bank to be part of a Palestinian state, along with Gaza.[48] During the last major round of negotiations, which began at Taba on January 21, 2001, the parties were just over 2 percent apart on territory, and both sides made progress on refugees and Jerusalem.

As these concessions unfolded, Arafat sought "to ride the tiger," said former Shin Bet head Ami Ayalon. According to him, Arafat had little choice: the Second Intifada arose from spontaneous anger over the failure to end the occupation and "Arafat could not repress it." Even if he had tried, Ayalon contends, "the Palestinians would end up hanging him in the public square."[49]

The tiger Arafat rode, however, changed as time went on. At first it was public anger at Israel after years of frustration at the negotiating table. As the Intifada continued, the tiger was anger at Israel's response to the Intifada itself.

Arafat's tactic of tolerating violence failed to recognize the nature of Israeli democracy: Barak and his predecessors could not simply impose a deal, and they could not sell the deal if no one trusted Arafat on terrorism.

His advisor Ghaith al-Omari believed that Arafat consistently underestimated the Israelis' sensitivities on security issues, and as a result thought he could raise or lower the level of violence without losing his long-term credibility. Years of Arafat's double-talk and deceit had exacted its toll. No longer was he viewed as a gentle grandfather. Israelis were now convinced that the Palestinian Authority "instigated, orchestrated, and directed the violence."[50] Wherever they sat on the political spectrum, all felt Arafat had successfully used violence to extract more and more concessions, and that this time they had to draw a line. Israelis—including many involved in peace talks—blamed Arafat personally for the failure at Camp David and subsequent negotiations. They came to believe that peace was not possible while Arafat held sway.[51]

This perception shaped the increasingly harsh Israeli response to the growing violence. In contrast to past flare-ups of violence, the IDF was ready. And it was determined to teach the Palestinians a lesson.

CHAPTER VIII

A MILLION BULLETS (2000)

IN ITS first few months of the Second Intifada, the IDF reportedly shot 1.3 million bullets. The precise figure is disputed, but to many critics the shorthand of "a million bullets" captures the scale of the Israeli response to the violence.[1] In Operation Field of Thorns, Israel's name for the military crackdown, the IDF displayed the tactical brilliance for which it is known. Yet in the end its supposed success only increased the violence.[2]

During the Second Intifada's first five days the IDF killed fifty Palestinians and wounded more than a thousand. In the first month of the conflict 109 Palestinians died and only ten Israelis—a result of the IDF's deliberate goal of having a casualty ratio that would demonstrate Israeli strength.[3] When the Palestinian security chief Mohammad Dahlan asked IDF Chief of Staff Shaul Mofaz, "How come we have 100 dead and you have none?" Mofaz saw it as a compliment to the IDF's skill. "When the army decides to make itself ready, that's what it does."[4] However, Dahlan's complaint underlined a political and cultural reality that Mofaz missed.[5] Avraham Sela, the Israeli expert on the Palestinians, believed that the "brutality and scope of the Israeli response" shocked the Palestinians, and honor demanded that they resist a ceasefire until they could strike a blow against Israel. The Mitchell investigation found that Israel's early decision to use lethal force was a key factor in the escalation of the violence.[6]

Much of the Palestinian violence initially consisted of unruly demonstrations. The Mitchell investigation found that "most incidents *did not* involve

Palestinian use of firearms and explosives" and castigated Israel for not differentiating between terrorism and protests.[7] Here Israel's broad definition of terrorism led to an overstatement of the threat the Palestinians initially posed and, as a consequence, a reaction that made the problem worse.

The exceptions mattered tremendously, however, as they were lethal. Snipers mixed among some demonstrators, and Palestinians began to attack settlers and army vehicles in the West Bank. As the IDF had feared, some among the tens of thousands of Palestinian police, armed and trained by the international community, joined in the violence.[8] An early Israeli casualty of the Second Intifada was Yosef Tabeja, the Border Police superintendant whose Palestinian counterpart killed him on September 29, 2000, while they were serving on a joint mission near Qalqilya.

Vital to understanding the full impact of the Israeli response is recognizing the schizophrenic nature of Israel's strategy at the time. Peres and several others called for strengthening Arafat because he was weak, while others in Israel blamed Arafat for the violence. Following the Rabin mantra of negotiating in the face of violence, Barak continued peace talks even as the violence began to soar. As the IDF cracked down harshly, negotiations soured even further.

To avoid taking casualties as it did during the 1996 tunnel debacle, the IDF had trained snipers to serve with regular units, reinforced its fixed military positions with better defenses, armored more of its vehicles, and provided body armor to soldiers; this approach was tested in April of 2000 in the drill "Frontal Gear." Because the IDF focused on armed Palestinians in its response, it did not plan for crowd control of riots and demonstrations and did not equip its forces with non-lethal alternatives. Chief of Staff Mofaz was worried lest Palestinians think that they could carry out violence without rebuke and prepared his soldiers to give a tough response. In addition to these deliberate decisions, the scope of the unrest overstretched the IDF, so units trained and equipped for crowd control were in short supply.[9]

It is difficult to criticize a military for operating effectively, or even ruthlessly, when it is being fired upon. As the former head of IDF planning Yossi Kuperwasser pointed out, "We shoot only at those who shoot at us." Nevertheless the broader political ramifications of the IDF's actions never entered into the overall equation. "Don't worry," said Mofaz to IDF soldiers. "We will defend you, and back you up in the face of politicians." The message he conveyed was simple: Do whatever you deem necessary, and don't worry about the consequences.[10] The Intelligence Branch officers jocosely called the field officers who complied with these directives "Mofaz's Tanzim."[11]

In contrast to their experience in the 1996 tunnel violence, the IDF intended to nip violence in the bud before it had any political impact. Knowing that negotiations were flailing, and seeing demonstrations like the May

15, 2000 "Nakba" demonstrations turn bloody, the IDF prepared for 2000 to be a "decisive year."[12] Indeed for officials like Bogi Yaalon, who headed Israel's Central Command when the Second Intifada broke out, and like-minded IDF leaders, the outbreak was an opportunity to "burn into the Palestinian mind" that violence was doomed to fail. Less ambitiously the IDF developed new measures to counter Palestinian tactics such as putting snipers among unarmed demonstrators, which had caused such trouble for Israel in the past. The IDF also sought to restore the credibility of deterrence, proving to groups like the recently triumphant Hizballah that Israel still had teeth.[13]

The IDF's plan, however, did not square with Barak's political strategy of restarting the peace process. Once again the day-to-day experience of counterterrorism was not in harmony with Israel's overall goals.

Civilian control over Israel's military, always weak, broke down almost completely in the early days of the Intifada. In addition to the post of prime minister, Barak also held the defense minister portfolio. It was simply too much to keep track of. Politically he was too weak to be seen as opposing any effort to fight terrorism, even if it backfired. IDF Chief of Staff Mofaz simply ignored Barak's peace efforts and aggressively targeted the PA police and security establishment. Mofaz spoke out publicly against the Clinton parameters even as Barak's government negotiated, warning that some of the proposed concessions would leave Israel vulnerable to attack. He and the IDF believed that Israel no longer had a Palestinian partner. Their goal was "Victory Value": every fight had to show an IDF victory rather than simply contain the demonstrators.[14]

The military too faced limits, as the hope of renewed peace talks and the expectation that the violence would soon end meant the IDF used force as punishment rather than as an attempt to hold territory. So tough operations like Field of Thorns were limited in their scope. Israeli military officers claim the IDF tried to avoid entering Area A, where the Palestinians had been granted authority for day-to-day governance, altogether. If they went in, they did so quickly and left immediately.

Mofaz's control over the IDF was unclear. Raids were often carried out by low-level commanders without central guidance. If a local brigade commander found someone wanted for anti-Israel violence at a police headquarters he might destroy the building, but his decision did not reflect—or violate—an official policy decision. Some parts of the military acted aggressively, others with restraint. Gal Hirsh, a colonel commanding a brigade in Ramallah, made his own decision to close Route 443, a key artery that connects several Israeli cities but was initially constructed to facilitate Palestinian traffic. Hirsch made it an Israeli-only road, which it would remain for most of the decade. Israeli negotiators promised Arafat they would reopen the Dahaniya airfield in Gaza; the IDF did open it, but then a local commander installed a roadblock on the access road, making it impossible to use. Deputy Defense Minister Ephraim Sneh wrote Barak, "From the CGS [chief of the general staff, Shaul Mofaz] to the last of the sergeants at the roadblock, not one of them carries out your policy."[15]

Destroying buildings and disarming security services humiliated potential partners and made them dig in even further. Most important the IDF did not appreciate risks of casualties. As the Israeli analyst General Shlomo Brom contends, when the goal is a peace settlement "the political logic is to kill fewer of the enemy." "Arafat turned the issue of casualties into an art form," contends General Amos Malka, an intelligence official.[16] IDF interrogators claim that militant groups deliberately worsened the problem, using children as shields to test the IDF's response.[17]

At a popular level the casualties provoked Palestinian outrage. One mother whose teenage son died in a demonstration mourned, "No mother in the world can cope with her son being killed in this way."[18] Palestinian funerals triggered violent demonstrations, which in turn resulted in more deaths and more funerals. U.S. negotiator Martin Indyk told me he believed that the lopsided casualties fueled anger on the street and made it even harder for Arafat to cut a deal. "That was the tiger" Arafat tried to ride in attempting to use violence to get a better deal. Hamas blasted Arafat for negotiating with Israel "at a time the blood of more than 100 martyrs . . . fell in the holy Aqsa intifada."[19]

Israel's interaction with foreign media, often problematic to put it charitably, compounded the country's problems. Although IDF commanders could mouth slogans about the importance of public relations, the army had not prepared its officers to talk to the media, and they often refused to do so when asked.[20]

Two iconic images loomed large in the early days of the Second Intifada. For Palestinians and much of the world, it was the story of the twelve-year-old boy Mohammad al-Dura and his father, Jamal. At a juncture near the Netzarim village in Gaza, where a small group of Israeli settlers lived, several hundred Palestinians had gathered to demonstrate. The violence began with rock throwing and Molotov cocktails, but a few demonstrators, including Palestinian policemen, fired guns. Israeli troops, who had been ordered to shoot only if fired upon, shot back.

Jamal al-Dura claimed that he and Mohammad were returning from a used-car market and were passing through the area. They were caught in crossfire between Palestinian rioters and Israeli troops on September 30. Jamal, who was injured but did not die, tried to save his son during the fighting. The video footage is painful to watch: as bursts of gunfire are heard, Jamal curls his body around his son and starts to yell. After another round Mohammad goes limp and collapses into Jamal's lap, blood spreading out from his shirt. The footage instantly became the symbol of Israeli brutality in the early days of the Intifada and resulted in protests around the world. In the majority of the coverage Palestinians are depicted as unarmed. Al-Dura's image appears on postage stamps in several Arab countries, and Osama bin Ladin even singled him out when he decried Palestinian suffering.

Several Israelis I talked to contend that the IDF did not kill Mohammad al-Dura, and some even claim that Palestinians staged his death to create such a haunting image. James Fallows, a respected American journalist, investigated and agreed that Israeli soldiers did not kill the boy.[21] Regardless of the truth, al-Dura's death came to symbolize the IDF's brutality.

For Israelis, the savagery of the new conflict hit home on October 12, when two IDF reservists in uniform accidentally drove into Ramallah, where PA police arrested them. A crowd gathered outside the jail, believing they were members of an undercover Israeli unit that dressed as Arabs and was responsible for killing Palestinians. The crowd then charged the jail and lynched the two soldiers. The most horrific image was that of Aziz Salha, one of the mob, proudly displaying his blood-covered hands from the jail's window to the crowd and an Italian TV network. "I've just killed your husband," one militant crowed in Hebrew to the wife of one of the soldiers, who was desperately trying to reach him on his cell phone.[22] Israelis were outraged. In response Israel attacked police stations and other targets in Ramallah with helicopter strikes and later used an F-16 to bomb a Palestinian prison.

At the end of the Intifada's first month the deadly escalation had only just begun. On October 26 PIJ launched its first suicide bombing. After negotiations on November 1, intended to move both sides back from the brink, Israel withdrew from positions near West Bank cities as a confidence-building measure. But on November 2, one day later, PIJ killed two in a bombing of the Mahane Yehuda market.[23] This attack, the first inside Israel proper—as opposed to attacks on settlements, army bases, and roads in the West Bank—was followed by another PIJ attack on November 21 in the town of Hadera. In response the IDF initiated measures to stop the bloodshed. On November 9 the IDF carried out its first targeted killing of the new Intifada. That same month, to create a security zone and reduce the risks of snipers and cross-border infiltration, the IDF began to demolish Palestinian houses and uproot thousands of trees along the Gaza Strip, thus destroying the livelihoods of many Gazans.

A New Front? The Return of Israeli Arab Violence

Israel's concerns weren't limited to the Palestinian population in the West Bank and Gaza. On October 1, with the image of al-Dura's death in the forefront, Israel's Arab community broke with decades of peaceful behavior and rioted against what they saw as IDF brutality. Demonstrations began in the Arab village of Umm al-Fahm, then spread to Arab villages in the Galilee, and ultimately to the area around Tel Aviv-Yaffo. With chants of "Death to the Jews," the rioters blocked a major traffic artery. Although warned that protests would occur, the police were not reinforced; the head of the subsequent investigation, Judge Theodore Or, said that they "stood helpless at the critical stage of the outbreak."[24] Compounding this initial lack of preparedness, Israel then overreacted and responded harshly, using snipers. Twelve Israeli Arab citizens died, along with a Jewish citizen and a Palestinian from the territories—the worst losses the Israeli Arab community had suffered at Israeli hands in almost 50 years.

Israeli Arab leaders had inflamed the community, claiming that Israel planned to massacre Palestinians and that fighting on the Temple Mount itself was still going on even though it had ceased. This incendiary rhetoric was in keeping with earlier provocations, such as the fiery speech that Azmi Bishara, an Arab member of the Knesset, delivered after Israel's May 2000 withdrawal from Lebanon. "We have tasted victory," he said, and claimed that Hizballah served as a model for all Arabs. Israelis considered this speech as evidence that he and other Israeli Arabs were on the side of the Lebanese terrorist organization, not the state of Israel.[25] Bishara later fled the country after Israeli security officials charged that he had been advising Hizballah in the 2006 war with Israel.[26]

As with the Intifada itself, one event could expose a large reservoir of anger. Although conditions for Israeli Arabs had improved considerably since the end of military rule in 1966, they remained second-class citizens. The Or Commission investigation found that discrimination and deprivation remained rampant. Moreover Israel's Arab community contains large numbers of young people, and they found the violence in the territories infectious. A poll taken shortly after the outbreak of the Second Intifada found that 66 percent of the community claimed they supported the Palestinian side, with only 13 percent supporting Israel.[27] The deaths of so many Israeli Arabs and the continuing violence further alienated the community. Israeli Jews, in turn, became vehement in their anti-Arab expressions. Jews often avoided Arab businesses and areas, thus worsening Arabs' economic status and reducing their integration into society.[28]

As the Intifada wore on, the Israeli Arab community became more involved in terrorism. A few Israeli Arabs surveyed targets for groups like Hamas and helped facilitate travel. In September 2001 Shacher Habishi earned the dubious distinction of being the first Israeli Arab suicide bomber when he blew himself up at a Nahariya railway station, killing three Israelis.[29]

Enter Sharon

Barak's efforts to make peace had failed completely, and the situation on the ground seemed to worsen by the day. Benjamin Netanyahu, the former Likud prime minister and the presumed party champion in the

2001 election, had a staggering nineteen-point lead in the polls. Recognizing his electoral dilemma, Barak sought to undercut Netanyahu by calling for a special election. Under Israeli law at the time, only sitting members of the Knesset could compete in a special election; Netanyahu, who had given up his seat after his loss to Barak in 1999, could not run. With Netanyahu sidelined, Ariel Sharon emerged as the Likud candidate. Barak wanted Sharon as an opponent, hoping his reputation as an extremist and his tarnished reputation from Lebanon would turn even right-wing Israeli voters against him. But the continuing violence instead led voters to embrace Sharon, and on February 6, 2001, he won a landslide victory: 62.5 percent of the vote.

In contrast to Barak, Sharon came to power on a platform that rejected peace negotiations with the Palestinians. "There will be no negotiations under fire. There simply will not be," Sharon declared. Only after security was restored would negotiations resume, and even then the offering would be far less than what Barak had offered: 42 percent of the territories, as opposed to over 90 under Barak.[30]

Power had also changed hands in Washington. U.S. officials would still come and utter platitudes about the need for peace talks, but the Bush administration did not believe a peace deal was possible with Arafat in power and did not press Israel for restraint to restart the negotiations. "There's no Nobel Prize to be had here," President Bush told U.S. negotiator Martin Indyk upon entering office.[31]

Although these political changes in Washington and Jerusalem were abrupt, the shift in Israeli counterterrorism policy was gradual. For much of 2001 some voices in the Shin Bet and the IDF still believe that Arafat could again be a partner for peace. Even without these voices, Sharon himself was initially cautious. His reputation for brutality gave him the political credibility to exercise restraint. Early on he continued Barak's policies, encouraging the PA rather than the IDF to crack down on terrorism. As had also been the policy under Barak, the IDF targeted terrorist leaders, conducted helicopter strikes, and razed Palestinian agricultural areas. Like Barak, Sharon continued talks with the Palestinians, albeit in his own way, initially using his son Omri as a backchannel to Arafat.[32]

However, as violence and skepticism over Arafat's intentions grew, Israeli use of force grew in scope and scale, and the push for negotiations became commensurately weaker. As he changed course, Sharon sought to balance strategy, international opinion, and public outrage. He had learned from his disastrous experience in Lebanon that Israel could not afford to alienate the United States, nor could the government leap ahead of public opinion. As Palestinian attacks continued, public demands for revenge began to influence Sharon's course of action. In a significant change from his earlier restraint, when he was unwilling to rouse international anger, he ordered the IDF to retaliate promptly after each attack.

Sharon attempted to counter Arafat's strategy of internationalizing the conflict. Israel did not want to alienate its few remaining European friends. Sharon particularly wanted to keep Egypt and Jordan from being forced to openly back Arafat.

Goading Sharon into action, and responding to Israel's gradual escalation, were numerous Palestinian militant groups: Hamas, PIJ, and the Tanzim in particular, but also new arrivals, including Fatah's al-Aqsa Martyrs Brigades and Gaza's Popular Resistance Committees. With Arafat's implicit support the Tanzim and other Fatah organizations began systematic attacks on settlers and IDF forces, and a Tanzim leader called for "the resumption of Hamas's martyrdom operations."[33]

At this point Arafat made a strategic mistake regarding Hamas: in the Intifada's early weeks he opened the PA jails and freed Hamas and PIJ activists, breathing new life into the organizations. His advisor Ghaith al-Omari believes that Arafat tolerated Hamas because he saw it as a defeated organization, and that his decision later came back to haunt him. For Hamas, long under the PA's thumb, this freedom to act independently was "like paradise. Everything was allowed," in the words of one expert.

Suicide Attacks Return

The extremists' deadliest tactic, and the one that had the biggest impact on Israeli morale, was suicide bombing. PIJ initiated suicide bombing almost immediately after the Second Intifada began, and Hamas joined in several months later. At the height of the Second Intifada there were more suicide bombings in a week than in all of 1996, the period when suicide bombings had halted the peace process and led to Netanyahu's victory over Peres. The Hamas leader Abdel Aziz al-Rantisi declared that these operations were "one of our most effective means, which can rival the impact of their F-16s."[34]

Training suicide bombers takes time and energy. To hide from Israeli intelligence, those picked for suicide operations were told not to share their status with anyone, a particularly difficult task as the would-be martyrs knew that if successful they would never see their families again. Mustafa Abu Sereh, a PIJ member, told no one before his attack. His mother later said she would have chased after and stopped him and then surrendered him to the Israelis to keep him alive.[35]

In the 1990s suicide bombing had at best mixed support from the Palestinian public, but during the Second Intifada "Palestinian society as a whole cultivated the suicide ethos as a weapon of defiance."[36] Terrorist organizations offered thousands of dollars as a reward to the bomber's family, an amount that peaked at twenty-five thousand dollars when Iraq's Saddam Hussein pitched in to help. Images of suicide bombers pervaded Palestine, dominating Hamas posters and artistic figures and inspiring even more to sign up.[37] After the attack the bomber and his family received a special place in society. Yet money and status alone do not explain the decision to be a suicide bomber, and self-interest does not really explain why individuals would risk their lives and join a militant organization.[38] Some bombers had a strong desire for revenge against perceived or real injustices. Others believed they were serving God and their nation. In some cases young people simply signed up because all their friends were doing so.

One of the worst terrorist attacks occurred on June 1, 2001, when a Palestinian suicide bomber stepped into a line of people waiting to enter the Dolphinarium disco in Tel Aviv. The bomber had talked with a group of teenagers before detonating the bomb, which contained metal screws and balls to increase its impact. The attack hit those waiting for the Dolphinarium and a club next door known as Pacha, wounding 120 and killing twenty-one, mostly teenagers from the former Soviet Union. This bombing led the Israeli government to openly charge Arafat with supporting terrorism, and Sharon stopped using his son as a go-between. Arafat condemned the bombing, but the Palestinian Ministry of Social Affairs gave the bomber's father two thousand dollars after the attack.[39]

When word of the Dolphinarium attack spread, crowds gathered and chanted "Death to the Arabs," in a reversal of the oft-used Palestinian chant "Death to the Jews." Support for house demolitions, town closures, and military operations grew. Yet contrary to expectations, and in face of the wave of anger rolling through Israel, Sharon boldly announced, "Restraint is strength."[40] Arafat, however, did not turn back. In Aaron David Miller's words, he "rode, exploited, and milked the violence to enhance his image, maintain his street cred, and demonstrate to Arab, Israeli, and Western leaders that he could neither be taken for granted nor blamed for Camp David without serious cost."[41]

The End of Cooperation

As both sides hardened in response to the bloodshed and destruction, some Palestinian police and security officials joined the violence, while most just went home. The militants the police pursued often were their blood relatives or old friends. Moreover with the breakdown in public order many of the wanted militants had more street power than the police themselves, and arresting them was perilous. Palestinian security forces had been trained for counterterrorism, but they—like their Israeli counterparts—lacked gear and doctrine for countering demonstrations. Further curtailing their role, Israeli military operations expanded in size and, in so doing, steadily reduced the areas in which the Palestinian services held sway. The biggest problem, however, was that Arafat did not push security officials to crack down. After the collapse of the peace process many security officials either openly sympathized with the militants or remained silent, concerned about being labeled Israeli stooges. A full-scale crackdown would require political cover that only Arafat could provide.

Once in a while the PA did crack down. After bombings in December 2001 the PA arrested almost two hundred Hamas members.[42] More often than not, recalls Israeli general Moshe Kaplinsky, PA security officials were "sitting with [the IDF] by day, planning attacks by night." Even the former PA security chief Mohammad Dahlan, feared by Hamas because of his heavy hand when cooperating with Israel in the 1990s, became involved in the violence. As Palestinian researcher Khalil Shakiki remarked, "Dahlan understood it was a matter of survival. . . . He probably learned that lesson from his boss, Arafat. If there's going to be a revolution, lead it."[43] Arrests, when they did occur, were often a sham. BBC filmmakers caught one of the heads of Palestinian intelligence negotiating with a man on a wanted list rather than arresting him. Many times the prison guards tried to protect prisoners against threats from rival groups and Israeli assassinations rather than treating them as criminals.[44]

As the Palestinian security services went from ally to adversary, Israel fell back on an old strategy: trying to coerce a hostile state (or, in this case, the pseudo-state PA) into action by threatening to destroy property and weaken its grip on power. Coercion focused on the traditional older leadership and the institutions it controlled. In August 2001, after Hamas bombed a Sbarro pizzeria in Jerusalem, killing fifteen, the IDF stepped up attacks on the PA infrastructure, striking security facilities in Ramallah, closing Orient House, the de facto PLO foreign ministry in Jerusalem, and launching a ground assault on security force posts in Gaza.

The destruction of the PA security forces and infrastructure "paved the road for Hamas," according to Israeli expert Matti Steinberg. Rather than leading Arafat to crack down, the destruction of the Palestinian security infrastructure reduced his power to impose his will. The lack of an Israeli partner for peace became a self-fulfilling prophecy.

New militants, both within Fatah and from rival groups like Hamas, began to dominate the agenda. In April 2001, when Arafat tried to dissolve the Popular Resistance Committees in Gaza, the Committees simply refused.[45] In 2001 the PA attempted to put Sheikh Yasin under house arrest, but Hamas fighters seized control of the area, and Gazans descended to defend him.[46]

Those hoping to end the violence could get little traction, and further escalation seemed inevitable. Then the horrific terrorist attacks of September 11, 2001 transformed the situation, offering hopes for a truce and perhaps even the return of peace talks.

CHAPTER IX

THE 9/11 CEASEFIRE THAT WASN'T (2001–EARLY 2002)

THE WHOLE world held its breath on September 11, 2001, when al-Qaʿida attacked the World Trade Center and the Pentagon. After the attacks the Bush administration renewed its attention to the peace process. On October 2 Bush announced his support for a Palestinian state—the first U.S. president to openly endorse it. On November 19 Secretary of State Colin Powell reiterated this call and dispatched a special envoy, General Anthony Zinni, to the region.

Although some Palestinians initially celebrated the 9/11 attacks, Palestinian leaders quickly condemned them, and the terrorist groups themselves laid low, fearing that they would be lumped in with al-Qaʿida if they continued. Arafat publicly called for "a complete cessation of military activities, especially suicide attacks." Given the chairman's record of empty rhetoric, Arafat's December 16 meeting with the leaders of the Palestinian militant factions was more significant. There he told them to stop the violence, and even more important he followed up and sent out lieutenants, among them Marwan Barghouti, to tell local cells to adhere to the ceasefire.[1] Even Hamas felt pressure after 9/11. Claiming to be "victims of constant Zionist terrorism," the terrorist group condemned the 9/11 attack and declared its sympathy with the victims.[2] Hamas leaders feared, correctly as it turned out, that continued attacks would lead Israel to reconquer the West Bank. One official admitted, "We didn't want to be depicted as responsible."[3]

In the three-week period after Arafat's declaration Palestinians killed one Israeli soldier in the West Bank, but there were no attacks in Israel proper. Under heavy U.S. pressure Israel stopped targeting Palestinian security posts and pulled its troops back from Area A.

Many Israelis, still stung by what they saw as Arafat's embrace of violence after Camp David, saw the decline in violence as only temporary, and the continued violence, even though it was at lower levels, fed this perception. On October 17, 2001, the Popular Front for the Liberation of Palestine, still a respected group though a shadow of what it was when it pioneered the skyjacking campaign in the late 1960s, killed Israel's tourism minister, Rehavam Zeevi, claiming revenge for the Israeli killing of PFLP's head Abu Ali Mustafa in August. Zeevi seemed to think of himself as invincible. He practically led the PFLP to his door by always checking into the same hotel in East Jerusalem. In the words of a senior Shin Bet operative, "He inflicted this murder upon himself."[4] Shortly before he was murdered he sent Shin Bet chief Avi Dichter away from a meeting about his own personal security, saying, "There is nothing to talk about," and he told guards assigned to the hotel, "Get the hell out of here."[5] Nevertheless for Shin Bet, the agency that was responsible for monitoring the security of the tourism minister, his murder was a watershed. Although an investigation found no direct blame for failing to prevent the assassination, Dichter, in typical forthright style, acknowledged Shin Bet's responsibility to stop it and later called it his biggest failure.[6]

In response to the killing of such a prominent political figure Israeli troops thrust deep into the West Bank, briefly occupying the major cities of Ramallah and Tulkaram. A month later Israelis killed Mahmud Abu Hanoud, a senior Hamas figure in the West Bank. Hamas retaliated with suicide attacks in Jerusalem and Haifa, killing twenty-six Israelis.

These attacks involved groups outside Arafat's immediate orbit, but Israeli suspicions of Arafat continued to grow, as he seemed to keep the option of violence at the ready. This suspicion appeared warranted when, on January 3, 2002, Israeli naval commandos intercepted the ship *Karine-A*, which was transporting a massive load of weapons from Iran to Palestinian fighters, hiding the goods among mattresses, sandals, and sunglasses.[7] The fifty or so tons of weapons included sixty-two Katyusha rockets; if shot from the West Bank, they could strike Ben Gurion International Airport and major cities. The *Karine-A* also contained antitank mines, C-4 explosives, sniper rifles, and various antitank missiles, in addition to rubber boats and diving equipment, which would have put Israel's coastal cities at risk from sea attacks.

The morning after the Israeli Navy intercepted the ship Sharon met General Zinni at his ranch. Zinni had come to persuade Sharon and Arafat to embrace a lasting ceasefire. Just before Zinni left to meet with Arafat,

Sharon received a note from his military secretary informing him that the operation to seize the ship had gone smoothly. "Tell Arafat that he should no longer worry about his consignment of weapons on board the cargo ship of *Karine-A*. It's in our hands," Sharon said with pride as he said goodbye to Zinni.[8]

Arafat himself was implicated in arranging the shipment, and for many Israelis this proved that the Palestinian leader wanted a ceasefire only so that he had time to rearm. Arms for the Palestinian Authority were supposed to be bought openly and provided via Israel and the international community, not shipped secretly from Iran, Israel's nemesis. Defenders of Arafat, however, contend that he was simply trying to defend his people during this violent period.

In contrast to Sharon, Arafat failed to recognize that 9/11 meant a sea change in U.S. policy: any hint of association with terrorism placed a person beyond the pale. Lingering U.S. hopes that Arafat would toe the line dissipated. Vice President Dick Cheney said the *Karine-A* proved that Arafat was "part of the global terrorist network,"[9] and Secretary of Defense Donald Rumsfeld said the ship linked Arafat to Iran, Hizballah, and Syria.

While the *Karine-A* seizure put the ceasefire on its deathbed, the killing of Raed Karmi on January 14, 2002, dealt the mortal blow. Karmi was only twenty-eight, but he was already the boss of Tulkaram in the West Bank, "a bully, a neighborhood gangster, who became famous." Israeli intelligence believed Karmi was involved in shooting at IDF posts after the Intifada began. They also saw him as culpable in the deaths of two Israeli restaurant managers in Tulkaram, who were murdered to avenge Israel's earlier killing of Fatah's leader, the dentist Thabet Thabet.

Under Israeli pressure the PA had jailed Karmi in Ramallah, but he soon escaped and returned to Tulkaram. From his home turf, where no one dared challenge him, he continued to orchestrate violence. Israel tried to kill him on September 6 with a helicopter strike, but Karmi sensed the attack and leaped from the car. He was injured and his two aides were killed. Driven now by revenge as well as hatred of Israel, Karmi continued plotting attacks after 9/11.[10] His attempted bombing of the house of a naval officer in Netanya on October 30, 2001, weighed heavily on the minds of IDF and Shin Bet leaders. Yet according to Palestinian journalist Wafa Amr, Arafat eventually convinced Karmi not to use violence. The Israeli analyst Matti Steinberg also endorses this view, noting that "he was entitled to be targeted before December" because of his clear involvement in terrorism, but after December he was holding his fire.

The IDF Central Command debated whether to kill Karmi when the ceasefire was holding. Karmi was thought to be a man who would inevitably return to terrorism, even though there was no intelligence indicating that he was planning any particular attack. Nevertheless Israel went ahead with the killing, in part because Shin Bet feared it would not again have the intelligence it needed to carry out the attack.[11] The organization's past director, Ami Ayalon, believes Israel killed him simply because the operational opportunity presented itself. After the strike Shin Bet claimed—the Israeli journalists Raviv Drucker and Ofer Shelah imply that Shin Bet fabricated—that Karmi had planned to kill a senior Israeli official and had an explosive belt in his house. Palestinian leader Marwan Barghouti later told an Israeli newspaper, "We convinced Hamas and PIJ to cease terror attacks. I personally held talks with them on this back in December. Twenty three days there was a cease fire, and then you wiped out Raed Karmi."[12]

Israeli officials did not want to be blamed for breaking the tentative ceasefire by killing Karmi. IDF Chief of Staff Yaalon relates that Israel designed an attack that would look like an accident: when Karmi went to see his mistress a bomb exploded from a wall in the local cemetery. (Ironically Karmi tried to walk underneath the wall to avoid being seen by IDF helicopters.) The Israelis hoped it would appear as though Karmi accidentally detonated the explosives himself. The planners had forgotten that it is hard to keep a secret in Israel. "Israelis could not keep their mouth shut," said Yaalon, and the IDF and Shin Bet took the blame for ending the ceasefire.[13]

Some Israelis believe Karmi's killing did have the hoped-for operational impact. One general told me that from reading intelligence you could "feel the fear" of the people in Tulkaram, as fathers tried to prevent their sons from joining the violence. But beyond this narrow operational sphere the killing shattered the post-9/11 ceasefire. A day later a Tanzim cell laid an ambush along Road 443 near a gas station. When Yoela Chen and a friend stopped for gas, Mohammed Matlah, a cell member, talked to her to make sure she was Israeli. Her identify confirmed, other cell members fired, killing her and injuring her friend.[14]

The carnage did not end there. "The Tanzim went mad," Matti Steinberg recalls. "The pragmatists within Fatah were totally frustrated." Leaders like Barghouti, who in the past led Fatah's political effort, now directed suicide operations. Given their past ties to Israel, Fatah political figures feared being labeled collaborators if they did not encourage terrorist attacks. On January 27, 2002, the al-Aqsa Martyrs Brigade, which had links to both Fatah and Tanzim, began to conduct suicide bombings in West Jerusalem.[15] These largely secular groups soon sponsored numerous suicide attacks, disproving the widely held belief that only religion could inspire people to kill themselves. March 2002 saw 17 terrorist attacks that killed 135 Israelis, with most of the deaths occurring within Israel itself, not among troops or settlers in the West Bank or Gaza.[16]

Looking back, Binyamin Ben-Eliezer, the defense minister, called the Karmi killing "the biggest mistake I made during my time in office."[17]

Several Shin Bet officers I talked to agreed. The analyst and retired general Shlomo Brom argued that this is a case of self-fulfilling prophecies. "Israel assumed the post-9/11 lull would fail and acted accordingly. Why lose an opportunity to act?"

It is easy to blame the failure of the peace process on the Karmi assassination. Yet the durability of any peace is questionable if killing a thug like Karmi can derail it so completely. The U.S. peace negotiator Aaron David Miller recalls that when he met with Arafat and Sharon in December 2001 they both said everything the U.S. wanted to hear but that "neither leader really wanted an agreement so much as they wanted to place blame on or to get rid of the other."[18] Some Israelis pointed out that the problem was Arafat, not Karmi: he never gave up on violence, and when the moment was ripe he would have resumed it. The *Karine-A* confirmed Israeli suspicions that the post-9/11 ceasefire was a lull, not a change of course. General Zinni pointed out that regardless of one's view of Arafat's intentions, Hamas and other violent groups used pauses in fighting to rearm and reorganize. Israel then faced the choice of letting them grow stronger while it did nothing or pursuing them and having it appear as if Israel fired the first shot.

Another impetus for continued violence came from the Palestinian people themselves. Popular support for suicide bombings was high, spurring the groups on and increasing recruitment. A poll conducted by the Palestinian Center for Policy and Survey Research in November 2002 found that 66 percent of those surveyed believed that violence helped Palestinians in ways that negotiations did not. The survey also found that 53 percent of Palestinians surveyed supported armed attacks against Israeli civilians in Israel proper and 91 percent supported attacks against soldiers.[19] Hamas was gaining strength, which suggested that there would be political consequences for Fatah if it made unpopular concessions to Israel.[20] With so many Palestinians backing violence the groups churned out a seemingly endless number of suicide bombers.

When the violence resumed, younger Tanzim fighters and Islamist radicals saw victory within their grasp. Peace overtures no longer worked. With the Hizballah model prominent in their minds, and with Israel reeling from attacks, the militants believed that they had the leverage to coerce Israel into ending the occupation. In fact the Israeli left's continuing willingness to offer concessions at the negotiating table in the face of growing bloodshed persuaded jailed Hamas leaders to encourage their followers to continue fighting. For Hamas and many younger members of the Tanzim, victory would be twofold: they intended to defeat the Israelis and end Arafat's old guard domination of Palestinian politics. The young militants, not the old apparatchiks, would then call the shots.

Palestinian terrorist groups competed with one another to conduct attacks, resulting in an astonishing escalation of violence. Hamas and PIJ initiated a campaign of regular suicide bombings, and Fatah became far more active after the death of Karmi in 2002. Other groups joined the fray. The PFLP's military wing, the Abu Ali Mustafa Brigades (named after its late secretary general), launched several strikes. Rivalry among factions led to competition to see who could deliver the largest number of martyrs. Jamal Hwaid, an al-Aqsa leader, said, "If I can compare this with football teams in Britain, like Manchester United, Liverpool, and Leeds United. When one team gets stronger, this drives the other teams to become stronger."[21]

The Palestinians' state sponsors added to the carnage. With talks on a peace deal over the Golan Heights only a memory, Syria had little incentive to rein in Palestinian groups; instead Damascus and Iran pressed Hamas and PIJ to increase attacks and trained their operatives to become more lethal. Money poured into Hamas. Saudi Arabia alone sent Hamas twelve million dollars in 2003, ostensibly for its charitable activities but indirectly strengthening the violent side of the organization.[22]

In contrast to the First Intifada, weapons seemed to be everywhere. The arms given to the Palestinian security forces were now used against the Israelis. When Israel destroyed police facilities in Gaza, officers simply brought the weapons home and shared them with their clans, transforming the clans into important armed factions.[23] Israeli criminals, at times working through Israeli Arabs, occasionally sold weapons from Israel for huge fees. When Shin Bet and the IDF found crude Palestinian weapons labs, the raw materials often had Hebrew letters on them.[24]

Despite the increase in violence—or perhaps because of it—discipline and strategic cohesion within the groups fell. Ghaith al-Omari, an analyst and advisor to Arafat and Abbas, contends, "There was no political management of the intifada." The violence was not calibrated to shape negotiations or even to distinguish between events in the occupied territories and Israel proper. Violence became a goal in itself.

New members were not wedded to past organizational rivalries. Tanzim members in particular began to conduct joint attacks with past rivals. In Gaza the Popular Resistance Committee formed, drawing members from Hamas, PIJ, Fatah, and PA security services. Over time, instead of referring to the Palestinian militant networks by organization—Fatah, Hamas, PIJ—the IDF started identifying them by geographical areas, "the Balata network," for example. The organization itself ceased to be an important binding force. Hamas's military wing also began to issue its own communiqués, highlighting its independence from and growing importance to the political wing of the organization.[25]

At the same time Arafat still made an occasional show of trying to cooperate with Israel. For Israel, this was only a token effort, and for Arafat, with Hamas encroaching on his authority, cooperation presented real danger. In Gaza many Palestinian Authority officials even hid from Hamas after PA police clashed with activists.[26]

As Palestinian groups began to fray and order collapsed, the early years of the Intifada also produced a crisis in Israeli society. An IDF report found that "citizens felt they'd become living targets."[27] The Israeli mood had darkened, and politicians felt the need to respond. Public pressure was particularly intense, as most of the casualties were within Israel itself.

As the militants hoped, Israelis felt the knife against their throats. But the attackers did not achieve their desired result, as the violence only stiffened Israeli resolve. IDF Chief of Staff Bogi Yaalon declared in an August 2002 interview that the Intifada was "an existential threat," and Israelis now saw the Palestinians as perpetually dedicated to violence.[28] The government of Prime Minister Sharon effectively abandoned negotiations, instead hoping to inflict enough damage to coerce the other side to stop the attacks. "We must cause them losses, victims, so they feel the heavy price, so they understand that they won't achieve anything through terror," he declared in March 2002.[29]

The killing of Karmi illustrates how difficult negotiations are when violence is rampant. The years of terrorism and the surge in attacks had soured Israelis of all political persuasions on negotiations. Under such circumstances restraint seemed foolish rather than prudent. Yet the Karmi killing also illustrates another, perhaps more painful truth about the Middle East: it can always get worse. When Israeli leaders decided to proceed with the operation they did not recognize that the existing situation, as abysmal as it was, would deteriorate further and require an even greater use of force.

After the killing of Karmi hope for a peaceful resolution of the violence did not return for many years. Israel discarded the constraints of Oslo once and for all and instead embraced a strategy to end the violence that relied on disruption and force, not negotiations with or cooperation from a Palestinian partner.

CHAPTER X

THE HORNET'S NEST: THE BATTLE OF JENIN AND OPERATION DEFENSIVE SHIELD (2002)

ON MARCH 27, 2002, Abdel-Basset Odeh calmly walked past the Park Hotel reception desk in the resort city of Netanya and entered the crowded dining area. Odeh had left the nearby city of Tulkaram disguised as a woman, and at the hotel he found two hundred or so Israelis enjoying a Passover dinner together. Most of those at the Seder went to the Park Hotel because they were not able to be with their families on this important Jewish holiday. Many were elderly Israelis who had lived through decades of war and terrorism. Several were Holocaust survivors. Odeh, a member of Hamas whom Israel had unsuccessfully asked the PA to arrest, exploded a bomb in his suitcase, killing himself and twenty-two Israeli civilians and wounding another 140.[1] Later eight more Israelis died from injuries. The attack was the bloodiest since the Second Intifada began in September 2000. "Suddenly it was hell," Nechama Donenhirsch, one of the wounded, told reporters. "We ran . . . over dead people, all in pieces."[2]

Although Israelis and Palestinians didn't know it at the time, the Park Hotel marked a watershed. Not only was this the single deadliest attack of the Second Intifada, but it also silenced any remaining hope that the peace process might be revived. As final proof of Palestinian perfidy, the PA condemned the Park Hotel attack in its English-language statements and glorified Odeh as a martyr in its official Arabic newspaper.

The Park Hotel attack was particularly grisly, but it was hardly an aberration. From the beginning of 2002 until this attack Israel had lost 101 civilians to terrorism, in addition to fifty-six security personnel.

Ninety-two of these attacks were carried out within Israel itself.[3] And the Passover attack was followed by what continued to be an exceptionally bloody year for Israel, which lost 277 civilians from terrorist attacks during 2002 and 149 security force personnel in clashes with Palestinian fighters. Suicide bombings were responsible for 188 of these deaths.[4]

As worrisome as the mounting death toll was the pace of attacks. In 2002 Israel would suffer a staggering fifty-three suicide attacks.[5] Hamas and other groups were launching suicide bombers every few days, shredding the fabric of daily life in Israel. Places like Tel Aviv and Netanya, which had been sanctuaries for many years, were now the front lines. Walking down the streets of major cities, strangers eyed one another warily. Restaurants and malls placed guards outside to search bags for bombs. People feared crowds and avoided busy areas. Describing the mood, Nahum Barnea, the Israeli journalist, noted, "Every kid had to have a cell phone, and his mother would call every few hours. Fear became embedded in the Israeli DNA."

The Park Hotel attack called for a tougher response, and Shin Bet believed it had the answer: abandon the restraint Palestinians and the international community demanded and destroy the infrastructure of terror. Israel responded with Operation Defensive Shield, a military operation that took place from March 29 to April 21, 2002, during which time Israeli forces reoccupied much of Area A, the area given to the PA to administer under the Oslo Accords. Defensive Shield began with the seizure of Arafat's headquarters compound in Ramallah, which also housed the headquarters of various Palestinian security forces that Israel believed had become a locus of resistance. The IDF followed the seizure with operations in the other key Palestinian population centers in the West Bank, such as Nablus, Tulkaram, Qalqilya, and Bethlehem. Prime Minister Ariel Sharon told the Knesset on April 8 that he had ordered the IDF "to catch and arrest terrorists—primarily, their dispatchers and those who finance and support them."[6] The bold language masked a subtle shift: Israel was no longer focusing on the suicide bombers themselves, but rather the broader infrastructure that recruited, trained, and protected them. Throughout the West Bank Israel imposed closures and banned vehicle traffic. This operation marked a sea change in Israeli policy. No longer would Israel even give lip service to relying on the PA to take measures against Palestinian militants. Instead the responsibility would rest on Israel alone.

In the wake of the Park Hotel attack the Israeli public clamored for action. The timing of the attack, on the eve of Passover, was seen as symbolic. A *Jerusalem Post* poll published on April 5, 2002, found 71 percent of those surveyed in favor of Operation Defensive Shield.[7] Many favored more extreme solutions that reflected Israeli rage at the carnage. A Jaffe Center for Strategic Studies poll in March 2002 found that 46 percent of Israeli Jews supported transferring Palestinians from the West Bank and Gaza.[8] Binyamin Ben-Eliezer, a retired general who became Israel's defense minister during the first years of the Second Intifada, declared, "The days are over when we were willing to negotiate in the morning and go to funerals of terror victims in the afternoon."[9] Public fury drove Israeli policy.

Diplomatically the Bush administration gave Israel a green light, and for Sharon this was vital. The 9/11 attacks had aroused U.S. sympathy for the terrorism threats faced by the Israelis. During the first three days of Operation Defensive Shield the U.S. Department of State talked only of Israel's "right to self-defense."

The operation marked a significant transition in IDF practice and procedure. The Israeli military was not keen on reoccupying Palestinian cities and refugee camps. Urban operations of any kind are nightmares for militaries. In cities advantages in skill and firepower, on which the IDF has traditionally relied to defeat Israel's enemies with few casualties of its own, are quickly lost. Traditional command and control break down as enemy fighters transform buildings, alleyways, and stairwells into killing zones. Radio signals are easily degraded, and units can get lost, confused, or delayed amid the unmarked warrens of the camps. IDF leaders also believed that if they attempted to gain control of the cities in Area A, troops would have to occupy the territory indefinitely. Occupation meant exposure: troops would be in close proximity to the Palestinians and risk attacks on a daily basis. The IDF also recognized that occupation would complicate a political settlement by increasing Palestinian anger.

The Israeli public is exceptionally casualty-sensitive, and the IDF feared hundreds of casualties from urban operations would sour the public on continued sacrifices. Within the military protecting the lives of soldiers is drilled into every leader, no matter how junior. Israel is a small, even intimate, country. "My biggest fear is to look to the parents of my soldiers if someone will die," said a lieutenant in Israel's elite Sayaret Golani unit, a concern I heard echoed in almost all my interviews with Israeli military leaders.[10]

Sharon's charge to the IDF to "destroy the infrastructure of terrorism" was operationally difficult. The infrastructure of terrorism is human; to destroy it you have to find and arrest people or, if you can't, kill them. To arrest the dispatcher or the bomb maker, however, you must first find him, seize him, and prevent him and his comrades from escaping and ambushing your own forces. These operations are far easier if you deprive terrorist groups of sanctuaries in which to organize. For the Israelis, removing the haven that Hamas, the Tanzim, and other groups enjoyed required cutting off and then occupying entire Palestinian cities.

Avi Dichter, who headed Shin Bet from 2000 to 2005, was perhaps the chief architect of Israel's counterterrorism policies in the Second Intifada;

he led the charge to build the security barrier that now separates most of the West Bank from Israel, pushed for reoccupying the West Bank, and helped orchestrate numerous targeted killings. Dichter believed that the best place to stop a suicide bomber was in Nablus, before he left, rather than waiting until he attempted to attack in Israel proper.[11] He explained that military forces first needed to cut off Palestinian cities so fighters could neither escape nor resupply. Then, when the territory was under control, security services could arrest the terrorists and their compatriots. The first arrest would create a spiral, producing more information that enabled further arrests. Shin Bet saw the problem not as an amorphous web of terrorism and its political and social sources but as a large but finite number of recruiters, weapons makers, and organizers. Take them out, and you crush the militant group's capacity to fight. The new strategy was not about making a deal with the Palestinians or forcing them to police themselves—the two prongs of Israel's strategy from the signing of Oslo until Operation Defensive Shield—but rather about imposing a settlement and eventually convincing the Palestinians that violence would not lead to victory. In essence Israel was giving up on its Palestinian partner.

In most of the Palestinian cities that Israel occupied as part of Operation Defensive Shield, Israeli forces swept in with little opposition. In three weeks of operations across the West Bank almost five hundred Palestinians were killed.[12] Other Palestinian fighters fled as the Israeli soldiers arrived, planning to fight another day.

There was one exception: the Jenin refugee camp. There perhaps two hundred fighters from different Palestinian factions stood their ground.[13] To Israelis and Palestinians, this was no surprise. "Of all the districts, Jenin boasted the greater numbers of fighters from Fatah and the other Islamic national factions," the Fatah leader Marwan Barghouti had written in September 2001. Jenin housed roughly fourteen thousand Palestinians and is only eight miles from the Green Line that separates the West Bank from Israel. Jenin sprawled; each apartment seemed to be piled on top of the next. IDF analyst General Giora Eiland, who was instrumental in the Jenin operation, claimed that before the operation twenty-eight suicide attacks had been planned and launched from Jenin, resulting in almost a hundred Israeli deaths. For Israelis, the sinister picture was complete when they found that one of the Jenin fighters had reportedly long answered to the nickname "Hitler."[14]

The al-Aqsa Martyrs Brigade, Hamas, and especially PIJ had a strong presence in Jenin, and the PA did little to curtail their activities. Barghouti concluded, "It is, as the other side calls it, a hornet's nest." Another al-Aqsa Martyrs Brigade leader, Jamal Hwaid, declared, "Jenin camp is the greatest source of martyrs for Palestine. It's the capital of martyrs."[15] IDF soldiers who went into the camp agreed. "This place is a factory for evil, a factory for terror," said Roy Mamluk, an Israeli reservist on the last day of fighting in Jenin. "We are talking about people who do not have any humane or democratic values. People who use civilians, their own brothers, as human shields by tying them or locking them in their homes."[16]

Before Defensive Shield, Israel had repeatedly taken military action in Jenin with little success. During 2001 it bombed administrative and police buildings and blocked roads to the town. In early 2002 the IDF sent troops to find and arrest militants and send a message to Arafat that continued fighting risked his control over refugee camps and cities. In these early attempts the IDF tried to avoid clearing the camp, fearing the casualties and the political damage.

Young Palestinian fighters hoped Jenin would prove to be what they called "our Karameh," referencing the 1968 battle that made Fatah prominent. They wanted to fight the Israelis block by block and, in so doing, inflict enough casualties to triumph through defiance.[17] Indeed to many Palestinian militants the Jenin operation must have seemed a dream come true, forcing the IDF to fight on the Palestinians' turf and terms. In the end Palestinian fighters also had more pragmatic motivations. One Fatah member noted, "The Israelis had put a cordon around the town; we had no choice. We had nowhere else to fight." Yet far from being another Karameh, Jenin was the Palestinians' Alamo.

The Fighting Begins

For Defensive Shield more than thirty thousand IDF reservists were called up for what would be Israel's largest military operation since the 1982 invasion of Lebanon. The escalating violence and the Park Hotel atrocity had galvanized the Israeli public, and reservists reported for duty enthusiastically at far higher levels than was usual for such a call-up.

Defensive Shield began by retaking Ramallah, where Arafat was headquartered and where the murderers of tourism minister Rehavam Zeevi were being protected. Arafat declared defiantly, "I will be a martyr, martyr, martyr."[18] But the IDF met little resistance at his headquarters. In Bethlehem the IDF failed to block off the Church of the Nativity and Palestinian militants took shelter there, along with several resident monks. The IDF feared a firefight in the site holy to the world's Christians. Eventually the militants agreed to surrender and accept deportation (but not custody in Israeli jails), a propaganda victory at best for them. In Nablus Israel saw successes as well. A Fatah member there commented that Israeli snipers were so accurate that it was impossible for Fatah fighters to move through the streets.

On April 2 Israeli forces began to enter Jenin, sparking a week of intense fighting that slowly petered out by the time the Red Cross entered the camp on April 15. Before the fighting began, Israel issued warnings for civilians to evacuate. Most residents fled, but more than a thousand, perhaps as many as four thousand, remained.[19] Some didn't hear the warnings; others ignored them. And some, of course, stayed to fight. As the IDF entered Jenin it again tried to get the civilians to leave, using loudspeakers to tell locals to surrender to IDF forces. "Everyone who surrenders is guaranteed medical treatment. Whoever does not surrender will bear the consequences. His blood shall be on his own head." However, the Palestinian fighters refused to surrender. The soldiers sensed something was different as they entered Jenin. The muezzin kept calling, "Itbach al-Yahud" (Slaughter the Jews). Later he switched to taunting disguised as persuasion: "IDF soldiers, return home. Your mothers are waiting for you."[20]

Hamas, PIJ, and Fatah fighters had all worked together to prepare for the IDF onslaught. Their leaders tried to anticipate Israel's preferred route of entry and the points the IDF would try to hold. Their goal was simple: inflict casualties on the IDF. With this framework in mind the militants decided that booby-traps, ambushes, and snipers would be the best way to confront the enemy. "Hanged bombs"—bombs dangling from trees and other high places—were particularly effective, they believed. As the Israeli invasion became imminent, a camp resident said, Palestinian fighters put bombs "inside cupboards, under sinks, inside sofas." Some of the bombs were as big as 250 pounds—ten times the size of a typical suicide bomber's payload.[21] PIJ's leader Abdullah Ramadan Shalah explained that they knew the IDF would go to the homes of suspected PIJ fighters, "so they evacuated the houses and booby-trapped them. They booby-trapped the doors, the furnitures, the book shelves and other equipment."[22] In all, thousands of bombs were placed throughout the camp.

Israel sought "intelligence dominance," to use former chief of staff Bogi Yaalon's term. When fighters were captured and civilians sought to flee, the intelligence officers would quickly interrogate them to learn the location of additional enemy fighters and other information. During interrogation Palestinian fighters often revealed where they had buried explosives.[23] One Palestinian source complained, "We were betrayed by the spies among us"; he said that collaborators cut many of the wires of the bombs militants planted.[24] Instead of the usual procedure—in which information is gathered, passed up the chain to intelligence headquarters, and then disseminated to those who need it—the processing was completed in the field and the results were almost instantaneous. Digital maps provided a precise guide to every house. Helicopters and unmanned aerial vehicles (UAVs) flew constantly overhead to scout out the enemy, orient troops, and provide information and firepower to commanders.

(Israel was a pioneer in the use of UAVs for reconnaissance and strike power, but in recent years the United States has caught up. Many of the U.S. strikes against al-Qa'ida targets in Pakistan have involved unmanned drones.)

As the information flowed in, snipers picked off Palestinian fighters. The IDF used *mistaravim* (Hebrew for "to become an Arab") units, in which Israelis dressed and acted as locals to gather intelligence. When the Israelis took over an area, troops went from house to house to collect the names, phone numbers, and other information from every resident. The use of UAVs and *mistaravim* units in conjunction with attacks from all directions proved deadly, disorienting Palestinian fighters and making it hard for them to move in response to Israeli attempts to flank them. Supplying fighters with food and water was almost impossible.

Yet for all the IDF's care and technology, Israel was not able to conduct the pinpoint operations in Jenin it had initially hoped for. Local leadership in Jenin was strong, and the Israelis found a well-prepared enemy. According to captured Palestinian documents and fighters, militants in the camp were aware of some Israeli signals intelligence capabilities; fighters were warned not to use cell phones when helicopters were nearby.[25]

On a particularly bloody day, April 9, 2002, Palestinian fighters ambushed IDF reservists in Jenin's narrow alleyways, opening fire from three different directions as young boys threw bombs. Palestinian sources claimed they lured the soldiers and trapped them: "We all stopped shooting and the women went out to tell the soldiers that we ran out of bullets and were leaving." The women then alerted the Palestinian fighters that the soldiers were now in the booby-trapped area. "When the senior officers realized what had happened, they shouted through megaphones that they wanted an immediate cease-fire. We let them approach to retrieve the men and then opened fire."[26] Thirteen died in the trap.

In his account of the battle the platoon commander Ofer Segal recalled the bloody moment. The radio receiver screamed, "Six [the radio code name for commander of platoon six], this is eight, we are wounded. Come rescue us." Segal started running toward the alley, where heavy fire came from all directions. Entering the alley, it dawned on him how deadly the ambush was. Palestinian fighters shot at the troops from windows above, and getting the wounded out seemed impossible. Because the soldiers and militants were mixed, helicopters could not fire without shooting their own.[27] As Segal watched, one of the soldiers trying to evacuate a friend stepped on a tripwire. In the massive explosion that followed the soldier died and two of his friends fell wounded. Rescue proved futile. It later became clear that bombs and trigger wires were everywhere in the alley. "They are all dead, there are no wounded," the radio receiver screamed.[28] Three bodies were taken by the militants, and a Special Forces unit went in to retrieve them. An Israeli UAV broadcast the ambush to IDF headquarters, where officers watched in horror.

In most West Bank cities the rapid Israeli seizure disrupted local Palestinian fighters and prevented them from mounting an effective response. Israeli military officials faulted the unit commanders in Jenin for moving too slowly and allowing local forces to regroup and concentrate. However, the soldiers who went to Jenin had little training in unconventional warfare, and they had never experienced operations in densely packed refugee camps. Segal's comments to his soldiers during the three-day training session before the Jenin operation reflects this lack of deep training: "Guys, we might need to take control of houses with civilians inside. This is something completely new for us."[29] IDF troops in Jenin also lacked proper equipment, and their overhead imagery of Jenin was more than five years old.

At the same time, the Palestinians had strong leadership and fought better than they did elsewhere in the West Bank. The fighters displayed a unity and determination their brothers elsewhere lacked. The fighters in Jenin were led by Mona Hazam, a fighter known as Abu Jandal who had fought the IDF in Lebanon and had served in the Iraqi Army. Mahmud Tawalba, the head of PIJ in Jenin who was at the top of Israel's terrorist list there, was a brave, charismatic, and demanding leader who had sent his own brother to commit a suicide attack in Haifa. Tawalba's widow recounts how her husband said goodbye to her and their children while carrying three explosive belts with him. She last saw her husband "urging his fighters by saying: 'go forward brothers, the keys to paradise are in your hands.'"[30]

The Quagmire Deepens

As the IDF stalled and casualties mounted, political pressure to take the camp quickly with few IDF casualties became overwhelming. Chief of Staff Shaul Mofaz ordered the IDF to "shoot five LAWs [antitank missiles] at each house before going in."[31] Although commanders toned down the order, it shows the intensity of the Israeli response.

After the reservists were ambushed, the IDF began to use D-9 armored bulldozers, twenty-foot tall machines that flattened everything in their path. (With no small irony they are called *dubi* in military lingo, literally "teddy bear.") Initially the IDF used the D-9s to smash holes in the walls of buildings, what the troops called "knock on the door," so the squad could then take the buildings by deploying in an area that was relatively undefended and without having to traverse the dangerous and booby-trapped alleys of Jenin. The bulldozers were also effective at exploding bombs, thus clearing a path so deploying soldiers could pass through without injury. A senior IDF intelligence officer and planner, Yossi Kuperwasser, described the D-9 as "the main tool for a war like Jenin." "It was a war to the pace of the D-9," explained platoon commander Ofer Segal. "We were supposed to cover for the D-9 while it was working and be ready to seize any terrorist who would expose himself or surrender as a result of the house demolition. He described a scenario where the D-9 approached a house containing nine terrorists. Eight surrendered. Their commander did not. The D-9 knocked the house on him and killed him.[32]

The D-9s gave Israel tactical superiority, but their use was questioned. "What human mind was able to invent such a machine of demolition?" wrote Segal. "The bombs squashed easily under the monstrous track joints. Every move of it made a jangly crashing sound. Anything that the D-9 merely touched was instantly deformed."[33] It enabled military forces to move freely and intimidate the fighters opposing them. "Either they come out or we keep rolling." Tabaat Mardawi, an Islamic Jihad fighter, put this plainly: "There was nothing I could do against that bulldozer. What could I do? Either surrender or be buried in the rubble." The PIJ commander Mahmud Tawalba died along with two other fighters when they tried to get close enough to a D-9 to place explosives directly on it; apparently the driver saw them coming and smashed a wall down on top of them.[34]

The D-9s took a devastating toll on the camp. One quarter of the camp's population, roughly four thousand people, became homeless from the destruction. An Amnesty International delegate found "parts of human bodies sticking out of the rubble of destroyed houses."

Despite shaping the battle to be sensitive to Palestinian casualties, the IDF came to be vilified for its actions in Jenin, specifically for using D-9s. To minimize civilian casualties Israel had avoided using combat aircraft and artillery, even though one division commander said, "[With such weapons] I could have finished it all in a whistle." Israeli leaders feared high civilian casualties would cost Israel politically and diplomatically and perpetuate the Palestinians' message that Israel was a heartless and brutal oppressor.

However, given the nature of Palestinian tactics, keeping civilian casualties low was exceptionally difficult because Palestinian fighters were mixed in among the general population. Unless a man had a gun in his hand, the difference between a fighter and a young male civilian was almost impossible to discern at first sight. One PIJ leader explained, "The camp's residents opened their homes for us. . . . We gained a lot of benefit from this experience because it gave us protection from the helicopters and the snipers."[35]

Further blurring these lines, Palestinian women and children also participated in the military action. Amnesty International reported that women and children helped supply the fighters and pass messages to them. Israelis claimed that women and children would open the door for entering Israeli fighters, "forcing them to hesitate just long enough to allow the terrorist to shoot first." Abu Jandal, the PIJ commander, bragged in an interview, "There are children stationed in the houses with explosive belts at their sides."[36] According to an article in the Lebanese journal *al-Intiqad,* some children reportedly also made bombs, while others hid them according to leaders' instructions. On the eve of the invasion hundreds of children assembled to swear they would fight until victory or death. When the IDF entered the camp, youths in the camps "stopped using stones, and attacked them with bombs, thus earning the name, 'the explosives' children." Rami, a child from Jenin, explained the shift with simple logic: "We switched the stones to bombs because their influence and efficiency are bigger." Another child put his bombs in his school backpack.[37]

Still, Israeli soldiers ended up killing some innocent Palestinians. In the heat of battle the IDF made mistakes. Fares Hassan al-Sa'adi, twelve years old, died when a bomb meant to destroy one house also led to the collapse of the adjoining one, where he lived. In another case Israeli soldiers let women go into a house to evacuate Jamil Fayid, a man who could not move, speak, or eat without help. Yet the approaching bulldozer driver did not hear his own comrades' yells to stop and demolished the house. The women escaped, but Fayid died in the collapse. Abd al-Karim Sa'adi, another resident, died because soldiers mistook his back brace for an explosive belt. The soldiers were reacting to one of the Palestinians' most feared tactics: sending suicide bombers against the soldiers to blow themselves up at close range. Other residents died for violating curfew, in part because of confusion as to when the curfew began and ended.

In addition to mistakes carried out by the IDF, Amnesty International reported that the IDF leveled the Hawashin district of the Jenin camp after most of the fighting, claiming this was done as "punishment for its inhabitants"; it was the same part of the camp where the Israeli reservists had been ambushed. Moshe Nisim, one of the D-9 drivers, boasted that he wanted "to demolish it all from top to bottom."

At times the Israelis did not allow civilians in the combat zone to flee as required by international law, and instead used them as shields to protect the troops. One camp resident, Maher Muhammad Hassan Salim, claimed that soldiers threatened to shoot his family unless he went first through "mouse-holes," entry points created between houses when soldiers went through walls rather than risking exposure in the streets. Another Jenin resident, 'Amer Muhammad 'Abd al-Karim, told human rights officials, "The soldiers would have us walk in front of them, sometimes with them resting their rifles on our shoulders." Kamal Tawalbi told Human Rights Watch that he and his fourteen-year-old son were in the line of fire for three hours. Segal explained that the IDF used to enter a house, concentrate all the inhabitants in one room, and then take one person to search the house. "We don't touch anything, he does everything we ask him to."[38] As one U.S. general told me, "Israelis inculcate a degree of ruthlessness among their junior officers that we don't."

Such methods, though ruthless, protected IDF troops. 'Afaf Disuqi, a fifty-two-year-old woman, died when soldiers had her open a booby-trapped door. One Palestinian militant explained why his group did not kill a large group of soldiers: "We would have had to kill the boys too. Their brother was with us and begged us not to. We had the chance to kill twenty-five soldiers, but we did not." However, the IDF planner Yossi Kuperwasser claims that Israel used civilians in this way to minimize casualties on all sides, as Palestinian militants wouldn't activate booby traps against their own people. It was "a dialogue with them in their language."

Despite the tactical effectiveness of these methods, the IDF discontinued the use of civilians as shields after the Israeli Supreme Court later ruled it impermissible on human rights grounds. Afterward the IDF came up with a new procedure, in which Palestinians supposedly had a choice to help or refuse soldiers' requests to go with them during operations. The Supreme Court later found that Palestinians in reality did not have an option to refuse (it is hard to refuse a request from a squad of men in full battle gear) and banned this method too. Today Israeli human rights officials believe the IDF has stopped using this tactic officially, though among some units it continues in a far more limited way without authorization.[39] This issue remains sensitive among IDF commanders, who regularly request the use of this tactic because it is so effective in keeping their men safe.

As with so many of Israel's actions, the question of whether or not their methods were unduly harsh depends on the alternatives. Israel paid for the decision to use ground troops, the far riskier option, with the lives of the reservists, a serious testament to the cost. "People claim the IDF is inhumane," said the deputy brigade commander responsible for the Jenin operation during the last days. "But the house-to-house method of fighting the warriors used, and the fact that thirteen of our friends were killed is a proof of our humanity. We could easily come with heavy armored vehicles or with fighter aircrafts and wipe out this area. But we didn't do it because we didn't want to harm innocent civilians."[40]

Assessments of the appropriateness of the devastation in Jenin depend on whether one views such operations as police or military actions. Clearly innocent are the twelve-year-old Fares Hassan al-Sa'adi and the disabled Jamil Fayid. Had this been a police operation against a domestic criminal group, such deaths would be unacceptable, even if a large number of criminals had been arrested. Amnesty International and other human rights groups excoriate the Israelis for failing their obligations to protect civilians and prevent the destruction of property; under international law Israel is under particular responsibility to protect civilians in the land it occupies in the West Bank. Human Rights Watch, which is often harshly and one-sidedly critical of Israel, has even gone so far as to declare some of the IDF's actions in Jenin "war crimes."[41] Yet in conventional military operations, where thousands of civilians perish in air and artillery fire, the death of innocents is accepted as an unavoidable reality. By this standard the death toll in Jenin was quite low. When I gave U.S. military officials a hypothetical situation similar to Jenin but set in Iraq, their estimate for civilian casualties was in the hundreds.

A Turning Point?

Initially Operation Defensive Shield seemed to make little difference in the toll of terrorism. In May and June 2002 another wave of violence hit Israel, killing sixty-seven civilians and twenty soldiers, numbers comparable to the period before the operation.[42] Other IDF operations followed Defensive Shield, including Determined Path, yet another massive operation in the West Bank. By now Israel had stopped thinking in terms of Areas A, B, and C and was simply holding territory in order to cleanse it of terrorist groups.

The cumulative effect of these operations was profound. Almost five hundred Palestinians died in the initial operations, many of them members of militant organizations. Jenin and other Defensive Shield operations proved an intelligence bonanza for the Israelis. With reportedly seven thousand arrested, interrogators amassed a staggering amount of information on virtually every member of the different groups. Many were released when officials determined that they posed little threat, but more than fifteen hundred stayed in detention.[43] As they put the missing pieces of information together intelligence officers steadily began to round up the groups' leaders, bomb makers, and recruiters, not to mention the day-to-day fighters. Some of those arrested and released were turned into Israeli agents in the process. As Israel consolidated its control, the militants' ability to evade security forces fell sharply. One intelligence official told me, "They need somewhere to sleep at night." The IDF and Shin Bet could now capture and interrogate suspects and use the information to stop other militants.

Information gleaned from these efforts was in real time. Intelligence officials might learn a suspect was in a nearby building or was otherwise accessible. Because forces were on hand, the area could be cordoned off with less danger of ambush and the suspect arrested before he had time to flee or summon other fighters to protect him. Now the IDF had excellent freedom of movement.

Israel's de facto control over the West Bank also fundamentally changed its ability to recruit sources. Daily life was now in the hands of the Israelis. Does your pregnant wife need to go to a nearby hospital? Fine, so long as she and her family provide information if asked. Want to see your mother in a neighboring village? Fine, provide information. Caught dealing drugs or committing some other crime? You can be punished, or you can become an informer.[44] In their endless interactions with Palestinians, Israeli forces did not always, or even mostly, seek information for counterterrorism, but the goal was always in the background. One informer claimed at a "trial" by Fatah that he betrayed his cousin, a Hamas bomb maker, with the excuse, "Israeli officers presented me with sexually compromising photos and threatened to show them to my family."[45] Others gave information because they feared a long prison sentence. Still others sought money or drugs. For some, a work permit was an inducement for cooperation. The IDF operations also provided a shield for collaborators, enabling them to interact with their Israeli handlers without standing out, and indeed with a degree of protection.

At first Hamas, PIJ, and the al-Aqsa Martyrs Brigades found new militants to replace those dead or arrested. But these new recruits were less skilled, and the difference showed. By 2004 Shin Bet was able to stop 95 percent of the attempted attacks on Israel, capturing almost every suicide bomber who dared attempt crossing into Israel. In the Tanzim and the al-Aqsa Martyrs Brigades, young and inexperienced fighters replaced old leaders, and many of the new recruits were more loyal to their family or local chief than to the Fatah leadership—a huge blow to the organization's long-term capacity.[46] The taking of Jenin devastated PIJ in particular, which had strong networks there before Defensive Shield and lost many members through subsequent arrests.

Soon it became clear that Israel had almost completely eliminated suicide bombing. In 2002 Israel suffered fifty-three attacks; by 2006 there were only six.[47] Groups like Hamas disintegrated into small cells. Defensive Shield did not stop terrorism altogether, but by reducing it Israelis could once again walk down the streets of Netanya and Tel Aviv without fear.

The operational benefits were not matched on the international political level. As Israeli forces went in, accusations started to fly. In a decision many Israelis later came to regret, the IDF banned the media from entering Jenin along with the troops. The IDF planner Yossi Kuperwasser explained that the IDF "didn't want the cameraman under a warrior's legs," and General Giora Eiland believed that the IDF assumed reporters would only report on supposed Israeli brutality. However, as the journalist and analyst Hirsch Goodman points out, "If you don't fill the information vacuum, others will do it for you." The D-9 bulldozers, used in part because they were less destructive and more discriminating than artillery or air strikes, were a Palestinian propagandist's dream. Claims that the IDF had killed thousands of civilians became known to Palestinians, Arabs, the human rights community, and other sympathizers as the so-called "Jenin massacre."

Predictably Arab voices criticized the Jenin campaign in the harshest terms, but so too did European audiences. Early (and unconfirmed) statements by Palestinian groups influenced European coverage, which greatly exaggerated the death toll. The left-leaning *Guardian* in Britain called Israeli operations in Jenin "every bit as repellent" as the 9/11 attacks, and a columnist for the *Evening Standard* talked of "genocide." Gerald Kaufman, a Jewish member of Britain's Parliament, declared that Sharon's actions were "staining the Star of David with blood." Zvi Shtauber, Israel's ambassador to Britain at the time, wryly noted that the newspapers didn't have bold headlines declaring their mistakes when the truth later became clear, and today the exaggerated figures are widely accepted.

The widespread perception of Israeli brutality in Jenin is particularly ironic as the total number of casualties on all sides was far less than was expected and initially feared. The United Nations later found that twenty-three Israeli soldiers and fifty-two Palestinians, up to half civilians, died in the fighting. The number of Palestinian civilian dead was quite small given the nature of the fighting—a reality that often surprises people—and flies in the face of the initial reports that described the Israelis slaughtering Palestinian civilians. (Ironically the UN believes that approximately twice as many civilians died in the Israeli takeover of Nablus, but that received little subsequent attention.)[48] The story of the Israeli campaign in Jenin is bound up in general beliefs about the nature of the Israeli military.

Yet regardless of the reality of the operation, the "Jenin massacre" is now part of the Palestinians' narrative of suffering and brutality at the hands of the Israelis. Al-Jazeera and other Arab media stations interviewed officials who spoke of thousands of casualties. *Jenin, Jenin*, a widely viewed film directed by Muhammad Bakri, an Israeli Arab, endorsed the view of the massacre of civilians no matter what the truth. One film segment, for example, is edited to suggest that a bulldozer drove over a row of Palestinians lined up on the ground, and another depicts the bombing of Jenin by the Israeli Air Force, which never occurred.

While the Jenin operation opened Israel to criticism, it also made clear, for those willing to listen, that the Palestinians lacked good faith in the peace process. Defensive Shield led to a massive intelligence take on the militant groups. Intelligence documents showed conclusive links between PA officials and groups like Palestine Islamic Jihad, proving what Israel had long argued: that Arafat and his subordinates were accomplices to the violence rather than helpless bystanders. In addition to identifying many militants and their support networks, the documents also showed the relationship between Fatah, PIJ, and Hamas and revealed the depth of the ties that linked the groups. It also revealed that Hamas's supposedly apolitical charitable organizations and mosques disseminated incendiary literature and helped manage the violence. One Shin Bet officer described it as "the wettest dream [he] ever dreamed."[49] This information even changed the beliefs of some European leaders, convincing them that many of Arafat's claims were lies.

Israel temporarily suspended Arafat's house arrest as a concession to the United States, which agreed in return to suspend an investigation into the Jenin military operation. But in September Israel resumed the house arrest, and once again Arafat was lionized (but probably less so than he would have been had Israel killed him). However, the Palestinian journalist Wafa Amr believes that at this point Arafat lost control: "When he was under siege, he didn't give a damn." As the Intifada wore on, Israeli leaders constantly debated whether to deport or even kill Arafat. Sharon feared the howls of protest that would come from the Arab world and European states if the IDF tried to deport him and, in so doing, got into a firefight with the bodyguards and aides who always surrounded Arafat. Indeed Arafat wore two pistols, and Israel intelligence feared he might try to go out a martyr. In the end Sharon promised President George W. Bush that Israel would not harm Arafat, effectively ending the debate.[50]

Defensive Shield and subsequent operations marked a new Israeli strategy; the goal was now to end Palestinians' capacity for terrorism and show them, painfully, that violence would never work. Peace would come, Sharon believed, when the Palestinians were "badly beaten."[51] When he became chief of staff, Bogi Yaalon phrased it as "the very deep internalization by the Palestinians that terrorism and violence will not defeat us." Until that time came, by default, Israel's strategy became "mowing the grass," keeping terrorist groups weak and off balance through arrests and strikes. General Moshe Kaplinsky described this approach as a recognition that grass will keep growing after you mow it, but the new grass is immature and easier to manage. To complete the metaphor, the new terrorists are greener—less experienced, less charismatic, and less dangerous. "Today in the West Bank there are no more Shehadas," Kaplinsky said, referring to the Hamas chief Saleh Shehada, whom Israel killed in 2002.

At the same time, mowing the grass is not expected to solve the problem completely; it requires constant attention to keep the danger manageable. However, Israeli security officials hoped they could reduce attacks to the point that they neither interfered with daily life nor influenced Israeli decision making on other issues. As one military official put it to me in 2009, "Ask an average Israeli what is happening in Judea and Samaria—he won't know. He would have known in 2001."

Because mowing the grass at best manages rather than solves the problem, it is often a pejorative phrase in U.S. military circles. Some U.S. officers see this phrase as a metaphor for the futility of Israeli operations; they see Israel as doomed to continued terrorism because its strategy today at best kicks the can down the road rather than aims at a lasting solution.

The most visible impact of Defensive Shield and other military actions at the time was on Israeli control over the West Bank and the political, diplomatic, and operational costs and benefits that ensued. After reoccupying the West Bank to stop terrorists, Israel was left with a conundrum: having crushed militant groups there, could it now leave without risking that the terrorists would return?

CHAPTER XI

OCCUPYING THE WEST BANK: THE PRICE OF SUCCESS (2003–TODAY)

SHORTLY AFTER the beginning of Operation Defensive Shield in 2002, U.S. National Security Advisor Condoleezza Rice demanded that Israel withdraw from the West Bank immediately. When asked if the United States would give Israel a few days to organize the withdrawal, Rice emphatically told CNN, "'Without delay' means without delay. It means now."[1] Israeli officials declined. One involved official claimed that they told Rice they would need a few months to secure the area. Soon after Sharon maintained that the Israeli presence in cities like Jenin and Nablus "will not last."[2] Nine years later Israel is still mired in the West Bank—and there is little sign that a withdrawal is around the corner.

The strategy embodied in Operation Defensive Shield effectively keeps the lid on a boiling pot; it does not remove the fire. Israel avoids painful decisions about how to exit the West Bank even though these might give it more security in the long-term. As the security analyst and retired IDF official Shlomo Brom told me, "The price of a bearable situation is its prolongation."

Most of the remaining violence is contained in Palestinian areas, so civilians inside Israel proper are far safer today, and Israeli soldiers and settlers still bear the brunt of the risks. Security officials also fret about the future. The spread of rockets, even short-range ones, from Gaza to the West Bank would be disastrous for Israel, far more so than the disruptive rocket attacks that have come from Gaza. All the while Israel faces demographic pressures of the Jewish population becoming a minority in the land under its control, making it ever harder to be both a Jewish and a democratic state.

Against this backdrop Israel's counterterrorism operations in the West Bank exact a costly toll against Palestinians. Though Jenin and other initial military operations were far less bloody than most believe, many of the counterterrorism measures used in the occupation are devastating in subtle ways. After Defensive Shield Israel created an extensive military presence outside Palestinian cities that includes a network of roadblocks and checkpoints, all of which is disruptive and humiliating for Palestinians. For several years the number of checkpoints rose even as violence decreased; only in 2009 did the numbers begin to fall significantly. During this period the Palestinian economy collapsed and society itself became fragmented. Meanwhile the occupation discredited moderate Palestinian leaders, who are perceived as Israeli flunkies, while Hamas and its rejectionist approach gained ground. A negotiated settlement seems more distant than ever.

Partners No More

In the years after Defensive Shield Israelis abandoned the idea of relying on a Palestinian partner. During Defensive Shield Israel destroyed the headquarters of Jibril Rajoub's Preventive Security Services headquarters outside Ramallah. Rajoub had been one of Israel's best partners in the 1990s, and the IDF's action humiliated him. Israel no longer distinguished between Palestinian security officials who might again prove partners and those who were irrevocably committed to violence. During one of the periods when Israel and the PA began negotiations again, Israelis criticized the PA security chief in Gaza, Mohammad Dahlan, for not arresting militants. Dahlan responded, "Where shall I put them? You've destroyed our prisons."

Perhaps the surest sign of the Israeli leadership's disdain for Palestinian capabilities was their response to what could have been a major shift in Palestinian leadership in 2003. After a June 18, 2002, attack on an Israeli school bus that left nineteen dead, Sharon told National Security Advisor Rice, "As far as I am concerned, Arafat is over." In a famous speech in the Rose Garden six days later President Bush finally put the United States openly behind the creation of a Palestinian state, but also made it clear that "peace requires a different Palestinian leadership [that is] not compromised by terror."[3] Facing concerted pressure Arafat caved and appointed Mahmud Abbas (often referred to as Abu Mazen) as prime minister on March 19, 2003. Abbas was openly pro-peace and against violent resistance, and his elevation was meant to weaken Arafat's power. Israel had finally found a Palestinian leader firmly committed to restarting the peace process.

In contrast to Arafat, Abbas had little money, no street power, no charisma, and no legacy as a revolutionary—in short, he was powerless.

His only hope was to prove he could deliver as a leader. Dov Weissglas, a close advisor of Sharon, later claimed that Arafat undermined Abbas as prime minister—a true statement, but one that captures only part of the problem.[4] Sharon did not take Abbas seriously. The American envoy General Anthony Zinni believed that Sharon's decision was personal, not political: "Sharon could not bring himself to play the Kabuki game" and openly bolster the Palestinian leader. Because Abbas could not deliver, his support plummeted.[5] Having weakened Arafat the Bush administration did little to fill the void. Bush himself was pleased that Arafat had been sidelined, but problems in Iraq quickly absorbed his administration's focus. Furthermore U.S. officials doubted that Abbas could impose his will.

The Apparatus of Control

Instead of relying on Abbas, Israel sought to ensure security through its own capabilities. But in contrast to the past occupation, it did not assume the responsibility of governance. Instead its forces largely withdrew from the heart of populated areas but controlled access points.

For most Palestinians, the occupation of the West Bank was measured by the number of checkpoints they faced in their daily lives; these were one of Israel's most important, and most disruptive, counterterrorism instruments. Checkpoints began in a makeshift way. To control access and stop potential bombers from carrying out their attacks, local commanders temporarily closed off entry to or exit from a town. Over time this ad hoc system grew massive. According to the United Nation's Office for the Coordination of Humanitarian Affairs, in June 2009 there were 613 closures within the West Bank, sixty-eight of which were permanently staffed checkpoints. In addition to these closures there were sixty-three crossing points along the barrier into the West Bank, known as "barrier gates," and on average seventy flying checkpoints a week during 2009.[6] (Flying checkpoints are road barriers that get moved from road to road as necessary.) There were also other obstructions, such as roadblocks, piles of dirt, iron gates, and trenches that blocked Palestinians' movement.[7]

From a counterterrorism point of view, movement restrictions served multiple and reinforcing purposes. Palestinian fighters found it difficult to obtain weapons when the IDF encircled every town, and it became harder for them to conduct meetings, send messengers, and coordinate their activities once they were unable to move from place to place without fear of arrest. Militant commanders who never left their home areas often lacked situational awareness. One senior military official claimed that 30 percent of Israel's counterterrorism arrests took place at checkpoints.

Although Israeli intelligence is far from perfect, Palestinian respect for it is high, and would-be terrorists feared their names might be on a list when they approached a checkpoint. Even when they have not been identified, their nervous behavior at a checkpoint would often give them away. If would-be terrorists try to avoid a checkpoint, it arouses suspicion. When messengers or operatives get stuck at checkpoints, they often pull out their phones. This enables Israeli signals intelligence to intercept the call and helps the IDF locate not only the operative but also the broader network and mastermind behind him. This system also enables Israel to recruit Palestinian collaborators, offering increased mobility in return for services as an informant.

An often overlooked but vital advantage of checkpoints, and of occupying territory in general, is time. In the past, Israeli intelligence would regularly learn about an attack while it was in progress but have only hours or even minutes to stop it. With checkpoints Israel can shut down movement on all or part of the West Bank, forcing the attackers to halt or risk detection, giving the IDF and Shin Bet additional hours to gather more information and find them. IDF General Giora Eiland offers a useful example: he recalls that in 2005 intelligence revealed that two unknown suicide bombers were about to go from Nablus to Ramallah, where they would meet a guide who would show them how to infiltrate and attack Jerusalem. Israeli intelligence did not know the bombers, but it did know the guide. Its assets followed him and observed him meeting with the bombers, and arresting troops swooped in to prevent the attack. Both the intelligence gathering and the arrest would have taken far more time if Israeli assets were not on hand for immediate action.[8]

Soldiers developed procedures to screen Palestinians to detect the approach of a potential bomber. Often they ordered Palestinian males to lift their shirt and expose their stomach to make sure the men were not wearing bombs. At times suicide bombers pursued soldiers at the checkpoints, but at least the threat moved away from Israeli civilian areas, a political victory even though the human cost remained high. Over time metal detectors and other technological measures minimized the threat to Israelis. Today the Qalandia checkpoint between Jerusalem and Ramallah is an imposing affair that resembles an international border. Soldiers manning the checkpoint examine travelers' documents, and individuals must pass through metal detectors. Iron bars and barriers are ubiquitous, restricting those going through to a controlled space.

Checkpoints are a constant aggravation and at times a location for abuse. One sergeant recalls that one of his officers beat up an old man in front of his little boy because the old man was not keeping the queue line straight.[9] One disillusioned soldier contended, "When you're human and you're upset, you take it out on yourself or you punch a pillow or wall. When you're a soldier in the West Bank, you take it out on the population."[10]

To reduce abuses and suffering Israel upgraded the checkpoints. In contrast to the Intifada's early years, at the major checkpoints there are now drinking fountains, bathrooms, and shaded areas where people queue, all of which make the checkpoints more tolerable. Most important the IDF professionalized checkpoint activity and personnel. Checkpoints now have electronic databases, and in many areas military police have replaced combat soldiers. The IDF also set up a code of conduct for the checkpoints that emphasizes the need to respect those passing through— even those arrested. Lt. Col. Amos Guiora, who helped design the code, wrote, "We stress that if you don't treat the Palestinian civil population according to these rules of conduct, they will go from being innocent civilians to terrorists."[11] Palestinians contend the rules are honored more in the breach, but they nevertheless represent a step forward from the Intifada's early days.

Detentions, Arrests, and Interrogations

Israel's experience in the Second Intifada exposes a fundamental gap in the current legal regime, one that U.S. administrations have grappled with since 9/11 but have not resolved. What can be done when a terrorist and guerrilla group, as opposed to an army, is engaged in a low-level but nearly constant war? The Israeli Supreme Court found that prisoner of war status is not appropriate, and they are backed up by the Geneva Convention articles, which maintain that if militias and resistance movements are to be treated as POWs, they need to carry arms openly, operate according to the laws of war (and thus not strike civilians), and wear some sort of recognizable uniform. Because Palestinian fighters don't meet any of these qualifications, prisoner of war status does not apply.

Israel has had to grapple with the unclear legal status of suspected terrorists, a question that became paramount after it reassumed control of the West Bank. In the Second Intifada Israel put thousands of Palestinians in jail, keeping them off the streets and thus preventing them from swelling the ranks of militant organizations. The Israeli human rights group B'Tselem reports that in January 2001 Israel imprisoned or detained 1,456 Palestinians. The figure peaked in early 2007 at more than nine thousand, then fell slightly to just under eight thousand by the end of 2008.[12] In May 2009 there were 7,669 Palestinians in Israeli jails. When the system works—and it still does today—it creates a benign circle: arrests and detentions of a few key operatives yield intelligence that enables further arrests and detentions, and so on to the point where the individual cells and the larger group cannot function. The detentions and arrests have devastated Palestinian militant organizations.

Of those detained, more than 250 were in administrative detention, a number that has waxed and waned over the years.[13] The administrative detention law itself is a relic of British emergency regulations, which were used against Jews fighting for independence after World War II. Israeli military laws that govern the West Bank allow detention, and in 1979 Israel passed an Emergency Powers detention law that gave the minister of defense the authority to detain a person "if he has reasonable grounds to presume that such detention is necessary for reasons of state security or public safety."[14] Under this law the state does not have to give material evidence to the defense team, but rather can give it directly to the court. Intelligence may also be used, including intelligence that might not be permissible in a regular court of law.

During the Second Intifada, however, the old system that required detainees to be brought before a judge within ninety-six hours of arrest was so overwhelmed with cases that the requirement was waived.[15] In 2002 the Knesset passed the Internment of Unlawful Combatants Law, allowing Israel to detain members of terrorist and guerrilla groups, "even the cook in the Hizballah kitchen."[16] Unlike prisoners of war, those interned may or may not eventually face criminal charges. Unlike those arrested on criminal charges, there is no fixed term limit for detention.

The IDF has two basic forms of administrative detention. First, the Ministry of Defense can issue an order for detention for six months, and that order can be renewed after review by a civilian district judge.[17] "You can detain someone for decades," Devorah Chen, the attorney who prosecuted Marwan Barghouti and several other senior Palestinians charged with terrorism, told me. But after that order a judicial review from the president of the District Courts (a senior judge) is still necessary, and the defendant has the right to a lawyer. However, witnesses are not called. Only the judge—not the defendant's lawyer—is allowed to see all the information. Although the prosecutor's responsibility is to reveal all information, there is no cross-examination to ensure this happens. A second form of administrative detention allows an IDF commander to issue a detention order, subject to review by an IDF judge.[18]

Human rights organizations have charged that legal procedures in these military courts, especially in the first few years of the Intifada, were often lacking. At times no Arabic translation was provided, so the defendants could not understand the charges they faced. About 60 percent were denied counsel in the first month of arrest. Of the 9,123 cases concluded in the military courts in the year 2006, for example, the defendant was found not guilty in twenty-three cases.[19]

Israel will at times use the traditional legal process rather than the military detention system. One such case was the prosecution of Marwan Barghouti. Barghouti rose to prominence as a young Fatah leader in the First Intifada, negotiated with the Israelis in the 1990s, and even today is considered a potential future Palestinian leader. He began to orchestrate violence during the Second Intifada, and Israelis believed that his prominence made it necessary to try him in a civilian court so that the verdict would be accepted internationally. Though the testimony of the victims was compelling, Barghouti put on a show before the world media, refusing to accept the court's jurisdiction and railing against the Israeli occupation. The court found that Barghouti "led, managed, and operated the Acts of Terror," "was active in obtaining arms and other weapons," played a major role in financing cells, and was aware of far more activities conducted by local commanders and their cells.[20]

Creating a legal system for detention that balances justice and security is problematic. Criminal court procedures are insufficient, because in criminal cases police must disclose sensitive information such as evidence of wiretaps and names of informants. Revealing the same information on collaborators and informants is far more serious for counterterrorism because these sources need to be tapped again and again, and some who cooperated with the security services would recant their confessions if called upon publicly.[21] The Supreme Court does review detentions, though the Court rarely questions intelligence judgments on an individual's guilt or innocence. Defenders of this system claim the Court does ask hard questions and occasionally issues rulings that shorten sentences, thus encouraging security agencies to take care in gathering and presenting evidence.

Despite this legal structure, abuses and tragedies occur regularly. There are stories of beatings and other mistreatment at checkpoints.[22] Many arrest attempts have turned violent. Military officials I spoke to claimed that killings happen only when the Palestinians use violence or refuse to surrender. However, IDF unit commanders and border police officers, reluctant to put their men at risk, at times shot first and asked questions later.[23] Human rights groups believe that some arrest attempts in the West Bank are really an unofficial means of killing suspected Palestinian terrorists: the soldiers go into the arrest ready to shoot at the drop of a hat. Jessica Montell, executive director of B'Tselem, argues that in many cases "there is just a fig leaf on arrests" and cites one case in which a man sleeping in a room was killed. In her view, there is at best a "Plan A" to arrest, "but Plan B comes in real quick" if there is the slightest risk of casualties.

Children have died when demonstrations turn violent or in crossfires when bullets hit them in the back or upper body, resulting in a small fine for an officer (say, twenty-five to fifty dollars) and no punishment for the regular soldiers.[24] In contrast to the First Intifada, when civilian deaths were consistently investigated, Human Rights Watch found the IDF rarely investigated allegations of illegal use of lethal force against civilians in the Second Intifada and issued only token punishments when it did find wrongdoing.[25]

The importance of arrest and interrogation highlights a bureaucratic shift in Israel: the rise of Shin Bet. As the locus of terrorism switched from outside Israel to Gaza and the West Bank in the 1990s, Shin Bet's role grew proportionally. This already large role became even more important during the Second Intifada, when Shin Bet became the brains behind Israel's day-to-day counterterrorism operations.

The Silent Occupation

Checkpoints, detentions, and the occupation itself made it hard for terrorist groups to strike Israel. They are also a constant insult to Palestinians' dignity, a disaster for Palestinian economic and social life, and at times a terrifying experience. "We debase the Palestinian," lamented the former Shin Bet head Avraham Shalom.[26] Daily life was a constant hassle. Iyad Haddad, a B'Tselem field researcher, wryly joked that Palestinians in the West Bank didn't need a car that went beyond third gear, as they would hit a checkpoint before they could go that fast. Sharif Waked, a Palestinian artist, created a video entitled *Chic Point* that models clothing "appropriate" for Israeli checkpoints, showing, for example, exposed midriffs, and juxtaposing these images with those of Palestinians going through Israeli checkpoints on the West Bank and Gaza.[27]

Such black humor was a rare escape from the difficulties of life under the occupation. Israel forbade Palestinians from entering areas where settlements were built, even if their lands were located there. Palestinians could not use Ben Gurion Airport. Restrictions were particularly harsh on young men, the most likely recruits for terrorist organizations.[28] The same checkpoints that prevented terrorists from mobilizing also prevented families from seeing their relatives and schoolchildren from attending their classes. Palestinians were prevented from holding on to jobs, carrying out their studies, or obtaining medical care.[29] On the days when Israel shut down the entire West Bank (and, before it departed in 2005, areas in the Gaza Strip), all previously issued permits were of no avail. There were 132 such days in 2005 and seventy-eight in 2006.[30]

Israeli policy squeezed the Palestinians administratively as well. Ramallah is surrounded by settlements and roadblocks. Even basic functions such as garbage removal required Israeli permission. Even worse, some urban Palestinian areas have exploded in population (Ramallah has almost doubled since Oslo was signed), but the size of Area A, where Israel has given the Palestinian Authority a degree of administrative autonomy, has not grown. As a result real estate prices have surged. "Even the graveyards are full," noted its governor Abu Ali.

The restrictions on Palestinian freedom of movement, the closures, and the checkpoints devastated the Palestinian economy: transportation costs increased, trade with Israel proper and with Jordan became difficult, and there was a decrease in the number and kind of goods produced because of lack of access to farming lands.[31] Palestinians attempting to travel to work or to leave their homes were prevented from departing or, if the closures were imposed only on vehicles, faced a trip of two or three hours rather than several minutes. How long it took to get from Ramallah to nearby Jerusalem, let alone from a location deeper in the West Bank, depended on the security climate of the moment and could take hours or minutes accordingly. As an example of the severity of the problem, it was often faster to deliver raw materials from China to the Ashdod seaport than from Nablus in the West Bank to Ashdod.[32] By the middle of 2006 two-thirds of the Palestinians were living in poverty, making less than two dollars a day.[33] Palestinian standards of living have yet to return to what they were in the days before the Second Intifada. The 2009 World Bank assessment of the Palestinian economy argued that it would not be able to bounce back until goods and people flowed freely.[34]

For all the talk of abuses at checkpoints, and for all their reality, the deeper problem is that they are designed for counterterrorism purposes, which by nature do not mesh well with the social and economic needs of the Palestinians, to say nothing of their political aspirations. For the soldier at the checkpoint, counterterrorism is the imperative. As the former IDF chief of staff Amnon Lipkin-Shahak pointed out to me, "The soldier has to explain why someone he let through exploded himself at a restaurant in Jerusalem." The problem is that "out of thousands of Palestinians coming to work, one can be a terrorist." Thus if soldiers err, they err on the side of caution, reacting harshly if necessary to safeguard the civilian population.

Terrorist groups have deliberately exacerbated this problem, taking advantage of Israel's sensitivities to humanitarian concerns. On January 14, 2004, a Palestinian woman killed four Israelis at a Gaza checkpoint by pretending to be disabled. Because of her condition, soldiers gave her a personal security check rather than using a metal detector; she then proceeded to detonate her bomb device. "I always wanted to be the first woman to carry out a martyrdom operation, where parts of my body can fly all over," she said in a message she videotaped before the attack.[35]

"Not everyone who appears to be pregnant is truly pregnant," notes one IDF official about the difficulties of running checkpoints. An ambulance speeding toward a checkpoint might be a ruse to deliver explosives or even a suicide bomber into Israel. Lipkin-Shahak told me that terrorist groups have used ambulances and babies' diapers as ways to smuggle explosives. In March 2002 the IDF and Shin Bet arrested a Tanzim terrorist working as an ambulance driver for the Palestinian Red Crescent. The ambulance he drove contained explosive belts and explosive devices destined for delivery to Tanzim activists in Ramallah. One explosive belt was discovered underneath the body of a child lying on a stretcher, whose family was with him in the ambulance at the time. In July 2004 the IDF arrested two members of the Palestinian security forces from Bethlehem who were also Tanzim operatives. The two were part of a plot to deliver a suicide bomber with an explosive belt into Jerusalem using an ambulance.[36]

That said, the vast majority of ambulances carry someone who urgently needs medical attention. At a checkpoint, however, the person is usually taken out of the ambulance and carefully scrutinized because, though it is unlikely, the patient might be a carefully disguised terrorist. The Israeli who makes this determination might be a soldier as young as nineteen.[37] Almost inevitably a sick woman and her baby on the way to a hospital are delayed and searched.[38] As General Zinni notes, "Everyone who goes through a checkpoint is treated as an enemy—he can be nine months old or ninety years old."

B'Tselem lists sixty-six Palestinians who died between the outbreak of the Second Intifada through 2008 because of denied or delayed access to medical care.[39] Isma'il Sa'id Ibrahim a-Sifi lived in Tell, a Palestinian town near Nablus. He died on December 12, 2006, of a heart attack. He was on his way to the hospital when he was stopped by a flying checkpoint and then redirected along dirt roads, making his trip to medical care much too long and ultimately too late. The World Health Organization found that between September 2000 and December 2004 thirty-six babies born at checkpoints died from complications that could have been prevented with appropriate medical care.[40]

Complicating the occupation further are the Israeli settlers, particularly those who took up residence deep in the West Bank. The settler movement exploited the Intifada and the consequent collapse of the peace process to expand existing settlements and build new ones. At the end of 2000 there were 191,600 settlers in the West Bank.[41] By June 30, 2009, that number had reached 304,569.[42] Palestinian deprivation stands out in stark contrast when compared with the lifestyles of Jewish settlers in the West Bank, who live on pristine hilltops in expansive accommodations dotted with swimming pools, while many nearby Palestinians live in cramped cities and refugee camps. Jewish settlers enjoy the luxury of traveling on a large network of well-maintained bypass roads connecting the settlements with one another and with Israel. The roads themselves are off-limits to Palestinians. Palestinian roads are sometimes unpaved and wind around circuitous routes. Closures were particularly common for towns near Jewish settlements, creating further misery. In Hebron some Arab areas were under curfew for months to protect the five hundred or so Jewish settlers living there.

Not surprisingly the settlements are inviting targets for attacks: one former security official claimed that half of the interceptions at roadblocks are related to attacks directed at settlers. Former IDF officers claimed that checkpoints are often set up to protect settlements and as a way to minimize contact between the settlers and the Palestinians.

House Demolitions, Permits, and Deportation

During the Second Intifada Israel began to again use one of the harsher tools of its past to pacify Palestinian areas: house demolitions. The program had petered out by 1998, but following the Dolphinarium Disco attack in

2001 the IDF demolished the home of Sa'id al-Hutri, the bomber. Four other houses were destroyed in October, and in 2002 Israel would destroy over two hundred and fifty homes to punish suspected terrorists and their supporters. The Israeli Committee Against House Demolitions, an Israeli human rights organization, reported that Israel demolished 669 houses from 2001 to January 2005, when it temporarily ended the policy.[43] (Israel resumed punitive house demolitions in 2009, when it destroyed the houses of the families of two Palestinians responsible for terrorist attacks in Jerusalem). The IDF described house demolitions as "a message to terrorists and their accomplices in terrorism, that their acts come at a price that will be paid by everyone taking part in hostile terrorist activity."[44]

Because the program involved punishing those not directly involved in terrorism, some Israelis criticized it, and governments overseas roundly denounced it. "How long does it take to demolish a house?" the Israeli author Yizhar Smilanski wrote. "Less time than is spent thinking about whether it should have been demolished."[45] B'Tselem criticized the program in part because a house was demolished *after* Israel had arrested the suicide bomber or after he had already committed his attack.[46]

Demolitions, however, are not meant to punish the perpetrator; they serve as a signal to other families who see that their homes too would be destroyed if their sons engaged in violence. Shai Nitzan, arguing for the Attorney General's Office before the Israeli Supreme Court, claimed that "the family is a central factor in Palestinian society" and through it terrorists can be deterred.[47] Regardless of its purpose, Israel's program does punish families and even neighbors whether or not they participated in an attack—a troubling tactic for a democracy. One Israeli Supreme Court Justice called the policy illegal, even citing Ezekiel's admonition that the father shall not bear the iniquity of the son. Furthermore B'Tselem found that almost half of the houses demolished "were never home to anyone suspected of involvement in attacks against Israelis."[48] For Palestinians, one of the biggest complaints is that house demolitions are used only against Arab terrorists. The house of Baruch Goldstein, who slaughtered Palestinians in the Cave of the Patriarchs, was never demolished.

The pain demolitions inflict on families is considerable. In an already impoverished area, losing a home means losing everything. Some families are broken up when they are forced to live with relatives or neighbors. The emotional impact, particularly for children, is devastating. The wife of one suspected terrorist whose home was demolished said that they spent the first night on the street: "My son Yassir, who is three and a half, was nervous and depressed for a whole month. He cried a lot, and kept saying he wanted our house."[49] Israelis retort that they are responding to militants taking lives, not homes.

Experts disagree on whether house demolitions are effective. The IDF cites several examples where family members turned in potential terrorists to stop their homes from being destroyed. However, a 2005 internal IDF report authored by retired Maj. Gen. Udi Shani concluded, "There is no proof of the deterrent effect of house demolitions." The report notes that terrorism rose after house demolitions began and further argues that the measure was ineffective: no more than twenty family members turned in their sons for fear of a demolition. Moreover the demolitions provoked hatred and hostility toward Israel.[50] Former chief of staff Bogi Yaalon cautions that house demolitions are effective only when Israel controls the territory. If Israel does not control the territory, the Palestinian groups simply build a bigger and nicer house for the family, so the supposed deterrent in fact becomes an incentive.

As this debate suggests, much depends on context. One Palestinian human rights official admitted that house demolitions do stop some people from joining a terrorist group, but it has the opposite effect on others: because they lost everything, their anger is greater.

Regardless of its effectiveness, the demolitions policy was a public relations disaster. Yaalon points out that "the need to demolish homes is difficult to explain while watching an old Palestinian woman looking for her belongings in the wreckage of her house."[51] In remarks that enraged other Israeli leaders, Justice Minister Yosef "Tommy" Lapid commented, "I saw on television an old woman picking through the rubble of her house in Rafah, looking for her medicine, and she reminded me of my grandmother who was expelled from her home during the Holocaust."[52]

In the international human rights community the destruction caused by house demolitions is captured by the image of a bulldozer running over twenty-three-year-old Rachel Corrie, an American member of the International Solidarity Movement, acting as a "human shield" on behalf of the Palestinians. On March 16, 2003, she was crushed to her death while trying to prevent a bulldozer from knocking down a house in the Rafah refugee camp. According to one witness, whose recollection is reprinted on a pro-resistance website, Corrie sat down in front of the bulldozer and started to yell and wave her hands. As the bulldozer continued ahead the ground beneath her started to pile up and she climbed on top of the mound. The bulldozer continued, pulling Rachel's legs into the pile of rubble under her and ultimately pulling her directly underneath the bulldozer. Badly wounded, she called out "My back is broken" as her fellow activists tried to help her.[53] It was too late. The belief that the soldiers deliberately killed Corrie is now gospel in many circles. The IDF claimed, and Israeli courts upheld, that the bulldozer driver was unable to see Corrie given the restricted vision from his perch, that Corrie died from being hit by debris rather than being run over, and that she acted recklessly by inserting herself into the path of the bulldozer.[54]

As it did in the early days of the occupation, Israel also deported Palestinians during the Second Intifada, often from the West Bank to the

Gaza Strip. Under the new deportation policy, thirty-two Palestinians were deported from the West Bank to Gaza between 2002 and 2004.[55] Deportations thus affected only a small number of Palestinians; for ordinary Palestinians a bigger problem was permits. Palestinians need Israeli permits to work, study, travel, and receive medical care. They need building permits or they can face house demolitions. They also need permits to go from the West Bank to the Gaza Strip. The separation barrier also forced Palestinians to get permits to work their land on the other side of the barrier. Israeli intelligence exploits the need for permits to gain information, but the cumbersome system makes life difficult for ordinary Palestinians.

Mohammad Jalud's frustrations illustrate the difficulties this system causes. Jalud lives in Izbat Jalud, south of Qalqilya, only a ten-minute walk from his fields. However, when the security barrier was constructed just on the edge of urban Izbat Jalud, his fields fell on the other side. The Israelis built a gate into the wall at Izbat Jalud, but Palestinians were not initially granted access to it. Jalud had to walk several miles north to another gate at Azun Atma before crossing over and walking back south to his fields. In 2004 Israel opened the gate by Izbat Jalud; however, because he had a permit to exit through Azun Atma he was not allowed to exit through either gate: at Azun Atma, he was told to go through the Izbat Jalud gate, and at Izbat Jalud he was told that he had a permit only for Azun Atma. It took him over a year to get the permit to cross at Izbat Jalud.[56]

Will Israel Reap the Whirlwind?

Checkpoints, permits, deportations, closures, and other tools have successfully inhibited terrorists and helped crush the Second Intifada. But is Israel only making things worse in the long term? Palestinians believe Israeli security measures make more violence inevitable. Zuhair Kurdi, a Palestinian journalist, commented, "The legal father of the suicide bomber is the Israeli checkpoint, whilst his mother is the house demolition."[57] Twelve retired Israeli commanders similarly denounced the checkpoints, and Ilan Paz, the former IDF administrator responsible for the occupation of the West Bank, contended that there is grave danger "in having the Palestinian people with its back to the wall, not seeing a light at the end of the tunnel, unable to improve their economy, unable to move from place to place. This creates a reality that creates terror."[58]

But does humiliation and anger lead to terrorism?

Assaf Moghadam, an expert on terrorism who teaches at West Point, examined the motives behind suicide bombers during the Second Intifada, looking at both the individual motives that would lead a person to become a suicide bomber as well as the motives that would lead groups to organize these attacks. He found a handful of personal motives that drive individuals, including the benefits to their family after their death in money and status, revenge for loved ones killed or injured by Israel, and the desire to overcome the humiliation of life as a Palestinian. Indeed some individual motives, such as Palestinian national aspirations, are sometimes intimately tied up with the sense of humiliation Palestinians suffer in their daily existence. Nichole Argo, another scholar, found that the bombers and militants she interviewed explained their decision to use violence by citing the deaths of children in Israeli military operations, the humiliation of women in searches, and other actions that led them to feel moral outrage.[59] This anger, however, becomes a grave danger to Israel only when terrorist groups themselves are given some freedom to function. Otherwise the frustrations fester and at times erupt, but they do not lead to sustained violence.

To lessen the anger Israel needs to reduce the intrusiveness of the occupation, and ideally end it altogether. Doing so, however, risks allowing militant groups more freedom to operate. Israel can square this circle if a Palestinian government comes to power that is both peaceful in its intentions and strong enough to make peace—and Israel is willing to cut a deal.

Making this dilemma even more difficult is the rise of Hamas. In the past Hamas complicated the peace process as a terrorist threat to Israel and as a rival to Fatah. These complications still hold, but now an even bigger issue dwarfs them: Hamas's rise to prominence near the end of the Second Intifada and its assumption of power in the Gaza Strip. The Israelis fear that if they end the occupation of the West Bank, Hamas will not only operate freely, but may even take power through democratic elections, as they did in Gaza.

CHAPTER XII

HAMAS TRIUMPHANT (2005-2008)

AFTER RETAKING the West Bank in 2002 Israel steadily began destroying the capacity of terrorist groups to inflict harm, especially Hamas and Fatah-linked groups like the al-Aqsa Martyrs Brigades. In the West Bank the costs associated with occupation seemed high, but as deaths from terrorism steadily fell, most Israelis felt it was a price worth paying.

As always, Gaza was harder. Hamas was far stronger in Gaza than in the West Bank, and Israel struggled to set the terrorist group back on its heels. A major blow to Hamas was the March 22, 2004, killing of the near-blind, wheelchair-bound Sheikh Yasin. One senior Israeli intelligence official argued, "You cannot say that Yasin was a religious man only, uninvolved in the decision making process; you simply cannot say it."[1] Israelis had delayed killing Yasin, concerned that his death would increase terror. They feared provoking the broader Arab and Islamic world, where Yasin drew wide respect. And indeed the rage Israel anticipated broke out: not only did Islamist groups around the world express their outrage, but so too did allies like Jordan's King Abdullah and Egyptian president Hosni Mubarak. Yet by the time Israel finally killed Yasin, his death had little impact on Hamas's intentions. For years the group had gone all-out against Israel, so killing its leader did not fundamentally change its orientation.

Yasin had been quite open in his enmity. As early as 1997 he had said, "Israel, as the Jewish state, must disappear from the map" and proclaimed, "The so-called peace path is not peace and it is not a substitute for jihad and resistance."[2] Shortly before his death, in the face of repeated threats by Israel to eliminate him, Yasin responded, "We do not fear death threats. We are seekers of martyrdom."[3] One Shin Bet figure who visited Yasin before he went to jail notes that Yasin had always declared, "There is no room for Israel in the Middle East." On the other hand, Tzvika Sela, the retired chief psychologist of the Israel Prison Service who spent dozens of hours talking with Yasin when he was in jail, argues that Yasin was in fact willing to acknowledge the existence of the state of Israel. Sela quotes Yasin as saying, "You established a state because of the military strength you had. The casualties I take of you are for the establishment of another state, while you just kill women and children in the sake of the occupation. You are filthy and hypocrites. I do not wish to destroy you, all I want is a state."[4]

Shortly after killing Yasin, Israel killed his longtime deputy and successor, Abdel Aziz al-Rantisi, when he broke his usual cautious routine and visited his home.[5]

As Hamas leaders fell, the tide began to turn. The year 2005 began auspiciously for Israel, when Hamas agreed to a temporary ceasefire without any significant Israeli concessions. Indeed it is plausible to argue that the Second Intifada ended with that ceasefire declaration. Later in the year, however, Sharon decided to withdraw Israeli settlers and soldiers from Gaza once and for all, uprooting settlements and pulling out the IDF. Gaza quickly fell into Hamas's hands. Yasin himself was dead, but his movement had triumphed.

Ceasefire

In February 2005, the PA "agreed to stop all acts of violence."[6] Around the same time, Hamas-linked militants agreed to a "period of calm" (*tahdiya*), tacit at first and then open by March.[7] The *tahdiya*, in contrast to a more formal and lasting ceasefire (*hudna*), denotes a temporary pause in hostilities, one that allows the group to respond should Israel attack. Some cells battled on, and Hamas at times planned and conducted attacks (often justified as a response to Israeli provocations), but for Israelis, but not for Palestinians, normal life began to resume. Israeli deaths dropped dramatically on both the civilian and military sides. In 2006 militants killed twenty-five Israeli civilians and seven members of the security forces, a sharp contrast with 2002, when 298 civilians and 155 security force members died.[8]

The causes of the *tahdiya* are debated. Hamas, to be clear, did not go so far as to recognize the legitimacy of the state of Israel. Yet the ceasefire largely held. Israeli counterterrorism officials point to policies like targeted killings and arrests that wore down Hamas. One intelligence official asked rhetorically, "Why did Hamas agree to the ceasefire? Because Yasin was dead, Abd al-Rantisi was dead, and other leaders of Hamas were dead. Hamas saw clearly that all of their leaders were either fugitives or were in cemeteries." Over time the constant stress of living on the run and the fear of being killed at any time proved difficult for the terrorists. Explaining Hamas's decision to endorse a ceasefire, the former Shin Bet head Avi Dichter contends, "Senior Hamas leaders decided they were tired of seeing the sun only in pictures."[9]

In 2005, following Hamas's lead, the Fatah-linked al-Aqsa Martyrs Brigade also agreed to a ceasefire. As the Second Intifada had gone on, Palestinians increasingly saw Fatah fighters as thugs rather than heroes of the resistance. "Extortion was the norm," one analyst told me, and Fatah's corruption stood in stark contrast with the relative honesty of Hamas. "Compared to others, we are living like kings," Jihad Ja'arie, a wanted al-Aqsa Martyrs Brigade leader, told the BBC.[10] Popular support for resistance fell, and ordinary Palestinians, now afraid of their own resistance groups, clamored for restoring law and order.

The ceasefire grew stronger in 2007, when the new Palestinian prime minister, Salam Fayyad, convinced the al-Aqsa Martyrs Brigade to disarm completely. Fayyad succeeded by playing up Palestinians' dissatisfaction with the violence and lawlessness and the sense that the fighting no longer had any chance of success. He also worked with Israel on another measure to bolster the ceasefire: amnesty. Israel removed names from its wanted list and the PA ensured that the men gave up their weapons. Some members were allowed almost complete freedom; others had to serve jail time but were assured by Israel that they would not be killed or arrested. Politically this amnesty offered the fighters an honorable way to resume a normal life and allowed the PA to focus on those who were simply thugs masquerading as freedom fighters.[11] The PA often even paid the former militants to prevent them from returning to violence simply to make ends meet. Shin Bet went out of its way to praise the amnesty program, or "wanted pact," saying that it "created an atmosphere that affected not only the wanted militants included in the pact . . . but those that were not."[12] Initially, in July 2007, only 170 wanted militants were listed, but by February 2008 two hundred additional names were included—a figure that would reach almost 500 by June 2010. Those who again took up arms paid a high price. The IDF killed Sudian Kandil, a member of the al-Aqsa Martyrs Brigades, because he apparently refused to give up his weapon.[13]

For Fatah members tired of sleeping in a different bed every night, the Israeli offer was too good to pass up. Palestinians even criticized Israel for not allowing a bigger amnesty program that would shelter some of the most violent militants. Those in the amnesty program often protested that they received only a pittance; said one former fighter, "1,050 NIS [roughly three hundred dollars] per month is nothing. How am I supposed to support a wife and two kids on that? I smoke that much."[14] But such grumbles did not lead him or other fighters to return to violence.

According to Rob Blecher, an analyst for the International Crisis Group, in 2002 or 2003 the same deal, had it been proffered, probably would have failed, as the passions of national liberation were high and groups were not yet convinced they would lose. Nor was there a functional Palestinian Authority to implement it. Now Palestinians seemed reluctant to engage in violence once again. Support for suicide bombings fell to less than 30 percent for the first time during the Second Intifada.[15]

The death of Arafat on November 11, 2004 brought new hopes for peace. Palestinians mourned Arafat even though he ended his career with a whimper rather than a bang. Israel allowed free access to Ramallah for the funeral from throughout the West Bank, but far fewer mourners turned up than expected.[16] And yet Arafat would be remembered as the man who put Palestine on the map. In an interview shortly before his death he declared, "Israel has failed to wipe us out. We are here, in Palestine, facing them. We are not Red Indians."[17]

On January 9, 2005, Abbas was elected to replace Arafat as president of the PA on an explicit platform of peace. As happened when Abbas became Arafat's prime minister, Israel did little to support Abbas as president. Rather than make concessions on Gaza (from which the IDF would soon withdraw) or reduce the number of checkpoints, Israeli officials often treated Abbas with contempt. The Bush administration was still embroiled in Iraq and skeptical that a renewed peace process would bear fruit.

While the world focused on the renewed chance of peace with Abbas's election, Arafat's death opened an opportunity for Hamas. For years Arafat the man, not Fatah, the party he led, unified Palestinians. When he was alive Yasin recognized Arafat's supremacy and urged his followers to avoid creating a schism within the Palestinian community. Abbas garnered no such respect. "Arafat's death was the thing that most influenced the decision to rethink our policies [regarding political involvement]," said one Hamas member.[18] Less directly the Hamas leader Khaled Mishal notes that Arafat's death "brought new conditions" for the domestic political arena.[19] With the death of Hamas's chief political rival, the attractiveness of political participation grew for Hamas, offering the Islamist group the opportunity to assume leadership of the Palestinian cause through the ballot box rather than through armed struggle.

Rob Blecher believes a mix of these factors explain the truce. "Sure, Hamas got the crap beaten out of it during the Second Intifada," he admits, but he also believes it was more than that: Hamas had already won all it could through violent resistance, and now was the time for it to consolidate its gains. Within Hamas voices pushing for participation in elections became stronger and stronger, a chorus made louder because many of the voices who opposed elections in 1995 were dead.

Withdrawal from Gaza

Five years of aggressive counterterrorism had battered Fatah and the PA. Still Israeli misgivings remained. This distrust reached its peak with the decision to withdraw troops and settlers from Gaza unilaterally (or "disengage") without a peace deal. Although Ariel Sharon had initially opposed unilateral withdrawal, he later warmed to it, and Israel pulled out the last of its settlements and soldiers from the Gaza Strip in September 2005.

The idea of withdrawal was contrary to the fundamental tenets of Israel's historic security strategy. For many years the West Bank in particular, but also Gaza, were depicted as shields for Israel against invading Arab armies and Palestinian raiders operating from neighboring countries. Shortly after taking office Sharon demonstrated his opposition to any relinquishing of Palestinian land, noting, "I see no possibility of separation [from the Palestinians]," and "Netzarim [an Israeli settlement in Gaza] is the same as Negba and Tel Aviv."[20] But the Israeli security establishment believed that occupying and patrolling the territories was costly and dangerous for the IDF.

Demographic arguments, combined with concerns about preserving Israel's democratic character, also drove the withdrawal. In 2009, if you excluded Arabs living in the West Bank and Gaza, Israel had just under six million Jews and almost 1.5 million Arabs; another 1.5 million Gazans and almost 2.5 million West Bank Palestinians made the overall numbers almost equal.[21] If not for the disengagement Jews would soon be a minority in historic Palestine due to higher Palestinian birth rates. As one official put it, "The danger is that the Palestinians would demand one man, one vote." For Israel to remain a democratic and Jewish state, its territorial makeup needed to change. The scholars Jonathan Rynhold and Dov Waxman say, "With a majority of non-Jews under its control, Israel could be Jewish *or* democratic, but not both."[22] Disengagement from Gaza removed more than one million Palestinians from Israeli control, helping reverse, or at least delay, the demographic tide.

The Israelis knew that disengagement would present security benefits because it removed the settlers from the "carpet of targets" in Gaza, as former Shin Bet head Avi Dichter described it. During the Second Intifada attacks on Israeli vehicles were one of the deadliest forms of violence. In Gaza settlers and soldiers were easy targets, as they needed to travel daily along roads surrounded by Palestinian areas. An entire infantry company and an armored platoon defended one settlement in Gaza that had only twenty-six families.[23] A whole battalion was designed to defend Netzarim's sixty families.[24] Retaliation against Qassam rocket attacks from Gaza would also be easier, as Israel no longer had to worry that Hamas would in turn escalate violence by attacking settlers.

Besides the risk of death that IDF soldiers faced, the miserable job of policing urban areas like those in Gaza damaged morale. Some six hundred members of the IDF, including some twenty-seven air force pilots and thirteen soldiers from elite army units, refused to serve in the territories.[25] Sharon feared that the country's will was being sapped and sought to lighten this burden.

Disengagement also eased the Israeli burden of caring for Gaza. Sharon believed it was not in Israel's interest to bear the ultimate responsibility for providing medical care, sanitation, and all the various administrative needs of Gaza.[26] And withdrawal was good politics. Sharon's disengagement plan helped bolster his sagging political position.[27] Dov Weissglas, Sharon's political advisor and one of the key figures in formulating the policy of disengagement, told Chief of Staff Bogi Yaalon that Sharon had to do something because his "political status [was] in decline." According to Yaalon, Sharon feared that the corruption indictments facing him resulted in his waning support. Disengagement, some believed, would lead leftist elites to "forgive" Sharon.[28]

For many Israelis, disengagement offered hope of security similar to what the peace process once did, providing a respite from the grinding conflict. As Vice Prime Minister Ehud Olmert put it in 2005, "We are tired of fighting, we are tired of being courageous, we are tired of winning, we are tired of defeating our enemies, we want that we will be able to live in an entirely different environment of relations with our enemies. We want them to be our friends, our partners, our good neighbors."[29] Finally, Israelis hoped withdrawal would take the wind out of the militants' sails by ending the occupation, the core Palestinian grievance, for at least part of the Palestinian population.

The debate over disengagement was fierce. There was opposition to both the idea of withdrawal and the unilateral manner in which it was enacted. Withdrawal of any variety meant abandoning some settlements and rejecting the "greater Israel" dream that motivated many on the Israeli right.[30] Begin himself had sworn to settlers in 1981 that Israel would not "leave any part of Judea, Samaria, [or] the Gaza Strip."[31] Withdrawal from Gaza was particularly contentious because it was coupled with the withdrawal from four isolated settlements on the West Bank. Dismantling these settlements and the possibility that more would follow meant the Israeli government was relinquishing the idea of Jewish control over the whole biblical land of Israel. Some Israelis claim that Sharon sought to give back Gaza to defuse pressure on the West Bank, which was ideologically far more important.

The unilateral nature of the disengagement was particularly conten-tious as Israel would be withdrawing under fire, thus undermining its overall deterrence capability. In 2002 Yaalon opposed even limited with-drawals on the grounds that "any such departure under terrorism and violence will strengthen the path of terrorism and violence"—a position he feels was vindicated.[32]

Many observers who wanted to restart the peace process called for a withdrawal agreement that would strengthen moderate Palestinian leaders like Abbas. Indeed Abbas had begged Sharon to negotiate the withdrawal and to attach conditions that would "prove" that negotiations, not violence, would result in peace for the Palestinians. The conditions would also give Abbas leverage to restrain Hamas, allowing him to raise the specter of Israeli reoccupation if violence was not ended. Sharon ignored him.

Withdrawing unilaterally enabled Israel to leave Gaza on its own terms. Sharon believed that terrorists would use violence to disrupt negotiations, so that Israel would be unable to complete the withdrawal as desired. Unilateralism was also in keeping with Sharon's personal style. He favored bold initiatives in politics as well as war, and boldness in this case meant acting unilaterally. He also made no secret of his distrust of and contempt for Arabs. He once told a reporter, "You know why we'll never have peace? Because the best thing that happened to Arabs in the last one hun-dred years is that they learned to pee standing up."

Mistrust among Israelis was so high that even concessions were pitched as punishments. Thus unilateral withdrawal was sold as a way of *not* mak-ing a deal with the Palestinians. Sharon's advisor Weissglas described dis-engagement as "formaldehyde" and contended that it was necessary to ensure "there will not be a political process with the Palestinians." Israel, he continued, now had U.S. support for refusing to engage in negotiations until "Palestinians turn into Finns."[33]

Israel had indeed secured support from the Bush administration for leaving Gaza unilaterally. The United States never pushed back on the unilateral nature of the withdrawal, believing (perhaps correctly) that negotiations would be interminable, whereas the political window for withdrawing Israeli troops and demolishing settlements was closing. The Bush administration's point man, Elliott Abrams, explained that given the circumstances, the administration did not feel that it could ask Sharon to withdraw as part of negotiations. As Abrams described it, President Bush had a tremendous amount of respect for democratic leaders who used their power to lead their people to take politically difficult measures. Bush recognized that Sharon had pushed his party as far as he could to accept the disengagement in the first place and could not push farther to ask for a negotiated withdrawal.

With the unilateral withdrawal proposal, former U.S. negotiator Martin Indyk explains, "the basic compact of the Arab-Israeli peace process—the exchange of territory for peace—was discredited and abandoned."[34] The Second Intifada convinced many Israelis that the Palestinians would never be ready for peace, or even for good-faith negotiations. In a 2004 letter to President Bush, Sharon explained his decision to pursue unilateral disengagement: "There exists no Palestinian partner with whom to advance peacefully toward a settlement." The U.S. reciprocated by praising the move as "a bold and historic initiative."[35]

Hamas Rises Again

Israelis now forged their own path. In deliberately sidelining any Palestinian partner, however, the Israeli withdrawal backfired in the long term. The moderates could claim no credit for Israel's departure, but Hamas and other radicals could. Moreover Hamas's political strength had grown during the Second Intifada while Fatah, especially after Arafat's death, was in disarray. Hamas would reap Gaza.

The IDF carried out the disengagement from Gaza and four West Bank settlements in August and September 2005 by forcefully removing those few settlers who did not leave on their own. On September 12 the last Israeli soldier left the Gaza Strip through the Kissufim border crossing, and the Palestinians celebrated their newfound freedom.[36]

Hamas propaganda boasted that "four years of sacrifices weighed more than ten years of negotiations"; in other words, violent resistance during the Intifada had gained more for the Palestinians than Abbas and other moderates had in over a decade of negotiations. Ghaith al-Omari, one of Abbas's advisors and a negotiator, bitterly agrees: "We the moderates cannot take credit for Gaza. Hamas can." Despite Sharon's rhetoric that the withdrawal should not be seen as a concession to Hamas, most Gazans agreed with Ismail Haniyeh, Hamas's leader in Gaza, who claimed, "Sharon cannot evade the truth. The Qassam [rocket] is what forced the enemy out."[37] A survey of Palestinians in both the West Bank and Gaza found that 84 percent of respondents saw the disengagement as a victory for "armed resistance."[38]

Throughout the Second Intifada Hamas had grown stronger politically and organizationally compared with its Palestinian rivals. Israeli counterterrorism had decimated the PA institutions and the Tanzim leadership, weakening the once dominant Fatah. Ideologically, Fatah's gamble on normalization with Israel had turned into a bust. Internal divisions within the traditional nationalist camp widened, particularly after Arafat's death. They had no leader to replace him. As the traditional order collapsed, Hamas steadily gained respect because its fighters waged what seemed to be an effective war against Israel, inflicting one body blow after another through suicide bombings. Khaled Hroub, director of the Cambridge Arab Media Project, argues that the various Israeli attacks seriously weakened

Hamas's ability to fight, but "with each new spate of killings, arrest sweeps, or institutional crackdowns targeted [at] Hamas, its popular legitimacy [grew]."[39] And Hamas had set in place a social service network that was now bearing political fruit. Its charities and hospitals dispensed aid without the incompetence and corruption of the PA bodies. Polls taken in February 2000 showed Hamas enjoying 10 percent support and Fatah 36 percent; in September 2005, immediately after the Gaza pullout, Hamas's support was up to 30 percent.[40]

By the time of the 2005 ceasefire declaration Hamas's leaders based outside of Gaza and the West Bank were playing a dominant role in the organization. In part, this was due to Israeli counterterrorism measures. Sheikh Yasin, Hamas's founder, was in jail for much of Hamas's history, as were key Hamas figures such as Saleh Shehada and Abdel Aziz al-Rantisi. Although Israel released many Hamas leaders during the Oslo period, the IDF and Shin Bet later hunted them ruthlessly. By the time of the Israeli withdrawal Yasin, Rantisi, and many other leaders were dead, while others were in Israeli jails or in hiding.

So by necessity Hamas's external figures, such as Abu Marzook, a key fundraiser, and Khaled Mishal, whom the Mossad had failed to kill in Jordan under Netanyahu, set Hamas's agenda and ensured that the organization remained robust. Part of their influence came from money. Hamas leadership outside the territories handled the flow of private funds from the Palestinian diaspora and sympathetic states; millions of dollars poured into their hands, and as a result they supported the politicians and policies they favored and financially starved those they opposed. In contrast to Hamas figures in the West Bank and Gaza, these individuals could organize, plan, and otherwise sustain the organization without constant fear of arrest or execution.

Hamas leaders often differ with one another on strategies and tactics and vie for primacy within the organization, but their rivalries should not be exaggerated. External leaders like Mishal were often more uncompromising, while West Bank and Gaza leaders like Ismail Haniyeh were forced to be pragmatic simply because they dealt with Palestinian rivals and Israelis on a day-to-day basis, and blind ideological stands would cost them dearly. But in the end Hamas is a consensus organization. There are often sharp disagreements, but its leaders share a commitment to work together. Indeed the diversity within Hamas is a reflection of its strength: it can work in multiple directions, favoring negotiations, social work, or violence (or all three) when it best suits its purposes.

A key Hamas decision was to aggressively contest Palestinian Legislative Council elections in 2006. Hamas claims they took this position, first, because PA corruption had reached intolerable levels; second, to prevent the PA from disarming Hamas; and third because the collapse of the peace process meant Hamas could participate in elections without validating negotiations.[41] Hamas also recognized its growing political power. On January 26, 2006, in a stunning turn of events, Hamas's Change and Reform Party, led by Ismail Haniyeh, won a relatively free and fair election, gaining seventy-four of the 132 seats in the Council. Fatah won only forty-five seats.

Israel and the Palestinian Authority had considered working together to block the elections. Sharon had proposed to Abbas that Israel would ban Hamas candidates from running in East Jerusalem, and then Abbas could use this as an excuse to postpone elections. Sharon's only requirement was that Bush not criticize this move. Bush himself, however, wanted the elections to go through because of his belief in democracy and his expectation that Hamas participation in government would make the organization more accountable to the Palestinian people.[42] Elliott Abrams agrees that the Bush administration's support for democracy was a significant piece of this decision. However, he also explained that Abbas did not want to ban Hamas from running because then the elections would look like a one-party shoo-in and Abbas would not have any legitimacy. Abbas said he could not tolerate those circumstances. In addition Hamas, Israel, and the United States all believed the polling that said Fatah would win.

Why did Hamas win? The victory caught everyone by surprise, including Hamas itself. In part the result was a vote against the PA. Support for violence against Israel and for Hamas's Islamist agenda also played a role, but these factors were secondary. Hamas campaign rhetoric emphasized the high crime rate, corruption, economic problems, and other governance failures of Fatah.[43] Almost half of the PA's civil servants voted for Hamas.[44] Violence, both criminal and political, had become extreme. "We have turned into Kandahar," noted one Palestinian security official in Gaza at the time, referring to the chaotic Afghan city.[45]

Hamas's role in resistance was an important part of the campaign, once again contrasting sharply with Fatah candidates, who, even if they had spent time in Israeli jails, were depicted as lukewarm in their opposition to Israel. One winning Hamas candidate was Miriam Farhat, "the Mother of Martyrs," who had lost three sons as suicide bombers and produced a campaign video showing herself helping her seventeen-year-old son into a suicide vest before he killed five Israelis.[46]

Fatah also lost because of poor electoral skills. Hamas's already existing network of religious and social services centers helped organize voters and ensure a high turnout among sympathizers. Fatah, on the other hand, ran multiple candidates in many districts, which split its voters, thus allowing the single Hamas candidate to emerge victorious by winning a plurality, not a majority. Sixty-three percent of Palestinians voted for non-Hamas candidates, but this vote was dispersed among the various Fatah and independent candidates. As one Fatah leader declared, "Hamas did not win the elections. Fatah lost them."[47] The Palestinian journalist Wafa Amr believes that if Arafat were alive he would have helped Fatah win outright, or at least made sure they rigged the voting properly.

The shock of the voting results led to chaos. In one of its closing acts the outgoing Palestinian Legislative Council gave PA president Abbas sweeping powers.[48] When the Hamas leader Ismail Haniyeh became the Palestinian prime minister, Abbas responded by trying to concentrate power in the president's office, especially control of the security forces, to ensure that all money went through him. Fatah and Hamas gunmen had regularly fought in Gaza's streets, and the Palestinian Authority (with international and Israeli contrivance) tried to isolate Hamas. Gazan Palestinians began to experience financial pressure from many sides. The Middle East diplomatic quartet, composed of the United States, the European Union, Russia, and the United Nations, stopped giving direct aid to the Palestinian government, with the caveat that they would resume giving aid if the government formally recognized Israel, renounced the use of terrorism, and respected previously signed Palestinian agreements with Israel—conditions meant to put Hamas in a box. For the world's democratic governments Hamas's election was a dilemma: a group they saw as undemocratic and violent had won fair and square.

The situation continued to deteriorate. In June 2006 Hamas deployed a new militia in Jenin in the West Bank, and they marched through the streets declaring that Fatah was in the thrall of foreign interests. PA forces arrested and harassed Hamas members in the West Bank. In October 2006 Fatah gunmen tried to kill Haniyeh in Gaza by attacking his car when he left a mosque.[49] Rumors spread that Israel, the PA, and the United States were working in tandem to help Fatah conduct a coup against Hamas in Gaza. By early 2007 Hamas and Fatah were regularly battling on Gaza's streets. In a particularly gruesome incident Hassan al-Bazam, one of Ismail Haniyeh's bodyguards, was captured by what appeared to be members of the elite Fatah unit Force 17. Al-Bazam reported that he had cigarettes extinguished on his back, gunshots fired between his legs, and hot wax dripped onto him. His eyebrows and beard were shaved off and the number 17 was shaved into his hair. Before he was released he was asked to turn in other members of Hamas and to curse God and Mohammad.[50] On the political level, in December Abbas tried to call for early elections to revisit Hamas's recent victory, a call that led to angry protests from Hamas supporters.[51]

In February 2007 Hamas and Fatah leaders came together under the Mecca Accord, convened under the auspices of King Abdullah of Saudi Arabia, and agreed to stop using violence and share power.[52] Still the violence continued. A report published by the Palestinian Independent Commission for Citizens' Rights (now the Independent Commission for Human Rights) in June 2007 found that Palestinian infighting had killed more than six hundred since the beginning of 2006.[53]

Bitter that Fatah was not truly surrendering power after having lost the election—and fearing that Fatah, Israel, and the West in general were trying to undermine their rule—Hamas leaders seized power in Gaza in June 2007. Fatah forces were larger than those of Hamas, yet many did not oppose the takeover, enabling Hamas to focus on those areas led by PA security chief Mohammad Dahlan, who did oppose it. In contrast to Fatah, Hamas was organized, well-led, and ruthless. One Israeli security official said, "Fatah was so weak, so corrupt, that the takeover was like wind blowing over a moth-infested structure."[54]

Yasin's prohibition against *fitna* (divisions within the community) fell by the wayside. A member of the Fatah-loyal Presidential Guard was reportedly thrown to his death from an eighteen-story building, and a member of Hamas's Executive Force met his death in the same manner.[55] Jamal Abu al-Jediyan, the senior Fatah official in northern Gaza, was killed by Hamas gunmen, reportedly "executed with 40 gunshots."[56] Fatah's Presidential Guards attacked Ismail Haniyeh's house with rocket-propelled grenades.[57] Directing its criticism against Palestinians rather than Israel for a change, Human Rights Watch took both Fatah and Hamas to task, declaring, "The murder of civilians not engaged in hostilities and the willful killing of captives are war crimes, pure and simple."[58] By June 14 Hamas fighters had consolidated their hold on Gaza, taking over Fatah's Preventive Security compound. Abbas, who could do little to change facts on the ground, announced that the national unity government was over.

Israel, the PA, and the world cried foul over the so-called Gaza coup and tried to isolate Gaza further. PA government officials in Gaza who had cooperated with Hamas were not paid. Police were told not to go to work. To encourage financial chaos, the PA declared a tax holiday in Gaza. Israel reduced supplies of food, fuel, and foreign currency that passed through the checkpoints, and the international community abandoned many of its humanitarian and reconstruction projects. Gaza's business community, often a voice for moderation, was devastated.

This isolation was meant to topple Hamas, but instead Haniyeh and his crew filled the void. The international community's refusal to provide aid in Gaza increased the importance of the social services Hamas provided. In a testament to the power of discipline over numbers, Hamas revamped the police and security forces, transforming them from fifty thousand members (on paper, at least) under Fatah to a small group of just over ten thousand. This small force then cracked down on local gangs and crimes. No longer did rival groups openly wear weapons or steal with impunity.

Suddenly government returned to Gaza. People paid their taxes and electricity bills, and in return the government picked up garbage and put criminals in jail. Gazans welcomed the end of chaos. "I can dial emergency services, and 100 police will come to my rescue," said one shopkeeper.[59]

Though economic conditions in Gaza are far worse than in the West Bank, Hamas's governance was, and remains, stronger than the PA's. The Israeli analyst Gen. Giora Eiland told me sardonically, "For the first time since the 1940s, someone controls Gaza and accepts responsibility."

The price of order was high. For Hamas it was payback time for Fatah's tough measures in the mid-1990s. Hamas channeled international humanitarian aid to its supporters, leaving Fatah cohorts high and dry.[60] Israelis might remember Fatah as passive and forgiving in the Oslo period, but Hamas leaders never forgot how Fatah tortured and humiliated their activists. Once Hamas wrested control of Gaza from Fatah, its fighters returned the cruelty, often crippling Fatah rivals by pumping bullets into their legs. All in all, in 2007 Israel killed 302 Gazans, while 454 died at the hands of fellow Palestinians.[61]

As a government Hamas had to arrange trash collection, pay municipal servants, handle the courts and police, and otherwise make 1,001 daily decisions. Sending each one up the chain of command and conferring with the external leadership would have been impossible. Now Hamas's political center shifted to Gaza. Under the most trying circumstances imaginable, Hamas was finally being tested on whether it could govern as well as resist Israel.

The Rockets of Sderot

Starting in 2001 Hamas, PIJ, and some Fatah-linked groups attacked Israel with rockets. These rockets received relatively little attention at first, given the havoc wrought by suicide bombers. But as other forms of violence fell, and as Hamas solidified its position in Gaza after disengagement, attacks from Qassam and other rockets went from a nuisance to a tremendous threat. The town of Sderot near the border with Gaza was a favored target.

The Qassam rocket, like the military wing of Hamas, is named after Izz ad-Din al-Qassam, the Palestinian guerrilla who led the Arab Revolt. Fatah and Tanzim militants, however, are miffed that Israel refers to the rockets from Gaza as "Qassams," their Hamas-given name, when they have their own name, "al-Aqsa" rockets; PIJ calls them "al-Quds" rockets, and the PFLP uses the label "Samud" rockets.[62] These rockets are often made from a lamppost section that is filled with explosives or other primitive devices. Hamas developed the Qassam in part because effective Israeli measures had driven up the cost of conventional weapons bought from "bloodsucker arms dealers," as one military leader claimed. Producing rockets from scratch, he said, cost only 1 percent of what it cost to buy the rocket from a dealer.[63]

In 2005 Palestinians launched over 800 rockets and mortars on Israel; by 2007 this figure had almost doubled (see Table 12.1). Even though the

Table 12.1: Rocket and Mortar Attacks Fired at Israel from Gaza

Year	Number of Qassam Rockets Launched	Number of Mortar Shells	Israeli Fatalities
2000	0	0	0
2001	0	510	1
2002	17	455	0
2003	123	514	0
2004	276	882	9
2005	286	574	6
2006	1247	28	2
2007	938	663	2
2008	1270	912	8 (4 during Operation Cast Lead)
2009	404	197	5 (All soldiers killed from mortar shells during Cast Lead)

These figures only include rockets and mortars that were discovered after the shooting. Israeli radar picked up hundreds more rockets and mortars that fragmented in flight, and they are not part of the official count.[67]

death toll was low, the daily bombardment was terrifying, in part due to the random nature of the Qassam. It falls on soldiers and children alike. A PIJ operative claimed, "If it hits a child, then naturally we are not happy," yet Sderot does not house any military bases and terrorists deliberately timed some of their attacks for the early morning.[64] So it appears that despite their protestations, they do indeed want to inflict harm on civilians, including women and children. One 2007 study found that over 25 percent of adults and between 72 and 94 percent of Sderot's children suffer from posttraumatic stress disorder as a result of the rocket attacks.[65]

Until 2008 the rocket attacks affected only the area within close range of Gaza, a relatively unpopulated area. However, over time Hamas learned to triple the rockets' range; in 2008 they used the 122mm "Grad" rocket, which carries 23 kilograms of explosives and has a range of 20 kilometers, greatly expanding its strike range. In March 2009 Israel destroyed a weapons convoy in the Sudan that was transporting Iranian "Fajr" missiles to Hamas—missiles that could have reached Tel Aviv from Gaza.[66]

After Hamas took power in Gaza the group launched (or allowed the launching of) rocket attacks on Sderot and nearby areas. Hamas refrained from a complete crackdown on PIJ, the al-Aqsa Martyrs Brigade, and the most extreme elements of its own movement, allowing attacks to continue. Through rocket attacks Hamas demonstrated that the culture of resistance remained alive and well. By allowing its own militant members to operate freely, it ensured their loyalty to the organization. Hamas newspapers showed pictures of Israeli civilians taking cover in Sderot and boasted about the fear that the Qassam rockets inspired.[68] One reporter told me, "When you talk to Gazans about why they launch Qassams that kill nobody but lead to deaths on their own side, you get a proverb like, 'He broke my legs but at least I spit at him.'" Hamas also tried to use rocket attacks to show its defiance in the face of IDF raids and force Israel to open the crossings into Gaza. Rockets offered Hamas the flexibility of targeting Sderot or even major cities like Beersheba and Ashkelon, and of executing two attacks or twenty.

Rockets were the most dramatic form of attack, but militants from Hamas and other groups regularly shot at IDF troops and Israelis working agricultural land near the Gaza border. From the outbreak of the Second Intifada through 2009 there were more than five thousand shooting attacks from Gaza. The vast majority of these were before Israel withdrew in 2005, but even after that Israel saw seventy-seven shooting attacks in 2006, ninety-eight in 2007, and eighty-two in 2008, though the number dropped off dramatically to four in 2009 (attacks during Operation Cast Lead are excluded), similar to the levels in the years following withdrawal.[69]

Although nearby kibbutzim and moshavim did not leave in the face of rocket attacks, many residents were forced to leave Sderot. Some Israelis fault poor local leadership and weak community bonds for the low morale in Sderot, but communities in northern Israel also became ghost towns when rockets threatened them during the 2006 Lebanon war.

In addition to the rocket assaults, Hamas continued with guerrilla and terrorist attacks. And they were not alone. Other groups also carried out operations against Israel, at times together with Hamas, at times in the face of Hamas's opposition, and at times without Hamas's knowledge. Israeli intelligence officials claim there were hundreds, even thousands of attempted and thwarted attacks, many involving incidents near the security barrier in Gaza.

Perhaps the most dramatic and significant attack was the June 25, 2006, kidnapping of IDF Corp. Gilad Shalit in an operation Hamas dubbed Dispelled Illusion. In a daring raid, Palestinian militants from Hamas, the Army of Islam, and the Popular Resistance Committees tunneled out of Gaza almost half a mile to the military base of Kerem Shalom and attacked an IDF post, killing two soldiers (and losing two of their own) and bringing Shalit back with them. This was the first Israeli the Palestinians had successfully taken prisoner in more than a decade. In 2003 Palestinian militants took Eliyahu Gorel, a cab driver, hostage and held him in East Jerusalem, where he was later rescued by Israeli commandos.[70] The Army of Islam, whose ideology is more akin to al-Qa'ida's than Hamas's, was a particularly surprising participant. Hamas took exclusive control of Shalit.

The Shalit kidnapping occurred against a backdrop of violence and negotiations. Eight Palestinian civilians who were picnicking on the beach in Gaza, including six members of the Ghaliyah family, died from what Palestinians reported to be an Israeli shell on June 9, 2006. (The IDF claimed it was caused by a device militants had planted near the beach.)[71] Israel's recent killing of Abu Samhadana, a Popular Resistance Committee leader who had been responsible for some of the rocket fire, also had outraged militants. Hamas ended its long truce and responded with more rocket fire, and Israel followed with a cross-border raid, infuriating Hamas by capturing two of its operatives.

Though some believe that internal Palestinian politics played a role in the Shalit kidnapping, this argument appears to be overblown. Hamas and Fatah had been engaged in a series of tit-for-tat killings for several months. The more radical members of Hamas may have arranged the kidnapping to undermine Haniyeh and stop any move away from confrontation. "It's Hamas against Hamas," one PA advisor said.[72] That explanation, though tidy, is overstated. The timing of the kidnapping was largely related to the escalation of violence in the preceding weeks; when Shalit was kidnapped, Haniyeh and Abbas were working together to build a unity government and were preparing to sign an agreement.

The Shalit kidnapping highlighted an area of intense Israeli vulnerability, as well as a motive that terrorist organizations well understand: the Israelis' desire to rescue their own prisoners. Israelis are often willing to trade hundreds of Palestinian prisoners for just one of their own, and they put intense political pressure on politicians to do so. When a soldier goes missing, the family "hires a PR company," according to one senior military official. After the Shalit kidnapping the families of Palestinian prisoners held rallies to celebrate and demand their sons in exchange.[73] From Hamas's point of view, seizing Shalit was a legitimate way to free prisoners. One Gazan involved in the negotiations with Shalit pointed out, "We did not take him from the market or from his family. We took him from a military tank on the Gaza border."[74] Even as the Intifada wound down, Israel would continue to hold thousands of Palestinian prisoners, an estimated 8,100 as of June 2009.[75]

Counterterrorism in Gaza

In Gaza, as always, the war was harsher than it was in the West Bank. Forty percent of Gazans lost a relative in the Second Intifada.[76] When patrolling Gaza some IDF units would be given open-fire orders, described by one sergeant as "Every person that is on the street—shoot to kill. Don't mind whether he has or has no gun on him."[77] Both before and after withdrawal the IDF routinely shot Palestinians approaching too near the security barrier in Gaza, which Israel declared to be a special security area.

After protests about the policy soldiers were told to find some evidence of hostile intent before shooting, but these orders were honored mostly in the breach. One Israeli officer argued, "The instructions surrounding the special security areas were almost war crimes."[78] Between the Israeli disengagement in 2005 and the 2008–9 war, Israeli security forces killed 1,270 Palestinians in Gaza.[79]

When Hamas seized power the counterterrorism situation changed dramatically—and Israel was caught flat-footed. Hamas gained the ability to operate openly, while Israel lost any hope of working with a local Palestinian partner. Individuals in Hamas's military wing, the Qassam Brigades, now became part of the police and other security services. "We're free and in charge," boasted one Qassam recruit, comparing it to the recent past when they "couldn't go out of the house for fear of Fatah and Israel."[80] Over time Hamas's security forces grew in size. In addition to the thousands of police, they still had several hundred operatives ready to attack Israelis, as well as internal security forces devoted to intelligence and protecting the coasts. Other radical groups, with perhaps as many as four thousand fighters, also joined Hamas in fighting the Israelis.[81]

Shin Bet and other Israeli intelligence organizations did their best to adjust, but because Israel did not control the territory it became harder to recruit informants. Entering the warrens of Gaza City was dangerous, and Israeli forces could not move swiftly or at night to arrest a suspected terrorist without grave risk. Daily life was now controlled by Hamas, not Israel, and the new regime used this control to ensure loyalty. One Israeli intelligence officer compared the challenge this way: "In the West Bank, if you dream an attack at night I am there in the morning to arrest you. In Gaza, you can't do that, things take much longer, you have to pay a big price to enter Gaza."

Despite these limits, Shin Bet thwarted hundreds of attempted attacks that Hamas launched from Gaza. Often Israeli forces destroyed bomb-loaded vehicles that Hamas intended to explode at Israeli checkpoints. In a display of confidence Shin Bet deliberately let the group waste their resources in preparing the attack before striking. Sometimes Shin Bet would also call the families of operatives, warning them to discourage their relative from executing an attack. Shin Bet and the IDF worked together closely to expedite the passage of intelligence, saving many lives with timely warning. Shin Bet also stopped Hamas attempts to send operatives to the West Bank to teach militants there how to launch Qassam rockets. Indeed the intelligence service was so successful that Hamas was forced to rely almost exclusively on the inaccurate Qassams to attack Israel.

This intelligence came in part from interception of communications, but also from unusual means of recruiting agents. Shin Bet recruited collaborators by phone, disproving the mantra in spy circles that personal contact is necessary for espionage. Palestinian officials claim that through its control of the waters off Gaza, Israel coerces Palestinian fishermen to act as infiltrators by refusing to grant them fishing permits unless they provide information to Israel.[82]

Beyond using unconventional means of gathering intelligence, Israel responded to Hamas's takeover with a mix of policies: limited coercive military strikes, shoring up the PA, sealing off Gaza, and economic pressure. Yet Israel had little sense of how to stop rocket attacks beyond lashing out militarily. After Roni Yichia, a forty-seven-year-old resident of Sderot, died from a rocket attack in February 2008, Israel launched Operation Hot Winter with ground and air assaults, killing more than a hundred on the Palestinian side.

To hinder Hamas's access to rockets, the IDF tried to destroy tunnels that crossed from Gaza to Egypt under the so-called Philadelphi route. Even before the First Intifada Palestinian criminals used tunnels to smuggle in drugs or prostitutes to Gaza, and their importance in smuggling both licit and illicit goods grew as Israel tightened the screws on Gaza's economy in the Second Intifada. Israelis called tunnels the "oxygen pipeline."[83] Now they were being used to smuggle ammunition, rockets, and people, including militants returning from training in Lebanon and Iran.

A contest began of innovation and desperation over the tunnels. Some tunnels were hundreds of meters long and dozens of meters below the ground, with concealed entrances, ventilation shafts, and even a phone line. Tunnels took months to dig and cost tens of thousands of dollars from start to finish, the price going up as Israeli demolition became more effective. A homeowner whose dwelling concealed an entrance would receive twenty thousand dollars, a small fortune in Gaza, in recognition of the risks he ran.[84]

The contest over the tunnels made the lives of Palestinian residents miserable. When militants shot at soldiers from houses near the Philadelphi route, the IDF unleashed heavy barrages, which led local residents to flee. The IDF would then declare the homes abandoned and demolish them, enabling it to widen its zone of control and increase the size of the corridor, thus forcing Palestinians to dig much longer tunnels.[85]

Israel never stanched the flow of military supplies and Qassams transported through the tunnels. One PIJ operative declared, "The Israeli blockade doesn't affect us; it's just intended to plunge the people into misery."[86] Indeed the IDF had actually predicted that after Israel withdrew from Gaza, Hamas would use tunnels to obtain longer-range rockets that would threaten Ashkelon and other major cities. Israeli officials worried that Hamas would repeat the Shalit operation, tunneling into Israel proper to attack IDF outposts or to send operatives to strike at civilians in nearby towns.

Tunnels to Egypt were the biggest problem. Smuggling had always occurred between Gaza and Egypt, but it skyrocketed after the Hamas takeover and the closing of various entry points. In June 2007 there were perhaps fifteen tunnels; nine months later there were 120.[87] Israel's efforts to squeeze Hamas in Gaza also depended on Egypt's patrolling its border. The town of Rafah spans the Egyptian-Gazan border, with families living on both sides. Smuggling and the massive construction of the tunnel industry are major sources of employment for the area.

Egypt's role in smuggling and ability to stop was contested under the Mubarak regime, which ended in February 2011. Cairo had successfully crushed a far larger terrorist threat from its own Islamist groups in the 1990s, and the Gaza stretch of border is short. Moreover an Egyptian police station has a clear view of many of the smugglers' tents.[88] The U.S. Army Corps of Engineers provided Egypt with special equipment and training to help it more effectively locate the tunnels. The United States also helped Egypt build a wall on the Gaza border, which went deep into the earth to stop tunnel building.[89]

Part of the problem is that Israel's closure of crossing points to Gaza has led to a significant rise in smuggling activity, thus rewarding smugglers and fostering corruption. Also some Egyptian police are complicit with Hamas out of ideological sympathy or simple bribery. The Mubarak government had its own terrorism problem in Sinai and did not have complete mastery over the area. The Mubarak regime worried about angering the Muslim Brotherhood, which has close ties to Hamas and is an important political force in Egypt. Yet Egypt moved more decisively in 2009, making progress on a barrier with Gaza that would go deep underground and stop most of the tunnels—to the point that Hamas itself was often quite pointed in its criticism of Cairo.

Israel executed military raids on Gaza, some of which were large in scale. The Shalit kidnapping led to Operation Summer Rain, which ostensibly sought to rescue Shalit by pressuring Hamas in Gaza, which is where he was held. However, Israel never possessed reliable intelligence on Shalit's whereabouts, so the operation was designed to make Hamas pay a heavy price for the kidnapping by killing its fighters and making life tough for civilians. In Gaza more than four hundred Palestinians died in the months after Shalit's kidnapping, including eighty-eight children.[90] Working with the PA, Israel arrested sixty Hamas ministers, parliamentarians, and other key figures in the West Bank. In subsequent operations, such as Hot Winter in February 2008, the Israeli Air Force bombed Hamas targets in Gaza. The IDF also sought to destroy tunnels and arrest or kill Hamas members in Gaza, as well as create a buffer zone that would stop Qassam rocket fire.[91] Israel arrested PA Cabinet members and attacked PA offices even though they were not complicit in the kidnapping.[92] "Pure politics" explained many of the strikes, according to the Israeli terrorism expert Boaz Ganor, who believed that Israel carried out the strikes despite the certainty that it was futile. As of February 2011 Shalit was still in Palestinian hands.

Despite Israel's difficulty in responding effectively to Hamas attacks, it was not without advantages in the wake of disengagement. Unilateral withdrawal, particularly the removal of the settlers, did simplify matters and offered fewer targets for Hamas and other Palestinian groups. As Eival Gilady, a senior IDF planner and aide to Sharon, noted in 2008, "Imagine if we still had 7,000 settlers in Gaza? The world would blame us for the Hamas-Fatah problems." Behind the scenes Israel also had some unusual allies in its struggle against Hamas: Arab governments. One Arab intelligence official told me that the entire Arab world, with the exception of Syria, opposes Hamas. All cooperated quietly with Israel to fight the movement.

For Israel, the balance between humanitarianism and security was always in question. In May 2007 Israeli security officials stopped two women, Fatma Zaq, a mother of eight who was again pregnant, and her niece Ruda Habib, a mother of four, at the Erez Crossing. Under questioning the two admitted that they carried forged medical documents that attested to their need for medical attention outside Gaza. In reality the two planned to stage suicide attacks in Tel Aviv and Netanya.[93] As this case demonstrates, Israel has cause to be wary about border crossings into Gaza. However, closing off Gaza pushed the humanitarian situation from bad to worse. Poverty, already high, became extreme, with 70 percent of Gazans living below the poverty line.[94]

In this period Israel repeatedly misjudged the political impact of its counterterrorism measures. Withdrawal from Gaza did not reduce the power of extremists; instead it led directly to Hamas's takeover of power. Efforts to isolate Gaza strengthened rather than weakened Hamas in relation to its rivals. For unilateral withdrawal to work, Israel had to revert to an old-fashioned deterrence approach, threatening Gaza with punishment if attacks resumed. However, as the Shalit kidnapping and Qassam attacks showed, Hamas could escalate in the face of Israeli pressure or undermine more moderate Palestinian rivals.

The tension with Hamas would fall and rise, but Israel could never solve the basic problem of a state controlled by a terrorist movement that refused to renounce violence against Israel. This tension would reach its peak at the end of 2008, when once again violence moved Israel to war.

CHAPTER XIII

WAR AGAINST HAMAS (2008–2009)

AFTER HAMAS seized power in June 2007 Israelis wrestled with the question of how to confront the terrorist organization that had become the government of territory on Israel's doorstep. Israel sought to end rocket attacks from Gaza, force Hamas to release Gilad Shalit, and, ideally, weaken Hamas's hold on power or at least stop it from becoming stronger. Israel arrested Hamas members in the West Bank, pressured Gaza economically, and conducted limited military strikes on Gaza itself. Israel also negotiated with Hamas indirectly and accepted a curious ceasefire for several months. Nothing worked. In December 2008, war returned with a vengeance.

In the eyes of the world the occupation of Gaza did not end with the Israeli withdrawal, even though no Israeli soldier or settler remained on Gazan soil. Israel retained control of Gaza's airspace and coastal area and all but one of its crossing points. Israel allowed some goods and currency to enter Gaza and did not prevent international and nongovernmental organizations from running social services. Although these supplies were not enough to save Gazans from economic disaster, they did prevent outright starvation.[1] One Israeli official complained, "[Israel is in an] absurd position whereby we are allowing goods to come into an entity whose rulers are continuing firing rockets at our civilians, and sometimes even using those goods—such as fuel and electricity—to carry on these attacks."[2]

For the PA, the tension with Hamas was even worse. Abbas and his cronies wanted Hamas to fail at governing the Gaza Strip. But in the name of Palestinian solidarity they had to appear as if they were helping Gazans even as they tried to undermine the government there.

Looking to Hizballah as a model, Hamas saw the Lebanese organization's self-proclaimed "divine victory" over Israel in 2006 as proof that the right combination of prowess and sacrifice would force Israel to surrender. A more immediate lesson for Hamas was the strategic value of rockets, even if they were inaccurate and short-range.

Hamas tried to reorganize and expand its fighting units to build a force similar to Hizballah's. Hamas had perhaps fifteen thousand potential combatants, along with the two thousand or so members of the Qassam Brigades, the military wing of Hamas, at its core. Israeli intelligence reported that Hamas forces began to train in conventional fighting, the use of antitank weapons, and the employment of improvised explosive devices. They acquired night-vision goggles, built bunkers and underground facilities, and constructed houses near the Gaza border with Israel to provide cover for snipers.[3] Hamas tried to ensure that, like Hizballah, it could continue launching rocket attacks on Israel even if the IDF invaded Gaza; the ground forces would protect the rockets and inflict casualties, eventually wearing down the IDF and the Israeli people.

To this end Hamas set up three lines of defense. First, in areas near the border with Israel, it placed mines and improvised explosive devices and sited mortars to fire in these zones. Second, it placed heavier weapons at the outskirts of major cities and prepared snipers and suicide bombers to attack along areas where the IDF would advance. In the third line of defense, inside the cities, Hamas laid numerous booby traps and erected a complex tunnel network. It planned to use the tunnels to move fighters and supplies, to position snipers, and to kidnap Israeli soldiers.[4]

To help fund these operations Iran provided roughly fifteen million dollars a month in aid to Hamas, including the "Grad" rockets, according to Israeli estimates.[5] Several hundred operatives went to Lebanon, where Hizballah, along with Iranian military officials, trained the militants. Additional training occurred in Iran and Syria, where hundreds learned advanced fighting techniques.[6] A Hamas commander from within the group's military wing, the Izz ad-Din al-Qassam Brigades, admitted this connection, saying, "We have sent seven 'courses' of our fighters to Iran"; there they trained for between forty-five days and six months. The commander disclosed that even more train in Syria, where they learn "high-tech capabilities, knowledge about land mines and rockets, sniping, and fighting tactics like the ones used by Hezbollah."[7]

Hamas worried, with good reason, that rocket attacks by PIJ, Hamas splinters, or other groups could lead Israel to escalate at a time when

Hamas itself wanted calm. Just as Hamas used attacks on Israel to embarrass the PA, now its rivals could do the same to Hamas. It regularly cracked down on these groups or tried to persuade them to stop attacks. In November 2007 PIJ agreed to stop attacks if Hamas brokered a ceasefire with Israel, and on June 19, 2008, Hamas declared another truce.

The Ceasefire Collapses

The truce did not bring true peace. Even with the momentary lull, divisions remained within Hamas on whether to embrace peace talks and how much to concede during this limited crackdown. Hamas still allowed low-level but regular rocket attacks on Sderot and other towns, and Israel continued raids in an attempt to destroy rockets and kill Hamas fighters. To pressure Hamas to end the rocket attacks Israel also closed crossings into Gaza. Also troubling to Hamas was Israel's attempt to arrest or kill its members in the West Bank, even when a truce existed that covered Gaza. Yet although the *tahdiya* did not eliminate rocket attacks, their frequency plunged. At the peak of the ceasefire (July 1 to November 1, 2008) there were twenty-six rocket attacks, still a significant number, but much lower than the previous six months, which saw over two thousand such attacks.[8]

The political fallout, however, was a different story. Even the trickle of rocket attacks after the ceasefire was damaging for Prime Minister Ehud Olmert. He was failing at the basic task of any leader—to defend his people—and also failing to meet the Zionist promise that Jewish life is sacred. For its part Hamas leaders misread the situation. They assumed that police investigations into Olmert for corruption, which seemed to dominate Israeli politics, would paralyze his government, not recognizing that public opinion on the shelling and on Shalit would not be affected.

Hamas accused Israel of violating the ceasefire when it killed six of its members during a November 4 raid on a tunnel to Israel—a tunnel Israel feared would be used for more kidnapping attempts like the Shalit operation or for smuggling terrorists into Israel. Palestinians also accused Israelis of timing the raid for the day of the U.S. election, when world attention would be focused far from Israel. Beyond this particular grievance Hamas faulted Israel for not fully opening the crossing points to keep goods flowing into Gaza. Not surprisingly Israel countered by pointing out continued mortar and rocket strikes. As if to reinforce Israel's point, Hamas launched more than thirty Qassams to protest the Israeli raid. In November almost two hundred mortars and rockets were fired, compared to one of each in October, when Israel closed the crossings into Gaza.[9] Critics began to slam Olmert and his government for inaction and for allowing Israel's deterrent capacity to lapse.

The always precarious ceasefire ended on December 19, 2008. Hamas launched dozens of rockets to mark its ending and the next day announced it would not extend it.

Hamas's logic in ending the ceasefire was a mix of hope and miscalculation. The organization thought Israel would not launch a sustained ground operation, in part because a new administration was about to take power in Washington and because it viewed Olmert as a lame duck prime minister. Hamas also believed the Qassam Brigades would inflict serious casualties on the IDF and that Hamas rockets would in turn make Israel sensitive to the risk of civilian casualties.[10]

Gaza's geography constrained many traditional military options, and the IDF entered the war with trepidation. Gaza is densely populated, with over 1.5 million people squeezed into an area of 139 square miles, much of it concentrated in Gaza City. Even creating a security corridor in Gaza is difficult, the former Shin Bet head Avi Dichter told me. Half the population lives in Gaza City, which is close to the border. A security zone deep enough to stop rockets would require evacuating the city. Because of overcrowding—and no ability to expand urban areas beyond the narrow strip—Gaza is a land of high-rise buildings. Such buildings populate the nightmares of military officers.

In addition to Gaza's hellish geography, Israel was well aware that Hamas had started shoring up its military forces and laying down booby traps in anticipation of a fight. One Givati Brigade intelligence officer said, "Before we were used to [being able to] operate anywhere in Gaza, with no resistance, and now, suddenly there is a new government there, an army, battalions, even missiles."[11]

The 2008–9 war between Israel and Gaza was not just another round in the Palestinian-Israeli conflict: the violence was off the charts. In a few short weeks, from December 27 to January 18, more than a thousand Palestinians died, many of them noncombatants. As always the specific numbers are disputed. The Palestinian Center for Human Rights claims that more than fourteen hundred Palestinians died, the biggest loss of life in so short a period since the Israeli occupation began in 1967. The Palestinian Ministry of Health reported that the dead included 431 children, but Amnesty International put that figure at three hundred.[12] The Israeli human rights group B'Tselem put the total figure at 1,387, of whom 773 were noncombatants. Israel's International Institute for Counter-Terrorism argues, however, that these civilian figures are overstated, as many of the people the Palestinian Center for Human Rights claims are civilians were later hailed as "military martyrs" by Hamas and shown in battledress. In addition the Palestinian Center counts policemen as civilians, but many Palestinian police were also members of Hamas's military wing.[13] The clash differed considerably from Israel's past wars, or even other limited military operations like Defensive Shield and the 2006 fight in Lebanon. This "war" was more like a raid, with most of the suffering and destruction being on the Palestinian side.

In addition to the body toll the operation destroyed or damaged thousands of homes and dozens of factories: twenty-two of Gaza's twenty-nine concrete factories suffered severe damage, as did 60 percent of its agricultural land.[14] Israel also hit Gaza's Legislative Council and the Ministries of Justice, Housing, and Labor.[15] Israeli casualties were far, far lower: thirteen in total, three of them civilians. Indeed friendly fire killed four of the ten soldiers who died.[16]

The IDF dubbed its operation Cast Lead. Few non-Israelis recognized this classic Israeli folk song reference to the tops spun at Hanukah, a holiday being celebrated as the fighting began. Cast Lead began with a disinformation campaign, announcing that Israel would open crossings from Israel to Gaza and claiming that Olmert was still holding more deliberations on a possible strike, even though the operation was already in motion. When the strikes came, Hamas was caught by surprise.[17] In the first wave of air strikes Israel hit Hamas bases, rocket launch sites, the homes of Hamas leaders, and the governing infrastructure, including police training camps and offices. Israel also struck hospitals, mosques, and schools, citing evidence that Hamas was storing weapons in or near these or otherwise using them for military purposes. The Israeli Air Force bombed the University of Gaza on the grounds that it was a symbol of Hamas's authority and a base for paramilitary activities. Several Hamas officials died in the bombings.

Israel also claimed that Hamas deliberately prevented civilians from leaving the strike zones, using them as shields. Hamas believed that if IDF continued to attack knowing they would kill civilians, it would still win the propaganda war by blaming Israel for murdering innocents.[18] One NGO reported that combatants they interviewed fired rockets from nearby Gazan homes "in the hope that nearby civilians would deter Israel from responding."[19] Human Rights Watch, often considered a reliable critic of Israel, reported, "Hamas forces violated the laws of war both by firing rockets deliberately and indiscriminately at Israeli cities and by launching them from populated areas and endangering Gazan civilians."[20]

On January 3, 2009, Israel deployed four brigade-size units with tanks and helicopters. The IDF cut Gaza in three parts and surrounded Gaza City, but did not try to penetrate deeply into the densely packed streets.

Israel's goal was to stop the shelling. How to do so was another question. Should the IDF thrust into Gaza until Hamas collapsed, a difficult endeavor to put it charitably, or should Israel attempt to maneuver Hamas into negotiations and force concessions on arms smuggling and rocket launching? Each of the three top ministers—Ehud Barak at Defense, Tzipi Livni at the Foreign Ministry, and Prime Minister Olmert—had different views. Keeping Israel's goals vague allowed Israel's leaders to avoid messy fights about what, exactly, they wanted to accomplish. Ambiguity also made it harder to paint the conflict as a failure should things go wrong. But it didn't make a coherent strategy likely.

This strategic confusion resulted in operational objectives that were just as murky. One IDF spokesperson described the first stage as an attempt "to strike a direct and hard blow against Hamas while increasing the deterrent strength of the IDF," an indeterminate goal at best. More specific objectives included destroying Hamas's "terrorist infrastructure" and reducing rocket fire against Israeli civilians by controlling the launching areas.[21]

Rocket firing continued throughout the conflict. All told, six hundred rockets hit Israel, killing three civilians and one soldier.[22] Some rockets had a forty-kilometer range, allowing them to reach the large southern city of Beersheba, with 213,000 residents. Many residents fled Ashkelon and other cities within range of the rockets. Schools were closed, except for those that were fortified against rockets. For Israelis living near Gaza, the fear was constant. "My five-year-old son always asks where the closest bomb shelter is," recalled one parent. "Little children shouldn't have such worries."[23]

As Israeli troops went in, they confronted not only the Qassam Brigades of Hamas, but also elements of Fatah and the PFLP. No Palestinian group in Gaza could sit this one out and maintain its credibility.[24]

The IDF vigorously attacked Hamas's rocket-launching capabilities, striking most of the places where the rockets were built and destroying a large number rockets and rocket-building material.[25] The IDF killed Interior Minister Said Siyam, a Hamas leader who was foolish enough to wander above ground and use a cell phone. In another strike the Israeli Air Force killed Nizar Rayan, the Hamas political leader, when it hit a weapons warehouse where Rayan happened to be hiding out.[26]

From an IDF perspective, one of the most encouraging things about the 2008 war was its performance at an operational and tactical level. After the 2006 failures in Lebanon the IDF had trained extensively on core conventional military skills such as combined arms fire and maneuver.[27] To counter the threat of mines and improvised explosive devices to approaching troops, Israel used its engineers and artillery and airstrikes to detonate the explosives in advance. The IDF created brigade task force teams to bring together engineers, forward air controllers, and infantry more effectively.[28] To avoid booby traps on roads the IDF moved its tanks and soldiers through fields and residential areas, warning civilians to leave and, if that failed, using firepower to move them along. Perhaps most important, commanders were leading from the front rather than trying to manipulate the battle from computer screens far away from the fighting.[29]

Cast Lead was an intelligence-driven operation. Shin Bet and other Israeli intelligence organs had prepared for the operation for months. This involved not only gathering intelligence, but developing procedures for it to be used in real time by military forces. Perhaps most important, information was quickly shared throughout the fighting forces. Shin Bet had worked hard in the lead-up to the operation to ensure that communication with military forces on the ground would be smooth, and this effort paid off in spades. In Cast Lead, intelligence-collecting units were embedded with IDF forces. One military leader declared Shin Bet's intelligence "extraordinary." One brigade intelligence officer recalled that intelligence poured in from surveillance balloons, unmanned aerial vehicles, and signals intercepts and that this information quickly went to military units, enabling them to thwart Hamas's traps.[30] As always, intelligence gaps remained; in particular, with the exception of Siyam, Israel was not able to hit Hamas's top leaders successfully.

Hamas appeared overwhelmed by the IDF. The intelligence officer of the IDF's Northern Gaza Brigade argued, "We need to remember that prior to Cast Lead, Hamas did not see a maneuvering army: It only saw limited operations—some were larger than others—but none resembled the power of a maneuvering armored brigade." The IDF's firepower, and its caution in exposing its troops to Hamas fire, made it hard for Hamas to do anything but fire mortars.[31]

The Price for Gaza's Civilians

Many voices in the international community condemned Cast Lead because of the tremendous suffering it inflicted on Gazan noncombatants. This criticism is accurate, but it ignores the complexities of military operations against a foe like Hamas.

Hamas's operations did not differentiate between civilians and combatants. The Palestinian organization stored weapons in civilian areas and commandeered civilian homes to use as bases to attack the IDF.[32] Later interrogations revealed that Hamas at times fired rockets from schools to avoid Israeli retaliation.[33] One Palestinian observed that almost all of the tall buildings in Gaza "had rocket launching pads on their roofs, or served as observation decks for Hamas."[34] A Hamas official boasted that Hamas "created a human shield of women, children, the elderly and the mujahideen" during the conflict.[35] Israel claims that many of the children who died in the conflict were Hamas spotters, not simply playing innocently, as human rights groups contended.[36]

To reduce civilian casualties the IDF broadcast warnings on the radio, dropped more than two million leaflets, and even phoned 165,000 home and cell phones in Gaza, warning people that their home would soon be a combat zone.[37] A new tactic for Israel was to "knock on the roof," firing a rocket with little or no charge at the roof of a building to scare the inhabitants into leaving, and then using a large bomb to bring the building down after they left. But predictably some residents did not leave because they thought they would be safer if they stayed indoors.[38] Others believed that they had no safe place to flee to, as Israel was also bombing targets in the center of Gaza.

One reason for the high number of Palestinian civilian deaths was a lesson the IDF learned from Lebanon in the 2006 war: that a high number of IDF casualties was tantamount to political defeat. Thus IDF operations tried to minimize their own casualties, even if it meant significantly increasing the risk to Palestinian civilians. Israel also feared that an operation, justified in part in the name of one kidnapped soldier, would lead to another kidnapping. Soldiers reportedly had orders to kill themselves rather than be captured.[39] Politically the operation was a risk. As one retired senior military official (who approved of the operation) told me, if there had been twenty or so soldiers dead in one operation or even one kidnapped soldier, public perceptions would be quite different. Israeli society will not stomach higher losses.

So rather than try to wind their way through streets infested with improvised explosive devices and booby-trapped buildings, the IDF limited its penetration and conducted longer-range strikes into Gaza. They used artillery and tanks rather than small arms, and as a result the devastation was greater and the high number of casualties among Gazan civilians predictable.

Concurrent with this decision was a fundamental change in the rules of engagement. One IDF major explained, "If there is a clear and immediate danger to our forces—then we don't have a shred of a doubt. This is one of the things we learned from the second Lebanon war: back then we were afraid to shoot and we were mostly busy with contemplating, and this is why we had casualties."[40] One soldier later told reporters, "From the first briefings before going in, it was clear the army had changed its entire mindset. Instead of getting the usual precautions on not harming civilians, we were told about the need to make a very aggressive entry."[41] Another soldier claimed his battalion commander told him, "If you are not sure—shoot. If there is doubt then there is no doubt."[42]

Documents left behind by the soldiers allow a glimpse into this change. A handwritten document in Hebrew dated January 16, 2009, probably written by a platoon commander, states, "Rules of Engagement: Fire also upon rescue. Not on women and children."[43] Another company commander was secretly recorded telling his soldiers during the operation, "We're not doing routine security work or anything like that. I want aggressiveness—if there's someone suspicious on the upper floor of a house, we'll shell it. If we have suspicions about a house, we'll take it down. There will be no hesitation, if it's us or them, it'll be them.

If someone approaches us unarmed, shoot in the air. If he keeps going, that man is dead. Nobody will deliberate—let the mistakes be over their lives, not ours."[44] The IDF issued a pamphlet quoting Rabbi Shlomo Aviner: "When you show mercy to a cruel enemy, you are being cruel to pure and honest soldiers."[45]

In the past IDF rules of engagement called for ground forces to seek further information before firing on suspicious individuals if soldiers were not sure if they were armed. Under the new policy soldiers did not need to seek additional information and could fire more freely. In addition the IDF allowed lower level officers and noncommissioned officers to make important decisions, such as whether or not to bring down a building suspected of housing militants, whereas in the past only more senior officers made such calls. Not surprisingly force was used far more often in far iffier circumstances.

Typically Gazans would be warned to flee a building as the IDF approached it. Residents would be given a few minutes to leave and be searched in the process. Those who remained were presumed to be Hamas fighters, even though soldiers knew some civilians had not fled. This led to some outcry from within the IDF. Recalling these rules, one squad commander claimed, "I call this murder. . . . In effect, we were supposed to go up floor by floor, and any person we identified—we were supposed to shoot. I initially asked myself: Where is the logic in this? From above they said it was permissible, because anyone who remained in the sector and inside Gaza City was in effect condemned, a terrorist, because they hadn't fled. I didn't really understand: On the one hand they don't really have anywhere to flee to, but on the other hand they're telling us they hadn't fled so it's their fault."[46]

The new rules increased the likelihood of accidental killings of civilians. Some members of Randa Salha's family were able to leave their house quickly after the first "knock," but Randa and four of her children only reached the bottom of the stairs and died. At times the system simply failed at a key moment. Eleven members of the Zeitoun family died when the IDF sent them to a warehouse and then inexplicably attacked it.[47] Saber Abu 'Aisha recalls that the IDF called him on his cell phone and told him to move his family to the back of his house because they were going to bomb the Hamas police post across the street. The IDF then called again later to ask him to tell his neighbor to leave his house. Then, to Saber's shock, the IDF bombed his house with no warning, killing his brother and four members of his family.[48]

"The amount of destruction there was incredible," recalled one soldier. "You drive around those neighborhoods, and can't identify a thing. Not one stone left standing over another. You see plenty of fields, hothouses, orchards, everything devastated. Totally ruined. It's terrible. It's surreal. You see a pink room with a Barbie poster, a shell that had gone through about a meter and a half below."[49] D-9 bulldozers, able to survive the mines that Hamas scattered in the Israelis' paths, were used to level buildings that held Palestinian snipers, tunnels, or booby traps, but they also created tremendous damage.

For most Israelis, Hamas's methods justified the destruction. One platoon commander in charge of several D-9s put it this way: "You arrive at a house, evacuate the women, children, and babies, and say to yourself 'God, these are some miserable people.' But then when you come to demolish the house, you suddenly see a body of a militant and a stash of weapons, and understand it was all justified."[50] Israelis would also point out that counterinsurgency against a foe with thousands of fighters is going to be bloody if the enemy decides to fight where civilians are present.

The contrast with previous operations is striking. The IDF took great pride in not using artillery during the 2002 fighting in Jenin because of the risk of civilian casualties, but in Cast Lead they used artillery and otherwise were more willing to risk civilian casualties.

Human rights groups believe there are numerous examples of deliberate targeting of civilians and, even more important, that the IDF did not do enough to avoid civilian casualties when striking suspected Hamas infrastructure sites. A controversial UN fact-finding mission led by Justice Richard Goldstone of South Africa—a Jew, which made Israelis especially sensitive to his criticism—faulted Israel for destroying a Gaza flour mill, chicken farms, and a waste treatment plant, none of which have an immediate military purpose.[51]

The IDF initially strongly denied that its soldiers deliberately targeted civilians at any time. Later IDF investigations found that abuses, perhaps inevitably, occurred but that this was not a matter of policy. A nine-year-old child, Majd, described what happened when soldiers dragged him from his mother: "I became very scared and wet my pants." They then forced him to try to open two small bags they thought were booby-trapped. Israeli military courts later convicted two soldiers for this abuse, and several other soldiers and officers have been indicted for crimes during the operation. Any military campaign in the midst of civilian areas is likely to involve such abuses—the key is whether a military tries to stop them or whether it tolerates or even encourages them—but Israelis believe they are being held to an absurdly high standard and that IDF efforts to minimize and punish abuses are ignored, with the world eager to believe the worst.[52]

In international opinion, though not in Israel, the destruction of the campaign made Israel look heartless. UN officials declared the suffering "shocking," and Amnesty International decried the destruction as "wanton."[53] Turkey, before the operation a strong ally, demanded that Israel not be allowed to enter UN headquarters since it would not conform to

UN resolutions. The IDF's disclosure that it had indeed used white phosphorous shells, which ignite on exposure to oxygen and burn what they land on, confirmed Israeli brutality in the eyes of the world.[54] The UN's Goldstone Report summed up international popular opinion by concluding that the Israeli operation "was a deliberately disproportionate attack designed to punish, humiliate and terrorize a civilian population."[55]

Part of the dispute revolves around the definition of a legitimate target. Amnesty International criticized Israel for killing policemen, but policemen were also members of Hamas's armed wing, so it is difficult to call these individuals "civilians" in the same way that children, women, and the elderly are. Even trickier is the question of what political and social institutions are valid military targets. The Goldstone Report criticized Israel's attacks on the Legislative Council building and Gaza's prison because these were not directly linked to Hamas's military effort.[56] Yet these civic structures were part and parcel of Hamas, enabling the group to sustain itself and control Gaza. The buildings and people were also part of the civilian governance structure. Hospitals with a Hamas affiliation were at times used to shield fighters and bolster the organization's strength and legitimacy, but they also cared for the sick in a territory with few private hospitals or doctors. Israel made an open decision to target Hamas as a whole rather than focus only on its military wing. As Deputy Chief of Staff Maj. Gen. Dan Harel reportedly told local Israeli authorities, "We are demanding government responsibility from Hamas and are not making distinctions between the various wings."[57]

To understand the severity of Israel's response it is important to be aware of the country's goal of deterrence. Deterrence depends on making the price too high for Hamas and its supporters to sustain. Casualties and destruction are part of this process. Israelis describe this as the "Dahiya doctrine," after the Hizballah-dominated neighborhood in Beirut that Israel flattened in 2006.[58] Deterrence moreover relies on disproportionate damage: if Israel is proportionate in the suffering it inflicts, Hamas wins because Hamas can tolerate casualties more than Israel can and its people do not expect them to inflict equal damage. When a reporter challenged Interior Minister Meir Sheetrit, "You imposed 100 times more casualties on Gaza than they did on you," he retorted, "That's the idea of the operation."[59] Israel's deputy prime minister Eli Yishai echoed this thinking: "It is a great opportunity to demolish thousands of houses of all the terrorists, so they will think twice before they launch rockets."[60]

Many Israelis reject any responsibility for civilian casualties and even argue that it may decrease the likelihood of future conflict. "Zero! Less than zero!" yelled one senior Israeli official when I asked him to discuss the IDF's responsibility. Once the enemy makes a decision to fight amid civilians, an army is not required to sacrifice its own soldiers.

Some current and former U.S. military officers I talked to are sympathetic to the Israeli position; others are vehement in their criticism. Sympathizers point out that urban warfare, even against a weak and lightly armed opponent like Hamas, is inherently bloody. Some believe that a similar U.S. operation would have caused a thousand civilian deaths or perhaps more. They point to operations in Fallujah or Sadr City in Iraq, noting that U.S. forces took far less care to minimize civilian casualties in these urban war zones. One former officer told me, "We've developed an unreasonable standard as to civilian casualties in modern combat based on conflicts like Kosovo and Gulf War One." These were not fought in urban areas and thus resulted in few civilian casualties. Others, however, believe that the Israelis should have done more to minimize civilian casualties, even if it meant military losses. "You're working for the enemy," is how one officer described operations that result in high civilian losses.

Although Israel was harshly criticized in the international media for the war, many Israelis believe they found a better balance for controlling the media story than they had in earlier conflicts. In Jenin during Operation Defensive Shield banning the media altogether led Palestinian propagandists to fill the void, creating sensational but false news about the "Jenin massacre." In Lebanon in 2006 near-complete openness to the media led to leaks on ongoing operations and a sense among policymakers that each misstep and casualty would be instantly reported as a way of keeping score. Cast Lead tried to walk the line between these extremes. The IDF confiscated soldiers' cell phones and issued strict orders that they not talk to reporters. Though the IDF banned most reporters, both Israeli and international, they did allow a handful to embed with units.[61] IDF officers also used YouTube and Twitter to disseminate Israel's message. Off-message footage still got out of course, and al-Jazeera, the Arab satellite network, continued to broadcast. Major networks used this footage, but they also complied with many Israeli restrictions and focused their reports on rockets raining on Israeli territory rather than on IDF destruction. As a result enough news was released to satisfy audiences (particularly at home), but not enough for Israel to lose control of the story as operations unfolded.

Aftermath

A definitive judgment on Cast Lead is difficult to make. Israel hoped to damage Hamas's hold on power, but it failed to recognize how strong the organization had grown in Gaza. The picture on deterrence looks more promising.

Politically Hamas did not lose out to its rivals despite its military defeat. Because the PA called for a ceasefire and not resistance, and because in general Palestinians knew that the PA was rooting against Hamas, the credibility of Abu Mazen and Salam Fayyad suffered. Polls taken after the war indicated that Hamas's leader, Ismail Haniyeh, would win a presidential race against Mahmud Abbas, while those before the war showed Haniyeh down ten points.[62] PA officials hoped this political blow was balanced by the points they scored with the Israelis for preventing any unrest on the West Bank, helping quiet Israeli doubts on PA competence.

After the fighting Hamas accused Fatah of spying for Israel, while Fatah claimed that Hamas rounded up its own supporters and imprisoned and tortured them. Both claims are justified. Israeli sources confirm that the PA helped the IDF gather intelligence for Cast Lead.[63] The Palestinian Center for Human Rights reported that "Hamas operatives killed six members of Fatah" and that another "35 were shot in the knees or beaten."[64] Amnesty International reported that in addition to killings and death threats, "scores of others [were] shot in the legs, knee-capped, or inflicted with other injures intended to cause severe disability."[65]

Although the fighting set Hamas back militarily, after it ended Hamas again smuggled weapons and tons of explosives into Gaza. It also used the lull in violence to build more tunnels and prepare for another round of Israeli strikes.[66] In short, it is unclear if Cast Lead altered Hamas's strategic situation. The organization remains firmly in power, its leadership alive and well. Gilad Shalit remains in captivity. Smuggling from Egypt continues.

Even so it is too simple to say Cast Lead had no impact; the decline in rocket attacks that followed Cast Lead suggests Hamas felt hard-hit by Israeli strikes and did not want to give Israel a reason to renew attacks on Gaza. Hamas's infrastructure, both civilian and military, took severe hits during the fighting. As the West Bank began to improve economically and Gaza remained destroyed, the popularity of Abbas and Fayyad began to increase at the expense of Hamas.

Perhaps most damaging to Hamas, it did not emerge with the aura of victory, as did Hizballah. Just before the war began the Hamas official Mahmud al-Zahhar warned, "Just let them try to invade Gaza. Gaza will be their new Lebanon."[67] Shin Bet officials rightly boast that during the operation no Hamas terrorist cells attacked Israel from the West Bank or within Israel proper. Israel did not lose a tank or a helicopter or suffer a kidnapping. Hamas suicide bombers either were a bluff or were unsuccessful, as they failed to kill IDF personnel. Hamas did continue rocket attacks, but they diminished as the 2008–9 war was in its closing days, in contrast to Hizballah's attacks, which grew in intensity as the 2006 war came to a close. This was in part because IDF military operations assumed control of launch areas and made it difficult for Hamas fighters to operate from others sites without grave risk. Several Hamas military commanders were fired because of the military wing's poor performance, suggesting its own displeasure with its performance.

Indeed some Israelis feel that Israel pulled back just as it was close to crushing Hamas once and for all. One lieutenant recalled, "We weren't far away from Hamas's breaking point," and a sergeant declared, "We wanted more Xs on our rifles," referring to the soldiers' practice of marking a kill by putting an X on their weapon.[68] Hamas, however, is a deep-rooted social movement as well as a regime; simply forcing its leaders farther underground or even killing several more of them would only have set back the group in the short term. In the long term Hamas would simply reemerge when the IDF left.

On the positive side of the ledger for Israel, the IDF restored the country's deterrence capability. Israel's weak performance in its 2006 clash with Hizballah weakened its credibility in Gaza (far more so there, ironically, than in Lebanon), but fear of Israel grew after Cast Lead. Operation Cast Lead was tough—even brutal at times—but in the months after it ended the number of attacks from Gaza plummeted. There were only four shooting attacks from Gaza into Israel in 2009, and rocket and mortar attacks fell to six hundred in total, a figure that actually overstates the activity, as most of the attacks were during the Cast Lead fighting at the beginning of the year and the numbers fell in the months that followed. As of July 2010 a comparatively low number of rockets have been launched from Gaza—few, if any, of which were launched by Hamas itself. As Ayman Taha, a former fighter and Hamas leader, noted, "The current situation required a stoppage of rockets. After the war, the fighters needed a break and the people needed a break."[69] Public opinion in Gaza was against a renewal of rocket attacks, as the population feared a return of the devastation.

Israelis see this effect as a rebuke to the criticism that they were too harsh in their conduct of the war. In the war's final days Foreign Minister Tzipi Livni declared, "Israel is not a country upon which you fire missiles and it does not respond. It is a country that when you fire on its citizens it responds by going wild."[70] One officer said that he had no problem with CNN and other networks covering the carnage in the aftermath of the conflict: "Let Arabs know this is what happens when you fuck with the Jews." This attitude may be growing more prevalent. After the war soldiers in a number of Israeli units sported T-shirts boasting of their ferocity. Sharpshooters from the Givati Brigade, for example, wore shirts showing a pregnant Palestinian woman with a bull's-eye on her belly and the words "1 shot, 2 kills."[71] One official I talked to attributed this to the rise of a new generation that had grown up amid suicide bombings. Half of the high school students in Israel oppose equal rights for Arabs in Israel.[72]

Gazans' misery did not stop when the shooting ended. After the war the International Committee of the Red Cross reported that Israel's partial closure of Gaza had led to "a dramatic increase in poverty," with more than 70 percent of Gazans living on an income of less than $250 a month for a family of nine. Unemployment is over 40 percent, and by some estimates much higher.[73] After the Gaza war only food, medicine, and detergent were allowed to enter the territory.[74]

Hamas is beset from all sides. Even though Fatah's credibility suffered because it sided against Hamas in Cast Lead, Hamas's rival is always in the wings, with Abu Mazen gloating over any Hamas weakness. Some Fatah elements in Gaza even worked with Hizballah to smuggle in rockets from Egypt in an apparent attempt to disrupt the postwar ceasefire.

A new confrontation reared its head in August 2009, when Abdel Latif Moussa, a Gazan preacher, declared in a mosque in Gaza that the strip was now an Islamic emirate—a direct challenge to Hamas's caution on this score. Hamas fighters surrounded the mosque, and twenty-eight died, including Moussa, in the shootout.[75] Moussa was part of a growing phenomenon of jihadists who look more to Osama bin Ladin than to Hamas for inspiration, though they are not directly tied to al-Qa'ida itself. For now these groups are small and disorganized; even the membership of the larger ones, such as Jaysh al-Umma, Jaysh al-Islam, Jaysh Ansar Allah, and Jaljalat, number only in the low hundreds.[76] They have gone underground for now, in response to the Hamas crackdown, but they will criticize Hamas if it fails to continue the fight against Israel or to further Islamicize Gaza. For now Hamas officials stress that they do not want to force Islamicization on Gazans. "Erdogan, not Taliban," is how the prominent scholar Yezid Sayigh described this view, referring to the moderate Islamist leader of Turkey.[77] But pressure from even more radical groups makes it hard for Hamas to drag its heels.

It is worrisome for Hamas that this extreme position evokes considerable sympathy among its rank and file, particularly its armed wing. Many joined the organization to fight Israel and to create an Islamic state. Bin Ladin–style jihadists now criticize Hamas for turning away from these goals. Al-Qa'ida has strongly denounced Hamas, some of its affiliates even calling for God to "destroy the Hamas state."[78] Al-Qa'ida leaders have always had a bitter relationship with Hamas's parent, the Muslim Brotherhood, seeing it as quick to compromise and willing to participate in elections and work with the host government rather than holding out for a more doctrinally pure solution. Any Hamas ceasefire or concession is thus held up to scorn. (They also criticize Hamas's rival and fellow traveler, Palestine Islamic Jihad, even though it remains in the fight, because of its ties to Iran, the hated Shi'a power.) Social conditions may favor these new groups. In Gaza Taliban-style dress is becoming more common.[79]

Israel's challenges have also grown since Cast Lead. While the ceasefire holds, Hamas can still build tunnels and extend the range of its rockets, all without blatantly violating a ceasefire. For deterrence to work in the long term Israel has to be willing to respond to even a small number of Qassam rocket attacks that kill no one. This is politically difficult, both at home and abroad. Inevitably critics will argue that a tough response imposes needless suffering and complicates any ongoing peace negotiations. Israeli policy will be confrontational against Hamas, and this will make it harder for more moderate figures in the West Bank to negotiate with Israel, as retaliation discredits them. In the words of one senior intelligence official, Israel must balance diplomacy in the West Bank while "one leg is deep in the shit of the Gaza Strip."

Equally notable is what Israel did not do in Cast Lead: reoccupy Gaza. As supportive as Israelis were of hitting Hamas hard and teaching it a lesson, there was no enthusiasm for stationing large numbers of troops in Gaza itself, even though they knew that Hamas was likely to stay in power and the threat of rocket attacks would continue. As one U.S. general told me, "The IDF did not want to go to Round 15."

Both sides recognize that another round of fighting might break out at any time. As one intelligence officer argues, "The battle now is over who learns faster—Hamas or us."[80]

Averting another war requires a long-term ceasefire and, ideally, a peace process that offers a political alternative. While outsiders look back to the end of the Oslo negotiations as the place to begin, this starting point is no longer realistic. For both Israelis and Palestinians, the Second Intifada and the rise of power of Hamas have fundamentally changed the shape of negotiations and the likely nature of any peace.

The Israeli bus ambushed by Arab terrorists at Scorpion's Pass on March 16, 1954.
Credit: Israel Government Press Office. Photographer: Fritz Cohen.

The King David Hotel, bombed by the Jewish group the Irgun in 1946.
Credit: Israel Government Press Office. Photographer: Hugo Mendelson.

Members of Unit 101, Israel's first military counterterrorism unit, posing with IDF Chief of Staff Moshe Dayan. Individuals include several future prime ministers, including Ariel Sharon.
Credit: Israel Government Press Office.

PLO Chairman Yasser Arafat addressing an audience after the signing ceremony of the Oslo II Accords at the White House.
Credit: Israel Government Press Office. Photographer: Saar Yaacov.

Leila Khaled, member of the PFLP who became a terrorist celebrity after she played a major role in multiple airplane hijackings.
Credit: Staff/Getty Images

One of the Black September Organization terrorists who seized members of the Israeli Olympic Team at their quarters at the Munich Olympic Village during the 1972 games.
Credit: Getty Images

A Japanese Red Army member standing trial for the 1972 Lod airport attack. The Popular Front for the Liberation of Palestine cooperated with the Japanese group to avoid Israeli security. Credit: Israel Government Press Office. Photographer: Fritz Cohen.

Red Cross personnel removing bodies after the massacre at the Sabra and Shatila Palestinian refugee camps.
Credit: Israel Government Press Office. Photographer: Yossi Roth.

Special Police firing gas grenades at the Temple Mount in response to the riots after the massacre at the Cave of the Patriarchs.
Credit: Israel Government Press Office. Photographer: Avi Ohayon.

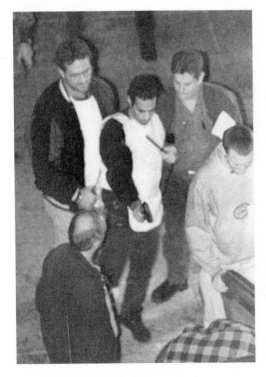

Jewish terrorist Yigal Amir reenacting his assassination of Prime Minister Yithzak Rabin for Israeli police.
Credit: Israel Government Press Office. Photographer: Nati Harnik.

Palestinian students at Al Najah University re-enact the Sbarro bombing.
Credit: Cam99/Getty Images

A France 2 television screen shot of Mohammad al-Durra and his father, shown protecting his son from the hail of bullets. The boy's became an icon of the second intifada.
Credit: AFP/Getty Images

A Palestinian displaying his bloody hands after the lynching of Israeli reservists who accidentally entered Ramallah.
Credit: Chris Gerald/AFP/Getty Images

The bombed Park Hotel in Netanyah.
Credit: Israel Government Press Office. Photographer: Sharon Noam.

A display of weapons and other military equipment confiscated from the Karine A ship, used in an attempt to smuggle weapons to the Gaza strip.
Credit: US Congress

A shot of the separation barrier outside Jerusalem. This section of the barrier is a wall.
Photographer: Sarah Yerkes

Israeli Prime Minister
Benjamin Netanyahu.
Credit: US Congress.

Avi Dichter, head of
Shin Bet during much
of the second intifada.
Credit: Israeli
Government Press
Office. Photographer:
Avi Ohayon.

Hamas leader Khaled
Mishal.
Credit: 20 Minutos,
Spain.

Israel's Chief of Staff
and later Prime Minister
Ehud Barak.
Credit: US Department
of Defense.

Israel's Chief of Staff
Shaul Mofaz.
Credit: Israel
Government Press
Office. Photographer:
IDF Spokesperson.

Palestinian leader
Mahmoud Abbas.
Credit: US Department
of State.

Jewish terrorist Meir
Kahane.
Credit: Israel
Government Press
Office. Photographer:
Nati Harnik.

Hizballah leader Hassan
Nasrallah.
Credit: humbleslave.
blogspot.com

Palestinians inspect damage at a mosque Jewish settlers set on fire.
Credit: Aafar Ashtiyeh/AFP/Getty Images

The Haret Hreik neighborhood in the Dahiye Section in Beirut after Israeli bombing.
Credit: UNHCR.

THE LEBANESE HIZBALLAH

CHAPTER XIV

THE BIRTH OF A MONSTER: HIZBALLAH'S CREATION (1982–1985)

I remember a giant ball of flames and then the blast. Or was it the blast first and then the flames? All the walls flew outward. We fell from the fifth floor almost to the ground, without being able to hold on to anything, because we were just dropping through the air. A metal fridge that was in our room fell against a chair, and my head was in the space between them. Thanks to that chair, I wasn't crushed to death. I lay there with my face down, unable to move, with almost my whole body except my head covered by tremendously heavy stones and walls. . . . Klein and Zada, two other CID investigators, were pleading for help in feeble voices, and I yelled to the rescue teams to save them first, because they had no air and could hardly breathe. I stretched my arm out to Zada and told him to reply to me by squeezing my hand if he could hear me, because I wanted to keep him awake until the rescuers reached him. After a while, the squeezing stopped.
—Aharon Halevy, quoted in Ronen Bergman, *The Secret War with Iran: The 30-year Clandestine Struggle against the World's Most Dangerous Terrorist Power*

ONE of the bloodiest single attacks Israel ever suffered is also one of the least known both in Israel and throughout the world. On November 11, 1982, in Tyre, Lebanon, a suicide bomber drove a car filled with explosives into the building where the IDF was running its Lebanon war operations. The attack killed seventy-five Israelis and dozens of Lebanese prisoners held in the facility. The Israeli government claimed the blast was an accidental explosion from gas cylinders, but the scholar Ronen Bergman points out that eyewitnesses had seen a car driving at high speed into the building, and that Israeli military police afterward found the leg of someone who. was neither an Israeli nor a Lebanese prisoner. Numerous other clues indicated that an attacker, not an accident, was behind the explosion.[1] On May 19, 1985, Hizballah claimed that Ahmad Qasir, who was fifteen at the time, had martyred himself by carrying out the attack, thus earning the sobriquet "the Prince of Martyrs."[2]

Confusing many observers, Islamic Jihad, a name unknown at the time, claimed responsibility for the attack. Islamic Jihad was a front organization for Hizballah, the terrorist organization that many deem the world's most capable. The Tyre attack was only the second suicide bombing in modern history, but it was the forerunner of many other bloody suicide attacks that followed. Early in 1983 similar attacks occurred on U.S. and French facilities, leading to the eventual withdrawal of European and U.S. peacekeeping forces from Lebanon. On November 4, 1983, another Hizballah suicide bomber struck at Tyre, killing twenty-eight Israeli soldiers and thirty-two Lebanese prisoners.[3] The body counts from these attacks made Hizballah infamous around the world. Groups like al-Qa'ida would later conclude from this experience that a dramatic strike against U.S. forces and facilities would lead the United States to withdraw military forces from the Middle East.

For over a decade Palestinian militants from Lebanon had conducted horrific attacks on Israel and shelled Israeli settlements, posing a constant danger to Israeli cities. Israel's 1982 invasion of Lebanon was meant to end the terrorist threat to Israel from Lebanon forever; thus beyond the casualties, the first Tyre attack was particularly painful, and perhaps the reason why the Israeli government sought political cover behind the story that the attack was an accident. Rather than the invasion producing an end to terrorist violence, the attack proved that a far greater danger was emerging.

The Birth of Hizballah

No one expected the Israeli invasion of Lebanon in 1982 to "uncork the Shi'i element," as the Israeli scholar and diplomat Itamar Rabinovich put it. With the fall of the PLO and the rise of Hizballah, Israel was not simply exchanging one enemy for another. Hizballah is recognized as one of the most formidable terrorist groups in the world. In 2002 Senator Bob Graham of Florida, then the head of the Senate Select Committee on Intelligence, declared Hizballah more lethal than al-Qa'ida. Then Deputy Secretary of State Richard Armitage echoed Graham's concern, noting that "Hezbollah may be the 'A team' of terrorists," while "Al Qaeda is actually the 'B team.'"[4]

Although Hizballah emerged from the cauldron of Lebanon's civil war, its roots go even deeper, tapping into centuries of poverty and desperation in Lebanon's Shi'a community. For most of the country's modern history its Shi'a Muslim community has been ignored and powerless, despite their numbers; they compose 30 to 40 percent of Lebanon's population, the largest communal group in the country, yet Lebanon's Maronite

Christian and Sunni Muslim communities have dominated the country. These two groups quarreled over who would lead, but not over whether the Shi'as deserved a greater say. The government spent money on Sunni and Christian areas, but aside from an occasional nod to traditional Shi'a leaders, they generally ignored the well-being of the community.

Beginning in the 1960s the charismatic cleric Musa al-Sadr challenged the traditional, politically quiescent leaders of Lebanon's Shi'as, organizing the community and demanding a greater voice in Lebanon's affairs. Sadr sought to arouse the Shi'a community, but his goal was limited and secular, despite his religious credentials: he sought to make the Shi'as a fully empowered community within Lebanon, not to foment an Islamic revolution.[5] As civil war engulfed Lebanon in 1975, communities that had not already formed their own militias quickly did so for self-defense. For the Shi'as, the key movement was Sadr's Amal, which the PLO helped arm and train. Still, in Lebanon's brutal power game, Amal remained a weak player. Many Shi'as initially fought for left-wing groups aligned with the PLO, and they suffered heavily when anti-PLO Christians attacked. Many of those who worked with the Palestinian groups also did so out of desperation: the Palestinians paid, and the Shi'a fighters were impoverished.[6]

The 1979 Islamic revolution in Iran shook Lebanon's Shi'a community. As its leaders took power in the name of their religion, the revolution became a tremendous source of sectarian pride. It also showed revolutionaries who once scorned religion as a force of stagnation that faith could be a vehicle for seizing power. In Lebanon the impact was particularly strong. Many young clerics had studied in the same seminaries (often in Iraq) that had educated Iran's new leadership. Some of Iran's revolutionary leaders had also trained at Palestinian camps in Lebanon.

Despite the significant Shi'a role among many Palestinian organizations and Palestinian aid to Amal, the relationship between the two communities was tense. In the south, near the border with Israel, Palestinians regularly lorded over Shi'a areas, using the excuse of fighting Israel to behave as thugs. As late as the mid-1980s Shi'a groups were still willing to kill thousands of Palestinians to prevent Fatah and other Palestinian organizations from returning. When the IDF went into Lebanon Shi'as welcomed the soldiers "with rice and with flowers."[7]

Nabih Berri, Sadr's rather lackluster but canny successor, cooperated with Amin Gemayel, who became president after his brother, president-elect Bashir Gemayel, was assassinated on Syrian orders in September 1982. Others in the Lebanese government also worked with the Israelis, hoping to exploit their presence for their own narrow goals or simply because they recognized Israel's power. Berri took over from Imam Sadr, who had disappeared mysteriously in 1978 on a trip to Libya; Israeli officials told me that they believe the Libyan leader Mu'ammar Qaddafi ordered Sadr thrown from a helicopter into the desert as a favor to Palestinian groups, who correctly saw Sadr as turning the Shi'as against them. Several local Shi'a factions, inspired by Ayatollah Khomeini's revolution, became disenchanted with Berri's leadership. They were already incensed over the Israeli presence in their country, and they rejected Berri's collaboration with Gemayel, arguing that the regime was nothing more than an Israeli puppet. Many Shi'as in Beirut and elsewhere saw Berri and Amal as weak defenders of the community, unable to stop rampaging Christian militias from evicting Shi'as from their homes during the civil war. Amal spurned many young Shi'as who had fought with Palestinian groups and had now lost their paymaster.[8]

The United States also entered the fray, albeit inadvertently. In 1982 the United States, France, the United Kingdom, and Italy all sent troops to Lebanon to oversee the evacuation of the PLO. The massacres at the Sabra and Shatila refugee camps led to an international outcry, and international forces stayed on, ostensibly to help keep the peace. At first they helped limit the violence, but soon they became a target themselves.

Enter Iran and Syria

Hizballah's formation and rapid emergence as Lebanon's dominant Shi'a movement is inseparable from that of its foreign patrons: Syria and in particular Iran, the intellectual father of Hizballah. Hizballah accepted Iran's supreme leader Rouhollah Mousavi Khomenei as the organization's guide, parroting Iran's rhetoric of jihad against foreigners and help for the oppressed. As Shaykh Subhi al-Tufayli, one of Hizballah's early leaders, declared, Hizballah's relation to Iran "is one of a junior to a senior. . . . Of a soldier to his commander."[9] Hizballah eagerly took on Iran's revolutionary hatred of Israel and participated as a junior partner in Iran's bitter struggle with Iraq. Sayyid Abbas Musawi, one of Hizballah's leaders who became its secretary general in 1991, declared that Israel was a "cancer" and that Hizballah would "wipe out every trace of Israel."[10]

But Iran did more than provide inspiration. Iranian officials were there to midwife the birth of Hizballah. In June 1982 Sayyid Hussein Musawi broke from Amal and founded Islamic Amal. Tehran's ambassador to Syria, Ali Akbar Mohtashemi, played a key role in encouraging this split. Iranian diplomats and paramilitary officials held senior positions in Hizballah's governing organization, particularly in its early years. Iranian officials worked to unite Amal splinters with the Islamic Students Union, the Association of Muslim 'Ulema, the Lebanese branch of the Dawa Party, and other small Shi'a groups operating at a local level, thus saving Hizballah from the fate of Fatah, which constantly contended with internecine killings and threats to its flanks.

Shortly after assuming power Ayatollah Khomeini declared, "We should try hard to export our revolution to the world. . . . We [shall] confront the world with our ideology."[11] Lebanon was his most successful effort. Iran sent perhaps fifteen hundred members of the Islamic Revolutionary Guard Corps (IRGC) to train and indoctrinate Hizballah recruits. (The IRGC presence, which later declined to around three hundred to five hundred, remains to this day.) Hizballah first established itself in the Bekaa Valley near the Syrian border, the territory where Iran's paramilitary forces eventually set up shop. It then spread to Beirut and finally to Lebanon's border with Israel, in most cases swallowing up local Shi'a militias that were already organized and fighting against Israel. In IRGC camps near the ancient Roman ruins of Baalbek recruits learned how to conceal themselves and ambush Israeli patrols, how to build roadside bombs and conduct psychological warfare, and how to infiltrate Israeli-held territory.[12] At camps in Iran itself Shi'a militants from Lebanon and around the world learned the finer points of terrorism and guerrilla war, such as building sophisticated explosives and forging convincing passports. To this day the military relationship is strong, and many Israelis would agree with Mossad's former head Shabtai Shavit's description of Hizballah to me as "an Iranian division deployed inside Lebanon."

In addition to teaching tactical basics such as marksmanship and how to set up an ambush, trainers from Iran's IRGC turned parts of Lebanon's Bekaa Valley into a microcosm of revolutionary Iran. Women wore veils, pictures of Ayatollah Khomeini were ubiquitous, and the debates in Iran were mirrored in Lebanon. Indeed Ayatollah Mohammad Hussein Fadlallah, the spiritual guide for many Hizballah members as he was Lebanese, initially called for defending the Islamic revolution before achieving the movement's aims in Lebanon.[13] After 1989 he hewed a more independent line from Tehran.

Equally important, Iran also provided money for Hizballah. Estimates vary, but Iran gave Hizballah perhaps five to ten million dollars a month for many years. Today Hizballah expert Shimon Shapira contends the figure is probably twice that, and that excludes military aid. Tehran gave perhaps a billion dollars to Hizballah to help it rebuild after its 2006 war with Israel. Hizballah fighters received a salary that enabled them to care for their families, no small accomplishment for many impoverished Shi'as living in war-torn Lebanon. Iranian backing also allowed Hizballah to establish schools and hospitals for its fighters and their families. Perhaps 90 percent of Hizballah's budget for these social programs came directly from Iran.[14] It's not surprising that many Shi'as gravitated away from Amal and other rivals to Hizballah. As the Hizballah scholar Amal Saad-Ghorayeb contends, "Even by Hizbu'llah's reckoning, it would have taken an additional 50 years for the movement to score the same achievements in the absence of Iranian backing."[15]

Iran went long on Hizballah, and it paid off. The group became Iran's loyal proxy not only in Lebanon, but around the world. Early in Iran's bitter war with Iraq, individuals who would later lead Hizballah dutifully pursued Iraqi targets in Lebanon at Iran's request. Hizballah attacked targets in Kuwait to push Kuwait out of Iraq's embrace and then bombed Paris in 1986 to punish France for its arms supplies to Iraq. Hizballah also served as a bridge for Iran to the Arab world, helping the Persian state portray itself as a leader in the Muslim world.

Yet confining Hizballah to a strategic asset of Tehran misses half the picture. The Syria-Hizballah relationship was less chummy than that of the Iran-Hizballah relationship, but in many ways it was more important. Although Iran inspired Hizballah and guided it, Syria was the dominant player in Lebanon, and Hizballah had to adjust to Syrian demands. Damascus saw Hizballah as a useful tool for wresting control of the Shi'as out of Amal's hands after Berri's forces did not fire on the Israelis. In addition, when Hizballah proved to be a dedicated foe of Israel it became useful to Syria in bloodying the IDF.

Syrian support of Hizballah is also bound up in the pariah status of the 'Alawis, who dominate the country's leadership. 'Alawis are a minority sect within Islam and are considered by many mainstream Sunnis to be near heretics. Like the Shi'as, the 'Alawis venerate 'Ali, the prophet Mohammad's cousin (and son-in-law) and the fourth caliph of Islam, but their views are even farther from traditional Sunni views of Islam. Because the Shi'as are generally more recognized and respected among Muslims, they could grant the 'Alawis legitimacy, and Amal's founder, the venerated Shi'a leader Musa al-Sadr, did just that.

Among Syria's leaders the ghost of 1967 binds their Lebanon policy. In that year the Syrians proudly tied themselves to the Palestinians' destiny, ratcheting up tension with Israel in the name of revolutionary solidarity. When war broke out, Israel quickly crushed Syrian forces and took the Golan Heights. After that Syria's new strongman, Hafez al-Asad (whose son Bashar took power when Hafez died in 2000) saw Lebanon as both a risk and an opportunity. On the one hand, Asad feared that Palestinian activity—and later Hizballah activity—could spin out of control to the point that Israel would intervene militarily and threaten Syria itself. Nor did Asad want Lebanon to fracture to the point of developing distinct enclaves where some, particularly the Maronite Christians, might reach out to Israel for protection.[16] On the other hand, Asad hoped to exploit militants in Lebanon to press Israel into making concessions, such as returning the Golan Heights.

Syria was a far more ambivalent sponsor than Iran, particularly during the rule of Hafez al-Asad. While Iran sought victory for Hizballah, Damascus wanted to control the group in Lebanon and use it against Israel. Asad also feared that the rise of the Shi'as in Lebanon could alienate

Sunnis at home, and Syrian forces have clashed with Hizballah in an effort to assert Damascus's dominance.

Iran's and Syria's roles in Hizballah's day-to-day operations are murky, but there is no question that both countries were deeply involved. Until Syria was forced out of Lebanon in 2005, Damascus was the landlord of Lebanon; little occurred there that did not have its tacit blessing. Any activity that went on without Asad's approval soon ended. Syria worked closely with Hizballah in devising its military efforts against Israel and its Lebanese client militia, the South Lebanese Army, as did Iran's IRGC. The attack on the U.S. embassy in Beirut, for example, occurred after the Soviet Union gave Syria the information that top CIA officials would be meeting there on April 23, 1983. [17]

Israel Fuels the Fire

It is difficult to imagine Hizballah's development without recognizing the key role Israel played. The Lebanese Shi'as in southern Lebanon, for years mistreated by Palestinian militias, initially welcomed the Israeli invaders.[18] Although most Shi'as were glad to see the PLO routed and removed from their villages, inevitably the Israeli occupation of Lebanon first grated on, and over time enraged, local Shi'a communities.

In southern Lebanon a series of blunders were particularly provoking. On October 16, 1983, during the important Ashura holiday, Israeli soldiers tried to drive through a religious procession in Nabatiyya. As the soldiers attempted to push mourners out of their path, the mood turned ugly and a riot began. The threatened soldiers then fired into the crowd and killed and wounded several of the rioters. Although the Ashura shooting was a grave error, such mistakes are almost inevitable during an occupation when there is a war or insurgency in the background because soldiers and civilians constantly rub up against one another. As the Israeli analyst and former policymaker on Lebanon Reuven Erlich contends, "If not Ashura, it would happen in another incident."[19]

These mistakes were predictable because Israel had no intelligence structure in Shi'a areas.[20] The Mossad had focused its activities on Palestinian groups and the Maronites. (Later Israel acquired a similar level of detail on West Bank and Gazan Palestinians.) The few Israeli analysts who focused on internal Lebanese politics knew little about the Shi'as, and most of their information on Lebanon came from the Maronite community, which disdained the Shi'as. Israeli leaders also thought the operation in Lebanon would be over quickly. "Pessimists said the operation would last months," Erlich told me. No one believed the IDF would operate in Shi'a areas for years.

Israel tried to reshape Lebanon, but in so doing discredited potential allies and created new hostile forces. As part of Israel's plan to place allies in charge, the IDF installed Bashir Gemayel's pro-Israel Phalange at Lebanon's helm. A 1983 accord brokered by the United States created the National Salvation Committee, which Gemayel headed. Other Lebanese parties were pushed into cooperating with it, including the Shi'a Amal, which joined in part because of its hostility to the Palestinians and because Berri thought the Israelis were the ascendant party. This collaboration with the quisling government led to a split in Amal and enraged many Shi'as, allowing Hizballah to accuse its enemies of collaboration.

Israel failed to recognize the bind it placed on Amal and other potential partners. Although Amal cooperated with the IDF against the PLO in the south, at the same time it fought the IDF in Beirut because there it needed to win over the Shi'as against rivals who were attracting recruits by fighting the Israelis. The IDF often blew up the houses of Amal supporters after Hizballah attacks on Israeli soldiers, conflating the two organizations and driving Amal members into Hizballah's arms. Even by the time of the second Tyre bombing, when the Hizballah front group Islamic Jihad had been active for a year, the organization seemed a shadow. So Israel responded to the attack by hitting Palestinian and Syrian positions—known targets, but the wrong ones.[21]

Israel dusted off the counterterrorism kit it had used successfully in Gaza and the West Bank, but the same weapons backfired in Lebanon. Shin Bet deployed to Lebanon to work with IDF intelligence, which had previously run the show. On February 12, 1984, Israel—or its local Lebanese operatives—killed Sheikh Ragheb Harb, the thirty-two-year-old leader of the religious resistance in the village of Jibshit, a hotbed of opposition. Harb had just returned from Iran, and Israel suspected him of murdering cooperative local leaders. Three bullets fired from behind a wall in his garden killed him.[22] Rather than hurting Hizballah's operational capacity, Harb's death only provided the movement with a martyr. In response Hizballah fighters began to drive explosives-laden vehicles into Israeli targets.

Perhaps ten thousand Palestinians and Shi'as went to jails in Israel and Lebanon in 1983.[23] Jailing suspects with only limited intelligence, however, can backfire. It radicalizes the innocent and those not fully committed. It also alienates people in their communities who usually know the guilty from the innocent. Because the Israelis did not control Lebanese territory the way they controlled the West Bank and Gaza, Hizballah had far better local intelligence than they. Even worse, Israeli intelligence sometimes worked at cross-purposes; military intelligence and Shin Bet both frequently ran the same local agents, who enjoyed a double salary without the spy agencies' knowledge.[24] Over time Hizballah developed its own counterintelligence capabilities, enabling it to weed out informers and to plant its own spies in communities that cooperated with the Israelis.

Hizballah Rises

Hizballah exploded into the consciousness of Israel and the West after conducting a series of dramatic and bloody attacks on the forces of both. In attacks in November 1982 and 1983 Hizballah suicide bombers destroyed the Israeli military and intelligence facilities in Tyre. In April 1983 a Hizballah suicide bomber killed sixty-three at the U.S. embassy in Beirut; on October 23, 1983, 241 U.S. Marines died when a suicide bomber struck their compound; fifty-eight French soldiers died a few minutes later in a similar attack in Lebanon. Despite evidence clearly implicating Hizballah figures in the attacks, the organization denies responsibility to this day.

The novel tactic of suicide bombing inspired particular fear. Israel and other governments that Hizballah targeted now had to devise means of defeating an organization whose members embraced their own death, a concept alien to Western thinkers. It would take the Palestinians ten years to emulate suicide bombings.

Concurrent with its use of suicide bombings, Hizballah also took hostages to frighten Westerners out of Lebanon. By 1988 Hizballah had already kidnapped eighty foreigners. In addition to Israelis and Westerners, operatives targeted Iraqis (the Iranians' mortal foes) and Saudis, after Riyadh killed Shi'a activists in the Saudi Kingdom. Hizballah mostly took hostages to advance its own agenda in Lebanon. However, it worked closely with Iran and Syria in abducting the hostages and during negotiations for their release.

In 1985 Hizballah released an official statement announcing its goals and acknowledging its existence after several years of hiding in the shadows. In this declaration the group acknowledged its loyalty to the directives of Ayatollah Khomeini. It declared its enmity to "the Phalanges, Israel, France, and the U.S." The manifesto was a litany of grievances that excoriated the UN security forces and claimed that the outsiders are invaders and oppressors who "slit the throats of our children." The manifesto also rejected group identity or, more derisively, "clannism," Hizballah's derisive description of the political system in Lebanon that allocates parliamentary seats according to sect and community. Against Israel Hizballah was uncompromising: "Our struggle will only end when this entity is obliterated. We recognize no treaty with it, no cease fire, and no peace agreements."[25]

Perhaps no one exemplifies Hizballah's professionalism and ruthlessness better than Imad Mughniyah, who led its terrorist wing until his killing in Damascus in 2008. Mughniyah was born in the Lebanese village of Tayr Dibba but grew up in one of Beirut's teeming slums, where so many Shi'as and (for a while) Palestinians lived. He was a son of Shaykh Muhammad Jawad Mughniyah, a leading Shi'a religious figure who reviled Ayatollah Khomeini's clerical system of government and condemned

Imam Sadr as an Iranian spy.[26] Before joining Hizballah the son studied engineering at the American University of Beirut, where he worked closely with Fatah to organize a student unit. As part of the PLO's Islamic wing he joined Force 17, Fatah's internal security unit, where he reportedly served alternatively as a sniper and a bodyguard for Abu Iyad, the head of PLO intelligence, and at times Arafat.[27] The Palestinian failures and the rise of the Iranian alternative inspired Mughniyah to make his switch. He initially joined the student wing of Lebanon's Dawa Party, which was later integrated into Hizballah. Some reports indicate that he switched to Hizballah with Arafat's full support.[28]

Evidence from trials related to a 1994 Hizballah bombing in Argentina places Mughniyah as the head of coordinating Hizballah's foreign operations and the training of guerrilla groups.[29] CIA reporting puts him behind several hostage takings in Lebanon and Hizballah's operations against U.S. and French targets in Kuwait in 1983. Mughniyah also masterminded the hijacking of TWA Flight 847 en route from Athens in 1985. The plane was diverted to Beirut, where Hizballah dumped the dead body of U.S. Navy diver Robert Stethem on the tarmac. The hostages were eventually released, probably after Israel agreed to release about 700 Lebanese Shi'a prisoners.

The CIA describes Mughniyah as "highly intelligent" and having "very close relations with Iran."[30] David Barkai, an Israeli military officer in charge of assessing Mughniyah for many years, described him as "one of the most creative and brilliant minds [he had] ever come across."[31] Robert Baer, a former CIA officer, reported that Mugniyeh "enters by one door, exits by another, changes his cars daily, never makes appointments on a telephone, never is predictable." The Israeli diplomat and scholar Itamar Rabinovich alludes to his skill by noting that Israel did not even learn of his importance to the organization until the 1990s. More bluntly a leading Israeli official described him to me as "a very capable son of a bitch." For Hizballah, as for most successful terrorist groups, competence is valued over ideology. Mughniyah was undoubtedly a true believer, but in a phone conversation that Israel recorded, Sheikh Naim Qassem reportedly noted, "He's no great saint when it comes to religion."[32] Nevertheless Mughniyah headed Hizballah's Central Security Apparatus and directed its terrorist activities.

Mughniyah had an exceptionally close relationship with Iranian intelligence. Israelis tell me that he spent much of his time in Iran, reporting directly to Iranian officials as well as Hizballah Secretary General Hassan Nasrallah.[33] Despite being one of the world's most wanted terrorists, he remained exceptionally active. In 2001 he was elected to the organization's leadership council, formalizing his always considerable influence.[34] His family was less lucky. His brother Jihad died in a car bomb attack in Beirut that was supposedly the work of the CIA. Another brother, Fuad, died in a Mossad-orchestrated car bombing in Beirut in 1994, an attack that many believe was done to punish his brother rather than because Fuad himself was a worthwhile target.[35]

The End of the Beginning

The year 1985 also marked the beginning of Israel's retreat from Lebanon and its abandonment of the dream of transforming the country, what Reuven Erlich labels "the end of the beginning." Even the invasion's defenders recognized that Israel was trapped in Lebanon, with no way to emerge victorious. However, because Israel had failed to install a friendly regime in Lebanon, it was caught on the horns of a dilemma. Leaving Lebanon meant risking a return of the PLO to Israel's border or allowing another foe to set up shop there; staying meant becoming an occupying power and slowly bleeding resources. Politically the revelations of the killings at the Sabra and Shatila refugee camps and the steady increase in IDF casualties led to a strong shift in Israeli public opinion against the continued war in Lebanon.

How to withdraw, however, was a thorny question, and Israel sought a way to minimize risks. Understandably it did not trust either the Lebanese Army or UN forces with its security. As the civil war intensified, the writ of Lebanon's government barely extended outside Beirut. Even before the war it had shown itself unable to stop Palestinian attacks from Lebanon. UN forces did little to change this. Thus Israel ended up trying to find a military solution without a political arrangement—a recurring problem for the country.

Although UN Security Council Resolution 425 called for Israel to withdraw completely, Israel set up a large security zone as it withdrew: 850 square kilometers, or around 10 percent of Lebanon's total territory. The zone was an expansion of the border strip established after Israel had invaded Lebanon in Operation Litani in 1978. As before, the IDF and the South Lebanese Army worked together to control the zone. The IDF paid and equipped the SLA, and in turn the SLA defended southern Lebanon on Israel's behalf. The SLA's officers were mostly Christian, with a few Druze officers and a very small number of Shi'as, but many of the movement's rank and file were Shi'a Muslims. By the end of Israel's time in Lebanon in 2000 the SLA manned forty-two of the fifty Israeli positions.[36] Although the size varied, the SLA forces numbered approximately twenty-five hundred, and the IDF had roughly one thousand to fifteen hundred troops deployed. The two forces established fortified and well-armed observation posts along the hilltops.

The security zone was set up despite several prescient warnings from Israeli intelligence. They first warned that the SLA would be able to maintain the zone only if the IDF actively supported it. This is a problem the United States has faced in recent years: its local allies' strength depends on a strong U.S. commitment, which in turn risks dragging the United States deeper into a conflict. The second warning cautioned that Hizballah and its rivals would feel compelled to fight Israel to maintain their resistance bona fides.[37]

The security zone was sold politically as a temporary measure. Yitzhak Rabin, then Israel's defense minister, claimed in May 1985 that Israel would remain in the security zone for only a month "to test Syrian intentions."[38] "We'll pull Israel out of the Lebanese mud," he and Prime Minister Shimon Peres promised.[39]

Israel's involvement in Lebanon led to its own soldiers being taken captive, which in turn led to prisoner exchanges. In 1983 Israel released almost five thousand captured Palestinians in exchange for six captured Israeli soldiers. As it withdrew to the security zone in 1985, Israel freed over a thousand more prisoners, most of whom were Palestinian, in return for three captured Israelis. In addition to getting its people back, Israel also wanted to dampen Palestinian grievances (for this was still seen as the main threat) and, Israeli leaders hoped, put Lebanon behind them. Thomas Friedman, the *New York Times* reporter who won a Pulitzer Prize for his coverage of the Lebanon war, wrote about the mixed feelings in Israel after the 1985 release:

> There was joy when the three Israeli prisoners of war stepped off the planes Tuesday at Tel Aviv airport and were reunited with their families after nearly three years in captivity. But there was also rage, the kind that makes a person want to kick his television set, at watching a smiling Kozo Okamoto, the Japanese terrorist who took part in the 1972 Lod Airport massacre that killed 26 people, join 1,149 freed Palestinian prisoners. There was fear that the newly released Palestinians, 600 of whom were let go inside Israel or the West Bank, would again take up acts of violence against Israel.[40]

On its own terms the security zone at first succeeded. Infiltration in particular was limited, and as a result citizens in northern Israel enjoyed some peace. The zone's creation made it harder to carry out short-range rocket attacks on Israel, and the withdrawal of the IDF from much of Lebanon greatly reduced casualties and otherwise created an illusion of normalcy for many Israelis. Over time Hizballah would shatter this illusion, but for several years the compromise measure appeared to work.

The zone, however, bolstered Hizballah. When Israeli forces withdrew to the security zone in 1985, Hizballah claimed an even greater accomplishment: it had forced back the mighty Israelis, the first time that Arab force of arms had accomplished that goal. At the same time Israel's continuing occupation cemented its control of southern Lebanon and gave it a reason to keep fighting the IDF. Many Lebanese, and increasingly much of the world, justified Hizballah's attacks on Israel in the name of legitimate national resistance.

Another problem was Israel's reliance on the SLA. By local standards the SLA was a competent fighting force, and as Ephraim Sneh, an Israeli politician who also held senior positions in the IDF working on Lebanon, points out, it fought hard "almost until the end." But the SLA was outmatched by Hizballah and was able to stay in the field only with considerable Israeli support. As part of the price for cooperation, SLA leaders demanded that their deployment include the Christian town of Jezzine, but doing so greatly stretched the size of the zone and made it far more vulnerable.[41] Because the Jezzine area is mountainous, the security zone had to be extended deep into Lebanon, well past the Litani River. This extension and the area's broken terrain provided Hizballah with many ambush opportunities and increased the number of Israeli casualties.

The Israelis also knew of—and tolerated—its proxy's legal and human rights abuses. Israel often relied on the SLA to run prisons that held Lebanese militants, including the notorious Khiam Detention Center. Because Israel controlled the territory and its intelligence services had full access to the facility this was a way of avoiding responsibility while still exploiting the information prisoners gave up to interrogators. (The United States faces similar temptations and risks when it works with authoritarian regimes against common terrorist foes.) SLA interrogations were often brutal. Human rights groups found that beatings and electric shocks were common.[42] Amnesty International reported that "detainees held [at Khiam] without charge or trial for up to 15 years were subjected to systematic torture, relentless interrogation through beatings, dousing with water and torture with electric shocks."[43] After Israel withdrew, Hizballah turned Khiam into a museum.

Israel's partial withdrawal from Lebanon was the first true military defeat the country had suffered. All in all four hundred Israelis would die in Lebanon during the war itself, and more than twice as many would perish before Israel pulled back to the security zone, more than it had lost in the 1956 war and almost as many it lost in its 1967 war.[44] Rather than cut bait Israeli leaders tried to minimize the country's loss with only a partial withdrawal. In so doing they only prolonged their country's suffering. For the next fifteen years Israel and Hizballah would spar repeatedly in clashes that enhanced the image of the Lebanese group and diminished that of Israel.

CHAPTER XV

THE RULES OF THE GAME: LIMITED WAR WITH HEZBOLLAH (1985-2000)

JEWS LIVING in Buenos Aires must have felt a world away from Israel's bitter war in Lebanon. Yet the war came to Argentina not once but twice: in 1992 Hizballah blew up the Israeli embassy and in 1994 it bombed the Jewish cultural center.

In planning these attacks Iran's minister of intelligence, Ali Fallahijan, worked closely with the Hizballah terrorist mastermind Imad Mughniyah. For the 1994 strike, Hizballah operative Ibrahim Hussein Berro drove a van filled with several hundred kilograms of explosives and parked it in front of the Asociación Mutual Israelita Argentina building. When the van exploded it killed eighty-five people and wounded at least 151 others.[1] Rosa Barreiro was walking in front of the building with her five-year-old son, Sebastian; she was severely wounded, and a blast fragment penetrated the child's skull.[2]

Hizballah's global reach appeared to be a major escalation in the conflict and astonished observers. Yet from Hizballah's point of view it was perfectly justifiable: Israel had provoked the Argentina bombings by breaking the unwritten rules of the conflict in Lebanon. On February 16, 1992, Israel had killed Hizballah's leader, Secretary General Sayyid Abbas Musawi, along with his wife and one-year-old baby and four other people. Musawi not only played a major role in founding Hizballah, but he also inspired, planned, and led many attacks. Israel hoped that Musawi's death would cripple the Lebanese organization, or at least cause a serious setback.

In contrast to many other Israeli killings of terrorist group leaders, the Musawi killing was done with little advance planning. One intelligence source told me that everyone in military intelligence opposed the operation, but that Chief of Staff Ehud Barak pushed for it anyway and convinced the defense minister and prime minister to proceed. Israel did not originally have a plan to kill Musawi, but the same intelligence official said that when Israeli intelligence learned he would be at a memorial service for Sheikh Ragheb Harb, whom the Israelis had killed at the outbreak of their war with Hizballah, they went forward with the operation. New optical surveillance platforms confirmed his presence, revealing that Musawi's four-car convoy of expensive Land Rovers looked different from the others in Jibshit, where the memorial was being held, and had special parking privileges. The information was processed in the late morning and the decision was made to go after Musawi. At 3:00 in the afternoon IDF helicopters swooped down and fired missiles that killed him and the others. As with so many Israeli attacks, the death of a legitimate target was disturbing because it included the deaths of innocents surrounding him. In part due to the speed required to make the decision, Israel was not able to gather the additional intelligence that Musawi's family was with him.

Killing Musawi violated the unwritten rules of the conflict, whereby both sides focused on the security zone. For several years Hizballah had largely refrained from launching rocket attacks on northern Israel. With Musawi's death this restraint ended, and Israel responded by bombing Lebanese villages. Hizballah also attacked a synagogue in Istanbul and blew up the car of an Israeli official in Ankara. It then launched the attack in Buenos Aires, which it saw as Israel's well-deserved punishment for the strike on Musawi. Perhaps Hizballah also believed the attack would serve as a deterrent to stop other Israeli strikes on its leaders.

In hindsight Israelis disagree on whether Musawi's killing was smart. One official involved in decision making at the time told me that no one expected Hizballah to retaliate as harshly it did. Some Israelis dismiss this criticism. Shabtai Shavit, who headed the Mossad at the time, contends, "If we had not killed Musawi, Hizballah would still kill Jews."

Musawi's killing and Hizballah's reaction highlighted the no-win situation Israel faced. Whenever the Israelis tried to break out of the stalemate and end the slow bleed it suffered in Lebanon with an innovative counterterrorism effort, Hizballah escalated its attacks on Israeli targets. In June 1994 Israel raided the Ayn Dardara training camp in the Bekaa Valley (well outside the security zone border), killing forty members of Hizballah with F-16 and helicopter strikes. In a different raid that same year Sayeret Matkal forces abducted Sheikh Mustafa Dirani to gain a bargaining chip in negotiations with Hizballah. Dirani was responsible for the capture of a downed aviator, Ron Arad, a navigator on an F-4 who bailed out of his plane in 1986, which probably was crippled after one of its bombs exploded prematurely under its wing.[3] (Israel hoped to gain information on Arad even if Hizballah would not negotiate for Dirani's release.)[4] In response (primarily to the attack on the training camp) Hizballah bombed the Israeli cultural center in Argentina.

Israeli law also began to make its weight felt. Initially Israel's Supreme Court had ruled that the Israelis could capture and detain individuals for reasons of state security, even if they themselves were not directly involved in violence, but in 2000 a judicial panel ruled that it was illegal to use detentions as "bargaining chips."

One unexpected long-term consequence for Israel was that Musawi's replacement as Hizballah's secretary general, Hassan Nasrallah, proved an exceptional leader. Israeli intelligence bitterly sings his praises too, though of course they also hope to kill him should the opportunity arise. One Israeli official described him to me as "a born leader of men." The replacement of Musawi by Nasrallah suggests an obvious though difficult lesson for all countries who kill terrorist leaders: know who will replace them. In addition, soon after the Musawi killing Iran began to provide Hizballah with long-range rockets.

Intelligence officials believed that killing Musawi was necessary because Hizballah was slowly gaining the upper hand. At first, Israel seemed to be winning. After Israel withdrew to the security zone, attacking Israeli targets became more difficult and Hizballah took many losses in reckless attacks on the IDF and the South Lebanon Army. The harsh Israeli reprisals alienated local residents from Hizballah. In contrast to Hizballah attacks before 1985, Lebanese civilians saw their suffering yielding little in return on the battlefield.

Israel also put in place a new set of defenses against Hizballah. Fences with sensors were placed along the border to stop infiltration, and sensors were used along potential guerrilla routes. Electronic countermeasures were used to jam or prematurely detonate improvised explosive devices (IEDs). Hospitals, police, and firefighters in Israel all were mobilized to respond to Hizballah attacks.[5]

Israel also reorganized its armed forces in Lebanon. Because there was little political support for operations in Lebanon, Israel wanted to keep casualties down at all costs, particularly among reserve units, about whom the Israeli public was exceptionally sensitive. To keep the pace of operations robust with less reserve involvement, in 1995 the IDF reconstituted a volunteer unit, Egoz (Hebrew for *almond* and an acronym for antiguerrilla and micro-warfare, *anti gerila ve-lohama zeira*) that was permanently based in Lebanon and conducted aggressive operations to disrupt Hizballah fighters and supply lines.

While many terrorist cells and groups—the Palestinians provide numerous examples—stagnated or collapsed in the face of such difficulties, Hizballah adapted and, over time, emerged as a more powerful and capable foe. Throughout the 1980s it consolidated its power in southern Lebanon near the security zone. It eclipsed the Palestinian groups, and later Amal, replacing "Fatahland" with "Hizballahland." Other groups still attacked Israel from southern Lebanon, but they did so only with Hizballah's blessing.

Nevertheless in the mid-1980s Hizballah was still a rag-tag military organization. "They failed every time," says the former intelligence official Barak Ben Zur in describing Hizballah's significant military operations against IDF posts in the mid-1980s. In the 1990s the group improved its forces in part by getting smaller, though gauging the exact size of Hizballah is difficult. Only a few of the organization's supporters are official members; the rest are "like supporters of a football club," according to the scholar Hala Jaber, who are loyal but not formally tied to the organization. As another Hizballah scholar Ahmad Nizar Hamzeh notes, "The fighter could be a carpenter, farmer, worker or student who is instructed at times to join his *majmu'ah* [group] to participate in fighting the enemy."[6] Still, in the 1980s Hizballah had perhaps five thousand full-time fighters and roughly the same number of reserves.[7] To fight Israel and the SLA it divided its forces into roughly five hundred to a thousand core fighters and three thousand to five thousand part-time fighters that included thousands more as volunteers who would join at short notice if necessary. By the time the Israelis withdrew from Lebanon in May 2000 Hizballah had approximately five hundred full-time fighters and another one thousand part-time cadres.[8]

Over time Hizballah became far more than a typical terrorist group, and terrorism was only a small part of its overall activities. It had specialists not only in guerrilla attacks, but also artillery, engineering, and communications. As one Israeli officer noted, "Hizb'Allah are a mini-Israeli army. They can do everything as well as we can."[9] Hizballah differentiated its terrorist actions from its guerrilla warfare organization. The Hizballah-run Islamic Jihad had a few hundred members under the control of Imad Mugniyeh, along with several other front groups such as the Revolutionary Justice Organization.[10] These smaller groups specialized in terrorism, planning suicide bombings, and taking hostages, thus allowing the broader movement the ability to deny its involvement in terrorism.

Militarily Hizballah's combat section became increasingly distinct. One part prepared for guerrilla warfare, one trained with rocket launchers, and another consisted of fighters who focused on surveillance and logistics. Hizballah also has an acclaimed sabotage unit, which proved superb at making roadside bombs. The IRGC helped with all these functions, and much of the advanced training occurred in Iran itself.[11]

Hizballah developed a sophisticated doctrine for fighting the Israelis. Haj Halil, an operational leader who promised "to pave South Lebanon with the skulls of Israeli soldiers," proclaimed thirteen principles that focused on guerrilla verities such as surprise, identifying Israeli weak points, slipping away "like smoke" in the face of Israeli responses, and wearing down the Israelis.[12]

To match this doctrine Hizballah changed its tactics. It had always used the standard guerrilla mix of light caliber weapons, roadside bombs, and surprise attacks but it now began to use heavy machine guns, mortars, and even surface-to-air missiles. Fighters could send tube-launched, optically tracked, wire-guided missiles through the windows of IDF and SLA outposts—impressive marksmanship.[13] Even so, Brig. Gen. Erez Gerstein, the commander of Israeli forces in southern Lebanon and an IDF legend, dismissed Hizballah, saying, "The bottom line is that the terrorists show films, but the bodies they leave with us."[14] He even claimed that Hizballah's ranks had so few veterans that it could not conduct sustained attacks on IDF forces.[15] Gerstein's underestimation of Hizballah cost him his life in 1999, when the Lebanese group detonated an IED as his car rounded a bend in southern Lebanon, sending it over the cliff in flames. Hizballah filmed the ambush and aired it on television.[16]

Hizballah responded to Israeli tactical changes by becoming increasingly adept at camouflaging its forces and the bombs they laid and using remote-controlled devices. Southern Lebanon is covered with shrubs and *wadis* (dried out riverbeds), both of which are ideal for ambushes.[17] Hit-and-run attacks against SLA positions caused steady attrition among those forces, and roadside ambushes against both the IDF and the SLA caused many casualties. Hizballah also used suicide bombers as a weapon in guerrilla war; from 1985 to 1999 it launched five suicide attacks on Israeli targets such as command posts, military camps, and motorcades.[18]

While Hizballah adapted, Israel was plagued by bureaucratic infighting. Shin Bet and military intelligence bickered, the latter accusing Shin Bet of being too harsh in its methods against the local population. At times the levels of brutality was high. Rafi Malka, a senior Shin Bet official, noted that in Lebanon, "in order to stay sane and stay alive, you had to do things that were unacceptable."[19] (Hizballah too was brutal, often executing informants for Israel.)[20] A particular bureaucratic problem was that Hizballah operated in the security zone, which was Shin Bet's responsibility, but was based outside it, where military intelligence held sway. Eventually a senior Israeli official with wide expertise on Lebanon and Shiism, Uri Lubrani, was brought in to coordinate activities; he improved cooperation but could not end the infighting.[21] One official involved claimed that even a decade later "everything was a mess."

As Hizballah's prowess grew, SLA members began to see themselves as "sandbags for an Israeli bunker," hardly an inspiring role.[22] Not surprisingly Hizballah penetrated the SLA. The organization's ranks were 50 percent Shi'a, and Hizballah coerced the families of those who refused to cooperate.

In 1997 twelve Israeli naval commandos died after Hizballah set an ambush for them at Ansouriyeh; some Israelis believe that an SLA member tipped them off, though this claim is disputed. Still, as the Israeli analyst Reuven Erlich noted, "It's Lebanon, and everyone was reporting to everyone." The IDF came to assume the SLA was penetrated even in cases where individual units were loyal, greatly complicating operations.[23] In January 2000 Hizballah assassinated Aql Hashim, an SLA leader, by putting a bomb inside his house. Defections grew as other SLA members, fearful of meeting a similar fate, began to cooperate.[24] When Lebanese anticipated the Israeli withdrawal Israel lost several important intelligence assets.[25]

Hizballah also gained the upper hand in a skill vital to any successful terrorist or guerrilla organization—counterintelligence—with a proficiency Fatah never achieved. With advice from Iran, Hizballah became expert at ferreting out potential infiltrators and ensuring secrecy within the group. Recognizing Israel's skills at signals intelligence, its members avoided, whenever possible, even encrypted phone calls.[26] By some estimates Hizballah now has more members dedicated to internal security than it does full-time fighters against Israel.[27] Family and tribe often form the basis for recruitment, particularly for the more elite units that carry out terrorism.

With cells around the world Hizballah has an external security section that operates so closely with Iran's intelligence that it is difficult to tell where one begins and the other ends. These cells form the core of Hizballah's global terrorism reach. In addition to the 1992 and 1994 Argentina attacks, in June 1993 they attempted to kill Jacques Kimche, a Jewish community leader, in Istanbul. Hizballah has also assisted others in terrorism, a mission that over time has become a core function. Besides the attacks in Buenos Aires, Hizballah and Iran worked together to conduct bombings in Paris in 1986 and shoot dissidents in Berlin in 1992.[28] The U.S. government concluded that a member of Hizballah assisted Saudi terrorists in making the tanker truck bomb that killed nineteen American soldiers at the U.S. military facility Khobar Towers in Saudi Arabia in 1996, a plot directed by Tehran.[29]

Hizballah cells have been found throughout Europe, Africa, South America, and Asia. Many of these networks are quite large; German officials estimate that there are nine hundred Hizballah activists in their country. Some of those who cooperate with Hizballah actively support the movement, and some simply fear it. Operatives in these cells provide logistical support for global attacks, raise money, recruit local operatives, and collect intelligence. For example, Hizballah has worked with the Lebanese Shi'a diaspora supporters in West Africa to raise money and identify potential operatives who receive further training in Iran and Lebanon.[30]

In 2001 U.S. investigators even uncovered a Hizballah cell in Charlotte, North Carolina, that was raising money for the organization. Many in the cell had grown up together in Beirut, and their families still lived there. Cell members purchased hundreds of cartons of cigarettes in low-tax North Carolina and resold them illegally in high-tax Michigan. They used the profits to buy night-vision devices, global positioning satellite systems, aircraft analysis and design software, and other sophisticated equipment.[31] The remaining profit was either sent directly to Hizballah or used to purchase items for it.[32]

Hizballah concentrated its efforts on fighting Israel and the SLA in Lebanon, but the group also continued to sponsor terrorist attacks inside Israel. In April 1996 Israel arrested Hussein Miqdad, a Lebanese citizen who infiltrated Israel with an explosive device hidden in a radio. While he was putting the bomb together it exploded, and he was seriously injured. In 1997, at a mosque in Germany, Hizballah recruited Steven Smyrek, a German convert to Islam educated in the United Kingdom. Smyrek traveled to Beirut, where Hizballah vetted him for his loyalty and then trained him in explosives. They sent him to Israel with money and a camera and orders to photograph potential targets. "The second stage should have been the suicide mission," Smyrek later said. "Two days before leaving Lebanon I was asked to be filmed on video. At the Hezbollah people's request, I spoke in English about how I was going to be a *shahid* [a Muslim martyr], and that the Zionists are our enemies." Smyrek was a perfect choice as an operative because he did not look like an Arab or come from an Arab country. Unbeknown to Hizballah, the Mossad had monitored Smyrek after he arrived in Lebanon, and Israel worked with Dutch police when Smyrek transferred to Europe in order to fly to Israel. In a shrewd move, Israeli officials deliberately let Smyrek enter the country rather than refuse him entry and have him strike elsewhere. They arrested him at the airport.[33]

Hizballah's military operations grew steadily. In the five-year period after Israel withdrew to its security zone in 1985, it conducted roughly one hundred attacks on Israeli forces. In the five years before Israel withdrew from Lebanon in 2000, Hizballah conducted almost five thousand attacks. These operations also became more effective and over time eroded Israeli public support for remaining in Lebanon. In the initial years of fighting Israel, Hizballah suffered a five-to-one or even higher ratio of losses to Israel; after 1995 their losses were two to one. Hizballah's operations became far more daring; they even planted IEDs near the Israeli border fence.[34]

Although Hizballah made its mark with suicide bombing, a new weapon entered its arsenal that became the symbol of the group to most Israelis: the Katyusha, which Fatah had used as early as 1968. The Katyusha rocket is an old Russian weapon system; its range is only twenty kilometers (twelve miles), and it is inaccurate. (Israelis often use the word "Katyusha" to describe a range of rockets, including the original system and more modern and long-range rockets such as the "Grad"). On the battlefield it doesn't offer much, yet as a weapon of terror against civilians it is highly effective. Indeed its very randomness is perhaps more frightening than an accurate weapon would be: a family in northern Israel never knows where the rocket will land.

Despite these many tactical changes, Hizballah's military strategy against Israel remained constant: inflict casualties, take hostages, and otherwise destroy Israel's will to fight. Naim Qassem, Hizballah's deputy secretary general, put this bluntly: "When an Israeli soldier is killed, senior Israeli officials begin crying over his death. . . . Their point of departure is preservation of life while our point of departure is preservation of principle and sacrifice."[35] This declaration is somewhat misleading: Hizballah does care about the lives of its fighters and personnel and does not sacrifice them wantonly.[36] Yet it also recognizes that it benefits politically from casualties, whereas Israeli leaders suffer from them.

Israel's classic strategy of hitting a government hard and forcing it to crack down on terrorism had little impact in Lebanon, where the government was too weak to move against Hizballah. Hizballah itself, however, did not offer an array of targets to strike as governments like Egypt and Syria did when Israel fought them. In 1994 Prime Minister Rabin criticized calls to get tough on Hizballah, saying, "There are no targets to retaliate against."[37] To reduce its casualties Israel started to fortify its positions and avoid patrols, a tactic that Israeli military professionals would later criticize as passive and against the spirit of the IDF. As a result Hizballah fighters found it even easier to penetrate the security zone and plant roadside bombs.[38] In response to attacks the IDF and the SLA shelled or bombed villages from which Hizballah operated.[39] Again, as with past efforts to turn the population against Hizballah, these attacks bolstered its popularity instead.

Israel tried to put pressure on parts of Lebanon outside the border areas, a move they hoped would force the Lebanese government to act decisively against Hizballah. The Israeli Navy blockaded parts of the coastline in southern Lebanon (and even Beirut during major flare-ups), a move that prevented fishermen from earning a livelihood. Israel demanded that Lebanese forces not search or harass cars going from the Israeli-controlled part of Lebanon to the rest of the country. To win over the Lebanese people, Israel gave money to newspapers to plant favorable stories. They supported a radio station, Mashrak, that broadcast into Lebanon, an effort they hoped would dramatize Israel's humanitarian efforts. They initiated a half-hearted civil aid program. To discourage popular assistance to the guerrillas, they dropped leaflets warning of retaliation for any attack.[40]

Over time the perception grew that Hizballah, not Israel, was winning, despite the body count in Israel's favor. The war that Israel would lose over and over again was the battle of propaganda. It was one that Hizballah and Israel's enemies grasped instinctively: in the fight against terrorism perception matters more than military results. For example, on October 27, 1994, IDF forces fled when Hizballah guerrillas stormed the Dabshe outpost in the security zone and replaced the Israeli flag with the Hizballah flag. Though the operation was militarily useless, it was a brilliant propaganda victory for Hizballah, and they filmed it to ensure it received wide attention. Even more devastating for Israeli soldiers, Hizballah hung banners on the Lebanese side of the border, just meters from Israeli military positions, showing gory images of the body parts of Sgt. Itamar Ilya, whom Hizballah killed in an ambush in 1997. Hizballah exchanged Ilya's body in 1998, but it continues to show these pictures as a warning to Israeli soldiers.

Describing Hizballah's propaganda tactics, Hizballah strategist Haj Halil said, "The media has innumerable guns, whose hits are like bullets," a point most Israelis failed to grasp.[41] Hizballah videotaped raids, but they only aired the successful ones. Their media trumpeted their successes, broadcasting in Hebrew to avoid any confusion. These broadcasts threatened Israelis, telling them that IDF strikes on Lebanon would lead to rocket attacks on settlements. More menacingly Hizballah launched a "Who's next?" series, showing photo after photo of Israeli casualties and ending with a question mark over the silhouette of another fallen Israeli.[42]

Beyond Terrorism

Hizballah is a terrorist group, but to use only that term is misleading. It is also a guerrilla force, a political party, a social service provider, and an ideology. Working with Iran, Hizballah has a vast social network of foundations and charities that expand its reach throughout Lebanon, providing money and other aid through the Martyrs' Agency, the Construction Jihad, and the Agency for the Injured, among other institutions. The Construction Jihad instructs farmers on how to improve their crop yields, and Hizballah provides daily drinking water to much of southern Beirut.[43] As in Hamas, the various wings work together. These organizations help Hizballah gain friends domestically and provide new venues for promoting its ideology of resistance. Its services are vital in Lebanon, particularly in the southern areas where the government does little for its citizens. Hizballah recruits from its social wing into its military units. Its politicians, who named their parliamentary bloc Loyalty to the Resistance, trumpet the group's battlefield accomplishments when they run for office.[44] During elections in the 1990s one political poster showed pictures of Hizballah fighters with the caption "They resist with their blood.

Resist with your vote."[45] Because of Hizballah's political strength it is difficult for the Lebanese government to crack down on, or even condemn, the group.

Hizballah's shift toward greater involvement in Lebanon's political scene began after 1990, when Syria consolidated power in Lebanon. Syria was always the dominant player in the country, but under the 1989 Taif Accord, which Arab powers negotiated to end Lebanon's civil war, Damascus's military presence and political dominance was sanctioned by the Arab League. Not all factions in Lebanon accepted this *pax Syriana*. Damascus formally exerted control when its troops crushed the forces of the last holdout, the Christian leader Michel Aoun, in October 1990. Syria deployed more than thirty-five thousand troops in Lebanon to impose its will and disarmed many of the militias.

Hizballah was the exception, but only partly so. Syria had long demanded that Hizballah toe the line, and Damascus carried a big stick to enforce its will. When Syria's leader Hafez al-Asad wanted to stop hostage taking in 1986 and 1988, Hizballah and Syria clashed directly over this issue.[46] But the power balance tilted further in Damascus's favor after 1990. In the late 1980s, when Syria attained its goals in Lebanon, Damascus sought more stability, or at least wanted to ensure that any violence directly served its ends. To weaken Hizballah Syria often backed Amal. Eventually a bloody battle between the two organizations led to Syrian forces joining the fray directly against Hizballah. Syria also interrupted and limited the flow of IRGC members and weapons from Iran, both of which transited Syria.[47] Indeed Israelis did not fully appreciate how much of the tentative normalcy depended on the Syrians. From 1993 on, Syria often blocked penetration from Lebanon to Israel to avoid an escalation and spoil peace talks.[48] As Human Rights Watch noted in a 1996 publication, "By controlling Hizballah's prime access to arms, Syria appears to hold considerable influence over Hizballah's ability to remain an active military force in the south."[49]

Hizballah's position on the disputed chunk of turf known as Shebaa Farms, a small strip of territory between Lebanon and the Golan Heights, is instructive. The UN accepted Israel's claims that Shebaa Farms is part of Syria, not Lebanon, and that Israel had completely withdrawn from Lebanon in 2000. Hizballah had never cared about Shebaa Farms, yet when Damascus sought a pretext to keep the pressure on Israel after it withdrew, Hizballah took up the cudgel and launched attacks ostensibly to drive Israel from the Shebaa Farms area.

Hizballah also lies low when Damascus wants to avoid a confrontation. When Syrian president Hafez al-Asad met with President Clinton in January 1994 Hizballah avoided attacks on Israel, and when U.S. pressure on Syria heated up before and after the war with Iraq, Hizballah also halted attacks on Israel, from January until August 2003, so as not to antagonize its patron.

Hizballah's military power, ties to Syria, and social network were enough to ensure that it could continue to attack Israel and pursue its goals with little interference from the government of Lebanon. When the civil war ended, however, the game inside Lebanon changed and participation in government—once an exercise in futility—now had new meaning. In 1992, after years of sneering at other Lebanese organizations for sullying their hands with daily politics and its inevitable compromises, Hizballah participated in elections even though the political system negotiated under the Taif Accord underrepresented Shi'as. The two most important positions under the new system went to the Sunni and Maronite Christian communities, and, as was true under the old system, the Shi'ia consolation was the speaker of the Parliament position, the third most important position in the government. Because the decision was so contentious, and because Hizballah's own leadership was split, the organization's leaders checked in with Iran, whose supreme leader approved the organization's open embrace of politics.[50]

For Lebanon's Shi'ia community, Hizballah was more than just an Islamist party. In 1992 only 13 percent of the Shi'as, who were not even a majority of Lebanese, wanted an Islamic republic in Lebanon. Yet Hizballah still did well in the polls.[51] Hizballah offered food and medicine to the poor, helped rebuild neighborhoods devastated by the civil war, and provided a safety net in a country where none existed. Most important its fighters had driven the Israelis out of much of Lebanon. The grinding struggle and the appearance of success of Hizballah against Israel gave credibility to the movement. Nasrallah's son Hadi died fighting the Israelis in 1997, a sacrifice that bestowed upon Nasrallah—in contrast to virtually every other Arab leader—the stature of personal sacrifice.

Surprisingly Hizballah also garnered the respect of Lebanon's non-Shi'as. Its leaders had a reputation for being less corrupt than other Lebanese elites (admittedly a low bar), and its extensive schools and hospitals for the poor won many friends in other communities. As one Christian who voted for Hizballah explained to a would-be rival, "Where were you when we needed emergency snow removal and fuel? In this village, everyone is going to vote for Hizballah."[52] When all of Lebanon's militias stained their reputation by shedding the blood of other Lebanese, Hizballah focused primarily on Israel; its participation in the civil war was primarily limited to an internecine struggle with Amal. Rather than calling for an Islamic state or imposing its interpretation of Islamic law over areas where it ruled, Hizballah emphasized concern for the poor and stressed its resistance activities. As a result many Lebanese saw it as a national movement rather than one that was focused only on the Shi'as.

Hizballah's fundraising reflects its multiple dimensions. Iran, as noted, regularly gives roughly two hundred million dollars a year to the organization. But Hizballah also raises hundreds of millions from charitable giving by Lebanese abroad and at home, taxes on businesses in Hizballah areas, criminal activity, and even Lebanese government financing of Hizballah-run projects.[53]

Perhaps the most important wing of Hizballah is its information operations. Although the quintessential American image of the group may be a suicide bomber launching himself against U.S. marines and diplomats, many Arabs see Hizballah as embodied by Hassan Fadlallah, the news director of its television station Al Manar, or Imad Marmal or Batool Ayoub Naim, the hosts of two popular television shows. Al Manar's primary purpose is to spread Hizballah's message throughout the Arab world, offering news and exhortations with a strong Hizballah slant. One Al Manar series, *The Diaspora*, detailed a supposed Jewish plot to dominate the world. Not surprisingly Al Manar is particularly popular in Gaza. In 1984 it launched a weekly newspaper, *The Pledge*, and several years later it launched its radio station, Al Nour.

This brief depiction of a multifaceted Hizballah suggests that the organization has moved beyond its early reliance on terrorism. But top Hizballah fighters still play key roles in the group's decision-making bodies, and as the scholar Ahmad Nizar Hamzeh contends, "Hizbullah is first and foremost a *jihadi* movement that engages in politics, and not a political party that conducts jihad."[54]

Israel's Response: Operation Accountability

As Hizballah became stronger and stronger Israel found itself fighting a grinding war of attrition against an increasingly capable foe.

In June 1993 the struggle that had long been in the background regained the headlines when Hizballah launched rocket attacks on Kiryat Shemona. In July an attack by the Popular Front for the Liberation of Palestine—General Command led to several IDF casualties. The soldiers of the Givati Brigade had been on a routine operation near the edge of the security zone, where gunmen from the PFLP-GC lay in ambush. Although the squad spotted the ambush, they took heavy casualties in defeating it.[55]

Israel responded by attacking a PFLP-GC base and shelling a Hizballah stronghold. Hizballah continued the fighting, attacking a joint IDF and SLA post that resulted in even more Israeli casualties, a total of five. From that point on, the back and forth continued, with more Israeli and SLA losses and heavy Israeli shelling of Lebanese villages. When Hizballah launched several Katyusha rockets at the Galilee in response, Israel decided to mount a more massive operation. No single act was excessive in the context of the now eight-year-long struggle over the security zone, yet taken together this was an extremely bloody toll for Israel, the worst it had suffered in such a short period in many years.

Israel responded with Operation Accountability (known in Lebanon as the Seven-Day War) from July 25 to July 31, 1993. It began with a heavy initial bombing effort; gunboats and warplanes blasted the outskirts of Lebanese villages, which had mostly been evacuated after Israeli warnings.[56] Helicopters attacked Palestinian refugee camps. Hizballah responded by firing more Katyushas at the security zone and Israel proper. One attack killed two civilians in Kiryat Shemona, a rare case of accuracy that, whatever satisfaction it may have produced in Hizballah circles, increased Israel's determination to respond.[57] Israel then launched a series of helicopter, fighter jet, and artillery strikes in the Bekaa Valley and southern Lebanon.

Israel sought not only to destroy Hizballah facilities and headquarters, but also to hit the organization hard enough to prevent it from launching future attacks of this scale. It hoped that Hizballah's use of civilian shields and the ensuing civilian suffering would turn the population against the organization.[58] The Israeli Cabinet declared, "Israel will not allow firing from within villages and will not permit Hezbollah to conceal itself among the civilian population and from there launch Katyushas at communities in the north."[59] The Israeli assault killed around 120 Lebanese and injured almost five hundred more. In addition 300,000 residents of southern Lebanon fled their homes during the operation, while Hizballah's rocket strikes in response killed two Israeli civilians and injured twenty-four; one soldier died when an antitank missile struck his tank. Israeli officials estimate that Hizballah lost between fifty and seventy-five guerrillas in the fighting, while Lebanese and international sources put the figure far lower, at eight.[60]

Israel tried to turn the population against Hizballah and force the government of Lebanon to quash the group. Deputy Defense Minister Ori Orr noted, "The Lebanese government can do more. It must understand that Lebanon's gross domestic product will not grow."[61] Prime Minister Rabin declared, "We have said repeatedly that, if security and quiet will not prevail in our northern towns and villages, there will be no security and quiet for residents of southern Lebanon north of the security zone." He made the point that it was up to the Lebanese government to end its people's suffering: "Your government has the option of empowering the Lebanese military to prevent Katyusha fire at Israel. Only if fire at Israel's northern communities will cease, will you be able to return to your homes in southern Lebanon."[62] Human Rights Watch found that by the end of the operation a thousand homes had been destroyed and another fifteen hundred partially destroyed; many more suffered light damage. For good measure an IDF helicopter also rocketed the grave of Sheikh Harb, punctuating his death by Israeli forces ten years earlier.[63]

Both U.S. and Israeli officials charge that Hizballah deliberately used civilians to shield its fighters from Israeli attacks. This practice, common in guerrilla warfare, poses a tremendous challenge for militaries like Israel's and America's. Guerrillas take advantage of the deaths of innocent civilians to portray Israel (or the United States) to the world as a brutal occupying force, which in turn decreases public support for military operations and helps Hizballah recruit new members. Human Rights Watch, which in general is highly critical of IDF operations, found at least one case where Hizballah stored weapons in a village. Though Israel did warn villagers to leave their homes, some civilians remained, particularly those without the means to leave, and human rights organizations contend that Hizballah's use of human shields did not justify the number of children and other noncombatants killed in Israeli attacks.[64] Indeed in the end Israel looked both ineffective and cruel, a devastating combination.

The problem with the approach by human rights organizations is that it does not allow Israel a low-casualty option for striking at Hizballah. The only way to discriminate carefully between Hizballah fighters and noncombatants is to send troops into each town in brutal urban operations, as in Jenin; the alternative is to allow the presence of civilians, to preclude any effective military response. Either way, Israel loses.

Throughout the operation Hizballah continued to lob rockets into northern Israel. For inhabitants of the region the random nature of the rocket fire made the continuation of normal daily life all but impossible. Hizballah's ambition was to use the continued suffering of Israeli civilians as a way to coerce Israel into stopping its attacks. Ironically this mirrored Israel's strategy with Hizballah, but with one important difference: Israeli politicians lost support when civilians suffered, whereas Hizballah gained support. For Hizballah, even the back-and-forth fighting was a form of success: no one expected the group to win, so just staying in the game was a victory.

Before Operation Accountability Israel had partially escaped from the "glass house" problem that had plagued its counterinsurgency and counterterrorism campaigns in Lebanon. As one IDF colonel noted, operations in Lebanon were far less constricted than in the West Bank: "In south Lebanon, there is nothing between you and God Almighty. The only question you ask yourself when you are going to blow up someone's house is whether to use 50 kilos of dynamite or 25 kilos."[65] Now more extensive operations such as Accountability focused media attention on Israel once again. One former Israeli journalist wrote that Accountability "seemed specially designed for Israel bashers. What could be better fodder than pictures of thousands of civilians abandoning their homes to the sound of Israeli cannons?"[66]

When both sides agreed to a ceasefire on July 31 Hizballah emerged as the victor. Despite Israel's military superiority, Hizballah proved superior in two crucial aspects: its ability to tolerate pain and its success in turning losses into a propaganda victory.

After the operation Hizballah and Israel informally agreed to a set of unwritten rules to limit the conflict. Both sides made their red lines clear.

For Israel, the red line was the cessation of rocket fire into Israel; for Hizballah, it was stopping all attacks on civilians in the south. Hizballah's deputy secretary general Sheikh Naim Qassem warned, "Whenever the Israeli enemy shells and harms civilians in our villages, we will shell northern Palestine and the Israeli settlements."[67]

War within the security zone, however, could continue without interruption. For several years the understanding seemed to work. When Israel bombed a house in the village of Deir al-Zahrani in 1994 and mistakenly killed seven civilians, it did not retaliate after Hizballah fired rockets at northern Israel, recognizing this as an acceptable response given the civilian casualties it had inflicted.[68]

Although the 1993 understanding limited the war, it did so in a way that favored Hizballah in the long term. The understanding recognized the Lebanese militant organization and Syria, not the Lebanese government, as key actors. The red lines of course protected Lebanon's civilian population from the often harsh Israeli attacks, thus reducing any potential backlash from Hizballah's supporters. Internationally the lines legitimated Hizballah attacks on Israeli soldiers. Because the war was limited to the security zone Hizballah could now control the rate of its own casualties: it could force the IDF to fight, but not the other way around. The war boiled down to a contest of attrition, which heavily favored the less casualty-sensitive Hizballah. Indeed success was now measured according to the metric of peace for northern settlements rather than fighting Hizballah. When Israel did not retaliate after the killing of nine soldiers in 1995 Prime Minister Rabin said, "Our main aim was to allow the Israelis and the children on summer holiday to enjoy themselves."[69] Perhaps most important the red lines enabled Syria to keep the cauldron bubbling while it negotiated with Israel without the risk of attacks spiraling out of control.

Grapes of Wrath

Although the lines drawn after Accountability seemed clear, in practice there was considerable ambiguity. Each side engaged in a tit-for-tat battle of retaliation when they disagreed and each reserved the right to retaliate against civilians. The possibility of violence spiraling out of control was enormous.

The responsibility for the spiral that led to the April 1996 Grapes of Wrath operation remains disputed. In the weeks before it commenced, a series of attacks and reprisals left seven Israeli soldiers, one Hizballah fighter, and three Lebanese civilians dead. After the IDF shelled the village of Yatar, Hizballah responded by conducting rocket attacks on Israeli civilian sites, which led to more Israeli artillery strikes.[70]

Yet for both Hizballah and the Israeli government, broader concerns, particularly the peace process with the Palestinians and, on a separate track, the Syrians, contributed to the fighting. For Israel, the horrific deaths from the Hamas bus bombings and the bloody Dizengoff Center suicide attack in February and March of 1996 created political pressure for tough action, but the continuation of peace talks with the Palestinians precluded retaliation in the West Bank or Gaza. During the tight race for prime minister that year, the challenger, Benjamin Netanyahu, lambasted Prime Minister Shimon Peres: "Our children are afraid to get on a bus. Many of you who are watching us now are getting up in the morning and asking yourselves whether the next attack will happen today. Mr. Peres, you brought our security situation to a nadir, and this is a direct result of your terrible policy."[71] So Peres found an enemy to demonstrate his toughness. Syria meanwhile was miffed that Israel was focusing on the Palestinian track and wanted to refocus Israel's attention on Damascus's concerns. Hafez al-Asad pointed out, "There can be no security for Israel while Arab land is occupied."[72]

For sixteen days in April 1996 Israel carried out Grapes of Wrath, an operation that killed 154 Lebanese civilians and only a few fighters, perhaps twenty-four in all. Once again Israel tried to target Hizballah leadership sites directly and put pressure on the Lebanese government by destroying the Lebanese infrastructure, and once again the Israeli attacks led to massive displacements, as 400,000 or so Lebanese fled the south to escape the war. Israel's goal was to make sure that Hizballah's supporters knew the price of backing the group.[73]

Grapes of Wrath came to an ignominious end after Israeli artillery shells hit a refugee compound at the UN post in Qana, killing more than a hundred civilians who had taken shelter there. The IDF claimed that Hizballah forces had fired from the Qana area and that in response the IDF mistakenly overshot the fighters' position; thus any resulting civilian deaths should be laid at Hizballah's door for cynically shielding their fighters with civilians. Several Israelis I talked to pointed out that, conspiracy theories aside, there was no reason for Israel to deliberately hit the UN compound. Other investigations, including one by the UN itself, reject this claim, contending that Hizballah's operations were sufficiently far from the compound (and that the compound's location was well known), so the strike was not legitimate. Moreover the UN report indicates that Israel fired seventeen projectiles at or near the compound, suggesting that the problem was not simply an errant shell or two, and that two or three Hizballah fighters had entered the compound, probably to see their families.[74] The UN report, however, does note that the IDF had been fired upon from an area near the compound and that a Fijian UN force member who tried to stop Hizballah was shot in the chest.

Hizballah and Israel struck yet another deal. According to the "April Understanding," Hizballah agreed this time not to carry out attacks into

Israel proper, and in response the IDF and the SLA agreed not to target civilians or civilian areas in Lebanon itself (that is, where Hizballah's base was).[75] One Israeli military officer involved in the monitoring explained that the goal in the late 1990s was to take Israeli civilians out of the equation. France, Syria, Lebanon, and the United States formed an International Monitoring Group to arbitrate should disagreements occur about the rules. For the most part both sides tried to honor these rules; Israel would apologize when it unintentionally attacked Syrian forces helping Hizballah, and Hizballah apologized for Katyusha attacks in 1998 that violated the understanding. Similarly Israel would at times accept that a Hizballah attack on Israeli soldiers followed the accepted rules.[76]

By any measure Grapes of Wrath was a failure for Israel. The 1996 ceasefire was in its essence similar to the 1993 ceasefire: Israel was still confined to a struggle whose rules favored its opponent. Although Israel killed few fighters, it did kill many civilians, including children, and these deaths were captured on film. And again, instead of rejecting Hizballah, the operation increased its popularity among the non-Shi'a Lebanese.[77] Reinforced by the images of civilian suffering, the Qana disaster created a perception of IDF incompetence and cruelty. In a foreshadowing of the 2006 war the IDF strikes not only failed to prevent Hizballah from launching rockets, but led to an increase in the number of attacks.

Israeli leaders should have learned several lessons from both Accountability and Grapes of Wrath and from its many years occupying southern Lebanon. But as Israel would demonstrate in 2006, these lessons did not stick. Israel has never seemed to recognize that victory is a matter of political perception as much as results on the ground. So long as Hizballah remained defiant, the casualty ratios or other standard measures of military effectiveness did not matter. Israel had to confront the unpleasant reality that it would be condemned for attacks on civilians even if Hizballah used them as shields for its activities. Moreover, as Israeli general Baruch Spiegel points out, "some bombs will always miss." Given how dense many populated areas are in Lebanon, "if you miss one bomb by a hundred meters, it becomes a strategic problem and you are finished."

The failed operations also revealed that Damascus called the shots in Lebanon, a reality Israel both accepted and ignored. As Amnon Lipkin-Shahak, who headed the IDF for part of the 1990s, told me, "Lebanon is not a government. Lebanon is a group of factions." A fundamental flaw in Israel's coercive strategy was that Syria was more than willing to fight to the last Lebanese: the Syrian regime didn't suffer when Israel hit its neighbor. Even in Lebanon blame for the suffering would fall first on Israel and then on the government in Beirut. So long as peace did not serve Syria's interests, the war would continue. Eitan Azani, a former intelligence officer in Lebanon, contended "Asad was willing to let all the Lebanese die."

Israel's attacks increased Hizballah's popularity because, unlike the Lebanese Army, it was fighting back. The organization had long promoted itself as a resistance group, and this image became popular not only among the Shi'as, but also among most Sunnis and Druze and even many Christians.[78] As a result even the government of Lebanon did not call for Hizballah to stop shelling Israel. Not surprisingly Lebanese civilians tended to blame Israel and its jets and artillery for the loss of their homes and the deaths of civilians rather than the Hizballah fighters who instigated the conflict.

This Syrian-Israeli-Lebanese drama played out while the United Nations watched. In the fifteen years of the security zone's existence, one thing became clear: the United Nations was not the solution. The United Nations Interim Force in Lebanon deployed close to five thousand soldiers from nine bases in Lebanon. Its mandate, however, was limited to overseeing the withdrawal of Israeli troops. It did not have the mandate or the military force to prevent Hizballah's attacks or the Israeli response. Instead UNIFIL looked on ineffectually as the violence continued.

Grapes of Wrath marked the last major IDF operation in Lebanon until the 2006 war. For the most part Israeli forces were on the defensive; only a few elite units conducted raids. At times artillery, attack helicopters, and aircraft were used to strike at Hizballah infrastructure. Israel became much more effective when it changed its military operations in the late 1990s. Amos Malka, who headed Israeli military intelligence for several years, points out that in 1999–2000 Israel improved its military operations and shifted from deep raids to active defense.[79] Before this period Israeli special forces attacked five to fifteen kilometers behind Hizballah lines using large units. Each operation was time-consuming, and Hizballah often attacked the troops with antitank missiles and IEDs as they went back and forth. With active defense, however, Israel concentrated on the existing security zone line, conducting more operations but integrating them effectively with intelligence to close down penetrations. Hizballah sputtered militarily, and Israeli casualties fell. This success, however, arrived too late to affect public opinion: in the 1999 election Ehud Barak ran successfully on a promise to end Israel's role in Lebanon.

In the background of Israel's military back and forth with Hizballah in the 1990s was the prospect of peace with Syria. According to Itamar Rabinovich, one of Israel's chief Syria specialists and negotiators, Rabin hoped that making a deal with Syria would solve Israel's Hizballah and Lebanon problems. Negotiations faltered after Rabin's death. Instead of a deal with Syria, Israeli leaders believed they could extricate themselves from the Lebanese quagmire simply by leaving.

CHAPTER XVI

THE FALSE PROMISE OF NORMALCY (2000–2006)

"THIS 18-YEAR tragedy is over," Prime Minister Ehud Barak declared as the last Israeli soldier left Lebanon on May 24, 2000.[1] With those words Barak fulfilled his campaign promise to end Israel's involvement in Lebanon. In all more than fifteen hundred Israelis died in Lebanon from the 1982 invasion until the 2000 withdrawal; more than three hundred of them fell following the withdrawal to the security zone in 1985.[2] Hizballah, however, would soon make Barak's words ring hollow.

The withdrawal itself was humiliating. Almost until the end the IDF reassured its Lebanese proxy, the SLA, that Israel would stay. Barak even avoided giving the IDF information on the precise date of a withdrawal in order to avoid a leak and a public dustup.[3] When the order came IDF officers told them, "From now on, your fate is in your hands."[4] SLA proxy units collapsed one by one. Several thousand officers, soldiers, and their families fled to Israel rather than risk retribution from Hizballah. Politically the withdrawal was a gift to Hizballah, which correctly touted its own role in forcing Israel to leave. Lebanese crowds gathered along the border to taunt the Israelis on the other side.[5]

A mixture of despair and hope led to Barak's decision. The IDF's presence in Lebanon had become a millstone around the neck of Israeli leaders. As Hizballah inflicted a steady stream of Israeli casualties the consensus behind the Israeli military presence in Lebanon crumbled.

A turning point in Israeli public support for continued operations in Lebanon occurred after two helicopters collided in February 1997, killing seventy-three soldiers. Though the accident was not due to enemy fire, the crash led to the formation of the Four Mothers group, which became the basis of a broader movement that questioned the IDF's role in Lebanon. The movement received further impetus in September 1997, after Hizballah's ambush of an elite Israeli naval assault unit resulted in eleven Israeli deaths. The raw casualty numbers and the growing sense that Israel had no strategy for victory eroded political support for the occupation. In 1997 79 percent of Israelis opposed withdrawing from Lebanon; by May 2000 70 percent favored leaving, even if it was a unilateral step. And unlike in the West Bank, there were no Israeli settlements in Lebanon.

More optimistically many observers also believed that an Israeli withdrawal would leave Hizballah with no agenda. A number of Israeli security officials emphasized what seemed to be obvious: Why would Hizballah risk its 2000 victory and Lebanon's economic prosperity by renewing the conflict with Israel? Moreover Barak hoped the withdrawal would build "an invisible wall of illegitimacy" that would lead Hizballah to refrain from attacking Israel.[6] In essence this logic pitted Hizballah's military wing against its political and social wings. Removing its military raison d'être would transform Hizballah into a more normal, less violent political movement. Or so Israel hoped.

Another part of this assessment was the decline in ferocity of Hizballah's state sponsors. When Barak took power in 1999, Syria and Israel were negotiating over the Golan Heights (though Israel had recently decided to focus on the Palestinian peace track over that of the Syria). Implicit in these talks was the assumption that if peace were achieved, Syria would prevent Hizballah from attacking Israel. Walid al-Mualim, Syria's ambassador to the United States, made the promise of peace clear, noting that Hizballah leaders understood "that every agreement accepted by Syria, Israel, and Lebanon [would] obligate it as well."[7] From Israel's perspective Hizballah's relationship with Iran also appeared to be changing for the better. After Ayatollah Khomeini died in 1989 Hizballah's leaders lost some of the veneration they felt for their Iranian sponsors, and Iran's leaders also sought more distance. In the mid-1990s the government led by President Akbar Hashemi Rafsanjani reduced funding for Hizballah and became less enthusiastic about exporting Iran's Islamic revolution.[8] The years that followed appeared even more promising. Iran, under the reformist leadership of President Mohammad Khatami who succeeded Rafsanjani, appeared to be moving toward the West. Hizballah's own rhetoric seemed to cautiously follow this moderate trend. In an interview shortly before the Israeli withdrawal Hizballah Secretary General Hassan Nasrallah claimed that although Hizballah opposed peace with Israel, it would not "make any turmoil out of it" if the Lebanese government signed a peace treaty.[9]

Unfortunately Israel's unilateral withdrawal sowed the seeds of later problems. Israel did not trust the United Nations to police the border, fearing that if it was forced to resume military operations in Lebanon it would be hampered by the UN presence. And Israel had contempt for the Lebanese government. So it did not hand over its security in southern Lebanon to any partner, but indirectly to Hizballah itself.

The success of this gamble depended on whether Israel could make deterrence work. As Israeli troops readied for departure, Barak swore, "I would like to see anybody dare to fire on our soldiers or settlements now. We will know what to do, the IDF is free to fight back," and he warned, "The land of Lebanon will be set on fire [should this happen]."[10] It was possible to make good on Barak's threats, but also quite risky: efforts to deter Hizballah in the 1990s had failed, and similar efforts to deter the PLO before that had also collapsed. Too much depended on transforming Hizballah into a moderate, nonviolent organization. For this policy to work it would be necessary for Israel to respond to Hizballah's provocations harshly—a threat easy to promise but hard to deliver, as Israel soon found out.

Yet this is a caveat drawn in hindsight. It is fair to say that in 2000 Hizballah was at a crossroads. The Lebanese resistance organization had to struggle with a problem that other terrorist groups would have envied: what to do when you've won. Looking back at Hizballah's founding, two key goals had been met: Western influence (exemplified by U.S. and French peacekeepers) had been brought to heel, and the dreaded Israelis had fled Lebanon. Hizballah's other major objective—spreading Iran's revolutionary credo to Lebanon—had over the years become a more remote principle rather than an immediate goal. Even the emotive Israeli-Palestinian issue seemed less important as peace loomed. In victory Hizballah had emerged magnanimous, treating most former SLA fighters and their families with leniency. When it did arrest SLA members it turned them over to the Lebanese government, which, after a trial, imposed fines on many and imprisoned some—not the mass executions that SLA members feared.

From an Israeli point of view, Hizballah's demands, though still unacceptable, were no longer categorical. By the end of the decade Nasrallah was focused on three things: an Israeli withdrawal from Lebanon and the Golan Heights, a return of Hizballah prisoners, and the Palestinian refugees' right to return (a sensitive issue for Lebanese Shi'as, who emphatically wanted the Palestinians out of Lebanon). These demands were a far cry from the uncompromising manifesto of 1985. Moreover Hizballah's willingness to adhere to the red lines and to focus on military over civilian targets led many Israelis to believe that pulling out of Lebanon would not result in Hizballah's targeting Israel proper.[11]

Despite these promising signs, a return to violence always loomed. To no one's surprise the Lebanese government never moved to disarm

Hizballah. Nor did Syria, Lebanon's landlord. As Israel withdrew, it was not the Lebanese Army but Hizballah that brought its fighters and weapons to the border and set up observation posts. Although Hizballah's ideological fervor waned, it never completely disappeared. According to Hizballah, Israeli-occupied land not only included Lebanon but all Muslim territory under non-Muslim control, particularly historic Palestine.

Resistance works—that was Hizballah's lesson. In a speech at Bint Jbeil after the Israeli withdrawal Nasrallah crowed that even though Israel has nuclear weapons and a mighty air force, "Israeli society is as weak as a spider web": it looks strong from far away, but if you reach out your hand you can sweep it aside. This statement is at the core of Hizballah's resistance: they believe that for all of Israel's technological superiority, it is morally weak, whereas Hizballah's steadfastness will allow it to prevail despite its material weakness.[12]

The withdrawal did not end Hizballah attacks on Israel. On October 7, 2000, just after the Second Intifada broke out, Hizballah staged a demonstration near the border of Shebaa Farms that turned bloody. While this was going on, Hizballah fighters ambushed an Israeli patrol at a poorly defended point in the Israeli defensive line and brought three of their bodies with them into Lebanon. (Whether the soldiers died during or shortly after the operation is not clear.) Hizballah artillery then shelled Israeli posts to cover the retreat. One militant involved in the operation claimed, "After 40 minutes, we already transferred the captives to a safehouse."[13] Just over a week later Hizballah, this time cooperating with Iranian intelligence, kidnapped Elhanan Tannenbaum, a reserve IDF colonel and Israeli businessman, whom Hizballah claims was an Israeli spy. Tannenbaum had huge gambling debts, so Hizballah lured him to a meeting with the promise of a lucrative drug deal.[14]

Nasrallah claims that Hizballah began to emphasize kidnappings of Israeli soldiers after the withdrawal because that was the only way to force Israel to release prisoners. Jawad Kasafi, a Hizballah prisoner in Israel, responded to the news this way: "I knew for sure that I had hope, that's it, we are going to be released."[15] Hizballah in 2004 traded Tannenbaum and the remains of the dead soldiers for 435 prisoners, many of them Palestinians. The released prisoners praised Hizballah and Nasrallah, recognizing that their military actions—not Arafat's negotiations—led to the release.[16]

In hindsight the October 7 kidnapping was a missed opportunity for Israel to demonstrate its commitment to deterrence. The withdrawal in 2000 in essence meant a strategic shift from prevention via the security zone to deterrence: Barak, after all, had threatened massive force should Hizballah continue attacks. Gen. Moshe Kaplinsky, who headed IDF forces in Lebanon during and after the withdrawal, points out that the IDF knew in 2000 that Hizballah would deploy its forces along the border after the

IDF withdrew and that it would continue to strike Israel. Israeli politicians, however, promised that the IDF would teach Hizballah a lesson by retaliating harshly after the first attack on Israel. This promise was not kept. After the kidnapping the IDF did conduct limited strikes on Lebanon, and the Israeli Air Force bombed the Syrian radar in Lebanon, but these attacks were pinpricks. At the time Barak claimed, "We are reserving the right to respond at the time we see fit,"[17] but more cynical Israelis believe he did not want to respond in a way that would suggest that withdrawal had been a mistake. So in the end momentum for teaching Hizballah a lesson or otherwise bolstering Israeli deterrence faded as Israeli politicians focused on the Second Intifada and the kidnapping disappeared from the headlines. In 2002, during Operation Defensive Shield in the West Bank, Hizballah launched a limited rocket attack as a show of solidarity with the Palestinians. Once again Israel failed to act.

For Hizballah, deterrence was only partial, though Israel acted as if it were complete. The former head of military intelligence Amos Malka writes that during this period "Israel successfully deterred Hezbollah from initiating strikes against civilian targets but failed to deter it from continuously striking military targets in northern Israel, involving itself in terrorism in the Palestinian theater operationally and logistically, and from acquiring strategic weapons [long-range rockets]. On the other hand, Hezbollah successfully deterred Israel from striking Lebanese civilians or infrastructures, and even from striking the organization's high-ranking figures."[18] Because the group knew Israel would always hesitate before escalating, the rockets made it difficult for Israel to threaten it.

Hizballah's demands for prisoners did not end with the 2004 exchange, as several other Hizballah members remained in Israeli hands. The group also claimed Samir Kuntar, a Lebanese Druze, as one of their own. Despite Kuntar's deliberate and brutal killing of a four-year-old and other members of the Haran family, Nasrallah declared him to be "a national treasure."[19] For Israelis, this was a particularly odious addition, though they would later stomach it and swap Kuntar. (The Israelis I talked to see Hizballah as an enemy, but their hatred is mixed with respect, in contrast to their views of terrorists like Kuntar.)

In November 2005 Nasrallah reiterated the "duty to capture Israeli soldiers and swap them for Arab prisoners in Israel," and the organization declared 2006 to be the "year of retrieving prisoners." Nabih Berri, Lebanon's speaker of the Parliament, later claimed that Hizballah had attempted eleven kidnappings.[20]

In the months and years that followed, Hizballah fired at and bombed IDF posts and convoys (usually in the Mt. Dov sector, in which Shebaa Farms is located). They rocketed an IDF post in the Reches Ramim area, fired mortars from across the border, and otherwise harassed Israel. Between the Israeli withdrawal and the 2006 conflict, Hizballah directly killed twenty-one Israelis (mostly soldiers) and injured thirty-six more.[21] For the most part it avoided constant strikes against civilians in northern Israel, using this threat as a deterrent should Israel choose to escalate.

Although it received little notice at the time, Hizballah also attempted several other kidnappings and conducted cross-border operations in addition to the October 7 kidnapping. In March 2002 Hizballah (or possibly PIJ) fighters shot across the border into northern Israel, killing six. Later in 2002 and in 2003 Hizballah mortar, rocket, and anti-aircraft fire killed one Israeli and wounded others. In 2005 a firefight along the border led to the death of one soldier.[22] Most ambitiously, on November 21, 2005, Hizballah tried to distract Israeli attention with a mortar barrage while an elite force crossed the border to attack a paratroop unit. Alerted to the crossing, the unit evacuated its post and one sharpshooter shot four Hizballahis.[23] Several weeks later Hizballah fired rockets into Kiryat Shemona, wounding three Israelis. However, the IDF seemed to ignore the broader lesson: that Hizballah was active and planning sophisticated operations. As the Winograd Commission, a group of experts charged with investigating Israel's performance in the 2006 war with Hizballah, later put it, "The next abduction was just a matter of time and it was doubtful it could be avoided."[24]

Israel's clandestine operations against Hizballah focused on the organization's links to the Palestinians. On July 19, 2004, Ghaleb Awwali, a senior Hizballah operative involved in support for Palestinian groups, was killed in Beirut, an operation Hizballah blamed on Israel. On May 26, 2006, Israel killed the Palestine Islamic Jihad liaison with Hizballah. Other attacks killed Hizballah liaisons to groups in the West Bank and Jihad Jibril, the son of the founder of the radical Popular Front for the Liberation of Palestine–General Command, who ran that organization's operations in the Second Intifada.[25]

Hizballah's state sponsors also changed. Each year after the withdrawal they grew more aggressive toward Israel. Talks between Israel and Syria on the Golan had collapsed, and with the Palestinian Intifada raging Israelis had little appetite for sitting down once more with the Syrians. But without peace talks, Syria now had an incentive to use violence to assure that the Golan issue remained on the agenda. In 2002 Syria began transferring to Hizballah 222mm rockets that have a range of between twelve and eighteen miles, several miles farther than the Katyushas, which have a maximum range of twelve miles.[26] Iran would transfer even long-range rockets to Hizballah as well.

Further complicating matters, politics in Lebanon changed completely. On February 14, 2005, Rafik Hariri, Lebanon's former prime minister and a critic of Syria, was assassinated. The assumption at the time was that Syrian agents killed Hariri, though in 2010 it would be revealed that Hizballah operatives played a major role. Syria had routinely killed

Lebanese politicians in the past, but this time Damascus went too far. The assassination led to a swift and sudden outpouring of Lebanese and international outrage. Syria had to backpedal and withdraw its troops from Lebanon, officially ending its fifteen-year occupation of the country.

Lebanon's government passed mainly into the hands of anti-Syrian, pro-Western forces, but Hizballah too was part of the equation. Pro- and anti-Syrian demonstrations and counterdemonstrations occurred regularly, as did Syrian assassinations of critics in Lebanon. For the Bush administration, the success of the so-called Cedar Revolution was vital to its call to support democracy in the Middle East and to isolate Syria. Israeli leaders were more cynical about the chances of anti-Syrian leaders in Lebanon, but they too did not want to take actions that would play into the hands of Hizballah and the Syrians, nor did they want to undermine what had become an important U.S. policy interest in the region.

After 9/11, as the United States geared up to invade Iraq in 2003, Iran temporarily became more cautious in its support for terrorist groups. Iran's foreign minister Kamal Kharazi told Hizballah in 2002 that it should avoid giving Israel excuses to strike, a caution Iran's president Mohammad Khatami reiterated in 2003, when he visited Lebanon. As the U.S. occupation of Iraq unraveled, Iran's fear diminished, yet its desire to counter U.S. influence remained strong. President Khatami lost power to the firebrand Mahmud Ahmadinejad in 2005, a move that signaled the rise of a more assertive, anti-Western leadership in Iran. Despite the incendiary anti-Israel rhetoric of Ahmadinejad, who declared that Israel "must be wiped off the map" and that the Holocaust was "a myth,"[27] he and other Iranian leaders did not use Hizballah as aggressively as Tehran had in the early 1980s. Yet they did not apply the brakes either, and they were far less cautious than they were under Khatami or in the months after 9/11.

Hizballah sought a way to continue the conflict against Israel and at the same time limit risk to its position in Lebanon and to its sponsors. Assisting other groups, particularly Palestinian ones, helped them walk this line. As the Second Intifada broke out, Hizballah collected money to help support the struggle and to assist the family members of dead fighters. While the violence continued, Hizballah tried to send its own operatives into Israel to train and arm Palestinians and to recruit Israeli Arabs. When Israel launched Operation Defensive Shield in 2002 Hizballah escalated its operations in the Shebaa Farms area to draw off Israeli fighters. In May 2003 the Israeli Navy stopped a boat sent by Hizballah complete with missile ignition switches and an explosives expert trained to help the Palestinians improve their rockets. Al Manar television beamed in instructional videos on how to construct explosive devices.[28] Because Palestinians were energized, Hizballah was able to fight to the last Palestinian and suffer few costs of its own.

Hizballah Prepares, Israel Dithers

As Hizballah engaged Israel in these limited and often indirect ways, it also prepared for the resumption of a more massive struggle. Israelis, however, tried hard to put Lebanon behind them and did not prepare accordingly.

Although the Israeli withdrawal in 2000 removed Hizballah's biggest justification for its fighting forces, it strongly resisted efforts to curtail its military strength, keeping thousands of fighters, regular and part time, under arms.[29] Iran heaped weapons onto Hizballah, greatly increasing its supplies of Katyushas and hundreds of longer-range rockets. With the departure of Syrian troops in 2005, pro-Western forces in Lebanon increasingly pressed Hizballah to disarm. But Nasrallah threatened, "[We will] cut off any hand that reaches out to our weapons."[30]

Hizballah also developed a coherent military strategy to exploit its expanded arsenal of Iranian-supplied weapons. It would use these rockets to harass and threaten Israeli civilians and send a clear political signal that it was unvanquished. At the same time it would engage IDF forces, not to hold territory but for the sole purpose of inflicting casualties. Hizballah leaders believed that, if a war came, Israeli public and international pressure on Israel would limit the length of any military campaign. Indeed the leaders believed that even limited casualties would result in Israel's backing down. For Hizballah, standing bloodied but defiant as it had done time and time again would be victory enough.

Hizballah was clever. The group studied and understood Israeli methods and used deception and concealment to its advantage. According to Israeli intelligence estimates, Hizballah had almost twenty thousand rockets.[31] The Katyushas and other short-range rockets were generally hard to detect and destroy, and so Hizballah scattered the rocket launchers around villages and other parts of southern Lebanon. The rockets were hidden underground in bunkers designed to survive Israeli air and artillery strikes, sites often referred to as "nature reserves." If battle was joined, lookouts would watch for Israeli aircraft, and when a zone was free separate groups would transport the rocket and prepare it for firing. Bicycles, hard to see on radar and therefore hard to target, were often used to transport crews. The process of setting up and launching a rocket took less than a minute.[32]

Hizballah placed medium- and long-range rockets farther away from the Israeli border. In addition to the Katyushas, it had roughly a thousand Iranian "Fajr-3" rockets with a forty-two-kilometer range, "Fajr-5" rockets, some of which had a range of seventy kilometers, Syrian rockets with a range of 115 kilometers, and longer-range Iranian "Zalzel 1/Zalzel 2" rockets that had ranges of 125 and 210 kilometers. Hizballah put many of these longer-range rockets in local homes. Activists were instructed to knock down a wall if the command came to fire them.[33] Although the locations of the rockets were a secret, their existence was not; to hearten his followers, Nasrallah announced that all of Israel's north was vulnerable. At the same time Hizballah prudently constructed deep bunkers in which leaders could hide from Israeli air attacks.

The civilian families and houses acted as shields. Nasrallah noted shortly before the war, "[Hizballah's operatives] live in their houses, in their schools, in their mosques, in their churches, in their fields, in their farms, and in their factories. You can't destroy them in the same way you would destroy an army."[34] Similarly Hizballah placed caches of explosives and arms in and near mosques and scattered up to five hundred arms caches in southern Lebanon.

To further protect the rockets, it established guerrilla forces and prepared positions. Squads were given considerable freedom to act on their own, a recognition that Israel might disrupt Hizballah's communications and that the man on the ground is best positioned to seize an opportunity in combat. Lebanon's rocky and hilly terrain in the south and its villages that could serve as fortresses would help Hizballah defenders.[35] The group would not try to hold territory. Hizballah's leader Naim Qassem explains, "Resistance work was essentially 'hit and run,' leaving the enemy surprised without any visible retaliation targets."[36]

Recognizing that Israel would be likely to enter Lebanon with armored forces, Hizballah fighters trained extensively with antitank weapons in Iran and Syria. Hizballah scouted out likely Israeli lines of approach and prepared firing positions in advance. Hizballah engineers built deep bunkers, almost six hundred of them. The important ones, which housed many Hizballah leaders, were forty meters deep; some even had air-conditioning. As with its rocket forces, Hizballah deceived Israeli intelligence, building false bunkers under the eyes of Israeli UAVs while taking great care to camouflage the real ones. It also made sure that only a handful of people knew the location of more than a few bunkers, so spies could not betray the entire network.[37] Israel later devoted considerable effort to destroying pretend targets yet often missed the real ones. Hizballah even developed counter–signals intelligence capabilities, monitoring the unencrypted cell phone communications of Israeli commanders.[38]

As Hizballah meticulously planned, Israel dithered. Israel did not develop a strong intelligence picture of southern Lebanon, nor did it enlist enough agents to provide information on Hizballah's dispersed military forces. Because Israel wanted to avoid escalating tensions with Hizballah, it limited low-altitude reconnaissance flights to gather information on the group's activities. When this limited intelligence collection was pitted against Hizballah's impressive deception efforts, Israel failed to learn where most rocket launch sites were located, where most arms caches were hidden, and where the advanced weapons systems from Iran (most notably antiship cruise missiles) had been stashed. They did not even know the identities of mid-level Hizballah commanders or the overall number of fighters.[39] Perhaps more disturbing, some of the information Israeli intelligence had gathered was declared "top secret" and not properly shared with the forces that entered Lebanon.

In the years before the 2006 war the IDF began embracing systemic operational design (SOD), a concept drawn in part from U.S. military thinking on effects-based operations and other topics. SOD drew on postmodern French philosophy, architecture, and psychology, among other influences; as a result many found it completely incomprehensible. The SOD-based doctrine was especially appealing to the IDF chief of staff Dan Halutz, who wrote in his introduction to the new doctrine, "Familiarity with and use of the concept of operation are the key to our success in warfare, in which the only option available is victory."[40] Halutz, an air force general, embraced the idea that airstrikes against crucial infrastructure systems alone could cripple an enemy. The Israeli military had moved away from its emphasis on taking territory as a bargaining chip, as it had in the country's early wars, because it now sought to avoid additional occupations and the risks of guerrilla war. In the end the IDF did not develop a coherent strategy for taking on Hizballah and fell back on airpower as a panacea.

Beyond this doctrinal confusion the Second Intifada left the IDF with its hands full. The IDF's readiness for more conventional conflicts, as opposed to fighting the Palestinians, declined precipitously. The intelligence services, the IDF, and the Israeli people as a whole all focused on the Palestinian arena. The economic downturn that came with the violence also forced the IDF to look for ways to cut its budget even as it expanded its role against the Palestinians. Tank crews did not train beyond their initial preparation; they and the artillery were then employed as light infantry and never gained mastery of their machines. Equipment for reserve units, which were necessary in a larger conflict, was often broken or obsolete. Reservists sometimes lacked bulletproof vests, radios, ammunition, and night-vision goggles. Air-to-ground liaison was weak. Many commanders did not operate combined forces correctly.[41] As one reserve soldier noted during the 2006 war, "For the last six years we were engaged in stupid policing missions in the West Bank. Checkpoints, hunting stone-throwing Palestinian children, that kind of stuff. The result was that we were not ready to confront real fighters like Hezbollah."[42]

Politics came into play too. While Barak was prime minister, resuming operations in Lebanon would have meant admitting that unilateral withdrawal was a failure. Ariel Sharon, for his part, had almost destroyed his career (and, for many, had forever destroyed his reputation) after the 1982 invasion of Lebanon. For both prime ministers, a return to Lebanon was not in the cards. Yet to be fair to both Sharon and Barak, later events would show that to operate in Lebanon Israel needed international (read, U.S.) backing and support from the Israeli people, neither of which was there before 2006. Sharon recognized this, and in the last meeting he held on Lebanon before his debilitating stroke, said, "Whatever doesn't have to be done over there—shouldn't be done."[43] More broadly, as the Israeli journalist Nahum Barnea points out, "quiet is the real objective of a democratic government." Beginning a war in the name of deterrence is not popular, and there is particular suspicion when a right-wing prime minister does so.

Israel had made a trade. For six years it enjoyed relative calm. The peace was far from perfect, but it was a better situation than the country suffered during the 1990s, when it averaged losses of well over a dozen soldiers a year. As one senior official involved in Lebanon decision making told me, "The security situation was excellent *after* the Israeli withdrawal." Hizballah attacked only soldiers, not civilians. Tourism in the north, an indirect measure of perceptions of the conflict, did well. Yet the shift in Lebanon had its price. Hizballah now emerged as a true military threat to Israel proper, particularly because of its growing rocket force, a threat Israel would discover when the fragile peace collapsed in 2006.

CHAPTER XVII

HIZBALLAH RETURNS (2006)

TWO FALSE assumptions guided Israeli policy: that the Lebanon problem was contained and that, should there be a conflict, Hizballah would prove easy to defeat.[1]

On July 12, 2006, Hizballah began to show Israel just how false its assumptions had been. In Operation True Promise Hizballah forces shelled Israel's border while its sharpshooters took out nearby observation cameras. These measures distracted and blinded the IDF, helping Hizballah raiders ambush a careless Israeli patrol driving along the Israel-Lebanon border, killing two soldiers. Hizballah fighters also pulled two wounded soldiers, Sergeants Ehud Goldwasser and Eldad Regev, out of their Humvee and kidnapped them, dragging them into Lebanon.[2] Many Israelis believe that Hizballah's terrorist mastermind Imad Mughniyah was behind the operation, though proof is elusive.

Some two hours later an IDF platoon-size unit entered Lebanon in the hope of retrieving the kidnapped soldiers. In anticipation of an Israel pursuit Hizballah forces placed a bomb on the road that destroyed an Israeli tank. Four died in the tank and a fifth was killed in a successful attempt to stop Hizballah from stealing the remains of his comrades.

Assessments of Hizballah's prowess must be balanced against Israel's slip-shod performance. The IDF soldiers who died were reservists serving their last day before going home. They made simple mistakes, ignoring standard procedures such as dismounting from their vehicles when approaching a potential point of ambush. In his study of the war the American analyst

Matt Matthews contends, "From the failure to disseminate intelligence, to the lackadaisical approach of the soldiers on patrol, and the failure to rapidly pursue Hezbollah fighters, the operation revealed a stunning ineptitude on the part of the soldiers and the leadership within the IDF."[3]

Hizballah justified its actions by claiming that it was following the unwritten rules of the game with Israel as it evolved after 2000. Its initial targets were military, not civilian, and it had attempted kidnappings in recent years (and successfully in October 2000) without a massive Israeli response. Why, then, did the July 2006 kidnapping spark such a massive war? One answer is that Israel believed the Intifada was ebbing, and the kidnapping was a reminder that Hizballah was overdue for a lesson. The war, however, cannot be understood without understanding Israeli politics. Both Prime Minister Ehud Olmert and Defense Minister Amir Peretz had low approval ratings. At the time of the abduction Israel was still reeling from the kidnapping of Corporal Gilad Shalit, who was snatched by Palestinian militants and transferred to Gaza less than a month before. Hizballah may have wanted its own kidnapping to be seen as a form of solidarity with the Palestinians, who were facing heavy Israeli military pressure. In response to Shalit's kidnapping Israel had launched Operation Summer Rain, in which perhaps 450 Palestinians died.

Not responding to the Hizballah kidnapping would have been politically disastrous. Initially support for the war was nearly unanimous among Israeli Jews.[4] And unlike Sharon or Barak, Olmert did not have political baggage (or, some would say, painfully earned experience) to weigh down his Lebanon policy. But by Israeli standards Olmert had limited security credentials. Though he had served in the IDF as a journalist and as a Knesset member had sat on the Foreign Affairs and Defense Committees, he was no Rabin, Barak, or Sharon; as the Israeli reporter Nahum Barnea points out wryly, "He had never killed Arabs." A successful war would make him look stronger on security issues.

War, Again

After the kidnapping and the failed rescue attempt, Israel proclaimed a set of ambitious objectives that included the return of the two hostages, the expulsion of Hizballah from the border area and its replacement with the Lebanese Army, the elimination of the long-range missile threat, and the disarming of Hizballah.[5] These goals, however, were not precisely or formally defined. At times Israel's goals seemed more like a wish list than a concerted plan of action.

Even though the military campaign was dubbed Operation Change of Direction, Israel dusted off its old playbook, using concepts it tried unsuccessfully in the 1990s with Operations Accountability and Grapes of Wrath, The IDF struck at Hizballah headquarters and command facilities, attempted to attack deployed forces directly, and bombed some of Lebanon's infrastructure to increase pressure on the Lebanese government. Yet the old playbook did not—and indeed could not—work. Israel was trying to simultaneously inflict pain and restrain itself, the worst of all approaches.

Before examining what Israel did, it is useful to consider what was off the table. Most important, Israeli leaders did not want to invade Beirut or otherwise get sucked back into the Lebanese quagmire of 1982. Planners were thus left with three unpalatable options: a limited air campaign focused on Hizballah, a broader air campaign that hit a range of non-Hizballah targets in Lebanon, or a more massive ground operation that occupied much of southern Lebanon. Israel could have struck Syria as Hizballah's sponsor, but Syria had long convinced the world that it could not be held responsible for what happened in Lebanon, and this claim was enhanced after its forces withdrew in 2005.

IDF chief of staff Dan Halutz vowed to "turn back the clock in Lebanon by 20 years," and Olmert declared, "Lebanon is responsible and Lebanon will bear the consequences."[6] The IDF proposed hitting Beirut to shut down the tourist season and put pressure on the government of Fouad Siniora, who had taken the reins in Beirut in 2005. Secretary of State Condoleezza Rice, however, told Olmert the United States did not want Siniora's government hurt—after all, Siniora had come to power on a wave of anti-Syrian sentiment in Lebanon—or Lebanon's civilian infrastructure destroyed. Olmert accepted these constraints, but they cramped the IDF plan. Yet even without U.S. pressure, the IDF plan was flawed. Past attempts to press the Lebanese government in the same way had failed. The result, as Nahum Barnea contended, was unacceptable: "In Beirut the lights are on; in Haifa, they are off."

At first Israel relied almost entirely on air power. In Operation Specific Gravity the Israeli Air Force hit the longer-range "Fajr" rocket launchers, effectively destroying much of the force—a tactical and intelligence success. It took out roads and bridges, and it also struck and devastated the Dahiye area of Beirut, a densely populated group of Shi'a neighborhoods, including Harat Hreik, where Hizballah's headquarters was located. (Hizballah guards this area carefully, searching suspicious pedestrians and monitoring vehicle traffic coming in and out of the neighborhood.) Israel justified the infrastructure strikes by claiming that roads and bridges might be used to smuggle the captured soldiers away from the Israeli border and to bring new fighters to the front. It seems more likely, however, that the goal was as much to put pressure on Hizballah and Lebanon by damaging infrastructure, for destroying the bridges and roads would not have seriously impeded the highly mobile Hizballah forces. Hizballah responded with rockets, striking deeper into Israel than ever before and in major population centers: Haifa on July 13, 16, and 17; Tiberias (twenty-five miles from the border with Lebanon) on July 15 and 17; and Afula (thirty-one miles) on July 17.[7]

At first the battle seemed to go Israel's way. The strike on the long-range rockets appeared successful: many rockets were destroyed and only twenty Lebanese civilians were killed. Politically Olmert had the full backing of the Israeli people for his response, achieving a 78 percent popularity rating while his rhetoric soared to Churchillian heights. The United States also welcomed a tough Israeli response and resisted (often with quiet Arab state support) international calls for a ceasefire. American neoconservatives wanted to punish Syria and hoped that by weakening Hizballah and Damascus Israel would bolster the pro-U.S. regime in Beirut.

The rest of the international community rallied behind Israel (a true rarity in recent years). A joint Jordanian-Egyptian statement blasted Hizballah's "irresponsible escalatory acts," and Saudi Arabia condemned its "reckless adventurism," stunning statements given these countries' long-standing policy of criticizing Israel in their public remarks.[8] Hizballah Secretary General Hassan Nasrallah admitted that the criticism was a surprise.[9] Perhaps most surprising, many Lebanese, including senior government officials, openly rejected Hizballah's actions.

Israel deliberately avoided striking the electric grid, water facilities, and other structures that would impose civilian suffering, including structures it had attacked in 1996. Yet from the start the media focused attention on the damage Israel inflicted in Lebanon, ignoring its restraint. Such biased media reporting, again inevitable for Israel, made the criticism of excess even worse. Israel was reported to have deliberately attacked schools, mosques, and hospitals even though it did not actually do so.[10] (When asked about the problem of killing civilians whose houses might be home to the rockets as well, Shin Bet's director Yuval Diskin suggested that bystanders are not innocent if they "go to sleep with rockets in their bedrooms.")[11] Foreign Minister Tzipi Livni put it even more bluntly: "When you go to sleep with a missile, you might find yourself waking up to another kind of missile."[12]

Israel had largely spared much of Beirut to concentrate on the Dahiye neighborhood. The devastation there, however, was horrific. One reporter described the carnage: "Some buildings looked like a vast creature had leaned down and bitten into them. Progress became more difficult as one faced a steeplechase of girders, blocks, spaghetti tangles of electrical wires, children's toys, books, beds, air conditioning units and other unidentifiable rubble."[13] Outside Beirut, villages near the front line were destroyed, as were many roads and bridges in the south. For much of the world this destruction was the war; Israel's restraint in other parts of the country didn't count. The decision to hit the Beirut airport, roads leading into Lebanon, and at times targets in anti-Hizballah Christian neighborhoods compounded this perception.

Often Israel's top officials thought only about what to do next rather than what they wanted in the end. When operations began Chief of Staff

Halutz predicted, "It'll be over tonight. A few hours. Maybe tomorrow morning."[14] With Hizballah politically and diplomatically on its heels and the Israeli Air Force apparently triumphant, Israel had a chance to call it quits and thus win the battle of perceptions. Diplomats even believed it was possible that Hizballah would hand the kidnapped soldiers over to the Lebanese government.

Success blinded the Israeli leadership, even though they did not have a plan to build on it beyond doing more of the same. IDF, political, and media officials all repeated overblown reports of success, drinking one another's Kool-Aid. Official statements and media reports that Israel had "destroyed all the Hizballah outposts in the border" and had "cut off southern Lebanon" were false.[15] The war steadily expanded, while Israel did not realize that the continuing destruction of infrastructure was playing into Hizballah's hands. As the damage to Lebanon grew, Hizballah's opposition in Lebanon and the Arab states was pressed to rally behind the organization against Israel. Even Israel's staunchest ally, the United States, could not unequivocally back Israel as the civilian destruction dominated the news coverage.

For Hizballah winning was much easier. It only had to remain standing, and its ability to do so increased as the Israeli operation wore on. Nasrallah told the Arab satellite station al-Jazeera that Hizballah did not have to down an F-16 or otherwise score an impressive military victory: "The victory we are talking about is whether resistance will survive." In an inspiring flight of rhetoric, he claimed, "As long as there is a missile that is fired from Lebanon and targets the Zionists, as long as there is one fighter who fires his rifle, and as long as there is someone who plants a bomb against the Israelis, then this means that resistance is still there."[16]

Hizballah's careful military preparation and Israel's disastrous neglect of its armed forces led to setbacks in several battles. The losses seemed particularly discordant when the IDF claimed that areas were conquered only to discover that Hizballah forces remained intact. In Bint Jbeil, for example, the IDF general Gal Hirsh declared that Israel was in "complete control" a day before a surprise attack there led to eight casualties.

As a measure of Hizballah's resilience both Israeli and outside observers focused on Hizballah's ability to conduct rocket attacks. Roughly one-third of Israel's population was within striking range of the rockets. Hizballah's huge stockpiles of rockets and launchers paid off, allowing Hizballah to increase its barrage even as Israel tried to destroy these systems. Perhaps four thousand rockets fell on Israel by the end of the war, most of which were short-range 122mm Katyusha rockets that were stationed near Lebanon's border with Israel. Almost a quarter of these rockets fell on Israeli cities, where fifty-three civilians died.[17] Many of the Katyushas were in "nature preserves," rural parts of the countryside, where they were positioned to take advantage of rough terrain for concealment. Lt. Col. Ishai Efroni, the deputy commander of one of the Israeli brigades fighting in Lebanon, remarked, "The Hezbollah fighter wakes up in the morning, drinks his coffee, takes a rocket out of his closet, goes to his neighbor's yard, sticks a clock timer on it, goes back home and then watches CNN to see where it lands."[18]

Though the IDF leadership recognized the difficulties of removing the short-range rockets without invading and occupying southern Lebanon, Chief of Staff Halutz dismissed these concerns as they went up the chain. Thus political leaders concluded that "the military" thought they could do the job without ground forces. Many ministers did not know what the IDF's actual recommendations were, as Halutz and Olmert often removed crucial points when transmitting them. The Winograd Commission later reported, "The ministers voted for a vague decision, without understanding and knowing its nature and implications. They authorized the commencement of a military campaign without considering how to exit it."[19] When he learned later that some of the more limited recommendations of the IDF were not presented to the Cabinet, Minister without Portfolio Eitan Cabel declared, "I wanted to wring somebody's neck."[20]

Casualty sensitivity also shaped plans. One IDF general recalled, "Every casualty was reported to the Chief of Staff, and there was a case in which an entire battle was stopped because of one casualty."[21] To minimize casualties the air force bombed from high altitudes and prohibited helicopters from flying deep into Lebanon.

As rockets continued to fall, Israelis began to flee northern parts of the country. Of the two million Israelis within range of rockets, as many as 500,000 left their homes, and another one million regularly took cover in bomb shelters. Eventually the pressure to end the rocket attacks grew too great, and Israeli leaders began a ground campaign. That campaign, however, was half-hearted and poorly conducted. The military that had reached Beirut in a week in 1982 penetrated into Lebanon only a few kilometers in 2006. The operation began on July 19, one week into the air war, with a move on the Lebanese town of Maroun al-Ras. The IDF quickly claimed to have taken the town, only to find that Hizballah forces remained intact and were continuing to fight. Indeed the IDF and Hizballah often fought from room to room in abandoned houses and buildings. Six Israelis died in the week it took to establish control over the town.

A week later the IDF moved into the town of Bint Jbeil; in both cases these operations led to tough firefights. Hizballah reinforced Bint Jbeil with more than a hundred fighters armed with antitank weapons. Some wore civilian clothing or even IDF uniforms and fought from the homes of civilians.[22] True to its doctrine Hizballah slowed the IDF down and inflicted casualties, creating a perception of IDF defeat.

The IDF continued operations, but these were more often raids than a serious attempt to control southern Lebanon, which would have been necessary to stop the rocket attacks. Such fighting did not correspond with standard IDF doctrine, which emphasized blinding speed and surprise attacks that would keep opponents off balance and unable to react effectively. The IDF often did not know where Hizballah bunkers were, making it impossible to strike them. Israel had not purchased "bunker-busting" munitions from the United States. [23] As the fighting continued, the IDF abandoned some of its goals, such as stopping the firing of Katyushas, in favor of more artificial, and achievable, objectives such as reaching the Litani River, though it eventually abandoned these objectives as well. Meanwhile, the IDF commanders failed to distinguish themselves, and communications within senior ranks were poor. Investigators later criticized the officers of Division 91, which played a major role in several battles, for not understanding their orders and failing to fulfill basic missions.

As the fighting wore on, the IDF tried to convince local Lebanese to help them. Doing this from afar, however, proved exceptionally difficult. Israel even resorted to calling the cell phones of Lebanese citizens. [24]

As the raids commenced, Hizballah's elaborate network of bunkers and careful deception efforts paid off. One member of the elite Israeli Maglan unit noted that early on in the fighting around Maroun ar-Ras, which is near the border, intelligence told them to expect "a tent and three Kalashnikovs," but his unit found instead "a hydraulic steel door leading to a well-equipped network of tunnels." Hizballah fighters swarmed from these tunnels and neighboring areas, trapping the Maglan unit.

On July 14, after two days of Israeli attacks, Hizballah scored a propaganda coup and Nasrallah displayed a brilliant sense of political theater. Augustus Richard Norton, an American scholar of Hizballah, wrote, "Nasrallah invited listeners to look to the sea, and with perfect theatrical timing an explosion on the horizon rocketed the INS *Hanit*, an Israeli naval vessel that was hit by an Iranian-produced C-802 Noor guided missile." [25] Nasrallah claimed that the hit on the *Hanit* meant that "the vessel that bombed Beirut [was] demolished." [26] Four Israeli sailors died.

Israel learned once again that Hizballah was far more formidable than Hamas or Fatah. When Palestinians shot at soldiers in the West Bank, the troops took shelter in nearby houses; when they tried the same tactic in Lebanon, Hizballah used antitank guided missiles to destroy the house. [27] One of the biggest Israeli disasters occurred when an airstrike accidentally wreaked havoc on the Qana area on July 30. Twenty-eight died, among them seventeen children. Beyond the human tragedy it was a political catastrophe for Israel as images of shattered bodies and children without arms and legs dominated news coverage. The recurrence of Qana as the location for a mistaken attack on civilians was a particular humiliation, reminding Israelis and Lebanese of the 1996 debacle in the same location. The disaster pointed to Israel's inability to find a solution for the Katyushas. The Israeli Air Force, desperate to strike the rockets, tried to identify possible launch locations and strike them despite limited information. Moreover when Israeli intelligence identified an area as the site of a Katyusha launch, air force doctrine called for bombing the buildings around that site with little or no further intelligence as to who or what was inside those buildings.[28]

It was clear that raids with ground forces were not enough. So on July 31, more than two weeks into the war, Israel's leaders initiated Operation Change of Direction 8, which was to establish a security zone along the entire border and required ten thousand troops, including reserve forces. Even as the IDF prepared for the ground assault, the rain of rockets continued. In one of Israel's greatest disasters in the war, a Katyusha killed twelve paratrooper reservists in Kfar Giladi, inside Israel, on August 6. The IDF soon penetrated into Lebanon more thoroughly and eventually had around ten thousand troops in southern Lebanon, with more deployed in support in Israel itself.[29]

On August 11 Israel launched Change of Direction 11, which was a westward drive parallel to the Litani River. During this operation part of an armored column from the 401st Brigade that had moved to join other Israeli troops was ambushed as it went through the Saluqi Valley. Hizballah blocked the route of tanks from the brigade by destroying a building and then used a mine or IED to block the road behind them. The trapped tanks then faced withering volleys of antitank missiles. In the ambush Israel lost twelve soldiers and eleven tanks. The IDF's focus on the Second Intifada and neglect of conventional ground operations were prominent explanations of a long list of mistakes, big and small. Artillery and infantry were supposed to support the armored column, but they were not present. Tanks often took the wrong routes, the IDF failed to employ elementary countermeasures such as smoke screens, and the infantry failed to understand that their mission was to eliminate antitank missile squads. Timur Goksel, who for many years advised UNIFIL forces, blasted the IDF, noting, "Anyone dumb enough to push a tank column through Wadi Saluki should not be an armored brigade commander but a cook."[30] During the weekend of August 11 a despairing Israeli officer lamented these losses, saying, "This was the Black Sabbath."[31]

Although Israel's performance deserves the widespread criticism it received, it is vital to recognize that at a tactical level, where Israel usually shines, it was unprepared for Hizballah's level of skill. This does not mean Hizballah's forces were perfect. Far from it. Hizballah fighters were poor shots with small arms and were unable to combine different weapons effectively. Nevertheless its fighters were far more impressive than Palestinian fighters or the Arab armies Israel has faced in the past. Hizballah fighters found cover in Dayr Siryan, where Israeli forces approached within one hundred meters but failed to see them. Hizballah fighters did not waste ammunition; they demonstrated first-rate skill in placing their mortars and antitank weapons. Even more impressive, they mined areas to force IDF armored forces to take certain routes and then readied prepared antitank guided missile ambushes to destroy them. Small units were well led, and Hizballah fighters fought bravely. As one Israeli soldier acidly commented, "Evidently they had never heard that an Arab soldier is supposed to run away after a short engagement with the Israelis."[32]

A constant challenge for IDF operations was the intermingling of civilians with fighters. Contrary to initial claims, later Israeli reports indicate that Hizballah did not use human shields extensively in the parts of southern Lebanon where it fought Israeli ground forces, and for the most part Hizballah fighters wore uniforms. Two American analysts of the war wrote that Hizballah "sought concealment chiefly via terrain rather than through civilian intermingling."[33] The IDF, however, had to plan and prepare for the use of human shields, but by the time IDF ground forces arrived, the villages were mostly empty, as the civilians had left.

Hizballah did, however, use civilian disguises for logistical purposes. Israeli intelligence claims that Hizballah operatives were carrying antitank missiles in backpacks when they were dressed in civilian clothes and carried white flags. They also reportedly used Red Cross vehicles and ambulances to transfer people and weapons, knowing the IDF would hesitate to target them.[34] Hizballah used civilian residences to launch rockets, according to the United Nations. More broadly some Hizballah organizational facilities were in civilian neighborhoods, making it difficult to destroy what belonged to the organization without also destroying the homes and shops of other Lebanese. UN Under-Secretary General for Humanitarian Affairs Jan Egeland condemned Hizballah for its "cowardly blending among women and children."[35]

Although the IDF suffered a host of problems, Israel's biggest weakness was at the top. The Winograd Commission reported that Olmert "made up his mind hastily" even though he had no detailed military plan. He also "made a personal contribution to the fact that the declared goals were overly ambitious and not feasible."[36] IDF Chief of Staff Halutz, the Commission found, failed to let his political masters know of the IDF's shortcomings. Olmert's and Defense Minister Peretz's limited military background meant they did not push Halutz for weaknesses in his approach even though Halutz was an air force officer whose understanding of the reality of ground combat appeared limited. Halutz had dismissed many of the traditional IDF tasks as outdated. In 2001 he declared, "We . . . have to part with the concept of a land battle."[37] Shimon Naveh, who headed the IDF Combat Studies Institute and whom others see as the architect of Israel's doctrine for this war, dismissed Halutz as "an idiot" and "a fool" because he never tried to learn about the challenges Israel was truly facing.[38] Naveh himself comes off remarkably high-handed and even narcissistic, claiming, "Normal human beings can't understand the complexity of my writings." While he disavowed his own responsibility, he contended that "most of the senior IDF officials should be executed."[39]

Although both sides suffered militarily and by some measures the war could be declared a draw, there is little question that Hizballah won a political victory, at least in the short term. As Israeli government official Dan Meridor argues, "If an NBA team plays a bunch of students and it is a draw, the students win." By Israeli standards the bill was high. Hizballah rockets killed fifty-three Israelis: forty-four civilians and twelve soldiers. In all Hizballah killed 121 Israeli soldiers, including Regev and Goldwassser, whose deaths were later confirmed as part of the postwar prisoner swap.[40] Hizballah's casualties were higher, but the precise number is not clear. Though it admits to 250, the IDF claims it has the names and addresses of more than five hundred dead Hizballahis (and believes it killed a couple of hundred it cannot account for); a UN estimate is closer to the higher Israeli numbers.[41]

In addition to the heavy losses suffered by the casualty-sensitive Israelis, Hizballah's command and control remained intact, with senior leaders defiantly surviving in the face of the Israeli onslaught. Israel was unable to stop the short-range rocket attacks; in fact by the end of the war, Hizballah was launching more than two hundred rockets a day, compared with one hundred at the start of the war. Hidden Hizballah teams would even launch rockets on Israel from behind Israeli lines. That the IDF had forced Hizballah to shift from longer-range to shorter-range rockets was a distinction without a difference to most Israelis and much of the world. One Israeli lieutenant remarked, "When a Katyusha falls on somebody's home, it's hard to tell them this is going well."[42] The result, as the Winograd Commission found, was that "the fabric of life under fire was seriously disrupted, and many civilians either left their home temporarily or spent their time in shelters."[43] Hizballah's propaganda later labeled their struggle a "divine victory." Israel's intelligence chiefs told Olmert, "The war was a national catastrophe, and Israel suffered a critical blow." [44]

Within Lebanon many Christians and Sunni Muslims initially condemned Hizballah. Over time, however, the devastation of the war brought many Lebanese to Hizballah's side. Outside Lebanon Hizballah's victory was even greater. For months after the war Hassan Nasrallah became the most widely admired man in the Arab world. His elevated status was a remarkable feat, not only because he is a Shi'a leader but also because the war occurred at a time when the civil strife in Iraq had heightened Sunni-Shi'a rivalries. Moderate Arab leaders who had initially criticized Hizballah, including Egyptian president Hosni Mubarak, King Abdallah of Saudi Arabia, and King Abdallah of Jordan, had to back away from their positions.[45]

As with so many of its counterterrorism operations, Israel ignored the political and informational aspects of the war. In the words of the American journalist Marvin Kalb, "the camera and the computer have become weapons of war."[46] In contrast to Jenin, Israel's media access was "more open than open," said the Israeli journalist and security expert Hirsch Goodman. Goodman went on to add that officers constantly briefed the media, giving Hizballah "hundreds of millions of dollars of free real-time intelligence." The IDF published daily numbers of its soldiers killed, and the Israeli media lavished attention on each casualty and funeral—not an approach designed to maintain public morale.[47] Compounding the problem, the IDF's inaccurate reports of progress discredited its overall claims with audiences at home as well as abroad. As casualties mounted and military progress stalled, the Israeli media became more and more negative, yet the country's political and military leaders had no plan to manage the media.

Hizballah, in contrast, understood the Israeli public's aversion to casualties and exploited it ruthlessly. When the Golani Brigade stumbled in southern Lebanon, Nasrallah proclaimed that "the elite force of the best unit in the Israeli army was totally defeated" and that this all occurred even as the Israeli Air Force, despite its "thousands of tons of bombs," was unable to stop Hizballah from shelling. Nasrallah taunted Israel and reassured his supporters that Hizballah retained missiles and rockets that could strike Israel and that Israeli intelligence estimates were wrong.[48] He also warned that Hizballah would strike "beyond Haifa and what is beyond beyond Haifa": Tel Aviv, in contrast to past disputes involving Lebanon, would not be safe.[49] In his first speech after the war commenced, Nasrallah even commented acidly, "You Zionists say in your opinion polls that you believe me more than you believe your officials."[50] In subsequent remarks he made it clear that Hizballah at least had learned from the military campaigns of 1993 and 1996. He noted that in those wars the Israeli public had at first rallied around the government but predicted that over time "this solidarity [would] begin to vanish"—a lesson that Israeli leaders would have been wise to heed.[51]

Israel also faced a double standard from the criticism leveled at Hizballah. Predictably Arab media showed a one-sided version of the war, portraying Israel as the unabashed aggressor.[52] Then, on August 3, Human Rights Watch charged Israel with war crimes.[53] William Arkin, an American defense analyst, writes that Hizballah fired more than a thousand anti-tank missiles inside of Lebanon and fought IDF forces tooth and nail, "and yet, when human rights organizations and much of the international community showed up or commented, they seemed to act as if the force Israel was battling was nonexistent."[54] Hizballah tightly controlled media access in Lebanon, refusing to allow foreign media to report on their own or even question the local residents. The organization was especially careful to ensure that photographers took the right pictures; in one case a dead boy's body was moved from location to location to help cameramen get a more effective shot.[55] Hizballah reportedly fabricated casualties, using photo editing software to add dead bodies to a scene. Israelis often point out the unfairness of this reporting bias, not recognizing that this is the reality in which they must operate.

Hizballah did not emerge unscathed from the war. In theory at least the Lebanese Armed Forces are now manning the Israel-Lebanon border, and there is a stronger UN presence as well. However, as Timur Goksel notes, withdrawal for Hizballah "means going home, putting your AK-47 under the bed, and changing your clothes."[56] Israeli intelligence reports that with Syrian and Iranian help, in 2008 Hizballah had three times as many rockets as it had in 2006, and the popular organization has had no problem finding new recruits to fill its ranks.[57] This too fits the pattern of past Israeli military actions. The publicity that attends the fighting, and Hizballah's ability to give Israel a black eye, give its sponsors an incentive to provide more support after the fighting dies down.[58]

As was so often the case in the Hizballah-Israel struggle, the Lebanese people suffered the most. Hundreds of thousands of Lebanese fled north during the fighting. The Lebanese government claims that the country lost more than a thousand civilians, with over three times as many wounded. Thirty thousand homes were totally destroyed or badly damaged, and far more suffered partial damage.[59] Quick to take advantage of the devastation, Hizballah reaped a political windfall by paying (with Iranian help) for many Lebanese to get temporary housing.

Aftermath: Did Hizballah Lose After All?

On February 12, 2008, a car bomb killed the master Hizballah terrorist Imad Mughniyah in Syria. The attack occurred in the Kfar Soose neighborhood near the headquarters of Syrian intelligence. In early 2008 the Mossad obtained photos of Mughniyah after the elusive terrorist had undergone plastic surgery in Germany. The Israeli newspaper *Yediot Ahronot* reported that when Iraqi security forces handed over a Hizballah operative they captured to U.S. intelligence, the Americans learned many details about Mughniyah, including his phone numbers. They in turn passed the information to the Mossad. The Israeli team sneaked into Syria, tapped Mughniyah's phone, monitored his activities, and learned the lay of the land near the Iranian Cultural Center. Israeli photo interpreters checked photos of individuals entering the Iranian facility in Damascus against the new pictures of Mughniyah, looking for a match. The Mossad also knew that Mughniyah would meet with Iran's new ambassador to Damascus on February 12 because that was the anniversary of the Islamic Revolution; a celebration would be almost compulsory for someone in Mughniyah's position. When they determined Mughniyah's identity, they exchanged the headrest of his Mitsubishi Pajero with another one filled with explosives. As soon as Mughniyah got into the car, they blew it up.[60]

Shortly after Mughniyah's death Azerbaijan's security services disrupted an attack on the Israeli embassy in Baku. Azerbaijani police also intercepted a car driven by two suspected Hizballah members who reportedly worked with the IRGC. The car contained explosives, cameras, and reconnaissance photos. In a follow-up raid on a safe house police found evidence of a plot to blow up the Israeli embassy in Azerbaijan.[61] Hizballah may have also considered attacking an Israeli target in Turkey. In 2009 an Israeli Arab, reportedly working for Hizballah, was arrested for plotting to kill the IDF chief of staff.[62]

Israel did not stop with Mughniyah's death. Hard evidence is elusive, but they may have also targeted Khalil Sultan, a senior Iranian official responsible for working with Hizballah, who was killed in May 2010 and had his laptop taken.

This bloody back and forth did not prevent Israel from cutting deals with Hizballah. In the hopes of preventing future conflicts, in 2008 Israel released several Hizballah prisoners and the PLF terrorist Samir Kuntar in exchange for the bodies of Regev and Goldwasser.

After the war Israel developed a new doctrine, the so-called Dahiya Doctrine, named after the Beirut neighborhood that the Israeli Air Force destroyed in the 2006 war. As the head of the IDF Northern Command, Maj. Gen. Gadi Eisenkot, explained, "What happened in the Dahiya quarter of Beirut in 2006 will happen in every village from which Israel is fired on." He went on to say, "We will apply disproportionate force on it [the village] and cause great damage and destruction there. From our standpoint, these are not civilian villages, they are military bases. This is not a recommendation. This is a plan."[63] In 2009 Defense Minister Barak warned the Lebanese that if Hizballah attacked, Israel would respond against "the state of Lebanon." Israel's use of heavy force in Gaza in 2008–9 made this threat particularly credible. To avoid a repeat of the IDF's poor showing in 2006, Israel also began retraining its forces and improving its intelligence collection on Lebanon.[64]

As was shown in the Cast Lead operation, Israelis also learned a lesson about the media and victory. For groups like Hizballah and Hamas, victory is what Israel cannot spin as defeat. So in Cast Lead, Israel would focus on minimizing its own casualties to avoid any claims by Hamas that it was punishing Israel.

Should Hizballah choose to continue the fight, it has plenty of pretexts. Shebaa Farms offers an example of how Hizballah can conjure up a nationalistic grievance where none existed before. Hizballah can always justify military operations in the name of the Palestinians or to prevent Israel from flying over Lebanese airspace to gather intelligence and "show presence." Yet these pretexts don't have the same emotional weight as defending Lebanese soil from Israeli occupation, the cause Hizballah championed until 2000. Over time Lebanese support for Hizballah's war with Israel is likely to diminish.

Lebanon too remains in crisis. In 2008, after taking over much of Beirut as a show of force against its domestic rivals, Hizballah gained the power to veto any opposing legislation. This move helped calm relations between the organization and more pro-Western and anti-Syrian Lebanese factions that composed much of the remainder of the government. Hizballah's narrative—that the Lebanese Army is too weak to defend Lebanon and thus an armed Hizballah is necessary—remains widely accepted. Yet Hizballah still finds it difficult to remain aloof from Lebanese politics: in the years after the war it killed several Lebanese in shows of force with the government, which was trying to clip its wings. These deaths played poorly on the domestic scene. For now there is an uneasy balance, though Lebanon remains susceptible to violence and instability.

Syria and Iran both remain active in backing Hizballah. Iranian representatives still work closely with Hizballah's senior leadership in the group's decision-making council. Iran poured money and arms into its proxy's coffers after the 2006 war and still views Hizballah as a major ally for advancing Iran's interests. Damascus is more cautious, using Hizballah to preserve its position as much as to advance it, but it too retains an interest in the ability of Hizballah to threaten Israel. In part because of this aid, Hizballah is again well-armed and again has long-range rockets that can hit deep into Israel. Although the 2006 ceasefire agreement forced the organization to withdraw its unconcealed forces from the border with Israel, the group has prepared to take up positions there in the event of renewed hostilities.[65]

Yet looking back on 2006 the war did accomplish one thing for Israel: its border is quiet, at least for now. The Shi'a community suffered terribly, and there is no enthusiasm for another round with the IDF. Hizballah, like Hamas, is a quasi government, and thus its leadership feels pressure when its people suffer. Although Hizballah may have won the 2006 war politically, it was a close call, and the organization is not eager to repeat the experience. Indeed Nasrallah later called the kidnapping operation that sparked the war a "terrible mistake"—a rare admission of error for an Arab leader and thus again distinguishing Nasrallah from other leaders.[66] Its losses in 2006, though not catastrophic, were still considerable. Hizballah fears the criticism it received in 2006, when many non-Shi'a saw it as Lebanon's destroyer rather than its savior.

Proof of Israel's success in deterring Hizballah was seen in 2008; when Israeli forces went into Gaza, Hizballah's guns remained silent. One former senior Israeli intelligence official sarcastically remarked that Nasrallah "will fight to the last Hamas soldier" rather than activate his own men. Nasrallah himself has avoided appearing in public, no doubt fearing an Israeli assassination attempt.

Israel has returned to the situation that prevailed before 2006, whereas Hizballah, at the very least, continues to train Palestinians, particularly Hamas, and maintains a strong armed presence. Israel in turn continues a low-level intelligence war against Hizballah trainers and liaisons with the Palestinian forces. If quiet continues on the border Israel can for now tolerate this uneasy situation. Hizballah has proven, again and again, that it can stand up to Israel, and the Jewish state has to live with this dangerous foe on its borders. As one Israeli told me, "We're not done with Hizballah, and Hizballah's not done with us."

Perhaps more than any group discussed in this book, the label *terrorist* doesn't do justice to Hizballah. The label is not wrong: the group has done many terrorist attacks in its past, and even today some of its activities fall under the rubric of terrorism. But for Israel, Hizballah's military capabilities are a more serious concern, while for Lebanese and U.S. policy in Lebanon, the organization's political influence is of most concern. When combating Hizballah, its broader dimensions must always be taken into account.

SECTION IV

JEWISH TERRORISM

CHAPTER XVIII

THE ENEMY WITHIN (1967–2000)

ON JULY 26, 1983, three members of a terrorist movement labeled the Jewish Underground fired automatic rifles at students at the Islamic College in Hebron, killing three and wounding another thirty-three.[1] Their motive was simple: revenge. On July 7 three Arabs in Hebron had murdered a yeshiva student, Aharon Gross, while hundreds of local Palestinians looked on. The Underground movement, which grew out of the religious Zionist settler movement, believed that the Israeli soldiers standing nearby could have stopped the killing, or at least shot the killers, but were afraid to use their weapons for fear of a court martial.[2] In the eyes of the Underground, revenge—and the hope that the killings would intimidate Palestinians and stop future attacks—justified murdering civilians.

Members of the Underground had attacked Arab leaders in the past, but this time the group went after less prominent community members. They claimed "they had to put fear into the hearts of Hebron's Arabs." The Underground members chose the Islamic College because they believed it was a PLO base: "One qualification for admission was identification with a terror organization."[3]

Opinions regarding the Hebron killings were mixed. The most important rabbis affiliated with religious Zionism refused to condone the attacks. Some objected outright; others simply would not give an opinion. Several members of the Underground claimed the rabbis knew nothing of the pending attack. Three less prominent rabbis, however, did sanction violence, arguing that because the government was not willing to defend the settlers, they must do it themselves.[4] Rabbi Moshe Levinger urged several Underground members to respond to the incident in an "appropriate" manner and to commit an act "so that the Arabs would learn a lesson." After the attack Rabbi Levinger declared that the killers had "sanctified God's Name in public."[5]

The Hebron attacks were violent, but they were hardly unique. Jewish terrorism has plagued Israel since the founding of the state. The zealots attacked ordinary Palestinians and tried to assassinate Arab mayors they believed were aligned with Palestinian militants. Jewish terrorists even considered blowing up Muslim holy sites on the Temple Mount, a plot that, if carried out, would have shattered any hope of peace between Israel and any Muslim country. Jewish terrorism reached its horrifying apogee in 1995, when a young Jew, Yigal Amir, killed Prime Minister Yitzhak Rabin to disrupt the peace process.

Defenders of these groups vehemently reject the terrorist label. They argue that the groups are trying to defend the state of Israel or that the violence is the act of unaffiliated individuals. Still almost all Israeli security officials I talked to readily employed the label *terrorist*, and the brutal acts they have committed fit the standard description of terrorism: political violence that seeks to instill fear in civilians.

Jewish terrorism, which helped drive the British out of Mandatory Palestine, continued even after Israel's independence in May 1948. On September 17, 1948, the small and radical Lehi organization led by the future prime minister Yitzhak Shamir, killed Count Folke Bernadotte, a Swedish diplomat who was mediating the Palestine issue for the United Nations. Lehi leaders believed that Bernadotte's goal was to end Israel's existence as an independent state and return it to England. The killing led to the passage of a strong antiterrorism law and the disbanding of Irgun and Lehi militias. The new government at first began with mass arrests of Lehi and Irgun members and a military crackdown, but then released most of the members and gave them and their leaders full access to the political process. But the government's attempt to find and punish the perpetrators was tepid at best. Israeli police did not seriously pursue the investigation, a policy that set the standard for future investigations of Jewish terrorists. No member of the Lehi hit squad ever faced justice. Indeed in 1960 a Lehi commander told Attorney General Gideon Housner that he was ready to reveal all. Housner quickly shut him down, declaring, "God forbid! Do you know the problems you will create for your country?"[6] Yehushua Cohen, one of Bernadotte's killers, even became one of Ben Gurion's personal bodyguards.

Although some left-wing groups flirted briefly with violence, most of the terrorism committed by Jews within Israel involved religious groups, such as the Covenant of the Zealots. They and some other small, like-minded religious radical groups opposed the socialism and secularism espoused by Israel's first leaders and fought instead to install a theocracy, a genuine Torah state. The Covenant of the Zealots attacked coffee shops and movie theaters that they believed were desecrating the Sabbath and even burned several restaurants. The group was shut down after its members tried to smuggle bombs into the Knesset and a military facility in Jerusalem. Later groups, such as Keshet, targeted newsstands that sold secular newspapers.

Another group, a prelude to more dangerous organizations that would later emerge, was the Kingdom of Israel. It began operations in 1951, drawing members from Lehi. These recruits, steeped in years of clandestine activity under British rule, formed a far more formidable cadre than the untrained and poorly led groups that preceded it. Like Lehi, the Kingdom of Israel defined its role as defending, or at least avenging, the spilling of Jewish blood. In response to Arab terrorism the group attacked Jordanian outposts. Later, after anti-Jewish purges in Eastern Europe, they struck the diplomatic missions of communist countries in Israel, though typically with little effect. In 1953 security forces cracked down on the Kingdom of Israel, and its members were given long jail sentences, sentences that were quickly commuted in 1955, a precedent for the state's treatment of Jewish violence.

At the time Israeli security officials viewed the threat of invasion by Israel's neighbors and cross-border raids sponsored by neighboring states as their major concerns. Jewish violence seemed a minor irritant at best, and they devoted little attention to it.

New Land and New Terror: Meir Kahane and His Legacy

Just as the stunning Israeli victory in the 1967 War fundamentally altered the nature of Palestinian terrorism, so too did it transform Jewish terrorism. Jewish terrorists sought revenge for Palestinian violence and wanted to intimidate Palestinians. The peace process and associated surrender of "Jewish" land also provoked their wrath.

Rabbi Meir Kahane and his followers created one of the first organized Jewish terrorist groups after the 1967 War. An American-born Jew, Kahane fled the United States in 1971 as the FBI began investigating him in connection with the vigilante violence of the Jewish Defense League (JDL). Kahane had founded the JDL in 1968 to defend Jews in New York against crime, and his methods included the threat and use of violence. The JDL later targeted neo-Nazis, Palestinian leaders, several African American leaders, and Soviet facilities and personnel in the West, all in the name of defending Jews. The JDL even attacked moderate Jews for their supposed betrayal of their people. The FBI would later characterize it as a terrorist group. In 2002 the Southern Poverty Law Center estimated it had at most a few dozen active members.[7]

After Palestinian terrorist attacks, Kahane's followers, many of them American immigrants to Israel, retaliated against ordinary Arabs and even tried their hand at international terrorism. A former Irgun operative, Amichai Paglin (who later became a senior advisor to Begin), worked with several extremists, including Kahane, in an attempt to seize the Libyan embassy in Rome and kill employees as retribution for the 1972 murder of Israeli athletes in Munich. Israeli security officers found explosives in Paglin's luggage and thwarted the plot. Kahane believed that violence against non-Jews was *Kiddush hashem,* the sanctification of God's name, because it saves Jewish lives by killing those who attempt to harm Jews. He also justified violence in the name of Jewish machismo, insisting that Jews should stand up and fight. For the most part these plots failed because they were inept and amateurish.

Kahane was also suspected of ties to the group Terror against Terror, known as TNT, formed in 1974. Many of the early TNT members were U.S. immigrants to Israel who had been indoctrinated in summer camps in the Catskill Mountains run by the Jewish Defense League. TNT attacked Arabs on the West Bank, Christian missions in Jerusalem, and Israelis who pushed for peace, and otherwise conducted revenge attacks and pressed for Jewish supremacy. Kahane expressed his logic: "Really, I don't think that we can sit back and watch Arabs throwing rocks at buses whenever they feel like it. They must understand that a rock thrown at a Jewish bus is going to mean a bomb thrown at an Arab bus."[8] A study by the terrorism expert Ehud Sprinzak found that individuals in groups affiliated with Kahane had conducted "countless violent operations against local Arabs since the mid-1970s."[9]

In 1984, much to the distress of moderate Israelis, Kahane was elected to the Knesset even though (or because) his platform openly called for expelling Arabs from the country. Under the Israeli electoral system at the time, a political party need amass only 1 percent of the vote total to be elected, and Kach, Kahane's party, received twenty-six thousand votes, enough for a win. As a Knesset member Kahane endorsed extreme measures, such as imprisoning non-Jews who had sex with Jews, using violence to frighten Arabs, and expelling Arabs from Israel. "I would only use force for those who don't want to leave," he proclaimed. He argued that Arabs should be allowed to remain in Israel only as alien residents (according to biblical law), deprived of any political rights. "Even the water commissioner cannot be a gentile," he explained.[10] He also questioned Israel's ability to be both a Jewish state and a democracy.[11] Embarrassed by Kahane's racism and open endorsement of violence—and perhaps alarmed by polls showing that his party's electoral strength was growing—the Knesset passed a law forbidding parties that incited racism from participating in elections, thus ending his career as a politician.

When the Arab extremist El Sayyid Nosair killed Kahane in New York City on November 5, 1990, his followers splintered in different directions. Some stayed in Kach and others formed Kahane Chai (meaning "Kahane lives" in Hebrew), the latter headed by Kahane's son. In 1992, on the anniversary of Kahane's killing, three Kahane Chai members threw a grenade into a market in the Muslim section of the Old City of Jerusalem, killing two Palestinians.[12]

El Sayyid Nosair, Kahane's assassin, was later linked to the 1993 bombing of the World Trade Center. He was also implicated in plots against Manhattan landmarks that same year. Osama bin Ladin helped pay for Nosair's legal defense.

Kahane himself died, but his movement lives on. His virulent anti-Arab teachings are admired and mouthed by a small but significant number of radical Israelis today, and the personal ties his network created endured.

The Jewish Underground

Just as the war changed the strategic balance of power, so too did it transform domestic politics. Israel now possessed the land of its three main adversaries: the Golan Heights, previously part of Syria; the Gaza Strip and the Sinai Peninsula, formerly under Egyptian rule; and the West Bank of the Jordan River, which had been controlled by Jordan. For many religious Zionists the decisive victory was God's sign that the Jewish state should be restored to its biblical (and thus true) borders, which included much of what was now the West Bank. The territories were liberated, not occupied. Religious Zionists believed that God had returned to their rightful owners Jewish sites such as the Cave of the Patriarchs in Hebron (where tradition holds that Adam and Eve, Abraham and Sarah, Isaac and Rebecca, and Jacob and Leah are buried), Joseph's Tomb in biblical Shechem (Nablus), and Rachel's tomb outside Bethlehem. Hebron was particularly sensitive. Aside from its being home to the Cave of the Patriarchs, Israelis remembered that in 1929 Palestinians had massacred sixty-seven Jews there and that the Jewish community had fled during the 1948 War. After 1967 the Israeli government officially named the areas Judea and Samaria, and after the Likud Party took power in 1977 these names were commonly used. The names derive from the Bible: Samaria was for a time capital of the biblical northern kingdom of Israel, and Judah was the name of the southern kingdom, whose capital was Jerusalem. Palestinians (and some secular Israelis) find this terminology offensive.

In the newly conquered territories Muslim, Jewish, and Christian religious sites overlap, almost begging for confrontation. The Cave of the Patriarchs, where Abraham is buried, lies inside a mosque. Both Muslims and Jews must go through the mosque to enter the cave. When the area was under Muslim control, Jews were allowed to advance only to the seventh step outside the cave.

More important than the Cave of the Patriarchs was the 1967 IDF capture of the Temple Mount in Jerusalem. This site houses the remnants of the first and second Temples built by Solomon and Herod, respectively; the famous Western (or "Wailing") Wall is a retaining wall of the second temple. On top of the Mount are two ancient mosques, the Dome of the Rock and the al-Aqsa Mosque, both of which are venerated by Muslims worldwide. Religious Jews and some Christians believe that the rebuilding of the Temple will occur when the messiah returns. A few Jews, however, believe that the final redemption of the people of Israel cannot occur until the mosques on the Temple Mount are destroyed and there is Jewish sovereignty in all the biblical land of Israel.

Although such radical Jews were and remain an exception, Jewish fundamentalism exploded after the war. Before 1967 secular elites had dominated the Zionist movement and the Israeli government. Religious organizations, on the other hand, remained largely apolitical. If they took a stand on foreign and security policy it was pragmatic. Following Israel's success in the 1967 War and the annexation of Jerusalem, movements emerged that called for a Jewish state in the "whole land of Israel" rather than Israel's internationally recognized borders.

The majority of the religious Zionist settler community opposes terrorism against Arabs. Yet most of today's Jewish terrorists emerge from this milieu, and its story is bound up in that of Jewish terrorism.

At first the settler movement was weak. Under the Labor government, with the war hero Moshe Dayan as defense minister setting the rules, the government was in theory firmly against settling the West Bank. A handful in the Israeli Cabinet favored settlements near the West Bank's borders with Israel for strategic reasons, but there was little support for settlements in the heart of the West Bank, in places like Hebron.

Would-be settlers, however, found wiggle room. Almost immediately after the 1967 War ended, Jews established a settlement at Kfar Etzion (next to Bethlehem), restoring the Jewish settlement destroyed in the 1948 war. In 1968, during Passover, a group led by Rabbi Levinger set up camp in Hebron, claiming they only wanted to celebrate a Seder in there. Then they sent Defense Minister Dayan a telegram wishing him a happy Passover in the name of "the Hebron Settlers" and refused to leave. A forced eviction was politically difficult given Hebron's religious and historical resonance. As a compromise Israeli political leaders allowed Levinger to set up shop at a nearby military base on Hebron's edge, and then in 1971 allowed the establishment of the Kiryat Arba settlement there. Levinger declared it to be "the onset of the Third Temple period."[13]

Levinger's methods in Hebron became a pattern: settlers took a yard when given an inch. Often they encamped without government permission but with the tacit support of some in the military and the government. Shlomo Gazit, the first IDF coordinator for the territories, later wrote that Dayan failed to recognize "the fanatic and militant nature of the settlers."[14] In Hebron and elsewhere settlers steadily pushed against the IDF and local Arabs to expand their settlements. In 1979 settler wives, led by Miriam Levinger, occupied the Beit Haddassah building and refused to leave after the government would not allow Kiryat Arba to expand. "Hebron will no longer be *Judenrein,*" declared Levinger.[15]

Over time the settlement project would discredit Arab leaders who sought to work with Israeli authorities. After taking power in Hebron, for example, the IDF had worked with the local leader, Sheikh Ja'bari, who had a strong anti-Israel reputation but proved surprisingly cooperative. The sheikh opposed terrorism and openly denounced Fatah.[16] Levinger's insertion of the settlers into Hebron, however, made leaders like Ja'bari look like Israeli stooges.

Rabbi Levinger was later a key figure in the 1974 founding of Gush Emunim ("Bloc of the Faithful"). Gush adopted the motto "The Land of Israel, for the People of Israel, According to the Torah of Israel." For Gush spiritual leaders "every clump of earth" of Israel's biblical land "is the holy of holies, as the Torah declares."[17] Gush counted between ten thousand and twenty thousand core members, many of whom were middle-class Israelis.

In contrast to the violent groups that would spin off the Gush movement, Gush's leadership itself did not question the government's legitimacy because the government advanced their own goal—the redemption of the land of Israel: "An IDF rifle and tank have the same value as the prayer shawl and phylacteries [the two small leather boxes that observant Jews wear when they pray]."[18] Gush opposed the killing of Palestinians and Arabs outside of self-defense, and thus tried to block Kahanists from settling in the West Bank, but Gush splinter groups often disagreed with opposition to violence. The disagreements came from three sources: extreme nationalism, anger at Palestinian violence, and frustration with the perceived passivity of various Israeli governments. All these factors led some Gush members to renounce politics and embrace violence.

The most important Jewish terrorist group to emerge was the Jewish Underground, founded in the late 1970s by a group of Gush members, several of whom had close ties to the Gush leadership. The Underground was not a formal group (the Israeli media gave it the name), but rather a network of like-minded people. Members entered and exited the network regularly, choosing to participate as they saw fit. All members believed that Jews should defend themselves against Palestinian violence. Yet they often disagreed on whom to target and whether it was right to risk the safety of apolitical Palestinians who might be hurt in an attack. Some Jewish Underground members were not informed of various attacks and did not support them when they heard the news of them. Most of Gush's leaders formally expressed their opposition to violence, but several gave at least tacit support to the Underground.

Carmi Gillon, who headed Shin Bet in the 1990s, recalls that the Jewish Underground members became operational after Anwar Sadat's historic visit to Israel and the Camp David agreement. The Begin government had transferred the Sinai to the Egyptians, and in so doing gave up territory on which Israeli settlements had been built—a gross affront to those who believed the settlers were carrying out God's will. The vague language in the agreement about Palestinian autonomy in the West Bank and Gaza was seen as a potential betrayal. While its members were extreme, they were also educated and accomplished, "the best of Israel," according to Gillon. Unlike the Kahanists, the Underground members were primarily native-born Israelis.

On May 2, 1980, Fatah terrorists killed six Jews returning from prayer in Hebron near the Beit Hadassah building. The IDF quickly deported Fahd Kawasmeh, the mayor of Hebron, and Mohammad Milhem of Halhoul. But that was not enough for the militants. On June 2 the Jewish Underground responded to the attack by bombing the cars of the Arab mayors of Nablus and Ramallah, crippling both men. Two other bombs had been incorrectly wired, and as a police demolitions expert tried to remove one of them the bomb exploded and he was blinded.[19]

The targeted mayors were part of the National Guidance Committee, a Palestinian nationalist organization that had ties to the PLO. The Committee members' fiery rhetoric convinced the Jewish terrorists that they were a threat to "the well-being of every Jew in Judea, Samaria, and Gaza."[20] Yehuda Etzion, who was involved in the attack on the Arab mayors, proudly declared that he felt "privileged to cut off the legs of some of the murderers."[21] Yitzhak Ganiram, an Underground member, later told Israeli courts that after Beit Hadassah "the government's incompetence could lead to more Jewish blood being spilled." Violence against Arabs was necessary to stop this ineptitude: "[It was] clear to me that saving lives took precedence over the state's laws."[22] In addition to revenge and a desire to intimidate Palestinians, the terrorists also sought to disrupt Israel's talks with Egypt and otherwise prevent a rapprochement with Arab states.[23]

Even many Jews not supportive of the Underground or the settler movement found satisfaction in these attacks. The paper *Ma'ariv* described the impact on Nablus after the attack on the mayors: "A population of 120,000 is terrified of terrorists." It went on to boast, "The tables have been turned: The Arabs are afraid of uninhibited Jewish terrorists."[24]

Some Israeli military officers endorsed these vigilante attacks. After the bombing of the mayors IDF Chief of Staff Rafael Eitan told two members of the Kiryat Arba town council whom he believed to be responsible for the bombings, "Next time you do something like this, coordinate it with us. Had we known, we wouldn't have evicted Kawasmeh and Milhem," referring to the mayors the IDF deported after the attack near Beit Hadassah.[25] Brig. Gen. Binyamin Ben-Eliezer, the military governor of the West Bank, commented on the attack, "It's a pity that didn't hurt them a bit farther up in there," referring to their genitalia.[26]

Several years later the Underground launched the attack on the Islamic College, demonstrating both their lethal capabilities and the inability of the government to stop them. Underground members entertained even more dangerous plots. One of their most ambitious schemes was to blow up the Dome of the Rock mosque in Jerusalem. Planning began in earnest in 1978, after Begin agreed to return lands to Egypt and made rhetorical concessions on Palestinian autonomy under the Camp David Accord. Yeshua Ben Shushan, one of the plot's leaders, believed, "Muslim control of the Temple Mount was at the root of the Jewish people's spiritual downslide, as manifested by the Camp David Agreements."[27] For a few Jewish Underground fanatics like Ben Shushan who sought to destroy the mosque, the hope was "to clear away the 'abomination [shikutz],'" their term for the Dome of the Rock, which would pave the way to rebuilding the Temple and the arrival of the messiah. Ultimately, they believed, it would lead to Jewish redemption. Most members, however, were not apocalyptic, believing instead that the destruction was a step that would galvanize the Israeli people and "torpedo the peace treaty with Egypt."[28]

The plotters included army officers trained to use explosives. They had stolen explosives from a military camp and studied the area in detail for two years. One member of the group, a French convert to Judaism, posed as a monk to gather information. The plotters carefully surveyed the Temple Mount from multiple angles to check the timing of patrols and examined old aerial photographs to ensure they understood the entire layout.

Enthusiasm for the plot plummeted when the evacuation of the Yamit settlement, located in the northern part of the Sinai, did not provoke mass opposition within Israel. Despite Gush's active opposition to the withdrawal, most of the plotters concluded that Israelis would not come together to support the mosque's destruction. Gush-affiliated rabbis also refused to approve the plan, and many plotters were reluctant to proceed without the rabbis' imprimatur. Some plotters also feared that international condemnation would force the Israeli government to rebuild the mosques, an act they believed was forbidden by their religion.[29] In addition security was much tighter after three Jerusalemites brought grenades to the Mount and the American Jew Alan Goodman killed two Arabs there. To succeed, the plotters would have to fight with the guards and risk shedding Jewish blood. Yehuda Etzion, the prime mover of the conspiracy, later commented that if they had blown up the Dome of the Rock they "would have been considered ordinary murderers [if they] wounded some guard."[30]

After the Jewish Underground members decided not to go forward with the Temple Mount plot, the same clique that carried out the bombing of the Islamic College decided in 1984 to bomb five Arab buses, a plot that, had it succeeded, would have been among the most lethal in Israel's history. The Underground felt duty-bound to respond to a number of Palestinian strikes: a bus bombed in Ashkelon, an attack in Jerusalem, and the takeover of Bus 300 on the Tel Aviv–Ashkelon route. One Underground member believed the attacks would "show Arabs that terrorism was a two-way street" and would also "alert the Israeli authorities to the need to enforce law and order, and to stop standing idly by while Jewish blood is spilled."[31] The plotters planned the attack for 4:30 on a Friday afternoon, believing that this would reduce Jewish casualties, as Jews would be home preparing for the approaching Sabbath.

This time Shin Bet was ready. After the attack on the Islamic College Begin pushed Shin Bet to find the perpetrators, and they did so quickly, in part due to a lucky break. During the polygraph of a Shin Bet applicant the machine went wild in response to the question "Were you ever a party, even if only by knowledge, to vigilante attacks on Arabs?" The applicant had been asked to participate in the Underground, and even though he hadn't joined, he had a guilty conscience. Shin Bet took advantage of his conscience and quickly tricked him into spilling information on several of the Underground members. Later, when Shin Bet learned of the plot to bomb Arab buses, they used other tricks to foil the plot. In one case, Shin Bet agents pretended to be soldiers who begged a ride from suspected Underground members, claiming a medical emergency. They used that opportunity to bug the car.[32] Shin Bet waited for Underground members to booby-trap all five buses, which they did on April 27, 1984, catching the members in the act. The Jewish Underground was now history—and headlines.

The Jewish Underground was the most significant and brutal Jewish terrorist movement of the time. Yet much of the violence emanating from the settler community did not involve the Underground. When Deputy Attorney General Yehudit Karp investigated settler violence against Palestinians he found that over a few months in 1982 settlers were involved in a range of harassment and intimidation, against both Arab property and Arabs themselves, particularly in Hebron. The true extent of the problem was difficult to discern, as some military administrators and police officials responsible for the West Bank did not cooperate with investigators.[33] Often this violence involved a tit-for-tat response, particularly when Arabs resisted settlers' attempts to seize land. The motives, the Commission believed, sprang "from the desire to demonstrate 'rights' on the ground."[34]

As the 1980s wore on, low-level violence between settlers and local Arabs became a constant problem. Palestinian stone-throwing, firebombing, and roadblocks increased, disrupting daily life. Many disruptions passed without a response, but often settlers would shoot at houses or break windows, and they forced some residents to leave.[35] At times the violence became even more extreme. On October 28, 1984, David Ben-Shimul, a Jew from Jerusalem, fired a LAW missile stolen from the IDF at a Palestinian bus in East Jerusalem, killing one passenger and wounding another ten. Ben-Shimul sought to avenge the killing of Jewish students in Bethlehem earlier in the month. He acted alone, but Kach lauded him as a hero. In the mid-1980s the Kahanist-linked Committee for Roads' Security began, ostensibly to protect Jews driving in the Hebron area. However, the organization also burned down Palestinian houses and damaged Palestinian cars. At times its members simply acted like thugs, charging through Hebron and turning over fruit stands while armed with submachine guns.[36]

During the First Intifada Gush members took it upon themselves to confront neighboring Arabs throwing stones, which resulted in many Arab casualties. Jewish violence continued as the Intifada waned. On May 20, 1990, a Jew killed seven Palestinians, later telling police that it was revenge for being raped by an Arab when he was a child. A few months later another Jew shot an Arab woman near Hebron, justifying his attack as revenge for Palestinian terrorism.[37]

The Double Standard: The Israeli Government's Response to Jewish Terror

The Karp report failed to dent the Israeli conscience, which suggests that Jewish terrorists lived by different rules than Palestinian terrorists. Jewish terrorists were not backed by foreign states determined to undermine Israel. They did not seek to drive Jews into the sea, and they rarely targeted Jewish civilians and soldiers. Rallies were held on a regular basis to demonstrate support. The Jewish terrorists fed upon the anger Israelis felt after Arab terrorist attacks, justifying their violence as a response to Arab violence. Even when they faced justice the punishment was not as swift or severe as when Arabs perpetrated the violence. Public surveys of the time showed that a majority of Israelis supported amnesty for Jewish Underground members.

Complicating Shin Bet's task was the radicals' relation to power; these were not people whose rights could be observed only in the breach. On one occasion, when Shin Bet sought permission to arrest a range of suspects and then "break them down during interrogation," a standard Shin Bet approach, Begin refused; he wanted arrests only if there was compelling evidence against them. When suspects were arrested, Begin would press for a quick release. In another case Shin Bet arrested Menachem Livni, a radical linked to the Jewish Underground and a friend of Yitzhak Shamir (prime minister from 1983 to 1984 and again from 1986 to 1992) from their days together in the anti-British terrorist group Lehi. According to Gillon, Shin Bet even tracked Livni's meetings to Shamir's office. When visiting the United States, Shamir refused to denounce the Jewish Underground's actions and referred to them as "unauthorized military acts." Members of the Knesset would show up at rallies in support of the Underground members.[38] Israeli security officials felt far more bound by the letter of the law in going after Jewish terrorists.

Part of the problem for Shin Bet was its own checkered history and its perceived linkages to the Israeli Labor Party. After the founding of the state Ben Gurion used Shin Bet to monitor former members of revisionist Jewish groups like Lehi and the Irgun, whom he saw as a threat to the new country's stability. He also pursued left-wing organizations thought to be tied to the Soviet Union. Shin Bet "was like the KGB," in the words on one intelligence official—an exaggeration of course, but one that highlights its internal role. Shin Bet eventually stopped spying on political figures. When Begin was elected it reduced its focus on the violent far right. Likud, which was far more sympathetic to right-wing causes, saw this kind of spying as an offense to the state's democratic character. This political shift occurred in tandem with the growth of the settler movement and Jewish militancy.

Many in the IDF, which administered the West Bank, viewed the settlers as a distraction and a danger. Still there was little reward for cracking down on them, and the IDF turned a blind eye to their activities. When Rabbi Levinger initially attempted to settle in Hebron, he paid a visit to Uzi Narkiss, the IDF commander in the West Bank. Narkiss exploded: "What do you want? To settle in Hebron? I don't care. I know nothing!"[39] It was easier to ignore the settlers and look for a short-term solution. Attempts to dismantle settlements were politically disastrous. Newspapers carried images of soldiers dragging off Jews, including covered pious girls, shouting patriotic and religious slogans. Settlers also timed the creation of new settlements for politically sensitive moments, when the government was loath to have a confrontation on the home front.

Likud encouraged the notion that the settlers were acting as government agents. In 1979 army reserve units incorporated Jewish settlers, giving them weapons and the responsibility for securing themselves. At times the army allowed them to patrol local Arab areas.

The government did still try to stop Jewish terrorism, but only up to a point. Israeli officials restricted the movement of Kahane's followers and arrested some of the more violent activists. In general, however, prosecutors were criticized as "overzealous" when they went after these individuals.[40] Kahane himself was administratively detained for six months in 1980 after Kach's plot to launch a missile at the Dome of the Rock was discovered. When Kahane was elected to the Knesset, however, Shin Bet could no longer track him, as Israeli law prohibited the organization from monitoring elected officials.

Even when individuals were arrested and convicted, the double standard was maintained. In 1988 Rabbi Levinger killed a Palestinian shoe salesman in Hebron, claiming that he was defending himself from stone throwers. At his trial he denied the charges but defiantly declared, "I wish that I had been privileged to kill a son of Ishmael."[41] For the killing he served thirteen weeks in jail. Most of the Jewish Underground members chose plea bargains that resulted in short sentences or were sentenced to jail terms of seven years or fewer, despite their bloody track record and lethal ambitions. One judge explained the limited terms by saying that the bombers were educated people who had fought in Israel's wars and were motivated by faith: "The transgressions of people like these are not like the crimes committed by others who aimed to destroy, kill, annihilate."[42] And even then, those with longer terms were released in 1990, when the Knesset passed a special law on their behalf.[43]

Before Oslo, national security forces looked upon Jewish violence an irritant but not a grave threat to the rule of law or the Israeli state. Jews, after all, would not harm other Jews.

The Dark Side of Oslo

The Oslo deal, accepted and promoted by Yitzhak Rabin, Israel's "Mr. Security," stunned the Israeli right wing. Settlers believed that the West Bank concessions were a betrayal of Israel's heritage, but Rabin saw the Israeli occupation of the West Bank as a grave risk to the Jewish and democratic character of the state. In an interview after signing the historic Oslo agreement on the White House lawn, he declared that letting the hundreds of thousands of Palestinians stay under occupation meant that Israel would either become undemocratic or, if Israel allowed them to vote, it would cease to be a Jewish state: "Whoever now speaks about the whole land of Israel [meaning its biblical boundaries] speaks either on a racist Jewish state which will not be Jewish or a bi-national state."[44] Nor did Rabin support settlements that were not motivated by strategic goals. He even declared Gush Emunim "a cancer in the body of Israeli democracy."[45]

Shortly after the deal Jewish terrorism raised its ugly head to challenge Oslo. On February 25, 1994, Dr. Baruch Goldstein, who was born in the United States and had been a follower of Rabbi Kahane, killed twenty-nine Palestinians and injured 125 who were praying in the Tomb of the Patriarchs in Hebron. This gave Hamas a pretext to launch attacks and proved a setback for Israeli negotiators on the peace process.

Guards at the Tomb had been warned to expect a terrorist attack—but from Hamas, not a Jewish extremist. Goldstein entered the Tomb wearing his IDF medical uniform. In the mosque he found some eight hundred Palestinians praying; he tossed a hand grenade in their midst and then opened fire with his machine gun, only stopping when his gun jammed and worshippers overwhelmed and killed him. A government commission investigating the massacre found the Israeli police performance "totally unsatisfactory." Equipment was in poor repair, tardiness was common, the number of personnel was insufficient, and orders from officers were confusing. Jewish settlers had permission to carry weapons, even into the Tomb of the Patriarchs, and Goldstein's IDF uniform served as an extra reason for security officials not to scrutinize him.[46]

Goldstein acted alone, but he was not a loner. Married and the father of four, he was well respected in his Kiryat Arba community. Goldstein believed that Palestinians had to learn that "Jewish blood is not cheap"; it was a theme of Jewish Underground- and Kahane-affiliated attacks in the past.[47] The Oslo Accords and the transfer of land to the Palestinian Authority in particular outraged Goldstein. After the Accords he wore a yellow star with the word *Jude* on it, likening the Rabin government to the Nazi regime. The massacre brought to a halt the peace process that had seemed near fruition. For Goldstein and his circle of Kahanists, however, the attack went beyond that: many of Goldstein's friends saw him as engaging in *Kiddush hashem,* sanctifying God's name by saving Jewish lives from the threat Rabin posed to Israel. A subsequent investigation into the killing found that he had acted under a framework that "fully justified anti-Arab terrorism." Kahane Chai, noting that the massacre fell during the Jewish holiday of Purim, praised Goldstein as a martyr who, like the biblical Mordecai and the Jews of Persia, "struck at all their enemies and did as they pleased with their foes."[48] His grave in Kiryat Arba is now a pilgrimage site for extremists.

The killing did not end with Goldstein's death. Palestinian protests turned violent, and dozens died in clashes with the IDF. In the town of Kfar Saba Palestinians axed an elderly Jew to death. Forty more people would die from the violence, more than Goldstein had killed.

For a brief period after the Goldstein massacre the Israeli government got tough with Jewish terrorists. In 1994 the government banned Kach and Kahane Chai, though the networks continued to function. The government made administrative arrests, issued movement restrictions against dozens of Kahane activists, and prevented suspected U.S. associates from entering Israel. Unlike Likud and the governments before it, the Rabin government was hostile not only to the terrorists but to the ideological currents in which they swam. Because the attack took place when the peace process was moving forward, the government also wanted to send a message to both Palestinian and U.S. audiences.[49] The Rabin government, however, did not evacuate the rest of the settlers in Hebron, despite the urging of Ehud Barak, the IDF chief of staff at the time.

The Goldstein killing was only a prelude to an attack with even more horrendous consequences: the murder of Israeli prime minister Yitzhak Rabin. Just as the prime minister was leading his country toward peace, his murder tore Israel apart, derailing the very process that promised an end to violence. On November 4, 1995, Rabin addressed a massive pro-peace rally in Tel Aviv; a young religious Israeli law student and right-wing extremist named Yigal Amir was waiting for him to emerge in a nearby parking lot. As Rabin appeared, Amir walked to within feet of him and shot him twice in the back. Although there were a thousand police and security officers deployed for the event, Amir, who had served in the elite Golani Brigade of the IDF, managed to pass himself off as a VIP driver and get near Rabin's vehicle. Initially Shin Bet failed to secure the area as planned. When the police finally did so, Amir was already inside the cordon. Immediately after the shooting he was caught and arrested at the scene. In jail for life, he expresses no regrets for the murder.[50]

To Amir, Rabin was a *din rodef* and a *din moser*, a person endangering innocent Jews by giving away Jewish land. Though he did not have links to the Kahanist movement or extremists within Gush Emunim, Amir believed the prime minister was inviting Palestinians to kill Jews by agreeing to pull back Israeli troops from the West Bank. Using this logic he invoked his perverted interpretation of Jewish law to sanction Rabin's murder. Amir had also planned to kill Shimon Peres, Rabin's foreign minister and another champion of the peace process, but he had the opportunity to shoot down only one of Israel's peacemakers.

Although only a small portion of Israel's Jewish community condoned the murder, a much larger segment had contributed to an environment of radicalization before Rabin's death. Anti-Rabin demonstrations had become increasingly nasty. Political opponents portrayed him in hateful terms, calling the hero of Israel's many wars a traitor. Posters showed him smiling at Arabs while washing his hands in blood, or they portrayed him as a Nazi or with his head on Arafat's body. A month before his death a group of extremists gathered outside his home in Jerusalem to issue the "Pulsa di Nura," a mystical death curse, against him.

For Shin Bet, the organization responsible for stopping terrorism and providing security for the prime minister, the killing was a nightmare. Although they had encouraged Rabin to wear a bulletproof vest before the rally he had refused, believing he wasn't in danger. Amir's plans, however, should not have surprised Israeli intelligence. He had mentioned to friends that he intended to kill Rabin and had tried to do so twice. The first attempt failed because Rabin cancelled the scheduled event, and the second because the security cordon stopped Amir from getting close. Shin Bet had infiltrated the ranks of right-wing extremists using a close friend of Amir's as an agent provocateur; however, that friend, Raviv, had neglected to tell Shin Bet that Amir had talked of killing Rabin. Indeed Raviv knew that his relationship with Shin Bet gave him immunity from most punishments, so he felt free to participate in violent demonstrations and other illegal activities, which should have raised red flags within the organization about his fidelity. A subsequent investigation led by Meir Shamgar, a former chief justice of Israel's Supreme Court, found, "The Shin Bet did not do enough to adjust its protection methods to the worsening threat, nor did they ensure that its bodyguards properly understood the severity of the danger."[51]

Carmi Gillon, who headed Shin Bet at the time, stepped down as a result of the organization's failure. He said he had been concerned before the assassination because of the demonstrations and overheated rhetoric, but he lacked specific information to arrest anyone. Shin Bet focused on radicals in the settlements, but Amir came from the bucolic suburb of Herzliyya outside of Tel Aviv and was a law student at Bar-Ilan University, also in a suburb of Tel Aviv.

Amir got what he wanted from killing Rabin. The former U.S. peace negotiator Martin Indyk believes that Jewish terrorism, along with Palestinian violence, "derailed the peace process." More than ten years later Amir's brother Amitai praised him, saying, "Amir sacrificed himself for all of us. He saved us from the Oslo Accords and Rabin."[52]

CHAPTER XIX

SETTLER VIOLENCE AND THE SECOND INTIFADA (2000-2009)

ONE of the most heinous plots in the history of Israeli-Arab terrorism was the April 2002 attempt to blow up a Muslim girls' school in Jerusalem. Jewish terrorists from the settlement of Bat Ayin placed explosives in a trailer next to the school and set it to go off on April 29 at 7:35 a.m., the time when students would arrive. Because this was the height of the Second Intifada, passing policemen became suspicious of two kippot-wearing Jews in an Arab neighborhood in the middle of the night. When the policemen saw the Jews in the parked trailer, they investigated, and as a result found the bombs and saved many lives.[1]

After the arrest and interrogation of one of the suspects, Israeli police and intelligence officials learned of a massive cache of weapons, including machine guns, grenade launchers, dozens of pounds of explosives, and other heavy weaponry.[2] The specter of an attack on the Temple Mount mosques loomed once again. After the discovery of the cache, Avi Dichter, who headed Shin Bet at the time, reported, "[the extremists,] dream of removing the 'abomination' from the Temple Mount." Doing so, he warned, might "transform the conflict between Israel and the Palestinians to a conflict between 13 million Jews and a billion Muslims around the world."[3]

The Jerusalem plot was not the movement's first attempt to kill children. On September 17, 2001, the same group set a bomb to explode in another Arab schoolyard at 10:00 a.m., during recess, but the bomb malfunctioned and exploded fifteen minutes early. It destroyed a water fountain and a tree, and though several were injured, none were killed. (The timing of the attack, six days after 9/11, shows how tone deaf the extremists are; success would have undermined the sudden surge in sympathy for Israel as a victim of terrorism.) In March 2002 another plot targeted a Palestinian boys' school, setting a pink ice cream carton as bait. Fortunately the curious children knew not to open the carton and alerted a principal, who called the police. The bomb exploded before the police arrived, injuring ten.

The Jewish would-be murderers caught after the Jerusalem plot received real sentences, between twelve and fifteen years in prison. However, the follow-up effort to jail suspects tied to the Bat Ayin group and the weapons cache failed. These individuals, many of whom had links to the Kahane movement, had read the movement's manual, *How to Confront a Shin Bet Interrogation,* and kept their mouths shut. In the end the suspects were released. Supporters threw a party during which guests distributed a new volume of the counterinterrogation manual and called for hunting down Shin Bet members.[4]

Like the Jewish Underground, the Bat Ayin movement was a violent splinter of the settler movement, more a network of individuals than a coherent group. Even as the Oslo negotiations continued, settlements in the West Bank expanded: more than one thousand housing units were constructed each year from 1993 through 1999; in 1998, the peak year, more than four thousand units were built.[5] These settlements would not only be a sticking point in peace negotiations, but they would be at the heart of Jewish terrorism during the Second Intifada.

Much of the construction was the result of so-called natural growth, the constant expansion of existing settlements well beyond the initial small core that had been authorized. In a story repeated in different forms, Ariel Sharon, the infrastructure minister in 1998, went to Harasha Mountain near Ramallah. Sharon declared the place "strategic" and told the water company to build a water reservoir there. He then turned to a local settler leader and said, "Put a guard in the water reservoir. The guard will probably feel lonely. He will marry and have a family. The kids will need company. More families will come. Later, there will be a *minyan* [the minimum ten adult males needed for communal prayer] and the *minyan* will need a synagogue. The women will need a *mikvah* [a ritual bath]. The kids will need a kindergarten and gardens. This is how we shall turn the Harasha outpost into a settlement."[6]

Because the violent fringe among the settlers receives the most media attention, many assume that all settlers are violent. That is not the case. The 300,000-strong settler community is diverse in its demographics and its ideology: some are religious, some are highly nationalist, and some are secular. Many live in the West Bank simply because it is cheaper than living in Israel proper. The two largest and most significant groups are "national-religious Zionists," who believe that God gave the historic land of Israel to the Jewish people for eternity, and the ultraorthodox. In 2009 30 to 40 percent of the total settler community were ultraorthodox, the largest single component; 22 percent lived in national-religious settlements; another 15 percent lived in largely secular settlements; and the remainder were in mixed settlements. The ultraorthodox often choose the West Bank for its cheap housing and are rarely involved in violence or protests. Most of these settlers live under the protection of the security barrier that runs along or near Israel's border with the West Bank. Significantly perhaps 80 percent of the settlers on the West Bank outside the barrier are national-religious.[7]

Pro-settlement voices such as the Council of Jewish Settlements in Judea, Samaria, and the Gaza Strip, known by its Hebrew acronym, Yesha, criticize the government when it opposes settlements, but they do so peacefully. Within the national-religious community most see the Israeli state as an instrument of Jewish redemption even when it is led by secular figures. For the settlers, Independence Day is a religious holiday. Binyamin Elon, a rabbi and a former parliamentarian affiliated with the national-religious trend, recalled, "At school we were taught the worst thing we could do was turn against fellow Jews," referring to the civil war that preceded the destruction of the second temple. However, unlike the mainstream settler movement or even radicals like the Underground, the Bat Ayin terrorists and others in their network see themselves as challenging the legitimacy of the Jewish state as opposed to defending it.

Having opposed the peace process, the settlers suffered tremendously during the Intifada that came in its wake. Palestinian groups often targeted settlers in revenge for settler violence and to disrupt negotiations and retaliate for their own losses.[8] The attacks were popular, as most Palestinians loath the settlers. A poll taken in December 2003 found that 86 percent of Palestinians surveyed supported attacks on settlers, while 48 percent supported attacks on Israel proper.[9]

Settlers offered close and convenient targets. Many settlements are in largely Palestinian-populated parts of the West Bank, leaving settlers vulnerable to shootings or stones as they drove to and from their homes. Their vehicles were unarmored, and they regularly drove by populated Palestinian areas.

In the Intifada's first three years 162 of the 852 total deaths were among the settler community, 19 percent, far larger than their percentage of the population. Israeli statistics list the following: from September 2000 until July 2003 there were approximately 18,135 attacks, including many non-lethal attacks (stone throwing, Molotov cocktails, and so on). Ninety-six percent of these attacks (17,405) were in the West Bank and Gaza. Four percent (730) were inside the Green Line, Israel's pre-1967 borders, though these were particularly lethal. There were more than two thousand reported incidents of shooting at settlers' vehicles and more than one thousand incidents involving improvised explosive devices. In addition, there were 739 incidents of shootings at settlements from neighboring villages; forty-three settlers died when attackers infiltrated their homes.[10] All in all, from the Second Intifada's start through the end of 2008, 237 Israeli civilians in the West Bank and Gaza died, along with 246 security force personnel.[11] Among the settlers the death toll was so constant that many women settlers reportedly cleaned their home every morning so that if their husband was killed the house would be tidy when mourners came to comfort them.

Even as Palestinian and Jewish violence flared, settlements continued to grow. The Israeli government channeled millions of dollars to settlements in the first years of the Second Intifada.[12] When expansion bumped up against private Palestinian land, the state often expropriated land to continue the building. In 2009 the Israeli newspaper *Haaretz* obtained a government database on settlements. It showed that a stunning 75 percent of the settlements were built without a permit.[13]

Settlers used violence to drive Palestinians off their land, then appropriated the land when the settlement expanded. The human rights group B'Tselem documented "cases of shooting, threats of shooting and killing, beatings with various instruments, stone throwing, use of attack dogs, attempts to run over Palestinians, vandalizing of farm equipment and crops, theft of crops, killing and theft of livestock and animals used for labor," often with Israeli authorities turning a blind eye to the abuse.[14]

The revenge attacks of the past continued as settlers retaliated against Palestinian terrorism. In the spring of 2001 Jewish squads in the West Bank killed eight Palestinians in drive-by shootings and bombing attacks.[15] In 2002 an underground Jewish organization using the cover name the Tears of the Widows and Orphans, part of the Bat Ayin network, killed two Palestinians in the name of revenge. For Jewish extremists, the violence of the Intifada confirmed their worldview that the only answer to the Palestinian problem was force.

In addition to conducting attacks independently, settlers demanded a harsh response to violence from the IDF. To force the IDF's hand, they declared they would act if the IDF did not. Their demands did not fall on deaf ears. Because their community had suffered, the IDF sympathized with the settlers, often arming them for self-defense. In the initial stages of the Intifada the settlers openly carried weapons. To protect them the IDF installed checkpoints on roads and increased their already large presence in the West Bank. One estimate made in 2003 during the height of the Second Intifada found that the cost of guarding the settlements came to over 500 million dollars a year.[16]

Many Jewish militants drew upon funding and other support from Jews outside Israel, particularly those in the United States. Most of these donations were for legitimate charitable and religious activities, but part of it went to help militants, often in the form of legal aid to Jews charged with attacks on Arabs. Perhaps the most famous organization, Honenu, maintains a twenty-four-hour hotline that offers legal advice for soldiers and civilians accused of violence against Arabs.[17]

A striking number of the militant settlers come from the United States, driven by a vision of divine destiny to return to the land that God bequeathed to Abraham. No matter that they need to spill blood to fulfill that dream. Kahane and many of his American followers, including Baruch Goldstein, who massacred Arabs praying in the Tomb of the Patriarchs in Hebron, shared that vision. Israel's former president Chaim Herzog declared the United States "a breeding ground for Jewish extremists."[18] One Israeli intelligence official told me that he thinks many of the settlers are delusional: "America is very smart to send these people to Israel. They are truly dangerous."

The Intifada Wanes, but Jewish Violence Continues

After various Palestinian groups accepted a ceasefire in 2005 the Intifada tapered off. Still the risk of Jewish terrorism continued to grow. At the time the Shin Bet director Avi Dichter estimated there were "several dozen" Jewish terrorists, a small number compared to Israel's Palestinian problem, but a large one given the access that Jews have to all targets in the state.[19] In 2008 that number had grown exponentially. Maj. Gen. Gadi Shamni, who then headed IDF forces in the West Bank, reported that the number of people willing to use violence had swelled from a few dozen to "several hundred."[20] A 2008 United Nations study found that settler violence against Palestinian civilians steadily increased after 2006, going from 182 in 2006 to almost 290 by October 2008; half of the attacks were against women, children, and the elderly.[21]

A small number of rabbis have now reiterated the *din rodef* and *din moser* laws that allow a Jew to kill another Jew if he intends to endanger Jews or give away Jewish lands; it is the same justification Yigal Amir used to kill Prime Minister Rabin. Some cells ask rabbis for rulings or, more often, to use their teachings to justify violence that would deter peace with Palestinians or the return of land on the West Bank. As one intelligence official told me, this system is "no different from Hamas." Even if explicit rabbinical approval is not forthcoming some militants deliberately seek out vague rulings, while others simply turn to a different rabbi if the first will not sanction an attack.

As always, many settlers endorse revenge attacks, which to a lesser degree other Israelis support. After a Palestinian killed eight students at the Merkaz HaRav seminary in 2008 several prominent rallies called for the government to retaliate, and some demonstrators endorsed revenge attacks. After a Palestinian axed a settler boy, settlers opened fire in Palestinian areas to intimidate local residents, occupied four Palestinian shops in Hebron, and burned farmland in the Safa area.[22]

Israeli security officials are most concerned when the settlers use violence against Jews and the state of Israel to force their policy demands on the government. When the government seeks to dismantle all or part of a settlement, residents sometimes block traffic and throw stones at the IDF. More commonly they throw stones at Palestinian cars, burn the crops of Palestinian farmers, cut down Palestinians' olive trees, and fire weapons to intimidate Palestinians. Settlers have learned that such attacks can influence the government and prevent it from cracking down on fringe parts of their movement.[23]

Radicals espouse a "price tag" doctrine, hoping to make the political and material price too high for the government to move against them. Because of the price tag doctrine, the 2005 evacuation of the Jewish presence in Gaza and of four small settlements in the West Bank—about eight thousand people in all—required extensive preparation by the IDF. At first the government's fears seemed unfounded, as little violence occurred. Gaza itself has little biblical significance, and the Gaza settlers were less militant than their brothers in the West Bank, although some extremists from the West Bank traveled to the Gaza settlements to show their support, and the IDF had to manage them as well. Only one related terrorist attack occurred, and that was before the withdrawal. On August 4, 2005, Eden Natan-Zada, an AWOL IDF soldier and a member of Kahane Chai, boarded a bus filled with Israeli Arabs in the town of Shfar'am and opened fire, killing four and wounding twenty-two. When he paused to reload, the survivors jumped and handcuffed him, and later beat him to death. No one will know exactly what motivated Natan-Zada, but he carried with him an orange ribbon, a symbol used by opponents of disengagement from Gaza. The attack occurred just before the evacuation of Gaza was to begin, and a number of observers believe that Natan-Zada hoped that by provoking riots security forces would be too busy to carry out disengagement.[24] The attack, however, appears to have been Natan-Zada's alone; apparently other Kahane Chai members were not involved.

In February 2006 Ehud Olmert's government removed several houses at an outpost of the illegal Amona settlement in the West Bank. One extremist declared that the Israeli people "have to decide whether they are on the side of the Torah or the state."[25] More than forty people, including two members of the Knesset, were hurt in the demonstration and the police crackdown. Some settlers had their children wear yellow Stars of David as they departed in order to invoke the Holocaust; such heavy-handed imagery angered many Israelis.[26] Still there was no terrorism during the actual withdrawal. Later in 2006 Asher Weizgan, a Jewish resident of the Shiloh settlement on the West Bank, murdered four Palestinians in protest over the withdrawal.

Hebron, as before, is perhaps the most sensitive flashpoint. One soldier described Palestinians who live near Jewish settlers as having "about the shittiest life you can have."[27] The IDF must protect Palestinian children from Jewish kids who threaten them, throw stones at them, and beat them up. Settlers also throw stones and bricks at the cars of the Temporary International Presence at Hebron, a group of observers from five European countries and Turkey who monitor the humanitarian situation in Hebron under the 1997 Wye agreement.

In 2008, when Israeli riot police removed several families from the House of Contention in Hebron after the Israeli Supreme Court ruled that the claimed purchase of the building by settlers was not legitimate, settlers rampaged neighboring Arab areas in response. More than one hundred Palestinians were injured as violence spread. Settlers desecrated graveyards and burned houses, olive groves, and a mosque. Prime Minister Olmert declared that the violence "has no other name than a pogrom." "As a Jew," he added, "I am ashamed."[28]

A particularly radical faction, the Hilltop Youth movement, grew tremendously after disengagement. (Hilltop Youth is a misnomer. Most members are over twenty-five and married.) In the early 1990s the father of the movement, Avri Ran, promoted the idea that Jews should populate empty parts of the West Bank in order to stop them from being handed over to the Palestinians. Toward the end of the decade Israelis began to heed his words.[29] Professor Shlomo Kainel found that most of the Hilltop Youth are living on hills in the middle of heavily crowded Palestinian areas, particularly in the Nablus and Hebron area. A typical settlement consists of thirty to forty people; they try to live simply, eating what they grow and raising animals, studying Torah, and often working in construction on the West Bank in order to live their credo of avoiding dependence on non-Jewish workers. In 2009 there were perhaps eight hundred or so Hilltop residents, and around five thousand more who embrace the ideology.[30] They are at best loosely organized, more a movement than an organization, but Hilltop Youth spawned the Bat Ayin underground, among other violent groups.

Members of Hilltop Youth believe that Palestinians are "raping the Holy Land" and call for their expulsion. They endorse revenge attacks. From their small outposts they threaten Palestinians with guns, uproot their olive groves and rustle sheep, and use whatever means available to intimidate them.[31] In contrast to almost all settlers and even some extremists, Hilltop Youth members reject the Israeli state's secular government. They believe a theocratic state should be declared and run according to Jewish religious law. Some even criticize the mainstream settler movement because it does not actively reject the Israeli state and because it is willing to cut deals with the government.[32] The government, they believe, is gentile, not Jewish, and therefore has no legitimacy.[33]

Rabbi Yitzhak Ginsburgh is perhaps the most important rabbi for the Hilltop Youth. He famously declared, "[It is] time to crack the nut," arguing that the Jewish people are a nut within the shell of the state of Israel. Initially the shell was necessary to protect the Jewish people, but now the state only hinders the salvation of Jews. He calls for establishing the State of Judea, a theocracy with its own judicial and educational system as well as government. He opposes conscription and does not recognize the authority of the Israeli government. Ginsburgh supported Goldstein's 1994 massacre in the Cave of the Patriarchs and condones revenge attacks on Palestinians.[34]

The Hilltop Youth and like-minded radicals hold secular Jews in contempt, and some militants talk about killing leftist Jews as a way of putting the country back on a religious track. In 2008 Professor Zeev Sternhell, a critic of Jewish settlements, was wounded in a pipe bomb attack. Near his home were fliers offering almost 300,000 dollars to anyone who would kill a member of the left-wing Peace Now movement. The flyer declared that Israeli leaders "want to erase the laws of God" and that "the time has come to set up a state of Jewish law in Judea and Samaria."[35]

The IDF argues that enforcing order in the settler community is a police duty, but settler groups have successfully opposed attempts to increase the Israeli police presence on the West Bank. Palestinian police are barred from responding to settler violence. This policy reduces friction between settlers and Palestinian authorities, but it decreases the overall credibility of the PA, which cannot defend its people from settler harassment and violence.

Some Israelis fear that cracking down on settlers and removing settlements will lead to problems in the military. After 1967 segments of the orthodox community that had shunned military service now embraced it. They worked with the IDF to set up special yeshivas where young men divided their time between Torah study and combat service.[36] The IDF, whose elite was once composed largely of secular leftists from the kibbutzim, now has a disproportionate number of leaders from the national-religious sector of Israeli society; a common estimate is about one-third of the officer corps. The presence in elite units is even higher.[37] The Gaza withdrawal went smoothly and did not lead to problems within the IDF, but fears of antagonizing the military persists.

Extremists also threaten Israel's leaders. During the unilateral withdrawal period in 2005 Israel's defense minister Shaul Mofaz was warned that settlers would seek revenge against him and his children. Even Sharon received mail threatening "death to traitors."[38] It is tempting to dismiss this as the ranting of a few disturbed individuals, but after Rabin's murder the threat became impossible to ignore. Settlers not only lash out at Israel's leaders, but they also intimidate Shin Bet personnel. In 2002 one high-ranking member of Shin Bet's Jewish Branch, who was himself a settler, had to leave after his neighbors discovered that he worked to stop Jewish terrorism. The wives of the Bat Ayin underground, the group suspected of plotting to blow up a girls' school in East Jerusalem, demonstrated in front of the man's house and harassed his family. His wife noted bitterly that after her husband had worked for years to stop Arab terrorism, it was fellow Jews who turned on them.[39]

The Double Standard Continues

The double standard for Jewish terrorists persisted after the Second Intifada began and continues to this day. Administrative detention is rarely ordered.[40] Settler homes are not destroyed if a member commits a terrorist act. Israel does not impose restrictions on Jewish religious institutions that turn out militants and violent propaganda. Some rabbis who justify violence even receive government salaries.[41]

Shin Bet does have the power to act against violent settlers, but it remains reluctant to do so. Because Israeli politicians are sensitive to any perception that they are targeting settlers and their supporters, they are averse to acting preemptively. Unlike Arab terrorists, Jews accused of violence know Israeli law well and they can pay for the best lawyers. The settlers are skilled at resisting the security agencies. Those involved in violence have read the Kahane movement's tract, *How to Confront a Shin Bet Interrogation,* and keep their mouths shut. Unlike their Arab counterparts, they wait out Shin Bet, knowing that interrogators are less aggressive toward their own. In the end they prevail in court by saying nothing.[42]

Even when convicted, Jewish extremists receive lenient sentences. Before the Second Intifada Nachum Korman, a Jewish settler, entered a West Bank village in search of children who had thrown stones at Jews in cars. There he found eleven-year-old Hilmi Shusha, whom he beat to death with a rifle. In January 2001 Korman was sentenced to six months of community service, a token sentence that enraged Palestinians.[43]

Indeed although individual Palestinians may have been deterred from violence by the threat of retaliation, settler violence has mostly backfired. It discredits moderates and provides a reason for Palestinian militants to recruit new members. The harassment and occasional murder of individual Palestinians enrages the community and only strengthens groups like Hamas and PIJ that carry out attacks on the settlers.

The Jewish terrorists are more interested in opposing the peace process than achieving a goal, and in that sense they are successful. Many people believe that Rabin's murder brought the peace process to a screeching halt, an exaggeration perhaps, but the murder certainly played a major role in disrupting progress at a crucial phase. Today the price tag doctrine of Jewish terrorists makes the Israeli government reluctant to dismantle settlements, including illegal ones, even as part of a peace deal. Yet despite the terrorists' ability to pressure the government and Shin Bet, their success is limited. In the face of Jewish violence Israel withdrew from the Sinai and later from Gaza; peace talks did continue after Rabin's murder; Israel has removed some illegal settlements and several legal ones. The threat of violent resistance has made withdrawal more difficult for Israeli leaders, but not impossible.

Indeed, Jewish terrorism may backfire in the end. If Jewish violence involves attacks on soldiers or other Jews, or if it becomes a consistent embarrassment to Israel's political leaders, it will strengthen calls to dismantle settlements and rein in these extremists.

SECTION V

FINDINGS AND CONCLUSIONS

CHAPTER XX

INTERROGATION DILEMMAS

CONSIDER the cases of Abdel Samed Harizat, Nasser Issa Shakher, and Nasim Za'atari, three Palestinian prisoners whose fates illustrate the complexity of harsh interrogation methods. Human rights officials charge that Harizat died on April 26, 1995, when his Shin Bet interrogators shook him so violently it led to a subdural hemorrhage. His death may have influenced security officials almost four months later, when they arrested Issa Shakher, who was a liaison between Yahya Ayyash, the "Engineer" who designed Hamas bombs and planned many attacks, and a Hamas network in Ramallah. In Israeli custody on August 19, 1995, Shakher confessed to involvement in terrorism but refused to reveal any information on future attacks. Interrogators were not allowed to subject him to "special means," such as violent shaking. Two days later, on August 21, Sufian Jabarin blew himself up on Jerusalem Bus 26. Shakher later revealed, after rougher treatment, that he had planned the bus bombing, and his subsequent confession led to the discovery of a bomb factory and thirty-seven arrests. This was too late for the three Israelis and the American who died on Bus 26. Nasim Za'atari had been a scout for Hamas who guided suicide bombers to their targets during the Second Intifada. Israel captured him and broke him in interrogation, using the information they gained to kill the Hamas recruiter caught in the middle of preparations for suicide bombing missions.[1]

Israel has long wrestled with this tension between vital intelligence and human rights. "What kind of attorney general are you?" Rabin once yelled at Michael Ben-Yair. "I need you to fight terrorism, and you are constantly telling me what not to do"—a sentiment familiar to policymakers world-wide who wrestle with legal restrictions.[2] Rabin and Ben-Yair had been quarreling about a fundamental issue for intelligence agencies in Israel and other democracies: how to balance human rights with security needs. In particular, how much coercion is acceptable? Israelis refer to coercion as "special means" or "moderate physical pressure," while Palestinians and human rights organizations simply call it "torture."

Critics argue that rough interrogation simply produces false confessions. If prisoners are tortured they will confess to anything to avoid pain. Proponents of rough interrogation claim that the information produced can be cross-checked for accuracy against other sources, enabling interrogators to separate fact from fiction. They also contend the threat of abuse probably deters other, uninvolved Palestinians from taking up arms, though this is difficult to prove either way. Critics counter that Israel's methods embitter Palestinians and, for some, justify a violent response.

Maintaining the balance between the security payoff and the human rights cost is problematic. When he was prime minister, Ehud Barak told the Knesset, "We are not Holland. . . . We are a state that is faced with a constant threat of terror." Nevertheless he added a caveat: "Yet on the other hand we are a democratic state that is part of the international community."[3] Israel is not alone in grappling with this dilemma. All true democracies wrestle with the difficulty of maintaining the dignity and rights of the individual in the face of terrorism.

The Security Payoff

Interrogations may take place during or after a military operation, a time when many suspects are detained. More often interrogation relies on spies or signals intelligence to tip off operators that an individual should be brought in for questioning. When that happens Israel has an opportunity to gain information. The detained individuals are psychologically and physically isolated, which makes them vulnerable and more likely to talk.

For Israel more than perhaps any other country, interrogation is part of a sophisticated process that is at the heart of its counterterrorism intelligence. Interrogations elicit confessions that provide information on the activities of a militant group, such as loyalties within a militant cell, the number of weapons and their locations, and the amount of funding available; all can be revealed in interrogation sessions. The amount of data produced by interrogating thousands of suspected militants is massive.

Just as important, interrogation sessions are places for recruiting agents. In jail an interrogator may have just extracted a confession from a known militant, one who has also agreed to serve as an agent. That individual must then be released and provided with a credible tale to explain his return. Afterward he may or may not keep to the agreement, but if he does, the potential to ward off future terrorist attacks is enormous.

Israeli interrogators use tools beyond threats and coercion. Former Shin Bet head Avi Dichter described the job as "[becoming] friends with someone who murdered a baby."[4] One senior interrogator described his job with a dose of humor, noting that a good cop/bad cop mix of fear and kindness is often effective: "One day I was good. Next day I was bad. The prisoner said, 'Yesterday you were good. What happened today?' I told him we were short on manpower."[5] He often flattered Palestinian suspects to get them talking, complimenting them on how they manufactured a bomb to be placed under playground benches. A former head of the investigations unit claimed that interrogations often involve reasoning with a subject, playing on his emotions, tempting him with small rewards, making deals—measures that do not involve violence.

Another of Israel's previous senior interrogators, Michael Koubi, believes that when a suspect is taken in, disorientation is a key tactic for getting information. Keeping an individual uncomfortable by waking him from his sleep or putting his head in a rancid sack will make him more likely to talk. Koubi told the journalist Mark Bowden, "People are afraid of the unknown. . . . Try to see what it is like to sit with a hood over your head for four hours, when you are hungry and tired and afraid, when you are isolated from everything and have no clue what is going on."[6]

Interrogators have found religious terrorists harder to crack than others, though one official told me that the PFLP members were still the toughest group he had to crack. Religious terrorists tend to have a more ascetic lifestyle, making them less open to bribes and other small rewards for information.

One senior interrogator stressed that terrorists are not criminals, and treating them as such is a mistake. Criminals are in it for themselves, and they are ashamed of what they do. Terrorists, in contrast, "are proud of what they do" and believe they are serving their nation, God, or their family (or all three). They do not work for money—"That's bullshit," he said. Not everyone talks, but most people do. Koubi contends, "In some cases men who are quite famous for their toughness were the most helpful to us in captivity."[7]

Interrogators can manipulate subjects in a way that can make cooperation more likely, which can accelerate the pace of a confession. Koubi describes gathering together dozens of hooded suspects and asking who will collaborate. He pretended he had many volunteers, which then convinced others that there was no point in remaining silent. The process of manipulation does not end in jail. Often those who collaborate are released early so they can continue providing information to Israeli intelligence. One former field officer told me that releasing them can be exceptionally dangerous because once free, they may be doubled by Hamas or another group and turn on their handlers, ambushing them when they come for a meeting.

Language skills are vital for interrogators; Koubi himself speaks several dialects of Arabic fluently and enjoys correcting his subjects on some of the finer semantic points. A good memory and attention to detail are also vital, as are integrity and self-discipline, because mistakes are common in interrogations and it is important to admit it when the wrong person has been arrested. In general interrogators enjoy an unusual status in Israeli intelligence compared with their role in foreign services; they are an elite and are treated on a par with agent handlers and other cadres at the center of the intelligence service.

Shin Bet interrogation is different from Israeli police interrogation and from interrogation by U.S. law enforcement services like the FBI. The goal of a law enforcement service is to gain a conviction. For Shin Bet, however, the goal is to disrupt the entire network. Jail time may be an objective, but it is not essential. So for Shin Bet, the task might be penetrating a Hamas network in Hebron rather than gaining a conviction of a particular individual for using violence. Thus when they interrogate suspects they are seeking far more information than responsibility for a particular crime. Shin Bet is ready to turn the suspect into an agent or otherwise delay a conviction for the sake of more information.

When Shin Bet passes a subject to the police and the court for trial, they almost always have a confession. Often people see these confessions as proof of Shin Bet abuses, but today's Shin Bet is reluctant to push for a conviction based on circumstantial evidence. If the wrong person is jailed, terrorism will continue. An interrogator who pursued a weak case would find his career damaged. One official told me that if you get a false confession from someone for throwing a grenade and you jail him even though the real attacker is still out there, "you are kaput in the organization when the next grenade goes off."

Israel must be careful, however, as militant groups often exploit prisons. Because thousands of Palestinians are in jail, Israel cannot simply keep each prisoner in isolation; some mixing is inevitable. However, when many Palestinian leaders are jailed, a prison can become over time the de facto headquarters of a group. Moreover when prisoners live together and participate in communal activities with no other company but each other, they grow much closer to their comrades-in-arms. Indeed for some groups prison experience is necessary for advancement because it shows a degree of commitment to a cause and demonstrates whether or not an individual will cave under pressure. Hamas in particular flourished in Israeli prisons in the late 1980s and 1990s.

Dark Beginnings

After Israel took over the West Bank and Gaza in 1967 its detention and interrogation of suspected terrorists was often extremely harsh, an approach that did not correspond to the benign image Defense Minister

Moshe Dayan tried to create within the territories, nor with the image Israeli officials promoted at home and abroad. Intelligence officials focus on results. The delays and missed opportunities that come with due process haunt them, as they fear these time-consuming efforts will cost lives. They are judged on stopping terrorism, not on ensuring human rights. Because there was little oversight of their activities, gaining a confession became paramount, regardless of the price.

Palestinian groups have a deliberate interest in exaggerating the scope and scale of Israeli mistreatment of prisoners. Thus it is difficult to rely solely on their claims for accuracy. Palestinians—particularly those who reveal information—often cite torture to excuse their confession or collaboration, even when torture did not occur. However, a detailed investigation by the London *Sunday Times* in 1977 found that "torture is organised so methodically that it cannot be dismissed as a handful of 'rogue cops' exceeding orders." The investigation found that some suspects were repeatedly beaten about their face and body, including genitals. To compel a confession members of the victim's family were at times brought in and beaten or threatened in front of the prisoner. Omar Abdel-Karim, a Palestinian whom the Israelis suspected of being a member of the fedayeen, told the reporters that he confessed (falsely, he claims) after an interrogator arrested his wife and began to slap her.[8]

Stories like Abdel-Karim's, while widely known among Palestinians, did not penetrate the Israeli conscience. For many years Shin Bet was able to keep itself out of the Israeli newspapers and operate in the shadows. The lack of public scrutiny meant the agency could bend or ignore the rules regarding the humane treatment of prisoners. This invisibility ended after four PFLP members hijacked Egged Bus 300 on April 12, 1984, taking thirty-five passengers hostage. The hijackers diverted the bus from the Tel Aviv–Ashkelon route, forcing it toward Gaza. The bus came to a stop near Gaza, where the hijackers demanded that Israel release hundreds of Palestinian prisoners. Israeli troops stormed the bus, killing one passenger and two of the gunmen. The controversy began afterward, when the other two gunmen died in Israeli custody. Security officials claimed that the men had died in the retaking of the bus, but there were pictures showing the terrorists walking off the bus in Israeli hands. Israeli military censors banned the photographs. An Israeli newspaper published the picture anyway and was briefly closed down by censors, but not before a furor erupted.

Years later Ehud Yatom, a retired Shin Bet agent, told the papers that he "smashed their skulls" with stones and a crowbar, on the orders of Avraham Shalom, who headed Shin Bet at the time. The men had been put on stretchers, but Yatom said, "I received an order from Avraham Shalom to kill the men, so I killed them."[9] After his fellow Shin Bet members criticized him, Yatom denied making these claims and the inquiry foundered as Shin Bet and others were instructed to lie to investigators. A subsequent investigation found that Shin Bet agents routinely lied to the court on the issue of abuse and that this was accepted by the agency. "Everyone knew—they knew we were lying," Ami Ayalon, the future head of Shin Bet, would later say. The government refused to reopen the Bus 300 investigation, and the president pardoned those involved before they were indicted. Shalom eventually resigned even though he had been implementing the wishes of his political superiors. Prime Minister Shamir himself, who took power after Begin retired in 1983, had said, "Do not take any terrorists captive."[10] The incident, however, left Israelis doubting the honesty and integrity of their courts and security services.

Some reports suggest that military intelligence has at times been exceptionally brutal, even more so than Shin Bet. Mustafa Dirani, a Lebanese Shi'a leader whom Israel abducted in 1994 to gain information about the downed pilot Ron Arad, later filed a lawsuit claiming that Israeli interrogators had sodomized him. One soldier allegedly raped him, while another reportedly thrust a stick up his rectum; a military doctor who examined him reportedly confirmed that he had been raped.[11] Others imprisoned at the same facility (which Israel later closed) described how they were often stripped naked and threatened with rape.[12] Israel is taking the allegation against one soldier seriously enough to launch an investigation, and the Supreme Court is considering whether the case can be heard in Israeli courts.[13]

In 1987 the issue of torture came to a head. A commission headed by the former Supreme Court president Moshe Landau examined Shin Bet interrogation methods and other related issues. The Commission argued that "the exertion of a moderate degree of physical pressure cannot be avoided," yet, as Landau later related, "if interrogations are not regulated by law, a 'twilight zone' is definitely created . . . [and] terrible things happen in the twilight zone."[14] Landau believed that the trick was to regulate physical pressure to ensure it does not become pervasive or excessive.

The Commission issued a set of guidelines that tried to split the difference; it was a unique attempt to square the rule of law and brutal interrogation procedures by regulating and codifying them but not abolishing them altogether. Electric shock was banned, but interrogators could force prisoners to stand for days, shackle them to stools in contorted positions, shake them violently, expose them to cold and heat, and force them to urinate and defecate in their clothing, methods that many would consider torture.[15]

The 1990s: The Gray Era

Interrogation became even more important for counterterrorism after the Oslo period, when Israel's ability to run agents in Palestinian areas declined. Agent handlers had less influence over Palestinians' lives because the PA, not the Israeli government, was now a key administrative player. Now that Palestinian intelligence was trying to root out collaborators, they could not work openly with Israeli officials. As violence took off in the 1990s information gleaned from detainees and prisoners became more and more important.

Throughout most of the 1990s Shin Bet used a variety of techniques on prisoners. Agents deprived them of sleep, shook them violently, tied them to chairs in painful positions, and placed them in the "frog crouch" (forcing suspects to squat on the tips of their toes for long periods of time). Several Palestinians died in interrogations. Rabin claimed that before 1995 Israeli interrogators had violently shaken some eight thousand Palestinians, suggesting the scale of these methods.[16] An overwhelming majority of Israelis supported their use.[17] Mousa Khoury, a Palestinian whom Israel repeatedly arrested and interrogated, described his experience to the journalist Mark Bowden: "My hands were cuffed behind my back, and a potato sack was over my head. My legs were cuffed to a tiny chair. . . . If you sit back, the back of the chair digs into the small of your back. If you slump forward, you are forced to hang by your hands. It is painful. They will take you to the toilet only after screaming a request one hundred times."[18]

The Landau Commission called for painful techniques to be used only in rare cases, but in practice their use became commonplace. The Israeli journalist Amira Hass reported that among the numerous Gazan ex-prisoners she interviewed, she was told that beatings, blows to the testicles, and sleep deprivation were common experiences.[19] The human rights organization B'Tselem found that in 1998 at least 850 Palestinians suffered harsh treatment in detention—85 percent of those interrogated that year, which had been a relatively low point for terrorism. A senior interrogator told me that during this period "harsh measures were used systematically and broadly—the finger was very light on the trigger." In some cases the Landau Commission guidelines were ignored. For example, Israeli interrogators used rough measures after picking up a Hamas operative in their search for the Israeli captive Nachshon Wachsman. Rabin contended, "If we had been following every single word of the Landau Commission in the investigation of Hamas terrorists, we would not have located the place in Bir Naballah where Nachshon Wachsman was held."[20]

Judicial intervention in interrogation and intelligence issues is a source of tension in Israel. Given the fact that the Israeli Supreme Court is far more involved in day-to-day security activities than its U.S. counterpart, intervention is not surprising. The concepts of "standing" and "non-justiciability," which in the U.S. system place limits on what courts review, are relaxed in Israel almost to the point of nonexistence. So almost any issue by almost anyone can be brought before the court. In Israel, which inherited its legal system from the British colonial administration, human rights petitions bypass courts of first instance, which historically were run by "the natives." The British did not trust the locals on such sensitive issues, so human rights issues went directly to the upper court, which in colonial times was dominated by the British. Though the court often employed human rights rhetoric, through the years it usually tilted in favor of security concerns. The court made its mark on almost every aspect of Israeli counterterrorism, including interrogations, the route of the security barrier, the use of human shields for military operations, and targeted killings. On core issues such as torture and the impact of antiterrorism measures on innocent people (including those related to or close to suspected terrorists) the court was usually a voice for human rights.

The Israeli Supreme Court contended that interrogation procedures meant to be exceptional had become the rule. Thus in 1999 the court decided that in most cases Shin Bet must now follow police standards for interrogation.[21] Aharon Barak, who headed the Supreme Court at the time, declared, "Human dignity also includes the dignity of the suspect being interrogated."[22]

For a while Israel ended up with the worst of all worlds: confusion. Shin Bet's head Ami Ayalon later described this time thus: "We tell the interrogator: 'Do what you feel is right to save lives and afterward, we will consider whether or not to indict you.'"[23]

Interrogation during and after the Second Intifada

Human rights organizations believe that detainee abuse has decreased. Michael Sfard, a human rights lawyer in Israel, says that in the 1980s and early 1990s "physical or psychological torture were routine," while today it occurs only in "exceptional and isolated cases of interrogations of necessity."[24] Jessica Montell of B'Tselem agrees. She says there was "an assembly line of torture" in the past, while today it is confined to only a few dozen instances— still intolerable in her opinion, but far fewer than in the past. For many in the human rights community, the greater involvement of the courts is a victory, as it inserts the rule of law into the interrogation process.

Not surprisingly Palestinians are more skeptical. One Palestinian human rights worker told me that "the Israeli High Court is propaganda" because it often takes a long time to make decisions, sometimes delaying implementation for years. However, he admitted that the interrogation methods used today are more psychological than physical. Prisoners might spend eighty days in solitary confinement with little food and infrequent showers. Palestinian militant groups instruct their members on how to withstand both psychological techniques such as disorientation and physical techniques such as tying a detainee to the wall and forcing him to stand, but they do not prepare them for practices like electric shock, because such extreme techniques are not used today.

The court left open one important exception to its call for more humane treatment of suspects: the "ticking bombs." When interrogators have weeks in which to question suspects, they can employ a variety of tricks to lull or frighten suspects.[25] But these methods will not work quickly enough to stop a bomb that is about to go off; in those cases more forceful physical interrogation may be employed. As several intelligence officials pointed out, ticking bomb situations are hypothetical in the United States and are often treated as a purely academic exercise, but they occur all the time in Israel; in the early days of the Intifada in particular security forces often arrested suspects who were part of an active plot. A ticking bomb exception is more likely to invite abuses, but Israeli lawmakers claim that only 2 percent of those arrested during the height of the Intifada were subjected to forceful methods. In 2007 Shin Bet officials told Knesset members that of those interrogated from Gaza, only one of six cases involved "extraordinary measures."[26] Even with the ticking bomb exception, systematic abuse is less of a problem now than it was in the 1990s or before.

Today physical pressure is reinforced by psychological pressure. A former head of the investigations division told me that after the 1999 court decision Shin Bet began to rely more on trickery, better integrated lie detectors, and field agent operations. Yet despite the improvements, a 2007 B'Tselem report found that interrogators still bound many detainees in a way that caused pain. During their incarceration some detainees were isolated even from their lawyers and Red Cross representatives. Also common was solitary confinement in windowless cells with only a hole in the floor as a toilet. Interrogators often shouted and spat at detainees and threatened torture. Sometimes a detainee's family members were invited to the facility to make the point that Shin Bet could also threaten relatives.[27]

Israel has put in place a set of procedures to prevent interrogators from going off on their own and abusing prisoners. Interrogators often work with partners, and sessions are often videotaped. Extraordinary physical pressure must be approved by senior officials, and it is regularly reviewed.

Indeed Israeli jail conditions are far better than the conditions under which Palestinian authorities treat members of rival groups in their own prison. Some Palestinian human rights officials decry the situation, and being in a Palestinian jail is far worse than being in an Israeli jail.[28] But perhaps it is unfair to compare incarceration practices in a democratic country with practices in regimes that lack judicial, public, and political oversight.

A politically tempting alternative is to outsource interrogation and detention. In Lebanon Israel's local ally the SLA ran the prisons, and in the 1990s the PA at times served as Israel's policeman. In both cases the locals were far more brutal than the Israelis, which enabled Israel to deflect much of the criticism. The United States has done much the same thing in its rendition program, which takes suspected terrorists off the streets by sending them to countries such as Egypt, allowing the United

States to avoid dirtying its hands with interrogation and detention. From a human rights point of view, however, this approach is far worse because the appearance of clean hands masks a more brutal reality.

The debate over interrogation continues in Israel. The former Shin Bet director Carmi Gillon claims that he "always took the right of innocent people on a bus over those being interrogated. Other officials I talked to stressed that morality as well as expediency must come into play. Some did not shy away from saying that scruples would probably cost Israeli lives in times of conflict but were still necessary.

Israel has tried to balance the rule of law with the exigencies of security. The result is a compromise that satisfies neither human rights nor security officials, and thus is worthy of close study by those who care about both. Though Israel's interrogation methods may be harsher than human rights groups favor, they are gentler than they were thirty years ago and are now generally in accord with the rule of law. As with most counterterrorism techniques, concerns about abuses must be balanced by an appreciation of the cost of the alternatives. Arresting two people and interrogating them for weeks is a tough approach, but it may not be as damaging as the alternative: setting up a roadblock that prevents people from going to work and otherwise destroys the natural rhythm of a community.

One problem Israel has long faced is what to do when it cannot arrest and interrogate a suspected terrorist. Fatah and PFLP members often operated out of Europe or in sanctuaries such as Lebanon and Syria, where Israel had no power to arrest them. In the Second Intifada this problem grew more pressing. Terrorist leaders often operated from deep in Gaza City or were protected by loyal fighters in West Bank towns, making it risky or impossible for Israeli security forces to arrest them. To solve this problem Israel often decided to kill rather than arrest the suspected terrorists. Israel would score some impressive successes, but this method often proved problematic and at times disastrous.

CHAPTER XXI

TARGETED KILLINGS: KILL OR BE KILLED?

SALEH SHEHADA was a marked man. As a founder and leader of Hamas's military wing, he had helped orchestrate fifty-two attacks that killed 220 Israeli civilians and sixteen soldiers. His victims included five religious students killed in a settlement in Gaza and nineteen passengers who died in a horrific Jerusalem bus attack. Before he was killed Shehada had been planning to truck-bomb Israeli settlers, launch explosives-filled boats on bathers on the beach, and send suicide bombers to a shopping mall.[1]

Sporting a thick beard and angry eyes, Shehada was, like most Palestinians, a refugee. His parents fled the city of Jaffa during the 1948 war, and Shehada was born five years later. Like many children of refugees, he took to radical politics; however, he did not adopt the secular Marxist and Arab nationalist credo of most of his fellow students. During his studies in Egypt he embraced Islamist politics, and when Hamas was founded in December 1987 he was a natural choice to be a leader of its military and terrorist wing. For several years he had been running a small violent group, the Palestinian Mujahedin that Hamas's future leader Sheikh Yasin had initiated. Shehada stood out because of his intelligence, discipline, and leadership ability.

Shehada first went to jail for two years in 1984; at the time, Israel controlled Gaza and found it relatively easy to locate and imprison him. In subsequent years he was arrested regularly; his final incarceration was a ten-year sentence that began in 1989, after the Israelis tied him to Hamas's military wing.

Micha Kobi, a retired high-ranking Shin Bet interrogator, claimed that Shehada was one of the most cooperative prisoners in Shin Bet's history. "He was the first to break. . . . He gave me all the ideology of what would become Hamas. Things that we had no clue that were going on under our noses," recalled Kobi. Shehada's information brought down numerous Hamas operatives. He revealed the role of Israeli organized crime in selling Hamas weapons, and he helped prevent dozens of terrorist attacks. Shehada provided a detailed description of a Hamas secret weapons cache, even drawing a map that led the IDF to the hiding place.

Shehada cooperated because he was afraid of violence, Kobi contends. "With all his size, in the end of the day he was a man that was terrified of physical violence, and I just used it to my own advantage. I didn't actually use violence. . . . Shehada was the kind of detainee that wanted to talk." Kobi gave Shehada small rewards for cooperation. "He liked good food, so I'd buy him a steak in pita or humus or some chicken with *Majadra*. I'd let him have longer family visits or extra time with his lawyers. . . . He wanted to please us."[2]

Though Shehada was pleasant, Kobi said, "you could also feel his hatred": "He was not ashamed of it. He always told me that though he is cooperating, he will always be for Jihad. We also talked about other things. He was very erudite, loved history. This is a man that read *The Revolt* by Begin and *Pinkas sherut* [Duty Notebook] by Rabin. And he really found this interesting."

Yet for all of the information he provided Shin Bet his hatred triumphed in the end. Kobi claims Shehada secretly operated the military wing of Hamas from his Israeli cell, conveying encrypted messages to visitors, lawyers, and other inmates. He even orchestrated the kidnapping and killing of two Israeli soldiers, Ilan Sa'adon and Avi Sasportas, in 1989, an operation that led to Yasin's arrest in 1989.

After his jail sentence expired Shehada spent another twenty months under administrative detention. Shin Bet officials feared that he would quickly return to his terrorist activity, but the Israeli courts eventually ruled that he could not be detained indefinitely despite the risks he posed. Confirming Shin Bet's fears, Shehada immediately returned to violence. Not only did he plan terrorist attacks, but he also pushed for the development of the Qassam rocket, which would later rain down upon Sderot and other southern Israeli towns. His continuing involvement in terrorism led Israel to repeatedly request that Yasir Arafat's Palestinian Authority arrest him—requests that were ignored. Not surprisingly, when the Second Intifada broke out in September 2000 Shehada headed Israel's Most Wanted list.

Shehada's time ran out on July 22, 2002, when an Israeli F-16 obliterated his apartment building and several other adjacent structures with a massive two-thousand-pound bomb. Ariel Sharon told his confidant Uri

Dan, "[It was] one of our greatest victories against those bastards."[3] Only a few bricks and concrete powder remained of Shehada's multistory building.[4]

The archterrorist was not the only one who died that day. The blast killed fourteen civilians, including Shehada's daughter and nine other children as well as Shehada's wife and aide. Some reports indicated that the IDF knew that the attack would kill civilians but saw it as a necessary price for saving Israeli lives. Next door Mahmud Huwaiti, whose home was made of exposed cinderblock with an asbestos roof, found only his hallway still standing. Huwaiti's wife and two youngest sons died in the collapse. Jamal Halaby, who also lived nearby, told a reporter, "I fell out of my bed and I found myself a minute later covered in dust and stones, and the sounds of my children screaming and crying."

The Shehada killing's moral complications are matched by its complexities on an operational level. When the Palestinian Authority refused to arrest Shehada, Israeli officials attempted to arrest him themselves. Shehada, however, constantly switched houses and trusted only a few associates with his whereabouts. He also tried to stay deep in Gaza, knowing that sympathizers there would forewarn him of any Israeli raid to capture him. When he realized Israel had decided to kill rather than arrest him, he tried to stay close to noncombatants, knowing that Israelis hesitate to kill innocents.

Nor did things become simpler once Israeli officials decided to kill him. Yaalon claims that Israel repeatedly avoided killing Shehada earlier because he was with his daughter. Eight times Israel planned a hit, but each time it was postponed.[5]

When Shin Bet learned from Akram al-Zotmeh, an informant, that Shehada would be in an apartment building with no innocents nearby, Israel decided to act. (Israel typically uses more than one informant or intelligence source to ensure it is not being misled.) When al-Zotmeh was a student at Al Azhar University in Gaza City intelligence officers got close to him by pretending to work as Canadian researchers. Over time they ensured his cooperation by using a mix of bribery and blackmail, threatening to expose pictures of him in sexually compromising positions.

Because the intelligence did not reveal exactly where in the building Shehada was located, Israeli officials rejected the use of a missile, fearing it would not kill him. The intelligence was wrong or, more accurately, incomplete: Shehada was present, but so too were his wife and daughter, and the surrounding buildings were occupied, not vacant, as al-Zotmeh had claimed. Palestinian squatters, impoverished and desperate for shelter in Gaza, had made their homes in the buildings.

The reaction to the attacks was swift and overwhelmingly negative. More than 100,000 enraged Palestinians chanting "Revenge," "Death to Israel," and "Death to America" marched to commemorate Shehada. One man carried the body of his neighbor's two-month-old child, Dina Matter, who died along with her mother and siblings. Dina's tiny face was the only thing visible from under the Palestinian flag wrapped around her. Bogi Yaalon, the IDF chief of staff at the time, told the journalist Laura Blumenfeld that when he heard the news of the deaths of the children it felt "like something heavy fell on [his] head." World leaders condemned the attack, and even the Bush White House, usually sympathetic to Israel's actions against terrorists, declared the act "heavy-handed" and announced that the president was "deeply troubled" by the killing. Hamas, to no one's surprise, declared it a massacre and distributed a leaflet saying that it would fight until "Jews see their own body parts in every restaurant, every park, every bus and every street." True to its word, Hamas carried out a bombing on July 31 in the cafeteria of Hebrew University, claiming that it was to avenge Shehada. Seven died in the attack, including five Americans studying at the university.[6]

For Israeli security officials, the legacy of the Shehada killing lived on. Five years later Avi Dichter, who headed Shin Bet during the attack and later became minister of public security, had to cancel a visit to the United Kingdom because of the risk of a lawsuit from a London-based human rights group that saw the Shehada killing as deliberate murder. Bogi Yaalon too faced arrest if he went to the United Kingdom, which he wryly told me was "a pity." In the eyes of these officials, the risk of a lawsuit in the West is of little concern compared with the risk of a suicide bomber in an Israeli bus or restaurant.

Israel temporarily became more careful in its targeting of terrorists, but this strategy brought different risks. Two months after Shehada's death Israeli intelligence learned that all of Hamas's senior leaders, "the dream team," as some Israeli officials later called them, were meeting in one location. Yaalon recalled his reaction when the Shin Bet agent in the command center called out their names—Ismail Haniyeh, Mohammad Deif, Adnan al-Ghoul, and Sheikh Yasin: "I pictured each one, and I pictured blown-up buses and disco bombings, and shootings, murders of children, and captured soldiers."[7]

The meeting, however, was in a crowded neighborhood with schoolchildren roaming the streets. A one-ton bomb, like that used against Shehada, would destroy many buildings and cause numerous civilian casualties. For Yaalon, the deaths of children in the Shehada killing hung over the discussion on whether to strike the dream team.[8] He asked those who wanted to use a bigger bomb, "How can we look in the eyes of our pilots if they kill innocent people?" Dichter responded, "And if the terrorists walk out alive, and tomorrow another bus explodes, how do we explain it to our people?" The debate also touched on the fundamental question of how to defeat terrorism. Dichter believes that if you disrupt enough terrorists through killings and arrests, you render groups themselves ineffective. Killing terrorists does not simply create new ones who replace them. Yaalon disagrees. He says there is no bottom to the barrel of terrorists: "Dichter thinks we'll kill, kill, kill, kill. That's it—we've won. I don't accept that."[9] The debate goes on.

Initially Israel called off the strike, leery of causing more civilian deaths. However, at the last minute Shin Bet reported that the meeting would take place on the building's top floor, so only a small bomb would be necessary. But the operation failed: the intelligence was wrong. The meeting was held on the ground floor, so the small bomb was not powerful enough to kill the leaders. In the months that followed, some Hamas leaders were killed or driven underground as Israeli forces hunted them down, but in the interim they plotted and carried out more attacks. Gen. Dan Halutz, who headed the Israeli Air Force at the time, recalled, "When I see [the Hamas leader] Haniyeh, I ask myself, how is he alive? He shouldn't be there."[10] Dichter lamented, "How many Israelis died as a result of this failed killing?" Prudence, it seems, is deadly too.

The burden on those who implement the killings can be weighty. One pilot said that when he launches a bomb, he just says, "Hit the target, hit the target, hit the target,' . . . You hope nothing comes into the cross hairs, like a person. When I take off my helmet, my hair is wet, my undershirt soaked with sweat. You feel like you lost 20 pounds. I can't say the feelings are good, even on a successful mission. You feel bad, but you know what you did was necessary."[11]

As the journalist Laura Blumenfeld details, both Yaalon and Dichter drew on the Holocaust to explain their views. Yaalon recalls that his mother, the only member of her family to survive the Nazis, taught him that not only should Jews not be killed, "but it also means that we don't kill others." Dichter's father, like Yaalon's mother, also was the only family member to survive the Nazis, and Dichter swore, "I'm not going to let anyone kill a Jew, just because he's a Jew."[12]

Although Israel called off more than half of its targeted killings for fear of noncombatant deaths, in the end the killing campaign proceeded on a remarkable scale. From the outbreak of the Second Intifada until December 26, 2008, B'Tselem records that Israel conducted 234 targeted killings. During the course of these operations 387 Palestinians died, 280 in the Gaza Strip and 107 in the West Bank.[13]

Sharon believed strongly in targeted killings (or, as Israelis call them, *sakum*, the Hebrew acronym for "focused thwarting"). Under him they became one of Israel's primary counterterrorism weapons.[14] Even without Sharon's enthusiasm, public sentiment seems to have decided this debate. General Eival Gilady, a key military planner during Sharon's time in office, pointed out that when the issue comes up of killing a terrorist when he is with his wife and kids, "Israelis ask, are their kids worth more than mine?"

Israel has used a variety of methods to kill. Helicopters fired Hellfire missiles at the cars and homes of suspected terrorists, and the Air Force used F-16s and more powerful platforms when it wanted to deliver bigger bombs. Over time armed drone aircraft grew more important than aircraft. Yaalon noted that the Hellfire caused too much collateral damage, so Israel invested in technology to build smaller warheads, enabling them to take out an individual or two in a crowded area without killing nearby civilians. Israel regularly uses snipers, though they receive less publicity. Israeli intelligence also booby-traps cars, places bombs in place of bricks in walls that terrorists pass by, and in one case put a bomb in a tiny model of the al-Aqsa Mosque.

The Shehada killing and its aftermath illustrates both the benefits and the risks of Israel's targeted killing policy. Critics condemn the policy as immoral, illegal, and ineffective; they argue that it often backfires by fueling Palestinian anger and providing fodder for militant recruitment. And killings have at times disrupted diplomatic attempts to broker a peace, not to mention incurring the worldwide censure of Israel.

Given all the drawbacks, why does Israel continue with targeted killings? The reason is simple: targeted killings work. The strikes have disrupted Hamas, PIJ, the al-Aqsa Martyrs Brigade, and other Palestinian terrorist groups; they have depleted the number of skilled operatives; and they have forced the remaining militants to spend more time in hiding than in plotting future attacks. Targeted killings are not the only important tool in Israel's arsenal, but when these killings are combined with the security barrier and an increased ability to arrest suspects, the number of Israeli deaths from terrorism declines precipitously.

Israel has long used targeted killing to pursue its enemies. Before the 1956 war Israel struck at Egyptian intelligence operatives who ran fedayeen operations, killing them in Gaza and Jordan. Most famously the Wrath of God campaign after the Munich Olympics established targeted killing as a core part—indeed a legendary part—of Israeli counterterrorism. Israel has not officially claimed responsibility for many attacks, but it is widely believed that it was responsible for strikes against proven terrorists, including Dr. Wadi Haddad, who masterminded many PFLP and PFLP splinter group attacks in 1978; Zahayr Muhsin, the head of the Syrian-backed Palestinian group al-Saiqa, in 1979; Fatah lieutenant Abu Jihad in Tunis in 1988; the head of Hizballah, Abbas Musawi, in 1992; the PIJ's founder and leader, Fathi Shiqaqi, in Cyprus in 1995; and Yahya Ayyash ("the Engineer") in Gaza in 1996. These attacks made it clear that Israel believed the elimination of terrorist group leaders and key operatives was vital to counterterrorism.

Several of these killings—of Haddad, Muhsin, and Shiqaqi particularly—dealt stiff blows to the terrorist groups they led. The PFLP and its fellow travelers were already in disarray before Haddad's death, but his killing further shattered its ability to conduct international terrorism, and Saiqa disappeared from the map after its leader Zuheir Mohsein died, probably at Israeli hands. PIJ eventually rebounded, but only after several years of disarray.

Israel continues to justify targeted killings, claiming they can be a form of prevention, killing a "ticking bomb" before he explodes or killing the facilitators who send others to kill. Officials also hope that they will deter terrorists from violence or, if that fails, make them live in fear, rendering them less effective. Over time, and with enough deaths, the killings can also reduce the total number of terrorists. Just as important, but seldom mentioned, targeted killings play well in Israeli politics, reassuring the people that their country is striking back.[15]

The deaths of innocents are inevitable in such operations, whether as accidents or as anticipated costs of killing dangerous men, and that is the nub of much of the debate. A failed arrest or arresting the wrong person is not a fatal mistake, but with targeted killing there is no second chance for innocent victims. Israel's attempts to fight Hamas are further complicated by Hamas's abuse of Israel's reluctance to cause civilian casualties; Israeli intelligence officials claim that many Hamas terrorists travel with children knowing this may stay the IDF's hand.

Perhaps surprisingly given the scale of the killings, there are few cases of mistaken identity. One Israeli Air Force official boasted, "The Americans had killed more civilians in their first week in Iraq than we have killed during all these years."[16] Yet still innocents do die. In 1973 the Mossad mistakenly killed Ahmed Bouchiki, a Moroccan waiter, whom they thought was a senior Black September leader. On June 11, 2003, Israeli aircraft attacked the car of Hamas's number two operative, Dr. Abd al-Aziz Rantisi, who leaped out and survived before subsequent missiles utterly destroyed the car. Amal Jarosheh, an eight-year-old girl whose father had allowed her out to buy candy, died from shrapnel wounds sustained as she was standing nearby. "She never got a chance to eat it," said her father.[17] Israel later caught up with Rantisi, who once declared that he would rather be killed by an Israeli Apache helicopter than die of a heart attack.[18]

Israel has never answered the question of what is an acceptable level of civilian deaths. A committee that looked at the issue considered a standard of 3.14 civilian deaths per terrorist (a smaller ratio if the dead are children), but no agreement ever emerged. Dichter cited Shin Bet studies showing that every time a suicide bomber died sixteen to twenty lives were saved.

Killings complicate diplomacy, at times disastrously. Many countries look the other way when the Mossad hunts terrorists on their soil, but the Bouchiki killing, in which an innocent man died instead of a wanted terrorist, infuriated Norway, the location of the debacle, and Canada, because the assailants used Canadian passports. In 1997 the botched killing of the Hamas leader Khaled Mishal in Jordan enraged King Hussein, perhaps Israel's closest ally in the Arab world and a close partner in counterterrorism. Sheikh Yasin gained his freedom as Netanyahu stumbled to appease the king's wrath.

Targeted Killing Evolves in the Second Intifada

In the Second Intifada targeted killing became a near-constant tool. The killings began as a way around Israel's initial reluctance to reoccupy Palestinian areas. When Prime Minister Ehud Barak prohibited the IDF from entering Area A with large numbers of forces, Palestinian militant groups operated from these areas with impunity. In Jerusalem this presented a particular problem, as Jewish neighborhoods could be attacked directly from Palestinian neighborhoods, such as the outskirts of Bethlehem. Israeli officials demonstrated one solution to this dilemma: on November 9, 2000, Apache helicopters blew up the Jeep of Hussein Abayat, the head of Fatah-Tanzim in Bethlehem who orchestrated some of the shootings.[19] "Suddenly, I heard a loud explosion," recalled one resident. "I saw a car fly about six meters in the air."[20] Two women also died in the blast. One of the officials involved in the operation told me that the killing was not meant to set policy, but was simply a way around the prohibition of moving military forces into Area A to carry out an arrest.

After the Abayat killing the policy went through several permutations, becoming more aggressive. On December 31, 2000, an IDF sniper killed Dr. Thabet Ahmad Thabet, a dentist and Fatah-Tanzim leader, whom Israel claimed headed operations in Tulkaram. (Israelis joked that Dr. Thabet was killed not because he was involved in terror, but because he was a dentist.) This killing raised the political heat. Thabet did not fit the classic terrorist profile: he had been active in peace negotiations, though he also said that "the guns will start shooting again" if there was no political progress.[21] Israelis labeled Thabet a "peace activist by day and a terrorist leader by night."[22] Ephraim Sneh, a senior defense official, said, "The fact of having a position within the Palestinian Authority confers no immunity on anyone."[23] The Israeli change of attitude happened rapidly, reflecting public concerns over the surging violence. Two weeks before his killing Thabet had gone through Ben Gurion Airport without arrest or incident.[24]

In Thabet's case, for the first time Israel turned to the legal system to justify the killing. A team of IDF lawyers wrote an opinion stating that the conflict had escalated to the point of armed conflict; in short, the restrictions were those of armies fighting other countries, not those governing the occupation of a territory at peace. International law traditionally has rejected this possibility, defining armed conflict solely as a conflict between states, a failure of international law to keep up with changing times. But the opinion was not meant to be a blank check, and the legal advisor Daniel Reisner drew up guidelines for a targeted killing. In the opinion Reisner contended that the killings were legal under the following conditions: the target is a combatant, the target cannot be arrested, the operation is approved by senior civilian officials, efforts are taken to reduce civilian casualties (that is, they must adhere to the principle of proportionality), and the operation occurs in areas Israel does not control. Perhaps most important the target has to be a future threat, not just someone who committed crimes in the past. Reisner's ruling was meant to regulate the killings, placing them within the context of law and ensuring political accountability for them.[25] In 2010 the Obama administration issued vaguer but related legal justifications for the aggressive targeted killing campaign it is conducting against al-Qa'ida in Pakistan, citing principles such as proportionality, the need to not make civilians the target of the attack, and the imminence of the threat.[26]

Thabet's case was also unusual in that it was overt. For many years Israel tried to disguise its involvement in killings, but during the Second Intifada officials were often blunt about using this tool. Rami Gershon, a founder of the elite Duvdevan unit, whose members often worked undercover and disguised themselves as municipal or utility workers, told a newspaper, "We liquidate. Yes, we liquidate. If I don't liquidate Abu Jihad or if I don't liquidate whoever I am supposed to liquidate with the Duvdevan unit, then I'd have a bus explode and I'd have 17 kids liquidated." Referring to Israel's campaigns such as Wrath of God, he declared, "What's the difference between Mossad agents and the guys at Duvdevan who deal with sewage? The Mossad guys wear suits, smell of aftershave, drive BMWs, and waste people in Europe."[27] The former Shin Bet head Carmi Gillon points out that you cannot prove that Israel killed the Hamas leader Ayyash, but when you use helicopters "you leave your fingerprints everywhere."

The fingerprints can also lead to the discovery of Shin Bet agents. After Thabet's killing, a Palestinian court tried several collaborators accused of giving Shin Bet information and sentenced three of them to death.[28] Such losses occurred regularly after targeted killings, leading to the loss of intelligence regarding future attacks due to the deaths of informants and the fear of other potential recruits that Palestinian officials or group members might arrest or kill them if they supplied information to Israel.

When it killed Thabet, Israel drew a line, saying it would not kill political leaders, only terrorists—meaning individuals directly involved in violence on a day-to-day basis.[29] Yet the policy on targeted killings evolved again, and in August 2001 Abu Ali Mustafa, the head of the Popular Front for the Liberation of Palestine, was killed. Mustafa, one of the five most prominent leaders of the PLO, was the first leader on the political as opposed to the operational side of a group. Sharon and the Cabinet approved the operation after Israeli intelligence convinced them that Mustafa himself was involved not only in the planning of PFLP terror attacks but also in a drive-by shooting of an Israeli family and a car bomb discovered near the police headquarters in Jerusalem. Shin Bet also believed Mustafa was linked to up to five other terror attacks inside Israel, including an attempt to booby-trap a watermelon and bomb a bus stop in Jerusalem.

On August 27 at 11:30 Mustafa was on the phone in his third-floor office in Ramallah. The caller appeared to be a reporter with a pronounced English accent, but the call had been designed to prove beyond a doubt that Mustafa himself was at the other end of the phone.[30] Marking his window with a laser beam, two helicopters fired missiles into the office, decapitating Mustafa. Five others, including three innocents, were wounded. A defense source at the time claimed, "This is the first time that we target a senior political Palestinian, but this hit does not mean that Israel has decided to start hitting political figures, such as Barghouti. The hit on Mustafa was done despite the fact he is a political leader, and not because of it. Because the PFLP is a small organization, Mustafa was also operating within its military wing, and personally orchestrated attacks against Israel."[31] The PFLP quickly responded, killing Rehavam Zeevi, Israel's minister of tourism, in October, a killing that made Israelis skeptical that the Palestinians would adhere to Arafat's post-9/11 call for a ceasefire.

The killing of Thabet, Mustafa, and other suspected terrorists seemed escalatory to many observers. "Targeted killings of Palestinians don't end the violence but are only inflaming an already volatile situation," U.S. State Department spokesman Richard Boucher declared in July 2001. The 9/11 attacks and the U.S. embrace of targeted killings would silence this criticism from Israel's most important ally.

In December 2002 Maj. Gen. Giora Eiland, who headed the IDF's powerful Strategic Planning Branch, asked Shaul Mofaz, who had become defense minister, to target all Hamas personnel, regardless of whether they were ostensibly political or military. In a significant shift from the IDF legal advisor's initial emphasis on targeting combatants only, Israel raised the stakes again when it began a comprehensive campaign against the military, organizational, and political leadership of its opponents.

Israeli proponents argue that peace can go forward only when radicals are afraid and unable to function. Killings disrupt groups operationally and deter future attacks. Ceasefires merely give Palestinians a chance to rearm.

Israel is criticized for radicalizing Palestinians, for showing a lack of understanding of internal Palestinian dynamics, and for killing more moderate leaders. In July 2001 Israel killed two key Hamas members in Nablus, Jamal Saleem and Jamal Mansour. Mansour was a Hamas political figure who had even published a book that advocated for Hamas to be part of a political process (depending on the approval of the Palestinians).

He was "the most moderate within the Hamas spectrum," according to Matti Steinberg, an Israeli academic expert on the Palestinians. Steinberg believes Israel killed him in response to several suicide bombings in Nablus—Israel officials felt the need to show they were taking action. IDF officials say that Mansour played a major role in Hamas operations in the northern West Bank, distributing money to operatives and running explosives labs.[32] Another official told the press that Mansour "provided the guidance, set the goals and the methods, created the organizational infrastructures and sent the people out to kill."[33] In an interview with the BBC on January 2001 Mansour said that Hamas saw no wrong in killing civilians whenever this was possible. Unfortunately for him, Mansour was under the light and thus easy to target. A crowd of 150,000 attended his funeral demanding revenge.

Arafat's advisor Ghaith al-Omari points out that killing cell leaders often leads to revenge and becomes harder for moderates to champion a political, nonviolent alternative without looking like collaborators. The killing of Raed Karmi, which contributed to the end of the post-9/11 reduction in violence, played a major role in the Tanzim's decision to embrace suicide bombing. On August 21, 2003, Israel killed Ismail Abu Shanab, one of Hamas's most senior leaders, in Gaza City two days after a Hamas suicide bombing on a Jerusalem bus that killed twenty-three people, including six children.[34] Abu Shanab reportedly had said privately to other Palestinians, "Let's be frank. We cannot destroy Israel. The practical solution is for us to have a state alongside Israel."[35] He was a leading pragmatist within Hamas who had called for an end to suicide bombings. (He even reportedly met regularly with Israeli officials in an informal exchange.) At the behest of Mahmud Abbas, the organization had agreed to a truce several weeks before his death. The Abu Shanab killing, however, undermined potential pragmatists in Hamas and weakened Abbas's credibility just as he was trying to orchestrate a ceasefire. Although Israelis tend to think of the operational advantages of targeted killings, Eiland notes that "a military operation can turn into a complete failure if it doesn't take into account the political aspects."[36]

The capstone of the shift to attacking Hamas political leaders was the 2004 killing of Sheikh Yasin. As Israel anticipated, Yasin's killing shocked the world. Israelis had long maintained that the distinction between Hamas's political, social, and military wings was only a bureaucratic fiction. Still it was another thing to kill the crippled and graying Hamas leader in his wheelchair as he left the mosque. The Yasin killing might have set off a political bombshell abroad, but it reaped political benefits for Sharon. Israel and Hizballah had recently swapped four hundred prisoners for three dead Israeli soldiers and an Israeli businessman, and the killing deflected criticism.

The killing of Yasin reflected a perspective that steadily gained traction as the Second Intifada progressed: a lack of concern for how Israeli counterterrorism affected inter-Palestinian politics. Sharon reportedly would silence debates on the repercussions of Israeli actions by declaring, "Think less about the Arabs and more about the Jews."[37]

New Legal Grounds

The legality of targeted killings is furiously disputed. Israeli government lawyers cite the need for self-defense and argue that the killings should be seen in the context of the low-level but near-constant war it fights with terrorist groups. Much of the international community rejects this argument.[38] Critics allege that Israel pronounces the putative terrorists guilty and kills them before they have a fair and legal trial. They charge that Israel is not in a state of war with the Palestinians, and that it uses killings to avenge rather than prevent Israeli deaths. Others question targeted killings because, as an occupying power, Israel has a duty to protect citizens in the West Bank. One option, they say, is to arrest and jail terrorists rather than kill them.[39]

Weighing in on this debate, the Israeli Supreme Court accepts that the Geneva Conventions apply to IDF activities in the West Bank, noting that concerns such as proportionality apply if civilians are at risk. The court observed that as of the end of 2005 more than thirty targeted killing attempts failed and approximately 150 civilians near the location of the intended attacks also died. However, the court rejected the idea that because Israel is the formal occupier of the West Bank it must use only law enforcement methods. The court defines direct participation in hostilities far more broadly than is typical for a combatant in an army, normally defined as someone who bears arms. The court expanded the criteria by including participation as a human shield, which exculpated the IDF for killing the relatives, recruiters, planners, and group leaders of a known terrorist when striking the terrorist himself. The court added that the future threat does not have to be imminent; the target can simply be a member of a terrorist group and thus presumed to be involved in attacks, because "the rest between hostilities is nothing other than preparation for the next hostility." Israel must first try to arrest, but if that is not feasible, killing is considered legal.[40]

The Israeli Supreme Court dodged a critical issue that has bedeviled the United States: the true legal status of terrorists and other nonstate actors who take up arms against a country. The government of Israel asked for recognition of a third category to differentiate terrorists from legitimate combatants and civilians: "unlawful combatants." The government claimed that because terrorists neither distinguish themselves from the civilian population nor obey the rules of law, they should not receive the treatment appropriate for prisoners of war. The court, however, decided to "take no stance" on this question, leaving open what rights suspected terrorists have.[41]

Operational and Political Support

At times as many as two hundred people are involved in targeted killing operations, including pilots, sources on the ground, individuals assessing potential collateral damage, and those monitoring a vehicle as it moves. Ehud Ya'ari, an Israeli journalist, noted, "Each one is a little war, with an operations room."[42] Israel has an entire apparatus of sensors, attack helicopters, strike aircraft, and other forces ready to act quickly on perishable information. Often the difference between a successful and an unsuccessful operation is not the calls made by the leadership but the strength of the intelligence. At the height of the Intifada this small army resulted in near-constant Israeli surveillance and strike presence over Palestinian areas. As former Shin Bet head Avi Dichter said, "When a Palestinian child draws a picture of the sky, he doesn't draw it without a helicopter. Hamas and other militant group members also understand that Big Brother is always watching and listening from above."[43] The terrorists' efforts to thwart surveillance by encrypting communications has thus far met with little success.[44]

Both the IDF and Shin Bet have a say in the final "go" of a targeted killing. Shin Bet approves the intelligence to make sure it is accurate and that there will be no (or few) deaths of noncombatants. The IDF decides whether or not to fire the missile. For many years Shin Bet and the IDF had considerable autonomy, but as the Supreme Court became more involved, so too did Israel's political leaders. Sharon himself was involved in the details of many attacks when he was prime minister. The decision, however, was often done rapidly and by phone. One former Israeli official claimed that Israel spends an average of ten hours planning the operation and twenty seconds on the question of whether to kill or not. That said, political leaders have at times rejected proposed attacks or reshaped them to reduce the risk to civilians.

This process remains controversial, as there is no judicial involvement in weighing the guilt of individuals; the court sets overall rules only. The court has weighed in on broad issues such as proportionality, and legal advisors are part of the military system, but Michael Sfard, an Israeli lawyer who has challenged the killings before Israel's Supreme Court, declared, "Today we execute people without trial. It's so simple. That's what we're doing. No one shows evidence to anyone."

From Shin Bet's point of view, once it obtains senior-level political support it does not need to check in constantly. This creates a strategic risk, however, as the killings can have profound political ramifications.

The Israeli journalist Hirsch Goodman claims that the head of Shin Bet does not say "We're in the middle of negotiations" or really care, for that matter. In part this is an institutional problem, because the head of Shin Bet does not focus on broader political activities; Shin Bet's job is simply to maintain security.

Judging Effectiveness

To understand the cumulative impact of these killings, it is useful to look at the legacy of Husayn Abayat, the Fatah cell leader whose slaying in Bethlehem marked the beginning of the Israeli targeted killing campaign in the Second Intifada. After Israel killed him his brother Atef Abayat took over. Israel pressed the PA to arrest Atef, but the Abayat family was powerful, and the PA police were afraid to take them on. When Alaistair Crooke, a former intelligence official who became the EU special envoy to the region, went to Bethlehem he found Atef duly in jail as promised. Crooke, however, concealed himself near the jail after the meeting and watched Atef leave shortly after he did—a classic case, in Israeli eyes, of PA duplicity. Atef had links to criminal networks, however, and Israel took advantage of this. When a car thief gave him a new car, the Israelis blew it up, killing him and two of his men. It was then difficult for the PA to explain how a man supposedly in jail was killed driving a car. Leadership then passed to a third family member, Ibrahim Abayat. Though the Palestinians respected him because of his family pedigree, he lacked experience, and his own subordinates had to guide him. Thus over time the quality of leadership declined.[45]

As the Abayat family example suggests, repetition matters. In the first two years of the Intifada Israel reportedly killed or arrested five people it labeled "the head of the military wing of Hamas in Hebron."[46] While this is often depicted as an IDF exaggeration it also suggests how difficult it is for local cells to operate with the constant loss of men. The former intelligence official Barak Ben Zur points out the operational costs to groups when they lose their leaders: "You make them hands without a head." Another analyst exclaimed, "I think violence works, at least in the short to medium term. That's the scary thing. And a lot of violence works better than a little."

From an operational perspective, much of the debate over counterterrorism stems from a simple question: Can you kill or capture enough terrorists to disrupt a terrorist organization even when the motivations for terrorism remain acute? (In this case, killing and capturing should be seen as complementary policies for disrupting a group.) Avraham Burg, a former speaker of the Knesset, contends, "We could kill a thousand ringleaders and engineers a day and nothing will be solved, because the leaders come up from below—from the wells of hatred and anger, from the 'infrastructures' of injustice and moral corruption."[47] Some observers claim that Israeli counterterrorism measures make the problem worse in the short term as well as the long term. Mohammad Dahlan, the senior Palestinian security official, argues that with regard to targeted killings, "whoever signed off on killing a leader among Hamas or any other leader on the Palestinian side should turn the page and should sign off on killing 16 Israelis."[48] Arafat's advisor Omari believes that Hamas and other groups have enough reserves to fill the gaps created by targeted killings and arrests. And there are numerous cases in which individual cells and networks, enraged by the death of a comrade, redoubled their efforts to conduct an attack.[49]

This objection, though intuitively reasonable, appears to be wrong, or at least overstated. If killings (and, even more important, arrests) are extensive and if effective defenses are put in place, targeted killings reduce terrorist attacks. To understand this it is useful to make a conceptual shift—from fighting "terrorism" in a broad, generic sense, to fighting "terrorists," a finite and defined group of individuals. Ben Zur sees the problem not as "Palestinian terrorism" in a generic sense, but rather one confined to between one and two thousand terrorists—a large number, but not an insurmountably large one. From this perspective, it is not a question of changing long-term hatred but of effectively disrupting a select set of individuals. As Shin Bet's former head Avi Dichter claimed, "There is a bottom to the barrel."

Militants' own demands suggest that targeted killing has severe repercussions for the group in question. Statements like that of the Hamas leader Ismail Haniyeh that "this is a nation of martyrdom and martyrdom-seeking" abound, but again and again Palestinian groups have called for an end to the targeted killings before they would make peace.[50] This steady demand suggests that, despite what critics contend, terrorists do not welcome these strikes. The eulogies of those killed often stress how important the individual was to the organization.[51] Before his death the Hamas head Abdel Aziz al-Rantisi even conceded that the killings of Hamas leaders had made things harder for the organization's operatives.[52]

As Palestinian passion and high hopes transformed into a sense of futility as the Intifada wore on, targeted killings, along with arrests, placed additional pressures on militants. Al-Aqsa Martyrs Brigades members found that owners of coffee and barber shops did not want their business, as they feared their establishments would be damaged or destroyed during a strike. Even more depressing for the militants, fathers would not let their daughters marry them, worrying that they would be making their daughters widows and risking additional Israeli pressure.[53]

Targeted killings are low-risk operations for IDF and intelligence personnel. In fact drones are an almost risk-free way of killing, though often UAV information is supplemented by more risky on-the-ground intelligence. Arrests are an alternative to killings, but in places such as Gaza the suspect is likely to be well guarded and surrounded by a sympathetic population. For Israelis, keeping their own casualties low is not only a goal but a political imperative: Hamas, Hizballah, and the Israeli public all agree that the terrorists win if Israel suffers significant casualties.

In addition to the security benefits, targeted killings also offer rewards for Israeli politicians. Those on both sides of the political spectrum support killings: justice and politics demand a response to terrorist attacks. The greatest impact of terrorism, after all, is psychological: it seeks to undermine confidence in government. Israeli politicians have found targeted killings immensely rewarding for a public hungry for revenge. Killings also satisfy a public demand to "do something" in the face of continued violence. One Israeli officer told me that even though targeted killings sometimes make things worse, often you have no choice: "We won't just stand there."

Still this political logic constrains politicians. It prevents them from considering broader political measures that may in the long run do more good. "Any Israeli prime minister is reluctant to say no to a proposal to take out a bad guy," argues Martin Indyk, a former U.S. ambassador to Israel. Part of this is a genuine desire to kill those who are killing Israelis. But part of it is political. Because Israel is a leaky ship, word would get out that the prime minister refused to take out a terrorist, and he would have trouble explaining his decision to the Israeli people.

One danger of targeted killings is that they are sometimes precipitated by revenge rather than political necessity. The IDF was told to kill several Palestinian policemen, even though these men had worked well with their Israeli counterparts. The IDF justified the killings because Palestinian security forces had recently conducted attacks and, because the institution as a whole was deemed guilty, any officers "became a legitimate target."[54] The website Breaking the Silence, which is affiliated with left-leaning Israeli organizations, has chronicled IDF soldiers' statements of anger and outrage at what the military has done in the West Bank. One of the troopers involved in the attack on the police asked, "What did they do?" and was told simply, "It doesn't matter; they took six of ours, and we are going to take six of theirs."[55]

This kind of action abuses the system and sanctions unnecessary violence. It is one thing to kill a terrorist who has blown up a busload of children; it is another to kill policemen who are not known to have targeted civilians. The unfortunate truth is that the public wants the government to act, and the appearance of decisive action will placate public anger, whether or not it is justified. What, after all, can politicians do to prove to a vengeful public that they are fighting terrorism? Occupy more Palestinian areas? Install more checkpoints? Full-blown military campaigns such as the Second Lebanon War or the 2008–9 campaign in Gaza takes far more significant tolls on Israel's neighboring societies than do targeted killings.

In theory the public support gained from a successful killing should enable politicians to take other measures to defuse a conflict, such as engaging in talks with more moderate leaders, without appearing weak. But these reasons do not justify using targeting killings for political reasons.

Politicians derive more rewards for a killing, but counterterrorism officials stress that arrests are almost always more productive. An arrested suspect can be interrogated and reveal ongoing plots and information about other wanted men. A dead man will tell no tales. So targeted killings should be seen as useful when arrests are not possible or would be too dangerous for military and security personnel to attempt, not as an ideal answer to fighting terrorism.

Targeted killings are a necessary tool of Israeli counterterrorism and can be useful for other countries fighting terrorists based out of sanctuaries they do not control. And they are not going away: in 2010 Mahmud al-Mabhouh, a Hamas operative who also liaised with Iran, was killed in Dubai, allegedly by Israel. If done cleanly, targeted killings disrupt terrorist groups and force those who survive to focus on hiding and security, not on planning attacks. To maintain the high moral bar that Israel, as a democracy, establishes for itself, the killing of civilians must be avoided, or at least minimized when possible.

Despite the satisfaction many Israelis derive from killing suspected terrorists, this tool, like any other tool, does not solve the terrorism problem by itself. Indeed no matter how good Israel's intelligence is, arrests and killings are not enough. Israel needs defense as well as offense. And no defensive measure is as controversial as the security barrier Israel constructed during the Second Intifada.

CHAPTER XXII

BUILDING THE SECURITY BARRIER

THE SECURITY barriers that run along or near Israel's borders with the Gaza Strip and the West Bank are a visible symbol of the Israeli-Palestinian struggle, a scar that reminds even the most romantic tourist that the Holy Land is rife with conflict. The barrier is a double-edged sword: on one hand, it serves as a highly effective counterterrorism device; on the other hand, it complicates peace efforts and creates enormous hardships for Palestinians. Other Israeli defensive measures are less visible and problematic, but they too often involve trade-offs, and their effectiveness is debated.

Popularly referred to as a *fence* by Israelis and a *wall* by Palestinians and most of the international community, the barrier is both a chain-link fence and a concrete wall. It is surrounded on both sides by an intrusion-detection system, which has a set of around sixty electronic and other systems that take up at least forty-five meters on its sides. At its center is a wire fence with sensors and video cameras. A military road runs along the Israeli side so patrols can speedily converge on any intruder. Also along the Israeli side are sand traps or a smooth dirt strip, where an intruder would leave footprints, designed to reveal the path of any Palestinian who crosses illegally. On the Palestinian side there is a ditch to stop vehicles. Both sides have a mini wall of razor wire. The United Nations reports that when it is completed the total barrier length will be over 700 kilometers long. As of July 2010, over 400 kilometers have been built.[1]

Only a small part of it, thirty kilometers or so, is a concrete wall.[2] The wall is high enough to protect Israeli homes and vehicles from the sniper fire they suffered during the first years of the Second Intifada. The concrete portion of the barrier looms large, however, because it is located in populated areas. For many Palestinians and Israelis, particularly those in Jerusalem, the concrete is all they see.

There is also a barrier along Israel's border with the Gaza Strip. Rabin's administration built the Gaza barrier in 1994 even as it gave control over Gaza to the new PA. That barrier, forty-seven kilometers in length, has four crossings: at Erez, Karni, Kisufim, and Sufa. The Kisufim crossing is for Israelis only.[3] When the Second Intifada broke out, Palestinians destroyed or stole much of the Gaza barrier. It was later replaced and upgraded with better sensors and overlapping observation posts. The Israelis also bulldozed potential hiding places on the Gaza side to make observation more effective. The new systems include remotely operated weapons systems, enabling soldiers sitting a few kilometers away to target suspected militants without exposing themselves to fire.[4] On both sides the IDF leveled and cleared a three-hundred-meter strip and installed watchtowers to monitor it.

The Israeli Defense Cabinet approved the West Bank barrier in July 2001, but the initial construction moved slowly, not gaining momentum until violence picked up in 2002. The organization Fence for Life, founded after the Dolphinarium Disco bombing in June 2001, pushed for the barrier's construction under the slogan "The Security Fence is the only way." As violence peaked in 2002 and 2003 the public clamor grew: 84 percent of Israelis favored it by February 2004.[5] The West Bank barrier was much harder to build than the Gaza barrier; the final route is over fifteen times longer and it must go through hilly parts of the West Bank as well as through urban parts of Jerusalem.

Avi Dichter, the head of Shin Bet as the violence of the Second Intifada surged, pushed hard for the barrier. According to one intelligence official I talked to, Dichter argued that the barrier was "crucial" (not the bureaucratically safer "helpful") for stopping terrorism. In Dichter's eyes, the barrier promised an end to suicide bombing by stopping bombers from entering Israel proper.

The Israeli leadership, however, was split on the issue. Sharon initially opposed the barrier. Yigal Allon, one of Israel's legendary military leaders, had once remarked, "No modern country can surround itself with a wall," and Sharon, one of Israel's most aggressive military commanders, shared Allon's skepticism that defense was the answer.[6] Sharon also did not want to give up on the dream of a greater Israel that would include all of the biblical Jewish lands. At the very least he didn't want to offend his right-wing supporters who believed in the biblical concept. The military leadership agreed with Sharon. They feared that the Palestinians would find ways to insinuate themselves around the barrier and that it would divert money and manpower the IDF needed. Shaul Mofaz, who served as chief of the general staff of the IDF and then defense minister, asserted, "We will build the fence during the day, and fight over it during the night."[7]

In the end public pressure prevailed, but only gradually. The barrier's construction moved slowly, beginning in the northern part of the West Bank, separating Jenin, Nablus, and Tulkaram—three West Bank hubs of terrorism—from Israel proper. Building accelerated in 2002, but work proceeded at a snail's pace. At the current rate, complained one official, "it won't even be finished in 2014." Areas around Ariel, Jerusalem, and Gush Etzion remain incomplete, as well as sections in the southern West Bank area.[8]

The IDF blamed human rights organizations for delaying the fence, claiming their petitions together with the Supreme Court's slow rulings allowed terrorists to continue to enter Israel. The IDF even blamed a lack of funding. But part of the problem remains political. The barrier for the West Bank at times follows the internationally accepted border along the Green Line that separates Israel from the West Bank, but much of it is built on the Palestinian side. The designers tried to maximize the number of Israelis within the walls by creating enclaves of Jewish settlements on the Palestinian side of the Green Line. The result, ironically, is that the Barrier's route increases Israel's security problems and the vulnerability of its citizens to militant attacks.

If the barrier became the final border, settlements outside it risked becoming part of Palestinian land. Shaul Goldstein, a settler leader, argued, "Whatever stays outside the fence would eventually not be ours."[9] Opposing the barrier was politically risky because it was overwhelmingly popular, and the settlers did not want to be seen as standing in the way of counterterrorism. So they tried to solve the problem by establishing the barrier as far east of the 1967 borders as possible, even if doing so included rather than excluded Palestinians. When Israel decided to bring the area between Jerusalem and Gush Etzion inside the barrier, it also brought in twenty thousand Palestinians.

Many critics both inside and outside of Israel see the barrier as a form of annexation. Although Israeli officials regularly stressed to critics that the barrier is not a political border and can be removed, they feared that if the barrier ran along the 1967 border it would create a de facto line that would grant Palestinians parts of the West Bank that Israel hoped to control through negotiations. Non-Israeli negotiators, however, feared the opposite: that Israel would build houses and facilities on its side of the barrier, creating demographic facts on the ground that would be hard to reverse in peace talks.

Is security or annexation the driver? Gen. Eival Gilady, one of the barrier's designers, told me that the line was drawn segment by segment according to security criteria, not government design. He explained that the 1967 Green Line border was the initial reference; he then considered the topography. High ground is preferred, as you don't want snipers shooting down at you, and in general you try to make it harder to hit vehicles. He also had to consider the legal status of the land, choosing public over private land when possible. Finally, the architects looked at access to the area in the event of an incursion. When pushed on the human impact of the barrier, Gilady countered, "You don't ask questions after you see a four-year-old girl trying to wake up her dead mom." For much of the barrier's route Gilady's point is valid, especially with regard to the initial decision to construct the barrier, but in its ultimate route politics played an important part, particularly in Jerusalem, where ideology mattered more than security. Sharon himself drove much of the barrier's design, supervising and planning every kilometer when he was prime minister. According to Amos Gil, who headed the Jerusalem-focused human rights organization Ir Amin, Sharon sought to create a greater Jerusalem, incorporating several settlement blocs.

From a legal point of view, the issue is not the barrier itself but rather building it on territory that is annexed or otherwise not within a state's recognized boundaries. If Israel built the barrier entirely within the 1967 borders, there would be grumbling but little legal ground for opponents. In its judgment on the barrier the International Court of Justice found that the driver of the barrier was not security against terrorist attacks, but rather Israel's desire to annex territory. The International Court argued that because Israel was not threatened by another state, it could not rely on Article 51 of the UN Charter as a security justification for needing a wall.[10] Although accurate in a literal sense, this legalism misses the true nature of the security threat Israel faced, failing to recognize that nonstate terrorism, especially during the Second Intifada, posed a serious threat to Israel.

In 2004 the Israeli Supreme Court found that "the fence is motivated by security concerns." The court also found that the initial route was "not proportionate" to the suffering that it brought to Palestinians and required the barrier to be rerouted in places in order to reduce the infringement on the rights of Palestinians and relieve some of the suffering it entailed.[11] The new route took approximately 15 percent less Palestinian territory, though critics point out that many of the areas in which the court called for changes did not occur.

Over time, however, the court came to see politics and annexation as important drivers. In the case of Bi'lin, an Arab village contesting the route of the barrier, the court endorsed the Palestinian claim and ruled, "There is no other way to explain this route other than the desire to include the eastern part of Matitiahu-Mizrah west of the fence. If this was not the case, there is doubt whether there is any security justification to set the route of the fence where it is now set."[12] The judges cited the route's poor topography and risk to the patrolling forces to justify their skepticism.[13]

The Security Impact of the Barrier

Years after the construction began most Israelis believe the barrier has been a tremendous success, as terrorist attacks in Israel proper have fallen precipitously. The barrier functions as the ultimate checkpoint, difficult to bypass and always active (though in its incomplete state it can still be circumvented.) Uzi Dayan, who was one of the barrier's champions when he served on Israel's National Security Council, argued that when there is no barrier, "every place is a crossing point." As the former IDF planner Yossi Kuperwasser puts it, before the barrier, there were checkpoints, but they were "doors in a house without walls." General Moshe Kaplinsky, who was IDF Deputy Chief of Staff, adds emphatically, "Where the barrier is in operation, no terror attack goes through it. Period." Perhaps most convincing is the admission of Ramadan Abdallah Shalah, the PIJ leader, in a March 2008 interview with *Al-Sharq* that the barrier "limits the ability of the resistance . . . to carry out suicide bombing attacks" within Israeli territory.[14]

The impact in Gaza is particularly clear. Israel claims that the barrier has stopped hundreds of infiltrations in the buffer zone. During the Intifada's first years, over half of Palestinian terrorist attacks were launched from Gaza, but the barrier prevented almost all of them from succeeding. It was not perfect. Two suicide bombers, for example, went through security in the false compartment of a cargo truck in 2004 and killed ten in Ashdod, and of course Gilad Shalit was kidnapped when terrorists used a tunnel to raid the local IDF post, but the barrier made infiltration far harder. Most of those killed from Gaza were soldiers, which also proves that the barrier reduced the danger to Israeli civilians.

As with checkpoints, time is one of the barrier's gifts. If Israeli intelligence learns about an impending attack it can effectively shut off much of Israel proper from the West Bank and Gaza. Attackers in the northern West Bank now need to travel south to get around the barrier. In doing so, different terrorist cells would have to work together, exposing themselves to Israeli counterterrorism in the process. "One plus one is eleven" when it comes to counterterrorism, Dichter contends, arguing that this expansion of the operation's circle from one cell to another offers exponentially more opportunities for disruption.

Despite the contortions of the barrier's route, many settlers still remain outside of it. Ensuring these settlers easy transit into Israel poses huge risks for those inside the barrier. The human rights group B'Tselem reports that as of the end of 2005, there were forty-eight settlements on the Israeli side of the barrier, housing 187,840 people. East of the barrier, however, there were sixty-nine settlements, housing 57,330 people.[15] Because many cars with Israeli plates are waved through, the border is not well sealed: an Israeli Arab driver who can pass for a Jew is all that is needed to get through, according to Yossi Alpher, an Israeli security analyst. These holes in the barrier increase Israel's dependence on checkpoints.

Critics of the barrier rightly point out that Palestinian groups have overcome the barrier with rocket and mortar attacks. But not all attacks are equal. Palestinian groups used rocket and mortar attacks, roadside bombings, sniper shooting, and other methods to kill Israelis, but none come close to suicide bombing in effectiveness. The scholar Bruce Hoffman found that suicide bombing produced more than twenty-five times as many casualties as other forms of terrorism.[16] Almost half of the Israeli death toll resulted from suicide bombings during the Second Intifada, even though this method constituted less than 1 percent of total attacks. Suicide bombers had the ability to penetrate every major Israeli city, while—for now at least—many are outside Hamas rocket range. In 2007 Israel suffered only one suicide attack, when PIJ and the al-Aqsa Martyrs Brigade dispatched a bomber who traveled the "Het Route" (named after the Hebrew alphabet letter *Heth*, which looks like an upside-down U) from Gaza to Sinai to Egypt and then back to Israel. The crossing from Egypt to Israel is relatively easy, compared with the difficult crossing from Gaza to Israel. But even this unusual path is now harder due to improved Egyptian security measures. In 2009 there were no suicide attacks. In 2010 Israel began moving forward with a plan to fence off several dozen kilometers on the northern and southern ends of its border with Egypt.

Because of this success, the barrier enjoys immense popularity among Israelis. The journalist Hirsch Goodman notes that even though "it is the worst-managed project in Israel" public support is high: "There is no criticism of this ugly, internationally condemned, poorly managed barrier."

The Human Cost of the Barrier

Much of the barrier is being constructed on Palestinian land, leaving isolation and economic ruin in its wake. Although the barrier's extension beyond the 1967 border (the so-called Green Line) brings Jews inside it, Palestinian villages and lands are often caught between the barrier and the border. Israeli government documents indicate that there are about seven thousand Palestinians who live in this area, though other sources claim the figure is even larger.[17] The result is that some Palestinians now find themselves or their property within the barrier. According to the United Nations, in January 2006 almost three-quarters of the barrier's length (including East Jerusalem) is on the West Bank side of Israel's pre-1967 borders. This has created closed "seam" areas: 10 percent of West Bank and East Jerusalem land lies between the barrier and the Green Line.[18] The route artificially separates Palestinian communities. The Palestinian cities of Tulkarem and Qalqilya are only about fifteen kilometers apart, yet the barrier in that area is 165 kilometers long, having been stretched to include the Kedumim and Ariel settlements. Thus Palestinians find it hard to travel from one city to the other.[19] To cross into their lands on the other side of the barrier, Palestinians in the "seam zone" must obtain special permits from the IDF. Palestinians in the rest of the West Bank must also get permits to visit relatives in the seam zone and vice versa.

By now even the most valued and long-standing workers often cannot show up for work on time due to the difficulties of crossing the barrier. In 1999 seventy-four thousand Palestinians worked in Israel, mainly in agriculture and construction; in 2008 only twenty-three thousand worked legally in Israel. Tens of thousands of Palestinians work in Israel without permits (and thus reside there illegally).[20]

The barrier's impact is particularly profound for Jerusalem's Palestinian community. As one reporter told me, "Jerusalem has more disputes per square inch than any other place in the world." Before the barrier there were roughly 250,000 Palestinians in Jerusalem, one-third of the population. They saw themselves as Palestinians for cultural and family reasons, but they enjoyed the material benefits of being Israeli. Today, however, Jerusalem's Palestinians are split into three categories. First, there are those on the Israeli side of the barrier, representing 130,000 to 140,000 people. Second, there are another sixty thousand who are still part of the Municipality of Jerusalem but on the Palestinian side of the barrier; they have the rights of Jerusalemites, though they enjoy fewer services. They must cross the barrier to enter their own city, making it hard for them to work within Israel proper. The third category consists of Jerusalemites who have left the city to find a home elsewhere.

Ironically the new restrictions have at times driven Palestinians *into* Jerusalem. Rather than risk losing their rights, and fearful of losing jobs because of having to traverse checkpoints, Palestinians who are able buy real estate within the Jerusalem barrier. Even some traditionally Jewish areas are seeing a growth spurt in the Arab population. At the same time Jews are moving into traditional Arab areas near the Old City in the "Holy Basin" area. This intermixing will make it much more difficult to achieve a political settlement on Jerusalem. Amos Gil, the human rights official, believes Israel's policies have effectively sealed in tens of thousands of angry Palestinians.

Radical organizations actively seek out Jerusalem's Arab population. Shin Bet claimed that in 2004 4 percent of Jerusalem Arabs age seventeen to forty-five were involved in terrorism, potentially a significant percentage given that most terrorist cells draw on only a small part of a total population.[21] Because they hold Israeli documents and vehicle licenses, they enjoy far more freedom of movement and are therefore useful as drivers and scouts. In addition they speak Hebrew and understand Israeli culture.

As attacks from the West Bank dwindled, the problem in Jerusalem grew among Arabs inside the barrier. During 2008 and the first half of 2009 there were six "run-over" attacks by East Jerusalemites with tractors and other vehicles, killing three Israelis and wounding eighty. East Jerusalemites also stabbed tourists, and in one incident shot people at a checkpoint. The most bloody attack was the 2008 shooting and suicide attack at a Jerusalem religious school the Merkaz HaRav Yeshiva, which killed eight Israelis. According to Shin Bet, "The Jerusalem terrorists take advantage of their intimate knowledge of the area of the attack and their freedom of movement resulting from their status as residents of the city."[22]

Crossing the barrier can be a dehumanizing experience for Palestinians. Lines are often long, particularly when there are spikes in violence. Because the barrier makes it harder to cross into Israel, militants have struck at the barrier itself, resulting in even tighter security measures. In 2004 Hamas used a female suicide bomber, a mother of two, to kill four Israelis at the Erez crossing of the Gaza barrier. Afterward Israel put into place security cameras, automated gates, and other remote-control devices that minimize contact between Israelis and the Palestinians coming through.

Although at times Palestinians seeking to work, sell goods, visit relatives, or obtain medical care can pass through quickly, delays are common. Soldiers fear mistakes. Hanadi Taysir Jaradat, a woman, did not fit the typical profile of a suicide bomber because of her sex and Jordanian passport, which helped her avoid scrutiny when she went through a checkpoint in 2003. Because she was not carefully searched she went to the Maxim restaurant in Haifa, where she blew herself up after fastidiously paying her bill, killing twenty-one Israelis, both Arabs and Jews.[23]

Israelis, including the barrier's champions, are very open about the human costs of the barrier. The security expert Baruch Spiegel, who praises the barrier's effectiveness, also admits, "Each *dunam* [one thousand square meters of land] and each olive tree is somebody's living," and the former IDF chief of staff Bogi Yaalon wrote, "Any defensive measures taken by Israel—including traffic checkpoints, closures, and curfews—inevitably led to Palestinian suffering and to violations of their civil rights."[24] The barrier also poisons communal relations. Uzi Dayan, who believes the barrier is effective, told me, "I don't think that good fences make good neighbors." Continuing the poetic reference, however, he smiled and added, "If Frost had terrorists for neighbors rather than irate New Englanders, he would build a fence."

The barrier also fundamentally changes the nature of any future peace settlement. The former Shin Bet head Avraham Shalom contends that the barrier "creates hatred, it expropriates land, and annexes hundreds of thousands of Palestinians to the state of Israel," all of which makes a negotiated two-state solution harder.[25] Palestinians always assumed peace to mean a market for goods in Israel and relatively open borders, but any conceivable peace would still include the barrier, even if its location were moved to reflect new negotiated borders. The barrier would inhibit the flow of goods, particularly produce and other agricultural items, and make travel difficult for Palestinians holding jobs in Israel.

For many Palestinians the barrier is a sign that Israel rejects a peace deal, as it adds yet another indignity imposed on them. The Palestinian journalist Wafa Amr said, "It makes Palestinians feel like they are in jail."

Layers of Defense

The barrier is the most visible (and controversial) defensive measure, but it is far from the only one. Israeli defenses must be thought of as a series of layers, none of which is impervious, but together they make the task of Palestinian militant groups far more difficult.

Israel armored its buses that took routes deemed dangerous. Some buses even have electronic explosive detectors that enable drivers to quickly shut down doors if an explosive is detected.[26] Special security units were created to patrol public places and buses. Shopping malls, bus and train stations, and other public buildings all are guarded. Near Palestinian areas Israeli homes often have bulletproof glass. In the early 1990s Israel placed armed guards in the schools; perhaps as important as the lives saved was the psychological reassurance the guards' presence gave to parents and the community.

Israel also tries to keep citizens alert to terrorism, both as a preventive measure and as a psychological remedy. Many Israelis volunteer for civil defense units, and civilians are on the lookout for suspicious packages and individuals.[27] During the height of the Intifada the IDF's Home Front Command sent a fifty-two-page brochure to every home in Israel that explained the rules for how to deal with emergencies. Soldiers visit schools to tell students how to protect themselves from terrorists and even chemical and biological attacks. Israelis believe that this knowledge will reduce anxiety so that people will feel ready to handle terrorism challenges that come their way.[28] Finally, Israel has expanded its medical infrastructure to accommodate a large number of sudden injuries from terrorism, a measure that saves lives even when terrorists are not stopped. Some of Israel's defensive measures, such as its systems to detect and defeat improvised explosive devices, are shared and further developed in cooperation with the United States.

Many Israeli defensive measures are expensive, especially the barrier. Israel's state comptroller estimates the total cost of the barrier at nine billion shekels (more than two billion dollars), a third of which is allocated to Jerusalem. That figure excludes the cost of fulfilling Supreme Court rulings requiring Israel to alleviate the humanitarian burden the barrier places on immediately affected Palestinians and the cost of maintaining and manning the barrier.[29]

A particular defensive challenge is stopping rocket attacks, which for groups like Hamas is now their primary means of threatening Israel. To guard against the Qassam rockets Israel is trying to develop a technologically sophisticated antirocket system, called "Iron Dome." The feasibility of the system for intercepting a rocket that has only to fly a few kilometers is questionable, and its cost may be too high.[30] The security analyst Shlomo Gazit points out that producing a Qassam rocket costs about fifty dollars (others claim even less), whereas an anti-Qassam rocket costs about fifty thousand dollars. This ratio is prohibitive even for Israel, which is a wealthy society. Shlomo Brom, a security analyst and former IDF planner, asks, "What is the value of thousands of Israelis guarding each shop and restaurant?" He worries that Israel is "committing fiscal suicide." Brom's points are valid, but they must also be weighed against the considerable cost, financial as well as human, that comes with the Israeli response to terrorism. If defenses work well, there is less pressure for Israel to use military force, which is deadly as well as costly.

Even outside of expensive systems like Iron Dome, judging the effectiveness of defenses is difficult. Between 1993 and 2007 security guards prevented an attack or forced a premature, and thus less lethal, detonation on fourteen occasions.[31] Yet most of the impact is hard to observe. In March 1996 a suicide bomber attacked the Dizengoff Center in Tel Aviv and killed fourteen Israelis in a horrific attack. The terrorism expert Boaz Ganor points out that because the Center was guarded, the attacker was forced to change plans and blow himself up outside, killing far fewer people as a result.[32] Were the guards a success in this attack? Yes and no, depending on the yardstick used. This is an analytic problem for other forms of defense too. Their value is often in the form of an attack averted or fewer lives lost and thus is difficult to observe directly.

Defenses also reassure citizens that the government is protecting them. When citizens participate in civil defense units they feel some measure of control over their lives and believe they are contributing to their nation's defense, both of which are vital to combating the psychological toll that terrorism exacts.

The barrier's effectiveness can best be seen when its role is understood in conjunction with arrests and targeted killings. Because the barrier and checkpoints give counterterrorism officials more time and force terrorists to work with cells farther from their homes, the IDF is better able to stop a bomber en route to an attack. Because targeted killings and arrests have eliminated many terrorists and forced others underground, new operatives are relatively unskilled, and their ability to work together is reduced.

Yet perhaps more than any other Israeli counterterrorism measure, the barrier's political and social impact must be weighed in addition to its security benefits—and here the barrier's current route is problematic. For Palestinians, the barrier shreds social and economic relations and sours them on Israel's ultimate intentions. In theory the barrier can be moved, but in practice the region's history illustrates how supposedly temporary borders often become permanent. Removing or even moving the barrier would require Israelis to trust their Palestinian partner on the other side, and that trust is nowhere on the horizon.

CHAPTER XXIII

REORGANIZING FOR COUNTERTERRORISM

WHEN ISRAELI intelligence convinced Mosab Hassan Yousef, the son of one of Hamas's founders, to spy, Yousef agreed only because he planned to exploit the opportunity to work for Hamas as a double agent. But after watching Hamas's brutality toward suspected collaborators Yousef lost his faith in the organization. "They tortured people brutally, burned them, jabbed them with needles, put cigarettes on them," he recalled.[1] Yousef's Shin Bet handlers exploited his disillusionment and at the same time made sure he kept up the appearance of loyalty. They encouraged him to maintain his posture as the son of a respected sheikh, even urging him to take prayer breaks during their meetings. Given his father's status, Yousef met with high-ranking figures in all Palestinian groups, which helped Shin Bet capture or kill them. He also passed along intelligence that led to the disruption of dozens of suicide bombing attempts. Yousef would eventually leave the area, convert to Christianity, and take up residence in California—as a souvenir of his past, he even owns an IDF T-shirt.[2]

To acquire and exploit sources like Yousef against militant groups, the IDF and Israeli intelligence were forced to change their modus operandi, abandoning what worked so well in the 1970s and 1980s. The challenge was particularly difficult because it went beyond a narrow definition of counterterrorism. Groups like Hamas, Hizballah, and the Fatah-linked Tanzim carried out classic terrorist attacks, including suicide bombings, but they also attacked Israeli soldiers in guerrilla-style operations and controlled mosques, charities, and government institutions. Both the IDF and Shin Bet changed in response and, bureaucratically, Shin Bet rose to become Israel's premier counterterrorism agency.

While the IDF and Israeli intelligence adapted to the evolving threat, Israel's broader political decision-making system remained stuck. The system is a poor one for national security, making long-term planning in particular difficult.

A New Type of Foe

The IDF found the counterterrorism mission particularly trying. Carmi Gillon, who headed Shin Bet in 1995 and 1996, said that during his tenure, "The mighty IDF doesn't know how to respond to two Katyusha incidents, or LAW rockets. It knows how to respond to three divisions marching from right to left, but that isn't helpful against Bedouin shepherds."[3] Almost a decade later an Israeli general pointed out that "there were no relevant doctrines and techniques" for the type of conflict the IDF would face in urban areas at the beginning of the Intifada.[4]

The IDF began to overhaul its tactics before the Second Intifada began and accelerated the pace of reform as the violence grew. In 2000 it upgraded the size and power of its intelligence component, creating the Field Intelligence Corps (renamed the Combat Intelligence Collection Force in 2009). In the past information went up the chain from intelligence collectors to a central analytic facility. Now select ground troops conducted on-the-spot interrogations and gathered their own intelligence, which they passed to other troops in the field; information no longer got delayed or stuck at headquarters. In urban areas like Jenin Israelis jammed Palestinian cell phones to inhibit communications; UAVs and helicopters gathered information on enemy locations to find and kill snipers on rooftops; and maps were made three-dimensional, so terrain was clearly identified to soldiers as they advanced.[5]

Military forces learned to isolate an area and control traffic coming in and out. Tanks shielded the infantry, but they did not attack and overrun enemy positions, as in a conventional conflict. Engineering forces, equipped with saws, hammers, and explosive charges, broke through walls and disarmed enemy booby traps. Because units often fought at the squad and platoon level rather than in large formations, the IDF empowered lower level officers, giving them far more freedom of action.[6] To strengthen this level of the officer corps the IDF established new training programs such as the Tactical Command College.[7]

Training changed fundamentally. In 2002 the IDF set up an urban warfare training center at the Tze'elim army base, a facility labeled "Chicago." Chicago now has 472 structures that mirror actual buildings in the West Bank and Gaza, complete with mosques, schools, shops, a casbah, a cemetery, and even burned-out cars on the street and laundry hanging from windows.[8]

Special forces units are the most important military force in Israel. They get the first pick from the pool of ground forces recruits, selecting potential leaders who are fit and mentally tough. Undercover units like Duvdevan look for smart and independent actors, particularly those with good language skills. Individual toughness and independence are highly valued, as soldiers operate in small units without much oversight from commanders.

Undercover units often operate at night. Rather than use Jeeps or armored personnel carriers, they use grocery supply or utility repair trucks. When an undercover unit is inserted in enemy territory tremendous care is taken, as the potential for casualties is high. The plan is carefully vetted, and backups are inserted nearby should any of the steps in the operation go awry. Troops are constantly trained to think "What if?" so they can respond quickly if or when the unforeseen occurs. Because of the high risk, a unit officer once told me, "the first option for an undercover operation is not to do it undercover." Whenever possible the IDF would simply cordon off an area and arrest the suspected terrorist.

After the 1974 Ma'alot massacre, when terrorists from the Democratic Front for the Liberation of Palestine seized hostages in an Israeli school, with twenty-seven innocents eventually dying during the rescue attempt. Israel established a special counterterrorism police unit, Yamam, the Hebrew acronym for Special Police Unit (*yehidat mishtara meyuchedet*), designed primarily for hostage rescue. All of Yamam's people served at least three years in the army, and most came from elite units; at times the entire unit is loaned to the army. During the Second Intifada the unit played an important role in making arrests and killing wanted Palestinians.[9]

When working as part of a larger military force such as Defensive Shield, special forces units would swarm in small groups rather than deploy in large formations, which enabled them to confuse the enemy and attack from all directions. Palestinian fighters no longer had one large target on which to focus their fire. To go through the densely packed refugee camps as they did in Jenin, the units avoided alleys where the Palestinians had set up killing zones. Instead they dynamited holes through the walls of buildings, enabling soldiers to pass from house to house.

When militants attacked the IDF they were forced to reveal their location, which exposed them to Israeli snipers.[10] The impact of a sniper hit is devastating and surgical. "When a bullet hits the head, where it hits is only a small hole and on the other side half the head is missing," commented one sniper. The target dies, and those around him—to say nothing of the buildings and other objects devastated in larger military operations—survive. This does not mean there is no cost. The sniper also added, "The mothers there cried next to the bodies." Still it is far less devastating to ordinary Palestinians than aerial bombardment, artillery fire, or the D-9 bulldozers used in Jenin.[11]

Counterterrorism concerns persist even after the operation is long over. They are evident in policies governing everything from work permits to architecture. After Defensive Shield, for instance, Jenin's alleys were widened to allow the passage of Israeli tanks.[12]

Organizing a military for counterterrorism can have huge costs for conventional readiness. Israeli reviews of its military performance in the 2006 Lebanon war, when Israeli forces had to undertake more traditional military tasks, were scathing. They found that forces did not operate effectively as large units, commanders did not train on the use of combined arms, and commanders for armored units did not perform well. Many of these problems can be traced to the emphasis on the counterterrorism methods the IDF used during the Second Intifada.

Indeed Lebanon revealed what may be a more common pattern of conflict, one that the United States faces in Iraq and Afghanistan: a mix of counterterrorism, counterinsurgency, and conventional conflict. While the IDF was fighting large, well-organized Hizballah military units, they were also trying to kill individual Hizballah leaders and uncover hidden guerrilla movements. No simple or traditional military profile met this task.

The question of casualties, both military and civilian, is perhaps the toughest issue. General Moshe Kaplinsky of the IDF put the dilemma clearly. At one point at the height of the Second Intifada he got a phone call from one of his division commanders, who requested permission to bomb a building where three terrorists were hiding out. Kaplinsky denied the request, fearing civilian casualties. Instead the IDF sent troops in to take the building, and one of the soldiers died. He then had to explain to the soldier's mother why he sent her boy into the building rather than an F-16. From a human rights point of view, B'Tselem's Jessica Montell contends, "the job of a soldier is to take risks." In Jenin the IDF took casualties in part because it was willing to close with Palestinian fighters in order to reduce civilian deaths. As the 2008–9 Cast Lead operation would show, the IDF became far less willing to risk its own soldiers to reduce civilian deaths.

A New Intelligence Profile

Intelligence is at the heart of counterterrorism. Without it success is impossible. As difficult as the Intifada was for Israel's military forces, it was an even bigger challenge for its intelligence services.

For counterterrorism purposes, there are three key intelligence agencies: military intelligence (Aman), domestic intelligence (Shin Bet), and foreign intelligence (Mossad). The Mossad was the tip of the spear in Israel's efforts against Palestinian groups operating in Jordan, Lebanon, and elsewhere in the Middle East. The Mossad also has an aggressive foreign liaison program and is the gateway for most intelligence sharing.

After the Israeli invasion of Lebanon in 1982 Aman handled Lebanon with only a limited Shin Bet role until Israel withdrew in 2000. Today Aman still plays an important role in Lebanon.

The role of military intelligence, the largest of the intelligence organizations, is vast. One former U.S. intelligence official told me, "It's like our Pentagon," in that it has more people and more assets than its sister intelligence services, as well as a huge analytic capacity. Perhaps most important (and least reported) it controls most signals intelligence and aerial reconnaissance assets, on which counterterrorism depends. Knowing the importance of military intelligence in Israel's history, the unit has for many years attracted the country's best and brightest. Military intelligence also works closely with Israel's foreign partners, particularly the United States and the United Kingdom.

The capabilities of Unit 8200 of the IDF Intelligence Corps are another important part of SIGINT. This unit, the Central Collection Unit, is the biggest in the IDF, with thousands of soldiers. Unit 8200 collects signals intelligence (and electronic intelligence) for the entire intelligence community, including Shin Bet. It also works on hacking into computer systems around the world. The Israeli high-tech industry relies heavily on the retired personnel from this unit.[13]

Shin Bet has played an important role in limiting violence among Israeli Arabs and, after the 1967 War, among Arabs in the West Bank and Gaza Strip. Shin Bet focused largely on young men in refugee camps who were linked to leftist groups or Fatah. Sometimes they encountered recruits trained in Syria or Lebanon, but these men did not have extensive networks so it was hard for them to communicate. If they had connections beyond their town it was with Palestinian organizations abroad, not local groups. Many Shin Bet officers worked openly, collecting information on who did what in the territories. "Everyone in Nablus could say who the Shin Bet officer was," the former head of Shin Bet Carmi Gillon recalls.

The Shin Bet official assigned to collect intelligence from an agent is an elite member of an elite service—truly the best of the best. He begins an interview with full knowledge about the potential recruit: his family, his beliefs, and his habits. A police operative described the first meeting as "a chess game in which one side has three queens and the other is playing only with pawns."[14] Once recruited, the agent handler typically has to spend many hours with the source. The ability to forge a personal relationship with the recruit is vital, and the agent handler must at times be a father or a big brother figure. The source may be giving out information that would hurt his family and friends, and he needs to be confident his handler will protect him.

One former agent handler told me that putting yourself in a potential source's shoes is vital. When the nature of the enemy changed and Shin

Bet began working against religious groups as opposed to secular nationalists and left-wingers, this kind of empathy became difficult. With Hamas as the focus, its operatives worried not just about betraying their movement and their cause, but also betraying God. The family ties that bind groups like Hamas and PIJ made them even harder to penetrate.

In the 1990s the situation changed fundamentally.[15] Because Israel no longer controlled the Palestinian population Israeli decision makers assumed Shin Bet would need fewer personnel. After Oslo Shin Bet released 40 percent of its interrogators. But terrorist attacks increased even as Shin Bet became smaller and could not use Israel's control over the lives of Palestinians to extract intelligence. With the suicide bombings of the mid-1990s and the Rabin killing, morale plunged. "Reality didn't cooperate with us," noted one senior Israeli counterterrorism official.

The local nature of these groups posed a challenge to Shin Bet. It is easier to run an agent against a Palestinian far from his home and family, in a place like Bangkok, than in Hebron; in Bangkok the Palestinian is isolated, and any suspicious contacts would not be immediately reported. Technology was yet another challenge. Twenty years ago, if a Palestinian in Ramallah called Damascus it was easy to track. Now new computer and cell phone technology allow communication to be anonymous and greatly increased the volume of communications. Terrorist operations that once took weeks to roll out now occur much faster. Yet this danger presented Shin Bet with a new opportunity to gather data. If the organization could improve its signals intelligence capabilities, a whole new trove of information would be open to them.

An extensive review in 1996 found that Shin Bet had not organized its resources properly for the new challenge. Intelligence integration was a key issue. Information came from sources in different parts of Shin Bet organized according to region: one division might advise waiting before protecting a source, while another would advocate nabbing a suspect and interrogating him immediately. There was no clear hierarchy for decision making, and it became difficult for operatives to work together. Each command had autonomy, which resulted in a mix of methods and philosophies. This made some sense when terrorist cells were local and were handled by separate parts of the organization, but Shin Bet's methods remained the same even though terrorists no longer confined themselves to one area. On top of that it was not clear where Shin Bet's responsibilities ended and those of the Mossad and the IDF (and which part of the IDF) began.

The review led to two big changes: an increase in central coordination and better information sharing. To resolve the coordination problem, Shin Bet headquarters became stronger and more centralized, bringing people together as needed. The deputy director, who in the past would "do all the shit" (in the words of one official) involved in keeping the wheels turning for the organization as a whole, now had responsibility for resource allocation and operational activity. Over time Shin Bet "broke all the walls of compartmentalization" (the intelligence practice of keeping information secret even within and between government agencies to avoid revealing sources or compromising the intelligence). Now the information was open to anyone who might need it. Unlike the presumption of compartmentalization in most Western intelligence agencies, in Israel today the presumption is for sharing. Shin Bet officials need approval of the deputy director or the director to compartmentalize information, rather than the other way around.

During the Second Intifada, with their Palestinian partner falling apart and the violence intensifying, the imperative for change intensified and Shin Bet scrambled to regain intelligence dominance. As early as 2002 Israeli officials claimed that they had stopped roughly 80 percent of attacks by using advance intelligence.[16] It was an impressive success rate, but still not good enough given the increased pace of attacks.[17] Palestinians had attempted 155 suicide bombings inside Israel (not including the West Bank and Gaza), of which 112 were stopped and forty-three were carried out. "We didn't provide the Israeli citizen with the protection against terror he deserves," confessed the former Shin Bet chief Avi Dichter.[18]

To meet the challenge Shin Bet reorganized. There are three geographic field offices that focus on Palestinian areas and Israeli Arabs. Another part of the organization works on al-Qa'ida, Hizballah, and other groups, at times in cooperation with the Mossad. A fifth division looks at Jewish extremism. Other parts of the organization handle counterintelligence and VIP security. Each division examining terrorism has four main parts: human sources, signals intelligence, interrogations, and the "desk," which analyzes and coordinates the activities.

During most of Shin Bet's history "the most interesting thing an analyst saw was a neon light." The key figure was a highly trained, self-sufficient field officer who worked in the same place for long periods of time. But this in-depth local knowledge was insufficient when militants from different parts of the West Bank and Gaza worked together with groups outside the territories. Now no single person in the field was able to put the pieces together.

To coordinate all the information, the "desk" at headquarters where analysts sat became Shin Bet's counterterrorism brain. The desk operative sees all interrogation reports, SIGINT, and field agent reports and directs different collectors to complete more of the puzzle and pursue new leads. The desk also is responsible for helping coordinate with the IDF, the air force, and the police and must go to court to argue that a detention should be extended. Empowering the desk meant changing the bureaucratic culture. In the past Shin Bet favored agent runners and interrogators. Desk officers were the geeks whose job was to support the macho parts of the organization. Today the desk operatives run the show, working closely with field operatives. Many of them spend time at the desk to provide a field perspective. Eventually they know their assigned area like the back of their hand.

The job is incredibly stressful. One senior official told me, "They won't take a woman planning to have a baby," but then added with a smile, "In general, women are better at this." Indeed gender issues were a huge challenge as the new system often empowered young women at the expense of the experienced, and male, field operatives.

Bureaucratic changes, however smooth, account for only part of Shin Bet's successes. From the start the agency has recruited an elite corps from Israel's youth. Potential recruits are carefully vetted with an extensive background investigation that includes counterintelligence, psychometric tests, drug tests, and psychological tests for overall stability. Personality factors are as important as intelligence. A field officer must be flexible and creative, says the former Shin Bet director Carmi Gillon, and be "able to befriend people he doesn't like." Family stability is also important as an unstable family situation can lead to erratic behavior and vulnerability to espionage. Personal networks matter tremendously, for friends recruit other friends. Often top students are brought in to work part time during an evaluation to see if they are worth hiring. Only a fraction of the thousands who apply each year are accepted.

Experience matters, so Israeli intelligence pays its agents well to ensure retention. Not every country, including the United States, does the same. One Shin Bet veteran told me that he worked incessantly but that the pay was high and he could retire as early as forty-five and get 70 percent of his salary. (An interrogator told me his pension was 50 percent.) Money is not why people join Shin Bet of course, but it is an incentive and explains why people stay on. Shin Bet officials believe that rotations, which are constant for U.S. personnel in many security organizations, are a mistake because intelligence officers lose touch with the details and as a result make life-or-death decisions with less insight. Shin Bet has found that a smaller organization that invests heavily in salary and training is better than a larger one that is spread too thin. The agency doubled in size between the period when Oslo began and 2008, but it still remains small, perhaps four thousand people.

The investment in training is significant. An agent handler trains for two years before he enters the field. For those working on Palestinian terrorism, particularly interrogators and agent runners, training begins with language and culture. The trainee must live on the Shin Bet campus, seeing his family only twice a week. Hours are from 8:00 in the morning until midnight: "First it's work, then it's family," said one senior official who admitted that divorce is a problem. After training there is an apprenticeship during which the trainee works with another agent or interrogator for six months to a year. Shin Bet trains well because it has found that young and inexperienced people make mistakes that cost the lives of agents, Israeli citizens, and other Shin Bet personnel.

In the mid-1990s Shin Bet's information technology capabilities were primitive, but then it began building its SIGINT infrastructure and its information processing, particularly for techniques like data mining, which connects different strands of intelligence. The agency now has impressive capabilities for intercepting Palestinian cell phone calls and other means of communication. Perhaps most important it brought in a younger generation eager to use technology, a costly measure because these tech-savvy youths had more lucrative options in the private sector and they needed an expensive information infrastructure to function at full capacity. Shin Bet was willing to pay the price. Although Israeli officials are reluctant to discuss signals intelligence, the technology has played a large role in counterterrorism. Israel can intercept Palestinian militia walkie-talkies and cell phones to track potential terrorists and learn about their activities.[19]

Shin Bet also serves as a bridge for information. Israeli police work on only one side of the Green Line, while the IDF works on the other; only Shin Bet covers both. Shin Bet began to work closely with special police counterterrorism units, employing their own small units that sometimes act as snipers. The IDF and police were brought inside Shin Bet's command center to ensure that they had access to all information. Local commanders could reach out directly to Shin Bet regional leaders, decentralizing (and thus speeding up) information sharing.[20] Indeed there are a few cases of SIGINT officers directly calling the cell phones of unit commanders to warn them of an impending attack. In Operation Cast Lead Shin Bet and the IDF demonstrated superb coordination. Soldiers received intelligence on the ground, often at the squad level and in real time.

The situation is hardly perfect. There is still fighting over scarce SIGINT assets, and Shin Bet relies on the IDF for aerial surveillance and other expensive platforms. The police, who are assumed to be a source of leaks, are often excluded from valuable information. Yet by the standards of U.S. intelligence, where coordination is more cumbersome, Israel's sharing of information is impressive.

Although the numbers may be exaggerated, Palestinian security services claim that Israel has more than twenty thousand collaborators working for it.[21] Sources are often acquired, used, and then ruthlessly discarded. After an arrest or targeted killing, groups like Hamas and the al-Aqsa Martyrs' Brigade were often able to pinpoint and execute the source of the fatal intelligence. According to one former U.S. official, Israelis are "more willing to burn a source" than is U.S. intelligence. However, Israeli intelligence officials stressed to me that burning a source is incredibly risky, as the death of one informer may discourage others, who ask, "Why would I put my neck in the same place to be cut?" Shin Bet runs a large department that attempts to rescue Palestinian collaborators under a death threat, giving them a new identity in Israel.

Yet in the end Israeli intelligence can be ruthless. A constant refrain from Israeli security officials is "We live in the arena." One official explained that Israel tried to avoid exposing its intelligence assets in Gaza during Operation Cast Lead, but added, "At the end of the day, the security of our forces is above anything else."[22] An Israeli military official told me, "There is a higher price for not using intelligence. I make a mistake and many soldiers die."

Israeli intelligence also tries to sow fear and dissension within Palestinian ranks and deliberately encourage "accidents" among fighters. In one instance when Israel learned of an arms shipment to the Palestinians, they didn't confiscate the weapons. Instead "the Israelis started to put two capsules inside the bullet. One type was a capsule made of steel. Which meant that once the needle in the gun hit it, the bullet exploded."[23] Israel's targeted killing campaign also led to a murderous purge within Palestinian ranks. Fearful and vengeful PA security personnel sought out collaborators, leaving hundreds dead, their bodies thrown by the side of the road.[24]

Despite failing to prevent the Rabin assassination and stop terrorism during the Second Intifada, Shin Bet acquired an enviable reputation among the public and senior Israeli leaders. In 2004 Israelis voted it the most respected government institution.[25] As Israeli journalist and analyst Hirsch Goodman contends, "The public believes in Shin Bet 100 percent."

With the new changes the IDF and Shin Bet became far more effective in fighting Palestinian terrorism. By themselves they do not stop violence completely, yet their effectiveness has transformed terrorism from a massive problem that pummeled Israelis to a manageable one, enabling ordinary people to live their lives without fear.

A System Designed for Chaos

In over sixty years of fighting terrorism Israel has at times empowered radicals at the expense of moderates, tarnished its diplomatic image, allowed terrorists to use propaganda to turn defeat into victory, and otherwise failed at a strategic level. Such failures are in part due to the difficulty of the challenge Israel has faced and continues to face. But many of these mistakes must be laid at the door of the country's poor national security decision-making system.

Israel's national decision making is as disastrous as its military and intelligence services are impressive. Indeed Israel's decision-making process makes America's boisterous democracy and cumbersome bureaucracies appear collegial, high-minded, and efficient. Much of the problem is due to Israel's unusual system of democracy, which has an extreme degree of proportional representation; political parties today need only 2 percent of the vote to be represented in the Knesset, and that is an increase from the 1 percent floor of the 1990s. Government ministers are rarely chosen for their expertise, but instead to ensure that the prime minister can form a coalition to stay in government. In contrast to the American system, Cabinet ministers owe their primary loyalty to their own party and not to the prime minister. Nimrod Novik, a foreign policy advisor to Shimon Peres, maintains that "the prime minister must strike a deal with the minister of defense every morning." As a result Cabinet turnover is frequent and political horizons are short term, driven by politics rather than the greater good. Chuck Freilich, Israel's former deputy national security advisor, describes the Cabinet as "almost entirely dysfunctional." When it meets to discuss options, information is a weapon to wield or, if it must be shared, presented "in a manner designed to obfuscate as much as to clarify."[26] Leaks are rampant in Israel—even more than in America—clouding the judgment of decision makers.

Coalition governments result in ministries controlled by rivals from the same party or heads of other parties. Because these rivals often want to tear down rather than enhance the stature of the prime minister, prime ministers tend to rely only on their own political advisors. No one trusts the bureaucracy. The result is a narrow vision that does not allow for different options or a cohesive strategy.

Israel is not a country that produces strategy documents, which may seem a relief to anyone who has been bombarded by American military PowerPoint slides. The lack of strategy documents, however, reflects Israel's difficulties in integrating the different components of its government. High-level policy and day-to-day operations often proceed along wholly different paths. Even within the IDF long-term planning is often difficult. While the IDF is recognized for its brilliance in improvisation, this same *bitsuist* ("doer") mind-set that emphasizes acts and performance tends to downplay formal rules and structures.[27]

Only the IDF has the ability to put together plans or policy options (though Shin Bet is improving its capacity in this regard). The Foreign Ministry has no ability to do long-term planning. Knesset members lack the staff to enforce oversight and coordination in the government. Even the Ministry of Defense, which is supposed to oversee the IDF, has little ability to formulate policy. Although Israel has a National Security Council, unlike its American counterpart it has no bureaucratic heft and few staff. Successive ministers of defense have fought off proposals to strengthen it, recognizing that doing so would be a threat to their dominant position. "The army takes the place of the NSC," notes one intelligence official.

Given this lack of unified policy, Israel's decision making is usually reactive rather than proactive. Instead of attempting to shape the future environment, the government operates on a seat-of-the-pants basis.[28] Government officials rarely think through the long-term implications of their approaches and do not explore how different government agencies might work together. "We are the best tacticians in the world, but Israelis don't understand the word *strategy*," argues the Israeli counterterrorism expert Boaz Ganor.

Key agencies and staff are often left out of the decision-making process. As a result the IDF, one of the few agencies that presents a plan, has more input and can emphasize military power over diplomacy or other instruments. Usually the IDF plan is presented to senior officials as a "take it or leave it" option rather than a series of choices. Military solutions tend to be prioritized because there is no available bureaucratic counterargument. Thus the IDF and the intelligence services play key roles in counterterrorism policy, but the Foreign Ministry does not. During the height of the Intifada one former intelligence chief argued, "The political agenda has become solely a security agenda" and claimed that Israel was focused only on "how to prevent the next attack."[29] Ironically the backgrounds of most Israeli leaders, many of whom were war heroes, exacerbate the problem of getting expertise into the system. Maj. Gen. Giora Eiland, who chaired Israel's National Security Council and headed the IDF's Operations Branch and Planning Directorate, points out that Israeli leaders are wrong to think they know everything and don't need additional expertise. Foreign policy advisor Novik noted that this contempt for the rules holds at all levels. When orders come down, he says, "every third-rank official here will say 'What does the minister understand?'"

Although its decision-making horizons are short term, one strategic issue dominates discussions: Israel's relations with the United States. In Washington there is a sense that Israel acts without concern for U.S. views, but in reality the opposite is true. Charles Freilich, the former deputy national security advisor, says that "what the Americans think" is a key concern in most Israeli policy discussions (though he is also clear that Israel does not always do what America wants). Israel in the end is a minor power and much of what it needs for its own security and economic interests (oil imports, pressure on Iran over its nuclear program, and so on) requires U.S. action. The Israeli people recognize that ties to the United States are vital for their own security, and damaging this relationship is generally viewed as irresponsible. One Israeli analyst told me that sometimes leaders go so far as to elicit U.S. pressure; then they can justify their actions domestically by claiming that they chose a particular course to preserve the U.S.-Israel relationship.

This disjuncture between Israel's superb military and intelligence services and its poor decision making shows up on almost every important issue related to counterterrorism. The clearest evidence of this dysfunctional relationship is counterterrorism's relationship to the most important security issue for Israel: the peace process.

CHAPTER XXIV

FADING HOPES FOR PEACE

IMAGINE, if you will, Kermit the Frog toting a machine gun. Or Miss Piggy encouraging Fozzie Bear to strap on a suicide belt and blow himself up on a bus. It may seem the stuff of late-night comedy, but for Israelis and Palestinians such shows are deadly serious. The Hamas-run kids' television show *Tomorrow's Pioneers* featured a Mickey Mouse lookalike with a high-pitched voice named Farfur, who would simulate using an AK-47 rifle. In a later episode an Israeli interrogator beat Farfur to death. Nahoul, the talking bee that replaced Farfur, derided "criminal Jews." Nahoul also died at the hands of the Israelis when, after he became sick, they refused him permission to cross into Egypt to see a doctor. Israeli shrapnel then killed yet another replacement, a talking rabbit named Assoud.[1] A current figure (alive as of this writing but, I suspect, not long for the animated world), Nassur the Brown Bear, explained his appearance on the show as his coming to Gaza to join the mujahedin, namely the Qassam Brigades, Hamas's military wing.

Such shows are part and parcel of what Hamas calls resistance. In 2007 Hamas TV broadcast a video of four-year-old Duha, the suicide bomber Reem Riyashi's daughter, singing to her dead mother, "My mother, my mother . . . Instead of me you carried a bomb in your hands; I know what was more precious than us," and promising, "I am following Mommy in her footsteps."[2]

Such propaganda, anathema in the West, is part of the broader context of counterterrorism today. Many terrorist groups—notably Fatah,

Hizballah, and Hamas—were or are also insurgencies and social movements. As the United States quickly discovered in Iraq and Afghanistan, fighting such hydra-headed movements requires not only swift and bold attacks on their terrorist wings, but also working with the local population, creating credible political alternatives, crafting a message that encourages the peaceful resolution of conflict, and addressing the deeper roots of the violence.

When a political settlement is proposed for the Palestinian-Israeli dispute, however, Israel faces a dilemma. In the abstract peace is the ideal counterterrorism solution. A peace settlement would empower moderate Palestinians and give Israel a partner for counterterrorism, as the moderates too oppose more radical forces. Peace would also allow Israel to retain its character as a Jewish and democratic state. Israel cannot continue to rule over a massive and growing Palestinian population that does not have full democratic rights. Yet Israel's history suggests that when terrorism is rampant, trust disappears and Israeli politics dictate a return to arms until the threat abates.

This return, however, involves aggressive tactics that make negotiations more difficult. In the past hard-hitting Israeli methods have at times weakened Palestinian moderates, empowered radicals, reduced Palestinian government capabilities for fighting terrorism, soured the Palestinian population on concessions, and created difficult facts on the ground for negotiators. Israel's international legitimacy also suffers. Successful counterterrorism requires squaring this circle: fighting terrorism effectively but at the same time curbing the side effects that make peace more difficult.

So why can't we turn back the clock and solve the problem of terrorism by picking up where the Oslo process ended, with the so-called Clinton parameters that outlined what settlement would look like? As former prime minister Ehud Barak said, "The nature of the final agreement will indeed be according to the Clinton Parameters, even if it takes 5 or 10 years till we get there, and even if on the way there, we, on both sides of the conflict, bury thousands of people."[3] The problem for peace today is not a vision of *where* to go, but of *how* to get there. Abu Ali, a Palestinian official, pointed out that, "Oslo does not exist today." Talks have stagnated, mired in mistrust and bitterness.

Could Terrorism Return to the West Bank?

On the surface hopes for peace appear brighter now that Arafat is dead and buried. When President Mahmud Abbas and his prime minister, Salam Fayyad, came to power, most Israelis believed that they genuinely sought peace. Fayyad is a pro-Western economist, educated at the University of Texas at Austin (when he first visited the White House in

2003, President Bush extended his index and pinky fingers – UT's "Hook em Horns" sign).[4] Unfortunately, despite their good intentions, Abbas and Fayyad lack Arafat's ability to mobilize the Palestinian people. And Fatah's fall from grace is so vast that it is not even respected by those within in its ranks. Marwan Barghouti, one of the few Fatah leaders who could command respect, is in an Israeli jail.

After the 2007 Hamas coup in Gaza, prospects for ending the occupation of the West Bank became even slimmer. Some senior Israeli security officials think that Hamas's shadow government on the West Bank might have been strong enough to seize control there had the IDF not been present to stop it, and that this danger could reemerge should the IDF depart. As one senior military official put it, without the IDF presence "Hamas would do a coup d'état." Israelis fear that Hamas would immediately resume suicide attacks and begin launching Qassam rockets from the West Bank into Israel, as they now do from Gaza. Rocket attacks were not a threat when Clinton negotiated with Arafat and Barak at Camp David. The result would be catastrophic: Israel's high-tech areas, its key roads, airports, and major cities would all be at risk. Intelligence officers believe it would then be too late to solve the problem. One told me, "When you see the first Qassam on the West Bank, it means they have a thousand."

A Hamas report dated before the organization took power in Gaza states that eventually Qassam rockets will be available to its operatives in the West Bank and "carry great hope for the future." The report added that if Israel withdraws partially from cities in the West Bank, "in that case Afula, Hadera, Beit She'an, Netanya, Tel Aviv, Jerusalem and many other cities would be in the range of the Qassam 1 rocket. There would be no need for the Qassam 2 rocket [because these cities are so close], which means that this once vilified rocket will soon be the 'weapon of the hour' just as suicide bombing was the 'weapon of the hour' in past years. The distance between occupied Qalqilya and occupied Tel Aviv is not more than 7 kilometers. The distance between Netanya and Tulkaram is not more then 4 kilometers. Ramallah and Bethlehem are attached to each other."[5]

During the Second Intifada the philosophy of the IDF and Shin Bet was security first, then peace. But in attacking PA security forces Israel also hit prisons, ministries, and other sites that are now necessary if the PA is to again be a partner. An unintended consequence of Israeli policy was the Palestinians' diminished capacity to fight terror.

Arafat's heirs inherited ruined institutions, a destroyed infrastructure, an increased military occupation of Palestinian areas, and, most important, the distrust Arafat had sowed among Israelis. As the PA crumbled in the last stages of the Intifada Palestinian society turned on itself. Kidnappings, robbery, and even murder surged, while the courts and police collapsed. The PA would often try to buy off clans with positions of power and money, which only increased their power. Various militias, particularly those affiliated with Fatah, acted more like marauding gangs than national liberation movements. As one Palestinian observer pointed out, "Arafat was not corrupt personally," in the sense that he did not accumulate wealth to build lavish palaces, "but he corrupted the system and individuals." With Arafat's death no one had the capability to deliver the Palestinian people.

Abbas and Fayyad, in contrast to Arafat, hoped that through competent governing, Israel would eventually loosen its grip on the West Bank and turn security over to them. Abbas shut down radio and television programs that incited hatred of Israel, and he discouraged depictions of suicide bombings as heroic. Fayyad restored law and order in the West Bank. Working with Israel he used an amnesty program to rein in groups like the Tanzim and the al-Aqsa Martyrs Brigade, which in 2006 operated with virtual impunity in the West Bank. Fayyad is also trying to build state-like institutions in the West Bank in the hope that creating a de facto, functioning state will make a de jure one more likely.

After Hamas ousted Fatah in Gaza in June 2007, the PA returned the favor in the West Bank by firing and jailing Hamas officials and purging them from the government and security services. In the three months after the crackdown began the PA, often working with groups like the al-Aqsa Martyrs' Brigades, arrested fifteen hundred Hamas sympathizers, eventually letting many go but keeping the core. The PA even went after Hamas preachers, arguing that "they are more dangerous than gunmen."[6] In 2008 and 2009, under Fayyad's leadership, Palestinian police imposed order in the West Bank. During the highly unpopular Operation Cast Lead in Gaza in 2008–9, the PA effectively contained all unrest and political protests. Because of heavy PA repression, Palestinian cities like Ramallah and Nablus saw smaller demonstrations than cities in Europe or even Israeli-Arab populated towns like Sakhnin.[7] The PA also cracked down on Hamas political, educational, and humanitarian infrastructure in the West Bank, shutting down almost 200 organizations and seizing control of mosques in the West Bank. Even skeptical Israelis now admit the PA is aggressively going after the Hamas infrastructure in the West Bank.[8] In 2009 there were over 1,000 coordinated activities, and by 2010, Israeli-Palestinian security cooperation on the West Bank was perhaps the best it had ever been, even compared to the high points of the Oslo period.[9] Reflecting this improvement, the IDF removed many of the fully manned checkpoints from the West Bank in 2009, allowing Palestinians there to enjoy fewer disruptions than they had since Israel retook the West Bank in 2002.[10] During Cast Lead Israel did not impose a closure on the West Bank in recognition of Fayyad's success in preventing unrest there.

To the regret of Israelis, the PA has not fully extirpated Hamas in the West Bank. Some Palestinian observers believe that the PA is not capable of this and that, in any event, the request is unreasonable given Hamas's deep social roots. Some Israeli security officials fear that PA leaders prefer to keep the threat alive to prevent Hamas from going after Fatah supporters in Gaza. From the police to the courts to the jail, the security system is corrupt, incompetent, and politicized. And despite the crackdown, Hamas remains popular and active—on August 31, 2010, just before the Obama administration began direct talks between Israeli and Palestinian officials, Hamas terrorists shot four Jewish settlers in Hebron.

Terrorist attacks also remain popular. Settlers are widely considered fair game, but attacks in Israel are also supported. More than three quarters of Palestinians said they supported the February 2008 suicide bombing in Dimona and a shooting in March of that year of eight yeshiva students in Jerusalem.[11]

Some Israeli security officials believe Abbas, Fatah, and the PA are taking tough action to uproot Hamas because they fear the organization, not because they are committed to peace with Israel. According to this view, Abbas and Fatah are fighting for their political lives, serving Fatah first and the Palestinian cause second. This may seem a distinction without a difference—terror is fought either way—but if Hamas and Fatah reconcile their differences, Hamas could grow stronger on the West Bank.

To maintain power the PA leadership has come to depend on the IDF, both directly and indirectly. Some Palestinian observers believe that Hamas would win a truly free election, but for now Fatah and Israeli pressure on the organization prevent it from increasing its strength. Because the PA brutally cracks down on dissent and criticism of all kinds, its democratic legitimacy is shaky at best. The Hamas leader Khaled Mishal's acid observation—"This faction is prepared to ride on the back of an Israeli tank"—is painfully accurate.[12]

On some issues, Abbas and the Palestinian security forces lose either way: if security forces team up with their Israeli counterparts, they look like quislings; but if they stand aside as Israel acts, they look feeble. Indeed, Palestinians ask if the PA is there to provide security for Israel or from Israel. But Abbas has also used security reform as an excuse to crush and restrict political activities of Hamas and other rival groups and thus shore up his political position. Many arrests of Hamas affiliates are done outside the rule of law, and many detainees suffer torture.[13]

Because there is little prospect of a peace deal, the legitimacy of those who champion talks is questionable. Many Palestinians do not respect the PA security forces. In the words of one Palestinian observer, "Their purpose is to protect Israelis or hide as Israel comes in [to do its own operations]." In contrast Hamas won respect because of Israel's unilateral withdrawal from Gaza, proving to its supporters that resistance, not negotiations, is the path to success. An Israeli security official told me, "We say the Arabs only understand force, but it is really Israel that only understands force."

Prisoners are a particular problem. There are still more Fatah than Hamas prisoners in Israeli jails, suggesting that Fatah cannot even protect its own people.[14] The release of prisoners is often the result of Hamas or Hizballah hostage-taking and violence, adding to the luster of these resistance groups.

While both the United States and Israel call for a buildup of moderate Palestinian forces, the IDF has objected to giving the PA police body armor and sophisticated weapons that could be used against them should conflict resume.[15] Although all Palestinians are subject to the IDF's rules, the Palestinian police cannot even ticket cars with Israeli license plates or ID cards, further reducing Palestinian respect for their own police. Israeli forces regularly conduct raids in the West Bank against terrorist suspects, ignoring Palestinian security forces. IDF personnel often publicly disrespect Palestinian security forces, searching their vehicles and, as one security officer put it, treating us "like dogs in public."[16] At the same time, because the IDF focuses on Israeli security, it often ignores Palestinian criminal activity in areas of the West Bank it controls. Some Israeli-controlled areas are now sanctuaries for drug lords and other Palestinian criminals.

PA humiliation is particularly acute regarding the most visible nature of the Israeli presence outside the IDF: the settlers. The settlers often act with a disturbing degree of impunity, and many have contempt for their Palestinian neighbors. IDF policing of settlers depends on the individual Israeli soldiers rather than law. As one reporter told me, "When an abusive settler calls a soldier about a dispute with a Palestinian, it matters if the soldier is eighteen or twenty-one, a right-winger or secular, if he knows the settler is a dick, and so on." The settlements undermine peace negotiations, incite Palestinian anger, and require a larger and more intrusive IDF and intelligence presence in the West Bank.

Today, because violence is down, a peace deal is less compelling for Israelis. The Israeli journalist Nahum Barnea notes that the occupation of the West Bank is "non-news" in Israel. Politically this is a government success. By managing the problem politicians do not feel compelled to find a long-term solution. This, in the end, is a paradox: when violence is high, Israelis do not want to negotiate under fire; when violence is low, there is less urgency to come to the peace table.

U.S. Gen. Keith Dayton, along with envoys from the European Union and Jordan, has spearheaded the international community's effort to build the PA's capacity. Together they have trained thousands of police and security forces, teaching them basic skills and instilling a sense of professionalism. This effort has paid off in spades, with areas like Jenin—once a hornet's nest— now quiet and orderly. One Palestinian remarked, "The only unrest you might see here in Balata will be over the World Cup."[17]

However, as Dayton himself emphasized, Palestinians who join the force do so in the hope of contributing to Palestinian independence. Dayton contends that, as in the past, they would rebel and turn their weapons on Israel if they believed a Palestinian state was not in the works.[18]

If Palestinian security forces tried to increase the scope of their activities, they would run afoul of Israel's settlers in the West Bank, inevitably bringing confrontations. A decline or even collapse of security cooperation remains a constant risk. In 2010, a police officer bragged to the International Crisis Group, "I look at myself in the mirror with pride, as I know that what I am doing is the only way to an independent Palestinian state." He is right—peace will not come unless Israelis are sure of their security—but he, like his predecessors during the Oslo period, might come to believe that the only way to maintain his pride is to fight Israel if the security he provides does not bring an end to the Israeli occupation. [19]

How long will the calm in the West Bank last? The corruption of many Fatah figures and the daily vicissitudes of the occupation would seem fertile ground for future fighting. Palestinians still glorify violence: Bogi Yaalon, the general who hoped at the start of the Second Intifada to burn into the Palestinian consciousness that violence would not work, admitted in a 2008 interview, "The aspiration to fight is still there." And there is another problem: demographics. The Palestinian population is growing faster than the Jewish one, and if Israel is to remain a democracy it cannot continue to occupy a large and growing population that is denied basic rights. The former Shin Bet chief Ami Ayalon pointed out a bitter irony: "Only a Palestinian state will preserve the Jewish and democratic character of Israel."[20] In 2010 Ehud Barak, now Israel's defense minister, declared, "As long as in this territory west of the Jordan river there is only one political entity called Israel it is going to be either non-Jewish, or non-democratic. If this bloc of millions of Palestinians cannot vote, that will be an apartheid state."[21] Even some Israeli politicians from the conservative side of the aisle refer to the "apartheid state" as the danger and acknowledge that the situation is a moral burden as well as a stain on Israel's reputation.

Nor will trust come from the daily interactions Israelis have with their Palestinian neighbors. Once Israelis and Palestinians regularly traveled to each other's areas; today there is little casual interaction. Palestinian children know only two types of Israelis: soldiers and settlers, and a new generation of Israelis may know Palestinian areas only from their tours in the military.

This same generation of Israelis grew up with weekly suicide bombing attempts seared into their consciousness. In the wake of Operation Cast Lead news broke of the vulgarity of the T-shirts IDF units designed as a show of unit pride. A shirt created in January 2009 by soldiers from a Golani platoon depicts a Golani devil blowing up a mosque. This is the generation that knows not Oslo. On the Palestinian side, where life is harder, the bitterness is even greater. The lack of a real peace process is likely to make Israeli counterterrorism even more aggressive. As one Israeli journalist told me, "If there is no chance of a deal, most Israelis say 'fuck them.'"

Hamas: Capacity without Will?

Hamas and Gaza are the antithesis of the PA and the West Bank. In contrast to Abbas, Hamas can claim a popular mandate from its rule after the 2005 elections. In the face of enormous Israeli, PA, and international pressure Hamas brought law and order to Gaza, disarming local militias and tribes and restoring social services. Indeed Gaza is perhaps governed more efficiently now than at any time in its history.

And history seems to be on Hamas's side. Looking at the Arab world more broadly, the secular nationalism that Fatah has championed since its founding has faded as a political force. In contrast, political Islam, in particular the political Islam championed by the Muslim Brotherhood, Hamas's parent organization, is a vibrant political force and the most credible alternative to existing regimes in most Arab countries.

Israel, unfortunately, cannot make peace with the Palestinians without Hamas. In addition to controlling Gaza the Islamists represent an important segment of Palestinian popular opinion. Hamas is always eager to lambaste Abbas and others for even the hint of concessions to Israel. Should negotiations progress, a spate of rocket attacks from Gaza or terrorism on the West Bank is likely to provoke a harsh Israeli response that would push Palestinian leaders from the negotiating table. At the same time, if negotiations do not prevent violence Israelis would once again doubt their value. To complicate matters, cutting a deal directly with Hamas undermines the moderate Palestinians like Fayyad and Abbas who have long called for an end to violence. So Hamas must moderate before there can be peace—but whether this will happen is questionable.

Hamas is caught in many traps, most of its own making. The organization is committed to violent struggle against Israel but is too weak to take on the IDF. Now that it controls Gaza, it operates not only as a revolutionary resistance movement, but also with the pragmatism that comes with exercising political power. To turn these logistics to its advantage, according to Matti Steinberg, an Israeli professor and expert on the Palestinians, Israel must hope that Hamas will assume Max Weber's "logic of responsibility." When faced with the requirements of governing, Weber argues, "the only way to neutralize Hamas is to create a 'positive' tension between its ultimate values and its responsibilities."[22] This would require, however, a fundamental change in Hamas's ideology. As Elliott Abrams noted, Hamas didn't get into politics because Fatah was bad at picking up garbage.

Hamas wants many things: international recognition, successful governance in Gaza, control of the Palestinian nationalist movement, and the creation of an Islamic state and society in historic Palestine. But it is also is a proud resistance movement, and parts of the organization are staunchly committed to violence against Israel. Israeli intelligence officials believe that, in their hearts, Hamas leaders view Israel as Islamic property. They envision a country where Jews are at best second-class citizens, their presence tolerated only if they recognize the superior position of Muslims. Some of these goals are contradictory, pulling the group, or at least different factions within the group, in different directions at different points in time.

Indeed there is a tension between the parts of Hamas that work in the West Bank and with Palestinian refugees and the Hamas-controlled government of Gaza. Hamas remains a resistance organization, but the Haniyeh government is not fulfilling this ideology. No longer can it blame Fatah for not pursuing armed resistance or for neglecting to Islamicize society; now that blame falls on the government, which places it at odds with some among its core constituents.[23]

Reflecting this uncertainty, Hamas's rhetoric can be read in multiple ways. Hamas's charter declares "so-called peaceful solutions, and the international conferences to resolve the Palestinian problem, are all contrary to the beliefs of the Islamic Resistance Movement." Some Hamas leaders, however, leave themselves open to a political deal based on the 1967 borders, as opposed to all of Israel, though they also claim to oppose any territorial concessions, particularly on Jerusalem. Others believe the term *occupation* defines all of historic Palestine, and still others believe it refers only to the areas captured after 1967, thus enabling the same word to cover internal disagreements and conciliate both radicals and moderates.

This linguistic ambiguity also applies to the terms Hamas uses for a ceasefire. Its preferred word is *tahdiya*, often translated as *ceasefire* but often denoting a pause to build up strength before resuming the struggle. As one imam in Gaza declared, "If we have a cease-fire with the Jews, it is only so that we can prepare ourselves for the final battle."[24] Although leaders like Mishal have said that a broad ceasefire that could last many years is at least theoretically possible, most Hamas members remain highly skeptical of the peace process.[25] The group has long maintained that Israelis will respect Palestinian rights only if Palestinians are strong; military parity, or at least enough strength to deter Israel, is the key, not peace talks. Hamas's experience with Israel's unilateral withdrawals from Gaza and Lebanon confirm their view that Israel only understands force. Hamas is now using lulls like the one following the 2008–9 clash to acquire more weapons, train its military forces and dig more tunnels that can be used to smuggle goods and infiltrate fighters into Israel. So if a ceasefire does not last, Hamas will emerge as far more formidable as a military opponent.

Israeli economic pressure constantly threatens Hamas, as it must govern well to stay ahead of Fatah politically. When Gaza came under Palestinian control in 1994 the poverty rate there was 16 percent, barely over that of the United States. In 2009 the UN reported that 70 percent of Gazans were living on less than a dollar a day.[26] The World Health Organization reported at the beginning of 2010 that the isolation of Gaza has left hospitals unable to deliver quality health care and doctors unable to receive training. Disease and malnutrition are climbing, and education is suffering. Gazans, who for decades took menial jobs in Israel, now have no work. The closures after the 2005 disengagement and then the more complete blockade following Hamas's 2007 takeover explain much of this collapse. The heady dreams of Islamic revolution gave way to mundane concerns about goods, medicine, and law and order. As one Palestinian aid worker put it, "People in Gaza are more concerned with Karni [the crossing point to Israel] than al-Quds [Jerusalem], with access to medical care than the Dome of the Rock."[27] Hamas has raised some taxes and is considering dramatic raises on cigarettes, gasoline, propane for cooking, and other basics, which would dent its popularity.

Though hoping to avoid precipitating mass starvation among the Palestinians, Israel uses economic leverage to pressure Hamas: "No prosperity, no development, no humanitarian crisis" is the motto.[28] Israel restricts items to Gaza on security grounds, but the list is long and has included children's toys and cilantro as well as chemical precursors. In 2010, under international pressure after the *Mavi Marmara* incident, when Israelis killed nine Turks aboard a ship intent on busting the blockade of Gaza, Israel refocused the list on military-related items. But they left in a loophole, "dual-use" items, which could include goods ranging from electronics to construction materials, depending on how it is interpreted.

The continued siege tarnishes Israel's image internationally, as most countries blame it more than Hamas for Gaza's economic problems. When UN Secretary General Ban Ki Moon visited Gaza in March 2010 he declared Israeli policy "wrong," contending that it causes "unacceptable suffering." Cutting trade and investment also hurts the small Gazan middle class and others who would otherwise have the resources to stand up to groups like Hamas. So while Hamas suffers in its ability to provide for Gazans, its rivals also suffer.

Hamas also began taxing the tunnel trade, even creating a Tunnels Authority. The scholar Yezid Sayigh has estimated that Hamas earned up to two hundred million dollars from tunnel taxes in 2009. The tunnels employ more than forty thousand people, creating an important "business" constituency for Hamas. And the Israeli blockade has made it easier for Hamas to raise money from Iran, which sees its support as part of its struggle against Israel and as a way of scoring points with Sunni Arabs, who, unlike their governments, admire Hamas.

Looking beyond pariahs such as Iran, Hamas is escaping its diplomatic isolation. Khaled Mishal, its external leader, in 2010 met with Russian president Dmitry Medvedev in Damascus, and in a joint news conference with Turkish president Abdullah Gül called for including Hamas in peace talks. The *Mavi Marmara* raid increased support for Hamas, with more and more countries casting Hamas as the victim.

It is wrong to view the possibility of Hamas coming to the negotiating table solely in the context of Israel. Far more important to Hamas's decision making is the infighting within the Palestinian community. "Palestinians are 80 percent of the problem," complained one Hamas member. Fatah has tried to undermine Hamas politically and even stirred up violence in Gaza to discredit it.[29] Hamas fears that embracing peace talks would allow the movement to be outflanked politically. Groups like PIJ are always willing to pounce should Hamas embrace conciliation. Perhaps most important, splinters within Hamas, particularly in its military wing, might turn against the peace talks and support the use of violence. In short Hamas could find itself in the same position Fatah was in after it moved from violence to negotiations: unable to deliver politically while losing its credibility as a resistance movement.

Al-Qa'ida-style Salafis, a small but growing presence in Gaza, also put pressure on Hamas. The organization has suppressed Salafis who destroy coffee shops or otherwise use violence. Although still a limited problem, al-Qa'ida-like jihadist organizations are a growing concern for Hamas and Israel alike. The so-called Army of Islam led by Mumtaz Dighmush is one such group, as is the Jaljalat Group. Israel captured one militant, 'Abd al-Rahman al-Talalka, who told his interrogator that Hamas was "not religious enough." He went to the Sinai in Egypt for training and indoctrination and planned to carry out a suicide attack on Israel. "I was searching for a religious organization solely, which will carry on what the Quran instructed—attacks and killing of Jews. Hamas are very moderate and that is their problem. If they continue in this way, and don't change, they would disappear."[30] If anything, Hamas is more concerned about these organizations than about Israel. In its bitter feud with al-Qa'ida-affiliated groups it has arrested and even tortured individuals linked to these groups, according to Israeli sources.[31]

To complicate matters further, Hamas's state sponsors, particularly Iran, have put Hamas in a bind. Hamas is not an Iranian puppet, but the large sacks of cash Tehran provides are vital for the organization's ability to govern and maintain its large military infrastructure. The money cannot help but influence Hamas, as Tehran pushes it to reject a lasting peace with Israel. Even if Hamas rejected this pressure, it would be hard to crack down on true Iranian puppets like PIJ that would try to attack Israel and disrupt negotiations without losing Iranian support.

Another hope, still at the testing stage, is that Israel's Iron Dome antirocket system will soon be in place and provide Israel with protection from short-range rockets.[32] The IDF claims that field tests have worked so far. If the system deploys successfully, and if it is not too costly, Israel need no longer feel threatened by Hamas attacks from Gaza or the possibility of strikes from the West Bank.

Changing Counterterrorism to Bolster Peace Negotiations

The peace process seems stuck in time. In the West Bank Israeli fears about rockets and renewed suicide bombing make it reluctant to strengthen the chronically weak Abbas, even though he and his prime minister have made considerable progress in proving both their intentions to make peace and their ability to govern. One Israeli officer remarked that Israel has a "winning formula" for fighting terrorism, and "nobody wants to experiment with change on their watch."[33] The Hamas regime in Gaza shows little sign of truly embracing peace talks. As a result Israel is left by default with a partial occupation on the West Bank and a messy mix of pressure and deterrence in Gaza.

Israel is no a stranger to this situation. For much of its history peace was difficult or impossible because many enemy leaders thought they could win through violence or because they refused to take the political risks of making peace. The best Israel could do was weaken its terrorist foes and hope that eventually they would learn that victory was impossible and war, with either conventional armies or terrorist strikes, was pointless. Israel's strategy of "mowing the grass" did not require trade-offs with the peace process or political compromises.

If and when Israeli and Palestinian politicians return to serious peace talks (which, as of December 2010, appears far off), how should counterterrorism policy be adjusted?

One step—rhetorically easy but difficult in practice—is to show that violence does not work politically. Israel of course tries exceptionally hard to punish terrorists and make life difficult for their supporters. But such measures undercut Palestinian moderates and provide a grievance that terrorist recruiters exploit. Prisoner swaps are a particularly tricky issue. It is hard to fault Israel or any other country for valuing the life of its soldiers and going to great lengths to return them. In Israel's case this often results in exchange ratios of more than one hundred to one. More difficult to justify are similar exchanges for the remains of soldiers. Understandably Israel wants to honor those who have fallen in its defense and respect the wishes of their families, but these swaps lead to the release of hundreds of prisoners, some of whom are still dangerous, and are touted as political victories for militants. The lesson is that violence pays. Israel can mitigate the effects of a prisoner swap by negotiating instead with moderate leaders like Abbas and Fayyad to give them credibility.

In Gaza Israel should continue to enhance Hamas's desire to govern and diminish its justification for violence. This means that Israel must give Hamas opportunities as well as pressure. In particular Israel should work with the international community to open crossing points and allow monitored goods to flow into Gaza for a sustained period. It would then be clear to Gazans and the world that Israel is giving Hamas a real chance to govern and deliver. Continued violence after this point would justify another closure and make it clear to all that Hamas will never accept a ceasefire.

Israel's use of targeted killing, an effective form of counterterrorism, would also change if the goal were to bolster peace negotiations. To be clear, these attacks would not stop completely until a Palestinian government could, and would, arrest the terrorists. However, Israel would take more care to minimize the risk of civilian casualties, as the deaths of noncombatants also weaken support for moderates. Israel would also respect any amnesty or other deal that its Palestinian partners had worked out. In other words, leaders like Raed Karmi, whose death contributed to the end of the 9/11 decline in violence, should not be killed if the peace process were making serious progress. Should a dangerous terrorist emerge, it would be PA security forces, not the IDF, that would make the arrest or otherwise disrupt the plot.

Defensive measures such as checkpoints in the West Bank and the security barrier would also change. Part of the change would be procedural, for the goal would be to show that as peace progresses the procedures become less onerous. Even more important would be a political deal to reduce the number of checkpoints and change the location of the security barrier to run along areas that are not generally seen as Palestinian. The latter is a particularly important signal. To bolster PA security forces' credibility, the management of some checkpoints could be handed over to them.

Israel must also enhance the status and capabilities of Palestinian security forces on the West Bank. When they are working well, they can fight terror far more effectively than Shin Bet at its best, simply because they know their own people and have legitimacy among them. When Israel bypasses or humiliates them, their legitimacy plummets. And if there is no peace deal on the horizon, their people see them as Israeli collaborators rather than security officers cracking down on terrorists. As Palestinian forces stand up, Israeli security can stand down, creating a benign circle: Palestinian credibility will grow, and their ability to fight terrorism will increase.

The international community can play an important role in helping the transition from Israeli to Palestinian security. In addition to continuing to train Palestinian security forces in the West Bank, international forces could assume control of checkpoints in parts of the West Bank, ensuring a modicum of security for Israel and at the same time lessening the opprobrium of occupation for Palestinians. Such a presence buys time. As security spreads, it strengthens both the political power of Israelis who champion the process and the political power of Palestinians who advocate peace with Israel.

Improving the Palestinian economy, particularly in the West Bank as a reward for its more moderate leadership, is often touted as a first step or even as a substitute for a robust peace process. The theory is that Palestinians, hopeful for jobs and economic advancement, will choose financial security above violence, and that progress will contrast the West Bank favorably with Hamas's Gaza. But experience has proven this theory wrong. Again and again improvements in the Palestinian economy did not promote political goodwill. In fact they sometimes produced leaders far more hostile than their predecessors. Even so economic improvement is desirable in and of itself, and it can help move Palestinians toward peace as long as its political impact is the focus. Hamas seeks to outgovern as well as outfight its Fatah rivals; an economically viable state without the Islamists is one means of weakening violent movements.

Strength also requires the PA to improve its legitimacy among its own people. Restoring law and order has bolstered Abbas and Fayyad, but they need to build Palestinian institutions, in contrast to Arafat's deliberate efforts to weaken any independent power centers because they might threaten his rule. While they should get credit for their record of restoring order, they have not restored the rule of law. In the years since Fayyad became prime minister, Reporters Without Borders has twice ranked the PA lower than any other Arab government in terms of press freedom – as low as a standard as can be imagined.[34]

Peace is risky. It can collapse, as it did in the 1990s, or never get off the ground at all. Israelis fear appearing weak in the face of adversity. A less aggressive counterterrorism stance may cost lives while peace is being built, a decision that appears foolish if peace fails to materialize. Some Israelis believe Palestinian anger is so profound that it goes beyond whether or not Israel undertakes counterterrorism measures. Clearly, counterterrorism is only one concern alongside high-profile issues like borders, refugees, and the status of Jerusalem. But dismissing its importance to the peace process can lead to a self-fulfilling prophecy, whereby counterterrorism measures are unnecessarily harsh and thus fuel more anger.

Today Israel can assume more risk, particularly on the West Bank. Terrorism from the West Bank has plummeted, and Abbas and Fayyad form a team that is dedicated to making peace with Israel. Bolstering them, even if it means more risk in the short term, is vital for peace to move forward. Such restraint has paid off for Israel in the past, and it can in the future.

In the quote from which this book takes its title, Israeli prime minister David Ben Gurion emphasized two words: *exist* and *survive*. Terrorism against Israel does not threaten Israel's survival. Today the Jewish state is a regional powerhouse that cannot be toppled by weapons of the weak: 2010 is not 1953. What does threaten Israel's survival in the years to come is *not* separating from the Palestinians. Israel cannot remain a democratic and Jewish state and continue to rule over a large and restive Palestinian community that seeks its own state. In November 2003 four former Shin Bet chiefs went public in *Yediot Ahronot,* Israel's largest circulation newspaper, an extremely unusual breach of the service's usual silence in the face of politics. In an article titled "We Are on the Way to a Catastrophe" they warned that in its struggle against the Palestinians Israel is "taking sure, steady steps to a place where the state of Israel will no longer be a democracy and a home for the Jewish people." They suggested that the government is focused only on the next attack when it should be focused on the future "how we get out of the mess we find ourselves in today."[35]

To maintain its true character Israel needs peace within its borders and with its neighbors. The challenge is to think beyond the narrow confines of counterterrorism: not only must Israel arrest and kill those who would kill its citizens, but it must foster the development of partners with the will and strength to negotiate.

CHAPTER XXV

WHAT ISRAEL CAN TEACH THE WORLD AND WHAT ISRAEL SHOULD LEARN

ISRAEL has fought terrorism for more than sixty years, at times brilliantly, at times disastrously. There are lessons to be learned here, none of them easy. While Israel's experiences at times serve as a blueprint for fighting terrorism, they also demonstrate the limits that democratic countries face. And Israel too can learn from other countries' experiences, both positive and negative, in their fight against terrorism and political violence. The street runs two ways.

The Growing Difficulty of Deterrence

Of the many conundrums that Israeli counterterrorism strategy faces, one of the worst is surely this: the prevention of terror attacks often relies on deterrence, which demands *disproportionate* responses to any attack. Reprisals must be severe enough so the attacker fears any provocation. Israel's attackers are usually authoritarian states or militant groups that are less sensitive to casualties than Israel and other democracies, so inflicting limited casualties or destruction tends to fail and allow the group to claim victory. Israel, in contrast, is a liberal democracy that subscribes to the Just War tradition, which dictates a *proportionate* response. Thus it must forever wrestle with this dilemma: whether to respond disproportionately to ensure immediate safety, or to respond proportionately, a move that encourages groups like Hamas and Hizballah to believe that violence works. Regardless of effectiveness, international opinion approves the proportionate response and condemns the disproportionate response.

Making this dilemma harder, the very *success* of Israeli deterrence against Arab armies led to the necessity of deterrence in the name of counterterrorism. After the 1948 war Egypt and Syria, among other states, encouraged fedayeen raids that blurred the line between violence against the Jewish state and outright war. To stop this support Israel threatened, punished, and quietly cut deals with neighboring governments. At times Israel did deter regimes from backing terrorists, or at least reduced the level of support. At other times, however, its deterrence attempts spiraled into war, as in 1956.

When a hostile government is strong—say, Syria after Hafez al-Asad consolidated power in the 1970s—the deterrence strategy is straightforward: inflict enough pain on the regime so that it caves. A strong regime can face down its domestic opposition and survive. Israel's most difficult dilemmas arose when the government it faced did not fully support the militant groups but had limited capacity to crack down on them. So when Israel confronted Lebanon in the 1970s, and when the PA became Israel's partner in the 1990s, terrorist attacks continued and Israel was unable to hold the government accountable. The PA dilemma in particular led to constant debate over whether Arafat was really a weak partner or a foe in disguise.

Particularly risky is the repeated Israeli attempt to try to create popular suffering in order to force regimes to stop supporting militant groups. As with most Israeli counterterrorism measures, this policy has been neither a complete failure nor a complete success. Some governments respond by cracking down on anti-Israeli groups, concerned that their continued inability to stand up to Israel will humiliate them with their public. Others simply claim incapacity, ensuring that the militants have even more freedom of action.

Much of the Palestinian terrorism against Israel is about competition between groups, and hostility toward Israel is only secondary. As with states, the success of deterrence against terrorist groups varies according to whether the group's leaders can control their fighters. After unsuccessful military operations in 1993 Israel found a way to contain its conflict with Hizballah, and for the most part Hizballah followed the rules. But when small groups have attempted to provoke an Israeli response, groups like Fatah end up in the middle, unable to denounce the violence without looking like collaborators, yet at the same time suffering from Israeli retaliation and diplomatic isolation because the bloodshed continues. In such circumstances deterrence fails.

Israel's troubled deterrence record is likely to grow spottier in the years to come. Today the country is in the media spotlight more than ever, and human rights groups, both domestic and foreign, now exert more influence over policy. Regardless of where Israel fights, al-Jazeera television and other Arab media will be there. A disproportionate response—the essence of deterrence—is difficult to square with the growing international view that military operations should not inflict undue suffering. This concern is particularly (and appropriately) high when it comes to civilian suffering. In Gaza today Israel is putting tremendous economic pressure on Hamas by reducing the flow of goods through access points. At the same time it is allowing international aid groups into Gaza and letting in enough goods to prevent mass starvation—a humanitarian necessity, but one that goes against the theoretical logic of economic strangulation that drove the policy in the first place.

Israelis decried the Goldstone Report and its criticism of Israeli operations in Gaza in 2008–9, believing that it was biased. Israel, they contend, got no credit for its efforts to avoid civilian casualties, and the report assumed a moral equivalency between Israeli soldiers defending their country and Palestinian terrorists shooting rockets at civilian targets. Right or wrong, this type of criticism is likely to shape Israeli deterrence in the future because it strikes at the international legitimacy of the Jewish state, a sensitive point for Israelis. It also encourages groups like Hamas, which believe that the criticism may check Israel's military and enable them to weather future storms.

Israeli casualty aversion further diminishes deterrence, and terrorist leaders like Hizballah's Hassan Nasrallah have promoted that sensitivity as a weakness to be exploited. Israel's willingness to trade hundreds of militants for the remains of its soldiers reinforces this perception. If the idea spreads, other terrorist groups can correctly assume that inflicting even a few casualties will result in victory. All democracies are concerned about the lives of their civilians and soldiers, but Israelis are more sensitive to military casualties than are other democratic countries because its military is a citizen army, not a volunteer force, and Israeli Jewish society is tight-knit. The loss of even a handful of soldiers is a source of widespread public criticism of Israel's leaders. And the only thing in Israel more powerful than the IDF is a Jewish mother.[1] So when Israel carries out a military operation that kills a hundred Palestinians after losing ten of its own, the Jewish state loses in two ways. At home the public decries the ten deaths as unacceptable, while abroad the international community blasts Israel's disproportionate response. Not surprisingly terrorist groups take encouragement from this and the chances of successful deterrence fall.

This suggests that Israel's reliance on the Dahiya Doctrine—the threat to destroy civilian infrastructure of hostile regimes, as Israel did to the Dahiya neighborhood of Beirut, where Hizballah was headquartered in 2006—will face serious challenges going forward, as will similar approaches that involve considerable destruction of civilian infrastructure and a risk of civilian casualties. The humanitarian criticism, and the possibility that Israel's enemies will fight back effectively, make the use of force in the name of deterrence a harder choice. Israel has tried to compensate for this weakness by striking terrorist leaders directly. At times this approach has been successful and terrorist leaders have agreed to a ceasefire. More often than not, however, either intelligence is lacking or Israel is politically and diplomatically unable to sustain the campaign of killings necessary to coerce the enemy successfully.

Sowing the Seeds of Future Hatred?

Aside from the diplomatic and economic fallout, the most damning charge against Israeli counterterrorism is that it fails on its own terms by fostering more terrorism. No less an authority than Ami Ayalon, a former Shin Bet head, contends, "War against terrorism is part of a vicious cycle. The fight itself creates . . . even more frustration and despair, more terrorism and increased violence."[2] Many observers around the world embrace the idea that fighting terrorism requires a political solution and that tough countermeasures backfire.

Ayalon is half right, but the half on which he is wrong is vital to understand. Palestinian hatred of Israel has remained strong over time and even grown, particularly in times of acute crisis such as the Second Intifada. Early in the Intifada the tough Israeli response to violence only fueled the anger on which terrorism feeds. Violence eventually fell, however, as Israeli counterterrorism became more effective. The number of deaths from suicide attacks peaked in 2002, and the lethality per attack peaked in 2003, as shown in figures 25.1 and 25.2. As the decade wore on, however, both the number of attacks and the lethality of the attacks fell, suggesting a precipitous decline in Palestinian groups' capabilities for launching attacks.

Thus Ayalon's charge that through killings, arrests, checkpoints, and other aggressive measures Israel has simply replaced one generation of angry Palestinians with another is true. But it also misses the point. The Second Intifada petered out with Palestinian anger high and the Palestinian people further away than ever from achieving their homeland. Israel simply destroyed, disrupted, and deterred individual terrorist cells and eventually whole groups, rendering them unable to function.

The critics' argument has a core fallacy: they believe that terrorist groups have an angry population from which they can cull members and replace lost fighters, and that their strength can be reduced only by ending their anger. However, simply swapping one militant for another does not work. The number of skilled terrorists is often quite limited. Generators of terror such as bomb makers, trainers, document forgers, recruiters, and leaders are both scarce in number and require many months if not years to perfect their skills. If these generators of terror can be eliminated through arrests or killings, the organization as a whole is disrupted. The movement may still have many willing recruits, but it is no longer effective.

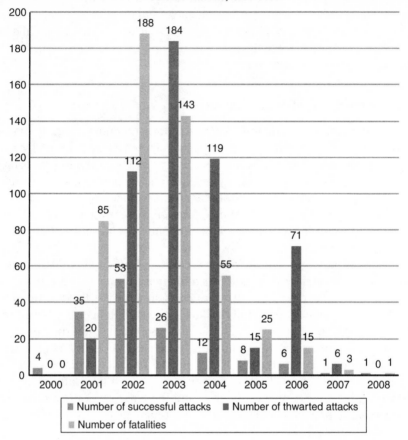

Figure 25.1 Suicide Attack 2000–2008. Note: numbers for 2000 start at the beginning of the second intifada, 9/29/2000.
Sources: The Israeli Security Agency, "Distribution of Fatalities from Palestinian-based terrorism in the 2nd Indifadah," http://www.shabak.gov.il/SiteCollectionImages/english/TerrorInfo/terror-victims-en.pdf; Intelligence and Terrorism Information Center at the Israel Intelligence Heritage & Commemoration Center, "Anti-Israeli Terrorism in 2007 and its Trends in 2008", May 2008, http://www.terrorism-info.org.il/malam_multimedia/English/eng_n/pdf/terror_07e.pdf
Credit: Graphic created by Sarah Yerkes.

Focusing counterterrorism efforts on a small number of skilled operators pays off. Even groups like Hamas, which have large social and political movements, depend heavily on a relatively small group of specialists to carry out a fast pace of attacks. Removing this small group does not destroy the broader political movement, but it can cripple its short-term operational capability.

Even if they cannot all be arrested or killed, an aggressive effort against this small group forces its members to spend more time ensuring their own

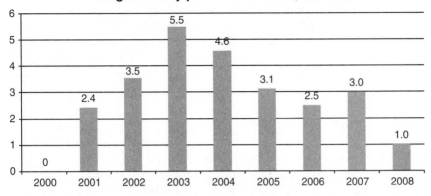

Average lethality per suicide attack, 2000-2008

Figure 25.2 Average Lethality per Suicide Attack, 2000–2008. Note: numbers for 2000 start at the beginning of the second intifada, 9/29/2000.
Sources: The Israeli Security Agency, "Distribution of Fatalities from Palestinian-based terrorism in the 2nd Indifadah," http://www.shabak.gov.il/SiteCollectionImages/english/TerrorInfo/terror-victims-en.pdf; Intelligence and Terrorism Information Center at the Israel Intelligence Heritage & Commemoration Center, "Anti-Israeli Terrorism in 2007 and its Trends in 2008", May 2008, http://www.terrorism-info.org.il/malam_multimedia/English/eng_n/pdf/terror_07e.pdf
Credit: Graphic created by Sarah Yerkes.

security than conducting operations. They must constantly change locations to avoid Israeli strikes. Because they cannot disclose their location to many followers for fear of being discovered, the flow of information is disrupted, making it difficult for leaders to communicate with and direct their followers. Over time Palestinian cells became increasingly autonomous, acting without guidance from leaders and unable to work together effectively. Within the organizations suspicion mounted. The al-Aqsa Martyrs Brigades executed tens to hundreds of Palestinians for treason, but only a few were the real collaborators.[3] The stress on terrorists becomes enormous. They cannot see their parents or children without risk of being killed. Hizballah, in contrast, never faced such a sustained campaign and was able to focus on operations against Israel as well as its own security.

Harder to measure, but plausible, is the possibility that the killings and arrests deter individuals from joining the group. IDF Gen. Moshe Kaplinsky argues that during a systematic campaign, over time the younger generation is less likely to join the group. Kaplinsky's argument must be qualified, for much depends on whether the population in general believes victory or defeat is likely. When Palestinian capabilities fell and success no longer seemed within their grasp, their willingness to sacrifice also declined. Sacrificing oneself in the name of imminent liberation is heroic; dying for a doomed cause is foolish. So early in the Second Intifada, when Palestinian hopes of victory were high, deterrence did not work; as the

Palestinian struggle languished and then clearly began to fail, the killings had far more of a deterrent impact. Among Palestinians, for now at least, there is little support for a third intifada. "Palestinians have learned their lesson," notes the Palestinian journalist Wafa Amr.

Ayalon's criticism, however, still contains important truths, particularly if you take a long-term view. At a tactical level Israel has devastated Palestinian militant groups. Today Palestinians are realistic on the costs of returning to terrorism, but they also admire Hamas leaders and others for standing up to Israel at the cost of their lives. The narrative of resistance remains strong and impedes efforts of moderates like Abbas to make peace. Militants thus fail militarily but often succeed politically. Hamas's steady growth in popularity during the Second Intifada came from its constant defiance, not its day-to-day effectiveness.

Another cost of focusing on destroying terrorist groups over negotiations is the loss of the high ground internationally. Americans are less aware of this as support for Israel in the United States remains robust, but the United States is increasingly alone among Western powers in its support for Israel. Israel's critics often ignore the reality of terrorism and focus on the harsh Israeli response. But that double standard does not change the perception, particularly in Western Europe, that Israel is the new South Africa: a pariah regime, morally unfit to be among the ranks of democracies. A BBC poll released in April 2010 ranked Israel as the fourth least liked country in the world; Israelis could take little comfort that they narrowly beat out Iran, Pakistan, and North Korea.[4] For Israelis, this shows up in ways both big and small: invitations to international conventions for scientists are withdrawn, would-be allies like Turkey publicly distance themselves, Israeli leaders cannot visit several Western countries for fear of arrest on "war crimes," and so on. Israelis can survive these snubs, but they are wearisome and go against the country's long-standing goal of becoming a respected and accepted part of the international community.

Perhaps most important, and as discussed in detail in the previous chapter, Israel's aggressive counterterrorism measures at times complicate efforts to negotiate a peace.

The Dangers of Sanctuary

Israel's history shows that no factor is more important to the success of a terrorist group than sanctuary. The sanctuaries the fedayeen enjoyed in Jordan, Lebanon, and other countries were vital to their survival and continuation of operations, particularly after Israel cleared them out of the West Bank after the 1967 War. Hamas used the toleration the PA provided after the outbreak of the Second Intifada to develop a vast apparatus for producing suicide bombers, and Fatah-linked organizations like the al-Aqsa Martyrs Brigades soon followed suit. Similarly Hizballah's use of parts of Lebanon outside Israel's control, such as the Bekaa Valley, enabled the group to train, plan, and operate with only limited Israeli interference.

The message is simple: if terrorist groups live in a friendly environment, they can build their organizations and carry out complex operations without outside interference, and thus become far more dangerous. And perhaps no action is more difficult for a state than having to operate in and remove a terrorist sanctuary.

Peace, of course, is the best answer to the sanctuary dilemma. Although Egypt and Jordan both supported or at least tolerated fedayeen raids into Israel in the past, they became effective counterterrorism partners as they embraced peace with the Jewish state. Unfortunately peace was often impossible. Israel's neighbors' hostility has often been unrelenting, many times because their domestic politics makes talks impossible. Israeli leaders often hesitated to make profound concessions to move the process forward. Some governments were simply too weak to crack down on terrorists on their soil.

As a result Israeli counterterrorism officials understandably felt compelled to act on their own against sanctuaries. Pressure on Jordan contributed to the Hashemite regime's decision to crack down on Black September, and Israel's invasion of Lebanon in 1982 effectively shattered the PLO there. The Lebanon invasion, however, played a major role in the creation of Hizballah, a far more formidable foe. Even when it hasn't resulted in disaster, occupations are miserable and costly. By 2002 terrorist attacks had forced a decisive response, and Israel once again occupied the West Bank. The move proved to be effective in reducing terrorism, but Israel has been in a grinding occupation of the West Bank ever since.

It is tempting, and often necessary, to work with local militias or other friendly forces to target a group in a sanctuary, as Israel did for many years with the SLA against Hizballah. In its counterinsurgency efforts in Iraq and Afghanistan the United States too has relied heavily on local warlords to do the fighting; locals have more intimate knowledge of the countryside and its people, and of course the fight is usually more theirs than America's, so they are more willing to sacrifice than the American people. The United States, however, should recognize that its local allies truly live in the arena, and their own interests understandably come first. Israel's Lebanese proxies often tried to kill IDF troops, or cut deals with foes, or lied to Israel. Only when their interests were in harmony with Israel's did they cooperate. These proxies are often more brutal as well, torturing prisoners, brutalizing civilians, and otherwise disregarding human rights.

A Model of Intelligence

Israel's intelligence services are fabled around the world (particularly in the Middle East) for their efficiency, skill, and seeming omniscience. As previous chapters have made clear, however, they are far from infallible;

Lebanon in particular was an intelligence and military debacle. Yet despite their many mistakes, they have often done an impressive job of gathering intelligence on terrorists and using this information to devastate terrorist organizations. Many lessons from Israel's experience seem obvious, but they often go unheeded in other countries.

Careful personnel recruitment is the first step. Israeli intelligence professionals, like their counterparts elsewhere, are carefully vetted and well educated. In Israel, however, intelligence is truly an elite profession, which is reflected in their high salary and lucrative benefit packages, Most important, however, is their attitude: they are encouraged to think of themselves as an elite within an elite. The workload is often tremendous, yet Israel has found it is more efficient to have a small, select number of people in intelligence rather than large numbers.

Specialization is also vital. Shin Bet devotes enormous attention to training its operatives on every aspect of Palestinian society, including language, culture, and economy. This intensive training prepares the agents to be effective in the field, the interrogation room, and headquarters, where they piece together the pieces of a problem. The Mossad also has its own division that focuses on liaising with foreign intelligence services, a crucial key to successful counterterrorism, as much of the vital information is held by allied services that are both partners and rivals. Contrast this system to the U.S. and many other intelligence services, where promotion often goes to managers and those who can move quickly from one responsibility to another, thus discouraging expertise.

Israeli intelligence and elite military units take more risks than their Western counterparts, but these sometimes backfire; the bungled assassination of Khaled Mishal in Jordan and the mistaken killing of Ahmed Bouchiki in Norway both cost Israel diplomatically and set back counterterrorism. Yet daring raids such as at Entebbe are not relics of the past, as Hizballah and Hamas operatives around the world are well aware. Israel is also more willing to use information from sensitive sources and risk exposing them as a result.

Intelligence success often depends on employing the full powers of a state to gather intelligence. When Israel controls a territory, it integrates its administration with intelligence gathering. Travel permits, permission to open a business, access to schools outside the area, and other components of daily life often involve contact with Israeli intelligence officers, who dole out these favors in exchange for information. This approach may be ruthless, but it does yield information.

Sharing at all levels is particularly important. When confronted with Hamas terrorism in the mid-1990s Shin Bet found that its ability to share information internally was poor, to say nothing of coordination with police and the IDF. Shin Bet solved the problem by removing barriers to the flow of information, which meant relaxing the controls on ownership even though doing so increased the chance that the information would leak or not be properly protected. On balance, however, Shin Bet found that the huge increase in information sharing more than offset the slight reduction in information security.

Operations like Cast Lead also show the tactical benefits of tightly integrating intelligence and military operations. Too often U.S. and other Western forces go blindly into a combat zone. Interrogators and other intelligence personnel also are often not integrated into low-level units, so when an area is taken from insurgents valuable intelligence is left uncollected. Israel's experience shows that counterterrorism and counterinsurgency both depend on the constant collection, analysis, and dissemination of high-quality intelligence.

Intelligence services' organization, training, and doctrine are by nature specialized and often impenetrable to nonspecialists. Yet these details often make the difference between effective counterterrorism and disastrous failure.

Maintaining Democratic Values in a Dirty War

When Israel first formulated its counterterrorism doctrine human rights concerns and legality played little or no role. After Israel's independence the shoot-to-kill policy along its borders led to the deaths of several thousand Palestinians, many of whom simply sought to return to their lands to harvest their crops and live in their old homes. Today a similar policy would lead to international outrage.

Over time, however, legality and human rights have shaped counterterrorism policy. Core aspects of Israel's policy—the level of coercion in interrogations, the use of hostage taking to extract concessions from terrorist groups, the creation and routing of the security barrier—all received scrutiny by Israel's Supreme Court, a victory for human rights groups like B'Tselem and for the rule of law. It is a victory for counterterrorism too, for such oversight and intrusions ensure that Israel's counterterrorism policies enjoy legitimacy among Israelis, enabling government after government, even those that disagree fundamentally on many issues confronting the Jewish state, to maintain a level of continuity in the counterterrorism struggle. As the Israeli prosecutor Devorah Chen argues, "The legal process is the foundation of fighting terrorism."

The United States is still early in this process of integrating legal and human rights perspectives into counterterrorism. Nowhere is this more true than the issue of detentions. So far lawmakers of both parties have avoided putting forward preventive detention legislation, liberals because they want to ensure the rule of law is not watered down, and conservatives because they do not want counterterrorism to become a criminal justice issue. The result, however, is that U.S. policy toward detainees often oscillates, with no clear set of rules governing the taking or holding of suspected terrorist prisoners.

The human rights community, for its part, should recognize that well-meant human rights concerns can backfire. When Israeli forces retook West Bank cities during the 2002 Defensive Shield war, Israeli forces used local Palestinian civilians as shields to prevent militants from firing at Israeli squads. Human rights groups and the Israeli Supreme Court viewed this action as a blatant disregard for innocent civilians and put a stop to the practice. But Israeli leaders still make the minimization of IDF casualties a priority. Thus in Cast Lead in 2008–9, when the IDF did not systematically use human shields to stop militants from shooting at Israeli forces, those forces were reluctant to go building by building to clean out Hamas fighters. So the rules of engagement became much more permissive, and without a human shield Israeli forces took down a whole building, resulting in higher civilian casualties.

While Israel is often the target of human rights organizations and legal criticisms, Palestinian abuses against other Palestinians are a profound and constant problem, under both the PA and Hamas leaderships. This should be no surprise, as Israel, the United States, and the international community winked at Arafat's autocratic ways and hollowed out Palestinian institutions. At first Israel saw Arafat's action as positive. Recall Rabin's glee that the Palestinian antiterrorism forces would not have to deal with a Palestinian B'tselem. But Arafat's methods turned out to be a double-edged sword; although they led to key arrests, they also convinced Palestinians that the PA was illegitimate and turned the security services into political creatures rather than professional agencies. All of these defects increased the respectability of militant forces, particularly those in Hamas, which were correctly seen as less corrupt. Today Israel and the United States both encourage the PA regime in the West Bank to extirpate Hamas, but in so doing the PA often disregards the rule of law, a short-term expedient that keeps Palestinian institutions weak.

Israel's experience shows the value of embedding counterterrorism methods, even controversial ones such as coercive interrogations and targeted killings, within the political and legal system. Maintaining them as part of the system is time-consuming and can sometimes lead to missed opportunities, but it ensures their sustainability and reduces the likelihood of abuses.

Resilience and Risk

Terrorism's power is psychological. Even in Israel, where a greater percentage of the population has died from terrorism than in any other democracy, an Israeli is far more likely to die in a car accident than in a terrorist attack. Terrorism, however, strikes at a nation's soul and undermines faith in the government. Winning the battle against terrorism is as much about shoring up national morale as it is about killing, arresting, or deterring a particular terrorist group. As Dan Meridor, an Israeli politician who has held several senior positions, remarked, "The only front is the home front." When a terrorist strikes, Israelis believe their country and their lives are at stake.

Whether the country's existence is truly at risk is debatable, particularly with regard to terrorism. Meir Elran, a retired Israeli general and an expert on resilience, said, "Perception has nothing to do with facts." He also noted that Israeli politicians always claim, "The next two years are the most dangerous in the history of the Jewish people." So while Israelis are resilient, they are also anxious. The Israeli novelist David Grossman believes, "Our army is big, we have this atom bomb, but the inner feeling is of absolute fragility, that all the time we are at the edge of the abyss."[5] For Elran, three factors drive this sense of fragility: "2,000 years of history" and associated persecution, the Holocaust, and the tendency of Israeli political leaders to play on people's sensitivity about survival. Other Israeli experts on resilience hit the same point. The Israeli journalist and analyst Hirsch Goodman also brought up the Holocaust in the context of domestic resilience, believing the Israeli national character is a mix of survival and "don't push me around." He emphatically added, "This six million ain't going nowhere. No more cattle trucks for us." Goodman notes that for Israelis many foreign policy issues involve a vague threat they don't fully understand, but terrorism is different: "They do understand when their kid doesn't come home from a birthday party." Thus terrorism leads to tremendous pressure on the government.

Domestic resilience neared the breaking point during the Second Intifada. For a brief period many Israelis changed the basic pattern of their daily lives. They stopped using buses, eating at restaurants, and shopping at malls, a sign that terrorism was working. Daily life began to return, however, as terrorist attacks in Israel proper fell. Restaurants and cafés, almost deserted in the dark days of 2002 and 2003, again filled with tourists and Israelis alike. The speed of the return to normalcy, said Meir Elran—how long, for example, it took for people to use buses after a bus attack—began to get shorter as Israelis become accustomed to regular attacks. Few Israelis felt that the stress of their daily lives made it necessary for them to seek professional help, though children sometimes suffered from posttraumatic stress disorder. Confidence in the security forces remained high even when violence was rampant. Despite the fears of many politicians, Israelis did not emigrate to escape the violence.[6]

Israeli governments get some of the credit. Israel involves its people in defenses, enlisting them to look for bombs, patrol the streets, and conquer their fear by joining the fight, even if these public measures have little actual benefit. Buses resume service within hours after a bombing, even along the same route. Israelis go back to business (often literally, in the case of attacks on shops) immediately after an attack, demonstrating that life goes on.

Americans in particular need to recognize the importance of resilience for counterterrorism. Immediately after 9/11 Americans focused on the first responders and how best to treat the wounded and prevent more lives from being lost. Afterward resilience was viewed as the restoration of infrastructure, whether buildings, transportation systems, and data storage would survive a bombing or other attack. Even more important, however, is psychological resilience: How can citizens move forward in the face of violence to reduce its effectiveness? Achieving this goal requires citizen involvement. As people join in the response they conquer the fear terrorists try to instill in them.

Governments often try to take immediate aggressive offensive actions, such as targeted killings or military incursions, to convince their people that their government is fighting back. "We won't just stand there," one Israeli intelligence official told me; action, even if you hit the wrong target, is better than lying down, he said. Hard-hitting actions, however, raise a dilemma for Israeli leaders and for leaders of other democracies. They need to act to shore up morale, but a strong response might escalate or inflame an already dangerous situation. In the early 1950s even relatively dovish figures like Prime Minister Moshe Sharett supported IDF punitive raids to calm an angry and fearful public desperate for action. Public anger more than strategic logic drove massive military operations against Hizballah in 1993, 1996, and 2006. These actions often failed to achieve their objectives and even backfired when neighboring states stepped up aid to terrorist groups and popular support for the terrorists grew. Politics can also lead to a neglect of valuable defensive measures. The scholar Ami Pedahzur has found that although Israel's defensive measures against terrorism are highly effective they are "less psychologically satisfying, take more time to take effect, and thus are less politically useful."[7]

Indeed because of the magnitude and frequency of attacks against Israel, it differs from most Western countries in that the public fully supports the use of force. In the United States and particularly in Europe politicians must work hard to gain support for a military response to a small-scale terrorist action; this is in sharp contrast to Israel, where politicians must generate the will not to use force after each provocation.

Counterterrorism professionals must account for this political reality when designing their policies. Politicians seek to uphold morale and defeat terrorism when they demand retaliation, even when its effects on the ground are limited. At the same time, however, they must push back against public sentiment, pointing out that some high-profile measures not only often fail but can also backfire.

Integrating Counterterrorism with National Security Policy

Israel has much to teach the world about counterterrorism. Even where it makes mistakes, these are often best explained by the difficulties inherent in counterterrorism operations. Yet Israel itself makes many mistakes that are avoidable, including several that are repeated again and again.

A persistent weakness of Israeli counterterrorism is the disconnect between day-to-day counterterrorism measures and broader strategic goals. The former Israeli National Security Council official Charles Freilich finds numerous "pathologies" in his study of Israeli national security decision making, including a contempt for experts who "see shades of gray," a lack of planning, constant media leaks, and a focus on the present to the exclusion of future problems.[8] In the United States the National Security Council staff and other bodies work to coordinate government security policy. Israel, on the other hand, has an organization with the same name but with little power. The resulting lack of strategy and coordination worsens during the inevitable decision-making confusion that arises in the dangerous and time-sensitive environment that follows a terrorist attack.

As a result Israel often works against itself. When the Second Intifada broke out, Prime Minister Barak and Israeli negotiators were trying to hammer out a final agreement with the Palestinians. At the same time tough IDF operations generated hundreds of Palestinian casualties, creating a backlash that made it far more difficult for Palestinian leaders to make concessions. There was logic to either negotiating or to responding harshly, but not to doing both simultaneously. The law of unintended consequences often kicks in as a result of this policy schizophrenia: eradicating the PLO from Lebanon produced Hizballah; weakening the PA produced a Hamas-run Gaza. Again and again a narrow, tactical focus has resulted in Israel's failing to anticipate the broader consequences of its actions. Often measures intended to be short term, like the reoccupation of the West Bank in 2002, become long term by default.

The diplomatic dimension also is sometimes ignored, resulting in Israeli counterterrorism measures that alienate allies. When Palestinians are killed, the Jordanian public's anti-Israel sentiment increases, a lesson Israel should have learned in the 1950s but seems to ignore even today. A Jordanian government official told me that open and aggressive Israeli actions create pressure on Amman to stand behind Hamas, which it loathes. Israeli relations with Turkey soured after the 2008–9 Cast Lead operation. At times the lack of attention to diplomatic consequences is mind-blowing, such as the attempt to kill Khaled Mishal in Jordan in 1997. Even if the operation had not been botched, responsibility would have inevitably leaked out, embarrassing Israel's closest Arab partner.

Institutionally Israel needs to shore up a functional interagency system to ensure that different parts of its political system work together and that long-term planning, including diplomacy, is incorporated into daily decision making on counterterrorism. Currently counterterrorism policies move forward from the IDF or intelligence services, and other parts of the system, such as the Foreign Ministry, have little input. The IDF's dominance of planning often means that civilian leaders are not presented with nonmilitary options. Too often decisions are made on a "take it or leave it" approach. To expand options Israel needs to bolster its civilian control and oversight of the IDF.

Israel's military and intelligence education systems need to include politics and strategy in the curriculum, not just operations. In the U.S. professional military education system the political elements of strategy—including the media, human rights, and the long-term political goals that conflict with tactical needs—are regularly discussed. Officers become aware of the tension between civilian and military officials and the need for effective political guidance and planning. With its emphasis on getting the job done, Israel often neglects this essential part of military education.

Thinking Counterinsurgency While Fighting Terrorism

One problem Israel has in common with other democracies is that it focuses narrowly on its foes' use of terrorism and ignores their wider strategies. To be clear, Hamas, Hizballah, and other Israeli foes discussed in this book have killed and terrorized civilians and therefore deserve the epithet *terrorist*. Yet most of the groups Israel has faced, particularly the most dangerous ones, are involved in much more than terrorism. Hizballah is also a political party, a social movement, and perhaps the world's most formidable guerrilla organization. Hamas too mixes politics, social action, and guerrilla proclivities. Today in Gaza Hamas is both a government and a state, so although the *terrorist* label is accurate, it is also limited and at times misleading.

When thinking beyond terrorism and in terms of political policy, the Israeli government should draw lessons from counterinsurgency, which addresses not only the military (or "kinetic," in American soldiers' parlance) dimensions but also the political, economic, and social ones as well. Core elements of counterinsurgency such as bolstering potential moderates and providing security are necessary to defeat movements like Hamas and Hizballah. The realm of counterinsurgency is vast, and with the U.S. military campaigns in Iraq and Afghanistan this broader outlook is prevalent once again.

Israel defines *terrorism* broadly—too broadly in fact. The Mitchell Commission's investigation into the causes of the Second Intifada criticized Israel for including actions such as stone throwing in its definition. On the other side of the spectrum, much of what groups like Hamas and Hizballah do is better described as guerrilla war, and a counterterrorism approach often does not address what makes these groups so strong. Both organizations have strong community support, for example, so it is easy for them to replace a low-level suicide bomber or guerrilla fighter. To defeat Hamas and Hizballah they must be attacked on all levels, from funding sources to alternatives to social services. Force is still necessary against the hard core of the organization, but even then, in the words of one IDF official, it should be "M-16s, not F-16s," referring respectively to the rifle and the fighter aircraft to make the point that discreet force is better that creating a swath of destruction.

A particularly important part of counterinsurgency is political action: supporting leaders who do not espouse violence. For all countries this is an exceptionally difficult task, but Israel's record is poor by any standard. Perhaps the most painful example is the 2005 withdrawal from Gaza. By 2005 Israel had decimated Hamas as a military organization, rendering it far less effective. At the same time the unrelenting Israeli campaign had created a crop of martyrs that increased popular admiration for Hamas. Israel's refusal to throw a bone to Mahmud Abbas, who, unlike Arafat, clearly sought peace, humiliated Palestinian moderates. Meanwhile the Israeli withdrawal enabled Hamas to claim credit for ending the occupation in Gaza through violence, in contrast to the PA's attempt to do so through negotiations. So when Israel pulled out of Gaza, Hamas was the logical victor in the subsequent elections and eventually took over the Strip. Israel's tactical success became a strategic failure.

This is not a unique dilemma. In 2006 in Iraq the United States and its local allies were headed for disaster. In the first years after the invasion the United States had tried to work with openly pro-American voices, few of whom had credibility among ordinary Iraqis. Led by Gen. David Petraeus, the United States fundamentally revised its strategy and, as a result, beat back the insurgency and shattered terrorist groups like al-Qa'ida in Iraq. Although the troop surge received the most attention, one of the most important shifts was America's new willingness to work with Sunni tribal groups and cut deals with some Shi'a militant groups, using the more moderate elements of these communities against the radicals.

Truly winning over Palestinian "hearts and minds" will be impossible for Israel. Given the long decades of suffering and dispossession and the bitterness of the Second Intifada, the best Israel can hope for at this point is to be hated less. That hope, however, should not be dismissed. If the Israeli occupation can be less harsh, and if Israeli leaders can be seen as trustworthy and peace seeking, moderate Palestinians are likely to come to the fore. In turn they can build the institutions and services that offer a counter to Hamas. As one senior Israeli security official told me, "The aim is not to close Hamas's social services, but instead to replace the management." With this modest goal in mind counterterrorism's political effects must be weighed with particular emphasis on how they affect moderate forces in the Palestinian community. Tactical successes that kill a particular leader or stop an attack can be invaluable, but if carried out at the wrong moment they can undercut a political force essential to Israeli security.

Israel also needs to do better at countering the informational and social service dimensions of a group like Hamas. For many years Israel focused almost entirely on militant group trigger-pullers, ignoring the broader infrastructure that supports them. Over time Israel began to go after the groups more comprehensively, but it still does not do enough to bolster alternative social service providers or promote credible messages to counter Hamas.

Also vital to a counterinsurgency approach is better coordination between Israeli political leaders and military officials. In the Second Intifada this link broke down when the IDF did not support attempts by political leaders to restart negotiations. It shows up today in ways large and small. The Givati Brigade T-shirts displaying a bull's-eye on a pregnant Palestinian woman can perhaps be dismissed as the unfortunate bad taste common to youth around the world, particularly in a combat environment. But because they offer an example of Israeli callousness such mistakes are catastrophic, as they are easily woven into the narrative of Israeli abuse and cruelty that militant groups try to spin. In the West Bank political leaders and senior IDF commanders should constantly attempt to minimize any abuses by soldiers. Not only are these abuses ethically abhorrent, but they also send a negative signal about the PA government's cooperation with Israel. Israeli political leaders should also develop clear guidance for when to impose closures on the West Bank. One military official described the IDF's fondness for closures as a "Pavlovian reaction" and noted that although they were necessary at the height of the Intifada, they are rarely if ever needed today, now that the security situation has improved.

An Information Strategy for Counterterrorism

Sixty years later Menachem Begin's description of Israel as a "glass house" still rings true. The world media are a constant presence in Israel, and Israeli counterterrorism is centered in their spyglass. The Israeli politician Dan Meridor points out, "Every child killed is on the TV screen at night." An event like the Qana disaster in Lebanon can stop an entire operation.

A democratic society cannot and should not prevent the media from operating. Israel has made widely different media choices, and its erratic policy shifts have been disastrous. In Jenin, for instance, Israel's effort to shut out the cameras allowed Palestinian groups to create a narrative of wide-scale brutality that is taken as gospel to this day, even though UN and other investigations showed it to be blatantly false. In Lebanon in 2006 Israel went to the other extreme, allowing access to the point where reporters disclosed potentially sensitive information, to say nothing of the political drain that the constant reporting of individual casualties created.

The irony is that Hamas and particularly Hizballah, knowing they cannot win militarily, focus largely on information strategies. Hizballah has been particularly adept at manipulating the media to show and report what the Lebanese group wants the world to see and know.

Israel improved its handling of the media slightly during Cast Lead, allowing limited access to trusted reporters and recognizing that Arab satellite stations like al Jazeera would continue to broadcast despite Israeli restrictions. The result was limited coverage of the devastation and enough information to prevent the world from believing wild conspiracy theories but not so much as to inhibit Israeli operations. This suggests that selectively embedding reporters may be an ideal compromise for Israel: reporters would get a sense of the ground truth, and the footage, often dramatic, would be useful to contrast that being shot by pro-Palestinian media figures. Yet Cast Lead highlighted a different problem: Israel did not factor in how the reporting of its operations would affect public and international perceptions when images of destruction—dead children, demolished factories and shops, and uprooted olive trees—appeared on television screens. Israel must also recognize that when it stops humanitarian organizations from providing medical assistance the public relations drawbacks, as well as the humanitarian impact, are considerable. Israel must plan to provide security for these aid organizations, even if they are critical of Israeli operations, while the fighting is going on.

During a conflict Israel must focus on disrupting the information strategy of the enemy. Hizballah's television station Al Manar and its website are as strategically important as, or even more important than its rocket launchers. Similarly Israel must press journalists to expose Hizballah's manipulation of the media to reduce the organization's credibility.

When an operation is planned, media officers need to be part of the process. The public relations outlook needs to be part of planning before an operation begins, not just there at the end to spin the facts. During the actual conflict a Cabinet member and a senior IDF official should be jointly responsible for media briefings. They would provide the public with regular briefings, including casualties, that would satisfy legitimate public and world interests without derailing the entire conflict.

Stopping Terrorism at Home

Although today most attention is focused on the West Bank, Gaza, or Lebanon, Israel is also running risks within its pre-1967 borders. Here Israel should draw lessons from the United States and several other countries that are trying to defuse potential dangers from terrorism at home.

An emerging concern is the Israeli Arab community. In contrast to the web of checkpoints and the security barrier that restrict Palestinians on the West Bank, Israeli Arabs enjoy freedom of movement. On September

9, 2001, on behalf of Hamas, Mohammad Shaker Habashi carried out the first suicide attack committed by an Israeli Arab, killing three Israelis. Israeli Arabs in 2003 assisted in several suicide attacks, and several others were arrested for planning more strikes. Additional attacks occurred in 2005, and the most bloody attack occurred on March 8, 2008, when an Israeli Arab killed eight yeshiva students in Jerusalem. In July 2008 Israeli security officials arrested an Israeli Arab youth group trying to create an al-Qa'ida-type cell within Israel.[9]

Israeli Jews, poor relations with Israeli Arabs, combined with the radicalizing pressure of satellite television and Israeli Arab leaders, all fanned the flames of extremism. This risk is likely to grow. As one intelligence official points out, "Israeli Arab and Israeli Jewish kids wear the same clothes and listen to the same music, but the Arab kids lack the opportunities that Jewish kids have." Politically the government has become more hostile to Israeli Arabs. Israel's foreign minister Avigdor Lieberman of the Yisrael Beiteinu Party won eleven Knesset seats in 2009, campaigning on the demand that Israeli Arabs swear loyalty to the Israeli state or lose their citizenship—in 2010, the Israeli cabinet approved a bill requiring Israeli Arabs swear loyalty to a "Jewish and democratic" state. Lieberman also called for banning traditional Israeli Arab marches commemorating the *nakba* (disaster) on Israeli Independence Day. A poll taken in 2009 showed that the percentage of Israeli Arabs who recognized Israel's right to exist had fallen to 53 from over 80 percent in 2003.[10]

To reverse this trend the broader Jewish community must recognize that almost 20 percent of Israelis—the Arab portion of the citizenry—are marginalized in the Jewish state today. Unfortunately Israel no longer has a coherent policy for this community. "Stupidity, stagnation, a mess" is how one informed official I talked to described the situation. Israel has ignored the recommendations of the Or Commission that investigated the initial outbreak of Israeli Arab violence in 2000, neither increasing development spending in Israeli Arab areas nor integrating this community.

Of equal or perhaps greater concern is confronting Jewish radicals. Given Israel's traumatic history of terrorism, it is disturbing that it has a double standard for Jewish violence and for Arab violence. For many Israelis Jewish terrorism is even worse than Arab terrorism, even though it is far less common. Israel's Jewish community can turn to its military, police, and intelligence services in response to Palestinian violence—in contrast to the Palestinians, who cannot turn to their own leaders when Jewish violence is leveled against them. After Rabin's assassination Shin Bet became more active in monitoring this community, but the focus remains on the risks to Jews.

A double standard for terrorists perceived as friendly but misguided and those directly hostile to the state is neither surprising nor uncommon. In the 1970s the United States tolerated Irish terrorists operating against the United Kingdom, allowing them to acquire arms, raise money, and find a safe haven. Today many countries tolerate ethnic diasporas or pro-government violence on their soil out of indifference or political interest. These countries often learned that such passivity can lead to disaster.

Israel should also expand its efforts to stop Jewish radicals who use violence against Arabs, including low-level violence such as intimidation of local Arabs and destruction of Arab property as well as outright murder. Jewish terrorists deserve long sentences for their crimes, and the Israeli government should make every effort to avoid their being treated as heroes. Such an effort would reduce a significant source of anger among Palestinians. It would also bolster moderate Palestinian leaders, as the Jewish radicals are viewed as operating with impunity. Finally, it would demonstrate that Israel is against all forms of terrorism, not just terrorism that kills Jews. Not punishing Jewish terrorists makes a mockery of government demands that other countries clamp down on terrorism and gives credence to the canard that one man's terrorist is another man's freedom fighter.

Even if the world learns all it can from Israel, and even if Israel adopts all the recommendations I suggest, terrorism will remain a threat. Much of what I address will be familiar to Israelis, and I wrote this book in the hope of informing those who fight terrorism outside Israel—soldiers, intelligence officers, and peacemakers in the United States, Europe, and elsewhere—so they can be more effective. I also hope the general public will understand the difficulties inherent in counterterrorism and subscribe to neither the myth of Israeli brilliance nor that of Israeli bungling. Counterterrorism, even at its most impressive, comes with trade-offs, and most of the time effectiveness simply means fewer attacks or less deadly ones rather than a complete end to violence. As Israel's experience shows, governments must often choose among bad options: the least bad is often the most to hope for. Realistic expectations of what democratic governments can and cannot accomplish is vital. Such realism enables leaders to fight or not fight, spend or not spend, and ultimately make sensible decisions about blood and treasure, knowing that citizens understand there are no easy answers.

NOTES

INTRODUCTION

1 For an account of the massacre, see "Massacre at Scorpion's Pass," *Time,* March 29, 1954; United Nations Security Council S/3252, June 1954. The Arab security official is General Glubb, the head of Jordan's army, and is quoted in Ilana Feldman, "Home as a Refrain: Remembering and Living Displacement in Gaza," *History & Memory* 18(2) (2006): 34. The quote from one of the raiders comes from the same article (37).

CHAPTER 1

1 For the period of the Yishuv, I drew on Ami Pedahzur, *The Israeli Secret Services and the Struggle against Terrorism* (New York: Columbia University Press, 2009); Benny Morris, *1948: The First Arab-Israeli War* (New Haven: Yale University Press, 2008); and Ami Pedahzur and Arie Perliger, *Jewish Terrorism in Israel* (New York: Columbia University Press, 2010).
2 Quoted in Avi Shlaim, *The Iron Wall: Israel and the Arab World* (New York: Norton, 2000), 18.
3 For a review, see Yoav Ben-Horin and Barry Posen, *Israel's Strategic Doctrine* (Santa Monica, CA: RAND, 1981).
4 Yael Yehoshua, "Abu Mazen: A Political Profile," *MEMRI*, April 29, 2003.
5 "Irgun, November 1948," www.betar.org.il/world/ideology/karoz003 .htm.

6 Thurston Clarke, *By Blood and Fire: The Attack on the King David Hotel* (London : Hutchinson, 1981).

7 *Palestine Post*, July 26, 1938; Arie Perliger and Leonard Weinberg, "Jewish Self-Defense and Terrorist Groups Prior to the Establishment of the State of Israel: Roots and Traditions," in *Totalitarian Movements and Political Religions*, ed. Leonard Weinberg and Ami Pedahzur (London: Frank Cass, 2004); Shmuel Katz, *Days of Fire* (Garden City, NY: Doubleday, 1968), 94.

8 Bruce Hoffman, *Inside Terrorism* (New York: Columbia University Press, 1998), 53.

9 Menachem Begin, *The Revolt: Story of the Irgun*, trans. Samuel Katz (Jerusalem: Steimatzky, 1972), 56.

10 Benny Morris, *1948: A History of the First Arab-Israeli War* (New Haven: Yale University Press, 2008), 101.

11 Quoted in ibid., 100.

12 Benny Morris, "Lashing Back: Israel's 1947–1948 Civil War," *Military History Quarterly* (2009), http://www.historynet.com/lashing-back-israel-1947-1948-civil-war.htm/1; Morris, *1948*, 102–3.

13 Morris, "Lashing Back."

14 Abu Iyad and Eric Rouleau, *My Home, My Land: A Narrative of the Palestinian Struggle* (New York: Times Books, 1981), 4.

15 As quoted in Aharon Bregman, *Israel's Wars, 1947–93* (London: Routledge), 20.

16 Benny Morris, *The Birth of the Palestinian Refugee Problem, 1947–1949* (Cambridge: Cambridge University Press, 1987), vii–xx; Ari Shavit, "Survival of the Fittest," *Haaretz*, January 1, 2004.

17 See Bregman, *Israel's Wars*, 30 and www.israeli-occupation.org/2009-11-27/tom-segev-the-makings-of-history-with-the-wave-of-a-hand/.

18 For background on cross-border wars, I drew on Michael B. Oren, "Escalation to Suez: The Egypt-Israel Border War, 1949–56," *Journal of Contemporary History* 24 (1989); Yezid Sayigh, *Armed Struggle and the Search for a State: The Palestinian National Movement* (New York : Oxford University Press, 1997); Benny Morris, *Israel's Border Wars, 1949–1956* (New York: Oxford University Press, 1997).

19 Iyad and Rouleau, *My Home, My Land*, 38.

20 Hillel Cohen, *Good Arabs: The Israeli Security Agencies and the Israeli Arabs, 1948–1967* (Berkeley: University of California Press, 2010), 95.

21 Like many modern groups, the fedayeen are difficult to pigeonhole. They conducted terrorist attacks, striking civilians and trying to instill fear, and also hit military targets and served as an adjunct to Arab state military efforts.

22 For a characterization of this as guerrilla war, see Moshe Dayan, "Israel's Border and Security Problems," *Foreign Affairs* 33(1) (1954/5): 260.

23 Morris, *Israel's Border Wars*, 145, 181.

24 Ilana Feldman, "Home as a Refrain: Remembering and Living Displacement in Gaza," *History & Memory* 18(2) (2006): 29.

25 Quoted in Morris, *Israel's Border Wars*, 145.

26 Quoted in Barry Blechman, "The Consequences of Israeli Reprisals," (Ph.D. Diss., Georgetown University, 1971), as quoted in Keren Fraiman, unpublished manuscript.

27 Quoted in Morris, *Israel's Border Wars*, 149.
28 Quoted in Cohen, *Good Arabs*, 67.
29 Quoted in Morris, *Israel's Border Wars*, 185.
30 Morris, *Israel's Border Wars*, 178.
31 Quoted in Hanon Alon, *Countering Palestinian Terrorism: Toward a Policy Analysis of Countermeasures* (Santa Monica, CA: RAND, 1980), 16.
32 Quoted in the documentary *The 50 Years War: Israel and the Arabs* (Virginia: PBS Home Video, 1999).
33 Quoted in Gil-li Vardi, "'Pounding Their Feet': Israeli Military Culture as Reflected in Early IDF Combat History," *Journal of Strategic Studies* 31(2) (2008): 302.
34 Morris, *Israel's Border Wars*, 257–76.
35 Isabel Kershner, *Barrier: The Seam of the Israeli-Palestinian Conflict* (New York: Palgrave Macmillan, 2005), 69; Morris, *Israel's Border Wars*, 262.
36 Quoted in Fraiman, unpublished manuscript, 32.
37 Morris, *Israel's Border Wars*, 86; Oren, "Escalation to Suez," 351.
38 Iyad and Rouleau, *My Home, My Land*, 24.
39 Oren, "Escalation to Suez," 355–56.
40 Iyad and Rouleau, *My Home, My Land*, 22.
41 Quoted in Feldman, "Home as Refrain," 36.
42 Oren, "Escalation to Suez," 350.
43 Ibid., 354.
44 Morris, *Israel's Border Wars*, 35.
45 Ibid., 355–90, 432, 438.
46 Yossi Melman, "Targeted Killings: A Retro Fashion Very Much in Vogue," *Haaretz*, March 24, 2004; Pedahzur, *The Israeli Secret Services*, 27–28.
47 Quoted in Mordechai Bar-On, "Small Wars, Big Wars: Security Debates During Israel's First Decade," *Israel Studies* 5(2) (2000), electronic version.
48 Cohen, *Good Arabs*, 68–93.
49 "Shadmi Zuka Me-Ashmat Retzach (Shadmi Was Acquitted from the Charge of Murder)," *Davar*, February 27, 1959.

CHAPTER 2

1 "Algeria: Skyway Robbery," *Time*, August 2, 1968; Terence Smith, "A Hijacked Plane Stirs New Tensions," *New York Times*, July 28, 1968. This section draws heavily on Yezid Sayigh, *Armed Struggle and the Search for a State: The Palestinian National Movement* (New York: Oxford University Press, 1997); Abu Iyad and Eric Rouleau, *My Home, My Land: A Narrative of the Palestinian Struggle* (New York: Times Books, 1981). "Pursema Mahut Ha-Mecheva Ha-Humanitarit: Yeshuchreru 16 'Aravim She-Histanenu Le-Yisrael Od Lyfney Milchemet Yuni" (The Essence of the Humanitarian Gesture Revealed: 16 Arabs Who Infiltrated Israel before the June War Will Be Released), *Davar*, September 4, 1968.
2 Bruce Hoffman, *Inside Terrorism* (New York: Columbia University Press, 1998), 67.

3 Quoted in Sayigh, *Armed Struggle,* 73.
4 Quoted in Bassam Abu Sharif and Uzi Mahnaimi, *Tried by Fire* (London: Warner Books, 1995), 59–60.
5 Iyad and Rouleau, *My Home, My Land,* 35.
6 Iyad and Rouleau, *My Home, My Land,* 36.
7 Andrew Gowers and Tony Walker, *Behind the Myth: Yasser Arafat and the Palestinian Revolution* (London: W. H. Allen, 1990), 13.
8 Barry Rubin and Judith Colp Rubin, *Yasir Arafat: A Political Biography* (New York: Oxford University Press, 2005), 11.
9 Fatah internal statutes, unpublished, cited in Andrew Gowers and Tony Walker, *Behind the Myth: Yasser Arafat and the Palestinian Revolution* (London: W.H. Allen, 1990), 31.
10 Bassam Abu Sharif, *Arafat and the Dream of Palestine: An Insider's Account* (New York: Palgrave MacMillan, 2009), 10.
11 Iyad and Rouleau, *My Home, My Land,* 107.
12 Quoted in Mehmood Hussain, *The Palestine Liberation Organisation: A Study in Ideology, Strategy and Tactics* (Delhi: University Publishers, 1975), 21.
13 Iyad and Rouleau, *My Home, My Land,* 43–44.
14 Sayigh, *Armed Struggle,* 120.
15 Michael B. Oren, *Six Days of War: June 1967 and the Making of the Modern Middle East* (Oxford: Oxford University Press, 2002), 81, 141.
16 Moshe Shemesh, "The IDF Raid on Samu'," *Israel Studies* 7(1) (2002): 139–67.
17 This section and the following on the West Bank and Gaza draw on Iyad and Rouleau, *My Home, My Land;* Shlomo Gazit, *The Carrot and the Stick: Israel's Policy in Judea and Samaria, 1967–1968* (Washington, DC: B'nai B'rith Books, 1995); Shlomo Gazit, *Trapped Fools: Thirty Years of Israeli Policy in the Territories* (Portland: Frank Cass, 2003); Ami Pedahzur, *The Israeli Secret Services And the Struggle Against Terrorism* (New York: Columbia University Press, 2009); Bard O'Neill, *Armed Struggle in Palestine: A Political-Military Analysis* (Boulder, CO: Westview Press, 1978); Shabtai Teveth, *The Cursed Blessing: The Story of Israel's Occupation of the West Bank* (London: Weidenfeld and Nicolson, 1970); Alain Gresh, *The PLO: The Struggle Within: Towards an Independent Palestinian State* (London: Zed Books, 1988); Barry Rubin and Judith Colp Rubin, *Yasir Arafat: A Political Biography* (New York: Oxford University Press, 2005).
18 Iyad and Rouleau, *My Home, My Land,* 51.
19 Quoted in ibid., 55.
20 Gazit, *Trapped Fools,* xii.
21 Rafi Man, *Lo Ya'ale Al Hada'at-Tzitutim, Bituyim Ve-Matbeot Lashon* (That's Unthinkable: Quotes, Phrases and Idioms) (Tel Aviv: Hed Arzi, 1998), 65.
22 Quoted in Gazit, *Trapped Fools,* 162.
23 Quoted in O'Neill, *Armed Struggle in Palestine,* 72.
24 Quoted in Neve Gordon, *Israel's Occupation* (Berkeley: University of California Press, 2008), 49.
25 Gazit, *Trapped Fools,* 5; Moshe Maoz, "Palestinian Leadership on the West Bank, 1948–1978," in *Hatnuah Haleumit Hapalestinit: Meimut*

Lehashlama?, ed. Moshe Maoz and B. Z. Kedar (Tel Aviv: Ministry of Defense, 1996), 231–40.

26 Gazit, *Trapped Fools*, 56.

27 Gazit, *The Carrot and the Stick*, 260.

28 Ibid., 242.

29 Quoted in Alon, *Countering Palestinian Terrorism in Israel: Toward a Policy Analysis of Countermeasures* (Santa Monica, CA: Rand, 1980), 74.

30 Ehud Yaari, *Strike Terror: The Story of Fatah* (New York: Sabra, 1970), 133–35, quoted in Alon, *Countering Palestinian Terrorism*, 43.

31 Gazit, *The Carrot and the Stick*, 252.

32 Iyad and Rouleau, *My Home, My Land*, 56.

33 Ann Mosely Lesch, *Political Perceptions of the Palestinians on the West Bank and the Gaza Strip* (Washington, DC: Middle East Institute, 1980), 39.

34 "Yehidat Rimon" (Rimon Unit), Fresh Internet Forum on the IDF, www.fresh.co.il/vBulletin/showthread.php?t=61602 (accessed December 28, 2009).

35 Gazit, *The Carrot and the Stick*, 260; Israel Ministry of Foreign Affairs, "Terrorism Deaths in Israel 1920–1999," www.mfa.gov.il/MFA/ Terrorism-+Obstacle+to+Peace/Palestinian+terror+before+2000/ Terrorism% 20deaths%20in%20Israel%20-%201920–1999 (accessed January 1, 2000).

36 Gordon, *Israel's Occupation*, xviii.

37 These sections on cross-border raids and the birth of international terrorism draw on Iyad and Rouleau, *My Home, My Land;* Sayigh, *Armed Struggle;* Abu Sharif, *Arafat and the Dream of Palestine;* Rubin and Rubin, *Yasir Arafat;* Pedahzur, *The Israeli Secret Services;* Yoram Schweitzer, "Innovation in Terrorist Organizations: The Case of the PFLP and Its Offshoots," in Maria Rasmussen and Mohammed Hafez, eds. *Terrorist Innovations in Weapons of Mass Effect* (Ft. Belvoir, VA: The Defense Threat Reduction Agency, August 2010), 86–98.

38 The Israeli paratroopers brigade association claims the CIA tipped off the Jordanians about the pending attack (www.paratroops.org.il/ siteArticle.asp?aid=56&cid=64). The Israeli Air Force claims the Jordanians learned about this from leaflets they dropped (www.iaf .org.il/Templates/FlightLog/FlightLog.aspx?lang=HE&lobbyID=40& folderID=48&subfolderID=321&docfolderID=828&docID=6835&doc Type=EVENT).

39 Abu Sharif, *Arafat and the Dream of Palestine*, 20.

40 Iyad and Rouleau, *My Home, My Land*, 59; Paul McGeough, *Kill Khalid: The Failed Mossad Assassination of Khalid Mishal and the Rise of Hamas* (New York: New Press, 2009), 24.

41 Benny Morris, *Righteous Victims: A History of the Zionist-Arab Conflict, 1881–1999* (London: J. Murray, 2000), 369.

42 Paratroopers Brigade Association, www.zanhanim.org.il/Info/hi_show .aspx?id=32431.

43 Iyad and Rouleau, *My Home, My Land*, 60.

44 Mouin Rabbani, "The Making of a Palestinian Islamist Leader: An Interview with Khalid Mishal: Part I," *Journal of Palestine Studies* 37(3) (2008): 62–63.

45 See www.pbs.org/newshour/bb/middle_east/jan-june99/ hussein_2-5.html.

46 Rubin and Rubin, *Yasir Arafat*, 28.

47 Pedahzur, *The Israeli Secret Services*, 35.

48 Quoted in Bassam Abu Sharif, *Best of Enemies: The Memoirs of Bassam Abu-Sharif and Uzi Mahnaimi* (Boston: Little Brown and Co., 1995), 59.

49 See Alon, *Countering Palestinian Terrorism*, 44.

50 Abu Sharif and Mahnaimi, *Tried by Fire*, 64–65; Oriana Fallaci, "A Leader of the Fedayeen: 'We Want a War Like the Vietnam War,'" *Life* 68(22) (1970): 31–35; Abu Sharif, *Arafat and the Dream of Palestine*, 18.

51 Fallaci, "A Leader of the Fedayeen," 33.

52 Leila Khaled, George Hajjar, ed. *My People Shall Live: The Autobiography of a Revolutionary* (London: Hodder and Stoughton, 1973), 21.

53 Quoted on "Hijacked," *American Experience*, PBS (n.d.) www.pbs.org/ wgby/amex/hijacked/peopleevents/p_crews.html.

54 Fallaci, "A Leader of the Fedayeen," 33.

55 Quoted on "Hijacked," *American Experience*.

56 Abu Sharif and Mahnaimi, *Tried by Fire*, 81–82.

57 "Hijacked," *American Experience*.

58 Donna E. Arzt, *Refugees into Citizens: Palestinians and the End of the Arab-Israeli Conflict* (New York: Council of Foreign Relations, 1997), 17. Some estimates go as high as 350,000. Most of these refugees went to Jordan.

59 Iyad and Rouleau, *My Home, My Land*, 57.

60 Joseph Nevo, "September 1970 in Jordan: A Civil War?," *Civil Wars* 10(3) (2008): 217–30.

61 Sayigh, *Armed Struggle*, 258.

62 Quoted in Alon, *Countering Palestinian Terrorism*, 38.

63 Amir Oren, "On the Brink in September," *Haaretz*, September 24, 2009.

64 Iyad and Rouleau, *My Home, My Land*, 81.

65 Fallaci, "A Leader of the Fedayeen," 33.

66 For background this section draws on Iyad and Rouleau, *My Home, My Land*; Simon Reeve, *One Day in September: The Full Story of the 1972 Munich Olympics Massacre and the Israeli Revenge Operation "Wrath of God"* (New York: Arcade, 2000).

67 "Arab Government Support for Black September Organization," U.S.*Department of State Telegram*, 047847 (1981).

68 Simon Dunstan, *Israel's Lightning Strike: The Raid on Entebbe 1976* (Oxford: Osprey, 2009), 7.

69 Alexander Wolff, "When the Terror Began," *Time*, August 25, 2002.

70 Ibid.

71 Ibid.

72 Terence Smith, "Arab Guerrillas Warned by Israel," *New York Times*, September 7, 1972; Reeve, *One Day in September*, 120–21.

73 "Will of the Munich Guerrillas," *Arab World Weekly*, September 16, 1972, 17–19.

74 Iyad and Rouleau, *My Home, My Land*, 112.

75 Dennis Ross, *The Missing Peace: The Inside Story of the Fight for Middle East Peace* (New York: Farrar, Straus and Giroux, 2004), 40.

76 U.S. Department of State, "The Seizure of the Saudi Arabian Embassy in Khartoum," Intelligence Memorandum (June 1973) http://history.state.gov/historicaldocuments/frus1969–76ve06/d217.

77 Bruce Hoffman, "All You Need Is Love," *The Atlantic*, December 2001.

78 Barry Rubin, *Revolution until Victory? The Politics and History of the PLO*, (Cambridge, MA: Harvard University Press, 1994), 40.

79 Duane R. Clarridge and Digby Diehl, *A Spy for All Seasons: My Life in the CIA* (New York: Scribner, 1997), 332–36; Ewen MacAskill and Richard Nelsson, "Mystery Death of Abu Nidal, Once World's Most Wanted Terrorist," *The Guardian*, August 20, 2002.

80 Jon Grinspan, "International Terrorism, 1985," www.americanheritage.com/articles/web/20061007-achille-lauro-youssef-majed-molqi-abu-abbas-terrorism-leon-klinghoffer-palestine-liberation-front-yasir-arafat.shtml; Sayigh, *Armed Struggle*, 354–55.

81 Riad N. El-Rayyes and Dunia Nahas, eds., *Guerrillas for Palestine: A Study of the Palestinian Commando Organizations* (Beirut: An-Nahar Press Services, 1974), 29.

82 Hussain, *The Palestine Liberation Organisation*, 23.

83 Pedahzur, *The Israeli Secret Services*, 47–50. A commission later found that the IDF units were not trained well enough in hostage rescue, leading in 1975 to the creation of Yamam, a company within the Border Police that was dedicated to antiterrorism.

84 Rubin and Rubin, *Yasir Arafat*, 33–34.

85 Iyad and Rouleau, *My Home, My Land*, 45; Sayigh, *Armed Struggle*; O'Neill, *Armed Struggle in Palestine*.

86 El-Rayyes and Nahas, *Guerrillas for Palestine*; Sayigh, *Armed Struggle*, 63; Rubin and Rubin, *Yasir Arafat*; Rubin, *Revolution until Victory?*, 30–31.

87 Iyad and Rouleau, *My Home, My Land*, 220–21.

88 Quoted in Rubin, *Revolution until Victory?*, 36.

89 Klein, *Striking Back: The 1972 Munich Olympics Massacre and Israel's Deadly Response* (New York: Random House, 2005) 123–28. This section draws on that book, as well as Reeve, *One Day in September*.

90 Reeve, *One Day in September*, 159.

91 Alon, *Countering Palestinian Terrorism*, 89–90.

92 "The New Arab Terror: Murder by Mail," *Newsweek*, October 2, 1972.

93 Quoted in Thomas Friedman, "Israel Turns Terror Back on the Terrorists, but Finds No Political Solution," *New York Times*, December 4, 1984.

94 Quoted in Reeve, *One Day in September*, 161.

95 Quoted in Reeve, *One Day in September*, 166.

96 Quoted in Reeve, *One Day in September*, 167.

97 Lisa Beyer, "The Myths and Reality of Munich," *Time*, December 4, 2005; Klein, *Striking Back*, 122–24.

98 David Ignatius, "PLO Operative, Slain Reputedly by Israelis, Had Been Helping U.S.," *Wall Street Journal*, February 10, 1983; Klein, *Striking Back*, 220–21.

99 David Ignatius, "Secret Strategies," *Washington Post*, November 12, 2004.

100 James Markham, "Life and Death of a Terrorist," *New York Times*, July 10, 1983; Ignatius, "PLO Operative."

101 "The New Arab Terror: Murder by Mail."

102 This section draws heavily for operational information on Dunstan, *Israel's Lightning Strike*, 10–59. It also draws on Pedahzur, *The Israeli Secret Services.*

103 David Kaplan, "A Historic Hostage-Taking Revisited," *Jerusalem Post*, August 3, 2006.

104 The quotes are from Dunstan, *Israel's Lightning Strike*, 14, 138.

105 Sharon Rofe-Ofir, "Hasifa: Ha-Mosad Tzilem, Mivtza Antebe Yatza La-Derech" (The Mossad Took Pictures and Entebbe Operation Was Launched), *Ynet*, July 1, 2006.

106 Pedahzur, *The Israeli Secret Services*, 61–62; Klein, *Striking Back*, 204–8.

107 Yossi Melman, "Targeted Killings - a Retro Fashion Very Much in Vogue," *Haaretz*, March 24, 2004.

CHAPTER 3

1 This section draws on Simon Reeve, *One Day in September: The Full Story of the 1972 Munich Olympics Massacre and the Israeli Revenge Operation "Wrath of God"* (New York: Arcade, 2000); Alain Gresh, *The Struggle Within: Towards an Independent Palestinian State* (London: Zed, 1985); Bard O'Neill, *Armed Struggle in Palestine: A Political-Military Analysis* (Boulder, CO: Westview Press, 1978); Daniel Helmer, *Flipside of the Coin: Israel's Lebanese Incursion between 1982–2000* (Fort Leavenworth, KS: Combat Studies Institute Press, 2007), 28; Ian Black and Benny Morris, *Israel's Secret Wars: A History of Israel's Intelligence Services* (New York: Grove Weidenfield, 1991); and Yezid Sayigh, *Armed Struggle and the Search for a State: The Palestinian National Movement* (New York: Oxford University Press, 1997).

2 Reeve, *One Day in September*, 180.

3 "An Eye for an Eye: Should the U.S. Use This as a Model?," *CBS News*, November 21, 2001; Reeve, *One Day in September*, pp. 182–83.

4 Julie Peteet, *Landscape of Hope and Despair: Palestinian Refugee Camps* (Philadelphia: University of Pennsylvania Press, 2009), 132–45.

5 Black and Morris, *Israel's Secret Wars*, 270.

6 Quoted in Rex Brynen, *Sanctuary and Survival: The PLO in Lebanon* (Boulder, CO: Westview Press, 1990), 95.

7 Rashid Khalidi, *Under Siege: PLO Decision-Making During the 1982 War* (New York: Columbia University Press, 1986), 32.

8 Quoted in Peteet, *Landscape of Hope and Despair*, 144.

9 Barry Rubin, *Revolution until Victory? The Politics and History of the PLO* (Cambridge, MA: Harvard University Press, 1994), 55.

10 Abu Iyad and Eric Rouleau, *My Home, My Land: A Narrative of the Palestinian Struggle* (New York: Times Books, 1981), 179.

11 William Claiborne, "Israelis Retaliate after Palestinian Rockets Hit," *Washington Post*, December 22, 1978.

12 "Lebanon Alleges Invasion by 15,000 Syrians," *The Times*, January 20, 1976.

13 Yitzhak Rabin, *The Rabin Memoirs* (Berkeley: University of California Press, 1979), 280.

14 According to one of the attackers, Khaled Abu Asba. See Avi Issacharoff, "Coast Road Terrorist Refuses to Apologize, Says Peace 'Important,'" *Haaretz*, August 5, 2009.

15 Itamar Marcus, "Encouraging Women Terrorists," in *Palestinian Culture and Society (Study #6—March 12, 2002)* (2002).

16 Israeli sources claim three hundred, while some of the more extreme claims range up to a thousand. See Joanne Tucker, "Israel in Lebanon," *Al Jazeera English*, August 12, 2009; "Operation Litani (1978)," *Ynet*, March 15, 2009.

17 Human Rights Watch, *Civilian Pawns: Laws of War Violations and the Use of Weapons on the Israel-Lebanon Border* (New York: Human Rights Watch, 1996), 42; Ahmad Beydoun, "South Lebanon Border Zone: A Local Perspective," *Journal of Palestine Studies* 21 (3) (Spring 1992), 35–53.

18 Human Rights Watch, *Civilian Pawns*, 40.

19 Chen Kots-Bar, "Kasha Li Li-Raot Yeladim Neheragim" (It Is Hard for Me to See Children Die)," *NRG*, July 8, 2005.

20 Nir Gontarz, "The Kuntar File, Exposed," *Yediot Aharonot*, July 14, 2008.

21 Kuntar claimed at his trial that he was wounded and rendered unconscious and said, "I didn't hurt the girl at all and I didn't see how she met her death." "Samir Kuntar," in *Terror Background Info*, Israeli Ministry of Foreign Affairs, 2008.

22 Ibid.

23 Christopher Walker, "60 Pc of Population Flee Kiryat Shimona: Despair Grips Front Line Town," *The Times*, July 21, 1981.

24 Black and Morris, *Israel's Secret Wars*, 371.

25 Menachem Begin, letter to Secretary of State Alexander Haig, quoted in Ariel Sharon and David Chanoff, *Warrior: The Autobiography of Ariel Sharon* (New York: Simon and Schuster, 1989), 451.

26 *Haaretz*, June 9, 1982, quoted in Eyal Zisser, "The 1982 'Peace for Galilee' War: Looking Back in Anger," in *A Never-Ending Conflict: A Guide to Israeli Military History*, ed. Mordechai Bar-On (Westport, Conn.: Praeger, 2004), 202.

27 Ze'ev Schiff and Ehud Ya'ari, *Israel's Lebanon War* (New York: Simon and Schuster, 1984).

28 Zisser, "The 1982 'Peace for Galilee' War," 206; George C. Solley, *The Israeli Experience in Lebanon, 1982–1985* (Quantico, VA: Marine Corps Command and Staff College, 1987).

29 Black and Morris, *Israel's Secret Wars*, 376.

30 For an excellent account of the military campaign, see Kenneth Pollack, *Arabs at War* (Lincoln: University of Nebraska Press, 2002), 524–51.

31 Israeli Air Force, www.iaf.org.il/Templates/Wars/Wars.IN.aspx?lang=EN&lobbyID=40&folderID=42&subfolderID=42&docfolderID=42&docID=3751.

32 Michael Bar-Zohar and Eitan Habe, *Massacre in Munich: The Manhunt for the Killers behind the 1972 Olympics Massacre* (Guilford, CT: Lyons Press, 2005), 228.

33 Quoted in Peteet, *Landscape of Hope and Despair,* 153.
34 Quoted in Peteet, *Landscape of Hope and Despair,* 164.
35 *The Accused,* BBC, London, 2001.
36 Leila Shahid and Linda Butler, "The Sabra and Shatila Massacres: Eye-Witness Reports," *Journal of Palestine Studies* 32(1) (2002): 38–40. The information is taken from the introduction by Linda Butler. The nurse's quote comes from p. 40 and the militiaman quotes come from pp. 45 and 56. The survivors' quotes come from pp. 45 and 50–51.
37 Shahid and Butler, "The Sabra and Shatila Massacres," 42.
38 Quoted in Schiff and Ya'ari, *Israel's Lebanon War,* 284.
39 O'Neill, *Armed Struggle in Palestine,* 92.
40 Jeroen Gunning, *Hamas in Politics: Democracy, Religion, Violence* (New York: Columbia University Press, 2008), 33.
41 Shlomo Gazit, *Trapped Fools: Thirty Years of Israeli Policy in the Territories* (Portland: Frank Cass, 2003), 22.
42 Quoted in Neve Gordon, *Israel's Occupation* (Berkeley: University of California Press, 2008), 116.
43 Gordon, *Israel's Occupation,* 1, 131.
44 Avraham Sela, "Authority without Dominion: The Path of the PLO from Armed Struggle to Political Settlement," in *Hatnuah Haleumit Hapalestinit: Meimut Lehashlama,* ed. Moshe Maoz and B. Z. Kedar (Tel Aviv: Ministry of Defense, 1996), 388–90.
45 Thomas G. Mitchell, *Native vs. Settler: Ethnic Conflict in Israel/Palestine, Northern Ireland, and South Africa* (Westport, CT: Greenwood Press, 2000), 127.
46 Sela, "Authority without Dominion," 367–74.
47 Reuven Aharoni, "The Palestinian Intifada, 1987–1991," in *A Never-Ending Conflict: A Guide to Israeli Military History,* ed. Mordechai Bar-On (Westport, CT: Praeger, 2004), 221. From December 1987 to February 1989 there were only twelve Israeli deaths.
48 Sergio Catignani, *Israeli Counter-Insurgency and the Intifadas: Dilemmas of a Conventional Army* (New York: Routledge, 2008), 81–83.
49 Shai Fogelman, "Present Trauma," *Haaretz,* March 4, 2010.
50 Catignani, *Israeli Counter-Insurgency;* quoted in Sari Nusseibeh and Anthony David, *Once Upon a Country: A Palestinian Life* (New York: Farrar, Straus and Giroux, 2007), 267.
51 Quoted in William V. O'Brien, *Law and Morality in Israel's War with the PLO* (New York: Routledge, 1991), 237.
52 Quoted in O'Brien, *Law and Morality,* 239.
53 Ze'ev Schiff and Ehud Ya'ari, *Intifada: The Palestinian Uprising—Israel's Third Front* (New York: Simon and Schuster, 1990), 50.
54 Gordon, *Israel's Occupation,* 158.
55 Betselem, "A Decade of Human Rights Violations, 1987–1997," *B'Tselem* report, 1998.
56 Quoted in Catignani, *Israeli Counter-Insurgency,* 85.
57 John Kifner, "Israel Detains 2 in Burial Alive of Palestinians," *New York Times,* February 16, 1988; Schiff and Ya'ari, *Intifada,* 136.
58 Aharoni, "The Palestinian Intifada," 220.
59 "Information Sheet: Update November 1, 1989 (English Version)," B'Tselem, 1989.

60 Amira Hass, *Drinking the Sea at Gaza: Days and Nights in a Land under Siege*, trans. Maxine Nunn (New York: Henry Holt, 1996), 23.

61 Ibid.

62 Nusseibeh and David, *Once Upon a Country*, 287–88.

63 Aharoni, "The Palestinian Intifada," 228.

64 Boaz Ganor, "Israel, Hamas and Fatah," in *Democracy and Counterterrorism: Lessons from the Past*, eds. Robert J. Art and Louise Richardson (Washington, DC: USIP, 2007), 291.

65 Zaki Chehab, *Inside Hamas: The Untold Story of Militants, Martyrs and Spies* (London: I. B. Tauris, 2007), 123; Azzam Tamimi, *Hamas: A History from Within* (Northampton, MA: Olive Branch Press, 2007), 68; Magnus Ranstorp, "The Hizballah Training Camps of Lebanon," in *The Making of a Terrorist: Recruitment, Training, and Root Causes*, ed. James J. F. Forest (Wesport, CT: Praeger Security International, 2006), 247.

66 Graham Usher, *Dispatches from Palestine: The Rise and Fall of the Oslo Peace Process* (London: Pluto Press, 1999), 21.

67 The text of the speech can be found at "Yasser Arafat, Speech at UN General Assembly," *Le Monde Diplomatique English Edition*, December 13, 1988.

68 William B. Quandt, *Peace Process: American Diplomacy and the Arab-Israeli Conflict Since 1967* (Washington, DC: Brookings Institution Press, 2005), 300–301.

69 Quoted in Klein, *Striking Back: The 1972 Munich Olympics Massacre and Israel's Deadly Response* (New York: Random House, 2005), 236.

70 Matti Steinberg, *'Omdim le-Goralam : ha-Toda'ah ha-le'umit ha-Palaṣtinit (Facing Their Fate: The Development of Palestinian National Consciousness 1967–2007)* (Yedi'ot Aḥaronot: Sifre Ḥemed, 2008).

71 Rabin's remarks can be found at "Peace Matters," *MacNeil/Lehrer NewsHour*, PBS, 1993.

72 Usher, *Dispatches from Palestine*, 13.

CHAPTER 4

1 Israel Ministry of Foreign Affairs, "Terrorism Deaths in Israel 1920–1999," January 1, 2000, http://www.mfa.gov.il/MFA/MFAArchive/2000_2009/2000/1/Terrorism%20deaths%20in%20Israel%20-%20 1920-1999.

2 Israel Ministry of Foreign Affairs, "Terrorism Deaths in Israel 1920–1999."

3 "Without Distinction: Attacks on Civilians by Palestinian Armed Groups," Amnesty International report, July 2, 2002, 3.

4 For a transcript of Rabin's remarks, see "Peace Matters," *MacNeil/Lehrer NewsHour*, PBS, 1993, online.

5 Aaron David Miller, *The Much Too Promised Land: America's Elusive Search for Arab-Israeli Peace* (New York: Bantam Books, 2008), 261.

6 Joel Greenberg, "Israel Bars Palestinian Officials from Gaza," *New York Times*, July 14, 1994; Ehud Ya'ari, "The Israeli-Palestinian Confrontation: Toward a Divorce," Jerusalem Issue Brief 2(2), Jerusalem Center for Public Affairs, 2002.

7 Clive Jones, "'One Size Fits All,' Israel, Intelligence, and the *al-Aqsa Intifada*," *Studies in Conflict and Terrorism* 26: 278.

8 Graham Usher, "Facing Defeat: The Intifada Two Years On," *Journal of Palestine Studies* 32(2) (2003): 23.

9 John Daniszewski, "Remarks on Terror Become Fighting Words," *Los Angeles Times*, March 11, 1998.

10 Quoted in Boaz Ganor, *The Counter-Terrorism Puzzle: A Guide for Decision Makers* (New Brunswick, N.J.: Transaction, 2005), 54.

11 Ed Blanche, "Israel Uses Intifada Informers to Abet Assassination Campaign," *Jane's Intelligence Review* 13 (2001), 22–24.

12 Martin Indyk, *Innocent Abroad: An Intimate History of American Peace Diplomacy in the Middle East* (New York: Simon and Schuster, 2009), 111.

13 Mouin Rabbani, "A Hamas Perspective on the Movement's Evolving Role: An Interview with Khalid Mishal: Part II," *Journal of Palestine Studies* 37(4) (2008): 3.

14 Michele K. Esposito, "The Al-Aqsa Intifada: Military Operations, Suicide Attacks, Assassinations, and Losses in the First Four Years," *Journal of Palestine Studies* 34(2) (2005): 104.

15 Amira Hass, "Israel's Closure Policy: An Ineffective Strategy of Containment and Repression," *Journal of Palestine Studies* 31(3) (2002): 8.

16 Neve Gordon, *Israel's Occupation* (Berkeley: University of California Press, 2008)

17 Amira Hass, *Drinking the Sea at Gaza: Days and Nights in a Land Under Siege* (New York: Metropolitan Books, 1999) 79, 84.

18 "Israeli-Palestinian Interim Agreement of September 28, 1995 (Oslo II Accords)," 1995, Annex I, Article 2, http://www.jewishvirtuallibrary .org/jsource/Peace/iaannex1.html#article2.

CHAPTER 5

1 Claude Berrebi and Esteban F. Klor, "Are Voters Sensitive to Terrorism? Direct Evidence from the Israeli Electorate," *American Political Science Review* 102(3) (2008): 279–301.

2 "Remarks to the American Israel Public Affairs Committee Policy Conference," *Weekly Compilation of Presidential Documents* 32(18) (1996).

3 Quoted in Clayton Swisher, *The Truth about Camp David: The Untold Story about the Collapse of the Middle East Peace Process* (New York: Nation Books, 2004), 8.

4 Clive Jones, "'One Size Fits All,' Israel, Intelligence, and the *al-Aqsa Intifada*," *Studies in Conflict and Terrorism* 26.

5 Dennis Ross, *The Missing Peace: The Inside Story of the Fight for Middle East Peace* (New York: Farrar, 2004), 265.

6 See Yoram Peri, *Generals in the Cabinet Room: How the Military Shapes Israeli Policy* (Washington, DC: USIP Press, 2006), 91.

7 Nicholas Goldberg, "Hawk to Dove? Netanyahu Says Reality Changed, Not His Politics," *Newsday*, January 19, 1997.

8 "Israeli Prime Minister's News Conference on the Hebron Accord," *Voice of Israel*, January 18, 1997.

9 Quoted in Akiva Eldar, "Popular Misconceptions," *Haaretz*, June 11, 2004.

10 Quoted in Graham Usher, *Dispatches from Palestine: The Rise and Fall of the Oslo Peace Process* (London: Pluto Press, 1999), 137.
11 See Dennis Ross, "Note for the Records," www.usembassy-israel.org.il/publish/peace/note_record.htm.
12 Ron Pundak, "From Oslo to Taba: What Went Wrong?" *Survival* 43(3) (2001): 33.
13 Quoted in "Without Distinction: Attacks on Civilians by Palestinian Armed Groups," Amnesty International report, July 2, 2002, 5–6.
14 Usher, *Dispatches from Palestine*, 136.
15 For a review, see Stuart Cohen, "Changing Societal-Military Relations in Israel: The Operational Implications," *Contemporary Security Policy* 21(2) (2000): 116–138.
16 Quoted in Zaki Chehab, *Inside Hamas: The Untold Story of the Militant Islamic Movement* (New York: Nations Books, 2007), 117.
17 Paul McGeough, *Kill Khalid: The Failed Mossad Assassination of Khalid Mishal and the Rise of Hamas* (New York: New Press, 2009), 2; Ami Pedahzur, *The Israeli Secret Services And the Struggle Against Terrorism* (New York: Columbia University Press, 2009), 107.
18 Quoted in McGeough, *Kill Khalid*, 128.
19 Efraim Halevy, *Man in the Shadows: Inside the Middle East Crisis with a Director of Israel's Mossad* (New York: St. Martin's Press, 2008), 165.

CHAPTER 6

1 Samuel M. Katz, *The Hunt for the Engineer: How Israeli Agents Tracked the Hamas Master Bomber* (Guilford, CT: Lyons Press, 2002), 106–98. For background, this section draws on Zaki Chehab, *Inside Hamas: The Untold Story of the Militant Islamic Movement* (New York: Nations Books, 2007); Matthew Levitt, *Hamas: Politics, Charity, and Terrorism in the Service of Jihad* (New Haven: Yale University Press, 2006);Azzam Tamimi, *Hamas: A History from Within* (Northampton, MA: Olive Branch Press, 2007); Paul McGeough, *Kill Khalid: The Failed Mossad Assassination of Khalid Mishal and the Rise of Hamas* (New York: New Press, 2009); Jeroen Gunning, *Hamas in Politics: Democracy, Religion, Violence* (New York: Columbia University Press, 2008); Khaled Hroub, *Hamas: Political Thought and Practice* (Washington, DC: Institute for Palestine Studies, 2000); R. Kim Cragin, "Palestinian Resistance through the Eyes of Hamas," PhD dissertation, Clare College, Cambridge, 2008; Avraham Sela, "Authority without Dominion: The Path of the PLO from Armed Struggle to Political Settlement," in *Hatnuah Haleumit Hapalestinit: Meimut Lehashlama*, ed. Moshe Maoz and B. Z. Kedar (Tel Aviv: Ministry of Defense, 1996).
2 Quoted in Chehab, *Inside Hamas*, 54.
3 Quoted in Chehab, *Inside Hamas*, 55.
4 Chehab, *Inside Hamas*, 60. See also Katz, *The Hunt for the Engineer*, 250–60.
5 Quoted in Serge Schmemann, "Palestinian Believed to Be Bombing Mastermind Is Killed," *New York Times*, January 6, 1996.
6 Muhammad Y. Muslih, *The Foreign Policy of Hamas* (New York: Council on Foreign Relations, 1999), 36.

7 Schmemann, "Palestinian Believed to Be Bombing Mastermind Is Killed."

8 Matthew Levitt, *Negotiating under Fire: Preserving Peace Talks in the Face of Terror Attacks* (Lanham, MD: Rowman & Littlefield, 2008), 137.

9 Schmemann, "Palestinian Believed to Be Bombing Mastermind Is Killed."

10 David Haham, *And the World Shall Fill with Violence: Sheikh Ahmed Yasin and His War with Israel*, trans. Eleazar Berman (Haifa: University of Haifa Press, 2006), 24.

11 Ibid., 12; Levitt, *Hamas*, 24.

12 Mouin Rabbani (interviewer), "Khalid Mishal: The Making of a Palestinian Islamic Leader," *Journal of Palestine Studies* 37(3) (2008), 59.

13 Erick Weiss, "Hoker Shabak: Mesigim Meida Be-Avoor Majadra" (Shin Bet Interrogator: We Get Information for a Dish of Majadra), *Ma'ariv*, January 24, 2009; Chehab, *Inside Hamas*, 23.

14 Chehab, *Inside Hamas*, 22.

15 See Hroub, *Hamas*, 265–66.

16 Hamas Political Bureau Memo, 2000 (just before the outbreak of the Second Intifada), reprinted in Hroub, *Hamas*, 279.

17 Rabbani, "The Making of a Palestinian Islamist Leader," 69.

18 "The Covenant of the Islamic Resistance Movement," August 18, 1988, http://avalon.law.yale.edu/20th_century/hamas.asp.

19 Memorandum of the Hamas Political Bureau, prepared in the late 1990s in Amman, reprinted in Hroub, *Hamas*, 268.

20 Mouin Rabbani, "A Hamas Perspective on the Movement's Evolving Role: An Interview with Khalid Mishal: Part II," *Journal of Palestine Studies* 37(4) (2008): 64.

21 Levitt, *Hamas*, 99–101.

22 Cragin, "Palestinian Resistance," 114. For information on what Hamas claims is its first attack, see Robert Kook, "Israel Returns to Deportation Policy for Arabs," *UPI*, December 16, 1990; Ghassan Charbel, "The Khaled Mishaal Interviews," *Dar al Hayat*, December 5, 2003.

23 Jerrold M. Post, Ehud Sprinzak, and Laurita M. Denny, "The Terrorists in Their Own Words: Interviews with 35 Incarcerated Middle Eastern Terrorists," *Terrorism and Political Violence* 15(1) (2003): 174.

24 Efraim Halevy, *Man in the Shadows: Inside the Middle East Crisis with the Man who Led the Mossad* (New York: St. Martin's Press, 2006), 177.

25 Amira Hass Maxine Nunn (trans.), *Drinking the Sea at Gaza: Days and Nights in a Land Under Siege* (New York: Metropolitan Books, 1999), 210.

26 Sara Roy, "Changing Political Attitudes among Gaza Refugees," *Journal of Palestine Studies* 19, no. 1 (1989): 77.

27 Graham Usher, *Dispatches from Palestine: The Collapse of the Oslo Agreement* (London: Pluto Press, 1998), 22.

28 Chehab, *Inside Hamas*, 43.

29 Quoted in ibid., 52.

30 Ghassan Charbel, "The Khaled Mishall interviews," *Dar al-Hayat*, November–December 2003.

31 Gunning, *Hamas in Politics*, 43.

32 Cragin, "Palestinian Resistance," 9. See also "Hamas Vows to Step Up Attacks on Settlers," *Mideast Mirror*, December 7, 1993.

33 Israel Ministry of Foreign Affairs, "Terrorism Deaths in Israel, 1920–1999," January 1, 2000, http://www.mfa.gov.il/MFA/ MFAArchive/2000_2009/2000/1/Terrorism%20deaths%20in%20 Israel%20-%201920-1999.

34 Quoted in Anat Berko, *The Path to Paradise: The Inner World of Suicide Bombers and Their Dispatchers* (Westport, CT: Praeger Security International, 2007), 14, 56.

35 Roger Gaess, "Interviews from Gaza: What Hamas Wants," *Middle East Policy* 9(4) (2002): 102–21.

36 See in "Without Distinction: Attacks on Civilians by Palestinian Armed Groups," Amnesty International report, July 2, 2002, 4.

37 Raphael Israeli, "Islamikaze and Their Significance," *Terrorism and Political Violence* 9(3) (1997): 113–15.

38 Post, Sprinzak, and Denny, "The Terrorists in Their Own Words," 172–78.

39 Berko, *The Path to Paradise*, 1

40 Berko, *The Path to Paradise*, 8.

41 Michael Horowitz, "The History and Future of Suicide Terrorism," Foreign Policy Research Institute, 2008, www.fpri.org/enotes/200808 .horowitz.suicideterrorism.html.

42 "A May 2002 Interview with the Hamas Commander of the Al-Qassam Brigades," Islam Online, 2002.

43 Levitt, *Hamas*, 52.

44 Amos Harel and Avi Issacharoff, *The Seventh War* (Tel Aviv: Yedioth Ahronot, 2004), 143–56.

45 Berko, *The Path to Paradise*, 8–9.

46 Yoram Schweitzer, "Palestinian Istishhadia: A Developing Instrument," *Studies in Conflict and Terrorism* 30(8) (2007): 670.

47 See, for example, "Armed Attacks, Peace Process, Elections, Unemployment," CPRS Polls, Survey Research Unit, 1996; "Armed Attacks, Palestinian-Jordanian Relations, Elections, and Other Issues of Concern," CPRS Polls, Survey Research Unit, 1995. http://www.pcpsr .org/survey/cprspolls/95/poll19a.html.

48 Yifrah Zilberman, "Developments in Radical Islam in the Territories since 1967," in *Hatnuah Haleumit Hapalestinit: Meimut Lehashlama?*, ed. Moshe Maoz and B. Z. Kedar (Tel Aviv: Ministry of Defense, 1996), 325–31.

49 Yezid Sayigh, *Armed Struggle and the Search for a State: The Palestinian National Movement, 1947–1993* (New York : Oxford University Press, 1997), 627.

50 Aaron Klein, *Striking Back: The 1972 Munich Olympics Massacre and Israel's Deadly Response* (New York: Random House, 2005), 227; Joel Greenberg, "Islamic Group Vows Revenge for Slaying of Its Leader," *New York Times*, October 30, 1995.

51 *United States of America v. Sami Amin Al-Arian, Ramadan Abduallah Shallah, Bashir Musa Mohammad Nafi, Sameeh Hammoudeh, Muhammed Tasir Hassan Al-Khatib, Abd Al-Aziz Awda, Ghassan Zayed Ballut, Hatim Naji Fariz*, paragraphs 27–29.

52 Ze'ev Schiff, "The Islamic Jihad Receives Additional Payment from Iran for Each Attack," *Ha'aretz*, July 31, 1997.

53 Martin Indyk, *Innocent Abroad: An Intimate Account of American Peace Diplomacy in the Middle East* (New York: Simon & Schuster, 2009), 176.
54 Gideon Levy, "They Won't Allow Us Not to Know," *Haaretz*, December 3, 2009, www.haaretz.com/hasen/spages/1130951.html. B'Tselem is the Israeli human rights organization.
55 Amnesty International, "Palestinian Authority: Prolonged Political Detention, Torture, and Unfair Trials," AI Index MDE 15/68/96 (1996).
56 Boaz Ganor, *The Counter-Terrorism Puzzle: A Guide for Decision Makers* (New Brunswick, N.J.: Transaction Publishers, 2005), 54.
57 *U.S. v. HLF, et al.*, Government Exhibit 016–0053, p. 4.
58 "Hamas Reportedly Agrees to Suspend Attacks against Israel," *Deutsche Presse-Agentur*, December 24, 1995.
59 Tahir Shuraytah, "Interview with Khalid Mash'al," *Al-Quds*, December 30, 1995.
60 Boaz Ganor, "Israel, Hamas and Fatah," in Robert J. Art and Louise Richardson, eds., *Democracy and Counterterrorism: Lessons from the Past* (Washington, DC: United States Institute of Peace, 2007), 271; "Oslo Is dead," *Washington Times*, March 25, 1996.
61 Moshe Yaalon, *Lessons from the Palestinian 'War' against Israel* (Washington, DC: Washington Institute for Near East Policy, 2007), 4.
62 Hass, *Drinking the Sea at Gaza*, 91–93.
63 Chehab, *Inside Hamas*, 49.
64 Quoted in ibid., 125.
65 Interview with Palestinian chief of intelligence Maj. Gen. Amin al-Hindi, *Al-Majallah*, November 30, 1996.
66 Khalil Shikaki, "Palestinians Divided," *Foreign Affairs* (81)1 (2002), 89–105.
67 Gershom Gorenberg, "The Collaborator", *New York Times Magazine*, August 18, 2002, 80.
68 Shai Fogelman, "Present Trauma," *Israel News*, April 3, 2010.
69 Quoted in Tamimi, *Hamas*, 189.
70 Hussein Hijazi, "Hamas: Waiting for Secular Nationalism to Self Destruct; An Interview with Mahmud Zahhar," *Journal of Palestine Studies*, 24 (3) (Spring 1995), 81–88.
71 Levitt, *Negotiating under Fire*, 130.
72 U.S. State Department, "Report on PLO Compliance," 2001.
73 Quoted in Akiva Eldar, "The Road to Hell," *Haaretz*, June 21, 2008.
74 Rabbani, "A Hamas Perspective on the Movement's Evolving Role," 62.
75 Muhammad al-Makki Ahmad, "Hamas's Shaykh Yasin Offers Israel Conditional Truce," *al-Hayah*, April 25, 1998.
76 Israel Ministry of Foreign Affairs, "Terrorism Deaths in Israel, 1920–1999."
77 See B'tselem, "1987–1997, a Decade of Human Rights Violations," *B'tselem*, January 1998.
78 Chehab, *Inside Hamas*, 52; Harel and Issacharoff, *The Seventh War*, 78–84.
79 Muslih, *The Foreign Policy of Hamas*, 25–27.
80 Isabel Kershner, *Barrier: The Seam of the Israeli-Palestinian Conflict* (New York: Palgrave Macmillan, 2005), 92.
81 U.S. State Department, "Report on PLO Compliance."
82 For a review, see a U.S. Congressional Research Service report on this issue: Aaron D. Pina, "Palestinian Education and the Debate over

Textbooks," Washington, DC, Congressional Research Service, 2005, 9. Ironically the textbooks were from Jordan and Egypt, the very nations that had signed peace deals with Israel. Textbooks produced by the PA did not have inflammatory material, though they were heavy on Palestinian nationalism. Fearing that PA-authored books would foster unwanted Palestinian nationalism, Israel allowed the more offensive Jordanian ones to be used in East Jerusalem schools, where it held sway, but refused to allow the Palestinian books. See Nathan Brown, "Democracy, History and the Contest over the Palestinian Curriculum," Prepared for Adam Institute, November 2001, http://www.mideastweb .org/Democracy%20in%20the%20Palestinian%20Curriculum.pdf.

83 Memorandum of the Hamas Political Bureau, prepared in the late 1990s in Amman, reprinted in Tamimi, *Hamas.*

84 Amos Malka, "Israel and Asymmetrical Deterrence," *Comparative Strategy* 27, no. 1 (2008): 8.

85 Rabbani, "A Hamas Perspective on the Movement's Evolving Role," 61.

CHAPTER 7

1 Ehud Barak, "Speech by Prime Minister Barak on the Presentation of the Government to the Knesset July 6, 1999," Jerusalem, 1999, http:// www.mfa.gov.il/mfa/government/speeches%20by%20israeli%20 leaders/1999/pm%20barak-%20presentation%20of%20 government%20-%20july%206-%20199. For his comments on Palestinian suffering, see also http://jpost.com/1999/Supplements/ Elections99/articles/Article-0.shtml.

2 "Arafat Says Accord Signing 'Beginning of a New Phase,'" *BBC Summary of World Broadcasts,* September 6, 1999.

3 For background, this chapter draws on William B. Quandt, *Peace Process: American Diplomacy and the Arab-Israeli Conflict since 1967* (Washington, DC: Brookings Institution Press, 2005); Martin Indyk, *Innocent Abroad: An Intimate Account of American Peace Diplomacy in the Middle East* (New York: Simon & Schuster, 2009); Dennis Ross, *The Missing Peace: The Inside Story of the Fight for Middle East Peace* (New York: Farrar, 2004); Amos Harel and Avi Isacharoff, *Ha-milḥamah Hasbiy'iyt: 'Eikh Nitzakhnu wa-Lamah Hifsadnu ba-Milḥamah 'im ha-Falasṭinim* (Tel Aviv: Sifrei Hemed, 2005). The latter title is also referred to as *The Seventh War.*

4 Jane Perlez, "U.S. Envoy Recalls the Day Pandora's Box Wouldn't Shut," *New York Times,* January 29, 2001.

5 Like so much else that is hotly contested in the Middle East, the Israelis actually put the outbreak of the Second Intifada one day earlier, on September 27, 2000, when an Israeli soldier was killed in Gaza.

6 John F. Mahoney, "Israel's Anti-Civilian Weapons," *The Link* 34(1) (2001): 1–13.

7 Axel Hadenius and Jan Teorell, "Elections as Levers of Democracy? A Global Inquiry," in *Democratization by Elections: A New Mode of Transition?,* ed. Staffan I. Lindberg (Baltimore: Johns Hopkins University Press, 2009). The Palestinian Center for Human Rights lists 2,828 Palestinians killed from the outbreak of the Second Intifada through the end of

January 2005, excluding Palestinians killed during armed attacks against Israelis ("Statistics," 2009).

8 Moti Basok, "Taktzov Ha-Bitachon Hu 50 Miliard Shkaliam, Aval Alut Ha-Bitachon Megia Le- 120 Milaird Sh'" (The Defense Budget Is 50 Billion, but the Defense Spending Is as High as 120 Billion Shekels), *Haaretz*, December 14, 2006.

9 See "Land Grab: Israel's Settlement Policy in the West Bank," B'Tselem, 2002. http://www.btselem.org/English/Publications/Summaries/200205_Land_Grab.asp.

10 "Report of the Sharm El-Sheikh Fact-Finding Committee ('the Mitchell Report')," 9. http://www.consilium.europa.eu/ueDocs/cms_Data/docs/pressdata/EN/reports/ACF319.pdf.

11 Robert Malley and Hussein Agha, "The Palestinian-Israeli Camp David Negotiations and Beyond," *Journal of Palestine Studies* 31(1) (2001): 62–85.

12 Aaron David Miller, *The Much too Promised Land: America's Elusive Search for Arab-Israeli Peace* (New York: Bantam Books, 2008), 269.

13 Ehud Barak, "The Myths Spread about Camp David Are Baseless," in *The Camp David Summit—What Went Wrong?*, ed. Shimon Shamir and Bruce Maddy-Weitzman (Brighton, England: Sussex Academic Press, 2005), 119; Ari Shavit, "Eyes Wide Shut," *Haaretz Magazine*, September 6, 2002.

14 Mohammad Dajani, "The 'Blaming Game' Is Wrong," in *The Camp David Summit—What Went Wrong?*, ed. Shimon Shamir and Bruce Maddy-Weitzman (Brighton, Portland: Sussex Academic Press, 2005), 29.

15 "Camp David Summit, Chances for Reconciliation and Lasting Peace, Violence and Confrontations, Hierarchies of Priorities, and Domestic Politics," in *Public Opinion Poll*, PSR -Survey Research Unit, 2000. http://www.pcpsr.org/survey/polls/2000/p1a.html.

16 Mouin Rabbani, "A Hamas Perspective on the Movement's Evolving Role: An Interview with Khalid Mishal: Part II," *Journal of Palestine Studies* 37(4) (2008), 64.

17 R. Kim Cragin, "Palestinian Resistance through the Eyes of Hamas," (PhD dissertation, Clare College, Cambridge, 2008), 172.

18 William J. Clinton, "President William J. Clinton, Statement on the Middle East Peace Talks at Camp David. The White House, the James S. Brady Press Briefing Room," Washington, DC, 2000. http://avalon.law.yale.edu/21st_century/mid027.asp.

19 Krishnadev Calamur, "U.S. Hopes Arafat Death Will Lead to Peace," UPI, November 11, 2004.

20 Ron Pundak, "From Oslo to Taba: What Went Wrong?" *Survival* 43(3) (2001): 31–32.

21 Quoted in Jeremy Pressman, "The Second Intifada: Background and Causes of the Israeli-Palestinian Conflict," *Journal of Conflict Studies* 22(2) (2003): 28; Graham Usher, "Facing Defeat: The Intifada Two Years On," *Journal of Palestine Studies* 32(2) (2003): 24.

22 Quoted in R. Kim Cragin, "Hamas and the Peace Process," unpublished paper (n.d.), 17.

23 Quoted in Sergio Catignani, *Israeli Counter-Insurgency and the Intifadas: Dilemmas of a Conventional Army* (London, New York: Routledge, 2008),102.

24 Giora Eiland, "The IDF in the Second Intifada," *Strategic Assessment* 13(3) (2010): 28.
25 Bassam Abu Sharif, *Arafat and the Dream of Palestine: An Insider's Account* (New York: Palgrave Macmillan, 2009), 4, 7.
26 Robert Malley, "The Arafat Enigma," *Washington Post*, November 7, 2004.
27 Indyk, *Innocent Abroad*, 345.
28 Pressman, "The Second Intifada," 117.
29 Quoted in ibid., 116; Amos Harel and Avi Issacharoff, *The Seventh War* (Tel Aviv: Yedioth Ahronot, 2004), 90–93.
30 Moshe Yaalon, "Lessons from the Palestinian 'War' against Israel," *Policy Focus* 64 (2007): 2.
31 "Report of the Sharm El-Sheikh Fact-Finding Committee ('the Mitchell Report')," 7.
32 Ari Shavit, "The Enemy Within," *Haaretz Friday Magazine*, August 30, 2002.
33 Indyk, *Innocent Abroad*, 123.
34 Quoted in ibid., 14.
35 Quoted in Barry Rubin and Judith Colp Rubin, *Yasir Arafat: A Political Biography* (New York: Oxford University Press, 2005), 232.
36 See Amos Gilad, "An Evaluation of Developments in the Israeli-Palestinian Context," in Yaacov Bar-Simon-Tov, ed. *As the Generals See It: The Collapse of the Oslo Process and the Violent Israeli-Palestinian Conflict* (Jerusalem: Leonard Davis Institute, 2004), 47–58.
37 Ruti Zooaretz, "Arafat Kvar Lo Matzhik" (Arafat Is Not Funny Any More), *Pnai Plus*, April 16, 2002.
38 Nahum Barnea, "Lirkod Im Arafat" (Dancing with Arafat), *Ha-'Ayin Ha-Shvi'ait*, January 1, 2002.
39 Na'ama Nehushtan and Ahmad Tibi, "Bleiser," *Ynet*, April 13, 2009.
40 Nadia Matar, December 28, 1997, quoted in "Ha-Radio Ha-Pirati Be-Yisrael: Tikshoret Alternativit Ao Sakana La-Democratia" (The Pirate Radio in Israel: Alternative Media or a Danger to Democracy), Keshev, the Center for Protection of Democracy in Israel, 1998, http://www.keshev.org.il/site/FullNews.asp?NewsID=24&CategoryID=14.
41 To see the puppet, go to www.youtube.com/watch?v=sW_LFi5tXuo.
42 Usher, "Facing Defeat," 25.
43 U.S. State Department, "Report on PLO Compliance," 2001.
44 Indyk, *Innocent Abroad*, 342.
45 "Report of the Sharm El-Sheikh Fact-Finding Committee ('the Mitchell Report')," 7.
46 "Israel Steps Up Assault: U.S. Envoy Sees Arafat; Suspect in Passover Blast Is Slain," *Boston Globe*, April 6, 2002.
47 Quoted in Indyk, *Innocent Abroad*, 352–53.
48 "Clinton Minutes," *Haaretz*, December 31, 2000.
49 "Former Israeli Shin Bet Head Speaks Up for Peace," *Le Monde*, December 22, 2001.
50 "Report of the Sharm El-Sheikh Fact-Finding Committee ('the Mitchell Report')," 7.

51 See, for example, many of the Israeli viewpoints in Shamir and Maddy-Weitzman, *The Camp David Summit*.

CHAPTER 8

1 Akiva Eldar, "Popular Misconceptions," *Haaretz*, June 11, 2004. The actual million bullets figure may be wrong. Ya'alon notes that when Amos Malka, as head of military intelligence, visited the IDF's Central Command, which oversees the West Bank, he was told they needed a million bullets total, not that they shot a million. An Israeli official points out that if you assume that bullets have even a one in twenty chance of hitting a person, then there should have been thousands killed; so if that many bullets were fired, most were fired into the air. Moshe Yaalon, *Derech Aroka Ktzara* (The Long Short Way) (Tel Aviv: Sifrei Hemed, 2008), 120–21.

2 For background, this chapter draws on Amos Harel and Avi Isacharoff, *Ha-milḥamah Hasbiy'iyt* ("The Seventh War"): *'Eikh Nitzakhnu wa-Lamah Hifsadnu ba-Milḥamah 'im ha-Falaṣtinim* (Tel Aviv: Sifrei Hemed, 2005); Yaalon, *Derech Aroka Ktzara*; Martin Indyk, *Innocent Abroad: An Intimate Account of American Peace Diplomacy in the Middle East* (New York: Simon & Schuster, 2009); Dennis Ross, *The Missing Peace: The Inside Story of the Fight for Middle East Peace* (New York: Farrar, 2004).

3 Eiland, "The IDF in the Second Intifada," 28.

4 Quoted in Harel and Isacharoff, *Ha-milḥamah Hasbiy'iyt* ("The Seventh War"), 46–47.

5 Quoted in Jeremy Pressman, "The Second Intifada: Background and Causes of the Israeli-Palestinian Conflict," *Journal of Conflict Studies* 22(2) (2003): 123.

6 "Report of the Sharm El-Sheikh Fact-Finding Committee ("the Mitchell Report")," (2001), 7, http://www.consilium.europa.eu/ueDocs/cms_Data/docs/pressdata/EN/reports/ACF319.pdf.

7 Ibid., 18–19, emphasis in the original.

8 Jeremy Pressman, "Israeli Unilateralism and Israeli-Palestinian Relations, 2001–2006," *International Studies Perspectives* 7 (2006): 361.

9 Eiland, "The IDF in the Second Intifada," 29.

10 Raviv Drucker and Ofer Shelah, *Boomerang* (Jerusalem: Keter, 2005), 55.

11 Ibid., 56.

12 Eiland, "The IDF in the Second Intifada," 28.

13 Yaalon, *Derech Arroka Ktzara*, 107.

14 Harel and Isacharoff, *Ha-milḥamah Hasbiy'iyt* ("The Seventh War"), 35.

15 Raviv Drucker; Ofer Shelah, *Boomerang: Kishalon ha-Manhigut ba-Intifada ha-Shniyah* (Jerusalem: Kesher, 2006), 30–31; Yoram Peri, *Generals in the Cabinet Room: How the Military Shapes Israeli Policy* (Washington, DC: United States Institute of Peace Press, 2006), 104–7, quote on 106.

16 Amos Malka, "Israel and Asymmetrical Deterrence," *Comparative Strategy* 27(1) (2008): 13.

17 I would like to thank Shay Hazkani for bringing this to my attention.

18 Wendy Pearlman, *Occupied Voices* (New York: Thunder's Mouth Press, 2003), 84.

19 Hamas communiqué, quoted in R. Kim Cragin, "Palestinian Resistance through the Eyes of Hamas " (PhD dissertation, Clare College, Cambridge, 2008), 176.

20 Eiland, "The IDF in the Second Intifada," 30.

21 See James Fallows, "Who Shot at Mohammed Al-Dura?," *Atlantic Monthly* 291(5) (2003): 49–56.

22 Harel and Isacharoff, *Ha-milḥamah Hasbiy'iyt* ("The Seventh War"), 38–39.

23 Moshe Yaalon, "Lessons from the Palestinian 'War' against Israel," *Policy Focus* 64 (2007): 17.

24 Theodor Or, "The Report by the State Commission of Inquiry into the Events of October 2000," *Israel Studies* 11, no. 2 (2006): 38.

25 See *MK Dr. Azmi Bishara v. 1. Attorney-General; 2. Knesset; 3. Nazareth Magistrates Court*, 47 (2006).

26 Jonathan Lis and Ilan Shahar, "Ex-Mk Bishara Suspected of Treason, Passing Data to Hezbollah," *Haaretz*, May 5, 2007.

27 Yosef Goell, "No Longer a Loyal Minority," *Jerusalem Post*, October 10, 2000.

28 For a review, see Rekhess, "The Arabs of Israel after Oslo: Localization of a the National Struggle," *Israel Studies* 7(3) (2002): 1–44.

29 See Washington Institute for Near East Policy, www.washingtoninstitute .org/documents/41ee9f4795e21.pdf.

30 Ari Shavit, "Interview with Ariel Sharon," *Haaretz*, April 12, 2001; Uri Dan, *Ariel Sharon: An Intimate Portrait* (New York: Palgrave Macmillan, 2006), 173.

31 Indyk, *Innocent Abroad,* 379.

32 Peri, *Generals in the Cabinet Room,* 112.

33 Quoted in U.S. State Department, "Report on PLO Compliance," 2001.

34 Quoted in Cragin, *Palestinian Resistance,* 185.

35 John Kampfner and Stuart Tanner, "The Ugly War: Children of Vengeance," *BBC Correspondent*, February 22, 2002.

36 Yoram Schweitzer, "Palestinian Istishhadia: A Developing Instrument," *Studies in Conflict and Terrorism* 30(8) (2007): 677.

37 Cragin, *Palestinian Resistance,* 187.

38 Nichole Argo, "Why Fight? Examining Self-Interested Versus Communally-Oriented Motivations in Palestinian Resistance and Rebellion," *Security Studies* 18 (2009): 651–680.

39 Intelligence and Terrorism Information Center at the Center for Special Studies, "Palestinian Authority Support of Hamas Suicide Terrorism," October 11, 2004, www.dailyalert.org/archive/2004-10/2004-10-11.html.

40 "On the Edge in the South," *Haaretz*, February 28, 2008.

41 Aaron David Miller, *The Much too Promised Land: America's Elusive Search for Arab-Israeli Peace* (New York: Bantam Books, 2008), 332.

42 Azzam Tamimi, *Hamas: A History from Within* (Northampton, MA: Olive Branch Press, 2007), 201.

43 Quoted in Isabel Kershner, *Barrier: The Seam of the Israeli-Palestinian Conflict* (New York: Palgrave Macmillan, 2005), 167.

44 Kampfner and Tanner, "The Ugly War: Children of Vengeance."

45 Graham Usher, "Facing Defeat: The Intifada Two Years On," *Journal of Palestine Studies* 32(2) (2003): 21–40.

46 Tamimi, *Hamas.*

CHAPTER 9

1 Shaul Shay, "'Ebb and Flow' versus 'the Al-Aqsa Intifada': The Israeli Palestinian Conflict, 2000–2003," in *Never-Ending Conflict: Israeli Military History*, ed. Mordechai Bar-On (Mechanicsburg, PA: Stackpole Books, 2006), 234; Sergio Catignani, *Israeli Counter-Insurgency and the Intifadas: Dilemmas of a Conventional Army* (London: Routledge, 2008); Graham Usher, "Facing Defeat: The Intifada Two Years On," *Journal of Palestine Studies* 32(2) (2003): 30.

2 Quoted in R. Kim Cragin, "Palestinian Resistance through the Eyes of Hamas " (PhD dissertation, Clare College, Cambridge, 2008), 177.

3 Hamas official quoted in ibid., 180–83.

4 Ben Kaspit, "Acholnu Limnoa Et Ha-Retzach" (We Could Have Prevented the Murder), *Ma'ariv*, October 31, 2003.

5 Yoav Limor, "Yoter Midai Meauvtechim, Pachot Midai Meavtechim" (Too Many Protected, Not Enough Protectors), *Ma'ariv*, November 9, 2001.

6 Israeli Knesset, Subcommittee for Intelligence and Secret Services, "Din Ve-Heashbon Be-Inyan Retzach Ha-Sar Rehavam Zeevi Zal" (An Account of the Murder of Minister Rehavam Zeevi), 2002; Menahem Rahat, "Ha-Kishalon Ha-Gadol Sheli—Retzah Gandi" (Dichter: My Biggest Failure—Gandi's Murder), *NRG*, May 4, 2005.

7 James Bennet, "Seized Arms Would Have Vastly Extended Arafat Arsenal," *New York Times*, January 12, 2002.

8 Uri Dan, *Ariel Sharon: An Intimate Portrait* (New York: Palgrave Macmillan, 2006), 198.

9 Aaron David Miller, *The Much too Promised Land: America's Elusive Search for Arab-Israeli Peace* (New York: Bantam Books, 2008), 341.

10 Amos Harel and Avi Isacharoff, *Ha-milḥamah Hasbiy'iyt* ("The Seventh War"): 'Eikh Nitzakhnu wa-Lamah Hifsadnu ba-Milḥamah 'im ha-Falaṣtinim (Tel Aviv: Sifrei Hemed, 2005),180–3.

11 Raviv Drucker and Ofer Shelah, *Boomerang* (Jerusalem: Keter, 2005), 166–74.

12 Yigal Sarna, interview with Marwan Barghouti, *Yedioth Ahronoth*, February 15, 2002, reprinted in Drucker and Shelah, *Boomerang*, 172.

13 Moshe Yaalon, *Derech Arooka Ktzara* (The Long Short Way) (Tel Aviv: Sifrei Hemed, 2008), 124.

14 *State of Israel vs. Marwan Barghouti—Ruling by Judge Zvi Gurfinkel*, 2002.

15 Rashid Khalidi, *The Iron Cage: The Story of the Palestinian Struggle for Statehood* (Boston: Beacon Press, 2006), 179.

16 Eiland, "The IDF in the Second Intifada," 31.

17 Harel and Isacharoff, *Ha-milḥamah Hasbiy'iyt* ("The Seventh War"), 186.

18 Miller, *The Much Too Promised Land*, 339.

19 PSR Survey Research Unit, "Results of Poll #6," 2002. http://www.pcpsr.org/survey/polls/2002/p6a.html.

20 PSR Survey Research Unit, "Palestinians Support the Ceasefire, Negotiations and Reconciliation between the Two Peoples but a Majority Opposes Arrests and Believe That Armed Confrontations Have Helped Achieve National Rights," Public Opinion Poll #3, 2001, http://www.pcpsr.org/survey/polls/2001/p3a.html.

21 John Kampfner and Stuart Tanner, "The Ugly War: Children of Vengeance," *BBC Correspondent*, February 22, 2002.

22 Matthew Levitt, *Hamas: Politics, Charity, and Terrorism in the Service of Jihad* (New Haven: Yale University Press, 2006), 181–88.

23 International Crisis Group, "Inside Gaza: The Challenge of Clans and Families," 2007, 3, http://www.prospectsforpeace.com/Resources/ICG_Report_inside_gaza___the_challenge_of_clans_and_families.pdf.

24 Kampfner and Tanner, "The Ugly War."

25 Cragin, *Palestinian Resistance*, 180.

26 "PA Security Office 'Gone Underground' for Fear of Hamas Retaliation," *Jerusalem Post*, October 9, 2002.

27 Harel and Isacharoff, *Ha-milḥamah Hasbiy'iyt* ("The Seventh War"), 135–42.

28 Ari Shavit, "The Enemy Within," *Haaretz Friday Magazine*, August 30, 2002.

29 Quoted in Ross Dunn, "Sharon Vows to Hit Palestinians Until It Is 'Very Painful,'" *Sydney Morning Herald*, March 6, 2002.

CHAPTER 10

1 Uzi Benziman, "A Breaking Point," *Haaretz*, March 29, 2002.

2 For background, this chapter draws on Amos Harel and Avi Isacharoff, *Ha-milḥamah Hasbiy'iyt* ("The Seventh War"): *'Eikh Nitzakhnu wa-Lamah Hifsadnu ba-Milḥamah 'im ha-Falaṣtinim* (Tel Aviv: Sifrei Hemed, 2005); Moshe Yaalon, *Derech Arooka Ktzara* (The Long Short Way) (Tel Aviv: Sifrei Hemed, 2008); Ofer Segal, "Az-K'ariel, 'Homat Magen' Sheli" (My Defensive Shield: Fighting in Jenin 2002), IDF Ministry of Defense Publishing House, 2006.

3 IDF, "Geut Va-Shefel—Sikum Netuney Shnat 2004 Ve-Hashva'aa Rav Shnatit" (Ebb and Flow—2004 Year Summary and Perennial Comparison), www1.idf.il/SIP_STORAGE/DOVER/files/4/37604.pdf.

4 Shin Bet, "Distribution of Fatalities from Palestinian-Based Terrorism in the 2nd Intifadah," 2009, http://www.shabak.gov.il/SiteCollectionImages/english/TerrorInfo/KReport130809_en.pdf.

5 Shin Bet, "Distribution of Fatalities from Palestinian-Based Terrorism in the 2nd Intifadah."

6 "PM Sharon's Address to the Knesset," April 8, 2002, www.mfa.gov.il/MFA/Government/Speeches%20by%20Israeli%20leaders/2002/PM%20Sharon-s%20Address%20to%20the%20Knesset%20-%20 8-Apr-2002.

7 Glenn Frankel, "Israelis' Hope for the Future Yields to Fear of the Past; Military Action Nonetheless Forges New Unity," *Washington Post*, April 7, 2002.

8 James Bennet, "Mideast Turmoil: The Overview: U.N. Chief Tells Israel It Must End 'Illegal Occupation,'" *New York Times*, March 13, 2000.

9 Quoted in Sergio Catignani, *Israeli Counter-Insurgency and the Intifadas: Dilemmas of a Conventional Army* (London, New York: Routledge, 2008), 109.

10 Quoted in Dominic Allan, "The Dirty War: Israel Undercover," BBC, Sunday 17 February 2002.

11 Raviv Drucker and Ofer Shelah, *Boomerang* (Jerusalem: Keter, 2005), 156–157.

12 United Nations Fact Finding Mission on the Gaza Conflict (The "Goldstone Report"), "Human Rights in Palestine and Other Occupied Arab Territories," 51, www2.ohchr.org/english/bodies/hrcouncil/docs/12session/a-hrc-12-48.pdf.

13 Palestinian accounts differ greatly on the number of PIJ fighters who were in the Jenin refugee camp as the IDF went in. Thabet Mardawi, who headed the PIJ effort in Jenin, claimed to have one hundred members; Bassam Al-Sa'aadi, another PIJ commander, claims the number is 250. The UN estimate is two hundred armed men. "UN Report on the Incident in Jenin," paragraph 45, www.qudsway.com/Links/Jehad/9/Html_Jehad9/9jihh3.htm; www.amin.org/news/issa_sharabati/2002/apr/apr29.html; Ghasan Nazal, *mukhïm Jinin—Astura hazat al-'ialam* (Aman, 2002), 19–20 in Yonatan Dahoach-Halevi, "Ha-Krav Be-Machane Ha-Plitim Be-Jenin—Nekudat Ha-Mabat Ha-Falastinit" (The Battle in the Jenin Refugee Camp—The Palestinian Point of View), 2003, www.terrorism-info.org.il/malam_multimedia/html/final/sp/jenin/jen_ys.htm.

14 Isabel Kerschner, "Palestinians Serenade Survivors in Israel," *New York Times*, March 25, 2009.

15 John Kampfner and Stuart Tanner, "The Ugly War: Children of Vengeance," BBC Correspondent, February 22, 2002.

16 Segal, "Az-K'ariel, 'Homat Magen' Sheli," 73.

17 Quoted in Graham Usher, "Palestine Militias Rising," *The Nation*, April 29, 2002, 5.

18 Barry Rubin and Judith Colp Rubin, *Yasir Arafat: A Political Biography* (New York: Oxford University Press, 2005), 6.

19 "UN Report on the Incident in Jenin," paragraph 51.

20 Segal, "Az-K'ariel, 'Homat Magen' Sheli," 17, 32, 34.

21 Matt Rees, "The Battle of Jenin," *Time*, May 5, 2002.

22 *Al-Hayat* (London), April 30, 2002, quoted in Dahoach-Halevi, *Ha-Krav Be-Machane Ha-Plitim Be-Jenin*.

23 Middle East Media Research Institute, "The Palestinian Account of the Battle of Jenin," 2002, http://www.freerepublic.com/focus/news/672071/posts.

24 Jonathan Cook, "The 'Engineer,'" *Al-Ahram Weekly*, April 18–24, 2002, http://weekly.ahram.org.eg/2002/582/6inv2.htm; Dahoach-Halevi, *Ha-Krav Be-Machane Ha-Plitim Be-Jenin*.

25 Dahoach-Halevi, *Ha-Krav Be-Machane Ha-Plitim Be-Jenin*.

26 Cook, "The 'Engineer'"; www.ezzedeen.net/Chat/htm/hawar01_04_02_1.htm; Omar Sa'adä, *Mukhïm Jinin al-majzara wa al-sumud* (Jenin Refugee Camp: The Massacre and the Steadfast) (Bisan, April 2002), quoted in Dahoach-Halevi, *Ha-Krav Be-Machane Ha-Plitim Be-Jenin*.

27 Ohad Hemo, Shani Haziza, and Li Bar-Leval, *Sheva Shanim Aharei—Tmunot Ha-Krav Hakashe Be-Jenin Nechsafot* (Seven Years Later—The Harsh Pictures of the Jenin Battle Are Revealed), Channel 10 News, (Channel 10 News (TV) Saturday Newscast, 2009).

28 Segal, "Az-K'ariel, 'Homat Magen' Sheli," 56–62.

29 Ibid., 12; "Tachkir Tzahal: Magad Hizhir Mi-Maarav Erev Ha-Krav Be-Jenin" (IDF Investigation: A Battalion Commander Warned of an Ambush the Night before the Battle), *Haaretz Online*, August 26, 2002, http://news.walla.co.il/?w=/0/273394&tb=/i/636637.
30 Quoted in Dahoach-Halevi, *Ha-Krav Be-Machane Ha-Plitim Be-Jenin*.
31 Harel and Isacharoff, *Ha-milḥamah Hasbiy'iyt* ("The Seventh War"), 256.
32 Segal, "Az-K'ariel, 'Homat Magen' Sheli," 75.
33 Segal, "Az-K'ariel, 'Homat Magen' Sheli," 51–52.
34 Rees, "The Battle of Jenin."
35 Sa'adä, *Mukhïm Jinin al-majzara wa al-sumud*, 22, quoted in Dahoach-Halevi, *Ha-Krav Be-Machane Ha-Plitim Be-Jenin*.
36 Middle East Media Research Institute, "The Palestinian Account of the Battle of Jenin."
37 *Al-Intiqad* (Lebanon), September 27, 2002, quoted in http://news.walla.co.il/?w=/0/273394&tb=/i/636637.
38 Harel and Isacharoff, *Ha-milḥamah Hasbiy'iyt* ("The Seventh War"),33.
39 See *Adalah v. GOC Central Command*, 2005.
40 Segal, "Az-K'ariel, 'Homat Magen' Sheli," 74.
41 A Human Rights Watch official even went to Saudi Arabia to raise money, citing the group's tough criticism of Israel as a sales pitch. See Jeffrey Goldberg, "Fundraising Corruption at Human Rights Watch," *The Atlantic*, July 15, 2009.
42 *Geut Va-Shefel*.
43 "UN Report on the Incident in Jenin," Report of the Secretary-General prepared pursuant to General Assembly resolution ES-10/10, June 30, 2002, paragraphs 30, 37(a).
44 Clive Jones, "'One Size Fits All': Israel, Intelligence, and the Al-Aqsa Intifada," *Studies in Conflict and Terrorism* 26(4) (2003): 273–288.
45 Ed Blanche, "Israel Uses Intifada Informers to Abet Assassination Campaign," *Jane's Intelligence Review* 13 (2001): 22–24.
46 Graham Usher, "Facing Defeat: The Intifada Two Years On," *Journal of Palestine Studies* 32(2) (2003): 34.
47 Israel Security Agency, "Analysis of Attacks in the Last Decade 2000–2010," http://www.shabak.gov.il/English/EnTerrorData/decade/Fatalities/Pages/SuicideAttacks.aspx.
48 "UN Report on the Incident in Jenin," paragraphs 43, 77.
49 Jones, "'One Size Fits All,'" 280.
50 Harel and Isacharoff, *Ha-milḥamah Hasbiy'iyt* ("The Seventh War"). U.S. officials, however, tell me that Bush never received a formal assurance that Israel would not kill Arafat.
51 Quoted in Jones, "'One Size Fits All,'" 274.

CHAPTER 11

1 Fareed Zakaria, "Colin Powell's Humiliation: Bush Should Clearly Support His Secretary of State—Otherwise He Should Get a New One," *Newsweek*, April 29, 2002.

2 Uri Dan, *Ariel Sharon: An Intimate Portrait* (New York: Palgrave Macmillan, 2006), 227.

3 President George W. Bush, June 24, 2002. http://georgewbush-whitehouse.archives.gov/news/releases/2002/06/20020624-3.html.

4 Ari Shavit, "The Big Freeze," *Haaretz*, October 8, 2004.

5 Yoram Peri, *Generals in the Cabinet Room: How the Military Shapes Israeli Policy* (Washington, DC: United States Institute of Peace Press, 2006) 131; PSR–Survey Research Unit, "While Support for Abu Mazin Drops, Support for a Ceasefire Increases with a Majority Supporting Ending the Armed Intifada and Agreeing to a Mutual Recognition of Israel as the State of the Jewish People and Palestine as the State of the Palestinian People," Public Opinion Poll #8, 2003.

6 Office for the Coordination of Humanitarian Affairs, Occupied Palestinian Territory, "West Bank Movement and Access Update," June 2009, www.ochaopt.org/documents/ocha_opt_ movement_ access_2009_june_english.pdf (accessed August 12, 2009).

7 B'Tselem, "Restrictions on Movement: Information on Checkpoints and Roadblocks," www.btselem.org/english/Freedom_of_Movement/ Statistics.asp (accessed August 12, 2009).

8 Eiland, "The IDF in the Second Intifada," 33.

9 Breaking the Silence, "Testimonies—Checkpoints, to Straighten up the Line," www.breakingthesilence.org.il/testimonies_e.asp?cat=16 (accessed January 9, 2010).

10 Sergio Catignani, *Israeli Counter-Insurgency and the Intifadas: Dilemmas of a Conventional Army* (London, New York: Routledge, 2008), 117.

11 Amos Guiora, "Balancing IDF Checkpoints and International Law: Teaching the IDF Code of Conduct," *Jerusalem Issue Brief* 3(8) (2003), http://www.jcpa.org/brief/brief3-8.htm.

12 B'Tselem: The Israeli Information Center for Human Rights in the Occupied Territories, "Detainees and Prisoners: Statistics on Palestinians in the Custody of the Israeli Security Forces," www.btselem.org/ english/statistics/Detainees_and_Prisoners.asp (accessed August 11, 2009); B'Tselem, *Administrative Detention: Statistics on Administrative Detention*, www.btselem.org/english/Administrative_Detention/ Statistics.asp (accessed August 11, 2009).

13 B'Tselem figures for January 2010, www.btselem.org/english/ Administrative_Detention/Statistics.asp.

14 As quoted by Dvorah Chen, "Prosecuting Terrorists: A Look at the Israeli and American Experiences," remarks before the Washington Institute for Near East Policy, November 14, 2006, http://www .washingtoninstitute.org/templateC05.php?CID=2531

15 Boaz Ganor, "Israel, Hamas and Fatah," in Robert J. Art and Louise Richardson, eds., *Democracy and Counterterrorism: Lessons from the Past* (Washington, DC: United States Institute of Peace, 2007), 292.

16 *A. v. The State of Israel*, 5–6 (2008). The quote is from Dvorah Chen, "Prosecuting Accused Terrorists in a Free Society" (unpublished paper, 2008), 7.

17 Chen, "Prosecuting Accused Terrorists in a Free Society."

18 The case can be appealed to the Israeli Supreme Court. IDF commanders have also used an "assigned residence" power to move

individuals from their homes on the West Bank to the Gaza Strip, ostensibly in order to disrupt their links with local terrorist groups, though many believe the true purpose is revenge and to put pressure on the bombers' families. This power has not been used in recent years.

19 See Yesh Din–Volunteers for Human Rights, "Military Courts Project," www.yesh-din.org/site/index.php?page=militarycourts&lang=en (accessed January 9, 2010); Yesh Din, "Backyard Proceedings: The Implementation of Due Process Rights in the Military Courts in the Occupied Territories," Volunteers for Human Rights, 2007, http://www.yesh-din.org/userfiles/file/Reports-English/ BackyardProceedingsfullreportEng.pdf.

20 *State of Israel vs. Marwan Barghouti—Ruling by Judge Zvi Gurfinkel*, 3, 5 (2002).

21 Chen, "Prosecuting Accused Terrorists in a Free Society."

22 Saree Makdisi, *Palestine Inside Out: An Everyday Occupation* (New York: Norton, 2008), 48–49.

23 Amos Harel and Avi Isacharoff, *Ha-milḥamah Hasbiy'iyt* ("The Seventh War"): '*Eikh Nitzakhnu wa-Lamah Hifsadnu ba-Milḥamah 'im ha-Falaṣtinim* (Tel Aviv: Sifrei Hemed, 2005), 203.

24 "Soldiers' Testimonies from Hebron 2005–2007," 32, 41, http:// www.shovrimshtika.org/UserFiles/File//Shovrim_Shtika_English_ Int.pdf.

25 "Human Rights Watch, 'Promoting Impunity: The Israeli Military's Failure to Investigate Wrongdoing,'" *Journal of Palestine Studies* 35, no. 1 (2005): 2–4.

26 "Former Heads of Shin Bet Reflect on Israel's Present and Future," interview reprinted in *Journal of Palestine Studies*, November 14, 2003, 178.

27 Sharif Waked, "Chic Point: Fashion for Israeli Checkpoints," *Nafas Art Magazine*, March 2005, http://universes-in-universe.org/nafas/ articles/2005/waked (accessed January 9, 2010).

28 Amira Hass, "Life under Prohibition in Palestine," *Haaretz*, January 22, 2007.

29 B'Tselem, "Siege: Imposition of Siege," www.btselem.org/english/ Freedom_of_Movement/Siege.asp (accessed August 12, 2009).

30 B'Tselem, "Closure: Figures on Comprehensive Closure Days," www.btselem.org/english/Freedom_of_Movement/Siege_figures.asp (accessed August 12, 2009).

31 B'Tselem, "Restrictions on Movement: Effect of Restrictions on the Economy," www.btselem.org/english/Freedom_of_Movement/ Economy.asp (accessed August 12, 2009).

32 Amira Hass, "Israel's Closure Policy: An Ineffective Strategy of Containment and Repression," *Journal of Palestine Studies* 31(3) (2002): 6, 10.

33 Makdisi, *Palestine Inside Out*, 7.

34 Economic Monitoring Report to the Ad Hoc Liaison Committee, *Palestinian Economic Prospects: Gaza Recovery and West Bank Revival*, World Bank, June 8, 2009, http://siteresources.worldbank.org/ INTWESTBANKGAZA/Resources/AHLCJune09Reportfinal.pdf.

35 Chris McGreal, "Human-Bomb Mother Kills Four Israelis at Gaza Checkpoint," *Guardian*, January 15, 2004.

36 Shin Bet (ISA), "Exploiting Israel's Humanitarian Policies for Terror Activities," www.shabak.gov.il/SiteCollectionImages/english/TerrorInfo/‫ניצול-מריניות-הומניטרית-אנגלית‬.pdf.

37 Guiora, "Balancing IDF Checkpoints and International Law."

38 For other incidents from recent years of attempts to use hospitals as hideouts and storage places for weapons, see Shin Bet, *Exploiting Israel's Humanitarian Policies for Terror Activities*.

39 B'Tselem, "Palestinians Who Died Following an Infringement of the Right to Medical Treatment in the Occupied Territories," www.btselem. org/hebrew/statistics/casualties_data.asp?Category=21&region=TERacc essed (accessed August 11, 2009).

40 Makdisi, *Palestine Inside Out*, 49–50.

41 Central Bureau of Statistics, *Israel Statistical Yearbook*, cited in Yehezkel Lein, "Land Grab: Israel's Settlement Policy in the West Bank," (B'Tselem), http://www.nad-plo.org/nego/permanent/colonies/related/BLandGrab.pdf. This figure excludes East Jerusalem.

42 Chaim Levinson, "IDF: More Than 300,000 Settlers Live in the West Bank," *Haaretz*, July 27, 2009.

43 Israeli Committee Against House Demolitions, "Statistics on House Demolitions (1967–2010)," http://www.icahd.org/?page_id=5508. These figures exclude houses demolished because they lacked a permit or during a military operation. For similar figures see also Ron Dudai, "Through No Fault of Their Own: Punitive House Demolitions During the Al-Aqsa Intifada," *Human Rights Quarterly* 28, no. (3) (2006): 20.

44 Quoted in Dudai, "Through No Fault of Their Own," 20. This chapter is focused on home demolitions in the West Bank, as opposed to demolitions in Jerusalem, which were usually not tied to terrorism. Israeli authorities claim that Jerusalem demolitions occurred due to missing construction permits, while Palestinians contend this is a thin excuse for a land grab.

45 Quoted in Ibid., 5.

46 Dudai, "Through No Fault of Their Own," 8.

47 Quoted in ibid., 20.

48 Dudai, "Through No Fault of Their Own," 7.

49 Quoted in ibid., 33.

50 From *The Seventh War*, quoted in Dudai, "Through No Fault of Their Own," 58. See also Amos Harel, "IDF Panel Recommends Ending Punitive House Demolitions for Terrorists' Families," *Haaretz*, February 17, 2005.

51 Yaalon, "Lessons from the Palestinian 'War,'" 13; Dudai, "Through No Fault of Their Own."

52 Jeffrey Heller, "Israeli Justice Minister Yosef Lapid Compares Demolitions and Destruction of Palestinian Homes in Rafah Refugee Camp to Nazi Atrocities against Jews During the Holocaust," Reuters, May 23, 2004.

53 See Joseph Smith, "Rachel Corrie: Detailed Eyewitness Account, Remembrance, and Thoughts about the Future," *Electronic Intifada*, March 21, 2003, http://electronicintifada.net/v2/article1284.shtml.

54 "State: IDF Not to Blame for Activist Rachel Corrie's Death," *Haaretz*, March 25, 2010.

55 "Deportation: Statistics on Deportation," B'tselem, http://www.btselem .org/english/deportation/statistics.asp.

56 Makdisi, *Palestine Inside Out*, 12–23; B'Tselem, "Planning and Building," www.btselem.org/english/Punitive_Demolitions/Index.asp (accessed August 12, 2009).

57 Matthew Gutman, "Destruction, Constructively Speaking," *Jerusalem Post*, January 9, 2003.

58 Quoted in Laurie Copans, "Ex-Israeli Generals Denounce Checkpoints," *Associated Press*, February 19, 2008.

59 Assaf Moghadam, "Palestinian Suicide Terrorism in the Second Intifada: Motivations and Organizational Aspects," *Studies in Conflict and Terrorism* 26 (2003):65–92; Nichole Argo, "Why Fight? Examining Self-Interested versus Communally-Oriented Motivations in Palestinian Resistance and Rebellion," *Security Studies* 18 (2009): 661.

CHAPTER 12

1 I would like to thank Adam Stahl for providing me with this information regarding his conversation with a senior intelligence official. The final discussion between Stahl and me on this issue was on January 20, 2010.

2 Quoted in Ami Isseroff, "Killing Ahmed Yassin: What Is the Point?," *MideastWeb*, March 22, 2004; "Sheikh Yassin: Spiritual Figurehead," *BBC News*, March 22, 2004.

3 James Bennet, "Leader of Hamas Killed by Missile in Israeli Strike," *New York Times*, March 22, 2004.

4 "Kobi Ben-Simchon, Ha-Psicholog Tzvika Sela, Hosef Sihot Nefesh She-Arach Ba-Kele Im Samir Kuntar Ve-Ahmad Yasin" (Psychologist Tzvika Sela Revels Heart-to-Heart Talks He Had with Samir Kuntar and Ahmad Yasin), *Haaretz*, April 17, 2009.

5 'Ali Waked and Hanan Grinberg, "Yisrael hitnaksha be-manhig ha-hamasRantisi" (Israel Assassinated Hamas Leader Rantisi), *Ynet*, April 18, 2004, www.ynet.co.il/articles/0,7340,L-2903854,00.html.

6 See his speech at the 2005 Sharm al-Sheikh summit, http://unispal .un.org/UNISPAL.NSF/0/082617960CDB7E168525707B0046A4C4.

7 Steven Erlanger, "Israelis and Palestinians Look to a Quiet Gaza and a Cease-Fire," *New York Times*, January 24, 2005; Steven Erlanger, "2 Sides in Mideast Resume Public Meetings," *New York Times*, January 27, 2005; Azzam Tamimi, *Hamas: A History from Within* (Northampton, MA: Olive Branch Press, 2007), 211.

8 Intelligence and Terrorism Information Center at Israel Intelligence Heritage and Commemoration Center, "The Nature and Extent of Palestinian Terrorism, 2006," March 1, 2007, www.mfa.gov.il/MFA/ Terrorism-+Obstacle+to+Peace/Palestinian+terror+since+2000/ Palestinian+terrorism+2006.htm (accessed August 12, 2009).

9 Quoted in Officer.com, "Ex-Shin Bet Chief: Israeli Assassination Policy Led to Period of Calm," June 3, 2005, http://forums.officer.com/ forums/showthread.php?t=31719.at (accessed January 10, 2010).

10 John Kampfner and Stuart Tanner, "The Ugly War: Children of Vengeance," BBC Correspondent, February 22, 2002.

11 International Crisis Group, "Ruling Palestine II," July 17, 2008, 6–8 www.crisisgroup.org/.../Israel%20Palestine/79_ruling_palestine_ii___the_west_bank_model.ashx.

12 "Heskem Ha-Mevukashim Nahal Hatzlaha" (The Wanted Pact Was Successful), *NRG*, February 10, 2002.

13 "divuh: mista'arvim patz'au mevukash sh-hefer heskem hanina she-nechtam aito" (Report: mista'arvim injured a wanted militant that broke the amnesty agreement he signed), *Haaretz*, 11 October 2007, http://haaretz.com/hasite/spages/911399.html?more=1; see also International Crisis Group, "Palestinian Security Reform under Occupation," September 2010, 6.

14 As quoted in International Crisis Group, "Ruling Palestine II," 16.

15 Jeroen Gunning, *Hamas in Politics: Democracy, Religion, Violence* (New York: Columbia University Press, 2008), 230.

16 Amos Harel and Avi Isacharoff, *Ha-milḥamah Hasbiy'iyt* ("The Seventh War")*: 'Eikh Nitzakhnu wa-Lamah Hifsadnu ba-Milḥamah 'im ha-Falaṣtinim* (Tel Aviv: Sifrei Hemed, 2005), chapter 15. Inevitably rumors swirled that the Mossad had poisoned Arafat, but a subsequent medical investigation found no credible evidence of this, though the precise cause of death was disputed.

17 Graham Usher, "Not Red Indians," *Al-Ahram Weekly*, November 4–10, 2004.

18 From Harel and Isacharoff, *Ha-milḥamah Hasbiy'iyt* ("The Seventh War"), chapter 15.

19 Mouin Rabbani, "A Hamas Perspective on the Movement's Evolving Role: An Interview with Khalid Mishal: Part II," *Journal of Palestine Studies* 37(4) (2008): 66.

20 Aluf Benn, "Kach Nolda Tochnit Ha-Hitnatkut" (This Is How the Disengagement Plan Was Born), *Haaretz*, December 29, 2006.

21 Motti Bassok, "Israel at 61: Population Stands at 7.4 Million, 75.5% Jewish," *Haaretz Online* (English ed.), April 27, 2009; "CIA World Factbook—Gaza Strip," https://www.cia.gov/library/publications/the-world-factbook/geos/gz.html; "CIA World Factbook—West Bank," https://www.cia.gov/library/publications/the-world-factbook/geos/we.html; Tani Goldshtein, "2007: Od 14 Elef Mitnachalim Be-Yehuda Ve-Shomron" (2007: 14 Thousand Additional Settlers in Judea and Samara), *Ynet*, January 20, 2008. The settler figure is from Chaim Levinson, "IDF: More Than 300,000 Settlers Live in the West Bank," *Haaretz*, July 27, 2009.

22 Jonathan Rynhold and Dov Waxman, "Ideological Change and Israel's Disengagement from Gaza," *Political Science Quarterly* 123(1) (2008): 24, emphasis in original. Thomas L. Friedman also makes this point eloquently in *From Beirut to Jerusalem* (New York: Farrar, Straus and Giroux, 1989), 234–55.

23 Rynhold and Waxman, "Ideological Change and Israel's Disengagement from Gaza," 30.

24 Imanuel Sivan, "Ha-Orot Shel Netzarim" (The Lights of Netzarim), *Haaretz*, July 11, 2003.

25 Molly Moore, "Israeli Army Engaged in Fight over Its Soul," *Washington Post*, November 18, 2003.

26 Uri Dan, *Ariel Sharon: An Intimate Portrait* (New York: Palgrave Macmillan, 2006), 239.

27 Rynhold and Waxman, "Ideological Change and Israel's Disengagement from Gaza," 31.

28 Moshe Yaalon, *Derech Arooka Ktzara* (The Long Short Way) (Tel Aviv: Sifrei Hemed, 2008), 159–60, 156–57.

29 Ehud Olmert, "Remarks by Israel's Vice Prime Minister Ehud Olmert," Israel Policy Forum Tribute Dinner, June 9, 2005, a partial transcript can be found at: http://www.jewishfederations.org/page. aspx?id=106962.

30 Rynhold and Waxman, "Ideological Change and Israel's Disengagement from Gaza."

31 Quoted in ibid., 15.

32 Ari Shavit, "The Enemy Within," *Haaretz Friday Magazine*, August 30, 2002; Yaalon, *Derech Aroch Katzar*, 156–57.

33 Avi Shavit, "The Big Freeze," *Haaretz*, October 8, 2004. In my judgment it is more likely that Weissglas's interview itself was the formaldehyde, a way of preventing opposition to the withdrawal from leading to the delay of the agreement.

34 Martin Indyk, *Innocent Abroad: An Intimate Account of American Peace Diplomacy in the Middle East* (New York: Simon & Schuster, 2009), 381.

35 See "Letter from Prime Minister Ariel Sharon to US President George W. Bush ," April 14, 2004 and "Letter from US President George W. Bush to Prime Minister Ariel Sharon," April 14, 2004. The text of both can be found at: http://www.mfa.gov.il/MFA/Peace+Process/ Reference+Documents/Exchange+of+letters+Sharon-Bush+14-Apr-2004.htm.

36 "Israel Completes Gaza Withdrawal," *BBC*, September 12, 2005.

37 Quoted in Aiza Hussain, "Quotes from Hamas Leaders on Hamas, Israel, Palestinian Politics," July 19, 2006, www.fmep.org/analysis/articles/ quotes_from_hamas_leaders_on_hamas _israel_and_Palestinian_ politics.html (accessed January 10, 2010).

38 "Palestinian Public Opinion Poll #17," September 28, 2005, www.pcpsr .org/survey/polls/2005/p17a.html (accessed July 30, 2009).

39 Khaled Hroub, "Hamas after Shaykh Yasin and Rantisi," *Journal of Palestine Studies* 33, no. 4 (2004): 22.

40 Poll results are available at Palestine Center for Policy and Survey Research, www.pcpsr.org/survey/cprspolls/2000/poll47a.html, www.pcpsr.org/survey/polls/2005/p17a.html, www.pcpsr.org/survey/ cprspolls/2000/poll46c.html, www.pcpsr.org/survey/cprspolls/2000/ poll46b.html. For 2009 data see www.pcpsr.org/survey/polls/2009/ p32e.html.

41 Rabbani, "A Hamas Perspective," 68.

42 See Indyk, *Innocent Abroad,* 382.

43 See "Election Manifesto for the Elections of the Palestinian Legislative Council 2006," reprinted in Tamimi, *Hamas,* 292–316.

44 Zaki Chehab, *Inside Hamas: The Untold Story of the Militant Islamic Movement* (New York: Nations Books, 2007), 7.

45 Quoted in Harel and Isacharoff, *Ha-milḥamah Hasbiy'iyt* ("The Seventh War"), chapter 15.

46 Paul McGeough, *Kill Khalid: The Failed Mossad Assassination of Khalid Mishal and the Rise of Hamas* (New York: New Press, 2009), 324.

47 Quoted in Graham Usher, "Hamas Risen," MERIP, "Year of Elections: Fact and Fiction," MER 238, Spring 2006, http://www.merip.org/mer/mer238/usher.html.

48 Tamimi, *Hamas*, 227.

49 "Gunmen Open Fire at Haniyeh's Convoy in Gaza," *Haaretz*, October 21, 2006.

50 Steven Erlanger, "Palestinian Premier Urges End to Factional Clashes," *New York Times*, June 9, 2007.

51 Tamimi, *Hamas*, 253.

52 "Text of Mecca Accord for Palestinian Coalition Government," *Associated Press*, February 8, 2007.

53 As cited in Isabel Kershner, "World Briefing Middle East: Gaza: One Dead in Factional Firefight," *New York Times*, June 8, 2007.

54 Quoted in Ethan Bronner, "Hamas and Gaza Emerge Reshaped after Takeover," *New York Times*, June 15, 2008.

55 Isabel Kerschner, "Israeli Airstrikes Hit Gaza Amid Palestinian Infighting," *New York Times*, June 11, 2007; Isabel Kerschner and Taghreed El-Khodary, "9 Die in Fierce Palestinian Factional Fighting," *New York Times*, June 12, 2007.

56 Quoted in Kerschner and El-Khodary, "9 Die in Fierce Palestinian Factional Fighting."

57 Steven Erlanger and Isabel Kershner, "Attacks Escalate as Palestinians Fight for Power," *New York Times*, June 13, 2007.

58 Human Rights Watch, "Gaza: Armed Palestinian Groups Commit Grave Crimes: Fighters Execute Captives, Attack Hospital, Put Journalists at Serious Risk," June 12, 2007, www.hrw.org/en/news/2007/06/12/gaza-armed-palestinian-groups-commit-grave-crimes (accessed August 10, 2009).

59 International Crisis Group, "Ruling Palestine I: Gaza under Hamas," March 13, 2008, 10, http://www.crisisgroup.org/en/regions/middle-east-north-africa/israel-palestine/072-ruling-palestine-I-gaza-under-hamas.aspx.

60 Israeli Security Agency, "Selected Examples of Interrogations Following Operation Cast Lead," http://www.shabak.gov.il/ENGLISH/ENTERRORDATA/ARCHIVE/OPERATION/Pages/cast-lead-Interrogations.aspx.

61 "Ruling Palestine I: Gaza under Hamas," 10.

62 Intelligence and Terrorism Information Center at the Israel Intelligence and Heritage Commemoration Center, "Rocket Threat from the Gaza Strip," December 2007, 22–26, http://www.terrorism-info.org.il/malam_multimedia/English/eng_n/pdf/rocket_threat_e.pdf.

63 Middle East Media Research Institute, "A May 2002 Interview with the Hamas Commander of the Al-Qassam Brigades," July 4, 2002, http://www.memri.org/report/en/0/0/0/0/0/0/703.htm; "Ruling Palestine II," 4, footnote 27.

64 Ulrike Putz, "A Visit to a Gaza Rocket Factory," *Spiegel Online*, January 29, 2008, http://www.spiegel.de/international/world/0,1518,531578,00.html.

65 United Nations Fact Finding Mission on the Gaza Conflict, "Human Rights in Palestine and Other Occupied Arab Territories," September 15, 2009, 32, http://www2.ohchr.org/english/bodies/hrcouncil/specialsession/9/docs/UNFFMGC_Report.PDF.

66 See Amos Harel, "In Bombing Sudan, Israel Sends Message to Iran," *Haaretz*, March 26, 2009.

67 Israeli Security Agency, "Analysis of Attacks in the Last Decade (2000-2009): Rocket Launching," http://www.shabak.gov.il/English/EnTerrorData/decade/Rocket/Pages/default.aspx ; Israeli Security Agency, "Analysis of Attacks in the Last Decade (2000-2009): Mortar Shell Launching Attacks," http://www.shabak.gov.il/English/EnTerrorData/decade/Mortar/Pages/default.aspx.

68 Itamar Marcus and Barbara Crook, "PA Gloats over Israelis' Fear of Missiles," *Palestinian Media Watch*, May 31, 2007.

69 www.shabak.gov.il/English/EnTerrorData/decade/Fatalities/Pages/Shooting.aspx.

70 Greg Myre, "Israelis Rescue Cabdriver after Kidnapping," *New York Times*, July 16, 2003.

71 Scott Wilson, "Israeli Airstrike Kills 10 Palestinians; Eight Civilians among Dead; Israel Denies Role in Last Week's Fatal Beach Explosion," *Washington Post*, June 14, 2006.

72 Quoted in International Crisis Group, "Israel/Palestine/Lebanon: Climbing out of the Abyss," 2006, 6, http://www.crisisgroup.org/~/media/Files/Middle%20East%20North%20Africa/Iraq%20Syria%20Lebanon/Lebanon/57_israel_palestine_lebanon___climbing_out_of_the_abyss.ashx.

73 Tamimi, *Hamas*, 243.

74 Lawrence Wright, "Letter from Gaza - Captives - A report on the Israeli attacks," *The New Yorker*, November 9, 2009.

75 United Nations Fact Finding Mission on the Gaza Conflict, "Human Rights in Palestine and Other Occupied Arab Territories," 28.

76 Richard Horton, "Palestinians: The Crisis in Medical Care," *New York Review of Books*, March 2, 2007.

77 Quoted in Breaking the Silence, "Testimonial Booklet 2", p. 42, http://www.shovrimshtika.org/UserFiles/File//ptihabeesh-englishforweb.pdf.

78 Quoted in Harel and Isacharoff, *Ha-milḥamah Hasbiy'iyt* ("The Seventh War"), 323–39.

79 B'Tselem, "Palestinians Killed by Israeli Security Forces in Gaza Strip," 2008, http://www.btselem.org/English/statistics/Casualties.asp.

80 "Ruling Palestine I," 6.

81 Intelligence and Terrorism Information Center, "Hamas's Military Buildup in the Gaza Strip," 11, http://www.terrorism-info.org.il/malam_multimedia/English/eng_n/pdf/hamas_080408.pdf.

82 Bayt Sahur International Middle East Media Center, "Israeli Intelligence Blackmails Gaza Fisherman," April 9, 2009, available at http://www.uruknet.de/?p=53272.

83 "Palestinian Terrorism in 2007: Statistics and Trends," 10, http://bern.mfa.gov.il/mfm/Data/131697.pdf.

84 Harel and Isacharoff, *Ha-milḥamah Hasbiy'iyt* ("The Seventh War"), 323–39.

85 Ibid.
86 Quoted in Putz, "A Visit to a Gaza Rocket Factory."
87 "Ruling Palestine I," 18.
88 Wright, "Captives."
89 See www.msnbc.msn.com/id/28546053/wid/18298287%20//.
90 Wright, "Captives."
91 See Moshe Yaalon, David Makovsky and Dennis Ross, "Hamas and Israel: From Isolation to Confrontation," *PolicyWatch* 1127, The Washington Institute for Near East Policy, July 20, 2006.
92 International Crisis Group, "Israel/Palestine/Lebanon: Climbing out of the Abyss," 7.
93 "Palestinian Terrorism in 2007: Statistics and Trends," 11.
94 Ziad Asali, "Testimony before the House Committee on Foreign Affairs, Subcommittee on the Middle East and South Asia" (Washington, DC: 2009), 7; Stephanie Nebehay, "Gaza Civilians Mired in Poverty after War—ICRC," *Reuters,* June 28, 2009.

CHAPTER 13

1 "International Crisis Group, "Ruling Palestine I: Gaza under Hamas," March 13, 2008, 4.
2 "Ruling Palestine I," 2.
3 International Crisis Group, "Ruling Palestine I: Gaza under Hamas," 7.
4 Cohen and White, "Hamas in Combat: The Military Performance of the Palestinian Islamic Resistance Unit," *Policy Focus* #97 Washington Institute for Near East Policy, ix, 6–10, http://www.voltairenet.org/IMG/pdf/Hamas_in_Combat.pdf.
5 Paul McGeough, *Kill Khalid: The Failed Mossad Assassination of Khalid Mishal and the Rise of Hamas* (New York: New Press, 2009), 366.
6 "Hamas's Military Buildup in the Gaza Strip," 47; Intelligence and Terrorism Information Center, "Senior Hamas Figure Tells London Sunday Times' Gaza Strip Correspondent about Iranian and Syria Military Aid," 2008, http://www.terrorism-info.org.il/malam_multimedia/English/eng_n/pdf/hamas_160308e.pdf.
7 Quoted in "Hamas Wages Iran's Proxy War on Israel," *Sunday Times* (London), March 9, 2009.
8 IICC, "Summary of Rocket Fire and Mortar Shelling in 2008," January 1, 2009, www.terrorism-info.org.il/malam_multimedia/English/eng_n/pdf/ipc_e007.pdf.
9 United Nations Fact Finding Mission on the Gaza Conflict, "Human Rights in Palestine and Other Occupied Arab Territories," September 15, 2009, 79.
10 Cohen and White, "Hamas in Combat," 5.
11 Tal Zagraba, "Achad She-Yode'a" (One Who Knows), *Ba-Mahane*, April 6, 2009.
12 Palestinian Centre for Human Rights, press release, March 17, 2009; Ziad J. Asali, "Testimony before the House Committee on Foreign Affairs, Subcommittee on the Middle East and South Asia," Washington, DC, 2009, 17; Amnesty International, "Operation 'Cast

Lead': 22 Days of Death and Destruction" (2009), http://www.amnesty.
org/en/library/asset/MDE15/015/2009/en/8f299083-9a74-4853-860f-
0563725e633a/mde150152009en.pdf.

13 Avi Mor et al., "Casualties in Operation Cast Lead: A Closer Look," ICT,
2009, http://www.ict.org.il/Portals/0/Articles/ICT_Cast_Lead_
Casualties-A_Closer_Look.pdf. One Israeli researcher, using open-
source intelligence, reported that 286 of the 343 "police officers" killed
were members of terror organizations, the vast majority of them
belonging to Hamas's military wing; see www.ynetnews.com/
articles/0,7340,L-3720759,00.html.

14 International Crisis Group, "Gaza's Unfinished Business," Middle East
Report No. 85, April 23, 2009, 3, http://www.crisisgroup.org/~/media/
Files/Middle%20East%20North%20Africa/Israel%20Palestine/85%20
Gazas%20Unfinished%20Business.ashx.

15 B'Tselem, "Guidelines for Israel's Investigation into Operation Cast
Lead," 2009, 11, http://www.btselem.org/Download/200902_
Operation_Cast_Lead_Position_paper_Eng.pdf.

16 "Ha-Lehima Be-Aza Kol Hamisparom" (Fighting in Gaza—All the
Numbers), *Channel 2 News (MAKO)*, January 18, 2009; Amos Harel,
"Four of Six IDF Soldiers Killed in Gaza Were Victims of Friendly Fire,"
Haaretz, January 7, 2009.

17 Barak Ravid, "Disinformation, Secrecy, and Lies," *Haaretz*, February 6,
2009.

18 For Israeli claims, see the IDF report at www.youtube.com/
watch?v=hRQa5-gmqys.

19 "Gaza's Unfinished Business," 3.

20 "Rights Group: Hamas Guilty of Gaza War Crimes," *Haaretz*, August 6, 2009.

21 See "Second Stage of Operation Cast Lead Begins," IDF press release,
2009.

22 Cohen and White, "Hamas in Combat," 13.

23 Quoted in "Operation 'Cast Lead': 22 Days of Death and
Destruction," 66.

24 The State of Israel, "The Operation in Gaza: December 27, 2008–18
January 2009: Factual and Legal Aspects," 33, http://www.altawasul.
com/NR/rdonlyres/E89E699D-A435-491B-B2D0-017675DAFEF7/0/
GazaOperationwLinks.pdf.

25 Intelligence and Terrorism Information Center, "The Gaza Strip after
Operation Cast Lead: The Rebuilding of the Civilian and Military
Infrastructure in the Gaza Strip Carried Out by Hamas. At the Same
Time, Hamas Continues Entrenching Its Control of the Gaza Strip,"
June 2009, www.terrorism-info.org.il/malam_multimedia/English/
eng_n/pdf/hamas_e074.pdf (accessed July 9, 2009).

26 Asali, "Testimony," 12; Hanan Greenberg, "IDF Admits Operational
Mishaps in Gaza," *Ynet*, April 22, 2009; Anshel Pepper, "Tachkirei
Mivtza Oferet Yetzuka: Lo Butz'aa Pgia Mechuvenet Be-Azrachim
Falastinim" (Cast Lead Investigations: There Wasn't Any Deliberate
Targeting of Civilians), *Haaretz*, April 22, 2009.

27 David Johnson, "Military Capabilities for Hybrid War: Insights from the
Israel Defense Force in Lebanon and Gaza," *RAND*, 2010, 6, http://
www.rand.org/pubs/occasional_papers/2010/RAND_OP285.pdf.

28 Alon Ben-David, "Israeli Offensive Seeks 'New Security Reality' in Gaza," *Jane's Information Group*, January 9, 2009, http://www.janes.com/news/defence/triservice/jdw/jdw090109_1_n.shtml.

29 "Gaza's Unfinished Business," 1.

30 Zagraba, "Achad She-Yode'a"; Yuval Halamish, "Modi'in Yatzuk Siya La-Oferet" (Cast Intelligence Helped the Lead), *Mabat Malam*, April 2009, http://dover.idf.il/IDF/News_Channels/bamahana/09/14/1401.htm.

31 Zagraba, "Achad She-Yode'a"; Dani Asher, "Bein Levanon Le-Aza— Modi'in Ha-Sade Ba-Hachanot Li-Krat Ve-B'at Ha-Lechima Ba-Hamas Be-Oferet Yetzuka" (Between Lebanon and Gaza—The Field Intelligence in the Preparations and Fighting Hamas in Cast Lead), *Mabat Malam* 53 (2009): 26–29.

32 Amnesty International, "Operation 'Cast Lead'," 75.

33 Israeli Security Agency, "Selected Examples of Interrogations Following Operation Cast Lead," http://www.shabak.gov.il/SiteCollectionImages/%D7%A1%D7%A7%D7%99%D7%A8%D7%95%D7%AA%20%D7%95%D7%A4%D7%A8%D7%A1%D7%95%D7%9E%D7%99%D7%9D/terror-portal/docs/english/Interrogations-en.pdf.

34 Quoted in "The Operation in Gaza: December 27, 2008–18 January 2009," 59.

35 Quoted in "The Operation in Gaza: December 27, 2008–18 January 2009," 69.

36 Lawrence Wright, "Letter from Gaza - Captives - A report on the Israeli attacks," *The New Yorker*, November 9, 2009.

37 "The Operation in Gaza: December 27, 2008–18 January 2009," 90; Ilana Dayan and Gilad Tukatly, "Roim Rachok, Roim Shakuf" (To See Afar, to See Transparent: An Interview with One of the Prominent Shin Bet Operatives Who Worked in Cast Lead), TV Channel 2, February 2, 2009, www.mako.co.il/tv-ilana_dayan/2009–29a8c3a93c82f110/Article-dfd2def2f673f11004.htm.

38 "The Operation in Gaza: December 27, 2008–18 January 2009," 145.

39 Wright, "Captives."

40 Zagraba, "Achad She-Yode'a."

41 http://news.bbc.co.uk/1/hi/world/middle_east/7878711.stm.

42 Quoted in United Nations Fact Finding Mission on the Gaza Conflict, "Human Rights in Palestine and Other Occupied Arab Territories," 13.

43 Amira Hass, "IDF Soldiers Ordered to Shoot at Gaza Rescuers, Note Says," *Haaretz*, April 28, 2009.

44 Amos Harel, "Testimonies on IDF Misconduct in Gaza Keep Rolling In," *Haaretz*, March 22, 2009.

45 Quoted in International Crisis Group, "Israel's Religious Right and the Question of Settlements," No. 89, July 20, 2009, 22, footnote 208, http://www.crisisgroup.org/~/media/Files/Middle%20East%20North%20Africa/Israel%20Palestine/89_israels_religious_right_and_the_question_of_settlements.ashx.

46 Amos Harel, "'Shooting and Crying,'" *Haaretz*, March 20, 2009.

47 Asali, "Testimony," 12.

48 "Operation 'Cast Lead': 22 Days of Death and Destruction," 3, 11, 13, 47.

49 Breaking the Silence, "Rules of Engagement," www.shovrimshtika.org/oferet/testimonies_e.asp?cat=4.

50 Quoted in Tal Zagraba, "Sipurei Dubim" (Bear Stories), *Ba-Mahane*, February 10, 2009.

51 "Operation 'Cast Lead': 22 Days of Death and Destruction"; Yaakov Katz, "IDF Probe: White Phosphorus Use Legal," *Jerusalem Post*, April 22, 2009.

52 Anat Shalev, "Child's Testimony Incriminates Soldiers," *YNET*, March 2010; Ethan Bronner, "Israeli Soldiers Convicted of Using Boy as Shield," *New York Times*, October 3, 2010.

53 "Operation 'Cast Lead': 22 Days of Death and Destruction," 54.

54 See "Israeli Troops Admit Gaza Abuses," *BBC News*, March 19, 2009. For detailed testimonies, see the controversial website Breaking the Silence, www.shovrimshtika.org/oferet/testimonies_e.asp?cat=4; Gal Beckerman, "New Government Gaza Report Cites International Law to Defend Actions: A Different Tactic in Response to Charges of Human Rights Abuses," *Forward*, August 5, 2009.

55 United Nations Fact Finding Mission on the Gaza Conflict, "Human Rights in Palestine and Other Occupied Arab Territories," 525.

56 United Nations Fact Finding Mission on the Gaza Conflict, "Human Rights in Palestine and Other Occupied Arab Territories." This is usually referred to as the "Goldstone Report."

57 Ynet, "Deputy Chief of Staff: Worst Still Ahead," December 29, 2008, http://www.ynet.co.il/english/articles/0,7340,L-3646462,00.html.

58 Quoted in United Nations Fact Finding Mission on the Gaza Conflict, "Human Rights in Palestine and Other Occupied Arab Territories," 329.

59 Jeremy Bowen, "Gaza Stories: Israeli Minister," *BBC News*, February 9, 2009.

60 United Nations Fact Finding Mission on the Gaza Conflict, "Human Rights in Palestine and Other Occupied Arab Territories," 332.

61 Steven Erlanger, "For Israel, 2006 Lessons but Old Pitfalls," *New York Times*, January 7, 2009; Anat Kam, "Barega She-Yikansu Le-Sham Matzlemot Yisrael Titztarech Latet Tshuvot" (Once the Cameras Would Go In, Israel Would Have Some Explaining to Do), *Walla!*, January 16, 2009.

62 Palestinian Center for Policy and Survey Research, "Palestine Public Opinion Poll Number 31," March 5–7, 2009, http://www.pcpsr.org/survey/polls/2009/p31e.html.

63 Ben-David, "Israeli Offensive Seeks 'New Security Reality' in Gaza."

64 Shahshank Bengali and Dion Nissenbaum, "Still in Charge," *Miami Herald*, July 31, 2009.

65 Amnesty International, "Palestinian Authority: Hamas' Deadly Campaign in the Shadow of the War in Gaza," February 10, 2009, http://www.amnesty.org/en/library/asset/MDE21/001/2009/en/9f210586-f762-11dd-8fd7-f57af21896e1/mde210012009en.html; Asali, "Testimony," 16–17.

66 Herb Keinon, "Yuval Diskin: Weapons Flowing into Gaza," *Jerusalem Post*, March 30, 2009; Intelligence and Terrorism Information Center, *The Gaza Strip after Operation Cast Lead*.

67 Umberto De Giovannangeli, "Hamas's Al-Zahhar Warns: 'Gaza Will Be Their New Lebanon,'" *L'Unita*, December 23, 2008, 27.

68 Quoted in Yarden Vintner, "Ma, Kvar Nigmar?" (What, It Ended Already?), *Ba-Mahane*, February 10, 2009.

69 Ethan Bronner, "Hamas Shifts from Rockets to Culture War," *New York Times*, July 23, 2009.

70 Quoted in Wright, "Captives."

71 Uri Blau, "Dead Palestinian Babies and Bombed Mosques—IDF Fashion 2009," *Haaretz*, March 20, 2009.

72 www.haaretz.com/hasen/spages/1155627.html.

73 Stephanie Nebehay, "Gaza Civilians Mired in Poverty after War—ICRC," *Reuters*, June 29, 2000, www.reuters.com/article/featuredCrisis/idUSLQ49576.

74 Amira Hass, "Israel Bans Books, Music and Clothes from Entering Gaza," *Haaretz*, May 17, 2009.

75 Nicolas Pelham and Max Rodenbeck, "Which Way for Hamas?," *New York Review of Books*, November 5, 2009, 36.

76 Yoram Cohen, Matthew Levitt, and Becca Wasser, "Deterred but Determined: Salafi-Jihadi Groups in the Palestinian Arena," Washington Institute for Near East Policy, 2010, http://www.washingtoninstitute.org/templateC04.php?CID=316.

77 Yezid Sayigh, "Hamas Rule in Gaza," Middle East Brief, Crown Center for Middle East Studies, 3, http://www.jmcc.org/documents/MEB41.pdf.

78 Intelligence and Terrorism Information Center, "The Struggle between Hamas and Jihadi-Salafist Networks in the Gaza Strip Affiliated with the Global Jihad," October 4, 2009, www.terrorism-info.org.il/malam_multimedia/English/eng_n/pdf/hamas_e084.pdf. For an excellent analysis of this phenomenon, see Cohen, Levitt, and Wasser, "Al Qaeda Inspired Groups in Palestine."

79 See Cohen, Levitt, and Wasser, "Deterred but Determined" for more on this point.

80 Zagraba, "Achad She-Yode'a."

CHAPTER 14

1 Ronen Bergman, citing an internal IDF investigation, contends that the IDF later determined the attack was a suicide car bombing. See *The Secret War with Iran: The 30-year Clandestine Struggle against the World's Most Dangerous Terrorist Power* (New York: Free Press, 2007), 64–67. For footage, see www.youtube.com/watch?v=pzSNvpz6B_0.

2 For background, this chapter draws on Jaber, *Hezbollah: Born with a Vengeance* (New York: Columbia University Press), 1997; Norton, *Amal and the Shi'a: Struggle for the Soul of Lebanon* (Austin: University of Texas Press, 1987); Ranstorp, *Hizb'Allah in Lebanon: The Politics of the Western Hostage Crisis* (London: MacMillan Press, 1997); Ahmad Nizar Hamzeh, *In the Path of Hizbullah* (New York: Syracuse University Press, 2004); Helmer, *Flipside of the COIN: Israel's Lebanese Incursion Between 1982–2000.* (Fort Leavenworth, KS: Combat Studies Institute Press, 2007).

3 William E. Smith, "New Bloodshed, New Hope," *Time*, November 14, 1983.

4 Rebecca Leung, "Hezbollah: A Team of Terrorists," *60 Minutes Report,*
April 18, 2003, www.cbsnews.com/stories/2003/04/18/60minutes/
main550000.shtml.

5 Martin Kramer, "The Oracle of Hizbullah: Sayyid Muhammad Husayn
Fadlallah," in *Spokesmen for the Despised: Fundamentalist Leaders of the
Middle East,* ed. R. Scott Appleby (Chicago: University of Chicago Press,
1997), 83–181.

6 Norton, *Amal and the Shi'a,* 49–51; Kramer, "The Oracle of Hizbullah";
Martin Kramer, "Hizbullah: The Calculus of Jihad," in *Fundamentalisms
and the State: Remaking Polities, Economies, and Militance,* ed. M. Marty and
R. S. Appleby (Chicago: University of Chicago Press, 1993), 539–56.

7 Quoted in Helmer, *Flipside of the COIN,* 46.

8 Kramer, "Hizbullah: The Calculus of Jihad."

9 Quoted in Martin Kramer, "The Moral Logic of Hizballah,"
www.geocities.com/martinkramerorg/MoralLogic.htm.

10 Quoted in Kramer, "Hizbullah: The Calculus of Jihad," electronic
version.

11 Quoted in Ehteshami, *After Khomeini: The Iranian Second Republic*
(New York: Routledge, 1995), 131.

12 Magnus Ranstorp, "The Hizballah Training Camps of Lebanon,"
The Making of a Terrorist published in *Parameters* (US Army War College
Quarterly) Winter 2006–07, 255.

13 Ranstorp, *Hizb 'Allah in Lebanon: The Politics of the Western Hostage Crisis*
(London: MacMillan Press, 1997), 46–49; Saad-Ghoreyeb, *Hizbu'llah:
Politics and Religion* (Sterling, VA: Pluto Press, 2002), 16.

14 A. Nizar Hamzeh, "Islamism in Lebanon: A Guide," *Middle East Review of
International Affairs* 1, no. 3 (Spring 1997), online.

15 Saad-Ghorayeb, *Hizbu'llah,* 14.

16 Itamar Rabinovich, *The War for Lebanon, 1970–1985* (Ithaca, NY: Cornell
University Press, 1989), 47.

17 Jaber, *Hezbollah,* 81–82.

18 Fouad Ajami, *The Vanished Imam* (Ithaca, NY: Cornell University Press,
1986), 200; Jaber, *Hezbollah,* 14.

19 Quoted in Helmer, *Flipside of the COIN,* 48.

20 Black and Morris, *Israel's Secret Wars: A History of Israel's Intelligence
Services* (London: Hamish Hamilton Ltd., 1991), 395.

21 Smith, "Middle East: New Bloodshed, New Hope." *Time,* November 14,
1983.

22 Christopher Walker, "Shaikh's Murder Fuels Shia Resentment over
Israeli Occupation," *The Times* (London), February 23, 1984.

23 Saad-Ghorayeb, *Hizbu'llah,* 12.

24 Yitzhak Latz, "HaSochnim nechsafu Beintifadat Al-Aqsa" (The Agents
Were Revealed in the Al-Aqsa Intifada), *Globes,* September 13, 2001,
www.globes.co.il/news/article.aspx?did=521979 (Lazar translation).

25 "An Open Letter: The Hizballah Program," www.standwithus.com/pdfs/
flyers/hezbollah_program.pdf.

26 Central Intelligence Agency, "Imad Mugniyeh: The Biography,"
December 29, 1989, Document 0615, Red no. 451188, XMX-111-89,
1988.

27 Bergman, *The Secret War with Iran,* 68.

28 Jaber, *Hezbollah: Born with a Vengeance* (New York: Columbia University Press, 1997), 116–17; AMIA Report, 544–51.

29 AMIA Report, 544–51.

30 Central Intelligence Agency, "Imad Mugniyeh."

31 Quoted in Bergman, *The Secret War with Iran*, 67.

32 Quoted in Bergman, *The Secret War with Iran*, 68.

33 See also AMIA Report, 188, 538–40, 544–51.

34 Borzou Daragahi and Sebastian Rotella, "Hezbollah Warlord Was an Enigma," *Los Angeles Times*, August 31, 2008.

35 Pedahzur, *The Israeli Secret Services and the Struggle Against Terrorism* (New York: Columbia University Press, 2009), 91.

36 Nicholas Blanford, "Hizbullah Attacks Force Israel to Take a Hard Look," *Jane's Intelligence Review* 11, no. 4 (April 1, 1999), online version; Norton, "Hizballah and the Israeli Withdrawal from Southern Lebanon," *Journal of Palestine Studies*, Vol. 30, No. 1 (Autumn 2000), online version.

37 Avraham Sela, "Civil Society, the Military, and National Security: The Case of Israel's Security Zone in South Lebanon," *Israel Studies* 12, no. 1 (2007), 53–78.

38 Jones, "Israeli Counter-Insurgency Strategy and the War in South Lebanon 1985–97," *Small Wars and Insurgencies* (1997), 88.

39 Quoted in Uri Dan and Dennis Eisenberg, "Sunk Deep in the Mud," *Jerusalem Post*, December 15, 1994.

40 Thomas Friedman, "Israel Makes a Bitter Deal," *New York Times*, May 26, 1985.

41 Sela, "Civil Society, the Military, and National Security."

42 Amnesty International, "Israel/South Lebanon: Israel's Forgotten Hostages: Lebanese Detainees in Israel and the Khiam Detention Center," July 1997, http://asiapacific.amnesty.org/library/Index/ENGMDE150181997?open&of=ENG-390.

43 Amnesty International, "Israel: Fear of Torture," May 30, 2000, www.amnesty.org/en/library/info/MDE15/021/2000.

44 Alex Fishman, "shel mi ha-chalalim ha-ele?," *Yedioth Ahronoth*, April 14, 2000, http://www.4mothers.org.il/articles/shel.htm. This figure includes soldiers who died from friendly fire, accidents, and disease in Lebanon in this period as well as those who died from enemy fire.

CHAPTER 15

1 Investigations Unit of the Office of the Attorney General, AMIA Case, no date—author's copy, 25–32. For background this section draws on Jaber, *Hezbollah: Born with a Vengeance* (New York: Columbia University Press, 1997); Ahmad Nizar Hamzeh, *In the Path of Hizbullah* (New York: Syracuse University Press, 2004); Clive Jones, "A Reach Greater Than the Grasp: Israeli Intelligence and the Conflict in South Lebanon 1990–2000," *Intelligence and National Security*, Vol. 16 Issue 1 (2001).

2 www.forward.com/articles/5040/.

3 See the website of his squadron, Patishim, www.planetnana.co.il/yonire/69vfs/real_squadron.htm (accessed June 30, 2009, translation by Eleazar Berman).

4 Pedahzur, *The Israeli Secret Services and the Struggle against Terrorism* (New York: Columbia University Press, 2009), 83–85.

5 Catignani, *Israeli Counter-Insurgency and the Intifadas: Dilemmas of a Conventional Army* (New York: Routledge, 2008), 67 ; Jones, "'A Reach Greater Than the Grasp,'" 21.

6 Hamzeh, *In the Path of Hizbullah*, 72.

7 Carl Anthony Wege, "Hizbollah Organization," *Studies in Conflict and Terrorism*, Vol. 17 Issue 2 (1994):155. See also Jaber, *Hezbollah*, 45–73.

8 Augustus Richard Norton, "Hizballah and the Israeli Withdrawal from Southern Lebanon," *Journal of Palestine Studies* 30, no. 1 (2000), online version. Magnus Ranstorp, "The Hizballah Training Camps of Lebanon," *The Making of a Terrorist* published in *Parameters* (US Army War College Quarterly), Winter 2006–07, 246. Magnus Ranstorp puts the full-time figure at five hundred. In "Declawing the 'Party of God': Toward Normalizing in Lebanon," *World Policy Journal*, summer 2001, 31–42, Steven N. Simon and Jonathan Stevenson say it is no more than one thousand. Jaber puts the entire Hizballah armed forces at around five thousand (*Hezbollah*, 38). Norton believes that by 2000 the full-time Hizballah figures were only five hundred, with another one thousand part-time fighters ("Hizballah and the Israeli Withdrawal from Southern Lebanon," 22–36, online version). Other sources put the number of full-time fighters even lower, at around three hundred. See Nicholas Blanford, "Hizbullah Attacks Force Israel to Take a Hard Look," *Jane's Intelligence Review* 11, no. 4 (1999), online version.

9 Quoted in Jones, "Israeli Counter-Insurgency Strategy and the War in South Lebanon 1985–97," *Small Wars and Insurgencies* (1997), 92.

10 Hamzeh, "Islamism in Lebanon: A Guide to the Groups," *Middle East Quarterly*, September (1997).

11 Hamzeh, *In the Path of Hizbullah*, 71–72.

12 Ya'ari, "Hizballah: 13 Principles of Warfare," *The Jerusalem Report*: 21 March 1996.

13 Matthews, *We Were Caught Unprepared: The 2006 Hezbollah-Israeli War*, (Fort Leavenworth, KS: Combat Studies Institute Press, 2008), 10.

14 David Rudgee, "IDF: Hizbullah Waging Propaganda War," *Jerusalem Post*, March 1, 1998.

15 Arieh O'Sullivan, "IDF–South Lebanon Liaison Commander: Calls for Unilateral Pullout Endanger Troops," *Jerusalem Post*, June 9, 1998.

16 Matthews, *We Were Caught Unprepared*, 5–6.

17 David Eshel, "Counterguerrilla Warfare in South Lebanon," *Marine Corps Gazette* 81, no. 7 (July 1997), 40–42.

18 Hamzeh, *In the Path of Hizbullah*, 84.

19 Quoted in Black and Morris, *Israel's Secret Wars: A History of Israel's Intelligence Services* (London: Hamish Hamilton Ltd., 1991), 399.

20 Black and Morris, *Israel's Secret Wars*, 398.

21 Pedahzur, *The Israeli Secret Services*, 72–75.

22 Jones, "Israeli Counter-Insurgency Strategy," 94.

23 Jones, "'A Reach Greater than the Grasp,'" 10–11; Ofer Shelach, "Ani zocher et atzmi be-matzav shek keos" (I Remember Myself in a State of Chaos), *Shisi*, Channel 10 News, September 19, 2008, http://news.nana10.co.il/Article/?ArticleID=583096&sid=126.

24 Matthews, *We Were Caught Unprepared*, 10.

25 Yitzhak Latz, "HaSochnim nechsafu Beintifadat Al-Aqsa" (The Agents Were Revealed in the Al-Aqsa Intifada), *Globes*, September 13, 2001.

26 Zeina Karam, "Hezbollah Fighters in Beirut Melt Away," *USA Today*, October 5, 2008, www.usatoday.com/news/world/2008-05-09-2834862695_x.htm.

27 Magnus Ranstorp, "The Hizballah Training Camps of Lebanon," 251. Ranstorp, citing Nizar Hamzeh, claims Hizballah's internal security branch has more than five thousand people.

28 Iran Human Rights Documentation Center, www.iranhrdc.org/httpdocs/English/pdfs/Reports/Murder-at-Mykonos_Mar07.pdf.

29 See *United States of America v. Ahmed al-Mughassil et al.*, United States District Court, Eastern District of Virginia, Alexandria Division, June 2001.

30 Martin Rudner, "Hizbullah: An Organizational and Operational Profile," *International Journal of Intelligence and Counterintelligence* 23 (2010), 226–46; Matthew Levitt, "The Hizballah Threat in Africa," *Policywatch* 823, January 2, 2004.

31 *United States of America v. Mohamad Youssef Hammoud et al.*

32 Sharon A. Melzer and Louise I. Shelley, "The Nexus of Organized Crime and Terrorism: Two Case Studies in Cigarette Smuggling," *International Journal of Comparative and Applied Criminal Justice*, spring 2008, 10.

33 Justin Sparks, "Freed Terrorist Vows He'll Fulfil Suicide Mission," *Sunday Times* (London), February 8, 2004; "Israeli Intelligence: Hezbollah Is Recruiting Europeans for Terrorist Attacks against Israel," *Middle East Intelligence Bulletin* 1, no. 9 (1999), www.meib.org/articles/9909_15.htm (accessed June 30, 2009).

34 Jones, "'A Reach Greater Than the Grasp,'" 10–13; Norton, "Hizballah and the Israeli Withdrawal from Southern Lebanon," 22–36; Noa Tzifer, "Hishvu 'al ha-korbanot" (Think of the Victims), *NRG*, June 11, 2007, www.nrg.co.il/online/1/ART1/593/680.html. The Israeli figure also includes losses to Amal and other groups in Lebanon.

35 Quoted in Jones, "Israeli Counter-Insurgency Strategy," 89.

36 See, for example, Haj Halil's teachings described in Ehud Ya'ari, "Hizballah: 13 Principles of Warfare," *The Jerusalem Report*, March 21, 1996.

37 Quoted in Uri Dan and Dennis Eisenberg, "Sunk Deep in the Mud," *Jerusalem Post*, December 15, 1994.

38 Blanford, "Hizbullah Attacks."

39 Human Rights Watch, "Civilian Pawns: Laws of War Violations and the Use of Weapons on the Israel-Lebanon Border," May 1996, 69.

40 Black and Morris, *Israel's Secret Wars*, 393–94; Jones, "Israeli Counter-Insurgency Strategy," 82, 96.

41 Ya'ari, "Hizballah: 13 Principles of Warfare."

42 Hamzeh, *In the Path of Hizbullah*, 59.

43 Sobelman, *New Rules of the Game: Israel and Hizbollah after the Withdrawal from Lebanon*, Jaffee Center for Strategic Studies, Tel Aviv University: Memorandum No. 69 (January 2004), 90.

44 Magnus Ranstorp, "The Hizballah Training Camps of Lebanon," 245.

45 Augustus Richard Norton, "Hizballah: From Radicalism to Pragmatism," *Middle East Policy,* Vol. 5, no. 4 (1998), 152.

46 Abbas William Samii, "A Stable Structure on Shifting Sands: Assessing the Hizbullah-Iran-Syria Relationship," *Middle East Journal* 62, no. 1 (2008): 39.

47 Ranstorp, *Hizb 'Allah in Lebanon: The Politics of the Western Hostage Crisis* (London: MacMillan Press, 1997), 189.

48 Sela, "Civil Society, the Military, and National Security: The Case of Israel's Security Zone in South Lebanon," *Israel Studies,* Vol. 12, no. 1 (2007).

49 Human Rights Watch, "Civilian Pawns," 22.

50 Nizar A. Hamzeh, "Lebanon's Hizbullah: From Islamic Revolution to Parliamentary Accommodation," *Third World Quarterly* 14, no. 2 (1993), online version.

51 The 13 percent figure is from Judith Palmer Harik, quoted in Saad-Ghoreyeb, *Hizbu'llah: Politics and Religion* (Sterling, VA: Pluto Press, 2002), 35.

52 Quoted in Harik, "Between Islam and the System: Sources and Implications of Popular Support for Lebanon's Hizballah," *Journal of Conflict Resolution,* Vol. 40 No. 1 (March 1996), 51.

53 Rudner, "Hizbullah," 232.

54 International Crisis Group, "Hizballah: Rebel without a Cause," July 30, 2003, 3; Hamzeh, *In the Path of Hizbullah,* 44.

55 David Rudge and David Makovsky, "Rabin: We Won't Tolerate Attacks in North; Message Sent to Assad after Three More Soldiers Die in Fierce Fighting in South Lebanon," *Jerusalem Post,* July 11, 1993.

56 Ethan Bonner, "Israeli Ships, Planes Continue Lebanon Raids," *Boston Globe,* July 27, 1993.

57 Human Rights Watch, "Civilian Pawns," 110–12.

58 Catignani, *Israeli Counter-Insurgency and the Intifadas: Dilemmas of a Conventional Army* (New York: Routledge, 2008), 68.

59 Storer Rowley, "Israel Pounds South Lebanon," *Chicago Tribune,* April 15, 1996, 3.

60 Human Rights Watch, "Civilian Pawns," 8–9, footnote 11; www. amnesty.org/en/library/asset/MDE15/042/1996/en/d971c8d1-eaf6-11-dd-aad1-ed57e7e5470b/mde150421996en.html.

61 Orr is quoted in Human Rights Watch, "Israel/Lebanon: 'Operation Grapes of Wrath,'" no. 8 (1997), 15. See also 5–6 and 14–15 for an overview of Israeli objectives.

62 "PM Rabin to Knesset: Political Statement on Action in Lebanon," July 28, 1993, www.mfa.gov.il/MFA/Archive/Speeches/PM%20RABIN%20 TO%20KNESSET-%20POLITICAL%20STATEMENT%20ON%20 ACTION.

63 Human Rights Watch, "Civilian Pawns," 152–55.

64 See ibid., 11, 19.

65 Quoted in Thomas L. Friedman, "No Pain, No Gain, No Peace," *New York Times,* March 31, 1996.

66 David Bar-Illan, "Lebanon Scenes," *Jerusalem Post,* August 6, 1993, cited in Helmer, *Flipside of the COIN: Israel's Lebanese Incursion Between 1982–2000* (Fort Leavenworth, KS: Combat Studies Institute Press, 2007), 56.

67 Quoted in Human Rights Watch, "Civilian Pawns," 59.
68 Human Rights Watch, "Civilian Pawns," 61.
69 Quoted in *Mideast Mirror*, October 17, 1995.
70 Catignani, *Israeli Counter-Insurgency and the Intifadas*, 70.
71 Marjorie Miller and John Daniszewski, "Peres Faces Off with Challenger in Feisty Debate," *Los Angeles Times*, May 27, 1996, 1.
72 Quoted in Judith Harik, "Syrian Foreign Policy and State/Resistance Dynamics in Lebanon," *Studies in Conflict and Terrorism* 20 (1997): 257.
73 Human Rights Watch, "Civilian Pawns," 26; IAF website, "Invei za'am" (Grapes of Wrath), www.iaf.org.il/Templates/FlightLog/FlightLog.aspx?lang=HE&lobbyID=40&folderID=48&subfolderID=324&docfolderID=390&docID=5542&docType=EVENT.
74 United Nations, *Report of the Secretary General's Military Adviser Concerning the Shelling of the UN Compound at Qana on April 18, 1996*, May 7, 1996.
75 "Lebanese-Israeli Cease-Fire 'Understanding,'" *Journal of Palestine Studies*, April 26, 1995, 138.
76 Norton, "Hizballah and the Israeli Withdrawal from Southern Lebanon."
77 Jaber, *Hezbollah*, 178–99.
78 Harik, "Syrian Foreign Policy," 254.
79 Malka, "Israel and Asymmetrical Deterrence," *Comparative Strategy*, Vol. 27 Iss. 1 (January 2008), 10.

CHAPTER 16

1 BBC News, "Barak: Lebanon 'Tragedy Is Over,'" May 23, 2000, http://news.bbc.co.uk/2/hi/middle_east/760062.stm.
2. Alex Fishman, "Shel mi ha-chalalim ha-ele?", *Yedioth Ahronoth*, April 14, 2000.
3 Sela, "Civil Society, the Military, and National Security: The Case of Israel's Security Zone in South Lebanon," *Israel Studies*, Vol. 12, no. 1 2007."
4 Harel and Issacharoff, *34 Days: Israel, Hezbollah, and the War in Lebanon* (New York: Palgrave MacMillan, 2008), 25.
5 For background, this chapter draws on Harel and Issacharoff, *34 Days*; Daniel Sobelman, *New Rules of the Game: Israel and Hizballah after the Withdrawal from Lebanon*, Jaffee Center for Strategic Studies, Tel Aviv, January 2004; Matthews, *We Were Caught Unprepared: The 2006 Hezbollah-Israeli War* (Fort Leavenworth, KS: Combat Studies Institute Press, 2008).
6 Harel and Issacharoff, *34 Days*, 22.
7 Quoted in Sobelman, *New Rules of the Game*, 29.
8 Ranstorp, *Hizb'Allah in Lebanon: The Politics of the Western Hostage Crisis* (London: MacMillan Press, 1997), 127.
9 "Peace Requires Departure of Palestinians," interview with Sheikh Hassan Nasrallah, *Middle East Insight*, March–April 2000, 32.
10 Quoted in Malka, "Israel and Asymmetrical Deterrence," *Comparative Strategy*, Vol. 27 Iss. 1 (January 2008), 19, note 2; Sagi Nir, "Ha'avoda:

Reshimat hisul" (Labor Party: Targets List), *Nana 10*, December 1, 2008, http://news.nana10.co.il/Article/?ArticleID=597491.

11 Molly Moore, "Israeli Army Engaged in Fight over Its Soul," *Washington Post*, November 18, 2003, A1.

12 Saad-Ghorayeb, *Hizbu'llah: Politics and Religion* (Sterling, VA: Pluto Press, 2002), 119.

13 See the transcript of *The Price of Freedom*, a coproduction of Article 2 (France) and LBC (Lebanon), broadcast on September 20, 2006, http://news.nana10.co.il/Articlle?articleID=394205&TypeID=1&sid=126.

14 "Tannenbaum: I Was in Lebanon for Drug Deal," *Jerusalem Post*, December 21, 2006, 8.

15 See Nasrallah's statements in *The Price of Freedom*.

16 Margot Dudkevitch, "Released Prisoners Praise Hizbullah," *Jerusalem Post*, January 30, 2004.

17 Harel and Issacharoff, *34 Days*, 40.

18 Malka, "Israel and Asymmetrical Deterrence," 2.

19 Hassan Nasrallah, "Hezbollah Victory, Fruit of Resistance," speech, July 17, 2008, www.aimislam.com/forums/index.php?s=5a78a63056dd7dc3 62deac1e89147abf&showtopic=457&st=100.

20 Quoted in International Crisis Group, "Israel/Palestine/Lebanon: Climbing Out of the Abyss," July 25, 2006, p. 10.

21 Israeli Ministry of Foreign Affairs, "Hizbullah Attacks along Israel's Northern Border May 2000–June 2006," www.mfa.gov.il.

22 Hanan Greenberg and Sharon Rofe-Nir, "Hayal tzhal neherag ve-'arba'ah niftz'au me-esh hizballah" (An IDF Soldier Was Killed and Four Were Wounded from Hezbollah's Fire), *Ynet*, June 30, 2005, www.ynet.co.il/articles/0,7340,L-3105782,00.html.

23 Sharon Rofe-Ofir and Hanan Grienberg, "Yom krav be-tzafon: 12 hayalim ve-ezrachim niftz'au" (Battle Day in the North: 12 Soldiers and Civilians Were Wounded), *Ynet*, November 22, 2005, www.ynet.co.il/ articles/0,7340,L-3172608,00.html.

24 Quoted in Harel and Issacharoff, *34 Days*, 8.

25 Ami Pedahzur, *The Israeli Secret Services and the Struggle against Terrorism* (New York: Columbia University Press, 2009), 128–29.

26 Michael R. Gordon, "Militants Are Said to Amass Missiles in South Lebanon," *New York Times*, July 16, 2006.

27 See Nazila Fathi, "Text of Mahmoud Ahmadinejad's Speech," *New York Times*, October 30, 2005; "Iranian Leader Denies Holocaust," *BBC News*, December 14, 2005, http://news.bbc.co.uk/2/hi/middle_ east/4527142.stm.

28 Sobelman, *New Rules of the Game*, 62; Israeli Security Agency, "Palestinian Terrorism in 2007: Statistics and Trends" (2008), 19–20; the full report can be accessed from the Ministry of Foreign Affairs at: http://www.mfa.gov.il/MFA/Terrorism-+Obstacle+to+Peace/ Palestinian+terror+since+2000/Palestinian+Terrorism+in+2007.htm; International Crisis Group, "Hizballah: Rebel without a Cause," July 30, 2003, p. 10.

29 Reuven Erlich, "Hezbollah's Use of Lebanese Civilians as Human Shields," Intelligence and Terrorism Information Center at the Center for Special Studies, November 2006, 30.

30 Quoted in Max Rodenbeck, "Lebanon's Agony," *New York Review of Books,* June 28, 2007.
31 See Erlich, "Hezbollah's Use of Lebanese Civilians," 28.
32 Matthews, *We Were Caught Unprepared,* 17.
33 Harel and Issacharoff, *34 Days,* 48–49; Erlich, "Hezbollah's Use of Lebanese Civilians," 139–40.
34 Erlich, "Hezbollah's Use of Lebanese Civilians," 34.
35 Exum, "Hizballah at War: A Military Assessment," The Washington Institute for Near East Policy: Policy Focus #63 (December 2006), 3–4.
36 Quoted in Matthews, *We Were Caught Unprepared,* 5.
37 Alastair Crooke and Mark Perry, "How Hezbollah Defeated Israel," Part 1: The Intelligence War *Asia Times Online* (October 12, 2006); Matthews, *We Were Caught Unprepared,* 21.
38 Shay Hazkani, "Be-tzhal hechrizu 'al milhemet horma ba-telephonim ha-nayadim" (IDF Waged a War on Cellular Phones), Channel 10 News, April 24, 2008, http://news.nana10.co.il/Article/?ArticleID=5512 06&TypeID=1&sid=126.
39 Yoaz Hendel, "Failed Tactical Intelligence in the Lebanon War," *Strategic Assessment* 9, no. 3 (2006), available at http://www.inss.org.il/publications.php?cat=21&incat=&read=90.
40 Alex Fishman, "Struck by a Virus," *Yedioth Ahronoth*, quoted in Matthews, *We Were Caught Unprepared,* 26.
41 Siboni, "The Military Campaign in Lebanon," in Brom and Elan, *The Second Lebanon War: Strategic Perspectives* (Tel Aviv: Institute for National Security Studies, 2007), 64–66.
42 Quoted in Matthews, *We Were Caught Unprepared,* 49.
43 Quoted in Harel and Issacharoff, *34 Days,* 70.

CHAPTER 17

1 For background, this chapter draws on Harel and Isacharoff, *34 Days: Israel, Hezbollah, and the War in Lebanon* (New York; Palgrave MacMillan, 2008); Daniel Sobelman, *New Rules of the Game: Israel and Hizballah after the Withdrawal from Lebanon,* Jaffee Center for Strategic Studies, Tel Aviv, January 2004; Andrew Exum, "Hizballah at War: A Military Assessment," Washington Institute for Near East Policy, December 2006; Stephen Biddle and Jeffrey A. Friedman, *The 2006 Lebanon Campaign and the Future of Warfare: Implications for Army and Defense Policy* (Strategic Studies Institute, U.S. Army War College), September 2008; Matthews, *We Were Caught Unprepared: The 2006 Hezbollah-Israeli War* (Fort Leavenworth, KS: Combat Studies Institute Press, 2008).
2 See www.haaretz.com/hasite/pages/ShArt.jhtml?itemNo=787670&cont rassID=1 on the claim that the patrol was not careful.
3 Matthews, *We Were Caught Unprepared,* 36.
4 Yehuda ben Meir, "Israeli Public Opinion and the Second Lebanon War," in *The Second Lebanon War: Strategic Perspectives,* ed. Shlomo Brom and Meir Elran (Tel Aviv: Institute for National Security Studies, 2007), 88–91.
5 See Israel Ministry of Foreign Affairs, "Behind the Headlines: The Second Lebanon War—One Year Later," July 12, 2007, www.mfa.gov.il.

6 "Hezbollah Warns Israel over Raids," *BBC News*, July 12, 2006, http://news.bbc.co.uk/2/hi/middle_east/5173078.stm; Roni Sofer, "Olmert: Medina ribonit takfa otanu ve-tisa ba-totzaot" (Olmert: A Sovereign Country Attacked Us, and It Will Bear the Consequences), *Ynet*, July 12, 2006, www.ynet.co.il/Ext/Comp/ArticleLayout/CdaArticlePrintPreview/1,2506,L-3274330,00.html.

7 William Arkin, "Divine Victory for Whom? Airpower in the 2006 Israel-Hezbollah War," *Strategic Studies Quarterly* (winter 2007), 118.

8 Harel and Issacharoff, *34 Days*, 102.

9 "Interview with Hezbollah Secretary General Hasan Nasrallah," *al-Jazeera*, July 20, 2006.

10 Arkin, "Divine Victory for Whom?," 102–3.

11 Quoted in Harel and Issacharoff, *34 Days*, 80.

12 Quoted in Marvin Kalb, "The Israeli-Hezbollah War of 2006: The Media as a Weapon of Asymmetrical Conflict," Joan Shorenstein Center on the Press, Politics, and Public Policy, Research Paper 29, February 2007, 9.

13 Richard Pendlebury, "Southern Beirut: Only the Dead or Insane Remain," *Daily Mail*, July 21, 2006, www.dailymail.co.uk/news/article-396821/Southern-Beirut-Only-dead-insane-remain.html.

14 Harel and Issacharoff, *34 Days*, 86.

15 Quoted in Arkin, "Divine Victory for Whom?," 109.

16 "Interview with Hezbollah Secretary General Hasan Nasrallah," *al-Jazeera*, July 20, 2006.

17 Biddle and Friedman, *The 2006 Lebanon Campaign*, 31; William M. Arkin, *Divining Victory: Airpower in the 2006 Israel-Hezbollah War* (Maxwell Air Force Base, AL: Air University Press, 2007), 55–56.

18 Quoted in Matthews, *We Were Caught Unprepared*, 33.

19 "The Main Findings of the Winograd Partial Report on the Second Lebanon War," *Haaretz*, April 30, 2007, paragraph 10c.

20 Harel and Issacharoff, *34 Days*, 86.

21 Quoted in Avi Kober, "The Israel Defense Force in the Second Lebanon War: Why the Poor Performance?," *Journal of Strategic Studies* 31, no. 1 (2008): 11.

22 Erlich, "Hezbollah's Use of Lebanese Civilians," IDF Center for Special Studies Intelligence and Terrorism Information Center, December 2006, 79–155.

23 The United States quietly shipped some in the later stages of the 2006 war, but the opportunity to strike had already passed. David S. Cloud and Helene Cooper, "U.S. Speeds Up Bomb Delivery for the Israelis," *New York Times*, July 22, 2006, http://www.nytimes.com/2006/07/22/world/middleeast/22military.html.

24 Harry de Quetteville and Colin Freeman, "Dawn Calls to Recruit Lebanese Informers," *Sunday Telegraph* (London), August 6, 2006, 26.

25 Norton, *Hezbollah: A Short History* (Princeton, NJ; Princeton University Press, 2007), 136. Some reports claim that Iranian forces operated the C-802s.

26 Harel and Issacharoff, *34 Days*, 101.

27 Kober, "The Israel Defense Force in the Second Lebanon War: Why the Poor Performance?" *Journal of Strategic Studies*, Vol 31 Iss. 1 (2008), 16–19.

28 Shay Hazkani, "IDF Knew There Was No Firing from the Building Hit in Qana," Channel 10 News (Israel), July 31, 2006, quoted in Keshev, The Center for the Protection of Democracy in Israel, "Milhama 'ad ha-rega ha-acharon" (War till the Last Second), July 2007, 135, www.keshev .org.il/FileUpload/reportweb.pdf.

29 Amos Harel, "Halutz, Olmert ve-Adam holchim le-hazia" (Halutz, Olmert and Adam Are Going to Sweat), Haaretz, January 25, 2007, www.haaretz.co.il/hasite/spages/817958.html.

30 Quoted in Matthews, We Were Caught Unprepared, 43.

31 Quoted in Harel and Issacharoff, 34 Days, 231.

32 Quoted in Matthews, We Were Caught Unprepared, 43.

33 Biddle and Friedman, The 2006 Lebanon Campaign, xiii, 44–45. See also Erlich, "Hezbollah's Use of Lebanese Civilians," 85. Erlich writes that Hizballah fighters intermingled with civilians extensively in rear areas, where rocket sites were present, and that its fighters often dressed as civilians. However, in battles in southern Lebanon most residents had fled the villages by the time fighting occurred.

34 Intelligence and Terrorism Information Center, "Hezbollah's Use of Lebanese Civilians as Human Shields," November 2006, 45, www.terrorism-info.org.il/site/html/search.asp?sid=13&pid= 167&numResults=7&isSearch=yes&isT8=yes.

35 "U.N. Chief Accuses Hizballah of 'Cowardly Blending' Among Refugees," Associated Press, July 24, 2006. www.foxnews.com/ story/0,2933,205349,00.html.

36 "The Main Findings of the Winograd Partial Report on the Second Lebanon War," Haaretz, April 30, 2007, paragraphs 12b, 12c.

37 Zeev Schiff, "The Foresight Saga," Haaretz, August 11, 2006. For an excellent discussion of new doctrinal concepts, see Eleazar Berman, "Meeting the Hybrid Threat: The Israel Defense Force's Innovations against Hybrid Enemies, 2000–2009" (MA diss., Georgetown University, 2010).

38 "Interview with BG (Ret.) Shimon Naveh," Fort Leavenworth, KS: Combat Studies Institute, November 1, 2007, 4.

39 Yotam Feldman, "Rosh nefetz" (Warhead), Haaretz, October 24, 2007, www.haaretz.co.il/hasite/pages/ShArt.jhtml?itemNo=916560.

40 Israeli Foreign Ministry, "Israel-Hizbullah Conflict: Victims of Rocket Attacks and IDF Casualties," July 2, 2006, www.mfa.gov.il/MFA/ Terrorism-+Obstacle+to+Peace/Terrorism+from+Lebanon-+Hizbullah/ Israel-Hizbullah+conflict-+Victims+of+rocket+attacks+and+IDF+casualt ies+July-Aug+2006.htm.

41 For the Israeli figure, see Abraham Rabinovich, "Retired Israeli Generals Vent; Chief of Staff of IDF Under Fire for Conduct of 34-day War vs. Hezbollah," Washington Times, September 27, 2006. For Hizballah's figure, see Jonathan Spyer, "Lebanon 2006: Unfinished War," Middle East Review of International Affairs, March 2008, http://meria.idc.ac.il/ journal/2008/issue1/jv12no1a1.asp#_edn31; Patrick Bishop, "Peacekeeping Force Won't Disarm Hizbollah," Daily Telegraph, August 22, 2006, www.telegraph.co.uk/news/1526970/Peacekeeping-force-wont-disarm-Hizbollah.html.

42 Quoted in Matthews, We Were Caught Unprepared, 33.

43 "English Summary of the Winograd Commission Report," *New York Times*, January 30, 2008, paragraph 11.

44 "War Was a Catastrophe," *Ynet*, March 30, 2007, www.ynetnews.com/articles/0,7340,L-3383151,00.html.

45 Alastair Crooke and Mark Perry, "How Hezbollah Defeated Israel: Part 3, The Political War," *Asia Times Online*, October 14, 2006.

46 Kalb, "The Israeli-Hezbollah War of 2006," 4.

47 Ben Meir, "Israeli Public Opinion," 87.

48 "Remarks by Hassan Nasrallah," *Al Arabiya TV*, July 18, 2006, translated by the Federal News Service, http://www.msnbc.msn.com/id/14953453/ns/world_news-mideast/n_africa/.

49 Amos Harel and Yoav Stern, "Lebanon Police: 15 Die in IAF Strike on Van in South Lebanon," *Haaretz* (English website), July 14, 2006, www.haaretz.com/hasen/pages/ShArt.jhtml?itemNo=738611&contrassID=1&subContrassID=0&sbSubContrassID=0.

50 See "Address of General Secretary of Hizballah, Hassan Nasrallah," 14 July 2006, translated by Eric Mueller, available at: http://electronicintifada.net/bytopic/historicalspeeches/447.shtml.

51 "Interview with Hezbollah Secretary General Hasan Nasrallah," *al-Jazeera*, July 20, 2006.

52 Kalb, "The Israeli-Hezbollah War of 2006," 13.

53 Deborah Howell, "A War of Images and Perceptions," *Washington Post*, August 13, 2006.

54 Arkin, "Divine Victory for Whom?," 101.

55 Kalb, "The Israeli-Hezbollah War of 2006," 18–26.

56 Harel and Issacharoff, *34 Days*, 131.

57 Matthew Levitt, "Hizballah's Military Wing under Pressure Despite Political Gains," *PolicyWatch* 1389, Washington Institute for Near East Policy, July 16, 2008.

58 Anshel Pfeffer, "WATCH: Lebanese Civilians Oust Hezbollah Men in Border Village," *Haaretz* (English website), August 25, 2009, www.haaretz.com/hasen/spages/1110035.html; Barak Ravid, "Israel to UN: We'll Continue to Gather Intelligence in Lebanon," *Haaretz* (English website), October 26, 2009, www.haaretz.com/hasen/spages/1123537.html.

59 Erlich, "Hezbollah's Use of Lebanese Civilians," 55; Harel and Issacharoff, *34 Days*, 249.

60 See "Report: Mughniyah's Israeli Killers Infiltrated to Syria from Kurdistan," *Yediot Aharonot*, February 7, 2009; "Mossad's Most Wanted: A Deadly Vengeance," *The Independent* (London), February 23, 2010.

61 Sebastian Rotella, "Azerbaijan Seen as New Front in Mideast Conflict," *Los Angeles Times*, May 30, 2009, www.latimes.com/news/nationworld/world/la-fg-shadow30-2009may30,0,2242157.story.

62 David Lev, "Released for Publication: Israeli-Arab Plotted to Kill IDF Chief," www.israelnationalnews.com/News/News.aspx/133188 (accessed January 7, 2010).

63 "Israel Warns Hizbullah War Would Invite Destruction," *Ynet* (English website), March 10, 2008, www.ynetnews.com/articles/0,7340,L-3604893,00.html.

64 See Nicholas Blanford, "Return to Arms: Hizbullah and Israel's Preparations for War," *Jane's Intelligence Review*, February 2010, 14–19.

65 Ibid., 14–19.

66 "Nasrallah: Soldiers' Abductions a Mistake," CNN.com, August 27, 2006, http://edition.cnn.com/2006/WORLD/meast/08/27/mideast .nasrallah/index.html.

CHAPTER 18

1 For background, this chapter draws on Ami Pedahzur and Arie Perliger, *Jewish Terrorism in Israel* (New York: Columbia University Press, 2009); Ehud Sprinzak, *Brother against Brother: Violence and Extremism in Israeli Politics from Altalena to the Rabin Assassination* (New York: Free Press, 1999); Ian S. Lustick, *For the Land and the Lord: Jewish Fundamentalism in Israel* (New York: Council on Foreign Relations, 1988); Gideon Aran, "Jewish Zionist Fundamentalism: The Bloc of the Faithful in Israel (Gush Emunim)," in *Fundamentalisms Observed*, ed. Martin E. Marty and Scott Appleby (University of Chicago Press, 1991); Segal, *Dear Brothers: The West Bank Jewish Underground* (New York: Beit-Shamai Publications, 1988).

2 Segal, *Dear Brothers*, 169.

3 Ibid., 173.

4 Nadav Shragai, "Yesh Lanu Efsharut Limchok Et Ze, Ma D'atchah Ha-Rav?" (We Have an Option to Wipe It Out, What Do You Think Rabbi?), *Haaretz*, May 31, 2007.

5 Pedahzur and Perliger, *Jewish Terrorism in Israel*. I would like to thank Arie Perliger for his assistance with this point.

6 Quoted in Sprinzak, *Brother against Brother*, 45–47.

7 See Southern Poverty Law Center, "Jewish Extremists Arrested in Failed Bombing Conspiracy," spring 2002, www.splcenter.org/ get-informed/intelligence-report/browse-all-issues/2002/spring/ anti-arab-terrorism.

8 Raphael Mergui and Philippe Simonnot, *Israel's Ayatollahs: Meir Kahane and the Far Right in Israel* (Atlantic Highlands, NJ: Saqi Books, 1987), 51.

9 Sprinzak, *Brother against Brother*, 211.

10 Mergui and Simonnot, *Israel's Ayatollahs*, 49.

11 Ibid., 31.

12 Knesset Research and Information Center, "Brief: Jewish Political Violence in Israel," www.knesset.gov.il/mmm/doc.asp?doc= m01268&type=pdf.

13 Segal, *Dear Brothers*, 19.

14 Gazit, *The Carrot and the Stick: Israel's Policy in Judea and Samaria, 1967–1968* (Washington, DC: B'nai B'rith Books, 1995), 166.

15 Segal, *Dear Brothers*, 2.

16 Shabtai Teveth, *The Cursed Blessing: The Story of Israel's Occupation of the West Bank* (London: Weidenfeld and Nicolson, 1970), 272.

17 Quoted in Aran, "Jewish Zionist Fundamentalism," 291.

18 Quoted in Aran, "Jewish Zionist Fundamentalism," 291.

19 Sprinzak, *Brother against Brother*, 166.

20 Segal, *Dear Brothers*, 94.

21 Lustick, *For the Land and the Lord*, 69.

22 Segal, *Dear Brothers,* 241.
23 Pedahzur and Perliger, *Jewish Terrorism in Israel,* 51–52.
24 Quoted in Segal, *Dear Brothers,* 116.
25 Quoted in Segal, *Dear Brothers,* 120–21.
26 Segal, *Dear Brothers,* 117.
27 Sprinzak, *Brother against Brother,* 156.
28 Segal, *Dear Brothers,* 60–62.
29 Ibid., 63. See Knesset Research and Information Center, "Brief: Jewish Political Violence in Israel"; Pedahzur and Perliger, *Jewish Terrorism in Israel,* 59.
30 Segal, *Dear Brothers,* 156, 243.
31 Ibid., 181–84.
32 Ibid., 178–87.
33 *The Karp Report: An Israeli Government Inquiry into Settler Violence against Palestinians on the West Bank* (Washington, DC: Institute for Palestine Studies, 1984), 35.
34 *The Karp Report.* The quote is from page 35.
35 Gazit, *Trapped Fools: Thirty Years of Israeli Policy in the Territories* (Portland, OR: Frank Cass, 2003) , 127–28.
36 Knesset Research and Information Center, "Brief: Jewish Political Violence in Israel."
37 Occasional violence against Jews occurred as well. Emil Grinzweig, a son of Holocaust survivors and a peace activist, was killed when Shalom Akhshav threw a grenade into a peace rally in 1983. Yet for the most part Jewish violence in this period focused on Arabs.
38 "Shamir on Jewish Terrorism: An Unauthorized Military Activity," *Ha'aretz,* September 7, 1984.
39 Segal, *Dear Brothers,* 17.
40 Ami Pedahzur, *The Israeli Response to Jewish Extremism and Violence: Defending Democracy* (Manchester: Manchester University Press, 2002), 85.
41 Quoted in Aran, "Jewish Zionist Fundamentalism," 293.
42 Quoted in Aran, "Jewish Zionist Fundamentalism,"302.
43 See Knesset Research and Information Center, "Brief: Jewish Political Violence in Israel"; Lustick, *For the Land and the Lord,* 69.
44 "Peace Matters," *MacNeil/Lehrer NewsHour,* PBS, 1993.
45 Yitzhak Rabin, *Pinkhas Sherut* (Tel Aviv: Ma'ariv, 1979), 550.
46 "Commission of Inquiry into the Massacre at the Tomb of the Patriarchs in Hebron," Israeli Government Press Office, 1994.
47 Sprinzak, *Brother against Brother,* 2.
48 Matthew Levitt, *Negotiating under Fire: Preserving Peace Talks in the Face of Terror* (Lanham, MD: Rowman and Littlefield, 2008), 30.
49 I would like to thank Arie Perliger for these points.
50 For a review of the assassination, see Michael Karpin and Ina Friedman, *Murder in the Name of God: The Plot to Kill Yitzhak Rabin* (New York: Metropolitan Books, 1998).
51 Eric Silver, "Shin Bet Informer Who Could Have Saved Rabin," *The Independent* (London), November 14, 1997; Patrick Cockburn, "Shin Bet Under Fire over Murder of Rabin," *The Independent* (London), March 29, 1996.
52 Yoel Marcus, "In Cold Blood," *Ha'aretz,* November 6, 2007.

CHAPTER 19

1 *Verdict of Yarden Morag, Shlomo Dvir Zelinger and Ofer Gamliel, Pae-Het 5034/02* (Jerusalem District Court); "Settlers Tried to Blow Up School," *The Guardian,* September 18, 2003. For background for part of this chapter, I draw on Ami Pedahzur and Arie Perliger, *Jewish Terrorism in Israel* (New York: Columbia University Press, 2009).

2 "Member of Jewish Terrorist Organization Jailed for 8 Years," *Haaretz,* December 6, 2004, http://www.haaretz.com/news/member-of-jewish-terrorist-organization-jailed-for-8-years-1.142695.

3 Efrat Weiss, "Dichter: Ma'arechet ha-bitachon nichshela ba-hagana 'al ezracheya" (Dichter: The Security Establishment Failed to Protect Its Citizens), *Ynet,* December 16, 2003, www.ynet.co.il/Ext/Comp/ArticleLayout/CdaArticlePrintPreview/1,2506,L-2841940,00.html.

4 "Shabak Criminals Should Be Hunted Down," *Ma'ariv,* February 9, 2003.

5 Dan Suan and Michael Shefer, *Shnaton Statisti Yehuda Ve-Shomron* 2002 (Judea and Samaria Statistical Almanac 2002) (Ariel: College of Judea and Samaria, 2003), 138.

6 Shaul Ariel and Michael Sfard, *Homa Ve-Mehdal: Geder Ha-Frada— Bitahon Ao Hamdanut* (The Wall of Folly) (Tel Aviv: Yedioth Aharonot, 2008), 52–53.

7 "Israel's Religious Right and the Question of Settlements," International Crisis Group: Middle East Report No. 89, July 20, 2009 1–2, 13.

8 See, for example, Joel Greenberg, "2 West Bank Jews Die," *New York Times,* December 7, 1993.

9 http://www.pcpsr.org/survey/polls/2003/p10a.html.; Questions and results found at http://www.pcpsr.org/survey/polls/2003/p10b.html.

10 Nadav Shragai, "24 Piguim Be-Yesha Le-Kol Pigua Be-Yisrael" (24 Terror Attacks in Yesha for Any Attack in Israel), *Haaretz,* September 23, 2003. Most of the 852 deaths were Israelis, and a few were citizens of other countries.

11 B'Tselem, "Israeli Civilians Killed by Palestinians in the Occupied Territories"; B'Tselem, "Israeli Security Force Personnel Killed by Palestinians in the Occupied Territories," http://www.btselem.org/English/statistics/Casualties.asp.

12 Ariel and Sfard, *Homa Ve-Mehdal,* 64–65.

13 Ibid.; Uri Blau, "We Came, We Saw, We Conquered," *Haaretz,* February 2, 2009.

14 B'Tselem, "Access Denied: Israeli Measures to Deny Palestinians Access to Land around Settlements" (2009), 7, http://www.btselem.org/english/publications/summaries/200809_access_denied.asp.

15 Amos Harel and Avi Isacharoff, *Ha-milḥamah Hasbiy'iyt* ("The Seventh War"): *'Eikh Nitzakhnu wa-Lamah Hifsadnu ba-Milḥamah 'im ha-Falasṭinim* (Tel Aviv: Sifrei Hemed, 2005), 116–19.

16 Amnon Barzilai, "Military Spending: An Extra Command and Several Brigades," *Haaretz,* September 23, 2003.

17 "Honenu," www.honenu.org.il/page.asp?ID=14.

18 Quoted in Avi Kay, "Citizens in Flux: The Influence of American Immigrants to Israel on Modes of Political Activism," *Jewish Political Studies Review* 13, nos. 3–4 (2001), http://www.jcpa.org/cjc/cjc-kay-f01.htm.

19 IsraCast, "Change in Command," May 15, 2005, http://www.isracast .com/article.aspx?ID=506&t=CHANGE-IN-COMMAND.

20 Matt Levitt and Becca Wasser, "Violence by Extremists in the Jewish Settler Movement: A Rising Challenge," The Washington Institute for Near East Policy: PolicyWatch #1434, November 25, 2008.

21 United Nations Office for the Coordination of Humanitarian Affairs, "Israeli Settler Violence against Palestinians and Their Property," December 2008, http://unispal.un.org/UNISPAL.NSF/0/665317F0F18D 199B852575230075076D.

22 "Israel's Religious Right and the Question of Settlements," 28–29.

23 "See Israel's Religious Right and the Question of Settlements" for a review.

24 "The Jewish Terrorist," Ynet, December 23, 2006.

25 Isabel Kerschner, "Radical Settlers Take on Israel," New York Times, September 26, 2008.

26 Conal Urquhart, "Settlers' Tactics Win Them Few Friends," The Guardian, August 19, 2005.

27 Breaking the Silence, "Soldiers Testimonies from Hebron," 2005-2007, 20, Available at: http://www.shovrimshtika.org/UserFiles/File// Shovrim_Shtika_English_Int.pdf.

28 "Olmert: I am shamed by Hebron settlers' pogrom," Haaretz, July 7, 2008, http://www.haaretz.com/news/olmert-i-am-shamed-by-hebron-settlers-pogrom-1.259015.

29 Kerschner, "Radical Settlers Take on Israel."

30 "Israel's Religious Right and the Question of Settlements," 8–10; Shay Hazkani, "Israeli Settlers in Focus," speech given April 14, 2009, Washington, DC, Georgetown University; and information provided privately to the author.

31 "Israel's Religious Right and the Question of Settlements," 28.

32 "The Generation That Didn't Know Zambish," Haaretz, July 22, 2008.

33 "Israel's Religious Right and the Question of Settlements," 7.

34 Hazkani, "Israeli Settlers in Focus."

35 Kerschner, "Radical Settlers Take on Israel"; Levitt and Wasser, "Violence by Extremists in the Jewish Settler Movement."

36 Aran, "Jewish Zionist Fundamentalism: The Block of the Faithful in Israel (Gush Emunim)," from Fundamentalisms Observed (Chicago: University of Chicago Press, 1994), 274.

37 "Israel's Religious Right and the Question of Settlements," 21.

38 Margaret Coker, "Israel Weighs Possible Crackdown on Jewish Extremists," Cox News Service, February 25, 2005.

39 Shay Hazkani, "Bachir ba-chativa ha-yehudit bashabak ulatz la'azov et tafkido" (A Prominent Shin Bet Operative of the Jewish Branch Was Forced to Resign), Galei Zahal Radio (Haifa), December 26, 2002.

40 There are exceptions. In 2001 nine settlers were put in administrative detention, and in 2006 a special military order prohibited nineteen settlers from entering the West Bank. See Roy Sharon, "Al Ha-Kavenet Shel Shirut Ha-Bitachon Ha-Klali" (On the Shin Bet's Viewfinder), NRG, November 2, 2006. In February 2010 Ephraim Hantzis was

arrested using detention powers, with Shin Bet citing evidence that was intelligence-based and not usable in court.

41 "Israel's Religious Right and the Question of Settlements," 1.
42 Shay Hazkani, "The New Jewish Underground Movement Investigation Collapses," Galei Zahal Radio (Haifa), 2003.
43 Suzanne Goldenberg, "Settler Fined for Clubbing Arab Boy to Death," *The Guardian*, January 22, 2001.

CHAPTER 20

1 For background, this chapter draws on Ami Pedahzur, *The Israeli Secret Services and the Struggle against Terrorism* (New York: Columbia University Press, 2009); Joseph Lelyveld, "Interrogating Ourselves," *New York Times Magazine*, June 12, 2005; Mark Bowden, "The Dark Art of Interrogation," *The Atlantic*, October 2003; Laura Blumenfeld, "The Tortured Life of Interrogators," *Washington Post*, June 4, 2007.
2 Quoted in Pedahzur, *The Israeli Secret Services*, 102.
3 Glenn Frankel, "Prison Tactics a Longtime Dilemma for Israel," *Washington Post*, June 14, 2004.
4 Quoted in Yorm Shalit, "Ha-Hakira Ke-Keli Modi'ini" (The Interrogation as an Intelligence Tool), *Mabat Malam* 49 (2007): 36–39.
5 Quoted in Blumenfeld, "The Tortured Life of Interrogators."
6 Quoted in Bowden, "The Dark Art of Interrogation."
7 Bowden, "The Dark Art of Interrogation," 65.
8 "Israel and Torture," *Sunday Times* (London), June 19, 1977, 17–19.
9 Patrick Cockburn, "West Bank Sealed Off after Two Israelis Are Shot Dead," *The Independent* (London), July 27, 1996; Israel High Court Ruling H.C.J. 4668/01: Supreme Court of Israel, "Yossi Sarid and Others Against Ehud Yatom and Prime Minister, Ariel Sharon" (Hebrew), December 27, 2001, http://elyon1.court.gov.il/Files/01/680/046/f12/01046680.f12.HTM.
10 Pedahzur, *The Israeli Secret Services*, 76.
11 Yuval Yoaz, "Hamedina: Dirani hu oyev, ein la-dun ba-'atirato" (Dirani Is an Enemy, the State Should Not Allow Him Proceedings), *Haaretz*, January 31, 2006, http://news.iol.co.il/?w=/9/851855.
12 Chris McGreal, "Facility 1391: Israel's Secret Prison," *The Guardian*, November 14, 2003.
13 Yitzhak Latz, "Hasochnim Nechsafu Beintifadat Al-Aqsa" (The Agents Were Revealed in the Al-Aqsa Intifada), *Globes* (Rishon Le-Zion), September 13, 2001.
14 "Interview with Moshe Landau," *Haaretz*, October 6, 2000.
15 Frankel, "Prison Tactics."
16 B'tselem, "1987–1997: A Decade of Human Rights Violations," Information Sheet, January 1998, http://www.btselem.org/english/publications/index.asp?TF=06.
17 Frankel, "Prison Tactics"; B'tselem, "1987–1997: A Decade of Human Rights Violations."
18 Quoted in Bowden, "The Dark Art of Interrogation," 64.

19 Amira Hass, *Drinking the Sea at Gaza: Days and Nights in a Land under Siege*, trans. Maxine Nunn (New York: Henry Holt, 1996), 212–15.

20 Quoted in Matthew Levitt, *Negotiating under Fire: Preserving Peace Talks in the Face of Terror* (Lanham, MD: Rowman and Littlefield, 2008), 82.

21 Yossi Melman, "The 'Torture Police': Every Shin Bet Move Is Watched by Its Legal Team," *Haaretz.com*, June 17, 2008. Human rights organizations criticized the court for not examining the IDF as well as Shin Bet, not examining the full range of Shin Bet techniques, and otherwise being willing to condone a certain level of coercion. See Nimer Sultany, "The Legacy of Justice Aharon Barak: A Critical Review," *Harvard ILJ Online* 48 (2007).

22 Quoted in B'Tselem, "Torture and Ill-Treatment as Perceived by Israel's High Court of Justice," http://www.btselem.org/english/torture/HCJ_Ruling.asp.

23 Quoted in Pedahzur, *The Israeli Secret Services,* 103.

24 Quoted in Melman, "The 'Torture Police.'"

25 The Supreme Court did not use the term *ticking bomb.* Instead the court describes "cases of extreme necessity" and left it to the attorney general to rule on whether a case fits that definition. This is usually done after the fact, as interrogators facing a ticking bomb prefer to ask for forgiveness rather than permission. For the use of this language by the court, see http://elyon1.court.gov.il/files/94/000/051/n15/94051000.n15.htm.

26 Shahar Ilan, "Shin Bet Use Emergency Regulations on 17% of Gaza Detainees," *Haaretz*, December 3, 2007.

27 B'Tselem, "The ISA Interrogation Regime: Routine Ill-Treatment," 2009, http://www.btselem.org/english/torture/interrogation_regime.asp.

28 See also Bassam Eid, "Jericho's Stasi," *Jerusalem Post,* June 24, 2009, http://www.jpost.com/Home/Article.aspx?id=146602.

CHAPTER 21

1 "Remarks by Maj. General Amos Yadlin," Jerusalem Center for Public Affairs, Jerusalem, November 25, 2004. For background, this chapter draws on Laura Blumenfeld, "In Israel, a Divisive Struggle over Targeted Killings," *Washington Post*, August 27, 2006; Amos Harel and Avi Isacharoff, *Ha-milḥamah Hasbiy'iyt* ("The Seventh War"): *'Eikh Nitzakhnu wa-Lamah Hifsadnu ba-Milḥamah 'im ha-Falasṭinim* (Tel Aviv: Sifrei Hemed, 2005); Moshe Yaalon, *Derech Arooka Ktzara* (The Long Short Way) (Tel Aviv: Sifrei Hemed, 2008).

2 Erick Weiss, "Hoker Shabak: Mesigim Meida Be-Avoor Majadra" (Shin Bet Interrogator: We Get Information for a Dish of Majadra), *Ma'ariv*, January 24, 2009.

3 Uri Dan, *Ariel Sharon: An Intimate Portrait* (New York: Palgrave Macmillan, 2006), 208

4 Press reporting on the number of stories of Shehada's building and the number of adjacent structures conflict. The building was three or four

stories, and between two and five adjacent structures were also destroyed.

5 Aluf Benn, "Sharon's Strangulation Strategy," *Salon.com*, July 30, 2002.

6 Laura Blumenfeld, "In Israel, a Divisive Struggle over Targeted Killings," *Washington Post*, August 27, 2006; Israel Ministry of Foreign Affairs, "Terrorist Bombing at Hebrew University Cafeteria," July 31, 2002, http://www.mfa.gov.il/MFA/MFAArchive/2000_2009/2002/7/Terrorist%20bombing%20at%20Hebrew%20University%20cafeteria%20.

7 Blumenfeld, "In Israel, a Divisive Struggle over Targeted Killings."

8 Ari Shavit, "The Enemy Within," *Haaretz Friday Magazine*, August 30, 2002.

9 Blumenfeld, "In Israel, a Divisive Struggle over Targeted Killings."

10 Ibid.

11 Ibid.

12 Ibid.

13 B'Tselem, "Fatalities," www.btselem.org/English/Statistics/Casualties.asp (accessed July 6, 2009).

14 Harel and Isacharoff, *Ha-milḥamah Hasbiy'iyt* ("The Seventh War"), 193–94.

15 An exception to this is Aharon Yaffe, "Selective Targeting: Risks and Prospects," International Institute for Counter-Terrorism, May 30, 2008, http://www.ict.org.il/NewsCommentaries/Commentaries/tabid/69/Articlsid/163/currentpage/9/Default.aspx.

16 Harel and Isacharoff, *Ha-milḥamah Hasbiy'iyt* ("The Seventh War"), 201–2.

17 Quoted in Molly Moore, "Israel's Lethal Weapon of Choice," *Washington Post*, July 29, 2003.

18 Hamas's Al-Qassam Brigades website, "Abd el-Aziz Al-Rantisi: The Doctor, the Martyr," April 20, 2004, www.qassam.ps/martyr-11-Abd_el_Aziz_Al_Rantisi.html.

19 Harel and Isacharoff, *Ha-milḥamah Hasbiy'iyt* ("The Seventh War"), 93–98.

20 Quoted in Yael Stein, "Israel's Assassination Policy: Extra-Judicial Executions," B'Tselem Position Paper, 4, http://www.crimesofwar.org/onnews/btselem_extrajudicial_killi.pdf.

21 Quoted in Isabel Kershner, *Barrier: The Seam of the Israeli-Palestinian Conflict* (New York: Palgrave Macmillan, 2005), 91.

22 Quoted in Adam Stahl, "The Evolution of Israeli Targeted Operations: Consequences of the Thabet Thabet Operation," *Studies in Conflict and Terrorism* 33(2) (2010): 122–23.

23 Quoted in Amnesty International, "Israel and the Occupied Territories: State Assassinations and Other Unlawful Killings," February 21, 2001, http://www.amnesty.org/en/library/info/MDE15/005/2001.

24 Raviv Drucker and Ofer Shelah, *Boomerang* (Jerusalem: Keter Publishing, 2005), 37.

25 For an excellent review of the Thabet case and its implications for Israel's targeted killing policy, see Stahl, "The Evolution of Israeli Targeted Operations."

26 Remarks of Harold Koh, "The Obama Administration and International Law," at the annual meeting of the American Society of International Law, Washington, DC. March 25, 2010.

27 Quoted in Ron Myberg, "Let's See Sylvie Keshet in the Slaughterhouse in Dizengoff Center," *Ma'ariv*, September 8, 2000.

28 Mark Lavie, "Palestinian Military Court Sentences Collaborator to Death," *Jerusalem Post*, August 3, 2001.

29 Amnesty International, "Israel and the Occupied Territories."

30 See Yitzhak Latz, "Hasochnim Nechsafu Beintifadat Al-Aqsa" (The Agents Were Revealed in the Al-Aqsa Intifada), *Globes*, September 13, 2001.

31 Zeev Schiff, "Ha-Pgi'aa Be-Mustafa Tehashev Ke-Haslama Yezuma Shel Yisrael" (The Hit on Mustafa Will Be Considered as an Intentional Attempt of Escalation by Israel), *Haaretz*, August 28, 2001; Ali Waked and Felix Frisch, "Halvayato Shel Abu Ali Mustafa Mitkayemet Be-Ramala" (Abu Ali Mustafa's Funeral Is Being Held in Ramallah), *Ynet*, August 27, 2001; Felix Frisch and Ali Waked, "Tzhal: Mustafa Achraai Le-Shurat Piguyim Be-Mechoniyot Tofet" (Mustafa Is Responsible for a Series of Attacks Using Car Bombs), *Ynet*, August 27, 2001; "Cohot Ha-Bitachon "Be-Konenut Piguyim Eliona" Me-Hashash Le-Nekama Falastinit Al Harigat Manhig Ha-Hazit Ha'amamit" (The Defense Forces Are in High Alert, Fearing a Palestinian Revenge for the Killing of the PFLP Leader), *Haaretz*, August 28, 2001.

32 Ali Waked and Elad Tene, "Sharon: Ha-Peula Bi-Shchem—'Ahat Ha-Mutzlachot Shel Yisrael" (Sharon: The Operation in Nablus—One of Israel's Most Successful Operations), *Ynet*, July 31, 2001.

33 "Ha-Bechirim She-Chuslu Hayu Tomhim Nilhavim Be-Piguey Hitabdut" (The Operatives Killed Were Avid Supporters of Suicide Bombings), *Ynet*, July 30, 2001.

34 Israel Ministry of Foreign Affairs, "Suicide Bombing of No. 2 Egged Bus in Jerusalem," August 19, 2003, www.mfa.gov.il/MFA/MFAArchive/2000_2009/2003/8/Suicide+bombing+of+No+2+Egged+bus+in+Jerusalem+-+1.htm (accessed January 11, 2010).

35 Quoted in Zaki Chehab, *Inside Hamas: The Untold Story of Militants, Martyrs and Spies* (London: I.B. Tauris, 2007), 111.

36 Dominic Allan, *The Dirty War: Israel Undercover*, BBC, February 17, 2002.

37 Dan, *Ariel Sharon*, 211.

38 William V. O'Brien, *Law and Morality in Israel's War with the PLO* (New York: Routledge, 1991), 113–14.

39 See Yael Stein, "By Any Name Illegal and Immoral," *Ethics and International Affairs* 17(1) (2003): 127-37; Amnesty International, "Israel and the Occupied Territories."

40 *Public Committee against Torture in Israel v. Government of Israel*, 2006, paragraphs 34–39, December 14, 2006, http://www.icrc.org/ihl-nat.nsf/46707c419d6bdfa24125673e00508145/d14f3f94989b702fc12572d80043927b!OpenDocument. The quote is from paragraph 39. For a critical analysis, see Kristen E. Eichensehr, "On Target? The Israeli Supreme Court and the Expansion of Targeted Killings," *Yale Law Journal* 116(8) (2007). Eichensehr is particularly critical of the temporal freedom the Israeli high court has given the IDF, as it allows uses of force that may prove unnecessary.

41 *Public Committee against Torture in Israel v. Government of Israel,*
    Case *HCJ* 769/02, paragraphs 27 and 28, elyon1.court.gov.il/files_
    eng/02/690/007/a34/02007690.a34.pdf. The quote is from paragraph 28.

42 Quoted in David Margolick, "Terrorism: Israel's Payback Principle,"
    Vanity Fair, January 2003.

43 "Ex–Shin Bet Chief: Israeli Assassination Policy Led to Period of Calm,"
    Officer.com, June 3, 2005, http://forums.officer.com/forums/
    showthread.php?t=31719 (accessed January 10, 2010).

44 In late 2005 Hamas bought an expensive Taiwanese encrypted
    two-radio communication system called "Senao" to try to prevent the
    IDF from listening. This achieved only limited success. See Israeli
    Software, "IDF Penetrated Hamas Secure Network," January 19,
    2009, www.software.co.il/wordpress/tag/crack-wep-key/ (accessed
    January 11, 2010); "Hamas Loses Gaza Cell Phone, Land Line
    Networks," *World Tribune.com,* January 7, 2009, www.worldtribune.
    com/worldtribune/WTARC/2009/me_hamas0020_01_08.asp
    (accessed January 11, 2010).

45 Harel and Isacharoff, *Ha-milḥamah Hasbiy'iyt* ("The Seventh War"),
    174–76; John Kampfner and Stuart Tanner, "The Ugly War: Children of
    Vengeance," *BBC Correspondent,* February 22, 2002.

46 Gideon Levy, "A Bankrupt Policy," *Haaretz,* September 14, 2008.

47 Avraham Burg, "A Failed Israeli Society Is Collapsing," Foundation for
    Middle East Peace, September 6, 2002, www.fmep.org/analysis/articles/
    failed_israeli_society.html (accessed January 11, 2010).

48 Margolick, "Terrorism: Israel's Payback Principle."

49 Yoram Schweitzer, "Palestinian Istishhadia: A Developing Instrument,"
    Studies in Conflict and Terrorism 30(8) (2007): 675

50 Middle East Media Research Institute, "Hamas PM: We Are a Nation of
    Jihad and Martyrdom," November 15, 2010, http://www.memritv.org/
    clip/en/0/0/0/0/0/0/2691.htm.

51 Hillel Frisch, "Motivation or Capabilities? Israeli Counterterrorism
    against Palestinian Suicide Bombings and Violence," *Journal of Strategic
    Studies* 29(5) (2006): 853.

52 Margolick, "Terrorism: Israel's Payback Principle."

53 See Alex Wilner, "Targeted Killings in Afghanistan: Measuring Coercion
    and Deterrence in Counterterrorism and Counterinsurgency," *Studies in
    Conflict and Terrorism* 33(4) (2010): 315–16.

54 Quoted in Ami Pedahzur, *The Israeli Secret Services and the Struggle against
    Terrorism* (New York: Columbia University Press, 2009), 121.

55 Breaking the Silence, "Testimonial Booklet #2, 'Yael'," http://www
    .shovrimshtika.org/UserFiles/File//ptihabeesh-englishforweb.pdf

CHAPTER 22

 1 United Nations, Office for the Coordination of Humanitarian Affairs
    Occupied Palestinian Territory, "Six Years After the International Court
    of Justice Advisory Opinion on the Barrier: The Impact of the Barrier
    on Health" (July 2010), http://unispal.un.org/UNISPAL.NSF/0/2C565C
    F02FA191128525775900613966.

 2 Isabel Kershner, *Barrier: The Seam of the Israeli-Palestinian Conflict*
    (New York: Palgrave Macmillan, 2005), 4; Amos Harel, "Ha-Bitachon

Mitkapelet: 2.4 Kilometers Me-Hagader Yu'atku" (The Defense Establishment Caves In: 2.4 Kilometers of the Fence Would Be Copied), *Haaretz*, July 28, 2008; Israeli Ministry of Defense, "Israel's Security Fence," January 31, 2007, http://www.securityfence.mod. gov.il/pages/ENG/purpose.htm. See also B'Tselem, "Separation Barrier: Statistics," http://www.btselem.org/english/separation_barrier/statistics.asp. For background, this chapter draws on Kershner's book as well as Doron Almog, *The West Bank Fence: A Vital Component in Israel's Strategy of Defense* (Washington, DC: Washington Institute for Near East Policy, 2004); Shaul Arieli and Michael Sfard, *Homa Ve-Mehdal: Geder Ha-Frada – Bitahon Ao Hamdanut* (The Wall of Folly) (Tel Aviv: Yedioth Aharonot, 2008).

3 Israeli Ministry of Defense, "Israel's Security Fence"; Yosef Amnon, "Hushlema Hakamat Geder Ha-Ma'arechey Bein Haretzu'aa Le-Yisrael" (The Building of the Fence between the Gaza Strip and Israel Was Completed), *Haaretz*, November 16, 1994.

4 Hanan Grinberg, "Hadash Be-Aza: Tzofim Ba-Mechabel Ve-Yorim Mi-Toch Ha-Chamal" (New in Gaza: See the Terrorist [from Afar] and Shoot from the HQ), *Ynet*, March 24, 2008.

5 Sergio Catignani, *Israeli Counter-Insurgency and the Intifadas: Dilemmas of a Conventional Army* (New York: Routledge, 2008); "Fence for Life: Public Movement for the Security Fence," www.hagader.org/English/about_hagader3_4.asp (accessed January 13, 2010).

6 Avner Yaniv, *Deterrence without the Bomb: The Politics of Israeli Strategy* (Lexington, MA: Lexington Books,1987), 17.

7 Arieli and Sfard, *Homa Ve-Mehdal*, 105.

8 Amos Harel, "The Delays in the Fence: Frozen by Lawyers, Budgets and Politics," *Haaretz*, July 29, 2008.

9 Arieli and Sfard, *Homa Ve-Mehdal*.

10 Daphne Barak-Erez, "Israel: The Security Barrier—between International Law, Constitutional Law, and Domestic Judicial Review," *International Journal of Constitutional Law* 4(3) (2006): 540–45.

11 *Beit Sourik Village Council v. The Government of Israel and Commander of the IDF Forces in the West Bank*, 2004, 44, www.elyon1.court.gov.il/files_eng/04/560/020/a28/04020560.a28.pdf.

12 Arieli and Sfard, *Homa Ve-Mehdal*, 363.

13 Along with Sharon, Col. (ret.) Dani Tirza was one of the barrier's main planners, and he often testified about the security considerations before the Israeli Supreme Court. There is growing evidence, however, that Tirza misrepresented the case to the court. He later told the court that he and his team "might have not been so accurate" when they testified that security concerns were what motivated the route of the barrier near the settlement of Tzofim. Dorit Beinisch, the court's president, was flabbergasted. She said, "I cannot believe it. I remember this session. It was in the middle of the terror attacks and the intifada. You said: Security, Security, Security." After the political nature of the barrier's route became clearer, the new IDF chief of staff, Gabi Ashkenazi, demanded that from then on the civilian authorities, not the IDF, should determine the precise route of the barrier, thus slowing its construction. He also demanded that IDF officers stop defending the barrier in court. See Arieli and Sfard, *Homa Ve-Mehdal*, 139–40; Amos

Harel, "Israel Agrees to Raze Part of West Bank Separation Fence," *Haaretz*, July 28, 2008.

14 See Intelligence and Terrorism Information Center at the Israel Intelligence Heritage and Commemoration Center, "The Leader of the Palestinian Islamic Jihad Again Admits That the Israeli Security Fence Built by Israel in Judea and Samaria Prevents the Terrorist Organizations from Reaching the Heart of Israel to Carry Out Suicide Bombing Attacks," March 26, 2008, www.terrorism-info.org.il/malam_multimedia/English/ eng_n/html/ct_250308e.htm (accessed January 13, 2010).

15 B'Tselem, "Separation Barrier: Statistics."

16 Bruce Hoffman, "The Capability of Emergency Departments and Emergency Medical Systems in the U.S. to Respond to Mass Casualty Events Resulting from Terrorist Attacks," written to the U.S. House of Representatives Committee on Oversight and Government Reform, May 5, 2008, http://cpass.georgetown.edu/documents/Hoffman_ Testimony_May52008.pdf.

17 The Israeli government claims that after the barrier is completed, only 6 percent of the West Bank will be a seam zone and only a few hundred Palestinians will live there. Israel also claims that it will have various accommodations to ease the humanitarian situation for those who remain, such as issuing special permits. See State response in HCJ 9961/03 and 639/04, 6, 8, 12, www.hamoked.org.il/items/6655.pdf.

18 United Nations Office for the Coordination of Humanitarian Affairs, "The West Bank Barrier," www.ochaopt.org/?module=displaystory& section_id=130&story_id=1456&format=html&edition_id= (accessed January 13, 2010).

19 Arieli and Sfard, *Homa Ve-Mehdal*, 64–65.

20 Israeli Knesset Information Center, "Mediniyut Hata'asuka Be-Anaf Ha-Binyan Ve-Hashlachoteya 'Al Ha-'Avoda Ve-'Al Ha-'Aovdim Ba-'Anaf" (Employment Policy in the Construction Field and Its Ramifications on Working and Workers in the Field), January 26, 2009, http://www.knesset.gov.il/mmm/data/pdf/m02180.pdf; Israeli Ministry of Defense, "Coordination of Government Activities in the Territories, Positive Trend in Economic Indicators for the West Bank," November 2008, http://www.mfa.gov.il/NR/rdonlyres/C1A9F626-4E6C-4271- B598-41C911A793CF/0/WBEconomyNov2008.pdf; Dani Rubenstein, "Ha-Calcala Ha-Falastinit: Shuvam Shel Ha-Po'aalim Le-Yisrael" (The Palestinian Economy: The Return of the Palestinian Workers to Israel)," *Calcalist*, February 9, 2009.

21 Herb Keinon, "Dichter: East Jerusalem Terror Reservoir," *Jerusalem Post*, July 5, 2004.

22 Intelligence and Terrorism Information Center at the Israel Intelligence Heritage & Commemoration Center, "The Lone Terrorist Attacks Still Continue in Jerusalem and in Other Areas. They Are Caused by a Combination of Factors, Including Incitement, Supportive Public Atmosphere, Economic Difficulties, and Frustrating Political Circumstances; However, They Are Probably Not Orchestrated by the Terrorist Organizations," May 7, 2009, www.terrorism-info.org.il/ malam_multimedia/English/eng_n/html/ipc_e028.htm (accessed January 13, 2010).

23 Kershner, *Barrier*, 44.
24 Moshe Yaalon, "Lessons from the Palestinian 'War' against Israel," *Policy Focus* 64 (2007), 6.
25 "Former Heads of Shin Bet Reflect on Israel's Present and Future," *Journal of Palestine Studies* 33(2) 2003: 184.
26 Jeffrey A. Larsen and Tasha L. Pravecek, "Comparative U.S.-Israel Homeland Security," The Counterproliferation Papers, Future War Series No. 34, Maxwell Air Force Base, Alabama, June 2006, 64, http://www.au.af.mil/au/awc/awcgate/cpc-pubs/larsen3.pdf.
27 Boaz Ganor, "Israel, Hamas and Fatah," in *Democracy and Counterterrorism: Lessons from the Past*, ed. Robert J. Art and Louise Richardson (Washington, DC: USIP, 2007), 238.
28 Larsen and Pravecek, "Comparative U.S.-Israel Homeland Security," 40, 80.
29 Israeli State Comptroller, "Ha-Michsol Ve-Hama'avarim Be-Otef Yerushalayim" (The Barrier and the Crossings in the Jerusalem Envelope)," 2009, 72.
30 Reuven Pedatzur, "Iron Dome Success Does Nothing to Ease Rocket Threat," *Haaretz.com*, January 13, 2010.
31 Ami Pedahzur, *The Israeli Secret Services and the Struggle against Terrorism* (New York: Columbia University Press, 2009), 124.
32 Ganor, "Israel, Hamas and Fatah," 284.

CHAPTER 23

1 Avi Issacharoff, "Israel's Man in Hamas Just 'Wanted to Save Lives'," *Haaretz*, March 2, 2010.
2 This chapter draws primarily on interviews for its information.
3 Quoted in Boaz Ganor, *The Counter-Terrorism Puzzle: A Guide for Decision Makers* (New Brunswick, NJ: Transaction Publishers, 2005), 74.
4 Quoted in Sergio Catignani, *Israeli Counter-Insurgency and the Intifadas: Dilemmas of a Conventional Army* (New York: Routledge, 2008), 3.
5 David Eshel, "Israel Hones Intelligence Operations to Counter Intifada," *Jane's Intelligence Review*, October 1, 2002 (online version).
6 Yaakov Amidror, "Winning the Counterinsurgency War," JCPA Strategic Perspectives, July 23, 2008, 24.
7 Tamir Libel, "Teaching Citizens to Be Professional Soldiers," in *The New Citizen Armies*, ed. Stuart Cohen (New York: Routledge, 2010).
8 Israel Ground Forces, IDF website, "37 uvdot al MALA" (37 Facts on MOUT), http://mazi.idf.il/4637-5184-he/IGF.aspx.
9 "Counter-Terrorism Unit Commander Revealed," *Ynet*, January 16, 2007, www.mfa.gov.il/MFA/Facts+About+Israel/Israel+in+Maps/1967-1993-+Major+Terror+Attacks.htm.
10 Amos Harel and Avi Isacharoff, *Ha-milḥamah Hasbiy'iyt* ("The Seventh War"): *'Eikh Nitzakhnu wa-Lamah Hifsadnu ba-Milḥamah 'im ha-Falasṭinim* (Tel Aviv: Sifrei Hemed, 2005), 251–53.
11 Quotes taken from Neta Bar and Eyal Ben-Ari, "Israeli Snipers in the Al-Aqsa Intifada: Killing, Humanity, and the Lived Experience," *Third World Quarterly* 26(1) (2005): 133–52 (online version).

12 Harel and Isacharoff, *Ha-milḥamah Hasbiy'iyt* ("The Seventh War"), 258–60.

13 Amir Kidon, "Unit 8200: In the Beginning,", IDF Website, September 1, 2008, http://dover.idf.il/IDF/English/News/today/2008n/09/0101.htm; Gil Kerbs, "The Unit," *Forbes*, August 2, 2007, http://www.forbes.com/2007/02/07/israel-military-unit-ventures-biz-cx_gk_0208israel.html; see also Shay Hazkani, "Yechida 8200 nechsefet" (Unit 8200 Exposed), Channel 10 News Tel Aviv, May 8, 2008, http://news.nana10.co.il/Article/?ArticleID=553324&TypeID=1&sid=126.com; see also Saul Singer and Dan Senor, *Start Up Nation: The Story of Israel's Economic Miracle* (New York: Twelve, 2009).

14 Gershom Gorenberg, "The Collaborator," *The New York Times Magazine*, August 18, 2002, 80.

15 After Oslo Israeli officials agreed that Shin Bet would have primary authority for gathering intelligence, though military intelligence would continue to gather and disseminate political intelligence, an agreement dubbed the "Magna Carta" by those involved. (In 1999 another agreement would be signed to give Aman's assessments preference.) Shin Bet, however, remained first among equals when it came to terrorism in Israel and the occupied territories and today is the most important service for counterterrorism.

16 Gorenberg, "The Collaborator."

17 "IDF, Geut va-shefel—sikum netuney shnat 2004 ve-hashva'aa rav shnatit," (Ebb and Flow 2004 Year Summary and Perennial Comparison), www1.idf.il/SIP_STORAGE/DOVER/files/4/37604.pdf; Amos Harel, "Me-40 piguyim be-shana le-5: kach mesaklim terror" (From 40 Attacks a Year to Five: This Is How You Prevent Terror), *Haaretz*, April 8, 2004, www.haaretz.co.il/hasite/pages/ShArtPE.jhtml?itemNo=413586&contrassID=2&subContrassID=1&sbSubContrassID=0.

18 "Dichter Speaks," *Mideast Mirror*, June 10, 2005.

19 Clive Jones, "'One Size Fits All:' Israel, Intelligence, and the Al-Aqsa Intifada," *Studies in Conflict and Terrorism* 26(4) (2003): 276.

20 Harel and Isacharoff, *Ha-milḥamah Hasbiy'iyt* ("The Seventh War"), 160–63.

21 Zaki Chehab, *Inside Hamas: The Untold Story of Militants, Martyrs and Spies* (London: I.B. Tauris, 2007), 69.

22 See The State of Israel, "The Operation in Gaza: December 27, 2008–January 18, 2009, Factual and Legal Aspects," July 2009, 90; Ilana Dayan and Gilad Tukatly, "Roim Rachok, Roim Shakuf" (To See Afar, to See Transparent: An Interview with One of the Prominent Shin Bet Operatives Who Worked in Cast Lead) TV Channel 2 (Tel Aviv), February 2, 2009.

23 John Kampfner and Stuart Tanner, "The Ugly War: Children of Vengeance," *BBC Correspondent*, February 22, 2002

24 Shai Fogelman, "Present Trauma," *Haaretz*, March 4, 2010

25 Harel and Isacharoff, *Ha-milḥamah Hasbiy'iyt* ("The Seventh War"), 160–63.

26 Charles D. Freilich, "National Security Decision-Making in Israel: Processes, Pathologies, and Strengths," *Middle East Journal* 60(4) 2006: 641, 649.

27 Catignani, *Israeli Counter-Insurgency and the Intifadas*, 9.
28 Freilich, "National Security Decision-Making in Israel," 643.
29 "Former Heads of Shin Bet Reflect on Israel's Present and Future,"
    Journal of Palestine Studies 33(2) (2003): 182.

CHAPTER 24

1 Lawrence Wright, "Letter from Gaza - Captives - A report on the Israeli
   attacks," *The New Yorker*, November 9, 2009.
2 Itamar Marcus and Barbara Crook, "Hamas Ideology of Hatred and
   Genocide," *Palestinian Media Watch*, May 24, 2007; Itamar Marcus and
   Barbara Crook, "Hamas Mouse: Blame the Jews," *Palestinian Media
   Watch*, May 13, 2007.
3 "Barak Le-Golshei Ynet: Medina Falestinit Zmanit—Pitaron Mesukan"
   (Barak to *Ynet* Surfers: A Temporary Palestinian State—a Dangerous
   Solution), *Ynet*, August 3, 2003, www.ynet.co.il/articles/
   0,7340,L-2715394,00.html.
4 Nathan Thrall, "Our Man in Palestine," *The New York Review of Books*,
   October 14, 2010.
5 Intelligence and Terrorism Information Center at the Israel Intelligence
   Heritage & Commemoration Center, "Ma'amar Be-Atar Ha-Internet
   Shel Ha-Hamas Meshakef Et Hatirat Ha-Tnu'aa Le-Ha'aatik Et Yecholot
   Ha-Yetzoor Shel Tiley Ha-Qassam Le-Yehuda Ve-Shomron . . ."
   (An Article on Hamas Website Depicts the Organization's Attempts at
   Copying the Abilities to Manufacture Qassam Rockets to Judea and
   Samaria . . .), June 28, 2005, www.terrorism-info.org.il/malam_
   multimedia/html/final/sp/6_05/qasam.htm (accessed January 12, 2010).
6 Quoted in International Crisis Group, "Ruling Palestine II: The West
   Bank Model?" Middle East Report N79, July 17, 2008, 26.
7 International Crisis Group, "Squaring the Circle," 9.
8 Nathan Brown, "Palestine: The Schism Deepens," *Carnegie Endowment
   for International Peace*, 2009, 3; "PA Security Commended for
   Anti-Hamas/Hizballah Actions," *Haaretz.com*, May 5, 2009.
9 International Crisis Group, "Squaring the Circle," 21–28; Thrall,
   "Our Man in Palestine."
10 Amos Harel and Avi Issacharoff, "Israel Removes Dozens of West Bank
    Checkpoints," *Haaretz*, November 1, 2009, www.haaretz.com/hasen/
    spages/1095231.html. According to UN figures from around the same
    time, there were thirty-two permanently staffed checkpoints not along
    the barrier (and thirty-seven along the barrier), along with twenty-one
    partial checkpoints. See www.ochaopt.org/?module=displaysection&
    section_id=125&static=0&format=html.
11 Thrall, "Our Man in Palestine."
12 Mouin Rabbani, "A Hamas Perspective on the Movement's Evolving
    Role: An Interview with Khalid Mishal," *Journal of Palestine Studies*
    37(4): 71.
13 This point is taken from the International Crisis Group, "Squaring the
    Circle," 4. See also 30–31.
14 Some forty-four hundred Fatah prisoners are in Israeli jails, compared
    with about twenty-six hundred Hamas prisoners. See IPS, "Asirim

Bitchoniyim Ha-Kluim Be-Sheirut Batei Ha-Sohar" (Security Prisoners Locked Up in Israeli Prison Service), 2007, www.ips.gov.il/NR/rdonlyres/B696DA63-1D78-4417-ABCC-0DE64B4E71D5/0/bitchonim_heb_2007.pdf (accessed January 12, 2010).
15 International Crisis Group, "Ruling Palestine II: The West Bank Model," 11.
16 International Crisis Group, "Squaring the Circle," 23.
17 As quoted in International Crisis Group, "Squaring the Circle," 38.
18 Keith Dayton, "Remarks at the Washington Institute for Near East Policy," May 7, 2009, www.washingtoninstitute.org/html/pdf/DaytonKeynote.pdf; Alex Fishman, "Ha-Ded Line Shel Dayton" (Dayton's Dead-Line), *Yediot Ahronot*, May 29, 2009.
19 International Crisis Group, "Squaring the Circle," 37.
20 "Former Israeli Shin Bet Head Speaks Up for Peace," *Le Monde*, December 22, 2001.
21 Rory McCarthy, "Barak: Make Peace with the Palestinians or Face Apartheid," *The Guardian*, February 3, 2010.
22 "Hamas Is Leading the Process: An Interview with Matti Steinberg," *Bitterlemons.org*, no. 12 (2005).
23 Yezid Sayigh, "Hamas Rule in Gaza: Three Years On," *Middle East Brief*, March 10, 2010, 2.
24 Quoted in Jeffrey Goldberg, "Unforgiven," *The Atlantic*, May 2008.
25 See, for example, Khaled Mishal, "Seven Questions: The World According to Hamas," *Foreignpolicy.com*, January 2008.
26 Wright, "Captives."
27 International Crisis Group, "Ruling Palestine I."
28 Quoted in Lawrence Wright, "Letter from Gaza - Captives - A report on the Israeli attacks," *The New Yorker*, November 9, 2009.
29 International Crisis Group, "Ruling Palestine I," 8. See also Kevin Peraino, "Fatah's War on Hamas," *Newsweek*, December 8, 2007.
30 Shimon Efergan, "Od Nita'age'a Le-Hamas?" (Will We Eventually Miss Hamas?), *Ma'ariv*, July 6, 2009.
31 Israeli Security Agency, "The Jaljalat Phenomenon in the Gaza Strip," www.shabak. gov.il/SiteCollectionImages/ופרסומים%20סקירות/terror-portal/docs/english/The_Jaljalat_en.pdf.
32 See "Israel's Iron Dome System Not a Silver Bullet," *Christian Science Monitor*, July 20, 2010, http://www.csmonitor.com/World/Middle-East/2010/0720/Israel-s-Iron-Dome-missile-defense-system-not-a-silver-bullet.
33 Quoted in International Crisis Group, "Ruling Palestine II," 12.
34 Thrall, "Our Man in Palestine."
35 For a summary, from which the quotes are taken, see Greg Myre, "4 Israeli Ex-Security Chiefs Denounce Sharon's Hard Line," *New York Times*, November 15, 2003.

CHAPTER 25

1 The point is taken from the following headline, though the story itself is about discipline issues in the IDF: Arieh O'Sullivan, "IDF Meets Formidable Foe: The Jewish Mother," *Jerusalem Post*, January 4, 1998.

2 Sergio Catignani, *Israeli Counter-Insurgency and the Intifadas: Dilemmas of a Conventional Army* (London: Routledge, 2008), 120.

3 Amos Harel and Avi Isacharoff, *Ha-milḥamah Hasbiy'iyt* ("The Seventh War"): *'Eikh Nitzakhnu wa-Lamah Hifsadnu ba-Milḥamah 'im ha-Falasṭinim* (Tel Aviv: Sifrei Hemed, 2005), 203.

4 BBC World Service Poll, "Global Views of United States Improve While Other Countries Decline," April 18, 2010, http://www.globescan.com/news_archives/bbc2010_countries/.

5 Quoted in Jeffrey Goldberg, "Unforgiven," *The Atlantic*, May 2008.

6 Nadav Morag, "Measuring Success in Coping with Terrorism: The Israeli Case," *Studies in Conflict and Terrorism* 28 (2005): 314.

7 Ami Pedahzur, *The Israeli Secret Services And the Struggle Against Terrorism* (New York: Columbia University Press, 2009), 8.

8 Chuck Freilich, "National Security Decision-Making in Israel," *Middle East Journal* 60(4): 654.

9 Yoram Cohen, Matthew Levitt, and Becca Wasser, "Deterred but Determined: Salafi-Jihadi Groups in the Palestinian Arena," Washington Institute for Near East Policy, 2010, http://www.washingtoninstitute.org/templateC04.php?CID=31.

10 "Israeli Arabs Defiant on 'Loyalty Laws' Plan," *BBC*, May 31, 2009.

INDEX

Index note: Arabic words and names beginning with the prefix "al" ("the") are indexed under the main word in the entry. For example, al-Qaida is listed under "Q."